OTHER BOOKS BY B. A. BOTKIN

THE AMERICAN PLAY-PARTY SONG (*Out of print*), 1937

Edited:

FOLK-SAY: A REGIONAL MISCELLANY, 1929 (*Out of print*),
1930, 1931, 1932

A TREASURY OF AMERICAN FOLKLORE, 1944

LAY MY BURDEN DOWN: A FOLK HISTORY OF SLAVERY, 1945

A TREASURY OF NEW ENGLAND FOLKLORE, 1947

A TREASURY OF SOUTHERN FOLKLORE, 1949

THE POCKET TREASURY OF AMERICAN FOLKLORE, 1950

A TREASURY OF WESTERN FOLKLORE, 1951

A TREASURY OF RAILROAD FOLKLORE
(with Alvin F. Harlow), 1953

SIDEWALKS
OF
AMERICA

Folklore, Legends, Sagas, Traditions,
Customs, Songs, Stories and
Sayings of City Folk

Edited by
B. A. BOTKIN

THE BOBBS-MERRILL COMPANY, INC.

INDIANAPOLIS   *Publishers*   NEW YORK

COPYRIGHT ACKNOWLEDGMENTS

The editors and publishers wish to thank the following authors or their representatives, folklore and historical societies, publishers and publications for special permission to reprint material credited to them at the foot of the page on which the material appears. An exhaustive effort has been made to locate all persons having any rights or interests in material and to clear reprint permissions. If any required acknowledgments have been omitted or any rights overlooked, it is by accident and forgiveness is requested:

Jane Addams estate; Herbert M. Alexander; Jack Alexander; American Folklore Society; *American Speech;* Wayne Amos; Appleton-Century-Crofts, Inc.; Merle Armitage; Arnold-Powers, Inc.; Herbert Asbury; *The Atlantic Monthly;* Bank of the Manhattan Co.; Hamilton Basso; Beechhurst Press, Inc.; Carl Biemiller; Bobbs-Merrill Co., Inc.; Albert and Charles Boni; Bookman Associates, Inc.; Brandt & Brandt; Florence L. Brown; California Folklore Society; Isabel Jones Campbell; Carl Carmer; Robert J. Casey; Caxton Printers, Ltd.; Bennett Cerf; Jacques Chambrun; Stoyan Christowe; Citadel Press; August Claessens; David L. Cohn; Columbia University Press; Crown Publishers (Covici Friede, Robert McBride & Co.); Curtis Brown, Ltd.; John Day Co., Inc.; DeSylva, Brown and Henderson; Dial Press, Inc.; Dietz Press, Inc.; Dodd, Mead & Co., Inc.; R. R. Donnelley & Sons Co.; Charles B. Driscoll; Doubleday & Co., Inc.; Duell, Sloan & Pearce, Inc.; E. P. Dutton, Inc.; Evan Esar; Jean Evans; Faber & Faber, Ltd.; Farrar, Straus & Young, Inc.; Erna Fergusson; Carl Fischer, Inc.; Edward G. Fischer; Funk & Wagnalls Co.; Garden City Publishing Co.; Genesee Book Club of Rochester; Stephen Graham; W. C. Handy; Harcourt, Brace and Co., Inc.; Harlem Book Co. (Penn Publishing Co.); Harper & Brothers; Hastings House; Harry Henderson; Houghton Mifflin Co.; International Publishers; King Features Syndicate; Alfred A. Knopf, Inc.; George Korson; *Latin Quarter-ly;* Ruth Laughlin; Isabel Leighton; Leslie Lieber; *Life;* Lipman Wolfe & Co.; J. B. Lippincott Co. (Frederick A. Stokes Co.); Littauer and Wilkinson; Little, Brown & Co.; Longmans, Green & Co., Inc.; Macmillan Co.; Edward B. Marks Music Corporation; Harold W. Martin; Harold Matson; Roy L. McCardell; David McCord; Tex McCrary and Jinx Falkenburg; McGraw-Hill Book Co., Inc.; Tom Meany; Julian Messner, Inc.; Mills Music, Inc.; Wiliam Morris Agency; Elise Morrow; William Morrow & Co., Inc.; *New Mexican;* New York Folklore Society; *New York Herald Tribune; New York Times; New York World-Telegram and the Sun; New Yorker;* Lewis Nordyke; Harold Ober Associates; *Oregonian;* Oliver Pilat; E. Alexander Powell; Henry F. and Katharine Pringle; G. P. Putnam's Sons (Minton, Balch and Co.); Random House, Inc.; Jo Ranson; *Record Changer;* Fleming H. Revell Co.; Rinehart & Co., Inc.; Selden Rodman; Rutgers University Press; Charles Scribner's Sons; Sam Shaw; Elie Siegmeister; Simon and Schuster, Inc.; William Sloane Associates; *Space;* Sigmund Spaeth; State Historical Society of Iowa; Wesley W. Stout; Texas Folklore Society; *This Week Magazine;* Mrs. William M. Thompson; *Time;* Roul Tunley; University of California Press; University of Chicago Press; University of Minnesota Press; University of Pennsylvania Press; William Hazlett Upson; E. S. Van Olinda; Vanguard Press, Inc.; Viking Press, Inc.; Charles Rumford Walker; Daniel K. Wallingford; *Washington Post;* Weekly Masses Co., Inc.; Wehman Bros.; Leigh White; A. A. Wyn, Inc.; M. Witmark & Sons.

"I must go and find out," I said, "what is the Voice of this city. . . ."
—O. Henry

Introduction

For years American folklorists from the cities have been going into the Kentucky mountains and other remote places to gather folk songs and stories, while all the time folklore was all around them on the sidewalks of America. To be sure, contemporary urban folklore is not always easy to recognize since it does not always fall into the conventional mold, and much of it is folklore-in-the-making. Moreover, it is often buried under the complicated overlay of modern industrial society. But it is time that we turned our attention from hillbillies to "city billies" and shared with the latter the excitement of making and transmitting the legends, anecdotes, yarns, sayings, blues and ballads of that continuous state of excitement that we call "the city."

The hero of this book—the city—has many faces and many voices. Not all of them are here, for there are as many as there are cities in the United States. But enough of them have been brought together to give a composite portrait, a folk's-eye view of urban America, of which we are all inescapably a part whether we live in cities or not.

The city of this book is the city not of history, sociology or literature (though all three have been drawn upon for material) but of folklore. The city is people, and wherever you find people you find folklore—that is, a body of traditions, collective symbols and myths, folkways and folk-say, rooted in a place and in ways of living and looking at life.

Wherever you find folklore you also find folk groups. A folk group is any group of people with common background, experience and interests that develops a body of custom and fantasy peculiar to itself. This book deals with the groups (the folk) as well as the lore of cities, the groups being the cities themselves, types of cities, their neighborhoods, occupations, nationalities, social classes, character types.

In the broadest sense, the folklore of cities includes all lore found in cities, regardless of origin. In a more specialized sense, it is the lore that is characteristic of cities and the urban way of life. It is also the "city in American folklore," the myths and symbols that have grown up about the city in American life.

The theme of this book—the impact of the city on the American folk imagination—grew out of a study of contemporary American folklore which attempted to answer the questions:

What happens to folklore and our notions of folklore in modern urban industrial America, in an age of print and mass media?

Do cities (individually and collectively) have a folklore of their own, which is partly a continuation of the folklore of the past and partly a new growth— as characteristic of today's mass living and thinking as earlier American folklore was expressive of frontier individualism and regional diversity?

To answer these questions fully would require an investigation not only of cities but of the whole field of contemporary folklore, including that of occupations, business, industry, mass media and the history of our own times. While these phases of the subject are touched upon in passing, the emphasis here is on the lore with a city locale.

To those used to thinking of folklore as something belonging to the past and to the country, "city folklore" may come as a surprise if not a shock. The antiquarian view of folklore that restricts it to the archaic or obsolete, the product of isolation and illiteracy, is part of the folklore of folklore scholarship, and is itself obsolescent. By now it is pretty generally understood that folklore is not the monopoly of any one class of society or stage of culture but is found in all classes and stages. "Survivals are folklore," wrote Joseph Jacobs in 1893, "but folklore need not be all survivals." By the same token, the educated and sophisticated as well as the uneducated and naïve have their folklore.

Though originally and in its purest form folklore is oral, much of it is embodied in written tradition. The relationship between written and unwritten traditions is a two-way flow, and the direction of the flow may be from above downward as well as from below upward. And since folklore, like the rest of culture, is the product of change and interchange, it is never found in a pure state but always in mixed and hybrid forms.

Strictly speaking, the "folk" is distinguished by limited acceptance and by diffusion through noncommercial and nonacademic media. The "popular," on the other hand, is characterized by wider usage and by circulation through such commercial media as press, radio, phonograph, stage, film, etc. However, there has always been an interchange between "folk" and "popular," as between written and unwritten traditions. Many of the popular or "lively" arts, such as burlesque and the comics, have a folk basis; and many folk songs (e.g., "Barbara Allen") originated as stage songs or were created by bards or minstrels (e.g., the English and Scottish border ballads). From the point of view of the dynamics of culture, more studies need to be made of the transition from folk to popular and vice versa, and of the techniques and media of communication. Nowhere can this process be studied to better advantage than in the city.

The disintegrative forces of city life are generally thought to be inimical to and destructive of folk along with other true community values. But the city also has its integrating factors, which create new group relationships, such as are found in city occupations and neighborhoods, and a new community spirit, which is different from the community spirit of the past as the folklore of cities is different from that of the country. For cities are made not by the survival of the old but by the creation of the new. The city is also a microcosm in which we can see in miniature and in focus what is happening all over the country as part of the acculturative democratic process.

The folklore of cities is thus a mixture or hybrid of the old and the new, the folk and the popular. It is also a mixture of the migratory and the local. In addition to the traveling stories that become attached to different places and persons, each city possesses a body of local or place lore that has grown up about its landmarks, streets, neighborhoods, place names, nicknames, local speech, foods, festivals, architecture, and the like. Since a city cannot be separated from its hinterland any more than it can be separated from its past, many of its folkways and traditions have a regional, provincial and rural basis. In fact, the city is the last refuge of rural folklore and, for that matter, of folklore itself. It is city people who are singing folk songs and collecting and studying folklore, and giving rural folklore back to the country, so that the country is becoming merely the reflection of the city. As part of the acceleration of modern life, the whole process is speeded up, with a shortening of the distance between collection and utilization, between the folk and the popular, and between the rural and the urban. Indeed, the rapid popularization of folklore has often bypassed the work of the folklorist.

An eloquent symbol of the ruralization of the city is seen in Henry Ford, who first brought about the breakdown of the separation between city and country by the "American road" and then started the vogue of collecting and preserving country dances and antiques to keep our rural heritage from being destroyed. Other signs and symbols of the ruralization of the city are the national costume of young people, jeans; the spread of outdoor cooking—the "barbecue"; the "ranch house" and the vogue of beamed ceilings and pine-paneled walls in restaurants and homes.

The differences between city and country and their reconciliation are part of city folklore. Some of these differences are differences that divide; e.g., the countryman's pride in the superiority of rural life and character, his disdain and resentment of fine city manners, his hatred of the big city's big business as symbolized by Wall Street. On the other hand, the city has attracted as well as repelled the small-town American, who is drawn to its pleasures and opportunities like the moth to the flame. Paradoxically, too, the city slicker pines for the country even as he feels superior to the hick.

The rivalry between city and country is matched by the rivalry among cities, with their boosting and knocking, cracks and slams, boom towns and ghost towns, fool towns and joke towns. Many city rivalries originate in the commercial and cultural competition of regional centers like Boston, New York and Philadelphia. Other rivalries reflect state and sectional prejudice, reinforced by the clannishness of first families and the old guard.

Cities take on the character as well as the prejudices of their region. Thus cities are distinguished by location (seacoast, river, prairie, mountains) and by activity related to regional resources (mining, milling, steel, wheat).

City folklore is further diversified and complicated by internal traits and differences (neighborhood, caste and class, high life and low life, native and foreign groups, residents and commuters or tourists); by city institutions (skyscrapers, apartment houses, big stores, subways); by the problems and tensions of city living ("too much of everything," hurry, congestion, the code of the street), culminating in flight from the city, which brings us back, full circle, to the country where we began.

In the selection and arrangement of the material in this book, an attempt has been made to represent as many cities, types, and aspects of city life and folklore as possible. But early in the course of the work it became apparent that within the limits of a single volume the value of such a collection would lie in the coverage of the main theme rather than of the minor variations. Therefore cities have been included not for their own sake but for their contribution to the pattern of the book, which is partly the pattern of city life and partly the pattern of folklore.

The aim of the book is somewhat different from that of its predecessors, beginning with *A Treasury of American Folklore*. Being interpretative rather than encyclopedic and also peotic rather than scientific in tone, attempts to create a mood—the mood of the city—as well as give a documented portrait of the city in the national picture. Wherever possible, preference has been given to storytelling, and discussion has been kept to a minimum, thus ruling out the purely local and temporal. The sources are as varied as the materials of city life—including biography, memoirs, historical and travel writing, reportage, as well as folklore and historical society publications, manuscripts, interviews and recordings.

"You walk around a corner," writes one New Yorker of his neighborhood, "and it's a different world." From the small world of the neighborhood to the larger neighborhood of the world, it is only a step, and the city is the link between them.

B. A. BOTKIN

Croton-on-Hudson, N.Y.
October 8, 1954

Acknowledgments

For advice, encouragement, criticism, assistance, and suggestion, contribution, or loan of material, I am indebted to the following:

Herbert M. Alexander, Pocket Books, Inc.; Cornelius B. Allen, Librarian, School of Commerce, Accounts, and Finance, New York University; F. Ivor D. Avellino, New York Public Library; Elsie Axelrod, Peekskill; Paul R. Beath, Washington, D.C.; Theodore C. Blegen, University of Minnesota; Oscar Brand, New York; Lukas Burckhardt, Basel, Switzerland; Jack Conroy, Chicago; Miguel Covarrubias; Sidney Robertson Cowell, New York; Rachel Davis DuBois, Workshop for Cultural Democracy; Louise Jones DuBose, director, University of South Carolina Press; Bob Duncan, Norman, Okla.; Fritz Eichenberg; Evan Esar, New York; Sam Eskin, Woodstock, N.Y.; Jean Evans, New York; Nathan Frankel, Croton-on-Hudson, N.Y.; Helen A. Fraser, assistant librarian, Albany Medical College; Tom Glazer, Ossining, N.Y.; Russel Goudey, Radio Music Service; Herbert Halpert, Murray State College, Murray, Ky.; Alvin F. Harlow, New York; Marion Charles Hatch; Harry Henderson, Croton-on-Hudson, N.Y.; Stewart H. Holbrook, Portland, Ore.; Pauline Inman, New York; Moritz Jagendorf, New York; Arthur Kober, New York; George and Rae Korson, Washington, D.C.; Aurora White Lea, Santa Fe, N. Mex.; Cornel Lengyel; Oscar and Leah Leonard, Croton-on-Hudson, N.Y.; Sam Levenson, Brooklyn; Benjamin A. Levett, New York; Ruben Levin, editor, *Labor*; Leo Manso, New York; David Stone Martin; James R. Masterson, Library of Congress; Raven I. McDavid, Jr., Western Reserve University; Mamie Meredith, University of Nebraska; George and Mary Milburn, New York; Evelyn Modoi, Peekskill, N.Y.; Harry Nestle, Croton-on-Hudson, N.Y.; Irving Nicholson; Abbe Niles, New York; Robert C. Notson, managing editor, The Portland *Oregonian*; Arthur H. Parsons, Jr., director, Omaha Public Library; Hyde Partnow, New York; Arnold Perl, Mamaroneck; Milton Plumb, the *C.I.O. News*; Sidney Reisberg, New York; Roaldus Richmond; Fred Rolland; Carl Rose; Gene Rose, Ossining, N.Y.; Terry Roth; Sam Schwartz; Tony Schwartz, New York; Charles Seeger and the late Ruth Crawford Seeger, Washington, D.C.; Ben Shahn; Edmond Sharrock; Grace Partridge Smith, Carbondale, Ill.; Joe Solman; Herman Spector; Bayard Still, New York University; May Swenson; Judy Toby, Provincetown, Mass.; Harold W. Thompson, Cornell University; Edward I. Ullman, University of Washington; Paul Vanderbilt, *Eye to Eye*; Sylvester L. Vigilante, Ossining, N.Y.; Ed Wallace, *New York World-Telegram and*

Sun; Clarence Weinstock; William E. Wilson, Indiana University; Ben L. Yablonky, New York University; George Zabriskie, Washington, D.C.

For their many services and courtesies I am grateful to the staffs of the following libraries: Baker Library, Harvard University; Columbia University Libraries; Croton Free Library; the Field Library, Peekskill, N.Y.; the Library of Congress (especially the Folklore Section and the Music Division); the New York Public Library; the Ossining Public Library; the White Plains Public Library.

Finally, I wish to express my thanks to the John Simon Guggenheim Memorial Foundation for enabling me to undertake research for this book on a fellowship grant in 1951-52; to my wife and daughter, Gertrude and Dorothy Botkin, for invaluable assistance in the preparation of the manuscript, proofreading, etc.; and to my editors, Hiram Haydn and Louis Simpson, and Walter J. Hurley and Helen Kayser of the Bobbs-Merrill production department in New York, for service beyond the call of duty.

Contents

VII. WAY BACK WHEN   229

VIII. FROM THIS THEY MAKE A LIVING   267

IX. HOW THE OTHER HALF LIVES   310

X. BRIGHT LIGHTS   368

XI. SOCIAL REGISTER   409

XII. GO FIGHT CITY HALL 438

XIII. THEY HAVE A WORD FOR IT 463

Contents   xix

Illustrations

SIDEWALKS
OF
AMERICA

I. Keys of the City

What makes a city a city? What makes it different from other cities? Humanly, not statistically speaking. To seek the heart of each city and, having won it, to carry in his mind "a concrete and clear conception of the figure that symbolized and typified each one" was the business of Raggles, the poetic and philosophic tramp in O. Henry's "The Making of a New Yorker." "A city to Raggles was not merely a pile of bricks and mortar, peopled by a certain number of inhabitants; it was a thing with soul characteristic and distinct; an individual conglomeration of life, with its own peculiar essence, flavor and feeling."

To Raggles a city was "she." Pittsburgh, for example, was a woman "homely, hearty, with flushed face, washing the dishes in a silk dress and white kid slippers, and bidding Raggles sit before the roaring fireplace and drink champagne with his pigs' feet and fried potatoes." From the folklore point of view, a city is "we"—you and I and everybody else, what people say, especially what they have to say about themselves in their own way and their own words, folk-say, and what they choose to remember. At one end of the scale—hearsay—folk-say and folk memory are embodied in proverb and anecdote—that is, in the apt, pointed saying or story that illustrates a trait of an individual or a community. At the other end—folk history—they take the form of "own" stories, in which a participant or eyewitness says, "I did or saw and heard these things myself."

Together these make up the voice of the city. And whoever seeks to know the heart of a city must listen to and for its voice, speaking in the individual voices of people talking, swapping stories, joking, wisecracking, bragging.

As a city begins with a place and ends with people, so the folklore of cities begins with the fact and ends with the symbol. From landmark, street, neighborhood, local trait, place name, personality, city folklore extracts essence, flavor, color, inflection. Customs become patterns, characters become types and stereotypes, and all become part of the legend of the city—composed of what a city thinks of itself, what it thinks of other cities and what they in turn think of it. More surely, more subtly than ticker-tape parades and welcoming speeches, the legends give us the keys of the city.

THE DEVIL AND THE WIND IN BOSTON [1]

High winds, especially on street corners, sometimes annoy [Boston] wayfarers. According to an old legend, the Devil and a Gale of Wind were once strolling along Winter Street. When they reached Tremont Street corner the Devil said to his companion, "Wait here a minute; I've got to go in there," pointing to the Park Street Church. The Devil went in and never came out; but the Gale of Wind is still waiting for him at the corner, where at times he becomes quite obstreperous!

[1] From *New England Colonial Life,* by Robert Means Lawrence, pp. 135-136. Copyright, 1927, by Robert Means Lawrence. Cambridge: The Cosmos Press, Inc.
Communicated by James M. Hubbard, Esq.—R.M.L.

BANKING IN BURLINGTON [2]

Lost in the mists of the decades is the real name of the elderly depositor who came to a window in the Burlington Savings Bank. Let us call him Elijah Winters. . . .

"Would you mind telling me," the supposed Elijah asked the teller, according to the oft-repeated tale, "how much my neighbor and dear friend, John Peabody, has on deposit in this bank?"

"Why, Mr. Winters," the teller protested politely, "that is quite improper, you know. We don't divulge information about our customers."

The old gentleman made similar inquiries over a period of weeks, always stressing the fact that Mr. Peabody was his close friend and would not care a tot of rum or maple sirup whether his account was disclosed.

"If Mr. Peabody is such a good friend of yours," the teller finally suggested, "why don't you ask him personally?"

"Heh! Heh!" then said the pretended Elijah Winters. "*I'm* John Peabody. I just wanted to make sure that you weren't telling other people."

"THE BEATITUDES" [3]

Sections of an older Albany have borne local names which many of the people who were raised in the particular vicinity still use in referring to the neighborhood. Michael Carey, the former poet laureate of this city, once penned a description of that part of the city which is now Lincoln Park. The final verses ran as follows:

> Oh, fare thee well, old Martinville,
> For you have had your day.
> Society has left you now,
> And gone to Gander Bay.

. . . Gander Bay . . . got its name because of the flocks of geese which roamed the sides of the enclosing hills. The South End was known by the German name of "Bonafettle," a corruption of the word "*Bohneviertle*," meaning "the place where beans are plentiful." Limerick was up in the North End, by the gas houses; Troubleville was the former Woodlawn avenue section. But did you ever hear of the famous four-corners down in the South End, known as "The Beatitudes"?

This section was so called because of the peculiar combination of business establishments which once graced this intersection. On one corner was Belser's store (They clothed the naked). On another was O'Connell's (They gave drink to the thirsty). On the third corner was Macwirth's (They fed the hungry),

[2] From "The Cities of America: Burlington, Vermont," by Henry F. and Katharine Pringle," *The Saturday Evening Post*, Vol. 224 (March 1, 1952), No. 35, p. 29. Copyright, 1952, by the Curtis Publishing Company. Philadelphia.
[3] From "Around the Town," by E. S. Van Olinda, Albany *Times-Union*, May 24, 1951.

and on the other corner was Barry's undertaking shop (They buried the dead). . . .

JIMMY WALKER AND THE KEYS OF THE CITY

I. How He Welcomed Gertrude Ederle[4]

It is probable that New York City will never again be as amusing, as full of unexpected belly laughs, as replete with startling spectacles, as during the administration of James J. Walker as Mayor. Certainly one of the grandest sights of those days, the City Hall reception for distinguished visitors, is seen no more, at least not in its perfect flower.

These affairs were held in the plaza in front of City Hall and on the steps leading to the entrance of that distinguished old building. Jimmy was always in the center of the picture, and seemed to enjoy it. The visitor might be really distinguished, somewhat notorious, or merely in tow of an alert press agent. All sorts of persons were thus honored—kings, prime ministers, Olympic swimming champions, channel swimmers, and stars of the radio, motion pictures and the stage.

The fact that it apparently made little difference whether the guest being honored was the Prime Minister of England or a butcher's daughter who swam the English Channel, each receiving the same sort of reception, finally led to sneers from critics that New York was deficient in dignity and taste. . . .

*   *   *   *   *

The first really big reception in the grand manner was on August 27, 1926, in honor of Gertrude Ederle, daughter of Henry ("Pop") Ederle, an estimable Amsterdam Avenue butcher and sausage maker. A few weeks before, Miss Ederle had made better time swimming the English Channel than the five men who had previously crossed it. Grover Whalen [sometimes called "The Black Hussar"] headed the group which went down the bay on the *Macom*, the city's official "yacht," to take her off the *Berengaria* and bring her to the Battery for the parade up lower Broadway to City Hall.

Down the bay two airplanes circled the *Berengaria*, two hydroplanes skimmed along the water, and a harbor full of tugs, excursion steamers, cutters, launches, motor boats, and sail boats joined in the welcome. Those having whistles tied them down. The din was terrific. The Fire Department band was on another city boat, the *Riverside*. Forty-two Ederle relatives were on the *Macom* and the *Riverside*.

Massed at the Battery when Trudy landed was a crowd of 15,000. Police charged the crowd with horses to protect the heroine from souvenir hunters who grabbed at her. Several worshipers were knocked down. Two policemen on the running boards of the Ederle automobile had to push their feet against the chests of some of the mob as the car moved up Broadway. Ticker tape,

[4] From *Mrs. Astor's Horse*, by Stanley Walker, pp. 31, 33-35. Copyright, 1935, by Stanley Walker. Philadelphia and New York: J. B. Lippincott Company.

telephone books, and old records were tossed from the windows along Broadway. On later occasions not only this sort of débris but toilet paper as well was thrown upon visiting notables.

Back of the automobile bearing Trudy came a posse of Boy Scouts, representatives from German societies, delegations from the Amsterdam Avenue section and the New York State Association of Butchers. Six persons were hurt painfully when a fence broke in City Hall Park, and a seventh, a girl, complained that a policeman's horse had stepped on her.

Governor Whalen had kissed Trudy when he met her down the bay. Mayor Walker, waiting at City Hall, was jokingly threatening to do likewise. In welcoming her the Mayor said:

"When history records the great crossings, they will speak of Moses crossing the Red Sea, Caesar crossing the Rubicon, and Washington crossing the Delaware, but, frankly, your crossing of the British Channel must take its place alongside of these.

"Of course," went on Jimmy, "the whole world has its eyes on you. I guess that is no exaggeration, but as the whole world is willing to pay you homage, you are after all just a New York City girl and an Amsterdam Avenue girl and that means more to us in New York City than anything that has ever been visited upon us."

When the party emerged from City Hall the crowd made another rush. A policeman had to pick up Trudy and carry her back to the hall, where she remained for thirty minutes until the crowd had thinned out.

Up in Amsterdam Avenue, there was a rousing neighborhood celebration, with much bunting and speechmaking. Late that evening things became a bit thick for the swimmer. She collapsed. . . .

II. Some Walker Asides [5]

. . . Mayor Walker . . . gave almost three hundred open-air receptions on the portico platform outside the [City] Hall, awarding the keys of the city, scrolls, and medals to honored guests. His speeches of welcome were extemporaneous, and the crowds greatly enjoyed the ceremonies, especially the Walker asides.

Upon one occasion a five-hundred-pound cheese arrived at City Hall accompanied by a delegation of Swiss admirers. Jim thanked his visitors for bringing the huge cheese, then said, "Will some one please run out and get me a cracker?"

To Guglielmo Marconi, the Italian physicist, Walker said, "It is gratifying to realize that you did not send a wireless, but came in person. Here we do not know much about transmission, but we have some mighty fine receptions."

When Commander Richard E. Byrd appeared for a third time at City Hall, Walker said, "Dick, this has got to stop; it's getting to be a habit."

* * * * *

Queen Marie of Romania was the first "crowned head" greeted by Walker. . . . Jim was attempting to pin a medal upon her coat. The lady from the

[5] From *Beau James*, The Life and Times of Jimmy Walker, by Gene Fowler, pp. 185-186, 187. Copyright, 1949, by Gene Fowler. New York: The Viking Press, Inc.

Balkans owned a splendid, although somewhat buxom, figure, and the place where the medal properly belonged—high up, and a bit to the left—suggested, among other things, a delicate target for a carelessly directed pin.

"Your Majesty," Jim said, "I've never stuck a Queen, and I hesitate to do so now."

"Proceed, Your Honor," replied the Queen. "The risk is mine."

"And such a beautiful risk it is, Your Majesty," Jim said in a low voice.

SHOOTING HELL OUT OF THE "CHILL" [6]

The Lucy Furnace, named for Lucy Coleman Carnegie, went into blast in May of 1872 at Fifty-first Street [Pittsburgh]. . . .

Taking raw ore and making it into pig iron was something new to the Klomans and Carnegies. They had always bought their pig ready-made. The new Lucy worked well for several weeks and then came down with a sudden "chill." A chill in a blast furnace is no joke. It means that the mixture of ore, limestone, and coke has been allowed to cool, through some breakdown of the machinery, and has formed a solid mass inside the brick stack.

The Lucy, it turned out, was chilled to solidity. The crew started in at the long slow job of digging out, from below, the mass of metal and flux. When the digging was perhaps six or eight feet up, Skelding, the Lucy's boss, remarked that if he only had a cannon he'd shoot all hell out of the chill.

The Allegheny Arsenal of the United States Government was nearby. Somebody went there and talked the officer in charge into loaning a small siege mortar. Skelding let out a whoop of joy. Putting the piece at the bottom of the stack, he shot three balls—all they could get—upward into the mass. Each ball served to bring down some of the chill, but much remained. The cannon balls were now stuck high up in the stack. With a magnificent oath, proper to the occasion, Skelding put an extra large charge of powder into the snub-nosed cannon, rammed it near full of cotton waste, and on top of this placed a fifty-pound hunk of hard iron ore that had come from the Republic mine in Michigan. Then he touched her off.

The ore shot did the trick. Down crashed tons and tons of the "hang" and the Lucy was soon clean and running on another blast. Skelding's feat gave blast-furnace men an epic to talk about for the next hundred years.

THE PHILADELPHIA ST. PETER'S SET [7]

. . . [A Philadelphia] society leader . . . , having it pointed out to her by the rector [of St. Peter's] that she really ought to call upon and thus recognize a newcomer, still demurred. "But you will have to meet her in Heaven!" he exclaimed. To which came the swift retort, "Heaven will be quite soon enough!"

[6] From *Iron Brew*, A Century of American Ore and Steel, by Stewart H. Holbrook, pp. 203-204. Copyright, 1939, by The Macmillan Company. New York.
[7] From *The Book of Philadelphia*, by Robert Shackleton, p. 21. Copyright, 1918, by the Penn Publishing Company. Philadelphia.

. . . [Another] woman, . . . dying, was leaving a life throughout every day of which every social duty had been punctiliously performed. "Don't ask my friends to my funeral," she whispered, to her grief-stricken husband, "because I could not return their calls!" . . .

THE LORD IN BALTIMORE [8]

A story illustrative of the great importance of family [in Baltimore Society] is told of the late Rebecca Shippen. Mrs. Shippen was born a Nicholson and descended also from the Lloyds of Wye House in whose veins flows the bluest blood in Maryland. She was sitting one afternoon with a friend over a cup of tea. "Rebecca," inquired the friend, "did it ever occur to you that if Our Lord had come to Baltimore we wouldn't have met him, since his father was a carpenter?" "But, my dear," replied Mrs. Shippen, "you forget. He was well connected on his mother's side."

PENTAGON HUMOR [9]

Almost before the roof was on, it was a butt of criticism, a begetter of jokes and a breeder of legend. There was the story of the Western Union messenger who went in on a Monday morning, got caught in the red tape, and walked out on Friday a full colonel. There was the man who sat down at an empty desk to rest his feet and forthwith found himself with a phone, blotter, desk set and secretary. And then there was the acutely pregnant woman who accosted a guard and urgently demanded the way out. "Lady, you shouldn't have come in here in that condition," he said. "But I wasn't, when I came in," she wailed.

*   *   *   *   *

The endlessly flowing paper is controlled by colored tags and big "buckslips." Congressional letters, of which the Pentagon gets about 300 a day, get a yellow "expedite" tag; an "urgent" tag is red, and one "rush-rush" marker is known as "the green hornet." An expert use of the buckslip—a small routing slip on which higher authority checks off directions such as "for action," "please brief for me," etc.—is an essential Pentagon skill. The classic story is one of a newly arrived Navy commander, snowed under with accumulating papers, who stumped over to an old hand behind a spotlessly clean desk and demanded to know how it was done. "It's easy," said the old hand. "I just write on the buckslip, 'Commander Smith probably would be interested in this.'" Roared the newcomer: "You b———, I'm Commander Smith."

[8] From *The Amiable Baltimoreans*, by Francis F. Beirne, p. 285. Copyright, 1951, by E. P. Dutton & Co., Inc. New York.
[9] From "The House of Brass," *Time*, Vol. LVIII (July 2, 1951), No. 1, pp. 16, 18. Copyright, 1951, by Time, Inc. New York.

THE SAINTS IN NEW ORLEANS [10]

The saints are very close to the Orleanian, who begs them to intercede in difficulties, to find jobs, to persuade evil women to stop annoying virtuous families. Because certain ones swear by one saint, and others have *their* favorites, jealousy often arises.

"Saint Rita—that's a stuck-up saint!" one woman cried to another. "What does *she* know about poor people?"

"Hunh!" her neighbor retorted. "Saint Rita's forgot more about the poor than your saint never knew. She's as plain as I am. I talk to her woman to woman!"

New Orleans is fond of Saint Expédite. Saint Rita is hailed as the "advocate of the hopeless." There may be "runs" on certain saints; if word gets out that one of them has done a particular service, the demand will be prompt, and overnight he will become a best-seller at the religious stores. Year in, year out, however, Orleanians retain their favorites. A continuing one is Saint Joseph. "Him, he can be a mean saint when he wants," an old woman says with a shake of the head. "But you get him in a good humor and he'll give you the shirt off his back." She has a method of countering his "meanness"; when he proves stubborn she stands him upside-down in his metal holder, and this, she says, brings him around!

In all this there is naïveté, of course, but also a direct simplicity. Who would wish to take from the devout the solace they derive from such faith? Their lively gratitude has been expressed for years through the newspapers' classified advertising columns in such items as these: "Thanks to the Infant Jesus of Prague in answer to the Flying Novena for favor granted." "Thanks to Holy Ghost for prayer answered." "Thanks to St. Anna. My dogs were all returned to me." "Thanks to St. Jude, Blessed Martin, Lily of the Mohawks, Blessed Mother and Her Son in helping my boy to walk." "Thanks to St. Jude Iscariot, St. Jude Thaddeus, Infant Jesus of Prague." When the phrase "Publication promised" is added, it means that, in praying, the petitioner pledged that the saint's name would be printed along with the thanks.

Mrs. Maud Ronstrom, in charge of want ads in the *Times Picayune-States*, recently made an appeal to the users of that column. It seems that too many were assuring the saints that she would run all such mentions of favors granted. "Please, ladies," she begged, "don't make such promises." There was simply not enough space to print them all, and nobody would want the saints to be disappointed.

[10] From *Queen New Orleans*, City by the River, by Harnett T. Kane, pp. 310-311. Copyright, 1949, by Harnett T. Kane. New York: William Morrow & Company.

MUD IN MID-CENTURY CHICAGO

I [11]

Lake shore sand, being the best material available, was early employed to top dress the principal business streets, and for a few moments made a neat and attractive appearance, but it was a delusion and a snare, being wholly insufficient to support any weight. The loaded vehicles cut through and mixed the yielding sand with the yielding mud.

The "signs of the times" placed in all the thoroughfares in spring and fall, were, "NO BOTTOM," "TEAM UNDERNEATH," "ROAD TO CHINA," "STAGE DROPPED THROUGH."

An old hat placed upon top of the mud to indicate where the wearer was last seen [and] the placard of "Man Lost" above it were familiar warnings where not to go; but where to drive could only be ascertained by repeating experiments like others, with probably similar results.

*   *   *   *   *

. . . In a general [Common Council] order passed December 14th, 1840, 2-inch plank walks, 4 feet wide, on 3 x 4 scantlings, were ordered on quite a number of downtown streets.

. . . Sometimes a recalcitrant log would tip over as it was stepped upon, or, sliding under the feet, would precipitate its disconsolate victim in the muddy abyss he was so laboriously striving to avoid.

It was one of these accidents, frequently befalling the wayfarer, that lent point to the joking remark of our esteemed friend, Thomas Church, that "He picked his second wife out of the gutter the first time he saw her."

II [12]

[During the mid-century] the mud was becoming too much for [Chicagoans]. Something would have to be done about it. Carts and carriages would be mired. Ladies, swinging a graceful hand to the rear to gather up their full skirts, would adventure forth at a crossing, walking tiptoe, only to sink deeply, losing a slipper, crying out for rescue. The jests no longer brought a laugh— not even the favorite one about the man who, seeing a hat lying in the mud, bent down to pick it up and on lifting the hat, saw a man's face staring up at him. "Say, stranger, you're stuck in the mud! Can I give you a hand to pull you out?" "Oh, no, thanks," the face replied, "I'm riding a good horse. He's got me out of worse spots—"

And some of the buildings were actually going down, sinking slowly by their own weight into the mire. The new Tremont Hotel, built of brick, four

[11] From *Reminiscences of Early Chicago and Vicinity*, by Edwin O. Gale, pp. 221-222, 228. Copyright, 1902, by Fleming H. Revell Company. Chicago.
[12] From *Chicago, Crossroads of American Enterprise*, by Dorsha B. Hayes, pp. 102-104. Copyright, 1944, by Dorsha B. Hayes. New York: Julian Messner, Inc.

stories high, which had replaced the old one when it burned down, was on the way to China.

They had tried planking the streets in '49, but that had proved a failure. Boards would teeter and come up and strike you in the face. Cobblestones were even more disappointing. They sank heavily into the ooze and disappeared. After some prolonged and worrisome speculation, a bold idea was hit upon— nothing for it but to raise the level of the streets, all of them! Just hoist up the land, make it higher so it would drain off properly. Cover up the slews. Pile on more earth. Sure, that would mean lifting the whole city, but what of it?— Chicago had to have good streets, didn't she?

It was a crazy-looking city while that task went on, and it lasted for ten years. As the level of the streets rose, what had been first floors became basements. Elevated wooden sidewalks had stairs descending at the end of each block and rising where the next block began. One Chicago lady who had been visiting in England returned with an enthusiasm for the fine pastime of walking, and having publicly declared herself, a cartoon of the day showed her busily engaged in climbing and descending endless flights of stairs. It was even said that Chicagoans could no longer walk on a level stretch. When they found themselves out strolling in another city, they would have to turn into a building every now and again and run up to the second floor and down again to get back into the swing of a stroll.

The downward trend of the Tremont was put to an end when a bright young stranger turned up in town and presented a plan for hoisting it. His plan was accepted, the hotel was raised, and George M. Pullman had begun his career in Chicago.

A TALL BEER IN MILWAUKEE [13]

Beer consumption has taken on a kind of Paul Bunyan quality in Milwaukee. . . . Capt. Fred Pabst—his rank was that of a lake-steamer captain and had no military significance—started the Pabst works toward greatness, and now, as a statue, looks benevolently on the towering ramparts of his domain.

LARGEST SCHOONER OF LAGER BEER IN THE CITY

5¢

[13] From "The Cities of America: Milwaukee," by Henry F. and Katharine Pringle, *The Saturday Evening Post*, Vol. 224 (September 15, 1951), No. 11, p. 111. Copyright, 1951, by the Curtis Publishing Company, Philadelphia.

The captain was very proud of his men, and especially of their capacity. One day, when some dignitary was visiting the plant, Pabst pointed to a fire bucket.

"Any of my boys," he said, "can fill that and drink it in one swallow."

The visitor was skeptical, so the captain called in Otto, a fine upstanding German. Otto excused himself for a moment, then returned and emptied the bucket. The guest left, vastly impressed, but Pabst was puzzled over his employee's momentary absence.

"I wasn't sure I could do it in one swallow," Otto explained apologetically, "so I tried it in the next room first."

DIZZY DEAN'S ENGLISH [14]

[In St. Louis] floodlight baseball has become a prime stimulus to night life. Nonattendants, walking along any street, can hear the radio play-by-play through open windows as Dizzy Dean recounts that "Slaughter slud to second," "Kurowski was throwed out," "Laabs swang and missed," or reminds his hearers, "Don't fail to miss tomorrow night's game."

A local legend is fast growing up around the Dean broadcasts. Schoolteachers are supposed to be combating the bad influence of the Arkansas righthander on the speech of their pupils. Dizzy responds that he "ain't goin' to change none," and thus far he hasn't.

One night, when the score was tied in the ninth, and the visiting team had the bases filled, Dizzy told his listeners that the situation "could be disastrous. Or," he brightened, "it could be goodastrous."

"Diz," a fellow announcer remonstrated, "there's no such word as 'goodastrous.'"

"There is now," said Dizzy serenely.

DENVER MORTICIANS [15]

They were a colorful lot, these Denver embalmers. Old Man Walley was the longest-lived and best known. His partner, Bob Rollins, was a machine politician, and the wordy rows between Rollins and Judge Ben B. Lindsey were *something* to hear. The gamecock Judge was as courageous physically as he was mentally, and many the time shook a fist in Bob Rollins' face at political meetings.

Old Man Walley came West in 1859 as a cabinet maker. When the city was founded no thought had been given as to who should bury the dead, until a lynching occurred and the vigilance committee found a corpse on its hands. So the lynchers called on Mr. Walley. He was a very handy man with the tape measure, as well as with hammer and saw. He measured the town's first cadaver and then fashioned a box. He had no ideas concerning an ornate casket,

[14] From "St. Louis: Boundary-Bound," by Carlos F. Hurd, in *Our Fair City*, edited by Robert S. Allen, p. 255. Copyright, 1947, by Vanguard Press. New York.
[15] From *Timber Line*, A Story of Bonfils and Tammen, by Gene Fowler, pp. 203-205. Copyright, 1933, by Gene Fowler. New York: Covici, Friede, Publishers.

still he was able to construct a form-fitting box, which later was called the "Pinchtoe Model." It got its name because Mr. Walley wished to save as much lumber as possible.

The lynched man was buried in a prairie hole. From that planting grew the town's first cemetery. Later it became Cheesman Park.

Walley conducted funerals thereafter for sixty years, and until a short time before his death walked two miles daily to and from his office at No. 1408 Larimer Street, across from old City Hall. He died at the age of ninety-four years.

One of Denver's undertakers owed his success to having been boycotted in Leadville during the gold-rush days. There had been an epidemic of pneumonia, and when a miner suffered that malady his chances in a high clime were those of a martyr among the Roman lions.

There was a shortage of caskets, the gold-seekers' ambitions having dispensed with the "Pinchtoe Model." As all caskets had to come overland by stage-freight, the undertaker was wondering what he should do about the problem of supply and demand. He struck on a brilliant procedure. He decided that caskets which he recently had buried would be in good condition. So he salvaged them at night and was doing a brisk business until the stage driver became suspicious— he had not been hauling that type of furniture of late. A committee kept watch at the cemetery and caught the undertaker *replenishing* his stock.

He left town at sunrise to become a leading figure in Denver's marble orchards.

THE HORSE IN THE SHAMROCK HOTEL [16]

[Glenn McCarthy] took the twenty-one million dollars and caused to be erected a hotel. Being rather fanatically Irish, Mr. McCarthy christened his baby The Shamrock. He built it some several miles, like about five, from the teeming center of Houston, the boom town. Mr. McCarthy had thoughtfully acquired most of the protective real estate around the site of his . . . monument.

The tongues started clacking in Houston.

"Jesse (meaning the poker-playing, hotel-owning, editor-fighting old man) will have it in a year, for six cents on the dollar," the kibitzers said. Mr. Jones himself was erroneously quoted as affirming the allegation. If he said it, he never said it for the record.

"Place is too far out," the kibitzers said. "Too far from town. Go bust in a year."

Contrary to the general betting, Mr. McCarthy's monument to Mr. McCarthy actually got built. Its color scheme (*Time* Magazine; the date escapes me) embraced 63 different shades of green. Its swimming pool by actual measurement was an acre larger than the Mediterranean, unless you throw in the Ionian

[16] From "Even the Midgets Stand Six Feet Tall," by Robert C. Ruark, *Esquire,* The Magazine for Men, Vol. XXXV (June 1951), No. 6, pp. 113, 114-115. Copyright, 1951, by Esquire, Inc. Chicago.

Sea and a portion of the Straits of Gibraltar. Its broad corridors were spangled with swank shops. Its Emerald Room was large enough to encompass an entire rodeo. Its air was conditioned. So were its switchboard operators, who spoke English instead of Texan.

*   *   *   *   *

Now the good people of Houston and outlying precincts suddenly started to fret over the publicity they had reaped before when they opened the sarcophagi of McCarthy's monument—the sneers that the Hollywoodians and the Easterners had showered on the conduct of the good rich folk who still bit the neck off their bourbon bottles from force of habit.

Having achieved distinction in three ways—The Shamrock, the Houston Social Register, and the Fat Stock Show—they lifted the fifth finger, right hand, when they caught a shot of panther sweat, and proceeded to live up to their new effeteness. They came to the first anniversary of King Glenn's monument determined to act like the descendants of diplomats.

Like when they brought the horse into the banquet room. Hell's bells, it was a big banquet room, and it was just there for McCarthy's pleasure. There was a saddle in the deal. The saddle cost $25,000 in beautiful, hard 60-cent dollars. It had 30 pounds of silver on it, and was generally accorded to be so pretty they figured that the horse would have to pay an income tax for the privilege of wearing it—unless McCarthy got it off the horse's back by declaring the usual depletion clause of twenty-seven-and-a-half per cent.

There were low hisses of disapproval from the guests when the horse came in. "Shhh—pssssss-shhhh—psss—a horse in the hotel. Fancy that!" somebody said. "Tsk, tsk, tsk!"

One stout cattleman remarked aloud: "Well, gahdammit, how else can you bring in a saddle that heavy if it ain't forked on a horse?" but he was cried down by his wife.

The point is that a year and a half ago nobody would have noticed the horse. McCarthy was aware that a horse in the dining room was a little *de trop*. He summoned the minions with brushes, and leapt astride the steed, a beautiful palomino, contributed by the gentlemen who bet, the year before, that Jesse Jones would own The Shamrock before its first birthday.

PHOENIX AND HEAVEN—AND HELL [17]

There is a classic witticism about Phoenix's climate which is usually attributed to the Rev. Bob Fisher, an eloquent preacher who filled a pulpit there in an earlier day. Fisher, to the bewilderment of his congregation, abandoned the ministry and became a lawyer. A few years later, Fisher was cornered by a group of amiable legal brethren who demanded an explanation.

"I preached Christianity here to the best of my ability," said Fisher. "But

[17] From "The Cities of America: Phoenix," by Milton MacKaye, *The Saturday Evening Post*, Vol. 220 (October 18, 1947), No. 16, p. 90. Copyright, 1947, by the Curtis Publishing Company. Philadelphia.

Christianity is based upon a system of rewards and punishments. Climate beat me. For eight months of a year the delights of heaven offer no special inducement to Phoenix residents. And for those who live through the other four months, hell has no terrors."

BETTER LUCK NEXT TIME [18]

. . . The Reno judges started out by being severe with divorce cases, so severe that the people of Nevada objected. For from the very beginning the Nevada people did not take kindly to the long-standing belief that divorce was a crime against man, woman and God. The judges, though, were not so sure. Or else they preferred playing safe. For ten years they used to cross-examine the divorce-seekers, but gradually the judges swung to the liberal procedure of today. This gradual swinging may best be personified, perhaps, by "Old" Judge Thomas Moran.

Years ago, he would cross-examine his witnesses with stock questions such as: "Do you believe in God?"

"Yes, your honor."

"Were you to meet your God would you be willing to say what you are saying on the stand today?"

"Yes, your honor."

"Decree granted. Better luck next time."

The ritual became in time such a sing-song that the Judge could ask it even while dozing, but always he would end with "Decree granted. Better luck next time." That is, until one day in court he met with minor disaster, the case being that of a woman who came right out and said she wanted a divorce because her husband was impotent.

The Judge, dozing, answered: "Decree granted. Better luck next time."

The answer not only broke up the courtroom. It changed the dear old Judge's routine. He never recited it again. And through the years the cross-examinations have undergone a complete metamorphosis. Today no curlicues are added to any hearing.

LOS ANGELES HORSE-RACE FEVER [19]

Los Angeles is hopelessly in the grip of horse-race fever and after each semester at Santa Anita and Hollywood Park the usual embezzlements and defalcations hit the papers. The degree to which the disease complicates the lives of the patrons was demonstrated at a film studio, which has its own bookie so employes won't waste too much company time telephoning their own bookmakers. A group of writers were waiting for the result of a race, and one of them who had wife trouble, as well as horse trouble, decided to call his attorney.

[18] From *Reno*, by Max Miller, pp. 15-16. Copyright, 1941, by Dodd, Mead and Company, Inc. New York.
[19] From *My L.A.*, by Matt Weinstock, p. 236. Copyright, 1947, by Matt Weinstock. New York: Current Books, Inc., A. A. Wyn, Publisher.

The attorney wasn't in so he asked the secretary if anything had happened in his pending divorce case. She told him the interlocutory decree had been granted.

The horse player hung up the telephone, danced a jig, and yelled: "I got the interlocutory! I got the interlocutory!"

One of his fellow writers, who had bet on something else, said sourly: "What'd it pay?"

ELEANOR ROOSEVELT AND THE ST. FRANCIS HOTEL [20]

The Powell Street side of Union Square [San Francisco] is taken up by one of the world's most famous hotels—the St. Francis, the first inn to introduce bed sheets to San Francisco [in 1851] and a fixture on Powell. This is the hotel toward which many of the world's great gravitate, among them Gen. Douglas MacArthur when he returned to this country in 1951 after being in the Orient for 13 years. The general arrived late, and the hotel, on that historic night, kept its head chef on duty all night to minister to the returning hero's appetite. The cook was prepared to plunge pheasant into boiling champagne, if necessary, to turn out something special for the general as his first meal on American soil. The chef was crushed, however, when the only order which emerged from the MacArthur suite was one for scrambled eggs.

[The following story] has been attributed, in varying forms, to other hotels, but I was solemnly assured by Dan London, the hotel's general manager, that it actually happened at the St. Francis.

During World War II, Mrs. [Eleanor] Roosevelt made plans to come to the city. She chose to make a reservation at the St. Francis. The manager was so pleased that he personally oversaw the preparation of the hotel's plushiest suite (drawing room, dining room, kitchen, two bedrooms, and two baths). Special furniture was moved in to create the most pleasant and luxurious effect, and the city's flower marts were ransacked for the choicest blossoms.

The wife of the President arrived after dark. A modest woman, she took one look at the lavishness of the quarters prepared for her, and asked if she couldn't have something simpler. Reluctantly, the management gave her a mere bedroom, the last in the house.

Several hours later, a sailor walked up to the hotel desk. He asked for a room, and was told there was none. Crestfallen, he explained it was his first and last night in San Francisco. He was going overseas to fight for his country the next morning, and he had hoped his last view of America wouldn't be from a park bench. The fellow must have had the eloquence of Demosthenes. He so touched the heart of the room clerk that the latter did something he'd never done in his whole life: He told the gob to take the empty penthouse suite—at minimum rates.

The sailor was as overwhelmed by the lavish layout as Mrs. Roosevelt, but

[20] From "Powell Street—The Spirit of San Francisco," by Roul Tunley, *The American Magazine*, Vol. 157 (February 1954), No. 2, pp. 41, 81. Copyright, 1954, by the Crowell-Collier Publishing Company. New York.

he reacted differently. He kept his mouth shut, closed the door, and then proceeded to call all his buddies on the phone. They came as quickly as they could, stopping only long enough to pick up a few bottles and whatever young ladies they could persuade to join them. The suite was obviously too dazzling to sleep in, and so they stayed up the whole night to enjoy it to the full. Because of its isolation, any noise they made was muted.

Early the next morning the sailor and his buddies folded their duffel bags and quietly slipped away. The suite, however, was a virtual ruin. A large mirror was broken, furniture overturned, cigarette burns scarred the rich damask of the chairs. Bottles trickled whisky on the high polish of the tables, and bits of torn clothing littered the thick carpets.

The hotel chambermaid arrived promptly at nine, and, as she timidly opened the door, she couldn't believe her eyes. When it finally dawned on her, she threw up her hands in horror and called the head housekeeper on the phone.

"If you ask *me*," she cried, "that Mrs. Roosevelt is *no* lady!"

THE BARKEEPER'S CANNON [21]

. . . The proprietor of a [Sacramento] bar across the street from the Southern Pacific Railroad station . . . was taken by surprise about three decades ago when a car jumped the tracks, bounced across the street, smashed in the side of his building and pinned him neatly behind the bar. He was extricated unhurt, but suffering from a towering, awe-inspiring rage that was directed at the wrecked car in particular and the railroad in general. He would never, he swore, be caught unprepared again.

When his wall was being restored a few days later, he appeared with an ancient Civil War cannon, which he had the carpenters imbed in the side of the building about eight feet above the sidewalk, the muzzle sticking out toward the railroad station and the lanyard hanging down inside the building within easy reach of the bar. The next time a car jumped the tracks, he explained angrily, he was going to be ready to blast it into fragments before it could cross the street. As far as is known, no car ever jumped the track again at that point; nor is there any record that the gun was—or could have been—fired. But for any who might doubt the barkeeper's intentions, the old cannon, zeroed in on the railroad tracks, is still there for all to see.

GENTILE KATE [22]

Near the Chapman House [in Ogden, Utah] was Gentile Kate's brothel, incomparably the leader of its kind. Kate was herself a respected part of the business life of the town, a speculator in real estate, the most liberal

[21] From "The Cities of America: Sacramento," by Joe Alex Morris, *The Saturday Evening Post*, Vol. 223 (April 21, 1951), No. 43, p. 138. Copyright, 1951, by the Curtis Publishing Company. Philadelphia.

[22] From "Ogden; The Underwriters of Salvation," by Bernard DeVoto, in *The Taming of the Frontier*, edited by Duncan Aikman, pp. 47-49. Copyright, 1925, by Minton, Balch & Company. New York: G. P. Putnam's Sons.

customer of the stores; she was, too, an unofficial great lady. When a railroad
dignitary or a visiting Cabinet member was to be banqueted, she was always
bidden to provide conversation and fine raiment above the reach of Ogden. No
one was ever swindled at her establishment; no one was ever disorderly there,
twice. A person of dignity was Gentile Kate, and of more than a little wit.
But her annoyance was Mormons—perhaps because she disliked their color-
lessness, perhaps because she felt that their multiple marriages were sabotage
against her profession, perhaps because she had knowledge of certain patriarchs
and bishops who, by day, denounced her in their meeting-houses. Doing almost
a bank's business in loans and mortgages, she never lent a penny to a Mormon; and the one unladylike expression in her vocabulary coupled a vivid
genealogy with the name of Joseph Smith.

Early in her career, Brigham Young died of overeating, and soon there was
an auction of his effects. Of late years he had taken to parading the streets of
Salt Lake in a new carriage—a barouche made for him in the East. One sees
the picture: Brigham at his portliest, at his most benignant, leaning back in the
wine-colored cushions, one arm bracing his paunch, his eyes straying over the
multitudes who uncovered and bowed their heads as the right hand of God
went by. An equipage of splendor, behind gray stallions; on one side, the all-
seeing eye, carved and glistening, on the other side, the beehive of Deseret, and
on the rear the angel Moroni ascending to heaven from audience with Joseph
Smith. But only a carriage, after all.

The Utah Central, one day, bore it up to Ogden. Next day, behind the
same gray stallions, bearing the same insignia of Mormonry, it rolled up and
down the streets of Ogden, and haughty in its cushions was Gentile Kate.

THE LEGISLATORS' MISTAKE [23]

. . . The Legislature went to Seattle to look into the whole disconcerting business [of the location of the University].

The Reverend Bagley handled the investigation splendidly. He welcomed
the legislators as pilgrims to a shrine of learning. Seattle was very proud of its
Territorial University and expected every one else to be proud also.

The visitors had to admit that the campus and buildings were fine. Everything seemed to have been done in accordance with the letter if not the intention of the law, and the university was an accomplished fact. There was very
little the Legislature could do.

About all the investigators did was to provide Seattle with a good story.
There was only one steamer a day, and the investigators stayed overnight at
the Felker House. The steamer left early in the morning. When a shrill whistle
sounded, the befuddled legislators dressed in the dark of early morning and
stumbled out with their carpetbags to Yesler's wharf. There they dived into

[23] From *Northwest Gateway*, The Story of the Port of Seattle, by Archie Binns, pp.
169-170. Copyright, 1941, by Archie Binns. Garden City, New York: Doubleday & Company, Inc.

the engine room and watched the engineer stoke the furnace with slab wood. After a while, when nothing happened, one of the legislators asked, "When are we leaving for Olympia?"

The engineer replied with dignity, "Sir, this sawmill does not run to Olympia."

II. My City, 'Tis of Thee

According to a former St. Louisan, Oscar Leonard, one citizen of St. Louis asked another how to make a city and was told, "Sell your hammer and buy a horn." This cryptic saying dates from the time of the Louisiana Purchase Exposition of 1904, when the boosters said it to music in "Meet Me in St. Louis, Louis," blowing their own horn louder than ever in an attempt to drown out the hammering of the muckrakers and the civic reformers. For in the same year appeared Lincoln Steffens' *The Shame of the Cities.*

The legitimate pride of the loyal citizen in his "fair city" was expressed for all time by Paul of Tarsus: "I am . . . a citizen of no mean city." In the United States every stage of town making, from the paper city and the boom town to the City Beautiful, has been accompanied by boosting—a peculiarly American combination of boasting and booming. According to Timothy Dwight, in *Recollections of the Last Ten Years* (1826), the Middle West was the "paradise of puffers. One puffs up, and another down." While the rich prairie soil gave promise of an actual "Ne Plus Ultra," the absurd claims and predictions of the town makers' advertisements were exploded in the following take-off, which Dwight cites from the St. Louis papers, in the genuine tall-tale tradition: "The name was 'Ne Plus Ultra.' The streets were laid out a mile in width; the squares were to be sections, each containing six hundred and forty acres. The mall was a vast standing forest. In the center of this modern Babylon, roads were to cross each other in a meridional line at right angles, one from the south pole to Symme's hole in the north, and another from Pekin to Jerusalem."

In the initial stages of town making municipal rivalry precipitated fierce battles over the location of townsites, railroads, ports, county seats and state capitals. Later, cultural as well as commercial rivalries (recalling the jealousies of older cities like Boston, New York and Philadelphia) have flowered in contests for civic honors. Thus, in 1926, when Dallas won out over Fort Worth in the competition for the Texas Centennial, Amon Carter, "Mr. Fort Worth," sought to rival the former's Cavalcade of Texas with Billy Rose's Casa Mañana, plastering the state with billboards and posters reading: "Go to Dallas for Education. Come to Fort Worth for Entertainment."

In 1917, when Colonel William H. Cody died, a couple of Denver officials, seeing the possibilities of acquiring a national shrine, immediately got his widow to agree to his burial in a park on near-by Lookout Mountain, which has since attracted millions of visitors. In 1921, when Mrs. Cody died and was buried beside her husband, the grave was secured, against grave robbing threatened by a rival claimant, Cody, Wyoming, with fifteen tons of concrete reinforced with steel rails. According to Roscoe Fleming, who tells the story, Buffalo Bill's grandson is still loyal to Cody: "If Grandfather were alive, he would say: 'It was my desire to be buried on Cedar Mountain at Cody. . . . Get me out from under these twelve feet of cold concrete if you have to quarry me out."

The "bigger and better" complex of city boosting is expressed in nicknames, slogans and totemic festivals celebrating local agricultural products, fruits, flowers, animals, etc. The nicknames of Philadelphia, for example, reflect various stages in its historical and economic development: "the Quaker City," "William Penn's Town," "Birthplace of the Republic," "City of Brotherly Love," "the Clydebank of America," "the Liverpool of America," "the Cradle of American Finance." Slogans may be bold (Chicago's "I will"), sententious ("In Detroit life is worth living"), idealistic (Kansas City's "Make it a Good Place to Live in"), complacent (as in the automobile license-plate mottoes of the Twenties: "Richmond and Proud of It," "Norfolk Where Prosperity Is a Habit"), or humorous (St. Louis' "First in Shoes, First in Booze, and Last in the American League"). The last points to the interesting possibilities of combining boosting and knocking in the same breath, as in Henry L. Doherty's line, "Denver has more sunshine and sons-of-bitches than any town in the country." "The more I read . . . books issued by commercial bodies," writes Julian Street in *Abroad at Home* (1914), "the more I am amazed at the varied things there are for cities to be first in. It is a miserable city, indeed, which is first in nothing at all."

Through booster clubs, trains, signs, songs and "weeks," the newer cities have striven to put themselves on the map. Typical signs noted by Stephen Graham on a tramp across the country in 1913 were: "Think of Newark" and "Boost for your own city and its industries. Make a habit of it." The habit became part of the "Creed of the American": "I remember always that I am a booster." As boosting joined hands with the "City Beautiful" movement, cities acquired "garden" nicknames—"The City of Elms" (New Haven), "The City of the Forest" (Cleveland). And school children took the following pledge: "I will try to make her cities beautiful and her citizens healthy and happy, so that she [America] may be a desired home for myself now and for her children in days to come."

Cities became afflicted with a new disease, known variously as "New Yorkitis," "Chicagoitis," etc. But as one Chicago paper put it, "Chicagoitis . . . is a thousand times better than Chicagophobia. Those suffering from Chicagophobia are as dangerous to society as those who have hydrophobia."

The virulence of the knocker is given an apocryphal origin in the following booster fable:

> When the Creator had made all good things, there was still more work to do, so he made the beasts and reptiles and poisonous insects, and when he had finished he still had some scraps that were too bad to put into the Rattlesnake, the Hyena, the Scorpion, and the Skunk, so he put these together, covered it with suspicion, wrapped it in jealousy, marked it with a yellow streak and called it a *knocker*.
>
> This product was so fearful to contemplate that he had to make something to counteract it, so he took a sunbeam and put it in the heart of a child and the brain of a man, and wrapped these in civic pride, covered it with brotherly love, gave it a mask of velvet and a grasp of steel, made it a lover of the fields and flowers and manly sports, a believer of equality and justice, and called it a *booster*.
>
> And ever since these two were, mortal man has had the privilege of choosing his associates.

But the knockers cannot be silenced by what Duncan Aikman calls the "blurbanity" of the "home town mind." And half of one town's boosting consists in knocking other towns. The quips and quirks of city rivalry have amused British visitors no end. In *Uncle Sam at Home* (1888), Harold Brydges cites the following as typical of the magazine and newspaper humor of the day: " 'But you will admit that our city is at least well laid out,' said a Philadelphia girl at Bar Harbor, playing her last trump in a

game with one of the elect from Boston. 'Well laid out? Oh yes; but Boston
would be better laid out if it were only half as dead!' " As city after city that
he visited declared that it was the "real America" and the other cities were
only impostors, Arnold Bennett compared the "healthy mutual jealousy
of the great towns" to the "gamboling of young tigers—it is half playful and
half ferocious." At the same time, he saw through this competitive aggres-
siveness as a defense mechanism to cover up a basic similarity and uniform-
ity. "The streets of every American city I saw," he writes in *Your United
States* (1912), "reminded me on the whole rather strongly of the streets of
all the others."

Cities also accuse one another of provincialism, of which each, in his
own way, is guilty. In the older cities like Boston this provincialism is
intensified and perpetuated by the clannishness of "first families" and the
old guard, resulting at times in absurd ignorance of and indifference to the
geography of the rest of the country, as illustrated by the comic maps of
Daniel K. Wallingford and others. Each city has inspired its citizens with
its own brand of local patriotism, from that of the New Yorker who arro-
gantly declares that "After New York every town is a Bridgeport" to that
of the Charlestonian, who, according to Elizabeth O'Neill Verner, feels an
"immediate bond" whenever he meets another Charlestonian, anywhere in
the world, regardless of race or class. Other cities, such as Brooklyn and
Peoria, become joke towns and seek to turn the joke on the jesters after the
fashion of Brooklyn Borough President John J. Cashmore in his reply to
Manhattan President Hugo Rogers, on the eve of Brooklyn's 300th anniversary, cited by John Richmond in *Brooklyn, U.S.A.* (1946): "Said Rogers:
'Believe me when I say that our right to rib you is born of genuine love and
pride in being neighbors to a borough whose very name alone can break out
a smile and light up the most solemn face.' Replied Cashmore: 'I can't say
why mention of the word "Brooklyn" makes even the most solemn smile—
it may be the whole world is pleased there is such a fine place as this?' "

THE HUB[1]

The Proper Bostonian is not by nature a traveler. . . . Basically he
remains adamant in his lack of geographical curiosity outside the suburbs of
Boston. The Beacon Hill lady who, chided for her lack of travel, asked simply,
"Why should I travel when I'm already here?" would seem to have put the
matter in a nutshell—also her compatriot who, arriving in California and asked
how she came West, replied, "Via Dedham." . . . When Cameron Forbes was
appointed governor-general of the Philippines many years ago, his brother Ralph
was congratulated. "I don't know," said Ralph, "it's kind of tough on Cam. He
won't know what's going on in Milton any more."

*   *   *   *   *

The Midwest has apparently always been Boston's bane. "A grand reservoir
for our excess population," declared a young Boston clergyman when the region
was first being settled. A more modern story grew up around two sisters from
Burlington, Iowa, who came to Boston to marry Bostonians. Declaring they
were from Iowa, they once received the astonishing rebuke, "In Boston we

[1] From *The Proper Bostonians,* by Cleveland Amory, pp. 23, 24, 27. Copyright, 1947,
by Cleveland Amory. New York: E. P. Dutton & Co., Inc.

pronounce it Ohio." Today a Boston businessman who is forced to travel in the West a good deal proudly declares he always keeps his watch on "Boston time" and computes the difference. In so doing, of course, he is following a travel tradition long established by the true Proper Bostonian.

*   *   *   *   *

The combined effect of Boston's lack of enthusiasm for crasser cities and its insistence upon homage at home has not been without its natural reaction. . . . To the salesman Boston and its environs have long been known as the graveyard circuit; it has been said that no worse fate can befall a traveling man than to have to spend a Sunday in that city. The New York businessman, referring to the cool breeze which blows in from Boston Harbor to end each summer hot spell and the special express which leaves the South Station for New York at five o'clock each weekday, has a stock expression for the unsophisticated little city north of him. "The best things about Boston," he says, "are the east wind and the Merchant's Limited." . . .

WHAT OUT-OF-TOWNERS BELIEVE ABOUT NEW YORKERS (ACCORDING TO THE LATTER)[2]

The average New Yorker (who just isn't, of course) and the average visitor from out of town (same) are traditionally opposite types. Neither is quite so strange and wonderful as he thinks he is, a fact which may be something to run up a flag about. The hinterlander's quaint delusions are no more *outré* than those of the New Yorker who believes that his country cousin believes that New Yorkers—

Have all been transplanted to the town. No one is really born here.

Know less about their city than visitors do.

Are the biggest hicks in the world, when you get right down to it.

Never get stiff necks looking at tall buildings.

All cherish a secret hope of one day owning a farm complete with Jersey cow, babbling brook, and no elevator service.

Whoop it up day in and day out. Are bears for night-clubbing, drinking, and assorted whatnot.

Dance in the streets at the sight of a horse.

Believe everything west of the Hudson is overrun by savages.

. . . New Yorkers who made the grade all came from Kansas or Iowa.

WHY WEEGEE WON'T MARRY A BROOKLYN GIRL[3]

. . . Weegee told us . . . he wants to get married. "So far I haven't been married as yet and I'm 47, but that wouldn't stop me. Of course," he

[2] From *Almanac for New Yorkers 1937*, Compiled by Workers of the Federal Writers Project of the Works Progress Administration in the City of New York, p. 121. Copyright, 1936, by Simon and Schuster, Inc. New York.
[3] From "Why Weegee Won't Marry a Brooklyn Girl," by Jean Evans, *PM, Picture News*, Sunday Magazine Section, April 21, 1946. Copyright, 1946, by *PM*. New York.

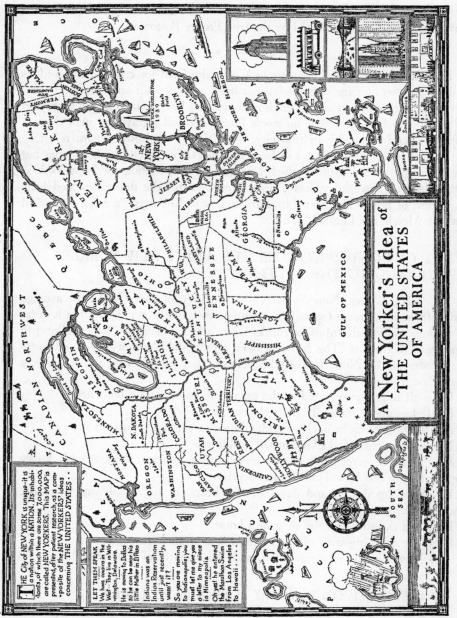

A New Yorker's Idea of THE UNITED STATES OF AMERICA

THE City of NEW YORK is unique—it is a nation within a NATION. Its inhabitants, of which there are some 7,000,000, are called NEW YORKERS. This MAP is presented, after patient research, as a composite of the NEW YORKERS' ideas concerning THE UNITED STATES . .

LET THEM SPEAK
We have cousins in the West. They live in Wilmington, Delaware.

He is moving to Dallas so he can be near his little Mother in Buffalo.

Indiana was an Indian Reservation until just recently, wasn't it?.

So you are moving to Indianapolis; you must let me give you a letter to my niece in Minneapolis.

Oh yes! he entered the Marathon Swim from the Los Angeles to Hawaii . . . . . .

added, "I don't believe in marriage. I'm a free soul. But I'd be glad to humor the girl along and marry her." He paused, then added, "One thing—I don't think I'll find her in Brooklyn."

We wanted to know why not. Weegee, who had been fingering the petals of a pink gladiola, picked up the cigar which had been smoldering on an ash tray beside his bed and puffed vigorously. "Well," he said, "those Brooklyn home girls all belong to the same kind of a society. They all ask the same questions: How much money have you got in the bank? How much do you make? What are your intentions? It tortures my soul," he commented, enjoying the sound of the phrase.

Weegee went on to say that when you take a girl out for the first time "you figure it isn't polite to ask right out, Where do you live?" By the time the evening is over, "you're caught like a rat in a trap. You know she comes from Brooklyn, and you've got to take her home.

"So the safari starts. You become an explorer. She's an Indian guide. She gives directions. You go over Manhattan Bridge. You get to the Flatbush Extension. You start making turns to the right, to the left, east, west, north, south. It's dark and there's no sign of life around you. You hope you're not going to get a flat tire. If you get lost here, nobody will find you.

"She gives you some more directions and then you're in a forest—Prospect Park. You figure, if worst comes to worse, you'll wind up in Coney Island. After all, that's as far as you can go.

"You get out of the wilderness and she tells you, now you got to make a few side trips. You go over roads that nobody has passed over for a hundred years, and then you find her stall. You know you've reached your destination because there's some kind of a house there, and it looks like people live in it.

"In Manhattan," Weegee pointed out, "when you bring a little babe home, you always get a good-night kiss or a little hug. You sit in the car a few minutes and hold hands, and watch the world go by. In Brooklyn"—he shook his head dramatically—"she shakes your hand, says, 'I've had a very pleasant evening,' and tschi, tschi, tschi—" He made a series of little mincing sounds and gestures to indicate her departure to her door.

"HONEYMOON CAPITAL" [4]

A goodly percentage of the citizens of Niagara Falls grow peevish when they hear their city called the Honeymoon Capital. They don't, of course, object to the millions of dollars left behind annually by adoring couples for food, lodging, and the incredible variety of knickknacks displayed in almost countless souvenir shops.

*   *   *   *   *

As long ago as 1850, Niagara Falls—then a small village—was already known as the Honeymoon Capital. Just how it became such an outstanding

[4] From "The Cities of America: Niagara Falls," by Henry F. and Katharine Pringle, *The Saturday Evening Post*, Vol. 221 (October 30, 1948), No. 18, pp. 24-25, 90. Copyright, 1948, by the Curtis Publishing Company. Philadelphia.

attraction for newlyweds is shrouded in mystery. The explanation is probably simple. Its location is central. Some 70 per cent of the population of the United States and Canada live within 500 miles of the Falls. And the cataract has been publicized for at least 200 years by writers, poets, musicians, travelers, and other assorted celebrities. In 1873 one visiting writer suggested a logical basis for the affinity between the Falls and honeymooners:

> The most obvious reason would seem to be that Niagara is the only place which by its vastness can equal the great happiness which is conferred upon those fortunate knights and ladies who have received Cupid's divinest accolade and that only its majestic monotone can be in accord with the blissful harmony which is purring in their united hearts.

Such illuminated prose is typical of those who write about the scenic wonders of Niagara Falls. The innumerable poets who have been inspired to hydraulic verse seem frequently to have lost all semblance of sanity. They tremble, shudder, and shake violently as they contemplate the Falls. Then the stanzas begin to spew in a surge that rivals the crashing flood. Here are some typical examples from an anthology of Niagara Falls poetry:

> Beauteous Queen of Cataracts;
>   Cruel as love and wild as love's first kiss.
>   Ah, God! The abyss.
> Nymph of Niagara! Sprite of the Mist!
> With a wild magic my brow thou hast kissed;
> I am thy slave, and my mistress art thou.
> For thy wild kiss of magic is still on my brow.
>
> Ye massive rocks! Ye rapids in your rush!
>   Ye trembling cataracts! Thou boiling surge!

*   *   *   *   *

An astonishingly large number of the tourists, today and as far back as history is recorded, are fresh from the altar. They stumble about, arm in arm, gazing soulfully at each other and taking pictures madly. The Chamber of Commerce smiles benignly on them and hopes that their numbers will increase still more. To this end it has organized a Niagara Falls Honeymooners' Club to which the qualified are admitted. A certificate signed by Mayor Lupton gives them life membership and declares them entitled "to all the rights and privileges of the organization as long as they both shall live while observing the rules for a happy marriage."

THE PROPER CHARLESTONIANS

I [5]

. . . There were . . . two dear old gentlewomen who were obliged to sell the milk of their cow. (There used to be cows in Charleston's back yards

[5] From *Charleston, A Gracious Heritage,* by Robert Molloy, pp. 9-10, 37-38. Copyright, 1947, by Robert Molloy. New York: Appleton-Century-Crofts, Inc.

not so many years ago before sanitary regulations put a stop to it.) These old ladies had devised a singular system of face-saving. The prospective purchaser of milk left a pitcher or other vessel before a kind of wicket, along with the necessary money. After a suitable interval, a hand would snatch (well, no, not snatch—no Charlestonian lady ever snatched anything)—would take the vessel away and the money, and would later return the former with the milk in it. But neither of these two ladies was ever seen engaging in trade.

* * * * *

Charleston is considered an excessively clannish city, and perhaps that is true now. One of the numerous stories told at the town's expense, and probably, like all good stories of the sort, the invention of a native, is that many years ago a ten-year-old boy was brought there. He grew up into a man, took his place in the community with some distinction, and found the salubrious atmosphere (Chamber of Commerce please note) so favorable to his well-being that he was well in his eighties before he breathed the last of it. When he was buried with proper ceremony, a headstone was erected over his grave. The inscription recited in detail all the interesting facts of his long career in his adopted city, and then, in a burst of approval, added: "Our Most Beloved Stranger."

It's a good story, but that headstone, like the grave of Rhett Butler, is one of the things you will seek in vain in Charleston. . . .

II [6]

When a Charlestonian dies, they don't bury him; they just stand him on the corner of Meeting and Broad.

If the South had only finished the job of seceding from the Union, South Carolina would have seceded from the South, the Low Country would have seceded from South Carolina, Charleston would have seceded from the Low Country, and Charleston below Broad would have seceded from Charleston.

CLEVELAND AND HEAVEN [7]

A story often told in Cleveland, the sixth largest city of the United States, goes like this: A group of Clevelanders have died and are going to heaven. They come to a crossroads. One sign reads: "To Heaven." The other sign says: "To Meeting to Discuss Going to Heaven." The Cleveland party takes the path leading to the meeting.

[6] As told to B. A. Botkin by Raven I. McDavid, Jr., Boulder, Colorado, July 18, 1950.
[7] From "The Cities of America: Cleveland," by Mary Ellen and Mark Murphy, *The Saturday Evening Post*, Vol. 221 (January 1, 1949), No. 27, p. 22. Copyright, 1949, by the Curtis Publishing Company. Philadelphia.

INDIANAPOLIS [8]

Indianap'lis is the city throughout the middle West
As an inland railroad center she is known to be the best;
She is hustling, bustling, thriving, and she's growing ev'ry day,
Indianap'lis, Indianap'lis, in the good old U.S.A.
In the center of our city stands a monument so grand
In mem'ry of the soldiers and the sailors of our land
Who bravely fought and risk'd their lives in battle and at sea
To save our homes, our people, and to set our country free.

CHORUS:

> (In) Indianapolis, (In) Indianapolis, "Indianap'lis no mean city," you can
> hear the people say;
> Indianapolis, Indianapolis, Indianap'lis, Indiana, U.S.A.

Indianapolis, in honor to our dear old "Hoosier State,"
Entertains this year in splendor, Nineteen Sixteen marks the date
Of her Hundreth Annivers'ry, with the good old U.S.A.
And invites you all to join her, in this festival so gay;
Indiana we are proud of you and cheer you One Two Three,
We have ev'ry reason for this pride, in which we all agree
In your cities, towns, and industries and in your people too.
And we, as Indianapolis, take off our hats to you.

Here we have our Hoosier poets, Mister Riley first we call,
As a writer of Child verses, he far excels them all;
Then there is Tarkington and Nicholson whose books are known too well
For need of further mention in this story that we tell.
There was General Lew Wallace, his masterpiece "Ben Hur,"
And close by our Charlie Major wrote "When Knighthood was in Flower."
Most all of them are living, though some have pass'd away,
But in memory they linger, and we think we hear them say—

EXTRA VERSES:

We've our Churches, Schools and Social Clubs, Our Institute of Art,
With Business Clubs, the Baseball League, the State Fair and our Parks,
Our Theatres, Subscribed Concerts, with the Movies, you'll agree—
All give to us the privilege Noted Artists for to see;
We don't lack in entertainment of any style or kind
And we've every opportunity to cultivate the mind;
There's not a better City in this whole United States
Than our *Dear Old Indianapolis,* the City UP-TO-DATE.

You have heard about our BOARD OF TRADE and CHAMBER OF
       COMMERCE—
These are "MEN BEHIND THE GUN," who fight to raise the purse,
To build our COLISEUM and boom our city right—
These are the men who persevere and always win the fight;

---

[8] Words and music by Stella Hall Millikan. Copyright, 1916, by Stella Hall Millikan.
Indianapolis: Published by S. H. Millikan.
    A Booster Song for the Capital of Indiana. Dedicated to "Indianapolis, No Mean City,"
and written in Honor of the Hundredth Anniversary of the admission of the "Hoosier
State" to the U.S.A.

They like to see our city grow, to prosper and to thrive—
To be a "CITY BEAUTIFUL," a City sure alive—
With progress and industry, and, a lot of hustle too—
A City you will sing about—And now it's up to you—

We've our INDIANAPOLIS BOOSTING CLUBS, who are always in the lead,
For boosting they are sure "some bunch" and we know they will succeed;
They are planning, scheming, working to have our city stay
Among the first of Cities in this good old U.S.A.
For *Lincoln Highway*, they did boost, in the interests of our town,
They also boosted for *Mars Hill*, a place of some renown;
They are pushing onward to the front, they're "Johnny on the Spot."
There's not a question in our minds, but what they've done a lot. For—

As a town of Automobiles, we are climbing, don't you know
And every little now and then, we have an AUTO SHOW.
At our last were represented, some hundred cars or more,
Headed by the HOOSIER MOTOR CLUB, of the City we adore;
And our SPEEDWAY auto races, on Decoration Day,
Are an event of interest, and you just can't stay away.
They're a test to motors, science, mechanism, mind of man—
Not alone our Home production, but those of foreign lands. In—

And in this Noted Speedway, that is known from Coast to Coast
We've had something to be proud of and of which we like to boast;
For 'twas said to be the finest and the best one in the land—
Anyway, we're very proud of it and think it very grand.
Built by Indianapolis Business Men of which there are a few,
Who are Natural Born Promoters, and are hustlers through and through.
Some are leading big industries for which our City's famed,
And we lift our hats to these men or at the mention of their name.

We have every kind of industry and factories galore
We have *Banking Firms* to help you save, Trust *Companies and Stores,*
Our daily papers are the NEWS, the TIMES, and morning STAR,
At which you only need to glance, to know *just who* we are:
We're a City of Conventions, and we're known both far and near,
For our Freedom, Hospitality, our welcome and good cheer.
If you're ever welcomed in our midst, for a visit, or to stay,
You will think of us in gladness and with pleasure you will say—

THE LORD AND SPRINGFIELD, ILLINOIS [9]

. . . From certain points of view Springfield was a very unlovely city. Abraham Lincoln often told a story which illustrated its uninviting character. One day a meek-looking man applied to Thompson Campbell who, as Secretary of State, had custody of the State House, for permission to deliver a series of lectures in the Hall of the House of Representatives.

"May I ask," said Campbell, "what is to be the subject of your lectures?"

[9] From *"Here I Have Lived,"* A History of Lincoln's Springfield, 1812-1865, by Paul M. Angle, p. 92. Copyright, 1935, by the Abraham Lincoln Association. New Brunswick, New Jersey: Rutgers University Press.

"Certainly," was the solemn reply, "they are on the second coming of our Lord."

"It's no use," said Campbell, "if you will take my advice you will not waste your time in this city. It is my private opinion that if the Lord has been in Springfield *once*, he will not come the *second time*."

THE PEORIA MYTH: "HICK TOWN" [10]

Except for Brooklyn, no community in the United States has been slandered so elaborately as Peoria, Illinois. Generations of comedians have vulgarized Peoria as the symbol of the rube and the boob, and have used the city's name to establish a suitable background for jokes about libidinous drummers. Peoria has become a companion word for "hayseed," an all-American common denominator, a municipal equivalent of the man in the street.

*   *   *   *   *

That the name of a city so fortunate and fruitful could have been taken in vain so relentlessly for so long is a source of wonder to most Peorians. Some serenely attribute it to the pure melodiousness of the old Indian word, Peoria, a little exotic, but entirely American, which rolls so nicely on the tongue; more are resentful of the implication that "Peoria" is synonymous with "hick town."

"We don't laugh when some one says 'Peoria,' " one of the city's first citizens remarked not long ago when the subject came up for discussion.

Many Peorians date their city's downfall in the national mythology to two masterpieces of libel visited upon them in the early '20's. The first is a scene in a popular play of the period called *Lightnin'*, in which an addlepated girl says mournfully that the only reason she and her husband got married was that they happened to be in Peoria and it rained all week.

The second is a gay little madrigal, written in 1925 by Billy Rose, which was still being sung by soldiers and sailors during the second World War. It is called *I Wish I Was in Peoria*, and it has eight stanzas, all equally derisive, but in several cases remarkably prescient. The last stanza says that "they trim their nails with guns in Peoria," a statement which would not have seemed, at times in the past few years, much of an exaggeration.

Earlier stanzas allege that:

> The present mayor of Peoria
> Works in a five-and-ten cent storia. . . .
> They chased the laundry out of Peoria,
> The legislature passed a lawria
> And bought a bathtub for Peoria.

⁰ From "The Cities of America: Peoria," by Elise Morrow, *The Saturday Evening Post*, Vol. 221 (February 12, 1949), No. 33, pp. 20, 21. Copyright, 1949, by the Curtis Publishing Company. Philadelphia.

MINNEAPOLIS VS. ST. PAUL

I [11]

One Sunday evening a Minneapolis minister started his sermon by saying, "I take my text this evening from St. Paul"; whereupon his congregation rose en masse and filed out of the church, refusing to listen to any such doctrine.

* * * * *

Outsiders still chuckle at the pass made by the Minneapolis business man, when the Chambers of Commerce met at a Twin-City banquet to bury the hatchet once for all. He rehearsed the essential unity of Minneapolis and St. Paul, and concluded, "Even the names of these cities might with advantage be combined. I would suggest, 'Minnehaha.' 'Minne' for Minneapolis, and 'Ha! Ha!' for St. Paul."

II [12]

Inevitably there was fierce rivalry among the frontier towns [of Minnesota]. Everybody considered his town the superior of all others, particularly of neighboring towns. Local citizens tried to promote town growth in every way. They worked for improved navigation on rivers. They subscribed to the building of roads and railroads. In order to entice new industries into their community they gave business sites, bought stock, and promised tax abatement. And they quarreled lustily with the people of nearby towns.

A classic illustration of municipal rivalry is the long-continued fight between Minneapolis and St. Paul. There are rumors that the rivalry has not altogether disappeared even today, but in any event it was active, even virulent, in pioneer days. St. Paul got the earlier start. It was the capital. It had the fur trade. It was the head of Mississippi steamboat navigation. It was a commercial center of great promise. But, ten miles away, St. Anthony and Minneapolis had the promise of the mighty power of the Mississippi tumbling over the rocky ledge at the Falls of St. Anthony, power for turning the wheels of industry in a great manufacturing city. In 1860 St. Paul, with more than ten thousand people, was the metropolis. Minneapolis and St. Anthony together had less than six thousand. Twenty years later, however, the picture had changed, for Minneapolis, which by that time had absorbed old St. Anthony, had 46,000 people to St. Paul's 41,000.

The rivalry of the two cities continued for many years and led almost to a municipal war when the United States census of 1890 was taken. The returns gave Minneapolis 182,967 and St. Paul 142,581. But there was something queer about the census. It turned out that in Minneapolis families had been greatly

[11] From *Adventure Under Sapphire Skies*, by Charles J. Finger, p. 52. Copyright, 1931, by Charles J. Finger. New York: William Morrow & Company.
[12] From *The Land Lies Open*, by Theodore C. Blegen, pp. 130-132. Copyright, 1949, by the University of Minnesota. Minneapolis: University of Minnesota Press.

increased by children and boarders who seemed later to have disappeared. Hundreds of houses were reported that nobody could find, and real houses had been filled with imaginary people. Another curious thing turned up: employees had been counted both at the shops where they worked and in their homes. Officially they led double lives.

St. Paul was virtuously indignant as these disclosures were made. It promptly proposed, as a nickname for its genial twin, the pleasant designation of "Pad City." Unhappily, investigations soon revealed that queer things had happened in St. Paul, too. It appeared, for example, that 275 persons resided in the St. Paul Union Depot. A family of appalling size lived in a downtown dime museum. Ninety-one lodgers resided in the building of an eminent St. Paul newspaper, and sixty-eight lived in a nearby bindery.

Minneapolis was now equally indignant, and its newspapers pointed the finger of shame at the city across the river. So the federal government had to act. The census was taken all over again in both cities, and the sad fact came out that in the first count there had been an exaggeration of 18,000 in the Minneapolis report and of 9,000 in the St. Paul report. One man was actually brought to trial on the charge of having overstated the number of people who lived in the St. Paul Union Depot. But he was tried before a jury of St. Paul citizens. After due deliberation they found him not guilty.

THE TULSA BOOSTER TRAIN [13]

. . . In . . . 1905 the Tulsans had run their first "booster train" to the "exhausted gas fields of the East to bring back factories." One hundred tickets were required for the special train and only eighty-five businessmen signed up. Charley Brown, cashier of the First National, liked to play cowboy and had a pal in Claremore, a rodeo cow hand, just then not working. Brown asked his friend to come along. The friend said he would if his expenses were paid, and the surplus tickets took care of that.

The friend put himself and Tulsa on the map. From St. Louis, the first stop, L. M. Nichols, city editor of the Tulsa *Democrat,* wired back: "The feature of the trip is Bill Rogers' fancy rope juggling. Mr. Rogers is an adept and his exhibitions show he is skilled beyond his reputation. He is the center of attraction in his cowboy outfit."

When the train reached Chicago, the Pullman company was outraged by the canvas banners defacing the exteriors of their sleepers, and haughtily commanded that these be removed before the train should be allowed to depart from the La Salle Street Station. The Tulsans would have complied meekly had not a Chicago reporter counseled them otherwise.

"Defy the Pullman people," he told them. "Issue indignant statements. Say you'll tie up the station. Go around to the Pullman Building and demand to see Robert Lincoln, the president. The longer they hold the train, the more

[13] From "The Cities of America: Tulsa," by Wesley W. Stout, *The Saturday Evening Post,* Vol. 220 (July 5, 1947), No. 1, p. 25. Copyright, 1947, by the Curtis Publishing Company. Philadelphia.

attention you'll attract. When you've had enough, yank the banner down and go your way."

So the Tulsans hoisted their band to the roofs of the Pullmans, directed it to play Dixie, jammed the station, and held the train for two hours. The Chicago evening papers had asked languidly, "What is Tulsa?" and "Ever hear of Tulsa?" on inside pages. The morning papers splashed Tulsa on Page 1.

HOUSTON VS. GALVESTON PORT

I [14]

First of the Seven Wonders of Houston[15] at the mid-point of the twentieth century was neither a building nor a man but an avenue of water, fifty miles long, connecting the Gulf of Mexico and the perspiring Port of Houston. To any one who ever thought about it, the importance to Houston of the Houston Ship Channel is as obvious as the sun on a clear June day. . . .

. . . Cotton and cattle and timber, the first roots of Texan wealth, were partly responsible for . . . lavish living; oil, the fat second root, was even more responsible, and by the 1950s it was enchantingly clear that a newer crop was every bit as responsible as these others. The newer crop was industry, and the Houston Ship Channel was its fertilizer, water, and sun.

For this last benefit, the barons of the bayou could spread their thanks as far back as a day in 1839 when a handful of the first families of Houston raised money through subscription and lotteries to start clearing snags, brush, and overhanging vines from the melting bayou that was to become a dredged, deepwater channel. Three years earlier a small steamer had actually sailed from Galveston to Houston, though it took three days for the tiny vessel to chop its way through the last twelve miles. . . .

*   *   *   *   *

Probably more than anybody else in the nineteenth century, a Yankee named Charles Morgan pivoted the bayou to the status of ship channel, and this mostly because he wanted to finish a fight he had started. The colorful, domineering Morgan owned a prosperous steamship line whose vessels had called at Texas ports since 1835. The Port of Galveston, in the 1860s, was incomparably more important than Houston's port, but by then Morgan was miffed by what he claimed were sky-high port and wharfage rates at Galveston. His feud with officials of the Galveston port looked hopeless for him until he decided to by-pass the island port and bring his ships to Houston. It was a daringly expensive threat, and Morgan carried it out. He bought the city of Houston's

[14] From *Houston: Land of the Big Rich,* by George Fuermann, pp. 142-145. Copyright, 1951, by George Fuermann. Garden City, New York: Doubleday & Company, Inc.

[15] The others: Glenn McCarthy, Hugh Roy Cullen, Jesse Jones, The Shamrock, Foley's, and the Sakowitz Store. Another candidate is the San Jacinto Monument, which honors the heroes of the state's last battle for independence in 1836. Texans, naturally, made their 570-foot monument taller (by fourteen feet) than the Washington Monument.—G.F.

stock in what was called the Houston Direct Navigation Company and forthwith began digging a deep-water channel.

In effect and within a few years, Morgan owned the Port of Houston. Though he died in New York City in 1878, his company continued its virtual ownership of the port and the channel to such a point that until September, 1890, a heavy chain was stretched across the channel and no ship got through without paying a toll to the Morgan interests.

Not all Houstonians were charmed with the idea of having a deep-water port. Opponents of deepening and widening the channel once called it "the most damnable outrage out of doors," but most of the opponents were in Galveston, where shipping interests had realized too late that Houston was draining Galveston's importance as a port in spite of the latter city's impressive geographic advantage. Sampson Heidenheimer, a Galveston merchant, once shipped six barges loaded with salt to Houston. When the whole cargo was washed overboard in a storm, the Galveston *News* gleefully headed its story:

> Houston at Last a Salt-Water Port;
> God Almighty Furnished the Water;
> Heidenheimer Furnished the Salt.

But it was too late for Galveston. An army engineer whose office was in Galveston saw to that. He was Henry M. Robert, a brigadier general who was U.S. division engineer for the Gulf of Mexico from 1895 to 1900, the same Robert who in 1876 had written a sensational best-seller called *Rules of Order*. In 1897 Houstonians asked Robert to recommend to Congress certain improvements to the Houston Ship Channel, and Congress later approved. The work was finally completed in 1914, though Houstonians first had to agree to pay half the cost when Congress fidgeted at appropriating so much money [$2,500,000].

Statistically, the Port of Houston was second in the United States in 1950 in tonnage of imports and exports. . . .

II [16]

As the steamer reached Aransas Pass [Houston], a Galveston man fell overboard. A lifebuoy was thrown him, but he thrust it aside contemptuously. A boat was hurriedly lowered, and reached him just as he came to the surface for the second time. Helping hands were stretched forth to rescue him, but he spurned their aid. He spat out about a pint of sea water and shouted:

"Go away and leave me alone. I'm walking on the bottom. You'll run your boat aground in a minute. I'll wade out when I get ready and go up to a barber shop and get dusted off. The ground's damp a little, but I ain't afraid of catching cold."

He went under for the last time, and the boat pulled back for the shop. The Galveston man had exhibited to the last his scorn and contempt for any other port that claimed deep water.

[16] From *Postscripts*, by O. Henry, with an introduction by Florence Stratton, pp. 29-30. Copyright, 1923, by Houston *Post*; 1923, by Harper & Brothers; 1951, by Sara Coleman Porter. New York.

THE BATTLE OF THE ARCHIVES [17]

. . . Austin, everyone knows, is the political hub of the state; a shining city; a city picturesque. Austin built a dam some twelve hundred feet long (which was carried away by a flood in 1900), and thus Lake MacDonald came into being, a lake on which international regattas were held, in one of which the Australian, Stansbury, won the world championship. And there is this, as an odd piece of history. Sam Houston did not approve of Austin as capital. He wanted the centre to be at Houston, and as President of Texas, in 1842, he called his congress together there. But the people of Austin would not give up their archives and commended Houston to go to the devil, sent his messengers back after treating them with contumely. Thereupon Houston, proud as Lucifer, took a high-handed way with Austin, and sent armed men and a six-pound cannon loaded with grape. The cannon was trained on the government building, and Houston's men went to work loading the archives into three wagons. A woman, experimenting, fired the cannon, and the noise set the citizens to running about like disturbed bees. So the archives were retaken from Houston's men and buried under a log house, and Sam Houston had to manage as best he could. Thus the Battle of the Archives, five days before Christmas in the year 1842. When Texas became a state, the matter of capital location was settled by popular vote. "In them there days," said a hotel keeper to me, "you couldn't put anything over on the people like you can now." He it was who told me the tale of the Battle of the Archives, though he held to a pronunciation peculiar to himself. Archivvies, he called it, nor did I argue that his reading of the word had led to erroneous and fanciful conclusions. . . .

THE ALAMO CITY [18]

San Antonio is called the Alamo City, or the City of the Alamo. The inhabitants are very proud of the Alamo. They consider it a sacred duty to let the stranger know that he is in the city of the Alamo, and ought to be grateful that there is such a place to come to. The first thing that I noticed, when I stepped out at the side-door of the hotel in the morning, was an ice-wagon. I noticed it because the street was not wide enough for both of us, and one of the wheels took a chip off my leg. "Alamo Ice Company" was painted on the side of the wagon. I walked across the plaza to the Alamo drugstore to get some arnica. An aged gentleman sitting in front of the store seemed to take a great deal of interest in my misfortune, and recommended a bottle of Alamo liniment—a medicine patented by the proprietor of the drugstore. The aged gentleman, knowing I was a stranger, volunteered a vast amount of information. "This

[17] From *Adventure Under Sapphire Skies*, by Charles J. Finger, pp. 232-233. Copyright, 1931, by Charles J. Finger. New York: William Morrow & Company.
[18] From *On a Mexican Mustang through Texas, from the Gulf to the Rio Grande*, by Alex E. Sweet and J. Armoy Knox, pp. 286-287. Copyright, 1883, by Sweet and Knox. Hartford: S. S. Scranton & Co., 1884.

is the Alamo plaza," he said, "and that square building in the center of the plaza is the Alamo meat market."

From where I stood I could see the Alamo livery stable, the Alamo cigar store, and the Alamo tin shop. I was told that around the corner I could find the Alamo bakery, the Alamo brewery, the engine house of the Alamo Fire Company, and the rooms of the Alamo Literary Society. The aged gentleman said there was some talk of building an Alamo monument, that the name and fame of the historic spot might be kept before the people; and I could not detect any sarcasm in the tone of his voice when he said it. . . .

MOVING THE ARIZONA LEGISLATURE [19]

The earliest tourists to Phoenix—tourists at the town's expense—were the members of the Territorial Legislature of 1889. This was the legislature which was persuaded to shift the seat of Arizona's government permanently from Prescott to Phoenix. Money had been raised in Phoenix to defray the expenses of moving the legislators and all legislative equipment. By stagecoach the two towns were perhaps 100 miles apart on the old Black Canyon Road. But the statesmen stubbornly disdained any mode of travel except Pullman car. As a result, they and their shabby gripsacks were hauled by rail to Los Angeles—with stopover—from Los Angeles back to Yuma, and from Yuma to Phoenix—a long detour but, by unanimous report, a pleasant and profitable excursion.

The story of the persuading of the legislature, I am told, has not been told fully in the history books. The ethics of the period were a little cloudy. For years the site of the capital had been on the auction block, and apparently Phoenix was able to dig a little deeper than Prescott or Tucson. Even by bald commercial methods, however, energetic Phoenix partisans were able to corral only enough support for a tie vote. One particular malevolent legislator from an outlying county was a sworn enemy, and he could not be bribed. It was a time, obviously, for more subtle planning.

The legislator was a man of forbidding and commanding ego, and he had a glass eye concerning which he evidenced a surprising amount of sensitivity. He was also a man of romantic predilection. A day before the crucial vote, the war council—or so the story goes—engaged a mercenary lady of the town named Jennie to assist them in their project. Jennie was intimately acquainted with the gentleman's habits. It was his custom, before retiring, to deposit his eye in a bedside tumbler of water. On the morning of the vote, he awoke somewhat the worse for the previous night's potations, and searched the tumbler with nervous fingers. It was empty. At once he roused his fair companion and questioned her.

"Oh, that glass!" she said sleepily. "I woke up thirsty in the night, and, do you know, I've been having a crazy dream ever since that I swallowed a marble."

[19] From "The Cities of America: Phoenix," by Milton MacKaye, *The Saturday Evening Post*, Vol. 220 (October 18, 1947), No. 16, p. 93. Copyright, 1947, by the Curtis Publishing Company. Philadelphia.

As the plotters had expected, the legislator refused to appear in public without the eye his false paramour had sequestered. And in the meantime, the vote on the moving of the capital was taken. For many years afterward there were annual stag dinners of the "Jennie Club" in Phoenix, and the uninformed never guessed what made the diners so raucously merry.

BOOM! BOOM! [20]   865704

[In the boom of 1886] the promoters' swiftest road to fortune lay in the "town site." From Los Angeles to the San Bernardino county line, a distance of thirty-six miles, twenty-five "towns" were laid out. Since they averaged more than a mile square, the entire distance was a series of theoretical municipalities. To lead their flocks into these barren pastures, to launch a subdivision where the coyotes howled and tarantulas and centipedes made whoopee, the promoters bought full-page ads in the town's three newspapers. Editors demanded and got cash in hand for these ads. The newspapers, especially the *Times,* reaped a golden harvest. Circulations doubled, quadrupled. Advertising rates went up with them. Machinery, printers, copy-writers, were rushed in. Here is a full page announcement:

Boom!	Boom!
ARCADIA
Boom!	Boom!

Another one begins:

HE OR SHE
That Hesitates is Lost
An axiom that holds good in real estate, as well as in affairs of the heart.
Selah!

Another:

Halt! Halt! Halt!
Speculators and Homeseekers, Attention!
$80,000—Eighty Thousand Dollars—$80,000
Sold in a Day at Marvelous
McGarry Tract

A whole newspaper page advertises a new "town" with a single word:

RAMIREZ!

Page after page, day after day, they appeared:

Catch on before the whole country rushes to Ferndale!
Every man who wishes a home in Paradise should locate
in this, the loveliest district in the whole of Southern
California.

Copy-writers grew delirious in describing the "Lily Langtry" tract at "Vernon."

[20] From *Los Angeles,* by Morrow Mayo, pp. 80-84, 85-86. Copyright, 1933, by Morrow Mayo. New York: Alfred A. Knopf.

Go wing thy flight from star to star
From world to luminous world, as far
As the Universe spreads its flaming wall—
One winter at Vernon is worth them all!

A man named Monroe started "Monrovia," by buying a piece of land and
building himself a house. On May 17, 1886, after appropriate propaganda had
been exerted, an excursion was run to this almost barren piece of mesa land
sloping down from the Sierra Madres, jammed with buyers. Five-acre tracts sold
at two hundred and fifty dollars the acre; lots measuring fifty by a hundred and
fifty feet went with a rush at a hundred dollars—thirty dollars down, the balance
in six months.

Another promoter started "Glendora," naming it after his wife, and at the
first days' sale auctioned off three hundred lots. Placards placed around the bare
land informed prospects.

This is where the orange groves are loveliest!
This is where the grapes are most luxuriant!
This is where the vegetation is grandest!
This is where the flowers are prettiest!

A group of Quakers from Indiana, Iowa, and Illinois started the town of
Whittier, selling four hundred thousand dollars' worth of lots in three days. One
newspaper said of it editorially: "Whittier is the coming place! It will dwarf
Monrovia and eclipse Pasadena. Nothing can stop it! The Quakers are coming
in from all over the United States!" The accompanying advertisement read:

WHITTIER! WHITTIER! WHITTIER!
Queen of the Foothills and Crown of the San Gabriel
Valley!

For every advertisement the newspapers threw in a "news story" to go with it.
Some poet tore off this full-page announcement:

THIS IS PURE GOLD! ! !
SANTA ANA,

The Metropolis of Southern California's Fairest Valley!
Chief Among Ten Thousand, of the One
Altogether Lovely!
Beautiful! Busy! Bustling! Booming! It
Can't be Beat!
The town now has the biggest kind of a
big, big boom.
A Great Big Boom! And you
Can Accumulate ducats by Investing!

Eighty thousand dollars changed hands in two hours when the sale opened. At
"Fullerton," ninety-two thousand dollars swapped owners in half a day.
Another read:

TUSTIN
The Beautiful
Unexcelled in charm and loveliness
An Earthly Eden Unsurpassed in

Wealth of Flower and Foliage.
However, Imagination Cannot Conceive It:
It must be Seen to be Realized!

They ran out of names. One tract was called "Azusa"—taking its name patriotically from the first and last letters of the alphabet, plus U.S.A. It is a pretty little community today, with a big banner across its main street, wishing one and all: "Welcome to Azusa."

Grand Railroad Excursion and Genuine
AUCTION SALE!
No Chenanekin! ! [sic]
Thursday, June 7, 1887.
Beautiful Palomares, Pomona Valley!
Lunch, Coffee, Lemonade, and Ice Water Free!
Full Band of Music!

Under the caption, "Veni, Vidi, Vici!" a full-page advertisement announced that an excursion, "Led by Bartlett's Seventh Infantry Band," would open up

Magnificent Monte Vista!
The Gem of the Mountains!
The Queen of the Valley!

Towns sprang up like mushrooms: Alosta, Gladstone, Glendora, Beaumont, Arcadia, Raymond, Glendale, Burbank, Lamar, Rosecrans, Bethune, Mondonville, Olivewood, Oleander, Lordsburg, Happy Valley, McCoy (advertised as "The Real McCoy!"), Busy Vista, Broad Acres, Ivanhoe, Alta Vista, Nadeau, Bonita, San Dimas, Ballona, Southside, Ontario, Walleria, Ocean Spray—a hundred more. The promoter who started Gladstone announced proudly: "A deed to one lot has been sent to the Prime Minister of England!" Gladstone sold like hot cakes, whereupon another master mind started St. James, advertising it as "extremely English." A hundred vehicles and five hundred persons were engaged in taking care of the mob which rushed to St. James when it opened; they bought forty thousand dollars' worth of lots in thirty minutes.

* * * * *

Maps and literature glorified the about-to-be-opened agricultural tracts. The promoters promised everything. The land would grow anything, and beneath the surface there was probably iron ore and oil, perhaps silver and gold. Brass bands rode through the streets in cable-cars, hay-wagons, and carriages, followed by fantastic parades a block long, with signs and banners announcing a new location. Martial music filled the air. Elephants and giraffes, lions and tigers, human freaks (the remnant of a stranded circus), were used as magnets. The blarings and blastings lasted all through the day and into the night. Hordes of prospects were loaded into buses and wagons and, preceded by the animals, the freaks, and the music, escorted out to where the virgin lots lay in the sun, marked off with American flags.

Here were long groaning tables, laden with free lunch—anybody could come and eat all he wished. Lots were raffled off, drawn by lottery, offered on wheels of fortune. Free music, free entertainment, free rides, and free food; it was the hobo's heaven. Sharpers and swindlers, gamblers and touts, prostitutes and evangelists, patent-medicine vendors and pickpockets bore down from the East and from the North along the coast, eager to share in the carnival spirit and the flow of loose money. . . .

SAN FRANCISCO VS. LOS ANGELES [21]

. . . The rivalry between San Francisco and Los Angeles is, of course, legendary. San Franciscans, however, don't like to think of themselves as competing with the city 400 miles to the south; they regard the latter as an upstart collection of villages. This was dramatized recently by a San Franciscan who went to Los Angeles for the weekend. When it came time to return, he went to the latter's railroad station and asked for "a ticket to town."

MINIMIZING SOUTHERN CALIFORNIA EARTHQUAKES [22]

It is not the desert that haunts the imagination of Southern California; there is an abiding fear of earthquakes. While taking elaborate precautions against earthquakes (such as ordinances limiting the height of buildings), Southern California amusingly minimizes the actual dangers involved. In a Santa Barbara booster book written in 1919, Lelia Weekes Wilson wrote that "a real earthquake has not been felt here for over a hundred years, so the danger from seismic disturbances need cause little worry." On June 29, 1925, Santa Barbara was nearly shaken asunder by a major earthquake. An investigator's manual, issued by a bondhouse in Los Angeles in 1939, glibly assures the investor that "California will not experience an earthquake exceeding materially the violence of that which occurred in San Francisco in 1906." Not only are earthquakes seldom mentioned in the history books, but, when mentioned, they are usually praised:

> We have an earthquake
> Now and again
> To let the people know
> God's greater than the men.

Let some Middle-Western city be inundated by flood waters, let some Florida community be devastated by a tornado, and the Los Angeles *Times* can be relied upon to publish a pious editorial stressing the fact that, after all, earthquakes are "not so bad." In an editorial of October 2, 1933, the San Bernadino *Sun* even contended that "an earthquake never killed any one." On one occasion when a flood in Tennessee had resulted in considerable loss of life and the wire services were carrying stories about "mangled victims being recovered from the turbulent waters," the *Times* ran a lengthy editorial pointing

[21] From "Powell Street—The Spirit of San Francisco," by Roul Tunley, *The American Magazine*, Vol. 157 (February, 1954), No. 2, p. 83. Copyright, 1954, by the Crowell-Collier Publishing Company. New York.

[22] From *Southern California Country*, An Island on the Land, by Carey McWilliams, pp. 200-202. Copyright, 1946, by Carey McWilliams. New York: Duell, Sloan & Pearce, Inc.

out that, while earthquakes do occasionally take human lives, the victims are never mangled. The editorial prompted Duncan Aikman to dash off the lines:

> The blessed dead of Tennessee
> Make blyther heads for you and me.
> Each Nashville babe in heaven that wakes
> Blows down the blurb of local quakes.
>
> This week the choicest news bears out
> That others catch it on the snout,
> And though our losses be more numerous,
> We find Confederate dead more humorous.
>
> Let storm and quake, then, leave us gory all,
> Cheer up and read our editorial;
> Tornadoes twist 'em; earthquakes mangle less
> The population near Los Angeles.

Following the disastrous earthquake of March 10, 1933, which caused $40,000,000 property damage and took many lives, the Los Angeles City Council adopted a resolution thanking the Almighty for a disaster which had demonstrated, once again, the warmhearted and generous character of the population of Southern California. The resolution went on to emphasize that the earthquake had overcome local civic rivalries and had created new bonds of friendship between Los Angeles and Long Beach. . . .

PAPER CITY [23]

. . . On May 1, 1890, according to the press of a goodly part of the new State of Washington, there ". . . sprang into being a city that will challenge the great ports and industrial centers of the Atlantic coast. . . . Three hundred city lots were sold on the day Ocosta threw open her gates to the world."

For at least three months before her gates were thrown ajar, Ocosta's name had been constantly in those daily and weekly papers which were, as the opposition papers had it, creatures of the Northern Pacific Railway interests. Such papers reported quite truthfully that Ocosta had been selected as the terminal city of the nearly complete Tacoma & Grays Harbor Railroad, a subsidiary of the Northern Pacific. The site was described as being "as logical as it is beautiful," and on the south shore of Grays Harbor on the Washington coast. This was truly a terrible piece of news to the citizens of Hoquiam and Aberdeen, both also on Grays Harbor; furthermore, both were going concerns, complete with mayors, police and fire departments, and schools. Both were doing a big business making lumber and shipping it to China and the Antipodes by seagoing vessels which could dock at any or all of the score of sawmills and shingle mills. Yet neither Hoquiam nor Aberdeen had a railroad.

Now came this new, this only railroad (in which, incidentally, a number of Hoquiam and Aberdeen citizens had purchased stock on the assumption that it

[23] From *Far Corner*, A Personal View of the Pacific Northwest, by Stewart H. Holbrook, pp. 133-136. Copyright, 1952, by Stewart H. Holbrook. New York: The Macmillan Company.

was to tap their towns), and elected to pass up, or by, those established cities and build its own metropolis. Wickedness could go no farther.

After three months of typical build-up, the promoters of Ocosta-by-the-Sea, as it was officially known, invited their friendly newspaper editors to visit the place "on the inclosed pass from the City Committee of Ocosta." Cut-rate transportation was offered to "all interested parties," by which was meant everybody who wanted to get in on the ground floor by buying a city lot or two, now, while prices were at rock bottom.

More than a thousand people arrived at Ocosta on that delirious 1st of May. (For months to come there would be other excursions.) Most of them must have noticed that while prices might be low, they could not be said to be at rock

THE CITY OF NEW BABYLON ON PAPER.

bottom. There was no rock bottom to Ocosta. It was all marsh, a wild, desolate expanse of reeds, coarse grass, seaweed and kelp, dotted, at low tide, with barnacled boulders. There were hundreds of acres of swamp. Indeed, Editor McDonald of the (unfriendly) Snohomish *Eye* declared the place should have been called the Great Dismal Swamp, and called it such in an editorial as soon as he returned to his sanctum.

The visitors to this metropolis saw that the swamp was lined and crossed with miles of raised plank walks. Starting near the end of the railroad, the planks seemed to stretch out to the horizon, and beyond. But what struck them more was that the wooden walks were lined, and most symmetrically, with handsome fir and cedar trees, not great trees, to be sure, but all of them ten or more feet tall. They looked mighty pretty. Skeptics, however, who were impressed less with the beauty of the saplings than with the fact that they should be there at all, in such terrain, and took the trouble to look, saw that the trees had been firmly spiked to the wooden stringers of the sidewalks at graceful intervals of about sixteen feet. They had been cut elsewhere than in swampy Ocosta, toted in by team, then raised and spiked one by one to the boardwalks. The trees were symbolic of Ocosta. They were rootless.

Yet more than three hundred of the visitors on that May day in 1890 believed in Ocosta as the City of Destiny, as advertised. They bought one or more city lots, or industrial sites, and went away, happy to be in on the ground floor, marshy though it might be. More gulls came later, by the cut-rate excursions, and they too bought Ocosta property. Men who described themselves as industrialists arrived to say they planned to build, respectively, a sawmill, a shingle mill, a brewery, a business block, a livery stable, a streetcar line, a gasworks. Man alive, it was wonderful the way Ocosta-by-the-Sea was going ahead. . . .

Whether or not Ocosta would have grown into Metropolis is to be doubted. In any case its fate was sealed presently by the he-men of Aberdeen, one of the two established towns which the railroad had by-passed. These stouthearted pioneers of Aberdeen set out to build their own one mile of railroad to connect with the Northern Pacific at a place they called Grays Harbor Junction. To do it, they salvaged rails from the wrecked bark *Abercorn*, which had providentially sunk in the harbor, and though the steel was pitted from six years in salt water it was still usable.

The spirit was cheering to behold. Pioneer Samuel Benn donated a city lot in Aberdeen to every man who helped clear the right of way and lay the rails. Pioneers Charles Wilson and A. J. West donated the ties. Pioneer J. M. Weatherwax salvaged and donated the rails. Citizens turned out by the hundreds and labored like beavers. Their wives fetched food, set up camp, and fed their men as the grade proceeded. And on went the rails. The one mile of track was laid without hitch, and at record speed.

By then the promoters of Ocosta were ready to quit. They dropped their paper city and were glad to run their trains to Aberdeen, and a little later to Hoquiam. The rails to Ocosta rusted a while, then were taken up.

Thirty years later, when I first saw the place, the wind swept wildly across the wastes called Ocosta-by-the-Sea. The only gulls there were sea-gulls. Two hulks of battered frame buildings leaned and shook to the blasts off the harbor. There was not even a windbreak of spiked trees to soften the ordeal. Complete melancholy blanketed the City of Destiny.

THE CITY OF NEW BABYLON IN FACT.

III. I'm a Stranger Here Myself

As individual cities have their legends, so the city in general has its mythology. Of the many myths that have grown up about the city as image and symbol, the oldest and most potent is the "lure of the city." Here belongs the myth of the city as a place of opportunity, of streets paved with gold, where the small-town boy hopes to make good and the immigrant seeks the promised land. Combined with the larger American "rags-to-riches," "get-rich-quick" myth, the "City of Golden Opportunity" (a new version of El Dorado) was a powerful factor in the rise of the city during the 1880s and again after World War I, when the theme song became "How You Gonna Keep 'em Down on the Farm after They've Seen Paree?" As in this song, however, the emphasis often shifts from dreams of wealth, success and power to dreams of pleasure and the related myth of the city as siren rather than magnet—the "Wicked City."

Rivaling the wide-open spaces as our national myth, the wide-open city took over many of the images and symbols associated with the frontier. About the figure of the stranger and the sucker has grown up the folklore of hick vs. city slicker, greenhorn vs. native-born or naturalized American, and dude or summer visitor vs. rustic. Variant themes are the country man who turns the tables on the city slicker and the city dweller who is just as gullible as the hick. Underlying these stereotypes are the older traditions of the comic "country man in the great world," the newcomer-fool and the trickster tricked.

Back of the battle of wits between greenhorn and sharper (who sells him variously a gold brick, the Brooklyn Bridge, the Woolworth Building, Grant's Tomb, the Information Booth in Grand Central Terminal for a fruit stand) is the deep-seated antagonism between the rural and urban ways of life. To the honest, simple, hard-working farmer the city has always appeared or been made to appear as a den of iniquity, luring the young and innocent to their ruin and the unwary into treacherous tricks and traps. In the United States rural-urban antagonism has also had a philosophical and economic basis in the agrarian tradition. Especially in the South and the West, with their colonial economy, the farmer's resentment of the city dandy's fine manners and fine living has been focused on bankers and monopolists and on Wall Street as their symbol.

With the metropolitan invasion of the country has come a second stage of urbanization, in which city folk and city folkways have been put in the country. Urban overcrowding and depression have increased the flight from the city to the suburbs and urban areas and "back to the farm," with the nation today divided not so much between city and country as between city and small town or suburb. About the commuter, the suburbanite and a new transient population on the move from city to city has sprung up a new folklore in the making—of an uprooted and schizophrenic America, midway between the nomadic and the settled, the metropolitan and the provincial.

For the uprooted immigrant the miracle of America and the synonymous wonders of the city have both often proved as illusory as alluring. And the disillusioned immigrant's resentment against America as a land of

42

"bluffers," "snobs" and "bums" became concentrated on cities. When the Macedonian immigrant in St. Louis writes of his fellow countrymen who had fallen victims to Americamania, "America put greed in their hearts and cleverness in their minds," "America" is synonymous with "the city." And "I'm a stranger here myself" gives way to "You'll always be a stranger here."

THE ROBBER INN [1]

As we drew near to New York I was at first amused, and then somewhat staggered, by the cautious and the grisly tales that went the round. You would have thought we were to land upon a cannibal island. You must speak to no one in the streets, as they would not leave you till you were rooked and beaten. You must enter a hotel with military precautions; for the least you had to apprehend was to awake next morning without money or baggage, or necessary raiment, a lone forked radish in a bed; and if the worst befell, you would instantly and mysteriously disappear from the ranks of mankind.

I have usually found such stories correspond to the least modicum of fact. Thus I was warned, I remember, against the roadside inns of the Cévennes, and that by a learned professor; and when I reached Pradelles, the warning was explained—it was but the far-away rumor and reduplication of a single terrifying story already half a century old, and half forgotten in the theater of the events. So I was tempted to make light of these reports against America. But we had on board with us a man whose evidence it would not do to put aside. He had come near these perils in the body; he had visited a robber inn. The public has an old and well-grounded favor for this class of incident, and shall be gratified to the best of my power.

My fellow-passenger, whom we shall call M'Naughten, had come from New York to Boston with a comrade, seeking work. They were a pair of rattling blades; and, leaving their baggage at the station, passed the day in beer-saloons, and with congenial spirits, until midnight struck. Then they applied themselves to find a lodging, and walked the streets till two, knocking at houses of entertainment and being refused admittance, or themselves declining the terms. By two, the inspiration of their liquor had begun to wear off; they were weary and humble, and after a great circuit found themselves in the same street where they had begun their search, and in front of a French hotel where they had already sought accommodation. Seeing the house still open, they returned to the charge. A man in a white cap sat in an office by the door. He seemed to welcome them more warmly than when they had first presented themselves, and the charge for the night had somewhat unaccountably fallen from a dollar to a quarter. They thought him ill-looking, but paid their quarter apiece, and were shown up-stairs to the top of the house. There, in a small room, the man in the white cap wished them pleasant slumbers.

It was furnished with a bed, a chair, and some conveniences. The door did

[1] From *The Amateur Emigrant: The Silverado Squatters*, by Robert Louis Stevenson, pp. 104-107. Copyright, 1895, by Stone & Kimball; 1905, by Charles Scribner's Sons. New York, 1923.

not lock on the inside; and the only sign of adornment was a couple of framed pictures, one close above the head of the bed, and the other opposite the foot, and both curtained, as we may sometimes see valuable water-colors, or the portraits of the dead, or works of art more than usually skittish in the subject. It was perhaps in the hope of finding something of this last description that M'Naughten's comrade pulled aside the curtain of the first. He was startlingly disappointed. There was no picture. The frame surrounded, and the curtain was designed to hide, an oblong aperture in the partition, through which they looked forth into the dark corridor. A person standing without could easily take a purse from under the pillow, or even strangle a sleeper as he lay abed. M'Naughten and his comrade stared at each other like Vasco's seamen, "with a wild surmise"; and then the latter, catching up the lamp, ran to the other frame and roughly raised the curtain. There he stood, petrified; and M'Naughten, who had followed, grasped him by the wrist in terror. They could see into another room, larger in size than that which they occupied, where three men sat crouching and silent in the dark. For a second or so these five persons looked each other in the eyes, then the curtain was dropped, and M'Naughten and his friend made but one bolt of it out of the room and downstairs. The man in the white cap said nothing as they passed him; and they were so pleased to be once more in the open night that they gave up all notion of a bed and walked the streets of Boston till the morning.

DANGEROUS NEW ORLEANS [2]

"They may talk of New Orleans," said a countryman, in our presence, just before the Jeff Davis Rebellion, "as a quiet city, and all that; but I look upon it as a *leetle* the most dangerous one that ever I made tracks in. To be sure I don't see many Bowie knives, except among the Thugs and the police, and I ain't got robbed yet; but I wish I may hoe corn with a cob-handled shovel if they ain't got something that touches the heart straight out afore I could split a shingle."

"What's that?" says Trap, as he stepped up. "Can I assist you in any way?"

"Halloo!" said the countryman, "who are you? I don't know you, but I like your face monstrous well. Give us your axholder!"

Trap gave him his hand.

"Wal, you see, stranger," continued the countryman, "I was thinking to myself, and bla-a-ting right out, I suppose, but no matter. I'm in a bad way, if I have got a flat boat and plenty of Tennessee money, for I have only tracked two streets in this town and my bosom is riddled like a sieve."

"Riddled!" exclaimed Trap. "Every man's bosom is a riddle for that matter. Can't you unriddle yours?"

"Maybe you mean fun," said the countryman. "If so, I mean fight!"

Trap said he meant just what was "right" in Kentucky.

[2] From *Wehman's Bits of Humor, or Drolleries of Human Nature,* Containing a Rich Lot of Comical Stories . . . , p. 9. New York: Henry J. Wehman. [N.D.]

The countryman cooled down. "Now," said he, "I mean just this: I've got a wife and several children to hum; wife's a good woman; and——"

"A very necessary article in every family," said Trap.

"Hush your meat trap!" said the countryman. "Wife's a good woman, and I love her next to the 'bar killer,' my old rifle. But if she ain't in just about as skeery a way as I ever seed a young fawn, there'll be no corn for the hogs next winter."

"How? What do you mean?" asked Trap.

"Why, stranger, I reckon I never drew a bead on quite so many handsome gals since Moses, as I have yesterday and today. I start 'em up all over the town. There they stand just like fat b'ars on the balconies, and by the winders, a-looking with their sweet eyes, something like wounded deer, all so pityful and sorrow-like. It makes my heart jump like a frightened rabbit. I'm afeared I'm a lost man. I don't care a cuss for my flatboat and bacon, and when I think about my cabin in the woods, I e'en a'most wish 'twas burnt up. I'm sure I wish I had never married and had no children, for I'm inclined to 'squat' somewhere near Orleans, if I could find some government land."

"Oh," said Trap, "you'd better give up thinking about our women. They wouldn't suit you nohow. There isn't one in forty that ever saw a deer, or could tell a fawn from a weasel. And besides, they paint their faces sometimes, just like Indians. Most o' their hair is false, they can't dress themselves, nor make a dish of hominy."

"Is that true?" asked the countryman, opening his eyes.

"As true and as strong as lye," replied Trap.

"Thank God!" replied the countryman. "Wife's safe, and all the little ones. And if I don't carry home a new rifle for my eldest boy and a new red petticoat for my Nabby Jane, my name's not Pipple. Let's liquor!"

And with this Trap and his rough and astonished friend parted. The countryman muttered to himself: "Gals painted like Injuns, false hair, can't cook—wife and little ones are safe, thank God!"

THE TWO NEVADA NABOBS IN NEW YORK [3]

In Nevada there used to be current the story of an adventure of two of her nabobs, which may or may not have occurred. I give it for what it is worth:

Col. Jim had seen somewhat of the world, and knew more or less of its ways; but Col. Jack was from the back settlements of the States, had led a life of arduous toil, and had never seen a city. These two, blessed with sudden wealth, projected a visit to New York—Col. Jack to see the sights, and Col. Jim to guard his unsophistication from misfortune. They reached San Francisco in the night, and sailed in the morning. Arrived in New York, Col. Jack said:

[3] From *Roughing It*, by Samuel L. Clemens, Vol. II, pp. 54-58. Entered according to Act of Congress, in the year 1871, by the American Publishing Company, in the Office of the Librarian of Congress at Washington. Copyright, 1899, by the American Publishing Company; 1899, by Samuel L. Clemens. New York: Harper & Brothers. 1903.

"I've heard tell of carriages all my life, and now I mean to have a ride in one; I don't care what it costs. Come along."

They stepped out on the sidewalk, and Col. Jim called a stylish barouche. But Col. Jack said:

"No, sir! None of your cheap-John turnouts for me. I'm here to have a good time, and money ain't any object. I mean to have the nobbiest rig that's going. Now here comes the very trick. Stop that yaller one with the pictures on it— don't you fret, I'll stand all the expenses myself."

So Col. Jim stopped an empty omnibus, and they got in. Said Col. Jack:

"Ain't it gay, though? Oh no, I reckon not! Cushions, and windows, and pictures, till you can't rest. What would the boys say if they could see us cutting a swell like this in New York? By George, I wish they *could* see us!"

Then he put his head out of the window, and shouted to the driver:

"Say, Johnny, this suits *me!*—suits yours truly, you bet, you! I want this shebang all day. I'm *on* it, old man! Let 'em out! Make 'em go! We'll make it all right with *you,* sonny!"

The driver passed his hand through the straphole, and tapped for his fare —it was before the gongs came into common use. Col. Jack took the hand, and shook it cordially. He said:

"You twig me, old pard! All right between gents. Smell of *that,* and see how you like it!"

And he put a twenty-dollar gold piece in the driver's hand. After a moment the driver said he could not make change.

"Bother the change! Ride it out. Put it in your pocket."

Then to Col. Jim, with a sounding slap on his thigh:

"Ain't it style, though? Hanged if I don't hire this thing every day for a week!"

The omnibus stopped, and a young lady got in. Col. Jack stared a moment, then nudged Col. Jim with his elbow:

"Don't say a word," he whispered. "Let her ride if she wants to. Gracious, there's room enough!"

The young lady got out her porte-monnaie, and handed her fare to Col. Jack.

"What's this for?" said he.

"Give it to the driver, please."

"Take back your money, madam. We can't allow it. You're welcome to ride here as long as you please, but this shebang's chartered, and we can't let you pay a cent."

The girl shrunk into a corner, bewildered. An old lady with a basket climbed in, and proffered her fare.

"Excuse me," said Col. Jack. "You're perfectly welcome here, madam, but we can't allow you to pay. Set right down there, mum, and don't you be the least uneasy. Make yourself just as free as if you was in your own turnout."

Within two minutes three gentlemen, two fat women, and a couple of children entered.

"Come right along, friends," said Col. Jack; "don't mind *us.* This is a free blowout." Then he whispered to Col. Jim: "New York ain't no sociable place, I don't reckon—it ain't no *name* for it."

He resisted every effort to pass fares to the driver, and made everybody cordially welcome. The situation dawned on the people, and they pocketed their money, and delivered themselves up to covert enjoyment of the episode. Half a dozen more passengers entered.

"Oh, there's *plenty* of room!" said Col. Jack. "Walk right in, and make yourselves at home. A blowout ain't worth anything *as* a blowout unless a body has company." Then in a whisper to Col. Jim: "But *ain't* these New-Yorkers friendly? And ain't they cool about it, too? Icebergs ain't anywhere. I reckon they'd tackle a hearse if it was going their way."

More passengers got in; more yet, and still more. Both seats were filled, and a file of men were standing up, holding on to the cleats overhead. Parties with baskets and bundles were climbing up on the roof. Half-suppressed laughter rippled up from all sides.

"Well, for clean, cool, out-and-out cheek, if this don't bang anything that ever I saw, I'm an Injun!" whispered Col. Jack.

A Chinaman crowded his way in.

"I weaken!" said Col. Jack. "Hold on, driver! Keep your seats, ladies and gents. Just make yourselves free—everything's paid for. Driver, rustle these folks around as long as they're a mind to go—friends of ours, you know. Take them everywheres—and if you want more money, come to the St. Nicholas, and we'll make it all right. Pleasant journey to you, ladies and gents—go it just as long as you please—it sha'n't cost you a cent!"

The two comrades got out, and Col. Jack said:

"Jimmy, it's the sociablest place I ever saw. The Chinaman waltzed in as comfortable as anybody. . . . B' George, we'll have to barricade our doors tonight, or some of these ducks will be trying to sleep with us!"

BILL NYE'S LETTER FROM NEW YORK [4]

Dear Friend—Being Sunday, I take an hour to write you a letter in regard to this place. I came here yesterday without attracting undue attention from people who lived here. If they was surprised, they concealed it from me.

I've camped out on the Chug years ago, and went to sleep with no live thing near me except my own pony, and woke up with the early song of the coyote, and have been on the lonesome plain for days where it seemed to me that a hostile would be mighty welcome if he would only say something to me, but I was never so lonesome as I was here in this big town last night, although it is the most thick settled place I was ever at.

I was so kind of low and depressed that I strolled in to the bar at last, allowing that I could pound on the counter and call up the boys and get acquainted a little with somebody, just as I would at Col. Luke Murrin's, at Cheyenne; but when I waved to the other parties, and told them to rally round the foaming beaker, they apologized and allowed they had just been to dinner.

Just been to dinner, and there it was pretty blamed near dark! Then I asked 'em to take a cigar, but they mostly cackillated they had no occasion.

[4] From *Remarks*, by Bill Nye (Edgar W. Nye), pp. 350-351. Copyright, 1891, by Edgar W. Nye. Chicago: Thompson & Foutz, Publishers.

I was mad, but what could I do? They was too many for me, and I couldn't coerce the white livered aristocratic mob, for quicker'n scat they could have hollered into a little cupboard they had there in the corner, and in less'n two minits they'd of had the whole police department and the hook and ladder company down there after me with a torch-light procession.

So I swallowed my wrath and a tame drink of cultivated whisky with Apollo Belvidere on the side, and went out into the auditorium of the hotel.

Here I was very unhappy, being, as the editor of the Green River *Gazette* would say, "the cynosure of all eyes."

I would rather not be a cynosure, even at a good salary; so I thought I would ask the proprietor to build a fire in my room. I went up to the recorder's office, where the big hotel autograft album is, and asked to see the proprietor.

A good-looking young man came forward and asked me what he could do for me. I said if it wouldn't be too much trouble, I wisht he would build a little fire in my room, and I would pay him for it; or, if he would show me where the woodpile was, I would build the fire myself—I wasn't doing anything special at that time.

He then whistled through his teeth and crooked his finger in a shrill tone of voice to a young party who was working for him, and told him to "build a fire in four-ought-two."

I then sat down in the auditorium and read out of a railroad tract, which undertook to show that a party that undertook to ride over a rival road must do so because life was a burden to him, and facility and comfort and safety and such things no object whatever. But still I was very lonely, and felt as if I was far, far away from home.

I couldn't have been more uncomfortable if I'd been a young man I saw twenty-five years ago on the old overland trail. He had gone out to study the Indian character, and to win said Indian to the fold. When I next saw him he was twenty miles farther on. He had been thrown in contact with said Indian in the meantime. I judged he had been making a collection of Indian arrows. He was extremely no more. He looked some like Saint Sebastian and some like a toothpick holder.

I was never successfully lost on the plains, and so I started out after supper to find my room. I found a good many other rooms, and tried to get into them, but I did not find four-ought-two till a late hour; then I subsidized the night patrol on the third floor to assist me.

This is a nice place to stop, but it is a little too rich for my blood, I guess. Not so much as regards price, but I can see that I am beginning to excite curiosity among the boarders. People are coming here to board just because I am here, and it is disagreeable. I do not court notoriety. I have always lived in a plain way, and I would give a dollar if people would look the other way while I eat my pie.

                                        Yours truly, E.O.D.

To E. WM. NYE, Esq.

P.S. This is not a dictated letter. I left my stenograffer and revolver at Pumpkin Buttes.   E.O.D.

NED UNDERHILL AND THE POCKETBOOK DROPPER [5]

No man, boy or green-horn was ever yet victimized by the Pocket-Book Droppers, the Thimble-Riggers, or the Patent-Safe men, who didn't have so strong a spice of the scamp in his own composition as to think he was coming a sure and profitable swindle upon some one not up to his own level of sharpness and treachery. These three games are all levelled at that particular trait of human nature which makes men desire to grab and pocket somebody's spare cash, without rendering an equivalent therefor; and the very reason why so many persons are losers by them, is that the great majority of mankind are so highly seasoned with roguery that it comes to the surface with the slightest provocation. There are hundreds of men pretending to be civilized, who although they wouldn't commit murder or highway robbery, and probably wouldn't pick pockets for fear of being detected in that fashionable recreation, would, nevertheless, pocket a man's last dime without remorse, if they could get hold of it under color of a bet or a bargain. One of the permitted amusements of a good Christian is to keep a sharp eye on these would-be-sharpers, and to laugh clean down to his toe-nails when he sees one of them out-sharped; and great is the rejoicing of his charitable heart when he beholds those who go out for wool come home shorn.

Pocket-Book Dropping may be almost considered as one of the by-gones; it being very seldom attempted except in cases of very aggravated verdancy on the part of the victim. It is always done in the same manner, and the tools necessary for the perfect performance of this little comedy are a green-horn, one, or perhaps two sharpers, and an old pocket-book full of counterfeit or broken bank bills.

Perhaps the best way to give an idea of the plan, is to detail the experience of an individual whom we will call Ned Underhill, and which one circumstance is only one of twenty years' series of verdant things in which Underhill aforesaid, has been engaged all his life.

When Ned first came to New York, in 1849, before he had got the hay-seed out of his hair, he was one day strolling up Chatham street, . . . when suddenly a pocket-book was dropped at his feet, and as suddenly picked up by a well-dressed young man who was apparently in a furious hurry.

The well-dressed young man asked Ned if it was his pocket-book. The devil in Ned's checked shirt-bosom suggested that he should say "Yes," and pocket the book without further question, but somehow he actually said "No," a piece of unpremeditated honesty which quite took him by surprise. The well-dressed young man walked by his side, and opened the treasure, disclosing to the astonished gaze of Ned a number of bills of the denomination of tens, twenties and fifties.

"Very strange," said the stranger, "here, I must leave the city on the first train, and what to do with this money I really don't know. There seems to be

[5] From *Tricks and Traps of New York City*, Part I, pp. 24-27. Brainard's Dime Books. Boston: Charles H. Brainard, 1857.

several hundred dollars of it; it will of course be advertised in the morning, and a large reward offered; it's too bad that I can't stay to get it; no one will think of offering less than one hundred dollars for the recovery, and I must go to New Haven on the next train, for my poor uncle is dying."

Ned couldn't volunteer any aid, for he didn't feel exactly delicate about offering to relieve the man either of his newly found treasure or his dying uncle. But a sudden thought came to the stranger, and he acted upon it instantly. Turning to Ned, he again spoke, "See here, friend, you look like an honest man, and I feel that I can trust this matter with you. I'll give you this money, and divide the reward with you. Give me fifty dollars, and in the morning you can restore it to the owner and pocket the full reward."

This suited Ned's complaint exactly, but he hadn't the fifty; however, he raked out twenty-seven dollars and a silver watch, which he passed over to the accommodating stranger, and received the pocket-book, while the man with the dying uncle made tracks into the dim distance.

The honest Underhill tucked the treasure under his checked shirt, hugged it to his heart, fully intending to appropriate the entire amount to his own private use, and hurried to his room at his cheap Greenwich street tavern, where he locked himself in and proceeded to count his treasure-trove.

The sequel can of course be imagined. There were bank-bills to the amount of two hundred dollars, Wild Cat Michigan money, broke all to flinders fourteen months before, and worth about a dollar and a half a ton. The remaining bulk was made up of fly-leaves torn out of a shilling Testament.

My gentle Edwin was sold; my gentle Edwin forgot his gentleness and swore fearfully; but no amount of profanity, however excusable under the circumstances, could bring back that twenty-seven dollars, good money—could restore that silver watch, or give him a single minute's private interview with the gentleman who was in such a hurry to get to New Haven to see his respected uncle kick the bucket.

This is the whole mystery of the pocket-book game; the complete thing reduced to a point—the entire secret boiled down to half a gill, so that it can be taken at a dose, and thoroughly cure our readers of any liability to be imposed upon and humbugged by New York Pocket-Book Droppers.

BUNKO STEERERS [6]

Sharpers may be found at every street corner, who assume the appearance of business men by rushing hither and thither as though some immense enterprise, beneficial to the entire world, was depending upon their activity.

The rural or provincial visitor who, with well-stored purse, goes down to New York on business or pleasure, is very liable to become a victim to the mendacity of sharks and his own egregious purblindness. This is how it is done:

[6] From *Metropolitan Life Unveiled:* or the Mysteries and Miseries of America's Great Cities, embracing New York, Washington City, San Francisco, Salt Lake City, and New Orleans, by J. W. Buel, pp. 129-131. Copyright, 1882, by Historical Publishing Co. St. Louis.

Brown, who is well-dressed but gawkish in manner, strolls down Broadway until he suddenly runs into a dapper young fellow of very gentle and sociable appearance. "Hello! Smith," he exclaims, "how are you, and how are all the folks out at Chicago?"

Brown is taken by surprise, and deferentially explains that his name is not Smith, nor is he from Chicago, but that he hails from Oshkosh, where everybody knows him as plain Jim Brown.

"Well, I was never so surprised in all my life; why, you are the very image of John Smith, of Chicago, who is one of the richest men of that place. Well, I'll declare, I've often heard it said that there are no two persons alike, but I don't believe in the saying. I used to know some people of Oshkosh, but it's been a long time since I was there. By the way, who runs the biggest bank in Oshkosh now? Tom Parker, did you say? Why, that's so, I remember now; he's got a nephew up here in Chatham Square, and he is at the head of a big business too; some of the finest paintings in New York are in his establishment. You ought to go up and see him, for I am sure he would be glad to learn directly from you all about his uncle."

The dapper young fellow has talked very rapidly with Brown, and before the conversation is concluded the names of many rich people of Oshkosh are made known to the bunko steerer, who finally parts with Brown, giving him a cordial shake and an invitation to call at the office before leaving town.

Brown continues his rambles a few blocks, thinking meanwhile of the singular meeting, until his meditations and observations are disturbed by another dapper young fellow who fairly rushes into his arms, exclaiming:

"Why, Mr. Brown, God bless you, I am so glad to see you; when did you leave Oshkosh? how are all the boys? how is Tom Parker, the rich old banker, and how is—" every other person mentioned by Brown during his conversation with the first confidence man.

This outburst of familiarity from a person who Mr. Brown is certain he never saw before causes some bewilderment, if not suspicion, but that feeling is very quickly dispelled by the protestations and assurances given him, and in two minutes more we observe Mr. Brown and his new acquaintance on their way to visit Tom Parker's nephew.

It is not necessary, perhaps, to tell the reader that these two bunko steerers are operating in conjunction. The first one, through an apparent mistake, makes the meeting serviceable by learning Brown's name and all about the people of Oshkosh; these facts are soon afterward communicated to a confederate, who then passes around the block to greet Brown familiarly, not forgetting to remember the story about Tom Parker's nephew.

Brown finds his companion very interesting, and follows him like a lamb led to the slaughter, for Tom Parker's nephew is certain to prove another confederate who keeps either a policy shop, bunko-den, mock auction store, or some lottery scheme. Whatever the means employed to fleece Brown, it is sure to be successful, for if credulity be not excited, violence will be used as a last resort.

SELLING THE INFORMATION BOOTH IN GRAND CENTRAL [7]

There are probably as many fictitious stories about city slickers selling the main information booth to new arrivals as there are about Brooklyn Bridge. But my favorite is one that old-timers swear by so vehemently I'm convinced it's true.

It seems that two prosperous Italian brothers who owned a chain of fruit stands were approached by two men who represented themselves as the president and vice-president of the Grand Central Holding and Real Estate Company, Incorporated. The information booth in the center of the concourse was being closed because people asked too many foolish questions, they said, and they were looking for a reliable firm to open what should become the world's busiest fruit stand. The brothers wanted to put a deposit on the deal then and there but the crooks waved the money aside. Other firms were being investigated, too, they said.

Finally, an appointment was made and the crooks met the brothers at the information booth and led them to an office in the Grand Central Building—a rarely used room reserved for long-distance train conductors. In return for a gilt-edge and very legal-appearing lease, the confidence men accepted a check for $10,000 for six months' rent in advance.

The brothers didn't know they'd been swindled until they arrived at the booth the morning their lease was to have begun. Behind them trailed a crew of carpenters to enlarge the counters and six helpers with hand trucks piled high with crates of oranges and apples.

HICK VS. CITY SLICKER [8]

I made my money from lumber and real estate mostly. I got started young and I worked hard. First I used my hands and muscle; then I started using my brain and letting other men work with their hands. A lot more strong backs in this country than there are sharp minds. Didn't take me long to figure it out neither. I was a young feller, in my twenties, and doing pretty well. I owned a sawmill and a store and a lot of land. I had some good timberlands, some of the best around. I always knew my lumber. I took to lumber like a red-headed woodpecker.

This big New York company wanted to buy some of my timberland. They sent men up here to look it all over, and they liked the looks of it first-rate. I made sure they saw the best stuff standing. Well, after fussing and fooling around they went back to New York to report. Had some correspondence with the company. I was supposed to go to New York to close the deal. I knew them fellers thought I was pretty green, so I thought I'd have some fun with 'em.

[7] From "Everything Happens at Grand Central Station," by Edward G. Fischer, with Wayne Amos, *Collier's*, Vol. 133 (March 5, 1954), No. 5, p. 89. Copyright, 1954, by the Crowell-Collier Publishing Company. New York.

[8] As told to Roaldus Richmond, Montpelier, Vermont. From "Yankee Businessman," Manuscripts of the Federal Writers' Project of the Works Progress Administration for the State of Vermont. 1939.

I bought a whole new outfit for the trip down to New York. I bought some overalls, a jumper, boots, sheepskin, leggings, and I dressed up in 'em and wore 'em down. Them city fellers liked to died when they see me come in the office!

I says to 'em: "Had a tarnation of a time finding this place. So many high buildings and so many people. You're way up in the air here, ain't you? How fur you s'pose it is down to the ground? I ain't used to all this commotion. Almost wish I had stayed to home!"

I says to 'em: "This is my best outfit I got on here. Only wear it to dress up for something special. Couple of years I'll buy me a new one, and I'll put this right on for every day. Up home we have to be sparing of our clothes."

I says: "What be them cars that run up on top of them tall poles and make such an awful racket? I wouldn't dare to walk under 'em, let alone ride in 'em. I never see such contraptions as you got here in the city!"

Well, by God, them city fellers was having more fun with me, you know. —but not half so much fun as I was having with them. Finally we got round to talking business. They wanted to give me $3000 down payment. I held out for $5000. They begin to sweat and squirm a little then. After quite a spell they got ready to write me off a check for $5000. I stalled 'em off some more, said I'd promised my wife not to close the deal till I talked with her. They wanted me to use the office phone, but I said I had to have a private telephone booth when I talked to my wife on account she had such a loud voice it might rupture folks' eardrums that wa'n't used to listening to it. So they let me go out. I stopped in a place I knew before and got a couple of drinks. I gave the bartender some more of that farmer lingo, and the fellers in there liked to died laughing at me. What I really went out for was to go to a bank and see if their check was any good. I found out it was and I went back to the office and picked it up. Them fellers didn't appear none too happy!

Then I asks 'em how I'm going to get back to the depot. I told 'em I was pretty apt to get lost in all the crowds and traffic and noise. I said I couldn't keep from looking up at the high buildings and it made me dizzy and I was apt to fall down and get run over. Well, by God, you know what they did? They sent a man right along with me clear up as far as White River Junction!

Well, in the spring them city fellers came up to take over, you know, and I collected the rest on the land. After they talked to some of the local lumbermen, they begun to think maybe they hadn't made such a good deal as they thought. They found out they hadn't stung Hank Davis a whole hell of a lot. And here's the best part of it all now. The company went bankrupt trying to get the lumber out of there!

A GREEN ONE IN THE LAND OF GOLD [9]

Ten minutes' walk brought me to the heart of the Jewish East Side. The streets swarmed with Yiddish-speaking immigrants. The sign-boards were

[9] From *The Rise of David Levinsky*, A Novel, by Abraham Cahan, pp. 93-95. Copyright, 1917, by Harper & Brothers. New York.

in English and Yiddish, some of them in Russian. The scurry and hustle of the people were not merely overwhelmingly greater, both in volume and intensity, than in my native town. It was of another sort. The swing and step of the pedestrians, the voices and manner of the street peddlers, and a hundred and one other things seemed to testify to far more self-confidence and energy, to larger ambitions and wider scopes, than did the appearance of the crowds in my birthplace.

The great thing was that these people were better dressed than the inhabitants of my town. The poorest-looking man wore a hat (instead of a cap), a stiff collar and a necktie, and the poorest woman wore a hat or a bonnet.

The appearance of a newly arrived immigrant was still a novel spectacle on the East Side. Many of the passers-by paused to look at me with wistful smiles of curiosity.

"There goes a green one!" some of them exclaimed.

The sight of me obviously evoked reminiscences in them of the days when they had been "green ones" like myself. It was a second birth that they were witnessing, an experience which they had once gone through themselves and which was one of the greatest events in their lives.

"Green one" or "greenhorn" is one of the many English words and phrases which my mother-tongue has appropriated in England and America. Thanks to the many millions of letters that pass annually between the Jews of Russia and their relatives in the United States, a number of these words have by now come to be generally known among our people at home as well as here. In the eighties, however, one who had not visited any English-speaking country was utterly unfamiliar with them. And so I had never heard of "green one" before. Still, "green," in the sense of color, is Yiddish as well as English, so I understood the phrase at once, and as a contemptuous quizzical appellation for a newly arrived, inexperienced immigrant it stung me cruelly. As I went along I heard it again and again. Some of the passers-by would call me "greenhorn" in a tone of blighting gaiety, but these were an exception. For the most part it was "green one" and in a spirit of sympathetic interest. It hurt me, all the same. Even those glances that offered me a cordial welcome and good wishes had something self-complacent and condescending in them. "Poor fellow! he is a green one," these people seemed to say. "We are not, of course. We are Americanized."

For my first meal in the New World I bought a three-cent wedge of coarse rye bread, off a huge round loaf, on a stand on Essex Street. I was too strict in my religious observances to eat it without first performing ablutions and offering a brief prayer. So I approached a bewigged old woman who stood in the doorway of a small grocery-store to let me wash my hands and eat my meal in her place. She looked old-fashioned enough, yet when she heard my request, she said, with a laugh:

"You're a green one, I see."

"Suppose I am," I resented. "Do the yellow ones or black ones all eat without washing? Can't a fellow be a good Jew in America?"

"Yes, of course he can, but—well, wait till you see for yourself."

However, she asked me to come in, gave me some water and an old apron to serve me for a towel, and when I was ready to eat my bread she placed a glass of milk before me, explaining that she was not going to charge me for it.

"In America people are not foolish enough to be content with dry bread," she said, sententiously.

While I ate she questioned me about my antecedents. I remember how she impressed me as a strong, clever woman of few words as long as she catechised

me, and how disappointed I was when she began to talk of herself. The astute, knowing mien gradually faded out of her face and I had before me a gushing, boastful old bore.

My intention was to take a long stroll, as much in the hope of coming upon some windfall as for the purpose of taking a look at the great American city. Many of the letters that came from the United States to my birthplace before I sailed had contained a warning not to imagine that America was a "land of gold" and that treasure might be had in the streets of New York for the picking. But these warnings only had the effect of lending vividness to my image of an American street as a thoroughfare strewn with nuggets of the precious metal. Symbolically speaking, this was the idea one had of the "land of Columbus." It was a continuation of the widespread effect produced by stories of Cortes and Pizarro in the sixteenth century, confirmed by the successes of some Russian emigrants of my time.

I asked the grocery-woman to let me leave my bundle with her, and, after considerable hesitation, she allowed me to put it among some empty barrels in her cellar.

I went wandering over the Ghetto. Instead of stumbling upon nuggets of gold, I found signs of poverty. In one place I came across a poor family who —as I learned upon inquiry—had been dispossessed for non-payment of rent. A mother and her two little boys were watching their pile of furniture and other household goods on the sidewalk, while the passers-by were dropping coins into a saucer placed on one of the chairs to enable the family to move into new quarters.

What puzzled me was the nature of the furniture. For in my birthplace chairs and a couch like those I now saw on the sidewalk would be a sign of prosperity. But then anything was to be expected of a country where the poorest devil wore a hat and a starched collar.

I walked on.

The exclamation "A green one" or "A greenhorn" continued. If I did not hear it, I saw it in the eyes of the people who passed me.

BEER AND BILLIARDS [10]

Ike and Mike, two young Russian-Jewish immigrants, took a walk on Grand Street on the third evening after their arrival in New York. They studied everything minutely and were attracted by an electric sign: Beer and Supposing we go in and try it."

They entered the saloon and ordered two glasses of billiards. The waiter Billiards.

"I drank beer in the old country," said Ike, "but I have never tasted billiards. sized up his customers immediately and brought two glasses of cold water. The boys drank it.

After leaving the place, Mike said to his companion: "What do you think of it?"

"It was all right," said Ike. "But do you know, if the waiter had not assured me that it was billiards, I would have sworn that it was plain water."

AMERICA BELLA! [11]

The problem of educating their children was easily solved by my relatives. If the children were females, there was no problem at all. To give a

[10] From *The Merry Heart, Wit and Wisdom from Jewish Folklore*, by S. Felix Mendelsohn, p. 193. Copyright, 1951, by S. Felix Mendelsohn. New York: Bookman Associates.

[11] From *Mount Allegro*, by Jerre Mangione, pp. 225-226, 229-231. Copyright, 1942, 1952, by Jerre Mangione. New York: Alfred A. Knopf, Inc.

daughter more education than that required by law was considered an extravagant waste of time and money. It was fine if you could afford piano lessons for her; that was something of a luxury, but it made sense, for a girl who knew some music was bound to be more *simpatica* than a girl who did not and, of course, every one knew that when a man wanted to marry he tried to choose a girl who was *simpatica*. But every one also knew that a man was not interested in a girl who knew much more than he did. So what was the use of spending money on her schooling?

Far better for her to learn to sew and cook, or to earn money for the family until the right man came along to marry her. Even if you imitated the Americans and sent your daughter to college, she would end up by marrying anyway, and what was the use of her education to her then? Look at the case of Dunnietta Palermo. Her mother ruined her eyes working in a tailor factory to send her through a teachers' school; then she up and married less than a month after she received her diploma. Now she had three children and spent most of her time in the kitchen. *America pazza!*

It was different with the sons. They had the world before them. Not the kitchen. In a country like *l'America*, which had *la Democrazia* they could go to high school and then to college with a little sacrifice on the part of the parents—and emerge a lawyer or a doctor. *Dottore, Avvocato*—magic words to any Sicilian. All other professions seemed insignificant to them. The *dottori* and the *avvocati* were the men most respected in their homelands—and they were the ones who made the most money.

America bella! Here a poor Sicilian who earned his bread shining shoes could, by shining more shoes, send his son through college and see him become an *avvocato* or *dottore*. It was wonderful because then, presto, the poor Sicilian was no longer poor. He could stop shining shoes and he and his wife could live comfortably for the rest of their lives, confident that the son for whom they had made so many sacrifices would support them and honor them. Not only that—but they would enjoy a great deal more "respect" among their *paesani*, regardless of whether he had been a shoe-shiner in Rochester or a *cafone* in Sicily. What more could a man want?

*   *   *   *   *

Our general attitude toward all Americans was bound to be distorted, for, not knowing any of them well, we could not make independent judgments and were influenced by the confused opinions our elders had of them. On one hand, my relatives were cynical about *Americani*: they had no manners; they licked their fingers after a meal and chewed gum and then played with it as though it were a rubber band. Also, *Americani* were *superbi* (snobs) and looked down on people who didn't speak their language fluently. On the other hand, they feared and respected *Americani* and there were times when they emulated them.

If a Sicilian began to behave like an *Americano*, they said he was putting on airs but, actually, they had great admiration for any one who achieved any degree of Americanization. After all, to be an *Americano* was a sign that you were getting on in the world. The bosses were Americans. The police were

Americans. In fact, nearly any one who had plenty of money or a good steady job was either an American or was living like one.

You had only to look at the example set by the sons of poor Italians who became doctors or lawyers in the community. As soon as they had established themselves, they married blonde American girls and moved as far as possible from their former neighborhoods. Some of them dropped the vowels from the end of their names, so that people would think they had always been American. They stopped associating with their relatives. Their wives got their pictures in society pages and, instead of having a raft of children, they bought wire-haired terriers and walked them around the block, like many other prosperous Americans. The only times they liked dealing with Italians was when it meant money in their pockets.

In spite of the fact that the word *Americano* was usually preceded by the Sicilian word *fissa,* meaning stupid, Americans were suspected of miraculous shrewdness and dishonesty. Yet once an *Americano* had shown his friendliness to a Sicilian in any way, however trivial, he could expect to be smothered with hospitality and love—never, of course, the love that one Sicilian relative has for another, but enough love to make an American regard his own relatives as so many cold fish for the rest of his life.

My relatives conceded that there were good and bad Americans, just as there were good and bad Sicilians, but they suspected that most of them were inclined to take advantage of a foreigner who could not speak their own tongue. Even before coming to the United States, Sicilians were educated to be suspicious of Americans. From their relatives in America, they received long pathetic accounts of how they had been robbed and cheated. Those who were planning to migrate were warned to beware of Americans from the moment they set foot off the boat.

The first supposedly English word many of my relatives learned even before they landed in America was *girarihir,* meaning "Get out of here." Immigrants were solemnly advised to yell this word at any stranger in America who approached them, for it was emphasized that if a Sicilian was identified as a *greenhorno,* some Americans would surely try to rob him of his money or belongings.

AMERICAMANIA IN ST. LOUIS [12]

"Yes, there's decent people in America." His voice was calm and even, as if he were not arguing but just thinking aloud. "There's people here who live good lives. Who have homes and wives and children. They were born here. This is their country. The bumbi [bums] have nothing to do with those Americans. The bumbi know only the gamblers and the bad women who take their money and give them diseases and. . . ." He suddenly checked himself, apparently becoming aware that he was giving voice to something which he had believed he was merely thinking.

[12] From *My American Pilgrimage,* by Stoyan Christowe, pp. 8-14. Copyright, 1947, by Stoyan Christowe. Boston: Little, Brown and Company.

"The Americans will never give us the easy jobs, my son." His voice changed, some warmth and animation coming into it. "It'll be coal shoveling, engine wiping for us. You don't want to do that forever, do you? You can't strike roots here. You'll always be a stranger here."

I stirred in my chair, hoping this would make him rise so we might go to the coffeehouse together for our regular Sunday visit. But he still had things to say.

"The bumbi think they're Americans because they learn a little English like parrots. How can they be Americans? Until yesterday they herded sheep and poked oxen and wore pigskin sandals [in Macedonia]. Because now they wear silk shirts and neckties, and brown shoes and pantaloons and have gold on their teeth, does that make them Americans? Clothes don't make Americans. You can put on the finest clothes you can buy on Sixth Street [St. Louis], and still under them you'd be what you always were. A silver saddle doesn't make a stallion out of a donkey. Americans! They! Americans! Until they came here they were lucky to eat corn bread and to sleep on straw mats on the ground. Now that they tasted white bread they want to eat in the restaurants. And to live on foornish [furnished rooms], and go to the theatricals, the electricals, and the live ones. Now I can understand how it might be amusing to go to an electrical once and see photographs that move, but to go to a live show like the Standard where women who have no shame come out without clothes on! That's bad, my son."

"It only costs a nickel at the electricals."

"It's not the money. A nickel. All right, a dime. Though I always like to remember that a dime saved here is ten dimes in the Old Country. It's what you see there that takes your mind away from the things you came here for. It don't matter how we live here. Nobody in our village will ask you how many times you went to the theatricals, or how many English words you know. How many gold napoleons you brought with you is what counts. Live like a miser in America that you may live like a vizier in your own country." He sat there in his chair with his head slightly tilted over his shoulder. There was a suppressed cry in his voice.

I felt sorry for my father. As soon as I had arrived in St. Louis I had noticed the change in him. A lean, wiry man with a small-featured face, but strong, there had always been about him a tough, tempered strength. Now he looked haggard. Two years in America with the tight routine of travail and thrift had dwarfed him. He seemed stripped of his patriarchal authority and innate dignity. He looked weak and helpless. For the first time I felt bigger and stronger than my father, and wondered whether it was my own growth or America that had produced the diminution in my father's stature.

"Aren't we going to the coffeehouse? It's getting late," I said at last, and rose.

"I don't think I'll come." He looked at his watch. It was an old Turkish watch he wound up with a little silver key that hung from the chain like a fob. The numerals on the dial were Turkish and the golden case was ornamented with Arabic scrolls. I had never thought of it before but now it seemed curious that that old Turkish watch should keep time here in America. Suppose you took out the movement from the Turkish case and set it in an American case with an American dial—who then would know that it was an old Turkish watch! Watches differed only outwardly. Inside there was something common to all of them. I began to think of human beings as being different only outwardly and inside all being the same, like the watches, and it was a matter of adjustment, but the comparison began to grow complex in my mind. I looked at my father and said, "Shall I go by myself then?"

"Yes, if you like. I had better get some sleep."

I started, with my hands in my trousers pockets. At the door I stopped and looked back but turned again and walked across the porch toward the stairway.

I could see my father sitting motionless in his chair just as I had left him, with his head still inclined over his right shoulder. I knew he was listening to my footsteps as I was descending the steps. I knew he felt terribly alone. I was his only son and I was going away from him, leaving him alone. Maybe I'd never come back; maybe I'd go to live "on foornish" somewhere on the West Side. Maybe Klement was right. My father had never wanted me to come to America; had written to me time and time again not to come.

Yet I had become a victim of the *Americamania* that had possessed the people in all the villages. Dollars, pantaloons, neckties, and silk shirts, pencils that needed no sharpening, and pens that wrote without being dipped in inkwells, had acted like magic, had disturbed the lives of thousands of people. Good people who had crossed themselves at mealtime, fathers and husbands, clean people. God-fearing people. America put greed in their hearts and cleverness in their minds. My father had become a victim of that epidemic. He saw the deception, but it was too late. He saw the dreadful things America had done to young men who had left the village with healthy bodies and clean minds. Look at them now! The blight's on them. He would go back to his own world, where he was a man, and he would build houses again.

Yes, houses! It seemed like a dream now, the engine wiper building houses. They were small houses, but they had windows and doors and some of them had balconies overlooking little courts paved with flagstones. He built these houses for people to live in, to live in like human beings, like God meant for them to live. The houses had cupboards in them, and kneading troughs, and weaving looms, and fireplaces. What's a house without a fireplace? A church without an altar. A man without a soul.

He would be a *Maistor* again and build houses, my father would. People would honor him and call him Maistor. He could lay bricks and stones and fit window frames into walls, rig up roofs, and do all kinds of carpentering. He could hew out a plow from the crooked branch of a beech tree or a wheel hub from a tree stump. And he could make wedding chests and flour chests, cart wheels, mill wheels, vats, wine barrels. His trousers might have been patched in the Old Country but his soul was intact. Here the pants must not be patched, even though the body may be fouled by disease and the soul moldering.

My father was here only with his body. His mind, his heart, his whole being were back in the homeland where life had meaning for him, where life was rooted in decency and dignity. The man he worked for there was his host and

not his boss. That was because he was building him a house to live in, or a
barrel to keep his wine in, or a wedding chest for his daughter. He could sit
down with him for a glass of brandy, or a cup of Turkish coffee.

This America was boring into his life like a worm into an apple, hollowing
out the soundness.

SAN FRANCISCO MELTING POT [13]

One of the town's perennial chuckles . . . is the fact that Tarantino's
restaurant on Fisherman's Wharf is owned by a pair of Irishmen named Gene
McAteer and Dan Sweeney. So one recent day a new crab stand opened on
the Wharf. It's called Hogan's—and its owner is an old-time Wharfian named
Tony Tedesco. "I jus' wanna show," grins Tony, "that the Italians are as gooda
sports as the Irishmen!"

* * * * *

. . . The New Italian Market on Battery near Green is owned by Herman
Quan, Walter Lai, Lee Suey How, Henry Fong, Wong Jan, King Choy Chai,
and Tim Fong. See? That's why they call it the Italian Market.

THE CABOTS AND THE KABOTZNICKS [14]

. . . One small poem which had its genesis in the social aspirations
of just two Boston Families has become what is probably the closest thing to a
social "folk song" any city ever had. Originally patterned on a toast delivered
by an anonymous "Western man" at a Harvard alumni dinner in 1905, it was
refined in 1910 by Dr. John Collins Bossidy of Holy Cross to be recited, apparently for all time, as follows:

> And this is good old Boston,
> The home of the bean and the cod,
> Where the Lowells talk to the Cabots,
> And the Cabots talk only to God.

* * * * *

. . . [The] Cabot case stands out above others [in which ordinary Bostonians
have seen fit to become Proper Bostonians by the simple procedure of having
their names changed]—as a classic of Boston Society. In this the judge allowed
the plaintiff, a man named Kabotznick, to assume the honored name, apparently
not foreseeing that his decision was also going to work a hardship on the
Lowells. He was shortly reminded of this fact by an anonymous newspaper poet.
Re-wording Boston's social "folk song," the poet wrote:

[13] From *Baghdad: 1951,* by Herb Caen, pp. 85, 86. Copyright, 1950, by Herb Caen.
Garden City, New York: Doubleday & Company, Inc.
[14] From *The Proper Bostonians,* by Cleveland Amory, pp. 13-14, 35. Copyright, 1947,
by Cleveland Amory. New York: E. P. Dutton & Co., Inc.

And this is good old Boston,
The home of the bean and the cod,
Where the Lowells have no one to talk to,
'Cause the Cabots talk Yiddish, by God!

'MERICAIN COQUIN [15]

There was a little song with which small boys used to taunt Anglo-
Saxons when they met them in the streets of the old quarter. Sung in Creole
patois, it went:

'Mericain coquin
Billé en naquin
Voleur di pain
Chez Miche D'Aquin!

Which translated meant that:

American rogues
Dressed in nankeen
Stole loaves of bread
From Mr. D'Aquin!

Monsieur D'Aquin was a Vieux Carré baker. The "Dressed in nankeen" indicated scorn for the Americans' lack of elegance and fashion.

On the other hand, mean little American boys used to torment Creole
gentlemen by shouting after them:

Kiskadee! Kiskadee!
Save a crawfish head for me!
Look all around a Frenchman's bed
You can't see nothing but crawfish heads!

THE "LITTLE FLOWER" AND THE ORGAN-GRINDER [16]

I . . . got my first glimpse of racial feeling born of ignorance, out
there in [Prescott] Arizona. I must have been about ten when a street organ-
grinder with a monkey blew into town. He, and particularly the monkey, attracted a great deal of attention. I can still hear the cries of the kids: "A dago
with a monkey! Hey, Fiorello, you're a dago too. Where's your monkey?" It
hurt. And what made it worse, along came Dad, and he started to chatter
Neapolitan with the organ-grinder. He hadn't spoken Italian in many years,
and he seemed to enjoy it. Perhaps, too, he considered the organ-grinder a
fellow musician. At any rate, he promptly invited him to our house for a
macaroni dinner. The kids taunted me for a long time after that. I couldn't
understand it. What difference was there between us? Some of their families
hadn't been in the country any longer than mine.

[15] From The Romantic New Orleanians, by Robert Tallant, p. 84. Copyright, 1950, by
Robert Tallant. New York: E. P. Dutton & Co., Inc.
[16] From The Making of an Insurgent, An Autobiography: 1882-1919, by Fiorello H. La
Guardia, pp. 27-29. Copyright, 1948, by J. B. Lippincott Company. Philadelphia and New
York.

I have heard Gilbert and Sullivan's *Pinafore* in almost every language, in many countries; and in the rendition of the song, "For He Is an Englishman," the traditional gesture mimicking the organ-grinder and the word "Eyetalian" always annoyed me.

Early in my first administration as Mayor, a traffic report by the Police Department showed that among the obstacles to free traffic was the nuisance of the street organ-grinder. It was with a great deal of gusto that I banned the organ-grinder from the streets of the City of New York. It caused some resentment among those who were sentimental about organ-grinders. One woman came up to me at a social function and berated me mildly for depriving her of her favorite organ-grinder. "Where do you live?" I asked. "Park Avenue," she said. "What floor?" "The fourteenth," she answered.

In addition to the fact that I never did like organ-grinders ever since my days of ridicule in Prescott when that one organ-grinder came to town, I felt that they made our traffic problem in New York more difficult. I was accused by some New Yorkers who liked them of having no sentimental feelings about organ-grinders, of having no soul, of oppressing the poor, of neglecting more important things to deprive old residents and young children of their pleasure. Some of my correspondents were genial and some were angry. Cornelia Otis Skinner, Beatrice Kauffman, Viola Irene Cooper were among the literary defenders of the hurdy-gurdy. Petitions were got up urging me to rescind the order. My answer to my critics was that there had been a time when the hurdy-gurdy was the only means of bringing music to many people. That was also the time before automobiles filled our streets. With the advent of the phonograph and the radio that time had passed. Free public concerts in parks, libraries, museums and other public places had given ample opportunity to hear music. But, more important, traffic conditions had changed. Children were endangered by trucks and other automobiles when they gathered in the middle of streets to hear and watch the organ-grinders. Also, the simple, sentimental hurdy-gurdy man had become a victim of a racket. My sentimental correspondents did not realize that the Italians' instruments were rented to them by padrones at exorbitant fees. Their licenses from the city were in reality licenses to beg. About a year before I banned the organ-grinders, I had terminated the contracts with musicians on city ferry boats on the grounds that these were merely licenses to beg issued by the city. Despite these reasons, which I gave to my correspondents in answer to their protests, the defenders of the hurdy-gurdy men kept on writing to me for over a year, and some of them warned me that they wouldn't vote again for a man without a soul.

QUEER PEOPLE IN PROVINCETOWN [17]

"You see an awful lot of queer people here," said a summer visitor to an old [Provincetown] resident, looking toward two fishermen in oilskins, tramping down the street, each with a big cod by the gills.

[17] From *Time and the Town*, A Provincetown Chronicle, by Mary Heaton Vorse, p. 80. Copyright, 1942, by Mary Heaton Vorse. New York: The Dial Press.

"Sure do," replied the ancient, looking toward a crowd of robust summer girls, shorts over their fat hams, "but come Labor Day they'll all be gone."

CRIME WAVE IN EVANSVILLE [18]

Southern Indiana is border territory, and as is always the case in border territory the people across the line—or, in that particular area, across the river—are a little suspect. My father was born in Mt. Vernon, Indiana, in 1870, and lived in Southern Indiana all his life. He was one time a Congressman from the old first district of Indiana, and a very tolerant man. But he had the usual Southern Hoosier's attitude toward Kentuckians.

During the second World War, one summer when I was home on leave, Father and I were sitting out on the front porch after supper. My mother and sister were in the back of the house washing dishes. The locusts were at work in the trees across the street, and it was a very pleasant evening.

Father talked about numerous things, and finally he said, "William, you know there's a crime wave on in Evansville here now. It worries me a great deal."

"A crime wave, Father? What do you mean?"

"Well, we've had some killings, and it's all due to these Kentuckians that come up across the river to work in our war plants here."

"Well, Father, as I remember, there have always been several murders a year in Evansville."

"I know, son. We've always had murders here in Evansville. I've lived here seventy-five years, and we've had two or three a year ever since I can remember. But not until these Kentuckians came up across the river in such numbers to work in our war plants, has anybody ever been killed in this town by anybody he didn't know."

THE DUDE IN SANTA FE [19]

There's the dude who bargains with an Indian for a turquoise necklace set in jet. He doesn't know that the "jet" is a melted phonograph disc, but he beats the Indian down from his price of forty dollars to twenty-seven fifty and offers him a ride to town to make up the difference. Says the Indian when he is on the front seat:

"Umh—Cadillac!"

"You know Cadillac, John?" says the dude, thinking "John" had never seen a motor before.

"Yes, I ride Cadillac in Detroit, Rolls-Royce in London, Hispano-Suiza in Paris, but I like Ford best. I travel everywhere with the Indian show."

And when the dude exhibits his necklace in town he finds the dealers' price is fifteen dollars.

[18] As told by William E. Wilson, University of Colorado, Boulder, Colorado, July 18, 1950. Recorded and transcribed by B. A. Botkin.

[19] From *Caballeros*, by Ruth Laughlin, pp. 116-117. Copyright, 1931, by Ruth Laughlin. Caldwell, Idaho: The Caxton Printers, Ltd. 1945.

I'LL TAKE NEW YORK [20]

[A private welfare] commission [in New York] was attempting to place each so-called "D.P." to the best advantage, not always with the co-operation of the D.P. One man in particular was well suited for farm work, but he would not leave New York.

"The trouble with you people," said the chairman angrily, "is that you all insist on staying here. If you would scatter out into the less densely populated parts of the country, you would all have a better chance."

The man who was being scolded looked out of the open window thoughtfully. He saw smoky air, smelled the gassy fumes, saw the harried thousands charging through the narrow streets. He turned to the chairman and smiled amiably. "*You* scatter," he said. "I'll stay here."

*   *   *   *   *

A New York tenement dweller was being coaxed by a former neighbor to visit the new house in the country. "Oh, it's grand!" said the former neighbor. "You'd love it, I know. All that fine fresh air—and such a view!"

The first lady was not impressed. "I've got the best view in the world right here in New York," she said. "Straight across the air shaft into somebody else's flat."

[20] From *Manhattan and Me*, by Oriana Atkinson, pp. 263, 265. Copyright, 1954, by Oriana Atkinson. Indianapolis and New York: The Bobbs-Merrill Company, Inc.

IV. Characters Make a Town

God made the country, man made the city and the devil made the small town, and all three are full of characters. Like cities, characters insist on being "different," on the right to be themselves.

While most of them succeed only in being queer, a few are destined to become heroes. While the more aggressive actually make or build a town, they all make it interesting and become part of its legend. And to a certain extent the town makes them. It might even be said that a city like New York breeds a distinctive type of character, as seen, for example, in Al Smith, Fiorello La Guardia and Jimmy Durante.

It is easy enough to be a character in a small town where everyone is a neighbor and everyone knows everyone else. One has only to do something unconventional that will start the neighbors talking. In the city, however, one has to work a little harder at the business of being a character. Where a premium is put upon novelty, showmanship and publicity, a character must have a touch of the spectacular, which will make good copy. And one way of standing out in a crowd is to attract a crowd—as in the case of the Brooklynite described by Meyer Berger who persuaded a water-front apple vendor to let him eat all the apples he could for a quarter. Before he was done—egged on by the longshoremen and loafers—he had eaten the entire stock of 257 apples and was something of a hero, carried off on the shoulders of his admirers who stood treat at a near-by saloon.

Almost every type of small-town character—rebel, atheist, fanatic, crank, crackpot, idiot, recluse, rake, ne'er-do-well, wastrel—is found in the city, the difference being largely one of degree. By the same token the urban zany and practical joker are only more sophisticated versions of the village wag and cut-up.

If a city like New York abounds in screwballs, it is because of the large element of irrationality that is present in the Big Town. If the New Yorker loves absurdities, it is because there are so many absurdities in the life around him

According to Cleveland Rodgers and Rebecca B. Rankin in *New York: The World's Capital City*, the quintessence of metropolitan heroes and hero-worship is the quintessence of New Yorkism. As a result of the modern urban division of labor, most New Yorkers are specialists, and suffer from the monotony inherent in specialization. This, plus the anonymity of urban mass living, creates an abnormal "avidity for diversion."

New York's constant crowds confer conspicuousness on those who step out of them. The stage is always set and an audience is assembled for any one who, willingly or otherwise, is caught in the glare of a spotlight. And how New Yorkers love solitary performers! These are eagerly accepted as surrogates by the millions who subconsciously aspire to imitate them. The Bronx bus driver, who, following an impulse, deviated from his route and drove his vehicle to Florida became a popular hero; most of his passengers would have gone with him without much urging.

In an age of mass living, mass production and mass communication, there has been an inevitable change in the styles of popular and folk heroes. If in the past our heroes have tended to be showmen, now our showmen tend to be heroes. Showmanship, however, is not limited to show business, from which a great many popular idols are recruited, but is also found in the worlds of business, politics, sports and crime, with an intimate connection between heroes, showmen and publicity.

Many city characters have their roots in the neighborhood (the urban counterpart of the village), especially Bohemia and Skid Row, which naturally attract extroverts and introverts. Not all exhibitionists or dreamers, however, live on the wrong side of the tracks. Nor are all city characters mere eccentrics. Many are men of solid reputation and achievement, city builders and leaders, who also happen to be a little crazy, because once they get hold of an idea they refuse to let go of it.

All are fabulous.

BIG MOSE[1]

. . . Oddly enough, he was by trade a printer; a compositor in the office of Beach's *Sun*—which doesn't seem logical. It is difficult to fancy those huge fingers picking tiny slivers of type out of a case and ranging them in neat rows. He should have been a blacksmith or a stevedore or a truckman. But he was what he was, the undefeated pride of No. 40, and one of the most vicious sluggers, eye-gougers, and hobnail-stampers in all New York's rowdy history. When not serving valiantly at a fire (and there were no braver men on a ladder or under a tottering wall than most of these brawlers) he was usually seeking honorable distinction against rival firemen or the gangsters of the Five Points. Rooster Kelly, of 30, claims that "I kin remember the night him and Orange County, our foreman, had it nip and tuck, and Orange County kinder got the bulge on him after a four-hours' tussle"; but no one else seems to recall this shading of the battle.

But Old Mose, like all other conquerors, finally met his Waterloo; met it at the hands of Henry Chanfrau in a great battle royal which was a landmark in fire department history and was talked of for sixty years thereafter. On one summer Sunday in 1838 a small fire occurred on South Street. Returning from it, the Lady Washington and Peterson companies trotted side by side up Pearl Street. All other crews were jealous of the Petersons, and there was particularly bad blood between them and No. 40. The ropes were fully manned, as always on Sundays; in fact, overmanned, for chroniclers assert that counting outside sympathizers who were pulling or pushing from behind, there were probably five hundred men in direct attendance on each machine; and in addition to this a crowd of partisans and the merely curious followed, hoping and expecting to see a fight. It had been rumored that 40 was spoiling to attack 15 and explode her boasted invincibility; and the presence at the Lady Washington ropes of several husky fighters from 30, 34, and 44 seemed to lend color to the belief that a conspiracy against 15 was on foot. Among the "ringers"

[1] From *Old Bowery Days,* The Chronicles of a Famous Street, by Alvin F. Harlow, pp. 207-210, 211-212. Copyright, 1931, by Alvin F. Harlow. New York: Appleton-Century-Crofts, Inc.

were Orange County of 30 and the giant Jeroloman of 44, who now for the first time appeared in 40's ranks.

The two machines wheeled into Chatham Street, and 15 turned eastward on its regular course towards Chrystie Street. The Lady Washingtons would ordinarily have turned off at Mulberry Street, but instead, they kept alongside the others into Chatham Square, which plainly revealed their hankering for trouble. The chaffing between the rivals became more venomous at every step. Foreman Colladay of No. 15 and Assistant Foreman Carlin, who was in charge of 40, passed up and down the line, ostensibly demanding peace, but in reality egging on their cohorts. "Now, boys, no fighting!" shouted Colladay, and then in a lower tone, "But if they will have it, give it to 'em good!" "Be quiet, men!" bellowed Carlin, and then *sotto voce,* "until they begin, then lam hell out of 'em!"

At the head of No. 15's rope was Country McClusky; opposite him on 40 was the formidable Jim Jeroloman. At the rear of 15's line Henry Chanfrau found himself opposite the mighty Mose Humphreys—a post calculated to pale the cheek of the hardest warrior. Henry Chanfrau was known as a sturdy fighter, but no one in the department would have believed that he could hold his own with Mose. It was his stout heart that carried him through.

Traversing Chatham Square it was evident that the conflict was imminent, and both sides began to "peel" for it, some even taking off their shirts. Jim Jeroloman removed his earrings and put them in his pocket. As they passed into the narrow bottle neck at the beginning of the Bowery, the pressure of the crowds on either side forced the two lines into collision. Instantly Jeroloman dropped his rope and swung at McClusky, and the battle was on.

Like a flash through a train of powder, the fray was joined all along the ropes, a distance of nearly a block, and near a thousand men were fighting. The din was frightful—curses, yells, the whack of huge fists against hard skulls and massive torsos, the roar of the onlooking mob, greedy for action and gore. The fighters were so crowded that a defeated brave scarcely had room to fall, and more than one man knocked cold was held upright by the jam around him. If he fell, he was in danger of being trampled to death by the boots of friend and foe.

For more than half an hour the battle raged. The Petersons fought like men inspired. At the end of thirty minutes a hitherto unknown champion named Freeland was getting the better of Orange County. And then suddenly Country McClusky bowed his head and butted Jeroloman in the stomach, doubling him up and sending him to earth like a closed jackknife—following this up, as might be expected, by jumping upon him and stamping him. It was the beginning of the end, and No. 40 began to give ground; for to the amazement of every one, Mose Humphreys had not been able to down Hen Chanfrau. While the conflict roared, Frank Chanfrau, then a boy of fourteen, watched it from the top of an awning post in front of Alvord's hat store, shrieking again and again in lulls of the battle, "Give it to him, Hen! Julia is looking at you!"

Julia, Henry Chanfrau's sweetheart, lived near by and was a spectator of the fray. Whether Frank's shrill cry reached Henry's ears or whether he saw Julia's pale face at the window and drew inspiration therefrom we do not know; but at last he landed a blow on the point of Mose's jaw which sent that burly champion reeling. Quickly he followed up his advantage—and then, to the horror of No. 40, the mighty Mose was down!—prone under the milling feet of the contending armies!

That was enough; the Lady Washingtons gave way, and some fled in disorder. Two of them dragged the fallen Mose to his feet and supported him away, tottering between them. And then the frenzied Petersons proceeded to wreak their vengeance on their fallen opponents' engine. It was dragged to a pump and deluged with water for hours, until its beautiful white and gold paint and its portraits of Martha Washington were almost completely washed off. Then it was taken in triumph to No. 15's engine house, and Carlin was later permitted to haul it away at the tail of a cart.

No. 40 never recovered from the disgrace of that defeat. Mose Humphreys vanished from his old haunts soon after the fight, and was next heard of as the proprietor of a pool and billiard hall in Honolulu and reputed chum of the Hawaiian king. He married a native woman and reared a family said to have numbered thirty children.

* * * * *

As years went by a folklore gathered about the Eocene figure of Mose. Pothouse vaporings over stale beer, yarns told in the engine houses at night between games of checkers and old sledge magnified his prowess until he became a sort of Achilles or Roland, like the Paul Bunyan of the lumber camps. He grew to be eight feet tall and crowned by a huge beaver two feet in height. His hands, actually as large as hams, hung on gorilla arms so low that his satellite, Sykesy, boasted that he could stand erect and scratch his kneecap.

His enormous boots were soled with copper, studded with inch-long spikes. In his belt was thrust a butcher's cleaver, and in summer a keg of beer for his refreshment also swung there. When going into action he was apt to carry a wagon tongue in one hand and a flagstone in the other; or he might simply draw a lamp-post from the earth and use that as a club. Once when the Dead Rabbits caught him unawares, he uprooted an oak tree and swept them as grain before the scythe. Again, he withstood a hundred of the most fearsome sluggers of the Five Points, pulling paving blocks and flagstones from the street and hurling them into the opposing mob with frightful effect.

As a jest he sometimes lifted a street car off the track and carried it for a few blocks on one hand as a waiter carries a tray, with the horses dangling from one end and Mose laughing thunderously at the terror of the passengers; or he would unhook the horses and draw the car the full length of the Bowery at terrific speed. Another favorite joke was to take his post in the edge of the East River, and as fast as vessels approached, blow them back with a few puffs from his mighty lungs. He could swim the Hudson with just two powerful strokes, and go clean around Manhattan Island with six. But his favorite method of crossing one of the rivers was to jump it.

CHUCK CONNORS [2]

Chuck Connors was the Bowery, the Bowery was Chuck. Of all its exponents of self-expression, and they were many and interesting, he, more than all, left his mark upon the Bowery, as the Bowery had left its mark upon him.

George Washington Connors was born and reared in Mott Street, of good hard-working Irish parents. His sister, Mrs. Margaret Miller, a most respected matron of the Bronx, speaks fondly of him to this day as Georgie. His brother James assured me that the most famous member of the family got his nickname as a newsboy because he was continually bumming out—those were Brother James' very words—and making his meals by cooking chucksteak on a stick over trash fires in the street. First his fellow gamins called him Chucksteak Connors. In due time they shortened the pseudonym to Chuck.

Chuck Connors was a stockily built, dark-eyed, dark-haired young fellow in 1890. A beloved vagabond, a mimic, a raconteur par excellence. He had been a newsboy, a street Arab, a harrier of the Chinese—known to their Occidental neighbors, the Irish especially, as monks.

Chuck Connors flourished in the Bowery and its environs all his careless years. At fifteen he was an engaging loafer, a clog dancer and singer of Irish songs betimes in the theatorium of the Gayety Dime Museum. Then he became a semiprofessional lightweight fighter and won consistently till he was twenty-five. A succession of defeats, because he did not keep in condition, turned him from the ring.

Then he fell in love and went to work. He got a job firing the dinky steam locomotives that hauled the L trains in those times. He married Annie Harrison, his beloved, a wistful slip of a blond girl. She thought to stir his ambition and educate him, but by the time she had him reading well and writing fairly, though careless of his capital letters, Annie died of consumption.

The story of Chuck's regeneration was engrossingly related in Owen Kildare's once best-seller novel of the Bowery, *My Mamie Rose*. Arnold Daly made a play of it. In the leading rôle, he made up as and imitated the mannerisms of Chuck Connors. [In 1924] *My Mamie Rose* was done as a motion picture, screen-titled "The Fool's Highway." The leading player in this feature film counterfeited the semblance of Chuck Connors too.

Chuck was a type—the type. All other Bowery boys imitated him. With no semblance of Chuck's costume, his mannerisms or his slang, Bowery boys had been known in life, in the newspapers, on the stage and in song and story for upwards of a hundred years. But the original type—and you will see it pictured in old Harper's and Leslie's weeklies—of the Bowery boy of the pre-Connorian period, was a six-foot genial ruffian, with an Uncle Sam chin whisker. He wore a battered plug hat, his trousers in his boots, chewed tobacco

[2] From "When the Bowery Was in Bloom," by Roy L. McCardell, *The Saturday Evening Post*, Vol. 198 (December 19, 1925), No. 25, pp. 80-82. Copyright, 1925, by the Curtis Publishing Company. Philadelphia.

and whittled a shingle on the street corners. In short, the type of the native American as London Punch still pictures him.

This Bowery boy was primarily a volunteer fireman. When the fire alarm sounded he grabbed an empty barrel from the nearest grocery store, and if it wasn't empty he emptied it. Then he ran to the fire plug nearest the burning building, turned the barrel over the fire plug and sat on it until the engine company he belonged to appeared upon the scene. Until his own fire company came that Bowery boy heroically defended that fire plug against all assaults, single or en masse, made upon him by members of rival companies arriving with or without their rope-drawn hand pump machines.

It was in 1888 that Chuck Connors utterly destroyed this traditional character and created the entirely new one in his own image. With the publicity and popularity accorded Chuck's creation, the old-time Bowery boy with his whiskers, his whittled shingle, his trousers in his boots, disappeared from mortal ken —as dead as Bill Pool, the last of his ilk of rough-and-tumble fighter, volunteer fireman, political ruffian; the New York draft riots of the Civil War being about the final conspicuous manifestation of this genus.

But at least this type of Bowery boy had been genuine as well as indigenous through and through. On the other hand, Chuck Connors' concept was partly synthetic and partly founded on the London costermonger.

After Annie Harrison died, Chuck Connors was shanghaied by a Water Street crimp. When he awoke from the effects of the drugged whisky he was on a British steamer bound for London, signed as a fireman. Chuck promptly deserted in London and spent two weeks in Whitechapel. He was intrigued by the costermongers, their dress and tricks and manners. When he returned to his native shores he habilitated him in a modification of the more conservative of coster costumes.

Chuck knew the Bowery would never accept him or anyone else in the full class-conscious costermonger holiday attire of velveteen and pearlies—the rows of buttons down the trousers seam, the rows of buttons on the peaked cap, the rows of buttons on the low-cut plaid waistcoat, or the gay silk neckerchief. Chuck had his tailor construct for him a hybrid sailor-ashore and costermonger costume—blue, wide-bottomed trousers, a blue-cloth, square-cut pea-jacket with a double row of the very largest size dark pearl buttons; beneath this a blue flannel shirt, a sailor's silk scarf.

Chuck attempted a costermonger's cap, conservatively pearl-buttoned, with this costume. But he was only to wear it for twenty minutes and two blocks. The Bowery rose against it, enraged. Chuck saved himself, but not the cap. The Bowery wore derbies only. Chuck went to Spellman and gave specifications for the low-crown style he was to wear all the days of his pilgrimage thereafter.

His novel attire, his expressive slang, his fund of stories, his homely philosophical observations of the slums and his rugged vigor in it all, gained for him the interest and even friendship of all he came in contact with. Chuck Connors, of the Bowery, had arrived; his personality was to become a tradition.

He played himself in melodrama when he would, was a manager of lesser prize fighters in a small way. He was sought after as guide to Chinatown and the Bowery and was more than satisfactory. Unless sight-seers had been ciceroned by Chuck, they suspected they hadn't seen the half of it. Chuck was copy for the newspapermen, they were his friends; for Chuck, with all his faults, was always interesting, always on the level.

The Chuck Connors Ball at Tammany Hall was a yearly event which the newspapers covered fully. When advertising it, Chuck coolly published the name of every notable New Yorker—he knew them all and they all knew him —among his patrons. None of them protested, many of them attended. Then, under the colored calcium lights, Chuck in all his glory would lead out the Rummager or the Truck—the reasons these ladies were so called are obvious— the ball was opened and the badged notables grabbed a Bowery girl in turn and joy was unconfined.

As an actor, Chuck was himself and excellent as such; but he had a profound contempt for the exigencies of the drama that compel actors to say and do the same things in the same place at cue. He would persistently speak new dialogues and introduce new business impromptu, and so cause the other actors to go up in their lines.

"You're a lot of cuckoos, saying de same t'ing an' doin' de same t'ings all de time," he would loudly protest.

Nor could he be depended upon to show up at the theater if there was a Bowery ball or a prize fight at hand, or if he met with congenial friends. He also had a disconcerting way of calling over the footlights to acquaintances in the audience and inviting them up on the stage to participate in the barroom or dance-hall scenes.

"Come on, bo!" he would shout. "It's real beer and plenty of it!"

He liked best to sit in Barney Flynn's place and tell cockney, Chinese, Yiddish, German and especially Irish stories of the tenements. Particularly was he graphic in describing scenes of his childhood in the Connors ménage; tales of his old tad of a father, of his shrewd and devoted mother.

Chuck composed and sang his own songs:

> My Pearl she has a golden curl,
>   She has a stylish strut;
> She wears the cutest bonnet
>   Upon her little nut.
> Oh, Pearlie is my girlie,
>   But, tut, tut, tut!

Chuck had his misadventures too. For a while he had a Chinese boy protégé named Sam Yip whom he was developing into a boxer. He brought him around to see me at the old Biograph studios in the early days of moving pictures. Chuck's idea was that a fight between him and the Chinese boy would be a big money-maker in the mutoscopes or penny-in-the-slot peep-show moving pictures.

"I'll make a mess of the monk," said Chuck, "and then all you need to do to cop de coin is to put a sign on the machines in the penny arcades: Drop in a Penny and See Chuck Connors Knocking Out Sam Yip, the Champion Light-weight of China."

The minute bout was staged before the camera with ring and seconds. But Sam Yip lost his temper when Chuck started to bash him about, and as an unexpected climax to the picture he knocked Chuck cold for the count at the end of the round.

"The monks was always bad luck to me," said Chuck when we brought him to and he had conferred angrily aside with his protégé. "Whatcha t'ink, dat Chink was willing to take five berries, and now he wants me to split fifty-fifty to take the picture over and do it right, wit' me knocking him out."

Chuck was getting twenty dollars and he had to divide it. The second bout, in which Sam Yip permitted his knock-out, is still a standard attraction in the coin mutoscopes.

Not because Chuck was mercenary did he protest, but, as he explained, ten dollars was too much money to give a monk, even for a murder.

STEVE BRODIE [3]

Steve [Brodie] jumped into fame off the Brooklyn Bridge where several before him had died in the attempt, or at least was credited with the desperate deed.

Whether Brodie took the chance, risking his life by that dreadful drop to the darkling waters of the East River for fame and fortune, or whether it was a fake, a publicity stunt, cunningly planned and carefully executed, is a matter of opinion. The world at large believed, a pessimistic few were always skeptical. A body was seen to fall as loud cries were heard from the river side. A head emerged from the water, a panting man was drawn into a boat. The cynics said a dummy was thrown from the bridge and that Brodie, a splendid swimmer, dived underwater from beneath a pier, for a hundred feet and more toward the spot where the weighted dummy sank.

Which story is true I do not know, but I was present in the gorge of Niagara two years later when Brodie, in a rubber suit, was scheduled to swim the rapids. He would not release his hold of a rope his helpers held alongshore, and after fifteen minutes of this he screamed to be drawn out; and he lay sobbing on the icebound shore, for it was bitter weather, and begged for a drop of whisky.

"I was kilt with the cold or I'd 'a' done it!" he kept repeating.

He was a shrewd showman, was Brodie. He was always merry and bright— save on this bleak day when he shivered and screamed by the icy, roaring waters of the rapids of Niagara.

Knowing him well, and even liking him greatly, I for one can never be convinced that Brodie took a chance.

In the days of Steve Brodie's prosperity when he lived in style, he persistently offered a fine home to his mother in his house or in a nice apartment of her own. Finally he refused to pay her rent and had her evicted with her few belong-

[3] *Ibid.,* pp. 82, 87.

ings. She sat on the sidewalk moaning and wailing, and then along came Steve.

"Now, mother, will you move into a decent place and a good neighborhood?" he asked.

"I will not!" she declared stoutly. "If I can't have me own old home where I married my man and where you was born, I'll die on the streets for all I'll go anywheres else, my lad."

And then she wailed and wept and the neighbors gathered round declaring what a shame it was she should be treated so, and Steve had her little sticks of furniture carried back into her three rooms, and lit the stove for her and made her a pot of boiled black tea.

"And the divil fly way wid you, Stevie," she said. "But I'll never go away from here till I'm waked and carried out."

Steve Brodie had no further thought than an engagement as a dime-museum attraction when he jumped—or feigned to jump—off the bridge. It may be seen that he was well aware of the value of newspaper notices. On his dime-museum engagements he would do publicity swimming and jumping feats, weather permitting and the jump being within reason. But though repeatedly offered large sums to leap in the presence of witnesses from the Brooklyn Bridge, he would only shake his head and say, "I done it oncet!"

He was a stocky, dark-eyed, dark-haired, pleasant-looking fellow with a peach-blow complexion. He was fastidiously neat in his personal appearance and dressed as became a prosperous man and a public character. He patterned his attire after great characters of the Bowery that he had envied as a boy—Owney Geoghegan, Harry Hill and John McGurk. He wore good clothes, faultlessly fine white shirts, white cravats and big diamonds and plenty of them. Diamonds on his plump manicured fingers, diamonds down his shirt front. Poor Chuck Connors had never a diamond in all his life. But Steve Brodie knew the well-dressed man has the advantage. He was a money-maker, thrifty, canny, and of all these things Chuck Connors had no notion.

The retirement from public life of Swipes the Newsboy, after he had accidentally killed a weak-hearted opponent in a prize fight, had the producers of the Bowery melodrama that had been written for Swipes looking for another star. There was Brodie. He was famous, he was smart. A brewer had set him up in a saloon, whereby, together with his theatrical engagements, Steve Brodie was to wax rich.

The producers of the melodrama waited upon Brodie. The canny Steve saw their need and his opportunity. He was no Swipes the Newsboy, to take a small salary. If he was worth anything to these men and their melodrama, he was worth something to himself. He asked an astonishing salary and declared himself in on the profits of the show.

"Can you act?" he was asked.

"Just can't I!" he replied confidently. "Haven't you heard me spiel on the dime-museum platforms? Don't you know I was always the best singer and dancer at the entertainments at the Newsboys' Lodging House, the Brace Memorial, on Duane Street, off Park Row? Can I act? I can eat it!"

And he could act. At least he could act well enough for a Bowery melodrama; and when he stood on the scenic Brooklyn Bridge and shouted, "I'll save the girl!" and jumped, closing his eyes from the showers of rock salt upthrown to simulate the spray to the roadway of Brooklyn Bridge from that mighty leap, the house roared and rocked. Nor would the audiences be content until he came before the curtain and bowed to the tumult, though strangely enough, for all his leaping into the river, dry as a dustbin.

When not out on the road in the money-making melodrama, Steve would stand in front of his bar and drink with the flattered sight-seers that thronged the place. He drank and they paid. But he was careful of what he drank. It would have been better far, however, in spite of his care, if he had never taken a single drop save the one that made him famous—the drop from Brooklyn Bridge. He took flats of beer—that is, beer in a whisky glass and mostly foam.

The ring of the cash register was music to the ears of thrifty Steve. He told me that he kept account of what it brought him a day when he took his flats at the expense of the constant line of hero worshipers who sought him out and shook his hand. His flat income, so to speak, from this averaged thirty dollars a day—and not the tenth of a cent's worth of beer in any one of the six hundred little glasses at five cents each!

Steve thought he was temperate. He never got drunk, and he was not standing in front of his bar drinking flats for more than six months of the year. But death lurked in the little flats of beer; he died of diabetes before he was thirty-five.

When custom fell off, Steve would do something to get his name in the papers. He was the first superlative publicity hound I ever met. To newspapermen he was courtesy, hospitality, generosity—everything. Steve Brodie was known to be so tight he had to turn himself around a corner with a wrench, but he'd offer to lend—yes, even give—money to newspapermen. He would enter into any sort of public appearance or take part in anything that would make newspaper notice for him. If he couldn't get good notices, he'd be glad to get bad ones.

"Say something about me—say I'm a crook, say I am a faker, that I never even jumped off a curbstone; say anything so you print my name!" he would cry. "I'll get arrested—anything! For when a story comes out about me, the hayseeds and sucker sight-seers come flocking in by droves."

Carrie Nation, the saloon smasher, in her heyday was brought to Brodie's saloon by a newspaperman, her famous hatchet in her hand. But Steve, with his bonny ways, his good appearance, his smiling gift of unctuous flattery, overcame the destructive intentions of the lady combatant of rum and rum sellers. Steve assured her that he intended to quit the booze business, close his mantrap, devote his ill-gotten gains to good works.

He pulled a large roll of bills from his pocket and said, "Mrs. Nation, here is a thousand dollars which I will gladly turn over to you to help you carry on your crusade."

She hesitated, but refused it.

"Take it," insisted the cunning Brodie. "Give it to foreign missions, poor ministers, struggling churches, temperance societies!"

But she said no, let Mr. Brodie contribute the money himself; she would send him a list of good causes. But it softened the erstwhile implacable lady from Kansas.

"You are a good man at heart," she said. "And you are a young man, Mr. Brodie. I am glad to see you realize the error of your ways in coining the tears of drunkards' wives and children into money in this hell hole. You may yet be saved, for you see the light."

The tears stood in Steve's eyes. He believed it all himself for the moment. He had not permitted one drop of liquor to be sold while the saloon-smashing crusader from Kansas was in his place. She withdrew, after giving him a hearty handshake and saying she would pray for him. But ten minutes later the tears came to his eyes again. This time copiously.

"Hully gee!" he cried aghast. "What a sucker I was to salve that old battle-ax, and I thought I was smart! Why look, if I had roughed her, she might have smashed the dump! I could get another lot of that junk she might have broken up and all the booze she might have spilled and scattered for a couple of hundred dollars—and I would have got first-page newspaper stories that would have brought the spending suckers in here by the million all the days of my life!"

It was the first and last time that Steve Brodie had overlooked a sure-fire publicity stunt.

HOW DIAMOND JIM GOT HIS NAME [4]

In New York Jim Brady's commissions [as salesman for the railroad supply house of Manning, Maxwell and Moore] were piling up. And there Jim let them stay; for while he was on the road he had no use for them. He was living and living well at the expense of the firm. What pocket money he may have needed he obtained in the faro games that could always be found in the smoking cars of trains and in the hotel lobbies.

He had a natural instinct for cards and scores of his friends have testified to his luck. Unfortunately, the records of this early period are lost. Most of the men who traveled with him in those first days are dead now. Too much heavy food and too many late parties cheerfully led the majority of them to early graves. The few who are still alive remember only that Jim Brady was a fine card player and that he would rather play for diamonds than for money.

All traveling men wore diamonds then. Sometimes, when short of money and seeking to recoup their losses, they would exchange a ring or a gem-encrusted watch fob for another pile of chips. The practice had started years before, and when Jim came along he found it such an excellent one and so in keeping with his own desire for diamonds that he naturally did everything in his power to

[4] From *Diamond Jim*, The Life and Times of James Buchanan Brady, by Parker Morell, pp. 26-30. Copyright, 1934, by Parker Morell. New York: Simon and Schuster, Inc.

continue it. Many of the diamonds in Jim's famous Number One set were won in pinochle or faro games played on lurching trans-continental trains and in smoke-filled hotel rooms.

In fact, his winnings at cards and dice formed the nucleus of his entire collection. While the men with whom he traveled made for the nearest bar-room, Jim would quietly slip off down the street in search of the local pawnshop. Walking in, he'd ask to see the unredeemed diamond rings.

"It's a bargain at one hundred and fifty dollars," the pawnbroker might say, of some particular gem.

"I'll give you seventy-five."

"To my own mother I couldn't sell it for less than a hundred and thirty."

"Eighty," Jim would serenely offer.

There were instances where his dickerings with pawnbrokers covered a period of several months. But in the end Jim would get his stone, and at a bargain. In an age when men boasted of their ability to drive a shrewd deal in a horse sale, Jim took an equally great pride in his ability to buy diamonds.

Sometimes the stones would be just little half-carat ones. Other times, depending on how rich he was at the moment, they might run as high as three or four carats. But diamonds they all were, never emeralds or sapphires or rubies. When he had completed his purchase, Jim always had the pawnbroker take the stones out of their mountings. These he would sell to the pawnbroker for their old gold value and then, putting the loose stones into a compartment in his wallet, he'd walk happily back to join his friends at the hotel.

Sometimes, too, his return to the hotel with a new prize would bring forth offers to exchange it for a stone owned by one of the salesmen or desk clerks. It was at a time like this that Jim's great persuasive powers received their acid test.

In tones that varied from honeyed sweetness to loud imperiousness he would alternately beg, plead, argue, and cajole to gain his ends. Sometimes the debate would continue for hours with all the drummers taking sides in the matter; sometimes it would be continued for the entire length of the trip. Often it would end with neither side being able to reach an agreement. But once in a while —and this happened more frequently than might be supposed—the battle would end with Jim possessing a stone bigger and better than the one he'd bought from the pawnshop.

It was not that he was dishonest. He never took unfair advantages. But he did like to drive a sharp bargain when it came to diamonds. And though there were many other traveling men who were his equal, the fact remains that with the passing of the years, the stones in his wallet grew bigger and bigger in size, and larger and larger in number.

Back of all this buying and bargaining was a purpose.

These diamonds were beginning to make money for him in another way. They gained him audiences with, and won the respect of, many of the lesser rail officials with whom he first had to do business. Some of these were petty despots who, full of their own importance, tried to impress the salesmen.

After a few minutes of general conversation Jim would swing the talk around.

"Speaking of diamonds," he would say, "I've got a few you might like to see—they're my hobby, you know."

Then he'd calmly take out his wallet (in a few years it grew to be a miner's belt) and spread a whole handful of precious stones before the astonished eyes of the railroad men.

Generally this display of affluence sufficed to reduce all beholders to a state of respectful awe. Diamonds alone were a rarity to most of them, and a man with a dozen or more was indeed a strange mortal. They'd ask him the value of each stone, then repeat the price in hushed tones, and tremble with the sensation of holding five thousand dollars in their palms.

There were times when Jim ran up against a man made of sterner stuff.

"Them ain't diamonds," the tough-minded one might say, "they're nothing but paste imitations."

Striding over to a window, Jim would take one of the stones in question and with it write the words, "James Buchanan Brady" in large and flowing letters on the glass pane. This never failed to clinch the argument. It was one of the great American Credos that a diamond, and a diamond alone, would cut glass. Jim had won his point and, what was more important still, had left his name written on the window of a railroad office where all could see it and remember the fat supply salesman whose word was not to be questioned.

It was undoubtedly one of the earliest and most effective forms of billboard advertising. Possessors of these personally autographed office windows became creatures set apart. They were respected and envied. People were forever wanting to hear about the itinerant Kimberley. Basking in the light of reflected glory, the owners of those office windows improved upon the story every time they told it. Jim's fame spread by leaps and bounds through the entire railroad system. It was inevitable for some one, sooner or later, to dub him Diamond Jim.

It happened this way. Early in the year 1884 a half dozen of Jim's cronies had planned to meet in Cincinnati for a week-end of card playing and general amusement. Some of the crowd arrived at the old Burnet House early Saturday afternoon and, after a drink or two, started to count noses. "Markie" Mayer, the short and fat star salesman for the cotton house of H. B. Claflin & Company, looked around the room and suddenly shouted: "Has any one here seen Diamond Jim yet?"

For an instant no one seemed to be able to recall any one by that name. Then another drummer cried: "Oh, you mean Brady—the big fat stiff who don't drink?"

"Yes," said Mayer, "he's the one—good old Diamond Jim Brady—the pawnbroker's curse."

Thus banally was born a cognomen that became the most famous (and valuable) nickname in America.

PICARESQUE MARIGNY [5]

Bernard's great-grandfather, François Phillippe de Marigny de Mandeville, was . . . a French gentleman of a noble Norman family. He went to Canada as an infantry officer in 1709 and later was transferred south as *Commandant des Troupes en Louisiane.* After helping Bienville found New Orleans in 1719, he became its *Major de Place* and stamped his line with his own qualities of hot-headed courage and arrogant pride.

His grandson, Pierre Enguerrand Phillippe de Mandeville, Ecuyer Sieur de Marigny, Chevalier de St. Louis, and father of Bernard, also became a soldier —a captain—but in the Spanish infantry, for Louisiana was a burden that the rulers of France and Spain seemed to be ever shifting, one to the other.

By this time the danger from Indians, floods, and snakes had decreased. New Orleans was growing and the time was ripe for development. Pierre saw and seized his opportunities, acquired plantations around the spreading city and sawmills, too, until he became the richest *milliardaire* in all Louisiana, with a reputed fortune of four million *pesos*—colossal for that day.

To Bernard he transmitted his venturesome blood, but did nothing to shape the boy's character, neglecting his education because he believed, with the soldier of his day, that shooting, fencing, and horsemanship were far more necessary to a gentleman than a knowledge of the three R's: that was fit only for priests and scriveners.

Surrounded from childhood by slaves eager to pander to his wishes and his every whim indulged by his father, Bernard grew up as wild and headstrong as an unbacked mustang. That he should also be a spendthrift was inevitable for he witnessed his father's extravagance.

*   *   *   *   *

[In 1800, at the age of sixteen] Bernard lost his father. His kinsman, Lino de Chalmette, became his guardian, but found his charge unmanageable—not surprising after such an upbringing. Finally, in desperation Lino de Chalmette shipped Bernard to Panton at Pensacola to learn English and business.

*   *   *   *   *

But even Panton's firm hand could not keep Bernard out of trouble and finally the boy so outraged the trader's Scotch Presbyterianism by seducing the female sacristan of the Catholic church that he sent the youngster back to New Orleans, a journey that then took from eighteen to thirty days.

This taste of dissipation only whetted Bernard's appetite and he continued his wild ways until Lino decided to send him to London to Mr. Leslie, Panton's associate in England. Influential noblemen were silent partners of Panton, Leslie & Company, among them Gordon, Lord Byron's father, and one of the Pitts; so at Leslie's house Bernard met the cream of British society. But he benefited little

[5] From *Creole City: Its Past and Its People,* by Edward Larocque Tinker, pp. 4-9, 61-62. Copyright, 1953, by Edward Larocque Tinker. New York: Longmans, Green & Co.

beyond obtaining a limited knowledge of the English language, which, to the day of his death, he spoke with a quaint French accent. He quickly discovered that Paris was much more to his liking than London and his trips across the Channel were more and more frequent. Europe became merely a larger field for his amorous adventures; and, as a consequence, back he was packed once more to Louisiana. Here he denied himself nothing, neither old wine nor young women, the taste of good food nor the tense thrills of gambling.

In the English coffeehouses, especially at Almack's, where Bernard had spent much of his time, he had learned a form of dicing, newly imported from the Continent, called *hazard,* and, although a similar game may have crossed the ocean with earlier adventurers, it was Bernard Marigny who, on his return, first made it the rage among the Creoles.

The nineteenth century had but begun and already energetic Yankees were swarming into New Orleans to the disgust of the pleasure-loving Creoles, who regarded them as rough, unmannerly interlopers, called them *Americains coquins* and despised them because of their willingness to work like "niggers." Returning this dislike, the Americans looked down on the Creoles as an effete, alien race and called them "Johnny Crapauds"—a term of reproach the British had long fastened upon the French because of their supposed predilection for frogs as an article of diet.

When the Yankees saw Creoles huddled about tables playing Marigny's new game of *hazard,* wagering slaves, plantations and even dull gold mistresses on the turn of a die, they slurringly referred to the pastime as "Johnny Crapaud's" game. But, as its popularity, spreading like yellow fever in a mosquito swamp, made it the obsession of Americans and Creoles alike, the former, it is said, deleted "Johnny" and renamed it "Crapaud's," which they later curtailed to "craps." Other explanations of its provenance are to be found in dictionaries, but none as picturesque and appealing.

Picaresque Marigny was the wildest gamester of them all, and was finally forced to subdivide his plantation in the Faubourg Marigny, just below the Vieux Carré, and to dispose of the lots piecemeal to meet his losses. One night he diced away a tremendous sum and the next morning ordered his man of affairs to sell sufficient lots to realize the necessary amount, for debts of honor had to be met within twenty-four hours. When the agent brought him the money, Marigny said, "Name the street those lots are on 'rue de Craps.'"

Craps Street it remained for over fifty years, until at last a church was built in the neighborhood and the good parishioners, too horrified to walk on Sundays through a thoroughfare with such an unregenerate appellation, petitioned the city fathers to change the name to Burgundy.

Tradition insists that Marigny had the proverbial compensation for ill luck at gaming and was a *succès fou* with the ladies. It was even whispered that he presented each of the frail objects of his attention with a small plot and cottage on the street below Craps and that this was why he saw fit to christen it "rue d'Amour." That "rue des Bon Enfants" should come next seemed only logical in a day when birth control was still unknown. Whether true or apocryphal these interpretations of Marigny's nomenclature are at least plausible, and the fact remains that "Love" and "Good Children" Streets are still to be found on the Anglicized maps of New Orleans and give rise to many quaint addresses in the old city directories, such as that of a certain *flâneur* who lived appropriately on the corner of "Love and Trifle."

* * * * *

. . . While Bernard was devoting his life to politics and pleasure, his business affairs were becoming more and more entangled. No fortune could stand the drain of his lavish entertainment, his gambling losses, his huge expenditure for political purposes, and his many other extravagances. He was so careless of money, so it was said, that he often twisted five-dollar bills into spills with which to light his cigars, and when a friend once remonstrated with him he answered, "Bah, it's a bagatelle!" Tradition has it that this inspired him to name the street in his *faubourg* where the incident occurred "rue Bagatelle"— a name that has since been translated into Trifle Street.

CHARLIE CROCKER'S FERRY RIDE [6]

The bay ferries came and went, and long after construction of the San Francisco-Oakland Bay Bridge, stories about these side-wheelers and stern-wheelers were among the City's favorites. San Franciscans always considered "the excursion to Oakland" a real adventure.

Almost from the beginning the ferryboats were equipped with restaurants, bars, blankets, and bedding—just in case they happened to have engine trouble and were forced to drift while repairs were made. Sometimes the ferries had Italian orchestras which included a couple of violinists, a harpist, and usually a dark-eyed Italian girl who played a tambourine and sang the songs of sunny Italy. They always passed the hat and collected nickels and dimes from the passengers.

There is an account of the time when Charles Crocker, the railroad magnate, crossed on one of these ferries after a lucky day at the races in Sacramento. The story goes that "Big Charlie" boarded the ferry in Oakland with his pockets jingling with more than twenty-five hundred dollars in five- and ten-dollar gold pieces. The big side wheels had barely started to churn before the Italian orchestra struck up "Tarantella" and Charlie began tossing gold coins at them. That inspired the orchestra to even livelier tunes, and the girl with the tambourine laughed and danced and sang as she had never done before. Charlie clapped and shouted and tossed more coins.

"Wine, women, and song!" mused Charlie. Then he suddenly remembered the wine was lacking, and he promptly ordered champagne brought from the bar and served to himself and the musicians.

The cabin was filled with ladies and gentlemen who began to scoff at such extravagance, but when Charlie invited every one to share his hospitality, the passengers became convivial and gentlemen began to swing their ladies to the

[6] From *San Francisco, Port of Gold,* by William Martin Camp, pp. 11-12. Copyright, 1947, by William Martin Camp. Garden City, New York: Doubleday & Company, Inc.

lively cadence of the waltz, the schottische, and any other dance the orchestra was requested to play.

Whether it was the dancing or the champagne, no one ever bothered to speculate, but the ladies and gentlemen came bounding off the ferry when it touched the San Francisco side and had to be hauled away in waterfront hacks. For this, so the story goes, Charlie Crocker laughingly paid the last few gold pieces remaining of his winnings. That was the most expensive ferry-boat ride Charlie Crocker ever had, but for a long time after that he still maintained it was worth every cent of that twenty-five hundred dollars.

RALSTON'S DIAMOND MINE [7]

One day . . . in 1871, Philip Arnold and John Slack, two weather-beaten prospectors, . . . wandered into the Bank of California [in San Francisco]. With them they . . . carried several sacks, which, they told a bank clerk, contained property of great value. For safekeeping they wished to deposit them in Ralston's bank. In making arrangements it was necessary to state what the sacks contained. "Diamonds, rough diamonds," the duo blurted out. They had found them in a deserted mountain section of the West. As soon as the receipt was in their possession, the prospectors shambled out of the bank.

Somehow or other news of those sacks of diamonds, reposing in a dark cranny of his vaults, reached Ralston's ears. Immediately his interest was stirred. With mines of gold and silver, and refineries bulging with bullion, the thought of diamond fields stayed Ralston's attention. Look what the Comstock had done for San Francisco. With a diamond mine what might he not accomplish for his beloved city? Ralston saw another chance to invest his Comstock wealth in something spectacular, and he sent for Arnold and Slack to come to his office.

A day came when the two roughly clad prospectors shuffled up to Ralston's desk. They seemed bewildered in his presence. Their attitude said plainer than words that accidentally they had stumbled upon a windfall. A windfall so monstrous that they did not know how to proceed. Being in doubt, they intended to remain silent. Arnold had made it especially evident that he did not wish to talk to Ralston. He was afraid of him, he claimed.

Ralston asked the bewildered duo where they had found the sack of diamonds.

But the prospectors were ignorant of their United States geography. Accidentally they had come upon them somewhere out in the great American desert. Arnold pointed a rough thumb towards the East: "Out there." Perhaps it was Arizona, or Colorado, or Wyoming. He didn't know. Anyway, it was about 1000 miles to the east of Ralston's office. Who knew, out in the great desert, where one wandered? Who cared? And the old prospector laughed. They were mining explorers. They had been looking for gold. By chance they had stumbled upon diamonds.

No! they did not want to sell out their rights. True: they had no resources.

[7] From *Ralston's Ring,* California Plunders the Comstock Lode, by George D. Lyman, pp. 190-201. Copyright, 1937, by Charles Scribner's Sons. New York.

To get a start, perhaps they would be forced to dispose of a small interest. But only perhaps. On no account would they part with the whole. They did not have money enough to secur title or develop their discovery. Perhaps on that account they would have to take a third party in with them. But they didn't want an outsider.

Ralston could make nothing out of the two, shy, cautious, bewildered men before him. So afraid were they of making some regrettable mistake that they didn't know what they ought to do themselves.

Several days passed and the miners, more amenable to reason, returned to Ralston's office. They would part with a half interest in their diamond fields, they told him, to men in whom they had implicit confidence. Patiently Ralston pointed out that negotiations were impossible until the location of the fields was disclosed and some sort of inspection permitted.

Then Slack and Arnold proposed a strange arrangement. On its face it seemed fair enough to Ralston. If anything, it made the offer more alluring.

They would conduct two men, to be selected by Ralston, to the diamond fields, and allow them to satisfy themselves of their extent, but only on one condition: when these men had reached the wild, uninhabited district where the diamond fields lay, they must submit to being blindfolded, both going and coming back.

Full of the adventure of the thing, Ralston agreed. For one of the proposed inspectors he selected David C. Colton of the Southern Pacific, one of the most prominent and level-headed men of big affairs in San Francisco. Ralston acknowledged that he would have absolute faith in Colton's conclusions.

One day Colton departed with the two prospectors. After some time he was back in Ralston's office. He had been to the marvelous diamond country. Both going and coming he had been blindfolded; but there he had unearthed more diamonds than he ever knew existed. There was no doubt of the genuineness of the fields or of their fabulous richness. There were acres and acres of precious stones; diamonds, rubies, sapphires, emeralds. The whole terrain sparkled with them. On hearing this rose-colored report from a sane official of the Southern Pacific, Ralston went absolutely wild. There was one spot to invest his "Belcher" millions. There millions would beget millions. There would be no end to what he could accomplish for San Francisco. Straightaway he cabled his old friend Harpending, who was in London on mining business, regarding the diamond discovery. The first telegram was so explanatory that it cost Ralston $1100. But he did not care. Ralston wanted Harpending for his general manager. Would he catch the next boat? Harpending demurred. Ralston burned up the cable with messages. Harpending, an unbeliever in American diamond fields, "felt assured his old friend had gone mad." Finally, at great personal sacrifice he gave up several lucrative London deals to go to his old friend's assistance. In the meantime rumors of Ralston's vast diamond field leaked out in London. No less a person than Baron Rothschild sought an interview with the departing Harpending. But the latter was non-committal, although he was still scouting the idea of diamond fields in his country.

"Do not be sure of that," commented the baron. "America is a very large country. It has furnished the world with so many surprises already. Perhaps it may have others in store. At any rate, if you find cause to change your opinion, kindly let me know."

When Harpending saw those sacks empty their contents on his billiard table he kept his promise.

Being a cautious investor, Ralston started an investigation. Who were these two prospectors? Philip Arnold, he discovered, was an old California miner. Originally a California pioneer of '49, he had come from Hardin County, Kentucky. Ever since his arrival he had been mining. Several times George D. Roberts, one of the best-known mining men in the West and a close friend of Ralston's, had hired Arnold to investigate mining properties for him. Never had he been dissatisfied with the honesty of his work. He was an honorable old-timer.

Harpending, too, had known Arnold, and had always found him reliable. As for Slack, he was a plain man-about-town of fair repute. In Ralston's mind there were no longer any doubts as to Arnold and Slack. They were well-known honest prospectors, "Old Forty-Niners." Still, all that mysterious hocus-pocus coming and going to and from the diamond fields deserved attention.

He decided to proceed carefully. The supply of diamonds might be quickly exhausted; only a "flash in the pan" as it were. That was not the sort of investment Ralston wanted for his Comstock winnings or for investors. Sensing Ralston's lack of enthusiasm, Arnold offered to go back to the diamond fields, collect a couple of million dollars' worth of diamonds, bring them back to San Francisco and allow Ralston to keep them in his possession as a guarantee of good faith.

That was fair enough. Ralston accepted. Slack and Arnold left San Francisco promising to be back in record-breaking time.

One night, shortly thereafter, Ralston received a telegram from Arnold. He was at Reno. He and Slack were on their return journey to San Francisco. He urged Ralston to have reliable persons meet them at Lathrop: "to share the burden of responsibility." The next morning, after a hurried conference, Harpending, who had just arrived from London, set out for Lathrop to meet the diamond emissaries and accompany them back to San Francisco. Before leaving, it had been agreed that Ralston, Rubery a London friend of Harpending, William M. Lent, and several others interested in the fields would await Harpending that evening in the billiard room of his home on Fremont Street to examine the diamond collateral.

That night an eager group assembled about Harpending's billiard table. Along about nine o'clock the rumble of carriage wheels and the crunching of gravel on the driveway could be heard. A moment later they heard the turning of a key in a lock and the shutting of a door. Then, all excitement, Harpending entered the billiard room. Under his arm was an awkward buckskin-covered bundle. He placed it on the table. He had a lurid tale to tell.

Ralston and Lent drew closer as Harpending began: When Arnold and Slack had reached the diamond fields they had struck an enormously rich deposit. With no trouble at all they had filled two packages, such as the one he laid upon the table, with diamonds, sapphires, emeralds, and rubies. Then they had started on their return. On their way they had been overtaken by a violent rainstorm. They had been compelled to ford a river on a raft. The river had been greatly swollen. Accidentally one package had been washed overboard and was irretrievably lost in the flood. But that had been no loss to the prospectors. There were millions more of precious stones on the fields. But time was pressing. They could not go back for more, so they had brought only one sack with them—the one on the table.

No time was lost in preliminaries. A sheet was spread over the green-baize covering. Ralston, Roberts, Dodge, Rubery, and Lent drew closer about the table. Harpending snipped the elaborate cord-fastenings about the bundle. Taking hold of the lower corners of the sack he turned it upside down. Out gushed a cascade of many-colored stones. How they flashed and scintillated in the dim light! As fiery as pieces of stars! They looked as if they would burn holes through the sheet. There lay at least a million dollars' worth of diamonds, rubies, sapphires, and emeralds. The ransom of a rajah! The loot of a dozen Burmah temples lay before Ralston's startled gaze. The flush on his cheeks turned a ruby red. Such a sight was worth a kingdom.

Having gorged their eyes to the full, Lent tied up the sack and locked the gems in Harpending's vault for safekeeping. After that, once a week on Sundays, the same group would lock themselves in Harpending's billiard room, spread a sheet over the green baize, open the safe, take out the bundle and spill out the gems. Then they would feast their eyes and speculate over each precious stone; descanting upon its size, beauty, brilliance, and value.

These men had only one fear: there would be a great depreciation in the value of all diamonds, all rubies, all sapphires, all emeralds, when the news of the contents of their sack and of the field of precious stones was given to the world. Sighing deeply, the owners would watch the gems put back into the sack and then into the stronghold until another Sunday should roll around.

So far, no attempt had been made at organization. It was generally understood that Ralston, Roberts, Lent, and Harpending, and one or two others, would be in on the deal by virtue of the large sums of money they had already loaned to the prospectors. For those advances there was ample security in the gems on hand, to say nothing of the unexplored diamond fields. Now without further delay Ralston determined to get the diamond fields on a business basis. For that purpose he called a meeting and outlined his plan of action.

First, a large supply of the precious stones would be sent to Tiffany & Co. of New York, the greatest authority on precious stones in America, for examination and appraisal. If their value were proved beyond peradventure, then a mining expert would be chosen to whom Arnold and Slack would be required to exhibit the diamond fields and permit a full examination. Those were the only conditions upon which Ralston would be willing to handle the situation.

To Ralston's preamble Arnold and Slack readily agreed. Pending the favorable reports of Tiffany & Co. and the mining expert, Ralston agreed to take care of all incidental expenses, which already amounted to several hundreds of thousands. Then Ralston looked up government laws regarding diamond fields. There was no existing one under which diamond lands could be located and held. Therefore a title must be procured and a law gotten through Congress. It would take plenty of money. But, as usual, Ralston shouldered it. Immediately a prominent Washington lobbyist was selected to engineer and pass an act through Congress that would cover the grounds on which their wonderful discovery had been made. After considerable delay and difficulty a bill was finally drafted, introduced, and passed. It was known as "Sargent's Mining Bill," and appeared May 18, 1872. In it the following passage was inserted, purposely to cover the field of precious stones: "Including all forms of deposit, except veins of quartz or other rock then in place."

In the meantime Harpending, who had taken a little bag of the gems to Tiffany & Co., New York, displayed the stones in the presence of Mr. Tiffany, Horace Greeley, General George B. McClellan of Civil War fame, and General Benjamin F. Butler, a lawyer of repute as well as a United States Congressman. Butler had been included because it was thought that he would be of aid in the legislation needed to acquire the diamond fields, as later proved to be the case.

"Gentlemen," said Mr. Tiffany, with the air of a connoisseur, as he picked up a huge gem from one of the piles of stones he had been building in front of him, and held it up to the light, "gentlemen, these are beyond question precious stones of enormous value. But before I give you the exact appraisement, I must submit them to my lapidary, and will report to you further in two days."

Within those limits, Tiffany presented his report before the aforementioned men. The stones were genuine. The lot was worth about $150,000. Ralston was stunned on receipt of that information, as the stones sent to Tiffany were a fair sample of the lot, but composed only about one-tenth of those still in Ralston's possession. It argued a total value of $1,500,000 for the whole.

All that remained now was the choice of an engineer. The name of Henry Janin suggested itself. Henry Janin was one of the best-known mining engineers then living. The John Hays Hammond of his day. As a consulting engineer he was without a peer in the world. His ultra-conservatism was his only known fault. He had experted something over six hundred mines. Never once had he made a mistake. Some complained that he never took a chance. He had not an iota of gambling instinct. This was just the kind of man he wanted to expert the diamond fields, Ralston explained. One couldn't be too careful with other people's money. Janin valued his services at $2500, an expense that Ralston readily shouldered.

So Henry Janin was dispatched to the region of many-colored gems and made an extensive examination. His report confirmed all that had been claimed for the field of precious stones.

Gems were so plentiful, Janin averred, that twenty rough laborers could wash out a million dollars' worth of diamonds a month.

At least, the uncut jewels were worth the value of all of "Crown Point" and "Belcher" stock combined. Some $65,000,000.

Ralston was so enthused over Janin's report that he telegraphed Harpending that he was ready to make the initial payment of $300,000 as per agreement, to Arnold and Slack. Not having ready cash, he made immediate arrangements to sell 100 shares of "Crown Point," which was then bringing $300 a share on the San Francisco stock market.

Ralston now cleared the deck for the formation of his great diamond company. After Janin's return from the diamond fields there was some talk of incorporating in New York, but Ralston would not listen to such heresy. "San Francisco stood ready to furnish any amount of capital required," he wired. Moreover, all gems should be brought to San Francisco. In San Francisco they must be cut. Ralston intended to move the great lapidary establishments of Amsterdam to San Francisco, a decision which caused the Low Countries "no small concern."

San Francisco was ripe for the new company: "The San Francisco and New York Mining and Commercial Company." It was capitalized at $10,000,000. Twenty-five gentlemen, comprising the cream of San Francisco's financial element, men of national reputation for high-class business standing and personal integrity, were permitted to subscribe for stock to the amount of $80,000 each. This initial capital of $2,000,000 was immediately paid into the Bank of California.

The London Rothschilds cabled that they were interested in the diamond discovery. As a result, A. Gansl, the Rothschilds' California representative, became a member of the company. Among other directors were: Samuel Barlow and Major-General George B. McClellan of New York, who were to be resident directors there, where a transfer office was to be maintained. Among San Franciscans, the directorate included: William M. Lent, Thomas Selby, whose daughter had married Ralston's brother; Milton S. Latham, Louis Sloss, Maurice Dore, W. F. Babcock, William C. Ralston, William Willis. Lent was chosen president; Ralston, treasurer; Willis, secretary. David D. Colton resigned his substantial position with the Southern Pacific Railroad to become general manager. Such were the men behind the diamond fields. The biggest names in California's Blue Book. The last word in the commercial and financial world. Men who only allowed their names to be used in 100 per cent concerns.

Handsome offices were engaged in San Francisco. Two or three secretaries were engaged to handle the voluminous correspondence.

The interests of Arnold and Slack were extinguished by a final payment of $300,000, making, with what had been already allocated, $660,000 in all. The capitalists congratulated themselves that $660,000 was an exceedingly small sum to pay for property capable of producing a million dollars a month, to say nothing of a million and a half dollars in value already in their possession. Without more ado, the honest prospectors received their money and faded into invisibility.

Not only in Ralston's office in the Bank of California but in nearly every financial center in the world, the public was keyed up to a point of high speculative craze. "Crown Point," "Belcher," Sutro, Mackay, Fair, and O'Brien retired to the region of limbo.

Suddenly, like a thunderbolt from the blue, came a telegram from a small Wyoming station. It was signed by the name of Clarence King, the noted scientist, head of the Fortieth Parallel Survey.

Taking assistants, King had visited the diamond fields in order to give official national significance to a notable local discovery. Readily he had located the fields and found diamonds, rubies, sapphires, and emeralds aplenty, scattered over a wide terrain. Immediately his admiration had been aroused by the sheer beauty of the ant-hills. Some were powdered with diamond and ruby dust, while others were sprinkled with pulverized sapphire and emerald particles. There were gorgeous things to behold. In the heart of every ant-hill he found a gem corresponding in color to the dust sprinkled over its surface.

On looking about more closely, King found diamonds and sapphires in rock crevices where nature alone could not have placed them. Several times he ran into rubies and emeralds in the forks of trees; but not a gem could he unearth in the underlying bedrock, where, had their occurrence been genuine, the inevitable laws of nature must have placed them.

But when he uncovered a large diamond with the marks of the lapidary's art still upon its face, he realized the moment had come to explode Ralston's bubble and he had sent his telegram: "The alleged diamond fields are fraudulent. Plainly they are salted. The discovery is a gigantic fraud. The Company has been pitifully duped." But how could Arnold and Slack have told that the expert King would examine their diamond field? With any number of unskilled workmen it would have passed muster.

Subsequently some of the "jewels" reached London, where they were recognized as South African "niggerheads." When Arnold's picture was displayed, there were those who remembered him as a buyer of low-grade diamonds and other jewels in the big centers of London and Amsterdam. Thus beyond a doubt the fraudulent nature of the jewel fields was exposed.

Cruel as the blow was to Ralston, as soon as he had been convinced that he and twenty-five other members of the high lights of the city's financial firmament had been duped, he called a meeting of the "San Francisco and New York Mining and Commercial Company." The Tiffany appraisement and the reports of experts Janin and Clarence King were both examined. Then a complete recital was prepared for the public, bringing out the confidence that Ralston and his trustees had reposed in Tiffany and Janin. In conclusion, a complete acknowledgment was made of the fact that every one had been cleverly duped. Ralston intended that not the least of his enemies should ever connect his name with a fraudulent procedure. Then he made up his mind that rather than endure the whinings of faint-hearted partners he would assume the burden of expense himself.

Philosophically he accepted the loss of his own investment. With magnanimity he restored dollar for dollar to the twenty-five stockholders, who had subscribed to the $2,000,000 capital funds. And they allowed him to do so. There remained incidental expenses for lobbying, experting, etc., and the $300,-000 that he had paid out of his own pocket to Arnold and Slack: an aggregate of loss not less than $500,000. Thus was expended a half million dollars of his

"Belcher" bonanza. This sacrifice Ralston cheerfully assumed. No person should ever even whisper that Ralston had gulled his friends. He would rather sacrifice his last dollar than let any man look him in the face and say: "I suffer through you."

At long last Ralston had the receipts-in-full framed. These he hung upon his office wall, where he might have a continual reminder alike of the faith and the duplicity of man.

Harpending did not get off so easily. Because of innocent activities in London, he was loudly denounced in San Francisco as having "put up the job" on Ralston and others. . . .

MARSHALL FIELD—"DO AS THE LADY WISHES"[8]

. . . By the Gay Nineties Chicago was fast becoming a grand market for luxuries. . . . As more and more of its men grew rich, some had started collecting expensive things, and not only things but expensive wives, who bought so much that more and more of them learned to distinguish the good from the bad. Many shopped in New York and some in London, Paris and Old Vienna and Rome. Back in Chicago they demanded architects who could build houses in better taste. On both the north and the south sides were appearing great houses of stone, many still awful but some of them good to look at, both outside and within, for our hostess knew about furnishings now. She gave large dinners of twenty or more, on glossy damask draped to the floor, on plates of silver and lovely old china, at each place half a dozen delicate high-stemmed glasses for wines. Chefs and butlers had appeared. In private ballrooms young people danced through long and colorful cotillions to the music of Johnny Hand and his orchestra. Strauss waltzes, Sousa two-steps, how Johnny could play when he'd had enough punch! Our own big brick house knew him well.

All this demanded clothes and furnishings of divers kinds; and though many still shopped in the East and abroad, all of them came to Field's store in Chicago. To keep them coming and better their tastes, his buyers ranged all over the globe for rugs, furs, laces, jewelry, tableware and costly clothes. Most of them sold, but I learned from a friend that in the linen department one day Field called the head and asked him:

"Where did you get this tablecloth?"

"Imported it from Italy, sir."

"Looks expensive. What's the price?"

"Eight hundred, sir."

"You'll never sell it." A week later he said to the same man: "Congratulations, Mr. B. I see your judgment was better than mine. I saw that Italian tablecloth while dining last night with Mrs. C." The department head ruefully replied:

[8] From *Giants Gone*, Men Who Made Chicago, by Ernest Poole, pp. 119-122. Copyright, 1943, by the McGraw-Hill Book Company, Inc. New York and London: Whittlesey House.

"I'm sorry to tell you, Mr. Field, that she took it yesterday on approval and this morning it came back!"

To avoid such costly errors and meet the local market needs, ingenious devices were worked out. A student at the Art Institute told me that he was one of a group employed in the nineties by Marshall Field to copy designs of old Persian rugs and adapt them in shape and size to suit Chicago customers. The designs were then sent over to shops in Persia, and so the rugs were made and sent back to Chicago for sale. And sell they did—and so did better things, rare treasures pouring into Field's store from abroad to give distinction to the lines of American goods. By the time of his death in 1906, with its seven thousand employees and thirty-six acres of floor space, it had become the great shopping center for women from all over the West.

Its lunch room seated two thousand and was crowded every day; for women came not only to shop, they lunched and wrote letters and rested, met friends; and as though it were a club, they showed the whole big place with pride to visitors from out of town. They loved the great show windows, the long vistas down broad aisles, the white columns and wide galleries and the glittering counters filled with luxuries of all kinds. Nobody ever urged them to buy; they could just wander about as they pleased—and that was something new in those days. They loved its atmosphere of wealth and the politeness everywhere. "The customer is always right," became the motto of the store. In earlier years, when disputes arose, often a clerk had heard the low voice of his chief at his elbow:

"Do as the lady wishes."

And the clerks had learned that lesson well. But as beneath its costly trimmings the immense shop was built of steel, so all this luxury and ease was built on an elaborate organization, cold, rigid and precise, working smoothly as a dynamo. And its commander was like that. Cleanly built and vigorous still, with hair and trimmed mustache turned white but blue eyes still clear and bright, voice low and gentle, an affable smile, he had lovely manners, the ladies said. A quiet, suave and courtly man. But if courteous, he was brief; the gentle voice held a dominant note and the eyes the cold clear judgment which had built in half a century the largest fortune in the West.

YOUNG JOHN ROOT BUILDS
THE FIRST CHICAGO SKYSCRAPER [9]

Until about 1880 the bulk of the city's buildings were four or five stories high. They might have been stretched two or three stories higher without any changes in building method, but these extra floors would have been vacant. Five stories was about the limit to which any ordinary man could lift himself on a hot day.

[9] From *Chicago Medium Rare, When We Were Both Younger*, by Robert J. Casey, pp. 15-16, 30-32. Copyright, 1949, 1950, by the Chicago *Herald-American*; 1952, by The Bobbs-Merrill Company, Inc. Indianapolis and New York.

Sometime just before the Civil War, Otis, or some other genius, had invented an elevator to help him lift iron parts for his factory. Shortly after the war he had added a device to keep it from falling, should the power cut off, and the world began to talk about a safe elevator for passengers. In the middle eighties it attracted the attention of the Chicago architects Daniel H. Burnham and John W. Root. Before 1890 they had built the Montauk Block, the Rookery Building, and the first section of the Monadnock Block—all of them ten or more stories in height. Before Root's death in 1891 they had hung the twenty-one-story Masonic Temple to the clouds. For many years it was to remain the tallest building in the world. The elevators worked perfectly.

The building of the first skyscraper made changes not only in Chicago but in all the growing cities of the United States. It made possible the concentration of hundreds of people over a ground space that twenty years before might have been crowded by a dozen. It gave quick access to the offices of people in associated professions. It slowed down the outward expansion of the original business district and made possible the Union Loop. And the hammering of steel and the piling of brick and stone has gone on ceaselessly ever since.

*   *   *   *   *

Built as it was on a swamp, the bottom of which had never been located since the establishment of Fort Dearborn, Chicago was the least likely place on earth to have developed a skyscraper. Conservative capitalists, backed by the opinions of some of the best engineers in the United States, shied away from the idea of lofty towers rising out of a jelly of water and sand. If you couldn't find a solid bottom for your foundation, they said, your buildings would have to float in this semicolloidal mass—and such a project was obviously nonsense.

It turned out, however, that all the capitalists in Chicago at that period did not follow the same rules of conservatism. Some of them were hidebound, no doubt. But there were plenty of them with gamblers' wits. Daring had been the principal factor in making them rich, and they were quite ready to take a chance, silly or not.

There was no lack of architects and builders who had new ideas and daring —William Holabird, John Root, Daniel Burnham, Louis Sullivan, Dankmar Adler and William Le Baron Jenney. Some of them may not have had much money—particularly at the beginning of their drive to put a new face on local construction. But every one of them was ready to hazard his reputation to prove that the city's unstable soil would support a tall building. So eventually they altered the appearance not only of Chicago but of San Francisco, Lima, Shanghai, Rio, New York, and, for that matter, most of the large cities in the world.

John M. Van Osdel and W. W. Boyington, whose impression was plain in the building trends that followed the fire, had made Chicago look something like a fairly raw Paris. There were stretches of four-story buildings along State Street with mansard roofs and chateau fronts, dignified lobbies and stairways that were grand to look at if not to ascend. The city was bowing with great dignity toward architectural tradition and was beginning to look uncomfortable.

Some newspaper engineer calculated in 1885 that an additional floor on each of the buildings in the downtown district would care for the growth of Chicago for fifteen years. But he admitted that the weight of an additional story would be a severe tax on the basic swamp. It might be better, he suggested, if Chicago were to move somewhere farther north—to Wilmette, for instance, or some place else where there wasn't any swamp.

The new architects, who had begun to raise a fine lot of argument about buildings of fifteen, seventeen, and twenty stories—fantastic conversation, their opponents declared—were uniformly a group that cared nothing for tradition. Until their coming, the foundations of buildings in the downtown area had rested on pilings or pillars of stone sunk deeply in the sand. Young John Root got the idea that taller structures could be erected on foundations that would have no stress to the sides, and as a sample, he invented a raft of railroad rails and concrete to be sunk considerably below the surface. The tall building, he argued, would be supported solidly by the raft.

His first venture with this construction was in Monroe Street. It was watched with leers and jeers by most of his contemporaries. A deep hole was dug with watertight wooden walls surrounding it. Steam pumps kept the excavation dry. A layer of cement some two feet thick was laid down as the construction's first step. Railroad rails were crisscrossed over it to a depth of a foot and a half, and cement was poured into the interstices. Another layer of concrete went in and another layer of crossed rails until the raft was some twenty feet deep. On top of it went the basement and ten stories of the Montauk Building, the first skyscraper that the world had ever seen.

Some of the skeptics remained, of course, and their voices were loud after La Salle Street and Michigan Avenue began to fill up with piles of masonry taller than most of the populace thought dignified, or safe, or even possible. Chicago was proud of new glories that brought astonished builders to its door from as far away as London, Paris, and Berlin. But a large contingent of the citizenry continued to go around with chins pulled well down into the protection of celluloid collars, mumbling about the day when all these ungodly structures would tumble down into the street. In spite of which, the floating foundation became a standard in Chicago building for the next twenty years.

"CRAZY CARL FISHER" [10]

Carl had told his friends in Indianapolis that he intended to spend seventy-five thousand dollars developing a winter playland for himself and his friends. The idea was not received with any great amount of enthusiasm in his home city. As for the Floridians, they looked with awe upon the phalanx of dredges pumping day and night on the shores of Carl's jungle kingdom on Biscayne Bay, and decided that public opinion had been right when, long before, it had judged Carl Fisher to be as crazy as a loon.

[10] From *Fabulous Hoosier*, A Study of American Achievement, by Jane Fisher, pp. 100-101, 102-103, 105-106, 126-127, 130-136, 146-147, 149-150, 155-156, 157, 159, 160, 166, 262. Copyright, 1947, by The McBride Company, Inc. New York.

[First] Carl sent in hundreds of Negroes with machetes to clear the jungle. Foot by foot, their backs dripping with sweat and covered with mosquitoes, they hacked away through the palmetto and mangrove, working only a couple of hours at a time in the killing heat.

The pigmy-high palmetto had slender roots that reached out like tentacles from the thick tap root, and these deceitfully delicate-looking roots turned the steel blades of the machetes. The palmettos were almost impossible even for mules to uproot with chains and grappling hooks. I have seen Carl tugging with his hands at a smaller palmetto, trying to break it free from the sand, cursing until I stopped my ears.

The mangroves, with their canopy of glistening green leaves, were fascinating; but steely roots showered from the tips to fasten the trees to the ground with a network strong as metal mesh. The iron-like roots defied the heaviest axes.

Men and mules fought slowly through tropical growth centuries old. The jungle strove hard to hold its own. The work was agonizingly slow, and the clearing of a single acre cost over fifteen hundred dollars.

I know Carl began to suspect he was licked. The jungle was stronger than man. Great as was his personal fortune, terrible inroads were being made on it by the building of this kingdom in the sand. And there was no let-up in sight.

Carl asked for bids for the dredging. The Miami Beach-to-be would not only have to be reclaimed, but actually created. Within a week the "fleet of Fisher dredges" was moving across the bay on heavy barges and hundreds of workmen were traveling to and fro across the new wooden [Collins] bridge [which he had helped seventy-five-year-old Quaker John S. Collins build across Biscayne Bay]. The dirt flew on the Beach, as Carl always loved to see it fly. Only now it was not soil, but sea sand sucked upward through pipes out of the bottom of Biscayne Bay to make land for a city yet to be born.

*   *   *   *   *

Among the engineering problems [his engineer] John Levi was facing was the need of three million cubic yards of dirt to fill in the swamp. The Fisher dredges—ugly, muddy objects—were pumping sand from the bottom of Biscayne Bay to fill it. One stretch of swamp, however, was a mile from the nearest shore, too far for any dredge to pipe its stream of water and sand. A dredge had to be set in the middle of Collins Canal.

The fill was like thick soup. We found the men working in mud and slime up to their knees. They wore hip boots to guard against the bites of snakes. From the beginning, the whole saga of the fill was one of minor tragedies and major setbacks. Dredges broke down and had to be repaired under the broiling sun. Pipes parted to let water and sand rush into the wrong channels, ruining weeks of work. Other pipes that were sunk in the bay clogged with weeds and had to be cleared by divers. There were times when a ladder of men standing on one another's shoulders was formed under water to hold the bottom man in place so that he could work clearing the pipe. When a shark came too near, they would tap one another's legs as a signal to shoot to the surface.

All the materials and supplies for the workmen had to be brought across Biscayne Bay and through Collins Canal on barges. If the barges were not perfectly balanced, they turned over. Many a laden barge somersaulted and lost its cargo. A dock was built on the canal where the barges were unloaded.

The mules working on the project presented difficulties uniquely mulish. Several fell into the soupy fill, trying to escape the bloodsucking insects. One landed in Collins Canal upside down and his rescue presented a new problem in engineering. Finally Carl had smudge pots placed where the mules were tethered at night, but the tormented animals backed into them trying to escape from the mosquitoes and some were severely burned.

Carl had planned to build a sea wall and fill up about two hundred acres of the marsh. John Levi warned him that this would be no trifling work. Carl had counted on spending no more than the estimated seventy-five thousand dollars on building the foundations of the city. Now he found these great dredges, sucking up the bottom of Biscayne Bay and spewing it through pipes over mangrove roots and palmetto, were pumping night and day into his great fortune. His bills were fifty-two thousand dollars a day.

*　　*　　*　　*　　*

Slowly the bottom of the bay was pumped and poured over the jungle marsh. Slowly the age-old mangrove swamps disappeared under the layer of sand that had been brought from the bottom of Biscayne Bay. Seven-hundred man-made acres of level whiteness lay over the land where not a blade of swamp grass nor a tree was left alive. Nothing but sand glittered there under the Florida sun.

For six months it lay idle, purified by sun and rain. To the eye, it seemed evanescent as snow. But under it, firmly upholding this new land, lay ageless coral as solid as the future Carl planned for Miami Beach.

*　　*　　*　　*　　*

The project seemed overwhelming when it first began back in 1913. The dredging and filling in of the swamp had been heartbreaking and costly work. But compared to the clearing of the land that started six months later, the dredging was child's play. Then the long wait for the broad sand expanse to sweeten.

Still no one wanted to buy this imperfect land, imbedded with dead trees, on a forsaken peninsula that could not even provide decent drinking water.

In the face of growing anxiety in 1913 we built and moved into our home, the Beach Shadows, at the very time when Miami Beach itself was being made. The new house, although it was isolated in wilderness, surrounded by cranes and dredges and hundreds of hard-working men and sweating mules, gave the entire undertaking a feeling of permanency. It was the start of the new city.

*　　*　　*　　*　　*

. . . Alton Beach was the name under which the city began, and not until 1915 would it be known as Miami Beach.

One morning Al Webb happened to drop into Carl's office in Indianapolis. Al was a leathery faced mechanical genius who had raced with Carl back in the barnstorming days as one of the "Big Four." Carl told Al of the heartbreaking labor of clearing the jungle by hand.

"I don't know how we'll ever grub out those goddam palmettos," he ended.

Al looked startled. "It's a funny coincidence, but I've been working on a plow to clear some land I have on the West Coast."

Carl slapped his hand on the desk in a wild burst of hope. "Build one for me, Al!" he exclaimed. "The biggest plow you can build."

Al set up his workshop in a garage in Gasoline Alley. There he constructed the powerful machete plow with a triangular blade fitted with kickers that could cut the toughest roots. The completed machine weighed tons.

Carl couldn't wait to try it out. "Ship it down to Florida," he ordered.

Al was shocked. "Why, Carl, it'll cost a thousand dollars to ship this plow!"

"Ship it!" was the response.

Al still hesitated. "You know, Carl, we're going to need a caterpillar tractor to pull the plow after we get it to Florida. That will cost five thousand dollars more."

Carl was always sent into a frenzy by any hint of delay. "Then goddammit, buy a tractor and ship it off tonight with the plow! And ship it by express," he added. "It'll get there quicker."

We reached Miami Beach ahead of the machines. When the tractor and plow arrived, it was discovered they were too large to be freighted across the Collins Bridge. A barge finally brought the heavy machines across Biscayne Bay and through the Collins Canal.

The first cuttings was made in the palmetto tangle near the canal. Carl sat on the tool box, his slouched hat pushed back as he eagerly watched Al Webb start the tractor. The steel cable tightened between tractor and plow. The three-cornered blade slipped deep into the land and ripped up the tough little palmettos as if they were ferns. Under the heaving palmettos, the upturned land fairly boiled.

Carl was on his feet whooping. "Look at 'em boil, Al, look at 'em boil!" He ran along beside the tractor like an excited boy. "Boil, you goddam roots, boil!"

The tired Negroes resting on their mattocks joined in jubilant chorus: "Boil, ol' roots, white man say boil!"

Of course, Carl had to climb aboard the tractor and drive it himself. The more excited he became, the louder he swore. "Gee-sus, look at 'em boil! Keerist-on-a-bicycle, look at 'em!"

Day after day he was out in the broiling sun watching the machete plow clear the land that was to hold the city. The big plow could clear ten acres in a single day. Thousands of hours of backbreaking labor and hundreds of thousands of dollars were saved.

The mangroves remained, many-rooted and formidable, as if defying modern machinery, but the different problem they presented was also solved by Al. He fastened a steel cable to the tractor and looped it to a hundred trees at a time.

Their trunks snapped with a sound like machine-gun fire as the matted mangroves gave.

All at last was cleared.

Soil from the Everglades, rich, centuries-old jungle earth, was brought across the bay on barges and spread over that blinding whiteness. The acrid smell of compost and fertilizer joined the brackish odors of seaweed.

Then planting began.

. . . The glory of Miami beach sprang from under the green thumb of Fred Hoerger.

Every tree, every flower, *every blade of grass* on Miami Beach had to be planted by hand. No seedling grass was strong enough to hold this newly made earth. Hundreds of Negroes, most of them women and children, crawled on their hands and knees over the earth, pushing ahead of them baskets of grass from Bermuda. Each sprig of grass had to be set out by hand. The Negroes had a quaint word for their work—"spriggin'."

Fred Hoerger sent all over the world for rare and bright-flowering and tropical plants—bougainvillaea, orchid trees, poinciana, hibiscus, and the thousands of oleanders—white, rose, apple-blossom pink and deep-red—whose perfume became the very breath of the new paradise. Thousands of coconut trees and stately royal palms and feathery Australian pines outlined the avenues and boulevards that as yet existed only on blueprints. The Australian pines shot up fourteen feet in one year to clothe the Beach with their glorious foliage. Small trees with trunks as dainty as fawn's legs hung heavy with papaya melons. Avocado trees dropped their rich, dark globes. Oranges were as large as grapefruit, and lemons as large as oranges. All these, planted at the same time, grew evenly. Within six months the Beach burgeoned into horticultural magnificence. Our home was hidden by palms and roses.

Overnight our man-built paradise was discovered by choruses of singing birds and brilliant clouds of butterflies. . . .

*   *   *   *   *

The little Quaker, John Collins, rocking away on his porch facing the sea, watched this beauty unfold beyond all his dreams. Its glory was complete when he told Carl with gentle happiness: "I'm ninety years old. I think that's a wonderful age."

It was a blossoming land. Not a sidewalk or a street marred its parklike beauty. Six months before, a ribbon of white sand had dazzled the eyes; now a wide ribbon of green was studded with gemlike flowers. "The Aladdin touch," people began saying; and, "More of Carl Fisher's magic." The criticism and carping died.

*   *   *   *   *

Carl had spent millions, and the building had not yet started on this city lifted from the bottom of Biscayne Bay. He told John Levi: "Let's get busy. Let's lay out some streets and get this city going."

Our flowery tropical paradise took on the appearance of an exotic American frontier as the actual building of Miami Beach was started. Derricks, cranes, mule and horse teams and steam shovels appeared under the newly planted palms. Skeleton frames of wood and steel lifted against the clear Florida sky. In his new flowering land small armies of engineers, carpenters, plumbers, and painters began building the first houses and the first larger buildings of the dream city on Biscayne Bay. The men who had come with Carl from Indianapolis grew lonely and discontented, and he brought their families down from the Hoosier city and built cottages for them—lovely little storybook houses set among scarlet, cinnamon and magenta bougainvillaea.

Barges weighted with crushed coral rock to crown the newly-laid out streets moved heavily across the bay and through the canal. Transporting the building material on land presented new problems, so Carl built a narrow-gauge railway to carry men, materials, tools, and soil. It was just one mile long. Carl solemnly sent passes for his midget line to presidents of all the big railroads in the United States. Many, amused, reciprocated with passes for their lines. A great deal of good-natured publicity followed. This was the opening wedge in "the most amazing publicity program in history."

Carl began the Miami Beach campaign with three-page newspaper advertisements in which he announced that, having built sea walls, cleared the land of mangroves and filled in the snake-infested swamps, he was preparing to lay out streets and build luxurious hotels, business stores, offices, banks, theaters, schools, and churches. In all, he promised to finance and build a beach—it was still being called Alton Beach at that time—that would be the play center of the world.

His plans made sensational news and were reprinted everywhere. Newspapers found good feature material in the fact that the "fabulous Carl Fisher" had discovered the true Fountain of Youth in Florida, and was building a playtime paradise in a jungle. The publicity kept ahead of the actual building because everything Carl did made news.

* * * * *

The ballyhoo methods that had served Carl in his bicycle and automobile selling days helped now at Miami Beach. A glittering publicity façade glamorized a city that was still in the making, concealing the makeshift scenery backstage.

The romantic posters that first brought Miami Beach to the attention of a nationwide public pictured Spanish palaces fretted with grill work, troubadours singing under palm trees, lovers drifting under sails on moonlit lagoons. This was the way Carl pictured it—this was the way it had to be.

* * * * *

. . . Carl was pouring out copy. Much of it he wrote himself. He had written ads for [the Indianapolis] Speedway. Later he would employ crack publicists—good-looking, smiling young fellows like Steve Hannagan and Joe Copps. From his publicizing of Miami Beach Steve would go on to become soon the world's most spectacular publicity man.

Slogans helped sell Miami Beach as a paradise for the sports lover, a playland for youth, a haven of peace and beauty for the aged. Northerners plodding through streets of frozen slush were maddened by posters of beautiful girls ocean-bathing in January, and there was drawing-power in the slogans:

It's always June in Miami Beach.
Where Summer spends the Winter.

Later there would be radio broadcasting stations with romantic names, such as (WIOD) "Wonderful Isle of Dreams."

Unwittingly, I was the original of the Miami Beach bathing beauty that was to help make our city famous.

* * * * *

. . . In 1915 Miami Beach became a town with thirty-three voters; between that date and 1920 Carl built his playland.

The magnificent yacht basin that had been created when the sand was pumped from the bottom of Biscayne Bay at last came into its own. Carl was essentially a sportsman. Having raced bicycles, automobiles, and balloons, he now turned with enthusiasm to speedboat racing. In 1915, he staged the first of the yachting regattas on the Flamingo course. Other sports followed.

. . . Before Miami Beach had a name he was building golf courses which he insisted would be "the finest in the world."

Polo was another game he gave his play city.

* * *. * *

The building of the chain of Fisher hotels, to hold the people he was certain would come to Miami Beach, was enough strain for an average man's lifetime. Carl envisioned these hotels rimming the ocean and the bay. He began the Lincoln Hotel on Lincoln Road, then the Flamingo, and then the Nautilus Hotel. . . . He built the Dade Hotel for his office help and later the King Cole Hotel on Surprise Lake, a sportsmen's hotel, where everybody appeared for breakfast in their riding togs and ate English-fashion, grilled dishes and such, from a sideboard. He housed the polo players and their families at the King Cole.

Now they were saying that Carl was a damn fool, risking the last of his millions at an age when most men are ready to coast through to the finish.

* * * * *

And still with land not selling, and people refusing to come to Miami Beach, when he was practically down to his last dollar, Carl completed the magnificent million-dollar Flamingo Hotel. The first financial help required by him since his bicycle-selling days was to complete the building of the Flamingo.

* * * * *

He brought . . . flamingoes to Miami Beach. Bright pink flamingoes in the gardens of the new hotel—black swans drifting in Indian Creek—Carl was indeed building his city to match the posters of his dreams!

[In 1920] the dream city was at last complete. The United States census allotted it a permanent population of 644 persons that year. It was all Carl had said it would be. It was paradise risen from swampland. It was "the only play city in the world."

*   *   *   *   *

The flamboyant twenties were opening before real estate began to move. Miami Beach started selling in 1920, slowly but in the right way. Much of it was vacant land. Some was plain sand. But most of it sold in single lots.

*   *   *   *   *

Now all who bought at Miami Beach joined in the building. The homes built were fashioned after those on Spanish haciendas. The Spanish trend predominated—the mellow walls, the iron fretwork, the pools gleaming in the palms, the tiled staircases leading to blue water were as Carl had portrayed in the first posters. This trend swept America from coast to coast within a few years. Yankee architecture had gone Spanish.

*   *   *   *   *

Under the palms at Miami Beach, erected by the citizens of the city, stands his sole memorial, the white cenotaph with the bronze bust of Carl. The dimpled, smiling face looks westward under the familiar battered hat. Under it are the words:

CARL GRAHAM FISHER—HE CARVED A GREAT CITY OUT OF A JUNGLE

PIGGLY WIGGLY MAN [11]

. . . In our time the Memphis man who has led the most adventurous life . . . [found] his romance [in] groceries. Out of his brain have come strange words like *Piggly Wiggly* and *Keedoozle* and store plans that have revolutionized the selling of food the world over. Clarence Saunders is a genius or a fool according to the man one is talking with. But everybody who knows his career, one of America's most spectacular stories of success and failure, will admit that the ex-millionaire is unique. Certainly no one in our day except Mr. Ed Crump has so jostled Memphis, added so much to its gayety, or contributed so greatly to it through success and failure.

In 1916, at 79 Jefferson Street, the first store of its kind in the world opened. The sign on it seemed appropriate for a carnival crazy house for tots: Piggly Wiggly! It was a crazy place. When you entered the door, you still were not in the store; you had to go through a turnstile—just like a game. After winding and clicking through the wheel, you found shelves with everything neatly tagged, but nobody to wait on you. Men in white coats went about refilling the vegetable bins and replacing stuff on the shelves. You were the clerk! Serve yourself. Get a basket. A cashier and a sacker finished your business, and

[11] From *Memphis Down in Dixie*, by Shields McIlwaine, pp. 268-270, 278-279. Copyright, 1948, by Shields McIlwaine. New York: E. P. Dutton & Co., Inc.

then you wound through a second turnstile. It was bewilderingly simple and satisfactory. And the groceries? Cheap as dirt.

An old friend of Clarence Saunders came to Memphis to see the new wonder store. He could not get into the front door because of the crowds. "It'll make millions!" the inventor told him; "I'll get a patent on it."

"Why, Clarence," said his friend, "you can't patent a turnstile." Sure enough, the patent office did reject the application. Then Clarence went into action and phoned the patent chief. "Will you give me a half-hour interview?" he asked. Clarence Saunders came back with his patent. Soon a factory with seventy-five workers was turning out Piggly Wiggly equipment. Orders for franchises and equipment came in from places all over the country. Clarence watched his trick stores multiply like tape out of a stock ticker: 25 stores, 1917; 52 stores, 1918; 162 stores, 1919; 1267 stores, 1923! Here was what he predicted—bonanza! But he did not spend his time shouting. Clarence Saunders was a natural efficiency engineer. Nothing escaped him. He made his system of selling groceries absolutely foolproof. In 1919 he issued a pamphlet which told how a Piggly Wiggly could be set up and run. If possible, locate your store on a corner, on a streetcar or bus line, on the right-hand side of a main travel route used by people going home from the downtown section. . . . With sales less than $2000 a week labor costs should not exceed $45, that is, $25 for a manager and $20 for an assistant . . . and a hundred other directions.

By 1917 Memphis realized that it had a business firebrand on its doorstep. Everybody had been making money in the prewar boom so that Clarence Saunders' 25 stores did not at first startle big money. But once the nation entered the war, labor became scarce and prices shot up; Piggly Wiggly stores, which used little labor and kept down food prices, seemed not only the work of a genius but a patriot's gesture. Electric signs with those two childish words flicked on in towns all over the land as if Clarence Saunders were playing with the switch of a magic projector. If this continued Memphis would soon have a new millionaire. Who was this merchandising fool, anyway?

Yet the spectacular success of Piggly Wiggly was incredible only to those who did not know its inventor. In 1904 when Clarence Saunders, age twenty-three, came to Memphis to work as a salesman for a wholesale grocery, he had been out in the world on his own for nine years. Son of a poor Virginia tobacco farmer, he did the backbreaking labor of a field hand. When he was eleven, he began working in a sawmill, stave and barrelhead factory. At fourteen he realized many an old-time farm boy's hope: he escaped the drudgery of the fields, in this case by crossing the mountains to Palmyra, a Tennessee village on the Cumberland River, where he became a clerk in a general store at a salary of $4 a month and board. In the tradition of more famous Americans, the boy clerk knew that his schooling had been miserable, that being nearly illiterate he could not rise in the world. He borrowed school books, and for three years he gave his nights to learning.

Then, after a year as night watchman at a coke oven in Alabama, and another in a sawmill, he got into the business that was to bring him a fortune. He became salesman at nineteen for the Hurst-Boillin wholesale grocery in

Clarksville, Tennessee. Quick, efficient, and positive, he doubled his salary in four years and left for the bigger field of Memphis.

* * * * *

In 1936, after the depression had twice sent him to the bottom, and Memphians had put Clarence in the past tense, he made their eyes spin with the most fantastic of all his fantastic ideas. A long Associated Press story went out to the country. Clarence Saunders said, "I'm not licked yet. I've got a great idea for a new chain. All I need is the money." People chuckled. No one would back him after his three failures. "Keedoozle Incorporated." That was his new idea. Keedoozle? Memphis laughed. The good old days were here again. Where did Clarence get such a cockeyed word? "I got it out of my noodle," he said, "just like I did Piggly Wiggly. It's not in the dictionary."

No matter. In March, 1937, the Keedoozle opened on Union Avenue with the typical crushing crowds. If the first Piggly Wiggly seemed like a side show this store was a three-ring circus by Rube Goldberg. It was a completely mechanized grocery, a robot store that did everything by electrical machines except sack your purchases and make change. "Electric service store" was Clarence's definition. It was like this.

On entering you were given a three-inch metal spike with a little ball on one end. All groceries were behind glass cases beside which were panels with sockets. You pushed your key into the socket for soap flakes, a bulb in the ball of the key flashed. You had made a purchase, for when the key flashed, backstage the $200,000 robot of 10,000 electrical connections, numerous chutes, and all manner of contraptions, dumped a box of soap flakes on a running belt and landed it in your basket at the cashier's desk. What fun! Simply walking about punching at the samples of what you wish, no baskets, no baby-carriage carts. Newsreel companies sent their men to photograph the new wonder store. "A year from now," Clarence vowed, jerking his head like a snorting, impatient pony, "I'll be worth ten million dollars."

But a year later with the crowds still coming for Keedoozle low prices Clarence began to call his store "experimental." He had rushed in where electrical engineers had feared to tread. With 10,000 electrical connections, his robot made only 2% of errors. But when the wrong stuff came down the belts, housewives raised the devil, and the cashier had to yell to the stockman for a rush hand delivery. Women could not remember what they had punched. "Machines can't think for you," Clarence said wearily, "and they can't explain to a customer." Sometimes a connection went dead and no matter how hard you punched no flash came; sometimes people dropped the keys and wrecked them. Housewives did not like being denied the privilege of pawing vegetables and haggling over meat. So these items were put outside in the old way, and a good deal of the machinery was junked or simplified. For absent-minded shoppers Clarence evolved a new key, really a pistol, with a roll of paper and an inker, which stamped the article and its price after you stuck its nose in a slot and pulled down. Now everything was foolproof. A full-page ad appeared beginning, "Let's Do Some Kissing, Let's Do Some Loving, Let's Go See

Keedoozle." This was Clarence's way of announcing the gala opening of his master store downtown. Into it he was putting all the wizardry and showmanship he had learned in a lifetime plus the Keedoozle robot. If he should throw away his machinery as a publicity stunt to put himself back into business, he would be launched once more into the game which for him was the most exciting thing on earth.

*   *   *   *   *

. . . No one was surprised and no one glad when Keedoozle closed its doors for good during World War II.

LA TULES, QUEEN OF THE SANTA FE GAMBLING HALLS [12]

. . . The story of "La Tules," the ragged peona from Mexico who became a power in New Mexico—whose gambling hall ran through the entire block from San Francisco Street to Palace Avenue, bordered by Burro Alley—who was reported to be the best monte dealer in the world—is one of the most fascinating in Santa Fe's history.

Gambling was a characteristic of the time—cards, betting on cockfighting, bullfighting, horse-racing, lottery, and tourneys on horseback, such as El Gallo [rooster-pulling].

Don Augustín Durán, a custom-house official, was such an inveterate gambler that after he had lost his money, mules, and clothing, he pawned himself in the excitement of the game. In the cold light of mañana he "confiscated" enough goods to redeem himself from his creditors.

In the midst of this fever of outpost gambling Doña Gertrudes de Barcelo, a comely girl, came to Taos, and, like every other courtesan, she soon drifted to the capital. Starting work in a small gambling place, she made some lucky bets on the side and purchased a gambling business of her own. This, together with her beauty, her challenging black eyes, her luck, and her shrewdness, gave her more influence than any other woman of her time.

When La Tules attended the fiestas in nearby placitas, four peons staggered under the load of her leather money-chests. With lavish grandeur she was known to scoop up a fanega of pesos from her chest and challenge the men to meet this bushel measure of silver.

Through Governor Armijo, who was one of her admirers, she practically ruled the province. Military maneuvers were planned and political intrigues born in the private salas of her magnificent quarters. Brussels carpets on her plank floors and heavy draperies gave an atmosphere of elegance. Sparkling chandeliers, where burned a thousand candles through the nights, lighted magnificent balls. Beautiful women, the chance to win fabulous money, gossip and scandal, brought generals, governors, clerks, and peons to this Southwest Monte Carlo. But they entered only at La Tules' invitation.

Every one, from the governor's wife down, visited her gaming tables. Monte,

[12] From *Santa Fe New Mexican*, Fiesta Edition, August 27, 1950, Section C, p. 21. Adapted from *Caballeros*, by Ruth Laughlin, pp. 59-61. Copyright, 1931, by Ruth Laughlin. Caldwell, Idaho: The Caxton Printers, Ltd. 1945.

faro, chusa, poker, and dice were played with stakes of gold piled on the tables. Rings, brooches, even rebosos edged with gold fringe, were a part of the stakes.

In the early days of the American occupation, when Col. David A. Mitchell was ordered to open communications with Chihuahua, he found himself without the necessary funds to supply his troops. Doña Gertrudes lent him a thousand dollars on condition that he enter the room at a formal ball, with her on his arm. The gallant colonel, so the story goes, "did his duty as an officer and a gentleman," and La Tules achieved her social ambition, the colonel received his money.

In her old age, though she wore a wig and false teeth, she maintained to the end her air of grandeur to the last. She added a respectable marriage to her experience, and in dignified obesity she became an imposing money-lender. Her will left exact instructions for one thousand six hundred pesos to be spent for candles, high masses, and prayers for her soul. When she died in 1851, she was widely mourned and, it is said, had a sixteen-hundred-dollar funeral.

THE LATER ADVENTURES OF ELFEGO BACA [13]

I. ELFEGO AND THE COLLECTOR

A gunman of note, whose formidable reputation had reached beyond the New Mexico borders, Elfego Baca came to Albuquerque to live out his declining years. In his vigorous youth Mr. Baca had made a reputation for courage and address as Sheriff of Socorro County, and he had also been known for other and less orthodox dealings with the law.

In Albuquerque he proposed to live a life of probity and to edit a newspaper to support his convictions and occasional political aspirations. So he bought a press from a Denver firm. Mr. Baca made a down payment, and there the matter rested for some time. Then a collector arrived from Denver. [This was in 1920.] Mindful of the debtor's fame, he called not upon Mr. Baca but upon Mr. William A. Keleher, Mr. Baca's friend if not his guide and philosopher.

"Quite all right," said Mr. Keleher. "Mr. Baca is now a solid citizen who will receive you as anybody would. Go right on over."

Over there the Denver city man faced a square-set man, alert and strong even in age. Tentatively he brought up the matter of the overdue payments on that press. Mr. Baca opened his desk drawer, reached in and pulled out an enormous sixshooter. The Denver city man waited no longer. By the time Elfego's twinkling gray eyes were raised, the collector was gone.

Back in Will Keleher's office he had a tale to tell. Threats. Menacing gestures. Will took up the phone.

"Now look here, Elfego, this won't do; we're living in a civilized world now. Rough stuff is out!"

[13] From *Erna Fergusson's Albuquerque*, pp. 74-75. Copyright, 1947, by Erna Fergusson. Albuquerque: Merle Armitage Editions.
For the life of Elfego Baca, see Kyle S. Crichton, *Law and Order, Ltd.* (Santa Fe, 1929).

"But what," countered Elfego plaintively, "what did I do? I wasn't threatening the little fellow. I just took my gun out to lay it on the desk while I found the papers on the case, and when I looked up . . . that man was gone!"

II. Interviewing Elfego

[In 1922] I called Mr. Elfego Baca on the phone. I had long known him by sight, but had never met him. I explained myself, giving my father's name as is a good idea in dealing with people of a certain generation in New Mexico.

"What's that you say?" came crackling back over the wire. "You're H. B. Fergusson's daughter? . . . Well, you come right on over here and we'll talk. Your father prosecuted me for murder three times and I got off every time!"

III. Elfego Baca's Insurance

[In 1924] Mr. Baca had gone to Juarez when the plant where he published *La Voz del Pueblo* burned down. Firemen in their zeal knocked type out of the fonts, smashed furniture, and completed the destruction with water. Mr. Baca, hastening home, filed claim for $1200 to compensate him for the severe loss.

The Insurance Adjuster, suspecting that Mr. Baca might have predicted that disaster, had the damage repaired. He hired a boy to pick up the type and sweep out, he paid for new wallpaper and fresh paint. But Mr. Baca was not satisfied. He called on a prominent lawyer, who was not his attorney but always a reliable go-between.

"Look here, Amigo," he said, "do you know that adjuster? . . . Well then you tell him that if I don't get my $1200 by noon today I'll kill him . . . And I mean it."

The attorney asked the Adjuster to call and explained. "By the mortality tables, you should have quite a few years to live. But it appears that something may intervene as of twelve o'clock noon today." He delivered Mr. Baca's message.

It was then 11:30. By 11:50 the lawyer had made it from his office to Mr. Baca's with a message from the Insurance Adjuster. The message, delivered just in time, was that if Mr. Baca would go to the First National Bank before noon he would find awaiting him a draft in full payment of his claim for insurance.

The business was closed by twelve.

JOHN PENNELL'S PLACE [14]

How [a Barbary Coast gentleman named John] Pennell came to desert San Francisco for Seattle is uncertain. Probably some seaman from one of the lumber ships told him of the yearnings of Puget Sound males; and with the supply in Pennell's line almost exceeding demand along the Barbary Coast, he

[14] From *Skid Road*, An Informal Portrait of Seattle, by Murray Morgan, pp. 59-61. Copyright, 1951, by Murray Morgan. New York: The Viking Press, Inc.

may have decided to prospect the virgin territory to the north. In the summer of 1861 Pennell debarked from a lumber schooner on the sandspit beside Yesler's Mill. A single glance at the pedestrians on the dusty reach of Front Street, who were as predominantly male as the crew of a ship, must have confirmed the reports he had heard in San Francisco. An examination of Seattle's economic base could only have made business prospects seem bright. Here was a town of bachelors, a town with no commercial entertainment, a town with an established payroll. Here was a town just waiting for the likes of John Pennell.

Within a month of his arrival there stood on the shore of the bay, not far south of the point where the logging road reached the mill, a pleasure palace of rough-sawed boards, the pioneer of a long line of establishments which were to give this part of town a distinctive character. The lot on which this bawdy house was built was "made land," a fill created on the tideflats by pouring in the sawdust from Yesler's Mill. It was not desirable land, for the flats stank when the tide was out; but Pennell could not be too particular, and the site had the advantage of being only a few minutes' walk from the mill and in plain view of the ships entering the harbor.

The Illahee, as Pennell named his house, was in the great tradition of the Old West. The oblong building of unpainted boards housed a large dance floor, which was flanked by a long bar. Along one side of the floor was a hall leading to a number of small rooms. Pennell imported three musicians (a fiddler, a drummer, and an accordion player) from San Francisco; the rest of his help was native. He traded Hudson's Bay blankets to local chiefs for a supply of Indian girls. These recruits were vigorously scoured; their long hair was combed and cut, they were doused with perfume and decked out in calico.

A girl would dance with any one without charge, but her partner was expected to buy a drink for himself and his companion after each dance. (The bartender usually substituted cold tea for whisky in the girl's glass, though the charge was for whisky.) When a man tired of purely social intercourse, he could always buy a couple more drinks and lead his partner down the hall to one of the little rooms.

There was no attempt to conceal what was going on at the water's edge. One historian has argued that it was the establishment of Pennell's place that led straight to Seattle's present-day dominance of the Northwest, the scholar's thesis being that word swiftly spread throughout the timberland about the type of entertainment offered at the foot of the skid road in Seattle. The town had, in that historian's words, "the best mouse trap in the woods; hobnails and calks were deepening all the paths to its door."

While this economic argument gives more importance to sex than even Freud would be likely to admit, there can be little doubt that Pennell drew his clientele from all over the Sound country, and that the men who came to town primarily to enjoy the girls also spent money in more legitimate trade. Some respectable members of the little community accepted Pennell's establishment as a necessary evil; others deplored it but failed to convince Sheriff Wycoff that he should close the place as a nuisance.

Somehow the name Illahee—which meant "homeland" or "earth" in Chinook

—didn't catch on. It may have been among the strait-laced that the establishment first came to be known as the Mad House, but the nickname stuck and was later applied to other houses whose stock-in-trade was of Indian origin. Those who did not call the brothel the Mad House sometimes referred to it as the Sawdust Pile or Down on the Sawdust. The inhabitants were known as Sawdust Women.

During a depression period in San Francisco at the end of the Civil War, Pennell rounded up a handful of out-of-work Barbary Coast girls and shipped them north. They were the first white women north of the Columbia to ply the oldest profession. Though it is doubtful that prostitutes unable to prosper in San Francisco were unduly attractive, their presence in the Illahee, according to a chronicle of the period, "had a powerful imaginative effect on the whole male population of the Puget Sound country, and old-timers still relate fabulous legends from those happy days." The legends were the standard ones of the red-light district. There was the tale of the ladylike whore who murdered the men she learned were carrying large amounts of money. There was the legend of the girl who fell in love and demurely denied her swain the favors she still sold, albeit unwillingly, to every one else. And, of course, there was the story of the girl who married a client and moved into one of the white clapboard houses on the hill.

DUTCH JAKE'S "HOTEL WITH A PERSONALITY" [15]

. . . "Dutch Jake" Goetz and his pal Harry Baer . . . had arrived [in Spokane] from the Coeur d'Alene shortly before [the great fire of 1889] with some two hundred thousand dollars of mining camp wealth and, as additional capital, possessed well-established reputations as gamblers and proprietors of bars and gambling joints.

Of the two, Dutch Jake was the better known because of his spectacular methods and an open-handedness that not only won for him the everlasting gratitude of the recipients of his bounty, but caused him to be regarded with a large degree of tolerance and even downright affection by others who had little use for his business. Wrote a newspaper friend, Dutch Jake "was one of the most reckless, indifferent, and big-hearted men that ever rode a mule or mixed a cocktail." Whenever or wherever a miner had appeared at Jake's bar with a pokeful of nuggets, he had quickly been helped to dispose of his hoard in ways highly satisfactory to his appetite if not always to his gambling instinct. But if luck went back on him the next time he spent a summer in the mountains with a pick and pan or rocker and returned broke to face a hard winter, Jake cheerfully extended credit and let him soak up the warmth of the saloon stove daily, and even nightly if financial embarrassment was such as to preclude even the slight comfort of a bed on the ground under the canvas roof of the camp "corral."

[15] From *Spokane Story*, by Lucile F. Fargo, pp. 168, 170-176. Copyright, 1950, by Columbia University Press. New York.

When Jake and Baer—and of course [Jake's wife] Louisa—arrived in Spokane Falls in the late eighties, the partners invested most of their two hundred thousand dollars in an ornate, four-story structure which they opened as bar, theater, dance hall and gambling resort de luxe. The fire wiped them out. All that remained was an inadequate insurance policy. However, Jake was not a gambler for nothing. He was ready with the motto that in time came to be embroidered on his shirt fronts and painted on the cover of his spare tire: "Don't tell 'em; keep going." With what insurance there was, he and Baer bought a tent which they set up on a likely corner and opened for business as usual.

The Spokane police force and members of the city council were not at that time spending sleepless nights over saloons and gambling resorts, and the proprietors of the tent establishments had little fear of interference. Both were old hands at the business. Down in Wallula where they had run a gambling joint before going into the Coeur d'Alene, Jake had been accustomed to open the evening's festivities by tossing a hundred silver dollars into the air about the bar. When the scramble for the coins subsided, the games began. Jake was not averse to joining in, and his participation was definitely to the advantage of the firm, since he had a habit of winning. For years he preserved as precious relics the famous poker hands which came his way in Wallula and elsewhere, each carefully tied up and labeled with date and place.

In the huge tent in Spokane Falls there might soon be seen upward of a thousand men playing at varied games of chance and making more or less frequent visits to the bar. If a steak promised to add the desired fillip to a game of faro, it could be ordered and devoured on the spot.

*   *   *   *   *

. . . Five years after the fire, [Goetz and Baer] had accumulated enough money to erect on the site of the present Coeur d'Alene Hotel a resort that made the headlines. It was of a lavish elegance never forgotten by those who saw it. From the basement quarters devoted to down-and-outers to the gorgeous dance hall on the fourth floor it was steam-heated and ablaze with gas and electric lights. French mirrors reflected the latest in fixtures above the polished, solid cherry bar on the first floor. The barroom was further adorned with a portrait of Jake's Coeur d'Alene friend, Jim Wardner, painted on a circular canvas three feet in diameter in a six-inch frame of variegated gold and silver. The description is furnished by the proud subject himself, who takes pains to add that the whisky dispensed at the bar was "as pure as Dutch Jake's character." . . .

In a clubroom on the third floor, Lady Luck could be wooed through every known game of chance, including keno run by electricity—in itself worthy of headlines. No minor was allowed here, and married men who, to Jake's watchful eye or those of his assistants, appeared to be wooing Lady Luck with a degree of recklessness inconsistent with the support of a family were advised to go home and stay away. Jake was a firm believer in good homes; he had a satisfactory one with Louisa as his life partner and was not going to allow any irresponsible husband to blame the Goetz and Baer establishment for failure to provide for his "vimmin-folks and schildren."

That no current form of amusement or entertainment might be lacking under their roof, the partners further provided a theater where vaudeville and fancy dancing—very fancy indeed—invited the tired businessman to laugh and relax.

The basement was an institution in itself—a kind of Salvation Army flophouse with salvation left out. Jake was never happy to cater to wealth alone. "I aind't got no use for millionaires," he was wont to say. On the contrary, he always made a place for those of empty purse, asking no questions and taking them as they were—especially if they were miners. In his basement the most bedraggled derelict was given a good meal at the lunch counter and if necessary provided with a blanket, in which, after a bath, he was privileged to roll up for the night on the floor.

Although Jake was inclined all his life to lump lawyers, millionaires, and preachers together as more or less useless excrescences on the social scene, his attitude toward all was tolerant. Jim Wardner was a periodic millionaire, but he was always welcomed, as were others in the same class. Preachers were welcome too if they wanted to come. In fact, on at least one occasion Jake personally invited a trio of them to do so. It was a Sunday afternoon in November when Jake's special guests, a visiting evangelist accompanied by a Methodist and a Presbyterian minister, arrived at the theater barroom to hold a religious service. Sunday afternoons in the winter had, as Jake noticed, become a bit tedious to the crowd loafing about, and a revival meeting would do no harm and would undoubtedly liven things up. So he had the mechanical pipe organ played to gather the crowd and provided further inducement by turning on the winking lights of the electrical fountain. When four hundred patrons had gathered to listen to the unusual guests, it seemed foolish to close the bar, so the service progressed to the clinking of glasses, the hurrying feet of waiters, and orders for assorted liquids given more or less *sotto voce*. Throughout, Jake took the part of kindly and gracious host. No heads were broken, everybody concerned got plenty of publicity, and Jake had added another to the already lengthy list of attractions sponsored by the resort over which he and Baer presided.

*   *   *   *   *

By 1910, the Goetz and Baer resort had become the Coeur d'Alene Hotel, a change in line with other happenings in a city by that time well on the road to respectability and definitely concerned with the habiliments of culture. Since Jake was a natural "greeter," who thoroughly liked meeting new people—and studying them—he was equally successful as hotel proprietor and as manager of a gambling parlor. The hotel business, he announced, was the nicest he ever got into. He continued his private flophouse in the basement. Above, in far more sumptuous quarters, he cheerily welcomed, housed, and fed more prosperous guests and on their departure presented them with his *The Hotel with a Personality,* a piece of literature in which he took extreme pride.

*   *   *   *   *

Jake lived to be seventy-three, happy in his hotel and in his homelife with Louisa and the son she had presented him. "The United Stadts has been goot to me so many years," he said, "I should be goot to her." . . .

THE "UNSINKABLE" MRS. BROWN [16]

Mrs. Brown was thirty-nine years old when she left Liverpool for New York on the Titanic's maiden voyage. Instead of a girlish slimness, she now was ruggedly and generously fleshed. Nevertheless, she still bubbled with a seldom-varying vitality.

She sang in the ship's concert and was popular with the traveling notables despite her growing eccentricities. She amused some and terrified others with pistol-feats, one of which consisted of tossing five oranges or grapefruits over the rail and puncturing each one before it reached the surface of the sea.

Although she spent great sums on clothes, she no longer paid attention to their detail or how she wore them. And, when she traveled, comfort, and not a desire to appear chic, was her primary consideration.

So, when Molly decided to take a few turns of the deck before retiring, she came from her cabin prepared for battle with the night sea air. She had on extra-heavy woolies, with bloomers bought in Switzerland (her favorite kind), two jersey petticoats, a plaid cashmere dress down to the heels of her English calfskin boots, a sportsman's cap, tied on with a woolen scarf, knotted in toothache style beneath her chin, golf stockings presented by a seventy-year-old admirer, the Duke Charlot of France, a muff of Russian sables, in which she absent-mindedly had left her Colt's automatic pistol—and over these frost-defying garments she wore a sixty-thousand-dollar chinchilla opera cloak!

If any one was prepared for Arctic gales, Mrs. Brown was that person. She was not, however, prepared for a collision with an iceberg.

In fact, she was on the point of sending a deck steward below with her cumbersome pistol when the crash came.

In the history of that tragedy, her name appears as one who knew no fear. She did much to calm the women and children. Perhaps she was overzealous, for it is recorded that she refused to enter a lifeboat until all other women and their young ones had been cared for, and that crew members literally had to throw her into a boat.

Once in the boat, however, she didn't wait for approval—she seized command. There were only five men aboard, and about twenty women and children.

"Start rowing," she told the men, "and head the bow into the sea."

Keeping an eye on the rowers, she began removing her clothes. Her chinchilla coat she treated as though it were a blanket worth a few dollars. She used it to cover three small and shivering children. One by one she divested herself of heroic woolens. She "rationed" her garments to the women who were the oldest or most frail. It was said she presented a fantastic sight in the light of flares, half standing among the terrified passengers, stripped down to her corset, the beloved Swiss bloomers, the Duke of Charlot's golf stockings, and her stout shoes.

One of the rowers seemed on the verge of collapse. "My heart," he said.

[16] From *Timber Line,* A Story of Bonfils and Tammen, by Gene Fowler, pp. 335-336, 336-339, 339-341. Copyright, 1933, by Gene Fowler. New York: Covici, Friede, Publishers.

"God damn your heart!" said The Unsinkable Mrs. Brown. "Work those oars."

She herself now took an oar and began to row. She chose a position in the bow, where she could watch her crew. Her pistol was lashed to her waist with a rope.

The heart-troubled rower now gasped and almost lost his oar. "My heart," he said. "It's getting worse!"

The Unsinkable one roared: "Keep rowing or I'll blow your guts out and throw you overboard! Take your choice."

The man—who really *did* have a fatty condition of the heart—kept rowing. Mrs. Brown sprouted big blisters on her hands. But she didn't quit. Then her palms began to bleed. She cut strips from her Swiss bloomers and taped her hands. She kept rowing. And swearing.

At times, when the morale of her passengers was at its lowest, she would sing.

"The God damned critics say I can't sing," she howled. "Well, just listen to this. . . ."

And she sang from various operas.

"We'll have an Italian opera now," she said at one time. "Just let any one say it's no good."

She kept rowing.

And so did the others. They knew she *would* throw any one overboard who dared quit, exhaustion or no exhaustion.

She told stories. She gave a history of the Little Johnny. She told of the time she hid three thousand dollars in a camp stove, and how it went up the flue.

"How much is three hundred thousand dollars?" she asked. "I'll tell you. It's nothing. Some of you people—the guy here with the heart trouble that I'm curing with oars—are rich. I'm rich. What in hell of it? What are your riches or mine doing for us this minute? And you can't wear the Social Register for water wings, can you? Keep rowing, you sons of bitches, or I'll toss you all overboard!"

When they were picked up at sea, and every one was praising Mrs. Brown, she was asked:

"How did you manage it?"

"Just typical Brown luck," she replied. "I'm unsinkable."

And ever afterward she was known as "The Unsinkable Mrs. Brown."

*   *   *   *   *

In April of 1912, the home town which had refused flatly to receive Molly as a social equal passionately acclaimed her as its very own celebrity. The S. S. *Titanic* had gone down, and Molly had been its heroine.

Suddenly her virtues were sung in nearly every paragraph of a front-page layout in the [Denver] *Post*. She became known as "The Unsinkable Mrs. Brown." The New York press called her "The Lady Margaret of the *Titanic*."

Now that Mrs. Brown had received the accolade in alien fields, her townsmen's praises resounded like songs in a beer stube.

The tardy cheers for Mrs. Brown were in keeping with the psychology of the provinces. Similarly, Eugene Field had been tolerated as an amiable prankster, a thistle-down jingler, and something of a sot during his Denver interlude. Then, his fame having been certified abroad, and death having corroborated his genius, Denver was the first of cities to rear a monument to his memory.

Perhaps it was an instinctive feeling for another free and generous soul that led Mrs. Brown to purchase Field's old Denver home and set it aside, a shrine for children.

*   *   *   *   *

Perhaps because it is the thing most lacking, heroism lifts any one above caste. Still, the Denver social tabbies would not admit Mrs. Brown to their select functions. But now she no longer cared. She went in for thrills.

She took world tours and explored far places, always meeting adventure half way. Once she almost perished in a monsoon in the China seas. At another time she was in a hotel fire in Florida. But the Unsinkable one was Unburnable as well. She rescued four women and three children from that fire.

In France she was given a Legion of Honor ribbon, with the rank of chevalier, in recognition of her charities in general and her work in establishing a museum for the relics of Sarah Bernhardt in particular.

She now was legally separated from old Leadville Johnny. But still he had not tied the purse strings. Molly could go where she wanted and do what she wanted. It was his way. As for him, he stayed in the parlor with his shoes off, or bent the elbow a bit with old-time pals. The Little Johnny continued to pour out gold as from a cornucopia.

Although her husband was a mine owner, Mrs. Brown always took the side of labor, and sent food, clothing, and money to the families of strikers.

During the World War she contributed heavily for the welfare of soldiers and for the hospitalization of wounded warriors of the Allied arms. If she had been hooted by a handful of social snobs in her home town, she now received the prayers of thousands of soldiers. The Allied nations awarded her all the medals it was possible for a civilian woman to receive. She was recipient of personal congratulations and the thanks of kings and princes.

After the war she took another of her world tours. When reporters met her in New York, she said:

"I'm getting to be more of a lady every day. In Honolulu I learned to play the uke. In Siam I mastered the native dances. In Switzerland I learned how to yodel. Want to hear me?"

And she astonished the customs guards by breaking into Alpine melody.

Rumors were circulated that the aged Duke of Charlot was planning to marry her—old Leadville Johnny having died in his stocking feet—and Mrs. Brown confirmed the report. Forty-eight hours later she declared the romance ended.

"Me marry *that* old geezer?" she said. "Never! Give me every time the rugged men of the West. The men of Europe—why, in France they're only perfumed

and unbathed gallants; in England, only brandy-soaked British gents. Pooh!
Pooh! Pooh! And a bottle of rum."

In keeping with his character, Leadville Johnny, a multi-millionaire, *left no
will*. There was an unpretty fight now. The Unsinkable Mrs. Brown was left
floating with little financial ballast. Her eccentricities were cited; her charities
construed as loose business affairs. She was awarded the life-income on one
hundred thousand dollars annually.

"Just to think," she said with a gay smile, "and I burned up three times that
much in one bonfire."

Mrs. Margaret Tobin Brown died in October, 1932. Apoplexy was the cause.
She had been singing in her town apartment at the Barbizon Club, in East
Sixty-third Street, New York City, then became dizzy and faint.

She was buried at Hempstead, Long Island, in surroundings that she loved
almost as well as she had loved her Colorado hills.

OOFTY GOOFTY [17]

. . . Oofty Goofty [was] a stringy little man who, for a while at
least, fancied himself as a dramatic actor. So far as journalistic or public knowledge went, Oofty Goofty had no other name than this singular appellation,
which he acquired during his first appearance before his San Francisco public,
as a wild man in a Market Street freak-show. From crown to heel he was
covered with road tar, into which were stuck great quantities of horsehair,
lending him a savage and ferocious appearance. He was then installed in a
heavy cage, and when a sufficiently large number of people had paid their
dimes to gaze upon the wild man recently captured in the jungles of Borneo
and brought to San Francisco at enormous expense, large chunks of raw meat
were poked between the bars by an attendant. This provender the wild man
gobbled ravenously, occasionally growling, shaking the bars, and yelping these
fearsome words: "Oofty goofty! Oofty goofty!" [18]

He was, naturally, immediately christened Oofty Goofty, and as such was
identified to the day of his death. For a week or so he was a veritable histrionic
sensation, the wildest wild man ever exhibited on the Pacific Coast. Then, since
he could not perspire through his thick covering of tar and hair, he became ill
and was sent to the Receiving Hospital. There physicians vainly tried for
several days to remove Oofty Goofty's costume without removing his natural
epidermis as well. He was at length liberally doused with a tar solvent and
laid out upon the roof of the hospital, where the sun finally did the work.

Thereafter Oofty Goofty eschewed character parts and decided to scale the
heights of theatrical fame as a singer and dancer. He obtained a place on the
bill at Bottle Koenig's, a Barbary Coast beer hall which also offered a low

[17] From *The Barbary Coast*, An Informal History of the San Francisco Underworld, by
Herbert Asbury, pp. 133-135. Copyright, 1933, by Alfred A. Knopf, Inc. New York.
[18] San Franciscans generally believe that Oofty Goofty originated this phrase, but, as a
matter of fact, a Dutch comedian named Phillips called himself Oofty Goofty Gus long
before the time of the San Francisco hero. Phillips was shot by his mistress in 1879.—
H.A.

variety entertainment. There he danced once and sang one song. He was then, with great ceremony, thrown into the street. In reality this was a very fortunate experience, as it indicated his future career, or, as he termed it, his "work." Oofty Goofty was kicked with considerable force, and landed heavily upon a stone sidewalk, but to his intense surprise he discovered that he was, apparently, insensible to pain. This great gift he immediately proceeded to capitalize, and for some fifteen years, except for occasional appearances at the Bella Union as a super, and a short engagement as co-star with Big Bertha, he eked out a precarious existence simply by letting himself be kicked and pummeled for a price. Upon payment of ten cents a man might kick Oofty Goofty as hard as he pleased, and for a quarter he could hit the erstwhile wild man with a walk-ing-stick. For fifty cents Oofty Goofty would become the willing, and even prideful, recipient of a blow with a baseball bat, which he always carried with him. He became a familiar figure in San Francisco, not only on the Barbary Coast, but in other parts of the city as well. It was his custom to approach groups of men, in the streets and in bar-rooms, and diffidently inquire: "Hit me with a bat for four bits, gents? Only four bits to hit me with this bat, gents?"

Oofty Goofty was knocked off his feet more times than he could remember, but he continued to follow his peculiar vocation until John L. Sullivan hit him with a billiard cue and injured his back. Not long afterwards Sullivan's pugilistic standing was impaired by James J. Corbett, the pride of San Francisco, and Oofty Goofty always felt that Corbett had acted as his agent in the matter. Oofty Goofty never entirely recovered from his encounter with Sullivan. He walked with a limp thereafter, and the slightest blow made him whimper with pain. With his one claim to distinction gone, he soon became a nonentity. He died within a few years, but medical authorities said that Sullivan's blow had not been a contributing cause.

SIMON RADILLA'S TOWERS OF JUNK [19]

Watts, the Negro district of Los Angeles where Simon Radilla staked out his pie-shaped claim to immortality thirty-one years ago, lies in the no-man's land of deteriorating bungalows that stretches interminably through the feature-less flats between Pasadena, the upper-middle-class Nirvana, and Long Beach, the end of the road from Iowa which has been called a cemetery with lights.

Crossing the tracks, the towers loom suddenly.

Simon, who also calls himself Sam, wanted it that way. He wanted the towers to be seen. A hill would have been better but the hills of Los Angeles had already been spoken for. At least by these tracks the towers would be visible from the trains. But who rides in trains any more, least of all through downtown Los Angeles? And for that matter who visits the heart of Los Angeles for any purpose, or believes it to have a heart? . . . Should one . . . venture as far as Watts, the chances are he would not see the towers at all. Though the tallest

[19] From "The Artist Nobody Knows," by Selden Rodman, *New World Writing, Second Mentor Selection,* pp. 152-157. Copyright, 1952, by the New American Library of World Literature, Inc. New York. Illustrated with line drawings by Pauline Inman.

is 104 feet, they are not conspicuous from five blocks off, and at ten, dwarfed by high-tension pylons and radio transmitters, they are invisible.

The wall around them was not part of Simon's plan. For all the obscurity in which they have grown, his will to communicate, to make their beauty available to every one, is as strong to-day as it ever was. But the local police saw a hazard to climbing children, so the walls were built. This was not Simon's first brush with authority. His dislike for the metropolis, one of the stimulants of his tireless energy, dates from 1921 when he applied to the city fathers for a building permit and was derisively turned down. The fact that the state government in Sacramento, whither he journeyed instantly to appeal the decision, overruled

Los Angeles, and that by some miracle of perception and generosity (which may be a fantasy in itself) has now promised to refund everything he has paid in the last thirty years, makes him more than ever certain he builds for time to come. Lacking a charter of recognition from the United Nations or from Washington, he might will his creation to the state but to the city—never.

Simon was born in Italy in 1898. He immigrated to the United States nine years later. Discharged from the Army Engineers in 1918 after service in France, he resolved to begin work on his contribution to peace at once. "Why so many people want to shed blood?" he asks. "You go boxing match. It's when nose is broken and blood flow over boxer's eyes that people clap for joy. That's why, my dear friend, I not turn on this radio my niece she give me." Simon prefers to play ancient Martinelli and Caruso records on the horn-phonograph that is the only piece of furniture besides the bed in his one-room shack behind the towers. Every cent he has made, over food and taxes, in the past thirty years has gone into his masterwork. In the early days he set tiles and bought junk. Nowadays he works off and on for the telephone company, crawling through their underground conduits to plug overhead leaks with handfuls of wet plaster; but to-day the junk dealers give him their broken bottles and tiles for free so that all his money goes for the steel rods and wire mesh that he thinks have made the towers earthquake- and bomb-proof.

How to describe them?

Jules Langsner, the hawk-eyed local art critic who guided me to Watts, calls them aptly "spider-webbed, Cambodian-like." Simon, a benevolent spider, was high in the webbing of the big tower my first visit. Attached by his window-cleaner's belt, he was adding a new series of flying buttresses—7-up bottles with their red labels facing out, embedded in mortar. This tower had been only twenty-five feet high in 1922. A fresh set of necklaces brought it up to fifty. And so on, to its present eminence. After the metal rods and mesh and a mixture of waterproof cement, come the artifacts of our civilization: orange-squeezers, bottle-caps, hub-caps, willow-ware; percolators, hair-setters, telephone insulators, burnt-out bulbs; tooth-mugs, pieces of old mirrors, a glass shoe, a three-fingered bowling ball. There is no conscious choice of objects just as there is no deliberate plan in their arrangement. The objects are whatever is discarded, available in quantity and resistant to time and tremor. The design is always mysteriously incomplete. Seventy-five thousand sea-shells embedded in the "stern" of this triangular ironclad would be overpowering (or pretty-like-a-tea-shoppe) if arranged symmetrically. As they are, in half-circles and broken spokes of low-relief, the effect is something like the awesome confusion of stars in the Milky Way. Only slightly more conventional are the volutes and cake-stamps stenciled into the pavement, the concave "fossils" of Simon's hammer, compass and chisel in the lunettes of the side walls, the rhythmic corncobs and ears of wheat like emblems of fertility above the fountains. These, too, are removed from the commonplace by being always sprained a little off their centers. Most astonishing is the seemingly unerring taste with which fragmented tiles of a thousand varieties are related in color-key and flow of design around the basins and stalagmite-like lesser outcroppings.

Whether Cambodia or any other exotic culture entered into Radilla's calculations is as doubtful as that he ever heard of the word "abstraction." That he saw San Marco or Monreale or Pompeii or the basilicas of Ravenna as a child is possible but not likely. The art of the mosaic is ubiquitous enough in bathroom and bistro, or was before the swarming democratic urinal gave way to the empty forums of the Fascisti.

If something like Jung's racial memory is not at work here, then whatever Simon brought with him from Italy is buried very deep indeed. Though his English is shaky, he speaks no Italian at all; and though he identifies himself with Giordano Bruno as well as Buffalo Bill, his historical sense is compounded of such encyclopedic misinformation as that Galileo built the Campanile at Pisa to prove to a skeptical world *that it could lean.*

The neighbors, most of whom are Negroes of the poorest class, have come to accept Simon and his proliferating steeples at their face value. But if pressed for an explanation of what rises in their midst, they tend to assume a melo-dramatic symbolism. One believes that the artist's wife (Simon insists that his work has never given him time for women, much less for marriage) is buried beneath the highest tower. "Some say," another neighbor added darkly, "that he murdered her and that this is his penance." Still another had heard that Simon was a drunkard when he came to Watts and only gave up alcohol when the towers began to sprout; presumably the truckloads of broken bottles now buried in the walls were to be interpreted as a warning to his fellow-men.

Simon himself answers such theorizings with the simplicity of the true artist. "I had in my mind to do something big and I did it."

When had the idea first come to him—and how? "My dear friend——" He shook his head as though searching for something too far back to be quite re-called, and launched into an account of a mysterious French "General of the Ocean" in Louisiana long ago who refused to sanction the slapping of a certain woman for stealing a skirt. This was connected in some way with the admiral's refusal to sell Louisiana to the British for ten million dollars; he preferred, it seems, to *give* it to the United States—to avert a war. The point, if there was a point, was that the Frenchman stopped people from seizing and punishing the girl because she was beautiful, and because in the stolen dress she looked even more beautiful. "You see, dear friend," Radilla added with his characteristic sweet smile, "she like the birds; they find grains of corn and eat them—who ask 'Whose corn?'"

History teaches us, he went on, that the "good-good" can be distinguished from the "bad-bad" by a simple test. "It is not enough to be President. Lin-coln, Jefferson, they leave behind monument like this" (taking in the towers with a sweep of his hand) "of words. They not sit with feet on big desk reading funny-paper. They not make speech written by clever judge for them. Take Jesse James, he bad-bad too, not like Buffalo Bill who always ride *ahead* of his men into unknown. Or Bruno, burn alive because he dare to say there be other worlds, million miles from here—and no proof of Heaven.

"I believe in God, dear friend," he added as if to reassure me, "but Christ He not crucified to build the power of the wealthy Church. That why I take down many years ago Cross that was on highest tower there. Why? Because priest come by and rub hands; he think Cross justify *him!*"

The deep furrows in Simon's leathery skin contract and he scratches his sparse graying hair when asked to supply logical connections between some of his statements. This bewilderment, and the obvious relish with which he de-scribes the torments of Bruno and St. Simeon and identifies himself with their martyrdom, raises the question of his sanity. The question would be answered in the negative by the average man, not on the basis of what Simon says but of what he has built. And its relevance depends upon one's opinion of the degree of sanity expressed by the architecture of the norm—from the clap-board shan-ties of Watts to the hygienic glass ranch-houses of Tarzana.

"If he had not been a great fool," said Macaulay of Boswell, "he would never have been a great writer." And the Italian painter Veronese, when haled before the Inquisition and ordered to substitute the Magdalene for a dog in one of his frescoes, refused with the words, "We artists take the same liberties as poets and madmen." The knowing artist in our time is inevitably the victim of his intelligence and his conscience. His conscience drives him in the opposite direction from the "poet and madman," making him deny pure fantasy as the most cowardly escape from social responsibility, while his torturing intelligence constantly reminds him that no rational protest can possibly counter the sensible degradation of the norm whether expressed in popular culture, the contemporary city or war. Simon Radilla, unlike Veronese and his modern counterpart, is a primitive. He is not conscious of "taking liberties" since intuition is his only daemon and censor. His gigantic protest against the community which epitomizes our materialism is effective precisely because it has no possible use save beauty and because its creator is content to live and die within what is intended wholly for the pleasure of others.

PROFESSOR SEA GULL [20]

Joe Gould is a blithe and emaciated little man who has been a notable in the cafeterias, diners, barrooms, and dumps of Greenwich Village for a quarter of a century. He sometimes brags rather wryly that he is the last of the bohemians. "All the others fell by the wayside," he says. "Some are in the grave, some are in the loony bin, and some are in the advertising business." Gould's life is by no means carefree; he is constantly tormented by what he calls "the three H's"—homelessness, hunger, and hangovers. He sleeps on benches in subway stations, on the floor in the studios of friends, and in quarter-a-night flophouses on the Bowery. Once in a while he trudges up to one of Father Divine's Extension Heavens in lower Harlem and gets a night's lodging for fifteen cents. He is five feet four and he hardly ever weighs more than ninety-five pounds. Not long ago he told a friend that he hadn't eaten a square meal since June, 1936, when he bummed up to Cambridge and attended a banquet during a reunion of the Harvard class of 1911, of which he is a member. "I'm the foremost authority in the U.S. on the subject of doing without," he says. He tells people he lives on "air, self-esteem, cigarette butts, cowboy coffee, fried-egg sandwiches, and ketchup." Cowboy coffee is black coffeee without sugar. After finishing a sandwich, Gould customarily empties a bottle or two of ketchup on his plate and eats it with a spoon. The countermen in the Jefferson Diner, on Village Square, which is one of his hangouts, gather up the ketchup bottles and hide them the moment he puts his head in the door. "I don't particularly like the confounded stuff," he says, "but I make it a practice to eat all I can get. It's the only grub I know of that's free of charge."

Gould is a Yankee. His branch of the Goulds has been in New England since 1635, and he is related to the Lowell, Lawrence, Storer, and Vroom families. "There's nothing accidental about me," he once said. "I'll tell you what it took to make me what I am to-day. It took old Yankee blood, an overwhelming

[20] From *McSorley's Wonderful Saloon,* by Joseph Mitchell, pp. 68-75, 85-86. Copyright, 1938, 1939, 1940, 1941, 1942, 1943, by Joseph Mitchell. New York: Duell, Sloan & Pearce, Inc.

aversion to possessions, four years of Harvard, and twenty-five years of beating the living hell out of my insides with bad hooch and bad food." He says that he is out of joint with the rest of the human race because he doesn't want to own anything. "If Mr. Chrysler tried to make me a present of the Chrysler building," he says, "I'd damn near break my neck fleeing from him. I wouldn't own it; it'd own me. Back home in Massachusetts I'd be called an old Yankee crank. Here I'm called a bohemian. It's six of one, half a dozen of the other." Gould has a twangy voice and a Harvard accent. Bartenders and countermen in the Village refer to him as The Professor, Professor Bloomingdale, Professor Sea Gull, or The Mongoose. He dresses in the cast-off clothes of his friends. His overcoat, suit, shirt, and even his shoes are all invariably two or three sizes too large, but he wears them with a forlorn, Chaplinlike rakishness. "Just look at me," he says. "The only thing that fits is the necktie." On bitter winter days he puts a layer of newspapers between his shirt and undershirt. "I'm snobbish," he says. "I only use the *Times.*" He is fond of unusual headgear—a toboggan, a beret, or a yachting cap. One summer evening he appeared at a party in a seer-sucker suit, a polo shirt, a scarlet cummerbund, sandals, and a yachting cap, all hand-me-downs. He uses a long ivory cigarette-holder, and a good deal of the time he smokes butts picked up off the sidewalks.

Bohemianism has aged Gould considerably beyond his years. He has got in the habit lately of asking people he has just met to guess his age. Their guesses range between sixty-five and seventy-five; he is fifty-three. He is never hurt by this; he looks upon it as proof of his superiority. "I get more living done in one year," he says, "than ordinary humans do in ten." Gould is toothless, and his lower jaw swivels from side to side when he talks. He is bald on top, but the hair at the back of his head is long and frizzly, and he has a bushy, cinnamon colored beard, which he says he trims every other Easter. He has a squint, and while reading he wears a pair of spectacles which slip down to the end of his nose a moment after he puts them on. He doesn't use his spectacles on the street and without them he has the wild, unfocussed stare of an old scholar, who has strained his eyes on small print. Even in the Village many people turn and look at him. He is stooped, and he moves rapidly, grumbling to himself, with his head thrust forward and held to one side. Under his left arm he usually totes a bulging, greasy, brown pasteboard portfolio, and he swings his right arm aggressively. As he hurries along, he seems to be warding off an imaginary enemy. Don Freeman, the artist, a friend of his, once made a sketch of him walking. Freeman called the sketch "Joe Gould versus the Elements." Gould is as restless and footloose as an alley cat, and he takes long hikes about the city, now and then disappearing from the Village for weeks at a time and mystifying his friends; they have never been able to figure out where he goes. When he returns, always looking pleased with himself, he makes a few cryptic remarks, giggles, and then shuts up. "I went on a bird walk along the waterfront with an old countess," he said after his most recent absence. "The countess and I spent three weeks studying sea gulls."

Gould is almost never seen without his portfolio. He sits on it while he eats and he sleeps with it under his head. It usually contains a mass of manuscripts and notes, a dictionary, a bottle of ink, his extra shirts and socks, a cake of soap, a hairbrush, a paper bag of bread crumbs, and a paper bag of hard round, dime-store candy of the type called sour balls. "I fight fatigue with sour balls," he says. The crumbs are for pigeons; like many other eccentrics, Gould is a pigeon feeder. He is devoted to a flock which makes its headquarters atop and around the statue of Garibaldi in Washington Square. These pigeons know him. When he comes up and takes a seat on the plinth of the statue, they flutter down and perch on his head and shoulders, waiting for him to bring out his bag of crumbs. He has given names to some of them. "Come here, Boss Tweed," he says. "A lady in Stewart's didn't finish her whole-wheat toast this morning and when she went out, bingo, I snatched it off her plate especially for you. Hello, Big Bosom. Hello, Popgut. Hello, Lady Astor. Hello, St. John the Baptist. Hello, Polly Adler. Hello, Fiorello, you old goat, how're you to-day?"

Although Gould strives to give the impression that he is a philosophical loafer, he has done an immense amount of work during his career as a bohemian. Every day, even when he is groggy as the result of hunger, he spends at least a couple of hours laboring on a formless, rather mysterious book which he calls "An Oral History of Our Time." He began this book twenty-six years ago, and it is nowhere near finished. His preoccupation with it seems to be principally responsible for the way he lives; a steady job of any kind, he says, would interfere with his thinking. Depending on the weather, he writes in parks, in doorways, in flophouse lobbies, in cafeterias, on benches, on "L" platforms, in subway trains, and in public libraries. When he is in the proper mood, he writes until he is exhausted, and he gets into the mood at peculiar times. He says that one night he sat for seven hours in a booth in a Third Avenue bar and grill, listening to a beery old Hungarian woman, once a madam and once a dealer in cocaine and now a soup cook in a hospital, tell the story of her life. Three days later, around four o'clock in the morning, on a cot in the Hotel Defender, at 300 Bowery, he was awakened by the foghorns of tugs on the East River, and was unable to go back to sleep because he felt that he was in the exact mood to put the old soup cook's biography in his history. He has an abnormal memory; if he is sufficiently impressed by a conversation, he can keep it in his head, even if it is lengthy and senseless, for many days, much of it word for word. He had a bad cold, but he got up, dressed under a red exit light, and tiptoeing so as not to disturb the men sleeping on cots all around him, went downstairs to the lobby.

He wrote in the lobby from 4:15 A.M. until noon. Then he left the Defender, drank some coffee in a Bowery diner, and walked up to the Public Library. He plugged away at a table in the genealogy room, which is one of his rainy-day hangouts and which he says he prefers to the main reading room because it is gloomier, until it closed at 6 P.M. Then he moved into the main reading room and stayed there, seldom taking his eyes off his work, until the Library locked up for the night at 10 P.M. He ate a couple of egg sandwiches and a quantity of ketchup in a Times Square cafeteria. Then, not having two bits for a flophouse and being too engrossed to go to the Village and seek shelter, he hurried into the West Side subway and rode the balance of the night, scribbling ceaselessly while the train he was aboard made three round trips between the New Lots Avenue station in Brooklyn and the Van Cortlandt Park station in the Bronx. He kept his portfolio on his lap and used it as a desk. He has the endurance of the possessed. Whenever he got too sleepy to concentrate, he shook his head vigorously and then brought out his bag of sour balls and popped one in his mouth. People stared at him, and once he was interrupted by a drunk who asked him what in the name of God he was writing. Gould knows how to get rid of inquisitive drunks. He pointed at this left ear and said, "What? What's that? Deaf as a post. Can't hear a word." The drunk lost all interest in him. "Day was breaking when I left the subway," Gould says. "I was sneezing my head off, my eyes were sore, my knees were shaky. I was hungry as a bitch wolf, and I had exactly eight cents to my name. I didn't care. My history was longer by eleven thousand brand-new words, and at that moment I bet there wasn't a chairman of the board in all New York as happy as I."

Gould is haunted by the fear that he will die before he has the first draft of the Oral History finished. It is already eleven times as long as the Bible. He estimates that the manuscript contains 9,000,000 words, all in longhand. It may well be the lengthiest unpublished work in existence. Gould does his writing in nickel composition books, the kind that children use in school, and the Oral History and the notes he has made for it fill two hundred and seventy of them, all of which are tattered and grimy and stained with coffee, grease, and beer. Using a fountain pen, he covers both sides of each page, leaving no margins anywhere, and his penmanship is poor; hundreds of thousands of words are legible only to him. He has never been able to interest a publisher in the Oral History. At one time or another he has lugged armfuls of it into fourteen publishing offices. "Half of them said it was obscene and outrageous and to get it out of there as quick as I could," he says, "and the others said they couldn't read my handwriting." Experiences of this nature do not dismay Gould; he keeps telling himself that it is posterity he is writing for, anyway. In his breast pocket, sealed in a dingy envelope, he always carries a will bequeathing two-thirds of the manuscript to the Harvard Library and the other third to the Smithsonian Institution. "A couple of generations after I'm dead and gone," he likes to say, "the Ph.D.'s will start lousing through my work. Just imagine their surprise. 'Why, I be damned,' they'll say, 'this fellow was the most brilliant historian of the century.' They'll give me my due. I don't claim that all of the Oral History is first-class, but some of it will live as long as the English language."

Gould used to keep his composition books in a dusty pile on the floor of a closet in a friend's photography studio in the Village. Whenever he filled a book, he would come in and toss it on the pile. In the winter of 1942, after hearing that the Metropolitan Museum had moved its most valuable paintings to a bombproof storage place somewhere inland, he became panicky. He made a huge oilcloth-covered bale of the Oral History and entrusted it for the duration to a woman he knows who owns a duck-and-chicken farm near Huntington, Long Island. The farmhouse has a stone cellar.

Gould puts into the Oral History only things he has seen or heard. At least half of it is made up of conversation taken down verbatim, or summarized; hence the title. "What people say is history," Gould says. "What we used to think was history—all that chitty-chat about Caesar, Napoleon, treaties, inventions, big battles—is only formal history and largely false. I'll put down the informal history of the shirt-sleeved multitude—what they had to say about their jobs, love affairs, vittles, sprees, scrapes, and sorrows—or I'll perish in the attempt." The Oral History is a great hodgepodge and kitchen midden of hearsay, the fruit, according to Gould's estimate, of more than twenty thousand conversations. In it are the hopelessly incoherent biographies of hundreds of bums, accounts of the wanderings of seamen encountered in South Street barrooms, grisly descriptions of hospital and clinic experiences ("Did you ever have a painful operation or disease?" is one of the first questions that Gould, fountain pen and composition book in hand, asks a person he has just met), summaries of innumerable Union Square and Columbus Circle harangues, testimonies given by converts at Salvation Army street meetings, and the addled opinion of scores of park-bench oracles and gin-mill savants. For a time Gould haunted the all-night greasy spoons in the vicinity of Bellevue Hospital, eavesdropping on tired internes, nurses, ambulance-drivers, scrub-women, embalming-school students, and morgue workers, and faithfully recording their talk. He scurries up and down Fifth Avenue during parades, feverishly taking notes. Gould writes with great candor, and the percentage of obscenity in the Oral History is high. He has a chapter called "Examples of the So-Called Dirty Story of Our Time," to which he makes almost daily additions. In another chapter are many rhymes and observations which he found scribbled on the walls of subway washrooms. He believes that this graffiti is as truly historical as the strategy of General Robert E. Lee. Hundreds of thousands of words are devoted to the drunken behavior and the sexual adventures of various professional Greenwich Villagers in the twenties. There are hundreds of reports of ginny Village parties, including gossip about the guests and faithful reports of their arguments on such subjects as reincarnation, birth control, free love, psychoanalysis, Christian Science, Swedenborgianism, vegetarianism, alcoholism, and different political and art isms. "I have fully covered what might be termed the intellectual underworld of my time," Gould says. There are detailed descriptions of night life in the Village speakeasies, basement cabarets, and eating places which he frequented at one time or another and which are all now out of existence, such as the Little Quakeress, the Original Julius, Hubert's Cafeteria, the Troubadour Tavern, Alice McCollister's, and Eli Greifer's Last Outpost of Bohemia Tea Shoppe.

He is a night wanderer, and he has put down descriptions of dreadful things he has seen on dark New York streets—descriptions, for example, of the herds of big gray rats that come out in the hours before dawn in some neighborhoods of the lower East Side and Harlem and unconcernedly walk the sidewalks. "I sometimes believe that these rats are not rats at all," he says, "but the damned and aching souls of tenement landlords." A great deal of the Oral History is in diary form. Gould is afflicted with total recall, and now and then he painstakingly writes down everything he did for a day, a week, or a month. Sometimes he writes a chapter in which he monotonously and hideously curses some person or institution. Here and there are rambling essays on such subjects as the flophouse flea, spaghetti, the zipper as a sign of the decay of civilization, false teeth, insanity, the jury system, remorse, cafeteria cooking, and the emasculating effect of the typewriter on literature. "William Shakespeare didn't sit around pecking on a dirty, damned, ninety-five-dollar dohicky," he wrote, "and Joe Gould doesn't, either." In his essay on insanity he wrote, "I suffer from a mild form of insanity. I have delusions of grandeur. I believe myself to be Joe Gould."

*   *   *   *   *

He is acquainted with hundreds of artists, writers, sculptors, and actors in the Village, and whenever he learns that one of them is giving a party, he goes, friend or enemy, invited or not. Usually he keeps to himself for a while, uneasily smoking one cigarette after another and stiff as a board with tenseness. Sooner or later, however, impelled by a drink or two and by the desperation of the ill at ease, he begins to throw his weight around. He picks out the prettiest woman in the room, goes over, bows, and kisses her hand. He tells discreditable stories about himself. He becomes exuberant; suddenly, for no reason at all, he cackles with pleasure and jumps up and clicks his heels together. Presently he shouts, "All in favor of a one-man floor show, please say 'Aye'!" If he gets the slightest encouragement, he strips to the waist and does a handclapping, foot-stamping dance which he says he learned on a Chippewa reservation in North Dakota and which he calls the Joseph Ferdinand Gould Stomp. While dancing, he chants an old Salvation Army song, "There Are Flies on Me, There Are Flies on You, but There Are No Flies on Jesus." Then he imitates a sea gull. He pulls off his shoes and socks and takes awkward, headlong skips about the room, flapping his arms and letting out a piercing caw with every skip. As a child he had several pet gulls, and he still spends many Sundays on the end of a fishing pier at Sheepshead Bay observing gulls; he claims he has such a thorough understanding of their cawing that he can translate poetry into it. "I have translated a number of Henry Wadsworth Longfellow's poems into sea gull," he says.

*   *   *   *   *

Gould's outspokenness has made him a lone wolf in the Village; he has never been allowed to join any of the art, poetry, or ism organizations. He has been trying for ten years to join the Raven Poetry Circle, which puts on the poetry exhibition in Washington Square each summer and is the most powerful organization of its kind in the Village, but he has been black-balled every time. However, the Ravens usually let him attend their readings. Francis Lambert McCrudden, a retired Telephone Company employee who is the head Raven, claims that Gould is not serious about poetry. "We serve wine at our readings, and that is the only reason Mr. Gould attends," he once said. "He sometimes insists on reading foolish poems of his own, and it gets on your nerves. At our religious-poetry night he demanded permission to recite a poem entitled 'My Religion.' I told him to go ahead, and this is what he recited:

In winter I'm a Buddhist,
And in summer I'm a nudist.

And at our nature-poetry night he begged to recite a poem entitled 'The Sea Gull.' I gave him permission, and he jumped out of his chair and began to wave his arms and leap about and scream, 'Scree-eek! Scree-eek!' It was upsetting. We are serious poets and we don't approve of that sort of behavior." In the summer of 1942 Gould picketed the Raven exhibition, which was held on the fence of a tennis court on Washington Square South. In one hand he carried his portfolio and in the other he held a placard on which he had printed: "JOSEPH FERDINAND GOULD, HOT SHOT POET FROM POETVILLE, A REFUGEE FROM THE RAVENS. POETS OF THE WORLD, IGNITE! YOU HAVE NOTHING TO LOSE BUT YOUR BRAINS!" Now and then, as he strutted back and forth, he would take a leap and then a skip and say to passers-by, "Would you like to hear what Joe Gould thinks of the world and all that's in it? Scree-eek! Scree-eek!"

V. Back Where I Come From

Back of every city and its legend are the region and its myth. It is from the region—its lay of the land, geology, climate, economy, communities of interest, etc.—that a city originally derives its existence and function, and continues to draw much of its resources, human and natural. Thus it is in terms of its region that a city is a Northern, Eastern, Southern, Western, Yankee, Creole, Hoosier, Mormon, coast, river, prairie, mountain, port, railroad, resort, capital, industrial, lumber, wheat, steel or oil city. Contrary to the accepted belief, "city life," according to Lewis Mumford, "does not diminish these relations [between man and the land]: it rather adds new ones."

Like cities, regions are obsessed with the idea that they are "different," and this "difference" is thought to have existed more fully in the past, before standardization set in, when the region was close to its sources. Thus the myth of the region arises as a restoration of the past and is perpetuated by a kind of compromise with history, retaining enough of the past, but not too much, to satisfy the desire for uniqueness and tradition.

This myth of the region is promoted and dramatized in regional festivals, etc., as tourist bait (for example, the Natchez Pilgrimage). The myth is also something a man carries with him when he moves to another region, like the Kansas neighbor of a California friend of mine whose "main goal in life is to make Malibu as much like Kansas as possible."

Regional influences and adaptations may be seen in architecture—for example, in the South, the use of porch or gallery, the "dogrun" house, the rear appendage for a kitchen, the sidewalk arcades in front of shops. The use of rice in Charleston is an eloquent example of the effect of the region on food and of food in turn on the culture of the region.

In the agricultural Midwest the rural heritage is still strong in the cities —so strong, in fact, that most Iowa cities are "overgrown country towns" and Minneapolis is a "farmer's city." By the same token the migration of retired farmers from the smaller cities of Iowa and other Middlewestern states to Los Angeles is said to be responsible for the city's "village spirit."

Also part of the regional heritage of cities is the culture of ethnic groups, for example, the Germans of St. Louis and Milwaukee, the Creoles of Louisiana, and the Spanish-Americans and Mexicans of Southwestern cities.

In *Back Where I Came From*, A. J. Liebling writes plaintively: "People I know in New York are incessantly on the point of going back where they came from to write a book, or of staying on and writing a book where they came from. . . . It is all pretty hard on me because I was born in an apartment house at Ninety-third Street and Lexington Avenue about three miles from where I now live." In spite of this complaint, New Yorkers live in a metropolitan region, composed of the five boroughs, Long Island, and Westchester County, and are constantly going back where they came from, if only to the Bronx, to observe and report on life among the natives.

THE PURPLE WINDOW PANES OF BEACON STREET [1]

. . . [A] well-known characteristic of some of the early houses [of Beacon Hill], notably in Beacon Street, [is] their much-cherished panes of purple glass. This embellishment is found only in windows dating between 1818 and 1824, and not by any means in all houses built or altered during that period, even in the same neighborhood or block. Although much prized today by those whose houses are thus distinguished, the color was purely a matter of accident. The builders of those houses had no intention of adorning them with windows of tinted glass, and it is not suspected that the manufacturers had any thought of turning out other than an article of the usual high-grade standard. Sunlight and time, however, developed a change which is said to be due to a gradual chemical transformation of one of the elements (oxide of manganese) in the particular batch of glass used in certain houses. Eventually these windows assumed a delicate lilac hue, and lilac they have since remained to the joy and pride, rather than to the chagrin, of their owners. This glass was not peculiar to Boston, though, for Robert Shackleton, in *The Book of Boston*, claims a similar distinction for certain old houses in Irving Place and Clinton Place, New York.

NEW YORK APARTMENT-HOUSE LORE [2]

Not long ago, a tribe of gypsies moved into a fashionable apartment house on Park Avenue, in New York—an event which the building's management was inclined to view as one of the major catastrophes in the history of real estate, along with the sack of Carthage and the destruction of Pompeii.

The tribe had resorted to a stratagem, of course, to get in, but once established, it was hard to dislodge. One of the building's owners described the basic problem as follows: "How," he inquired fretfully, "does one go about suing a gypsy?"

Their space was at street level and had large display windows, designed for rental to an aristocratic commercial tenant, such as a modiste or a high-priced furrier. When it was vacant one fall, the owners leased it to what they understood was a very exclusive firm of Christmas-card designers. How the gypsies ever got such a recommendation was never made clear, but the management was horrified when they moved in, hung some blankets at the windows and settled down to life among the gentry.

[1] From *Beacon Hill*, Its Ancient Pastures and Early Mansions, by Allen Chamberlain, pp. 290-291. Copyright, 1924 and 1925, by Allen Chamberlain. Boston: Houghton Mifflin Company.

There are but few remaining examples in Boston, the present proud possessors being 39, 40, 63, 64, and 70 Beacon Street and 29A Chestnut Street.—A.C.

According to Eleanor Early (*And This Is Boston!*, 1930, p. 54), "The manufacturers determined to duplicate the delicate shade. After years of experiment they succeeded in producing a similar glass. But it is woefully lacking in tradition, which is all that counts on Beacon Hill."

[2] From "The Curious Ways of Manhattan Cliff Dwellers," by Rufus Jarman, *The Saturday Evening Post*, Vol. 224 (April 19, 1952), No. 42, pp. 38-39, 104, 109, 112, 114. Copyright, 1952, by the Curtis Publishing Company. Philadelphia.

Males of the clan took seats in openings between the blankets to smoke their pipes, sip wine and meditate upon passing society women and their dogs. The gypsy women, arrayed in shawls and earrings, infiltrated nearby apartment buildings, offering their services as fortunetellers.

At first, the management undertook to discourage its new tenants by shutting off the electricity in their quarters—a fruitless move, because they had come equipped with candles. Next the water was turned off, but that wasn't effective either. The gypsies appeared to have little use for water, being addicted to wine as a beverage and not to bathing as a regular custom. Finally, the management paid the tribe to break camp and its lease and move away.

These events are remarkable, in the first place, because the elegant atmosphere of the Fifth and Park Avenue sector is perhaps the last place in the world that one would expect to find a tribe of gypsies in residence. The incident may also be significant when regarded as a minor one of numerous indignities that have befallen "luxury" apartment living on Manhattan's fashionable East Side over the years since the panic of 1929 and particularly since the close of the last war.

The gypsy episode illustrates how residents too colorful to be desirable, in the view of owners of exclusive properties, may advance upon elegant areas when a check is not made on their social background before admission. Renting agents for such properties generally investigate also the economic history and credit rating of applicants for apartments, regardless of how affluent they may appear. Otherwise, a landlord may be faced with an unhappy situation such as happened two or three years ago, when a renting agent became so impressed by one young man's expensive automobile and stylish clothing that he neglected to make the usual check when renting a small apartment in one of the better houses.

The new tenant employed a valet and spent several thousand dollars redecorating his quarters. Then he launched upon a season of wining, dining and entertaining that became the talk of the neighborhood. This went on for seven months, after which he disappeared, leaving two months' rent unpaid. He turned out to be a store clerk who had won $100,000 betting on the Irish Sweepstakes. It had taken just seven months for him to spend his winnings.

Most owners of apartment buildings on Manhattan's fashionable East Side are more interested these days in a prospective tenant's rating in Dun & Bradstreet than his listing in the Social Register. Rent controls, towering costs of building and other factors of these materialistic times have made owners more realistic than some years ago when they thought in terms of thirty-room apartments, inhabited by families dating back to Peter Stuyvesant.

Nowadays, so long as a tenant is well regarded in commercial circles, East Side landlords do not much care whether he frequents the horse show or prefers the horse tracks. Some years ago when the social checks were stricter, the gypsy band would probably have been identified before it moved in. As far as apartments themselves are concerned, builders of exclusive houses are no longer preoccupied with making penthouse palaces, but rather prefer the efficiency apartment, sometimes known as the "parlor, bedroom and sink."

New apartments for the upper classes are usually not more than a third the size they were built twenty-five years ago. Eighteen-room units used to be standard for large, well-to-do families. Nowadays, according to one well-known builder, banks or insurance companies probably would not make a loan for a building containing apartments of more than seven rooms. Lush apartments of the 1920's usually had a servant's room for every family bedroom. Now they have one servant's room for the whole apartment, if that. Many units haven't even regular dining rooms. Dining is done in one end of the living room, sometimes made into an alcove—the same system used in the low-rent public-housing projects.

Apartments were not only built big during the 1920's, but some were very tricky. The apartment, on East 78th Street, of a prominent yachtsman, for instance, was designed like a yacht. The entrance was a gangplank over a moat of water, and rooms were arranged like cabins, with companionways, hatches, ship's bells, coils of rope, a binnacle and a poop deck.

Bathrooms were favorite spots for ingenuity of the 1920 vintage of apartment builders and owners to blossom. A group of newspaper real-estate editors, invited some years ago to inspect the East 67th Street apartment of actress Doris Keane, were surprised to find two large bathtubs sitting side by side in each bathroom. After advancing some interesting but implausible theories, the editors learned that Miss Keane believed the human body benefited from violent temperature contrasts. The idea was to fill one tub with hot and the other with cold water. The bather would then leap from one tub to the other, absorbing stimulation and invigoration with every plunge.

Because of the size they're building some high-priced apartments these days, a family is lucky if two people, let alone two bathtubs, can be got into a bathroom. Some wealthy New York families, who have moved into new demi-luxe apartments, but want the traditional splendors of the past, have created some strange effects by installing chandeliers and carved mantels, designed to fit foreign palaces, in four-room apartments intended for simple modernistic furniture and a couple of roll-away beds.

In Schwab House, a flashy new apartment building on Riverside Drive, a woman lacking a lot of rooms to decorate has painted her living room seven colors. In another building a lady spent five days supervising an expensive painter, shading her living-room walls so they would have a constant hue all day, even with more light striking them nearer the windows. Some families have put $75,000 worth of new furniture in three-room apartments. One woman in Schwab House has replaced the hardwood in her four-room apartment with marble floors, and a two-and-a-half-room apartment there is reported to have carved doors from an Italian monastery.

*   *   *   *   *

"The New Yorker's theory of apartment living used to be 'Never live in one place longer than necessary,'" an editor of one of that city's dailies was remarking at a cocktail party recently. "I came to this town from Kansas City twenty-five years ago, married a typical New York gal, and she proceeded to move us so often that I was never quite sure where we were living at the moment. We'd get comfortably settled someplace, and six months later we'd be moved again. She usually had about fifteen good reasons why we ought to go. She didn't like the neighbors, or the kids across the street were hoodlums, or the janitor looked like a crook. Of course, we had to move every time I got a raise or promotion. 'You're making more money now,' my wife would say. 'We can't live any longer in a dump like this.'

"There was one bright spot in all this, as far as I was concerned. She looked after the moving. Your native New Yorker relishes the sport of the apartment hunt the way the English gentry love to hunt foxes. She would say to me, 'You don't have to find an apartment. I will.' And she would. A few mornings later when I was leaving for work, she'd say: 'Don't come back here tonight. Come to 482 Clayton Avenue, Apartment 4-A.' And I'd go to this strange place that evening, and here would be our furniture all arranged in the living room, with our kids playing around. My wife would be in the kitchen cooking dinner, just like we'd lived there ten years.

"Even today I can look down the want-ad pages at addresses of apartments for rent, and I can describe the buildings. I ought to know. I lived in most of them. Manhattan, the Bronx, Greenwich Village, Staten Island, Flatbush, Yonkers, Hastings-on-the-Hudson, Sheepshead Bay, Long Island City, Jamaica, Jackson Heights—I've lived everywhere. . . ."

BALTIMORE BRICK HOUSES AND MARBLE STEPS [3]

. . . There are some Baltimoreans who believe that a part of the stability of Baltimore working folk can be attributed to ground rent and the row house.

Most of these row houses, which are one room wide, contain six rooms, three upstairs, and three down. They originally cost their owners something like $2500, often with a down payment of as little as fifty dollars. This low price was possible because they were mass-produced by the row and because the purchaser only rented the land beneath them, usually with an option to buy it outright at the end of five years. This amounted to a kind of uncallable mortgage. For if, at the end of five years, the householder found himself not in a position to buy the land, he could go right on renting it. Through this device, the majority of Baltimoreans came to own their own homes.

To-day some of these rows of houses are seventy or eighty years old, yet, being constructed of brick, they still stand firm and strong. Sandwiched in, as they are, there is no leakage of heat through the side walls, and there is nothing to paint except the front door and the window frames. Therefore, a ten-dollar paint job on the outside woodwork and a little soap and water on the marble steps perks them up wonderfully. And most Baltimoreans take the trouble to do just that.

[3] From "The Cities of America: Baltimore," by George Sessions Perry, *The Saturday Evening Post*, Vol. 218 (May 11, 1946), No. 45, p. 55. Copyright, 1946, by the Curtis Publishing Company. Philadelphia.

ST. PETERSBURG—THE CITY OF GREEN BENCHES [4]

At St. Petersburg, Florida, we checked in at a hotel and I sent my suit out to be pressed. When it came back there wasn't any bill on it. "Compliments of Valentine Cleaners," the bellboy said. "No charge." You could have knocked me over with an ironing board. I don't know whether that sort of thing would have gone on indefinitely or not. Having only one suit of clothes, and not wanting to send it right back again, I didn't experiment further.

The St. Petersburg *Times,* which ran my column, got a call from a woman reader. She said she had read that I was flat broke, and she would gladly lend me a little money. She had misread the piece. I had written of somebody else's being flat broke. (As for me, I married money, and am so rich I can't sleep at night.) So we called back and explained to the woman, and thanked her.

That kind of good old Midwestern friendliness is the keynote of St. Petersburg, and the green sidewalk bench is its symbol. The green bench is to St. Petersburg what the lei is to Hawaii, the gondola to Venice, the rolling chair to Atlantic City, the sidewalk cafe to Paris. The green benches are where the winter residents sit in the sun and talk to each other and watch all the other visitors sitting and talking and sunning. When I was there the latest count showed 4,697 of these benches. About twelve hundred of them were owned by the city, and were in parks. The rest were owned by merchants.

The St. Petersburg sidewalks are very wide, and the benches are on the outer edge, at right angles to the street. One after another, like rows in a theater, for block after block. By ten o'clock of a warm morning it's almost impossible to find a seat. And it is an unwritten law that you may sit down beside any stranger on a green bench and start talking to him. If he doesn't respond and talk pleasantly back, he is rude and we hope nobody ever speaks to him again as long as he lives.

It is a city law that all public benches must be green, and made of wood. And they must be repainted once a year. They're more than just something to sit on.

St. Petersburg has probably taken more drubbing from us writing fellers than any other city in Florida. That's because so many elderly people go there for winters. St. Petersburg has been referred to as "The City of the Living Dead," and "The Old People's Home," and such things as that. This burns the civic leaders up. Of course, what they want to get over to the public is that you can whoop and holler in St. Petersburg as much as in other Florida cities. You can bet and go night-clubbing and fish and yacht and look at palm trees and parade in your sports roadster. But personally I'm at the point where I can yell "hotcha" about twice and then I want to go sit down somewhere. I think it's mighty nice to have a place like St. Petersburg where you don't need either a Blue Book status or eighty billion red corpuscles to have a good time.

A historical note: St. Petersburg's existence is due to two men—General John

C. Williams, of Detroit, who chose this spot as a healthful place to retire to, and Petrovich Demenscheff, an exiled Russian who built the first railroad into the area in 1888. Each wanted to name the town. Williams was for Detroit, his home town, and Demenscheff held out for St. Petersburg, his home city in Russia. So they flipped a half dollar. Demenscheff won. General Williams died in 1892. And as for Demenscheff—it's a dirty trick to be telling this—he left for California in the 1890s, and never came back.

THE SANTA FE STYLE OF ARCHITECTURE [5]

Santa Fe's heart is its tree-shaded Plaza and the squat adobe Palace of the Governors—now a museum—which has faced it on the north side since 1610, a full decade before the Pilgrims came to Plymouth. Here shops and office buildings of the modern business district crowd the narrow streets of the oldest part of the city. And here Santa Fe's ruling obsession, its own long history, finds its most spectacular outlet in the so-called "Santa Fe" style of architecture. Architect John Gaw Meem, master of the style, calls it the direct descendant of the ancient Indian pueblos and the colonial buildings, the haciendas and mission churches—which the Spaniards in New Mexico erected. Thus the Art Gallery and Auditorium of the Museum of New Mexico, close beside the Palace of the Governors, is the ingeniously composite reproduction of six famous Mission churches.

Diagonally across the Plaza stands the Fred Harvey hotel, La Fonda, in large part the design of John Meem himself. It raises its four stories—which make it, incidentally, a giant in the city—in the terraced manner of a pueblo, while its interior is a hotelman's dream of Spanish Colonial sumptuousness. Stores, office blocks, garages, warehouses, filling stations, theaters—all adhere faithfully to the Santa Fe style, and residential Santa Fe follows suit.

[5] From "The Cities of America: Sante Fe," by John Bishop, *The Saturday Evening Post*, Vol. 221 (September 18, 1948), No. 12, pp. 21, 128. Copyright, 1948, by the Curtis Publishing Company. Philadelphia.

Old adobe has the faculty, gained from years of weathering, of fading into a landscape as if it had been camouflaged. That quality has been built into modern Santa Fe along with the Santa Fe style. An incidental result, therefore, is that Santa Fe, even at a short distance, all but vanishes into its gigantic setting. In its oldest sections, the low buildings and the houses with their patios and walled gardens sprawl in hiding under cottonwoods and willows, the rich and the poor together. Where they straggle out upon the plain or reach tentaclelike into the draws and arroyos and out upon the shoulders of the hills, their soft lines and colors give them almost the look of natural features of the land.

There are, to be sure, glaring exceptions to the Santa Fe style which harshly refuse to efface themselves—the white-domed, brick State Capitol and matching Governor's Mansion; the French Romanesque sandstone Cathedral of St. Francis; a few uncomfortably red-brick store fronts around the Plaza and a scattering of gawky red houses along the winding streets near by. With those few exceptions, Santa Fe succeeds in making itself as nearly invisible as a modern American city of some 25,000 people can be invisible.

FOOD IN BOSTON [6]

Any school child in South Dakota can tell you that Boston is the home of the bean and the cod, though not many Boston school children can tell you that South Dakota in turn has its own formula for an inland herring salad. Boston has more in her refrigerator than the average American may think. Her immediate neighbors know it for a fact. She is the capital of a state bounded by Atlantic seafood and by five other states, each fiercely jealous of its own produce or its own way of cooking it. Boston is not wholly unmindful of the New Hampshire blueberry, Vermont maple syrup, New York cherry pie, Connecticut corned-beef hash, Rhode Island johnnycake, and cranberry juice from the red bogs of the Cape. . . . The beans . . . come in individual pots just a shade lighter in color than the companionable brown bread, which ought to be toasted, but generally is not. The cod industry has so grown and flourished that fish cakes are now as broadly American as rice pudding, though most of our countrymen have not yet learned to pour a thimbleful of cream on top.

Of course, when it comes to be served, it actually isn't cod but scrod. Thousands of visitors to this city are annually fooled into thinking that they have avoided the sand-white symbol of the state and depart with the happy notion that they have, on the other hand, discovered an entirely new variety of fish [whereas scrod, of course, is merely the young cod]. . . .

Boston is a great tripe center. With the passing of the old Adams House and Young's Hotel, two legs of the tripod have disappeared; but the Parker House still serves it in its pseudo-waffle shape, without syrup; and many other places carry it clandestinely on the menu. Of course it has a Rotarian function in Philadelphia pepperpot. Boston cream pie is a kind of institutional dessert, some-

[6] From *About Boston*, Sight, Sound, Flavor & Inflection, by David McCord, pp. 30-34. Copyright, 1948, by David McCord. Garden City, New York: Doubleday & Company, Inc.

what overfeatured in the dining halls of local schools and colleges. The Parker
House roll is almost as famous as the Bunker Hill Monument, though not so
easily placed geographically; and the Porterhouse steak, a name full of juice
and priority, has long outlived its forgotten proprietary tavern in the city across
the Charles.

Baked Indian pudding is a delicious Boston specialty, particularly when
mildly warm and topped with a Durgin-Park quality of vanilla ice cream.
Doughnuts and pie for breakfast are still possible and even popular factors on
the greater Boston bill of fare. If doughnuts at eight o'clock in the morning
seem odd to the uninitiated, that opening wedge of squash or apple is actually
something that the most hardened tourist can scarcely take. Which is why Boston sightseeing begins in the railroad lunch-room. Here the doughnuts are
under glass, the pie is under the counter, and the man who orders simply bacon
and eggs is under suspicion.

Bostonians are conscious of the enchanting quality of their fish chowder. A
good Boston fish chowder is hard to beat on Monday or Tuesday, and impossible to beat or even substitute for on Friday. Boston clam chowder—to wade in
shallower water—is the pure elixir from the sea. It bears no resemblance to the
Manhattan transfer which involves a powerful tomato base reflecting the presence of stiff or wire-haired variety of clam: a dish wholly unpalatable to any
one living within gunshot of Dorchester Heights, the Hill, or the Fenway.
Quahog chowder is simply clam chowder seen through a magnifying glass. It
is ordered, eaten, and understood largely by natives of the fifth generation.

Across the country, wherever cooking is held to be an art and not an industry, the food which Boston prepares and consumes is sometimes thought of as
ruggedly simple and ingeniously unflavored. Such is far from the truth. The
market of Boston is the market of the nation. It may not include the Pacific
sand dab, the Gulf-borne pompano, the Oregon blue grouse, and such; but you
will find there nearly everything else from the small and delicious Malpeque
oyster and Gilfeather turnip to Philadelphia scrapple, samp, and Wisconsin
cheese. Boston restaurants are among the most praised eating places of the land.
Durgin-Park, the Union Oyster House, Locke-Ober's, and Jacob Wirth's—to
name but four, conspicuously unconnected with hotels—are as unlike as they
appear to be remarkable in atmosphere and culinary delight.

And one thing more. At a time when bookstores everywhere are flooded with
cookbooks of general, local, regional, foreign, offshore, barbecue, and highly
specialized interest, it is still the home of the bean and the cod which sponsors
the daddy of them all. Fannie Merritt Farmer's *Boston Cooking-School Cook
Book* of nearly nine hundred well-seasoned pages has lately celebrated an anniversary with a golden jubilee edition. First published in 1896, and currently
edited not by the Farmer's daughter but by the Farmer's niece, the house of
Little, Brown (the more than century-old publishers up on Beacon Street) record a total sale through the years of well over two million and a half copies.
The sales of this cookbook, in fact, have been exceeded only by such lively
competitors as the Bible, *Uncle Tom's Cabin, Gone With the Wind,* and *How*

to Win Friends and Influence People. Herself the "Mother of Level Measurement," Fannie Farmer gave America the teaspoon clue to creative cooking.[7] . . .

EAT![8]

As I went down Belmont Avenue [in Brownsville], the copper-shining herrings in the tall black barrels made me think of the veneration of food in Brownsville families. I can still see the kids pinned down to the tenement stoops, their feet helplessly kicking at the pots and pans lined up before them, their mouths pressed open with a spoon while the great meals are rammed down their throats. *"Eat! Eat! May you be destroyed if you don't eat! What sin have I committed that God should punish me with you! Eat! What will become of you if you don't eat! Imp of darkness, may you sink ten fathoms into the earth if you don't eat! Eat!"*

We never had a chance to know what hunger meant. At home we nibbled all day long as a matter of course. On the block we gorged ourselves continually on "Nessels," Hersheys, gumdrops, polly seeds, nuts, chocolate-covered cherries, charlotte russe, and ice cream. A warm and sticky ooze of chocolate ran through everything we touched; the street always smelled faintly like the candy wholesaler's windows on the way back from school. The hunger for sweets, jellies, and soda water raged in us like a disease; during the grimmest punchball game, in the middle of a fist fight, we would dash to the candy store to get down two-cent blocks of chocolate and "small"—three-cent—glasses of cherry soda; or calling "upstairs" from the street, would have flung to us, or carefully hoisted down at the end of a clothesline, thick slices of rye bread smeared with chicken fat. No meal at home was complete without cream soda, root beer, ginger ale, "celery tonic." We poured jelly on bread; we poured it into the tea; we often ate chocolate marshmallows before breakfast. At school during the recess hour Syrian vendors who all looked alike in their alpaca jackets and black velour hats came after us with their white enameled trays, from which we took *Halvah*, Turkish Delight, and three different kinds of greasy nut-brown pastry sticks. From the Jewish vendors, who went around the streets in every season wheeling their little tin stoves, we bought roasted potatoes either in the quarter or the half—the skins were hard as bark and still smelled of the smoke pouring out of the stoves; apples you ate off the stick that were encrusted with a thick glaze of baked jelly you never entirely got down your throat or off your fingers, so that you seemed to be with it all day; *knishes*; paper spills of hot yellow chick peas. I still hear those peddlers crying up and down the street—*"Árbes! Árbes! Hayse gute árbes! Kinder! Kinder! Hayse gute árbes!"* From the "big" Italians, whom we saw only in summer, we bought watremelons as they drove

[7] A persistent myth reports that in a new edition of the *Cook Book* appearing a few years ago the publishers were anxious to include recipes for cocktails. The revised copy was ready for the press when some one discovered that the formula for a Dry Martini began: "To one cup of gin add. . . ."—D.M.

[8] From *A Walker in the City*, by Alfred Kazin, pp. 32-34. Copyright, 1951, by Alfred Kazin. New York: Harcourt, Brace and Company.

their great horse-smelling wagons down the street calling up to every window
—"Hey you ladies! *Hey ladies! Freschi* and good!"—and from the "small" ones,
who pushed carts through the streets, paper cups of shaved ice sprinkled before
our eyes with drops of lemon or orange or raspberry syrup from a narrow water
bottle.

But our greatest delight in all seasons was "delicatessen"—hot spiced corned
beef, pastrami, rolled beef, hard salami, soft salami, chicken salami, bologna,
frankfurter "specials," and the thinner, wrinkled hot dogs always taken with
mustard and relish and sauerkraut, and whenever possible, to make the treat
fully real, with potato salad, baked beans, and french fries which had been
bubbling in the black wire fryer deep in the iron pot. At Saturday twilight, as
soon as the delicatessen store reopened after the Sabbath rest, we raced into it
panting for the hot dogs sizzling on the gas plate just inside the window. The
look of that blackened empty gas plate had driven us wild all through the
wearisome Sabbath day. And now, as the electric sign blazed up again, lighting
up the words HEBREW NATIONAL DELICATESSEN, it was as if we had entered into
our rightful heritage. Yet *Wurst* carried associations with the forbidden, the
adulterated, the excessive, with spices that teased and maddened the senses to
demand more, still more. This was food that only on Saturday nights could be
eaten with a good conscience. Generally, we bought it on the sly; it was supposed to be bad for us; I thought it was made in dark cellars. Still, our parents
could not have disapproved of it altogether. Each new mouthful of food we
took in was an advantage stolen in the battle. The favorite injunction was to
fix yourself, by which I understood we needed to do a repair job on ourselves.
In the swelling and thickening of a boy's body was the poor family's earliest
success. "Fix yourself!" a mother cried indignantly to the child on the stoop.
"Fix yourself!" The word for a fat boy was *solid.*

PHILADELPHIA DISHES [9]

Somewhere at the back, or forefront, of almost every Philadelphia
custom, or organization, or meeting of any kind, annual or otherwise, you will
find an excellent supper or superb dinner, frequently featuring especial Philadelphia dishes and usually accompanied, whatever else there is to drink, and
as a rule there is plenty, by Philadelphia's historic wine, Madeira. Public eating
in Philadelphia is unbelievably bad; private eating still maintains a high, historic standard. All during colonial times, when Philadelphia was a capital and
a crossroads, and until comparatively recently, Philadelphia had a fine tradition
of food, as fine as New Orleans, and this tradition persisted until about four
decades ago, when American food everywhere began to break down under the
infiltration of bastard Franco-Italian cooking. At one time Philadelphia had
dozens of excellent restaurants, large and small, some of which, like the old
Bellevue, Green's, the old Continental, were world famous. Today in all the
city there is not a single first-class restaurant, although there is one excellent

[9] From *Philadelphia: Holy Experiment,* by Struthers Burt, pp. 364-366. Copyright, 1945,
by Struthers Burt. Garden City, New York: Doubleday & Company, Inc.

and historic sea-food place, and one excellent chophouse. Outside of these, the majority of Philadelphians, when not at home, eat in strange frowzy teashops or, if they are rich, in restaurants where the marvelous products of the native cornucopia are disguised or ruined by Mediterranean self-conviction. In many of Philadelphia's private houses, however, in the city or in the suburbs, you can still find what William Penn talked about, and the generations that followed him. It should be so, for the city is a middle city, exactly placed to receive the benefits of both the North and South, and at its back door is the richest farm land in the United States.

Philadelphia, then, has, or could have, superb mutton and beef, and so it still has if you want them, and know how to cook them, for, whatever may have happened to the city's restaurants, traditional and matchless markets remain. As for vegetables of every kind, fruits, dairy products, the town is golden and green with them. "Philadelphia butter" is everywhere spoken of with reverence, and so are "Philadelphia capons." Philadelphia cream cheese is a local invention and, incidentally, the best thing in the world for your teeth; it is filled with calcium. . . . The American love of cottage cheese, *Schmierkäse,* is due to Philadelphia, or rather, the neighboring "Pennsylvania Dutch." Philadelphia ice cream and ice-cream meringues, and Philadelphia's especial soup, pepper-pot, invented in colonial days, are things to be talked about. Philadelphia terrapin is a delight and its cousin, Philadelphia stewed snapper, is equally good. And with these can now be listed Philadelphia's éclairs, unlike any other éclairs in existence, and Philadelphia lady-fingers, lady-locks, white-mountain cake, and above all, Philadelphia cinnamon buns. In just one place in New York can you get real cinnamon buns, and there the Philadelphia recipe is followed.

Philadelphia has presented many dishes to the rest of the country, and in almost every instance the rest of the country ruins them. Few Americans, for instance, know what cinnamon bun is—not the glacéed, brown celestial kind. Nor do they know coffee cakes, which, in Philadelphia, owing again to the "Pennsylvania Dutch" influence, are flaky *croissants,* iced with sugar, raisins inside to make your mouth water. Philadelphia is one of the few places where you can get real doughnuts; those without a hole in them, and which are as light as thistledown. The list is endless.

Philadelphia not only has a perfect gastronomical latitude, but two ancient strains of cooking: Quaker cooking, the Quakers being the only English who ever understood cooking, and "Pennsylvania Dutch" cooking. The pretzel is a "Pennsylvania Dutch" invention; although, even if you are a Philadelphian, unless you know one or two hidden-away shops, you have to go to Reading to discover what a pretzel is. In Reading, they are large, but thin and crisp. Golden brown from butter; and with just the right sprinkling of salt. Not common salt, but salt crystals. And in Reading they still fold their arms symbolically across their breasts, seraphim in adoration, as the Moravian monks, who first made them, meant them to do.

Nor does any one north of Philadelphia know what an oyster is; a statement that will cause unbelief in the minds of New Yorkers and rage in the breasts of Bostonians. But Philadelphians, except in restaurants ruined by alien influence, do not eat the white, unhealthy, broken-spirited creatures found in New York, first cousins of liver-fed mountain trout, whose only taste is supplied by the horse-radish or tomato catsup furnished on the side. . . . To the real Philadelphian an oyster cocktail, unless one is forced to eat the debased sea creatures described, is an abomination. Why disguise the taste of an oyster? A touch of lemon; a touch of horse-radish—that is all.

Philadelphians eat slim and lovely gray oysters, caught far from the wicked ways of cities. When you swallow them, you taste the native salt, and if you close your eyes, you hear the tide on the shingles of lonely islands.

Scrapple, or *pon-haus,* which is not a "Pennsylvania Dutch" discovery, as is so generally supposed, but dates from the even earlier real Dutch and Swedish settlers, need not be gone into too deeply because it is a bitter nation-wide controversy: Philadelphians on one side, all the rest of the United States on the other. But Philadelphians who have married maidens from the barbarous outer forests speedily show them what a delectable dish scrapple is when properly cooked. It is not slimy, it should not be greasy, it should not be thick; it should be thin, piping hot, crisp as an October day, and as golden brown as a Reading pretzel. It should crunch. Correctly cooked and served, it will woo even the most reluctant breakfast appetite.

On that statement, like all others reared in Philadelphia, I will take my stand. Let the forest dwellers rave!

BALTIMORE CUISINE [10]

. . . Though in recent years the price has declined along with the demand, diamondback terrapin is still expensive. Preparation of the meat is a tedious business which finds few volunteers. Terrapin, therefore, is not for the masses who probably wouldn't appreciate it even if they could afford it. Even persons who like it find it hard to explain its subtle and seductive charm. Very likely a taste for it is based on a child's recollection of never hearing the word mentioned by its elders except with a smacking of the lips.

The only terrapin whose flavor meets the exacting specifications of the connoisseurs is the diamondback. Local restaurants occasionally offer lesser breeds to their patrons; the diamondback is seldom met outside the Maryland Club, or the supper which is a feature of The Assembly, or the private homes of the wealthy. The Maryland Club has long enjoyed distinction for its terrapin. The secret is said to lie in the fact that it is cooked with sweet butter. Usually sherry is added just before serving, and a cruet of sherry also accompanies the terrapin to the table. According to well-authenticated reports, Mrs. Miles White personally inspects and chooses every terrapin that is to appear at the Assembly as carefully as the committee on invitations scrutinizes the list of potential guests before sending out bids to the ball.

Philadelphia, too, is a terrapin city. But to the horror of Baltimoreans, Phila-

[10] From *The Amiable Baltimoreans,* by Francis F. Beirne, pp. 344-348, 352-353. Copyright, 1951, by E. P. Dutton & Co., Inc. New York.

delphians serve their terrapin with a cream sauce! At least such is the scandalous report in Baltimore.

On occasion terrapin appears at debutante parties, to the great distress of older guests who hate to see it wasted. At one such party, two elderly gentlemen barely escaped apoplexy when they heard a youth inquiring of a waiter, "Have you got any more of that soup?" There wasn't any more. It was all gone because the youth and others like him had eaten it all up thinking it was bouillon.

Twenty-five years or so ago, because the open season for ducks was longer and the permitted daily bag larger than at present, duck hunters frequently returned with more ducks than they could possibly use themselves. These surplus ducks made welcome gifts to friends who delight in eating duck but lack the moral courage to sit exposed in a ducking blind on a cold winter's day. Or, better still, the hunters invited friends in to eat the ducks. Wild duck, too, in those halcyon days was found along with terrapin on the bill of fare at the Maryland Club. With the passing of years, however, the ducks have grown scarcer. To reverse the trend the season has been shortened, the legal bag limited, and sportsmen have contributed generously to improving conditions on the breeding grounds in Canada. These heroic efforts seem to be having the desired effect, though progress is gradual. So to-day in Baltimore the highest compliment one person can pay another is to make a gift of wild duck or invite him to come and eat it.

Local tradition calls for a vastly different treatment of wild duck from that accorded the ordinary barnyard duck which appears on menus as "Long Island duckling." The barnyard duck is stuffed with bread and roasted until well done. It then is served with thick gravy, apple sauce, and very likely mashed potatoes to soak up the gravy.

The story is told of a Baltimore bride who received a gift of a pair of wild ducks and seized the opportunity to entertain an elderly friend she knew would appreciate them. Looking in her cookbook, she came upon a recipe for duck and gave instructions to the cook she had hired for the occasion. She went to a nearby golf course for a bit of relaxation before time for dinner.

The little bride ran into her prospective guest on the course. "Hope you are not cooking those ducks too long," he remarked, as he passed her. "Have you got currant jelly?" he inquired on their second meeting. Piece by piece he let her know that wild ducks should not be stuffed, that they should "fly through the oven," that currant jelly and not apple sauce should be served with them, and that wild rice or creamed hominy, not mashed potatoes, are the preferred vegetable. The bride did not wait to finish her match but rushed home to countermand the orders given and rescue the ducks from the tragic fate she had unwittingly prepared for them.

Because of its proximity to Chesapeake Bay Baltimore has always enjoyed a reputation for seafood and, in particular, for oysters. Poor conservation practice and the tendency of oystermen to ignore the advice of the scientists and to blame God for a dwindling supply have played havoc with the industry. The bay now produces virtually no oysters. So "Baltimore on the Chesapeake" is forced to the ignominious practice of importing its oysters from rivers contiguous to the bay, from Chincoteague, Lynnhaven Bay, and other alien waters.

Baltimore observes the custom of eating oysters only in those months which have R in their names. Ships reach the local market on September 1st with the season's first oysters and the gourmets lose no time sampling them and expressing expert opinion on the flavor and quality of the new crop. From then on oysters appear regularly on local menus. They are to be had raw on the half shell at oyster bars where patrons sit on high stools. They are to be had in soup, in stews, broiled on toast, panned, and in fritters. Most popular of all are oysters dipped in egg, rolled in cracker crumbs, and fried.

A fine old local custom is the oyster roast. A popular time for it is a moonlight night in October or November. It can be held at any house with an acre or more of land around it; if the property looks out over a body of water, so much the better. Guests come in warm sweaters, tweeds, and other sports clothes because a good deal of time is spent out of doors. Inside the house of the persons giving the party an open fire and a choice of drinks help to get things going.

At a convenient spot outside a pit will have been dug and a hot wood fire started. The oysters make their appearance in gunnysacks holding a bushel each. A metal grill is placed over the fire and on it the oysters are roasted in their shells. Oyster knives are provided for opening the shells and each guest has also a saucer of melted butter in which the roasted oysters are dipped before eating. An oyster bar also is rigged up where guests may eat their fill of raw oysters out of the shell before beginning on the roasted oysters. Bottled beer too is on hand.

When the guests have eaten all the oysters they want, they return to the house for a spread of cold cuts, sandwiches, potato salad, cheese and crackers, doughnuts, pie, and hot coffee.

* * * * *

An altogether characteristic item of food is the Maryland biscuit, which to-day is all but obsolete. When it does appear it is as an accompaniment to terrapin or Smithfield ham. The Maryland biscuit, as a matter of fact, is nothing more than the beaten biscuit of the entire South, from which it differs only in size and shape. The beaten biscuit is round and flat with a diameter of from two to three inches. The Maryland biscuit, on the other hand, is about the size and shape of a pullet egg. The recipe calls for nothing more than flour, salt, lard, milk, and water worked into a dough and dumped on a floured biscuit board.

Then begins the pounding of the dough with a rolling pin for a solid half hour, which gives the biscuit its unique quality. Nothing less, say the experts, will do. They scorn short cuts such as passing the dough through a meat grinder. In the old days it is said that one could tell the hour before breakfast by the sound of cooks beating biscuits all the way down the block. One no longer finds cooks who will take that much trouble. There are a few people in Baltimore who turn out Maryland biscuits wholesale for the market, but the biscuits have passed out of the ken of the ordinary family kitchen.

No dissertation on characteristic Baltimore food should omit mention of that most delectable of desserts—the Kossuth cake. Local tradition holds that it was created by an East Baltimore Street confectioner on the occasion of the visit of Louis Kossuth, Hungarian patriot, in 1851, and named in honor of him. Kossuth was the leader in his country of a revolt against Austrian rule that was part of the wave of revolutions which swept over Europe in 1848. For a time Hungary achieved its independence and Kossuth was its governor, but, with the aid of imperial Russia, Austria regained control. Kossuth was imprisoned temporarily and, upon his release, accepted an invitation to visit the United States. Here for a time he was hailed as a popular hero and champion of freedom. Kossuth's hope was to raise money for a new revolt.

Baltimore gave him a cordial reception and made him the chief figure in a grand parade. But when it came to contributing hard cash the Baltimore public held back. Kossuth's total take was a trifling $25.00. Even the dedication of so sublime a dessert as Kossuth cake could hardly have assuaged his disappointment. Ironically enough, any one who has partaken of this food feels in anything but a revolutionary mood. Nothing could be more conducive to complete acquiescence to the status quo.

The Kossuth cake is a particularly proud member of the Charlotte Russe family. A sponge cake about three inches in diameter and two inches high is hollowed out and filled with thick whipped cream. On top of the whipped cream is a thick cap of chocolate or strawberry icing. Each Kossuth cake sits in a pleated paper cup. It is served slightly chilled. No local cookbooks mention Kossuth cakes, which obviously have been the monopoly of confectioners and caterers. There still are one or two old establishments which make them, but an order has to be given in advance. A pseudo-Kossuth cake sometimes finds its way on to a local bill of fare. In this spurious version a dip of vanilla ice cream is substituted for whipped cream. It is inevitable that in so fraudulent a concoction the sponge cake should be stale and the chocolate cover thin and anemic. The true Kossuth cake must be made of the very best ingredients, and you must be prepared to pay for them.

RICE IN CHARLESTON [11]

. . . Rice in Charleston is more an institution than a cereal, and . . . until you subscribe to that belief, you will never altogether understand the history of the town. Outlanders will scoffingly tell you that the Charlestonians, like the Chinese, spend their lives eating rice or worshipping their ancestors. But the reverse is more true than the original. For, if since 1865 many Charlestonians have in one way or another eaten their ancestors, from time out of mind the most of them have always somewhat worshipped rice. Dine with one and you at once recognize that there is a ritual of rice he celebrates daily. In the first place you will find on every proper Charleston dinner table a spoon

[11] From *Charleston: Azaleas and Old Bricks*, photographs by Bayard Wooten, text by Samuel Gaillard Stoney, pp. 11-13. Copyright, 1937, by Bayard Wooten and Samuel Gaillard Stoney. Boston: Houghton Mifflin Company.

that is peculiar to the town. Of massive silver, about fifteen inches long and broad in proportions, it is laid on the cloth with something of the reverential distinction that surrounds the mace in the House of Commons at Westminster. And their functions are not dissimilar, for if you take away the bauble, as did Cromwell, the Commons of England are a mob without authority, and if you take away the rice-spoon from the Charleston dinner table, the meal that follows is not really dinner. In fact, it's hardly worth calling a meal; so little worthy of notice that one family, who, though only Low-Country Episcopalians were noted for their piety, would never ask a grace before a meal without rice, even when their parson was at the table, thinking it hardly worth thanking the Lord for.

You will, by trial and error, be shown that there are certain things that simply don't go with rice, as, for example, fish. But worst of all contacts are those with sugar or anything sweet. Whistle 'Marching Through Georgia' in St. Michael's Churchyard, proclaim on steps of the City Hall your admiration for John Brown or General Sherman, but don't ask for sugar when you've helped yourself to rice. The Charlestonian when not aroused is a courteous creature and inclined to make allowances, but there are limits beyond which he will not be tried.

And there is little excuse for not eating rice as the Charlestonians do when it is cooked as they want it. The way a Low-Country Negro handles a rice-pot is the sheerest black magic. It is all in the amount of water they put in with the grain, just enough to boil the rice sufficiently soft and then to start passing off at once in steam to leave grain separate from grain and the mass ready for the gravy that should be its sole concomitant. Of course, a Charlestonian will admit to you that in other places and with foreign rices a pudding may be the only way to get rice down the human gullet; but Carolina Rices, Gold Seed or White, from tawny, black-water, or salt rivers, are all of them too sacred to be treated lightly or inadvisedly, and when you get to know Charleston, you will find there people who know these rices as Burgundians know wines, maybe even a little better, for the rice-taster's palate must be subtle.

Two of the old rice-mills of Charleston are left to show you that not in eating alone was rice treated reverentially. West Point Mill on the Ashley, now become an office building for a trans-Atlantic airway terminal, is more austere than Bennett's Mill on the Cooper, but both of them have had too much architectural care expended upon them to be classed as mere mills. There is something of the temple in their design, and designedly so, for was it not through them that the Low Country sent out its great, its eminently respectable, staple to two worlds?

The homes, the histories, the manners and the morals of the Rice Planters have filled Charleston with much of her character, her romance, and her beauty. But the Low Country has been even more permanently marked by them. Consciously or unconsciously you will come everywhere upon their traces. Almost every river has in some of its stretches the monumental banks and canals that were necessary in rice culture. And on certain streams, as on the Santee near the ocean, you will see from the highway the stupendous systems of irrigation that were perfected for the crop. It was not only the oldest but always the most eminent staple of the Low Country. Indigo came, flourished, and vanished. Cotton took the country where rice wouldn't grow and spread like wildfire to become the crop of the rest of the South. But rice moved only once, and then as if by a beneficent Providence, it merely shifted from inland swamp land, half played-out and never properly watered, to the richness of the river marshes and the certainty of the tidal irrigation. And it made the move, too, just after the Revolution when the Low Country was most in need of new prosperity. But it was a laborious crop to serve, taking many hands, and those trained and patient. The rivers gave and the rivers took away. When after 1865 Low-Country purses became short and the discipline of the days of slavery relaxed, the march of one good hurricane tide up a river often meant the end of a whole system of plantations. For others were not so choosing of the rice they eat as the Carolinians, and lesser breeds of the grain could be made at smaller expense in the West. But even so, the crop survived the World War in the Low Country, and now it is being revived on the plantations by their new sportsmen-owners. It is natural bait for wild ducks, and with admirable economy many a hunter follows the old practice of the country in making his duck lands give him a rice crop of which the unharvestable gleanings feed his game.

It is not necessary to search deliberately for the traces of the old planters, for you will come on them wherever you go. Only remember when you walk the terraces of Middleton Place that if the Ashley was never a rice river of any importance, the great garden was the work of men whose wealth came for the most part from rice plantations elsewhere. In the Cypress Gardens the touch with rice is far more intimate, for the Dantesque beauty of the sombre waters and buttressed tropic trees springs directly from the needs of the rice-fields of Dean Hall Plantation out of whose 'reserve water' for irrigation the gardens have been contrived.

In the Low Country there was supposedly something occult in the effect rice had on the people who planted it. Maybe it was the crop's connection with tidewater that was accountable for its especially refining effect on the blood of those who lived by it as well as on it. Sea-island cotton was its only rival in this respect, maybe because the delicate, highly bred plant also hugged the margins of the ocean, on the big islands that gave it its name where a special breed of gentry bred special strains of cotton seed almost as plastically as if they had been animal instead of vegetable. Rice, though, was senior to cotton and held its primacy while eight generations of Low-Countrymen were born to eat it and respect it.

There was nothing in the other North American colonies that quite approached the status of rice in and around Charleston. Undoubtedly there were Virginians (certainly among their womenfolk in the days before the cigarette advertisement) who never used tobacco. The most ardent of Bostonians, however he might profit by the sacred cod, ate fishballs usually but once a week. And no Louisianian heaped a daily dinner plate with sugar. But in the Low Country there were extra-pious people who could go on eating rice in one form or another thrice in every twenty-four hours, year in and year out. And the mass

of the people used it not only as a basis of diet, but with somewhat the belief
of the African cannibals who think that virtue can be absorbed by the digestive
juices, and the more heroic the fed-upon has been, the more splendid the
feeder must become.

LOUISVILLE MINT JULEPS AND HOT-BRICKS [12]

An invitation to breakfast [in Louisville] may set a time anywhere
between 10:30 and 12:30 and the menu may vary from simple "vittles" like
country sausage and lacy corn cakes to elaborate viands such as broiled spring
chickens with mushrooms and strawberry mousse. The one item on the menu
that is a "must" is the mint julep. This noble "sippage" attains its full glory
in silver mugs (preferably family heirlooms), frosted and fragrant. Each host
has his own theory for the concoction of the drink and many have been the
arguments which have sprung up on the vital issue of whether or not the mint
should be bruised.

Marse Henry Watterson, the great Louisville editor and famous host, had
his own method for making the ambrosial beverage. His recipe, according to
legend, went like this: "Pluck the mint gently from its bed, just as the dew
of evening is about to form upon it. Select the choicer sprigs only, but do not
rinse them. Prepare the simple syrup and measure out a half-tumbler of whisky.
Pour the whisky into a well-frosted silver cup and throw the other ingredients
away and drink the whisky."

In cold weather, particularly during the hunting season, hot-bricks or stirrup-
cups are a popular beverage. These are made with boiling water, plenty of
"likker" and a butter-ball. Old-timers, in this part of the country, always drink
Bourbon. Scotch is produced for "visiting firemen" but is not a Kentucky favorite.

NEW ORLEANS PRALINES [13]

Cook's Praline Confectionery is on Chartres and Toulouse Streets
[New Orleans]. I go inside.

"Where'd the praline come from?" I ask Mr. Cook, an elderly vigorous man
with graying hair.

"Everybody talks of the praline. In New Orleans, up to ten or twelve years
ago, the praline was a quality product. All these old French families, the
Creoles, the real Southern aristocracy, they accumulated fortunes here and
didn't consider anything but real quality. It had to be quality," he says proudly.
"They made the praline. Praline means *sugared*. This old family, the Favre
family, they settled back here from Paris one hundred and fifty years ago. The
old Mrs. Favre died at the age of one hundred and two. . . . She remembered

[12] From *Louisville: The Gateway City*, A Cities of America Biography, by Isabel
McLennan McMeekin, pp. 155-156. Copyright, 1946, by Isabel McLennan McMeekin.
New York: Julian Messner, Inc.

[13] From *The People Talk*, by Benjamin Appel, pp. 448-449. Copyright, 1940, by E. P.
Dutton & Co., Inc. New York.

the praline as a child. She remembered when the boats came in from the West Indian Islands with cocoanut pralines. That's where the idea of the praline came from. I remember the old colored mammy we had. She had a camel's hair brush and she would select the halves of the pecan and brush them off to be sure none of the bitter wood was left. After making pralines for a good many years, she discovered that if she greased a piece of brown paper, it'd keep longer. She spooned the pralines out on the brown paper. Now we take the Canadian maple sugar out of New York in seventy pound bricks. We also use the brown cane sugar and blend them. To eliminate the molasses flavor, we use white granulated sugar."

He nods reflectively. "I grew up with the Favre family. My father followed the sea. . . . All my relatives are downeasters." In his blue coat sweater, he seems like a second mate himself. But behind him, the shelves are full of cans: SOUTHERN CONFECTIONS MADE FROM THE RECIPE OF AN OLD LOUISIANA FAMILY. PECAN PRALINES. "My children asked me to make some pralines. I changed the cooking pro-cess. . . . They all have their formulas!" he derides his competitors. "The Mexican praline made in San Antonio is just a sugar patty! Now over a century past sugar was made in the West Indian Islands. . . . I remember when I was a child, and Royal Street was the business street, we used to have the fireman's parade on the 17th of March. We'd come down to Jackson Square and the firemen'd circle the Square and there'd be fifty mammies with a palmetto fan in one hand, a basket of pralines in the other." He takes down one of the yellow, red, and black cans from the shelf. "I drew this myself. There's the church and Jackson, and the iron fence around the Square and the oil lamps. . . ."

SAZERAC AND THE DEVIL [14]

Old, honorable, and extraordinary is the Sazerac, the golden-brown drink that many insist is [New Orleans'] most glorious contribution to the art of drinking. Two small, heavy tumblers are required for it. While the first is being chilled with ice inside, the mixer works on the other. In it he crushes a lump of sugar moistened with water, then pours in a jigger of rye or bourbon, a half-jigger of vermouth, a dash of bitters, and a dash of orange bitters. In go several pieces of ice and the mixture is stirred with a spoon.

Now back to the first glass. Removing the ice, the mixer drops in a touch of absinthe, swishing the glass in his hand until the liquoricelike stuff has caressed all the inside, then throwing out the drops. Into this scented glass the mixture is now poured, lemon peel is twisted over it, and voilà—a small drink but a magnificently potent one. Once upon a time the following dialogue was current:

"When you go to New Orleans, my son, drink a Sazerac cocktail for me and one for yourself."

"And a third one?"

[14] From *Queen New Orleans, City by the River,* by Harnett T. Kane, p. 320. Copyright, 1949, by Harnett T. Kane. New York: William Morrow & Company.

"*That* must be for the Devil, my son, for no mere mortal could down it!"
(However, there have been courageous Orleanians who have tried to. . . .)

SAN ANTONIO CUISINE [15]

. . . The traditional cuisine of San Antonio is the humble fare of any
Mexican peon: *tamales*, chili peppers, *frijoles*, and *tortillas*. These unpreten-
tious dishes have only the remotest kinship with the innocuous "chili con carne"
that turns up on the bill of fare in Yankee hash houses. Chili con carne as
Americans know it is nothing but stew seasoned with a mild chili sauce. Mexican cookery is plainer and more fiery, simpler in essence and a good deal more
exotic. Even in San Antonio most Mexican food is not indigenous to Mexico.
Its flavor is Mexican, but its origin is as American as chop suey.

The staple diet of all true Mexicans—the bread of Mexico—is the tortilla.
It is a sort of flat, round, grayish pancake, made of white corn, mashed and
baked on a hearth. Tortillas were made by the Aztecs, long before Hernando
Cortes looked down on the walls of Tenochtitlán. It is a full time job for the
Mexican housewife to keep the family supplied with tortillas. The whole corn
is first soaked in lime water and then boiled. The wet grains are crushed
laboriously by pounding them with a stone on a *metate*—a rock mortar. The
mash is then baked. The result is a thin, tough, tasteless disc that scarcely jus-
tifies the trouble of making it.

A Mexican rolls his tortilla like a crêpe suzette, and sprinkles salt on it to
take the place of butter. Tortillas fried in liquid grease, known as *fritos* or
tostados, are crisp and hard. They can be used like a spoon to scoop up gobbets
of *guacamole*—aguacates crushed into a paste and seasoned—or munched like
potato chips. Or they can be folded around a salad of chopped lettuce, meat,
and tomatoes, to make *tacos*—a succulent dish invented by Americans. Another
Mexican delicacy that originated in Texas is the *enchilada*—a corruption of
ensalada, which means simply a hodgepodge or a salad. An enchilada consists
of chopped meat and chopped raw onions covered with a gooey mess of grated
cheese, all rolled up in a dripping tortilla. If anything will give you indigestion,
enchiladas are guaranteed to do it.

Tamales are something else again. They really are Mexican. Like tortillas,
tamales are made of mashed corn. Ground meat is wrapped in *masa*—corn
mash—like a tubular pie or an eclair. Then the whole tamale is wrapped in
corn shucks and steamed. It's a mighty savory morsel. Frijoles (short for *frijoles
refritos*: refried beans) are Mexican, too, and ancient as tortillas. They are big,
red, ranch beans, boiled first, then mashed and fried. To make them even
more fascinating, you can scatter chopped raw onions on top. A Mexican eats
frijoles for breakfast, frijoles for lunch, frijoles again for dinner. They are rich
and nourishing as meat, and a good deal easier to come by.

On all these dishes a good Mexican spreads *salsa piquante* with a liberal

[15] From *San Antonio: City in the Sun*, by Green Peyton, pp. 139-145. Copyright, 1946,
by Green Peyton. New York and London: Whittlesey House, McGraw-Hill Book Company, Inc.

hand. It is simply a hot sauce (and I mean *hot* sauce) made of chopped chili peppers and other fiery condiments floating in water or vinegar. There are all sorts of chili peppers, ranging from the kind that scorch your throat a little to the kind that burst into white flame like an atomic bomb as they go down. The hottest you can buy is the *chili jalapeño*—chile of Jalapa. Mexicans eat it raw, and claim that it's good for digestion. God help you if you try to do the same without a long tactical training period in Mexican cookery.

To wash these torrid viands down, a Mexican drinks quantities of beer. Some of the best beer in the world come from Mexico. In New York you will pay up to a dollar a bottle for Carta Blanca or Bohemia. They cost about the same as the best American beer in San Antonio. Both are products of the same brewing company, but Carta Blanca comes from Monterrey, Bohemia from Mexico City. They are light, cool, and dry, and they make a soothing antidote for throats parched by a pungent Mexican repast. For gullets craving a more volatile liquor, there are those potent products of the maguey plant: tequila, pulque, and mescal. In Mexico (but rarely in San Antonio) the cantina supplies a salt shaker filled with dried, crushed maguey worms, to ease them down. You gulp the tequila, sprinkle the mummified condiment on the back of your hand, swallow it, suck on a small slice of lime, and then sit down for a while to recover your senses.

* * * * *

A few years ago it wouldn't have been so hard to find good Mexican food in San Antonio. In fact, you could have picked up a snack of hot tamales or tacos on mighty near any street corner. From time immemorial San Antonio was famed for its "chili queens," Mexican crones who set up their tamale stands in the plazas downtown every morning and whisked them away when the last stroller departed, late at night. After dark, when the produce trucks were gone, chili stands flourished in the market plaza, over in the Mexican Quarter. The dusky women cooked tamales and frijoles on open braziers, glowing like little fires of hell in the warm, smoky darkness. You took them to a pine-plank table and ate them sitting on a bench, listening to the Mariachi singers wailing their hoarse laments and strumming their guitars. The plaza was pervaded with the faintly acrid smell of charcoal and corn husks that hovers on the air throughout Mexico.

Then, in 1937, with an election coming on, Mayor Charles Kennon Quin conceived a sudden passion for civic reform. His city health officer announced that the chili stands were unsanitary (as if any germ could survive in a bath of *salsa piquante*) and his burly police ran them off the streets. A few wandering chili vendors now have tacos and tamales for sale in glass-inclosed carts. A few small, indoor chili shops remain around the market plaza. But the earthy air and pungent odor of the plaza are gone. The singers still gather around your car and serenade you. But without the chili queens to exchange the anatomical insults with them in sonorous Spanish, they seem a bit lackadaisical and depressed.

COPPER TOWN CUISINE [16]

The [Butte] old-timer, when in a retrospective mood, will tell you that the first pasty made its appearance in the camp simultaneously with the arrival of the first Cornish housewife who followed her husband to the mining city direct from her hearth in Cornwall. And that is many score years ago. . . .

The camp at once adopted the pasty as its own. Today it is as much a part of Butte as the ore dumps. There are few other cities where it may be found. Possibly among the copper mines of Michigan or the Coeur d'Alenes. Elsewhere it is alien. Restaurant keepers and waitresses look bewildered when a native of Butte asks for it. They have never heard of it.

Neither the making of a pasty nor its ingredients are complicated. Your true pasty maker will insist, "It is not so much what you put into them as how you put it in."

*   *   *   *   *

The meat in a pasty is of vast importance. It must be beef of an excellent grade, Montana preferred. The finest cuts, tenderloin or sirloin are insisted upon. The meat should be diced to approximately the size of the third joint of a Cornish woman's little finger. It should weigh about three or four pounds. You do not make pasties in infinitesimal quantities.

Enough for the meat. Next, eight or ten fair sized Irish potatoes, peeled and diced—never sliced—into cubes of a size similar to the meat. The same procedure for whole, firm onions, in about half the quantity of the potatoes. . . . These are the ingredients.

And now the crust. The usual pie crust made with the addition of a breathed prayer or two will suffice. Keep praying. Mix thoroughly the meat and vegetables. Now, take generous heaps of the latter and wrap with dough that has been cut in the shape of a semi-circle about four inches in radius. Crimp edges and place in hot oven, not forgetting an added sprinkling of more prayers.

That is all there is to it. Sounds simple—but in the hands of the inept— or if sufficient prayers are forgotten—the result might turn out to be but a soggy mess. Expertly handled, however, the finished product is something to cause the true gourmet to contemplate on thoughts, ethereal and unworldly. A real pasty does those things to a human.

Serve it piping hot, with lashings of brown gravy, and it would indeed be an incurable dyspeptic who could not consume three or four at a single sitting. Served cold as a midnight snack, or at luncheon, a pasty always speaks for itself.

Fortunate indeed is the miner so steeped in connubial bliss as to possess a better half who in her loving care, as a token of her affection, places a pasty

[16] From *Copper Camp*, Stories of the World's Greatest Mining Town, Butte, Montana, compiled by Workers of the Writers' Program of the Work Projects Administration in the State of Montana, pp. 243-246, 250. Copyright, 1943, by the Montana State Department of Agriculture, Labor and Industry, Albert H. Kruse, Commissioner. New York: Hastings House Publishers, Inc.

or two in the lunch box of her miner spouse. "A letter from home" is what the miners term such a setup.

A noted breakfast dish introduced in the late nineties was referred to as "stirabout," simply old-fashioned oatmeal mush, thinned with milk to the consistency of a medium-heavy gruel. It was, no doubt, the thousands of Irish miners who followed Marcus Daly to the town, who first introduced this acclaimed cereal.

In the early days, the single men of the camp far outnumbered the married, and it was for the unmarried that the many large miners' boarding houses sprang up. Famous among them was the Florence Hotel, known to the miners as the "Big Ship," the Clarence, dubbed the "Mad House," and the Mullin House in Centerville. Each of these hostelries fed several hundred miners daily, and prominent in the kitchen of each was the huge "stirabout" pot from which countless bowls of the gruel were ladled out each morning. At the Big Ship, an ingenious cook contrived a sort of chute arrangement on the copper "stirabout" pot from which the breakfast bowls were filled by simply pulling a lever. A one-time manager of the Big Ship tells that in the early days of the hotel, the daily consumption of "stirabout" was never computed in pounds but in tons. Nearly every boarder, he says, consumed at least two or three bowls of the succulent gruel at a sitting. Naturally, this custom added to the profits of the dining room, as the average miner who paid his board by the week, when fortified by several bowls of the filling cereal, had little appetite for the hot cakes or ham and eggs. At the Big Ship, this former manager claims, the time and services of a special cook were needed for the preparation and serving of the oatmeal. The miners were very particular, and were not above registering loud complaints if the "stirabout" was burned or not properly prepared.

So popular was the food that many of the miners insisted on having a bowl of the mush included in their dinner bucket for consumption down in the mine. The custom was to add the "stirabout" to their tea and drinking water, the miners believing that the mixture would act as a deterrent to weakness or heat cramps that often attack a miner underground. A pinch or two of salt was often added. That there was a certain amount of preventive value in the salt at least has been later proven by scientists who have discovered that the cramps are caused by a loss of salt from the system due to the excessive perspiration. Butte miners who worked in the 100-degree "hot-boxes" also had the custom of salting their beer long before science learned the sound reason for the practice.

A story is told of one of the early-day miners, who upon taking his lady friend to one of the higher-class cafes for an after theater bite, became indignant and departed from the place in a huff because he could not find his beloved stirabout listed on the bill of fare.

Another food peculiar to the early-day Cornish, Welsh and Irish and to which a certain amount of superstition was attached was "boxty." As it is told, boxty was made from the first milk taken from a cow immediately after calving. This milk, a thick, clabber-like substance was strained thoroughly and then mixed with eggs and cornstarch or flour and steamed into a kind of pudding.

At that period many families owned their own cow, and boxty was an annual treat. The eating of the pudding was supposed to bring luck to the eater, strength and virility to the males, and a degree of fecundity to the female members of the family. It was another Copper Camp food that had its origin in the old country.

*   *   *   *   *

A sacred tradition in a town of traditions, the Shawn O'Farrell cannot properly be termed a single drink. It is two drinks for the price of one, a full ounce glass of whisky followed by a pint-sized scoop of beer. Both are served in the saloons that cater to the miner's trade for a thin dime.

Shawn O'Farrells are not served at any hour of day or night, but are reserved for the hours when the miners are coming off shift, and to be eligible to purchase one the buyer must have a lunch bucket on his arm to prove that he has spent the day working in the mines.

The "Shawn O' " as it is often abbreviated, is the miners' cure-all for the fatigue of the working day. As they explain it, the whisky is to cut the copper dust from their lungs, and the cooling beer is to slack the thirst accumulated during eight hours spent in the "hot-boxes."

One Shawn O' is refreshing tonic. Two makes a new man of the miner and calls for a third for the new man. Imitations of the Shawn O' have bobbed up in other industrial centers where they are sometimes referred to as "boilermakers."

ST. PATRICK'S DAY IN NEW YORK [17]

Townsfolk who shake in cold Fifth Avenue blasts as they watch the St. Patrick's Day march each year must know that icy winds have been part of the parade tradition in this city for more than 100 years.

The first parade on record was on March 17, 1779, when 400 "Volunteers of Ireland" tramped from Lower Broadway behind a British (Heaven forgive it) band to a restaurant on the Bowery for a St. Patrick's Day feast. They were led by their colonel, Lord Rawdon, himself Irish-born, but then in the King's service, fighting Washington's men. He had enrolled the volunteers with the help of a Lieutenant Colonel Doyle, who had his recruiting station at 10 Wall Street.

After the parade, The New York Mercury noted, the Volunteers of Ireland sat down to "the enjoyment of a noble banquet . . . of 500 covers," but Lord Rawdon found later he had wasted the King's funds. The Volunteers went over to General Washington in great numbers, which enraged his lordship. He offered ten guineas bounty for their heads; half that for any brought to him alive. He got no takers.

There were St. Patrick's Day breakfasts in the city before the parade tradition began. The earliest, held in 1756 at the Crown and Thistle that was conducted by Scotch Johnny Thompson in Whitehall Slip, was attended by Sir

[17] From "About New York: First St. Patrick's Day Parade Here in 1779 Was Led by (of All Things) a British Band," by Meyer Berger, the *New York Times*, March 17, 1954, p. L-33. Copyright, 1954, by the New York Times Company.

Charles Hardy, Governor of New York, with members of his Council and General Assembly. In 1774, the breakfast was at Hull's Tavern in Lower Broadway, "attended by the principal gentlemen of this city," and the next year was held there again by the Friendly Brothers of St. Patrick. They continued through most of the British occupation.

Throughout the Revolution there lived, at 218 Pearl Street, a gentleman delightfully named Hercules Mulligan, who had come to New York in 1746, as a child. He was General Washington's secret agent in the city, a dangerous assignment. Hercules had his reward after the last British soldier left Manhattan Island in November, 1783. The Commander in Chief, after reviewing his troops at Bowling Green, went to the Mulligans' house to dine.

It was not until the Eighteen Fifties that the St. Patrick's Day parades in New York assumed large proportions. By that time, immigration from Ireland was at flood and good-sized Irish county units were available. Marchers wore costumes that still smelled of native peat.

In 1851, when the parade formed in downtown Manhattan, icy winds cut at the assembled buckos and ice and sleet tore at their hats and jackets. But Col. Mike Phelan of the old Ninth Regiment, struck up the band and they fell in bravely behind him. Again, in 1852, bitter winds knifed down and a blizzard swept the marchers' ranks as they assembled in Third Avenue at Eighth Street, but the pipers' shrill call and the boom of the drums got them stepping and they plodded full route through the storm.

The route in those days was up Third to Twenty-third, to Eighth Avenue, to Hudson Street, down to Canal, to West Broadway, to Chambers, to Broadway, to Park Row and then up to St. Patrick's Cathedral in Prince Street.

Mayor Ambrose C. Kingsland reviewed the 1852 parade and Archbishop Hughes celebrated High Mass at St. Patrick's. Eighty of the Friendly Sons of St. Patrick had dinner that night at Keefe's Racket Clubhouse in Broadway. Oratory and red grape flowed freely. There were toasts to "Ireland, the Land of our Fathers," to "The Day, and to all who honor it," to "The Land of Our Adoption," to "The President of the United States," to "The Army and the Navy of the United States," to "The City of New York," to "The Harp of Innisfail"—and that was just a beginning. Henry Raymond of The New York Times responded to a toast to "The Press," a scholarly response that brought the guests to their feet with applause. It was not a quiet evening.

FIFTH AVENUE EASTER PARADE [18]

The Easter Parade tradition in New York isn't as old as many people seem to think. It started, in a small way, about 100 years ago, down around Old Trinity when the city had not begun to spread. Ladies and gentlemen in spring finery usually strolled up Broadway toward Canal Street, or down to the Battery after church, and took the new sun with neighbors until it was time for the noonday meal. There was a great carriage turnout, too.

Newspapers in the Eighteen Fifties paid little attention to the strollers. There

[18] From "About New York," by Meyer Berger, *ibid.*, April 14, 1954, p. L-31.

were short pieces about Easter Sunday sermons and masses; never a word about who wore what. By 1869, though, the parade was pretty firmly established. It made the last page of some of the local dailies. The city line had surged northward quite a bit by then, but the larger churches were still down near the island's tip.

Easter Sunday, March 28, was balmy that year. The New York Times was delighted to report next morning: "The day being pleasant, the streets and parks were filled with pedestrians gladly enjoying the first airs of spring. The ladies were out in full force, looking doubly charming under the influence of those genial skies." This was before the advent of the fashion reporter. Nothing was written, even then, about what women and their escorts wore at the Easter Sunday service.

It wasn't until the Eighteen Eighties that this note crept into newspaper reports about Easter Sunday. By that time the strolling area extended from around Madison Square into the Fifties on Fifth Avenue. In that year The Times found the roadways lined with "elegant equipages at church doors, manned by pompous footmen." "The fashion parade," it said, "went on until the shades of night began to fall. The throng was almost exclusively composed of churchgoers," the reporter wrote. "Young men of the genus vulgarly yclept 'dude' were out in force in high hats and brilliant gloves." He noticed "a group of Italian immigrants in dirt and rags who were dazzled and awed by the splendor of the throng." The writer decided that with all the "prancing horses, glittering harness, shining carriages thronging the thoroughfare" he could venture the statement that the show was "as splendid and beautiful a procession as could be found in the wide world."

In 1881 the Easter Sunday strollers made front page for the first time. Again the Avenue from Madison Square to Central Park looked from above like flowing flower beds. Jay Gould, newsmen noticed, peeked at the passing show from his Fifth Avenue windows, and the Vanderbilts' houses farther uptown were decked with fresh greenery and blossoms. The tradition was fixed by then.

*   *   *   *   *

. . . The after-church stroll is no longer an impromptu fashion display. Commercialism in the past few years overreached itself by sending professional models into the throng and even posed them on church steps. That drove the gentry out of it. They have withdrawn from the day-long promenade, so the only significant display of the newest fashions by such folk is on opening night at the opera.

JACKSONVILLE CAKE-WALK [19]

. . . During the summer months we went almost every Monday on an excursion to a [Jacksonville] seaside resort called Pablo Beach. These excursions were always crowded. There was a dancing-pavilion, a great deal of

[19] From *The Autobiography of an Ex-Coloured Man*, by James Weldon Johnson, pp. 84-87. Copyright, 1912, 1927, by Alfred A. Knopf, Inc. New York.

drinking, and generally a fight or two to add to the excitement. I also contracted the cigar-maker's habit of riding round in a hack on Sunday afternoons. I sometimes went with my cigar-maker friends to public balls that were given at a large hall on one of the main streets. . . .

* * * * *

These balls were attended by a great variety of people. They were generally given by the waiters of some one of the big hotels, and were often patronized by a number of hotel guests who came to "see the sights." The crowd was always noisy, but good-natured; there was much quadrille-dancing, and a strong-lunged man called figures in a voice which did not confine itself to the limits of the hall. It is not worth the while for me to describe in detail how these people acted; they conducted themselves in about the same manner as I have seen other people at similar balls conduct themselves. When one has seen something of the world and human nature, one must conclude, after all, that between people in like stations of life there is very little difference the world over.

However, it was at one of these balls that I first saw the cake-walk. There was a contest for a gold watch, to be awarded to the hotel head-waiter receiving the greatest number of votes. There was some dancing while the votes were being counted. Then the floor was cleared for the cake-walk. A half-dozen guests from some of the hotels took seats on the stage to act as judges, and twelve or fourteen couples began to walk for a sure enough, highly decorated cake, which was in plain evidence. The spectators crowded about the space reserved for the contestants and watched them with interest and excitement. The couples did not walk round in a circle, but in a square, with the men on the inside. The fine points to be considered were the bearing of the men, the precision with which they turned the corners, the grace of the women, and the ease with which they swung round the pivots. The men walked with stately and soldierly step, and the women with considerable grace. The judges arrived at their decision by a process of elimination. The music and the walk continued for some minutes; then both were stopped while the judges conferred; when the walk began again, several couples were left out. In this way the contest was finally narrowed down to three or four couples. Then the excitement became intense; there was much partisan cheering as one couple or another would execute a turn in extra elegant style. When the cake was finally awarded, the spectators were about evenly divided between those who cheered the winners and those who muttered about the unfairness of the judges. This was the cake-walk in its original form, and it is what the coloured performers on the theatrical stage developed into the prancing movements now known all over the world, and which some Parisian critics pronounced the acme of poetic motion.

THE STRIKERS' BALL [20]

. . . With all its outward semblance of calm, Mobile is gayest of American cities. Its free spirit, less commercialized than that of New Orleans,

[20] From *Stars Fell on Alabama*, by Carl Carmer, pp. 237-239. Copyright, 1934, by Carl Carmer. New York: Rinehart & Company, Inc.

has kept its Gallic love of the fantastic and amusing. Behind the ornate balconies and long French windows that sedately face the streets live a people to whom carnival is a natural heritage.

While Mobile waited the coming of the new year, 1833, candles burning in the windows, the horses of dandies clopping daintily along the cobblestones of Dauphin Street, a band of young men in whom the liquors of many a bar rioted, descended upon a hardware store—accoutered themselves with rakes and cowbells—and turned the night into a bedlam. Thus the society of *Cowbellian de Rakian* was born. For a hundred years thereafter Mobile has had its mad, bad time of Carnival. Until the War Between the States, New Year's Eve witnessed its revels. Now the Cowbellians are no more; only the Strikers, a similar carnival organization, celebrate the birth of the year with a ball, and all the other social groups make merry on Shrove Tuesday at the annual Mardi Gras festival.

It is difficult for most residents of America to understand the social processes of a Southern coast city. The rigid formality that was once natural to the aristocratic émigré has now become a game that must be played as strictly according to the rules as bridge or chess. The Strikers' Ball given annually in Mobile at the old Battle House is a revelatory example of the quality that makes the survivals of social rituals in American life so charming. The Strikers are the oldest mystic society in Mobile. It is a popular fiction that no one knows who its members are, though there is hardly a distinguished gentleman in the city who can truthfully deny membership. The origin of the name is explained variously. Some say that the first Strikers were markers of cotton bales; others that they were a group which broke away from the Cowbellian Society.

As New Year's Eve approaches an atmosphere of tension and mystery settles over the homes on Government Street and its environs. Débutantes look anxious, though they know that they at least will be present and be danced with. The hearts of post-débutantes and wives grow lighter when an envelope bearing the cherished "call-out" card, a masker's request for the honor of a dance, appears. The men of the house disappear frequently to attend unexplained "conferences" over costumes, favors, procedure. The younger men and the male visitors in town importantly make engagements for the "black-coat" dances that maskers unselfishly allow them.

The lobby of the old Battle House, as nine o'clock of New Year's Eve approaches, is filled with an excited crowd in full evening dress. They enter the ballroom to discover that curtains have been hung from the balcony to shut off the dance floor and the stage at the far end. Four or five rows of chairs, close to the curtains, are occupied by ladies, happy ladies who carry big bouquets of flowers, débutantes, sweethearts, wives who have received the "call-out" cards. Behind them sit the other guests of the Strikers.

At nine o'clock the band strikes up a march and the curtains are drawn. On the stage, grouped in striking tableau, stand the maskers. They may be in the laces and knee breeches of the court of Louis XIV, in the regimentals of the American Revolution, in the buckskin and beads of Indians, in the attire of any one of countless picturesque periods. Suddenly from the back of the stage the Captain of the Ball, in more elaborate dress than any other, leads out to the center of the tableau the girl who has been chosen by the Strikers as the princess of the night's revel. She wears a white gown and her arms are filled with red roses. There is a burst of applause as the two bow and then the Captain leads the girl down the center of the floor. Spotlights play on the couple from the balcony, sequins sparkle from their costumes, the applause grows deafening, almost drowning the blare of the band. Marching in single file the maskers follow the couple. At the end of the hall, while the Captain and his lady wait, they find their partners for the grand march—the first call-out. The Strikers' Ball has begun.

In the old days the guests were entertained at eleven o'clock with a champagne supper in the main dining room of the Battle House. The maskers had their supper in another room—a secret chamber where they might unmask without fear of being recognized. . . .

BASIN AND RAMPART STREET BLUES [21]

. . . At the very time when the famous [Basin Street] Blues came out, Basin Street already belonged to the past:

> That's where the light and the dark folks meet.
> Heaven on earth, they call it Basin Street.

Even in its glory it was a short street to have spread so much joy and jazz abroad. But I was not ready for its change of name to North Saratoga Street; after Canal and Rampart, what New Orleans street could be more widely known than Basin? Only a stone's throw away from the notorious section it magnetized is now the Lafitte Housing Project, trim and model. Across the iron picket fence the Southern Railroad trains rumble "down the line," but the street itself is quiet, with warehouses and commercial buildings where the bordelloes and gaudy saloons flourished. Sole memento of the vanished era of plush and lace, mahogany furniture, long mirrors and costly paintings, is a semi-pretentious white house, graying in the railroad soot.

Behind these long arched elegant windows, boarded now, reigned that internationally known purveyor of octoroon and quadroon beauties, Lulu White, whose diamonds and other gems made her resemble the "electrical display of the Cascade at the late St. Louis exposition." This had been a showplace of Storyville, the red-light district, where over a hundred musicians, white and black, were regularly employed in the restaurants and cabarets. Many of the bandsmen later became drawing cards in the cities of America and Europe. In the palaces, however, the piano was the favored instrument, and the pianists, so frequently Negro, were called "professors." "Professor" Tony Jackson was legendary, famous for his version of the "Naked Dance"; he is dead now, and so, more recently, is "Jelly Roll" Morton, who started as a mere "winin'" boy and whose memoirs recapture much of the lost resplendence and ribaldry. A third "professor," Spen-

[21] From "Farewell to Basin Street," by Sterling A. Brown, *The Record Changer*, December 1944, pp. 8-9. Washington, D.C.

cer Williams, composed *Mahogany Hall Stomp* to celebrate Lulu White's place, *Shim-Me-She-Wabble* to celebrate one of the entertainments provided there, and *Basin Street Blues* to celebrate the whole region.

> Don't you want to go with me
> Down the Mississippi. . . .

Rampart Street—and I thought of Ida Cox's plangent blues of the old times:

> I want to go down to Rampart Street.
> I want to hear those colored jazz bands play. . . .

Across Canal to South Rampart, where Louis Armstrong, before finding harbor at the Waif's home, had sat on a coal cart skatting out his wares in what he hoped was a bass voice, where he and Sidney Bechet later played on the same advertising wagon, where Clarence Williams, backed by some of the best young musicians, played piano at the Red Onion Cafe, and laid up memories for *Red Onion Blues, Gravier Street Blues,* and *Baby, Won't You Please Come Home?* Gravier Street was still ramshackly enough to stir a blues feeling, but the jazz bands weren't around. Rampart was a busy street, lined with offices, perfume stands, beer-joints, clothes stores, groceries, and record stores. But it wasn't the Rampart Street of hot jazz. In one juke-joint, packed and jammed on Saturday night, the favored records were schmaltzy; one souse put nickel on top of nickel in order to hear

> When the lights go on again, all over the world. . . .

The sentiment was fine, but I am afraid that it was the falsetto that got him. And it was on Rampart Street that I ran into a tall white man selling a song of his composing, a hymn of which, as unbelievable as it may sound, the second line of the chorus ran, "And we shall all be as white as snow." Dr. Livingston, I presume.

MARDI GRAS INDIANS [22]

[On a] Mardi Gras afternoon [in New Orleans], there appeared on a street corner a lone figure of an elaborately garbed Indian. He stood there, a lighted lantern in one hand, the other shading his eyes, as he peered into the street ahead, first right, then left. This Indian's face was very black under his war paint, but his costume and feathered headdress were startlingly colorful. He studied the distance a moment, then turned and swung the lantern. Other Indians appeared, all attired in costumes at least as magnificent as the first, and in every conceivable color.

A second Indian joined the first, then a third. These three all carried lanterns like good spy boys must. Then a runner joined them, a flag boy, a trio of chiefs,

[22] From *Gumbo Ya-Ya*, A Collection of Louisiana Folk Tales, compiled by Lyle Saxon, State Director, Edward Dreyer, Assistant State Director, Robert Tallant, Special Writer, pp. 17-21. Material Gathered by Workers of the Works Progress Administration, Louisiana Writers' Project. Copyright, 1945, by the Louisiana Library Commission, Essae M. Culver, Executive Secretary. Boston: Houghton Mifflin Company.

a savage-looking medicine man. Beside the first or head chief was a stout woman, wearing a costume of gold and scarlet. She was the tribe's queen, and wife of the first chief.

A consultation was held there on the corner. The chiefs got together, passed around a bottle, and argued with the medicine man until that wild creature, dressed in animal skins and a grass skirt, wearing a headdress of horns and a huge ring in his nose, jumped up and down on the pavement with rage. When, at last, it was decided that since there was no enemy tribe in sight, they might as well have a war dance, Chief "Happy Peanut," head of this tribe of the Golden Blades, emitted a bloodcurdling yell that resounded for blocks, "Oowa-a-awa! Ooa-a-a-awa!"

Tambourines were raised and a steady tattoo of rhythm beat out. Knees went down and up, heads swayed back and forth, feet shuffled on the pavement, as they circled round and round.

The Queen chanted this song:

> The Indians are comin'.
> Tu-way-pa-ka-way.
> The Indians are comin'.
> Tu-way-pa-ka-way.
> The Chief is comin'.
> Tu-way-pa-ka-way.
> The Chief is comin'.
> Tu-way-pa-ka-way.
>
> The Queen is comin'.
> Tu-way-pa-ka-way.
> The Queen is comin'.
> Tu-way-pa-ka-way.
> The Golden Blades are comin'.
> Tu-way-pa-ka-way.
> The Golden Blades are comin'.
> Tu-way-pa-ka-way.

The songs the Mardi Gras Indians sing are written in choppy four-four time, with a tom-tom rhythm. The music is far removed from the type usually associated with Negroes. The Indians never sing a blues song, but chant with primitive and savage simplicity to this strange beat, which has an almost hypnotic effect. The beating on the tambourine and rhythmic hand-clapping are the only accompaniments to the singing. Most of the words have little meaning, though some display special interests of the tribe, such as

> Tu-way-pa-ka-way.
> Tu-way-pa-ka-way.
> Get out the dishes.
> Tu-way-pa-ka-way.
> Get out the pan.
> Tu-way-pa-ka-way.
> Here comes the Indian man.
> Tu-way-pa-ka-way.
> Tu-way-pa-ka-way.

Sometimes the chief of the tribe sings alone a boastful solo of his strength and prowess.

> Oowa-aa!
> Tu-way-pa-ka-way.
> Oowa-a-a!
> Tu-way-pa-ka-way.
> I'm the Big Chief!
> Tu-way-pa-ka-way.
> Of the strong Golden Blades.
> Tu-way-pa-ka-way.

The dances are wild and abandoned. Unlike the songs, there may be detected traces of modernity, trucking and bucking and "messing-around" combined with pseudo-Indian touches, much leaping into the air, accompanied by virile whooping. All this is considerably aided by the whiskey consumed while on the march, and the frequent smoking of marijuana.

The tribes include such names as the Little Red, White and Blues, the Yellow Pocahontas, the Wild Squa-tou-las, the Golden Eagles, the Creole Wild Wests, the Red Frontier Hunters, and the Golden Blades. The last numbers twenty-two members, and is the largest and oldest of those still extant.

The Golden Blades were started twenty-five years ago in a saloon. Ben Clark was the first chief and ruled until two years ago, when a younger man took over. Leon Robinson—Chief "Happy Peanut"—deposed Clark in actual combat, as is the custom, ripping open Clark's arm and gashing his forehead with a knife. That's the way a chief is created, and that is the way his position is lost.

Contrary to the casual observer's belief, these strangest of Mardi Gras maskers are extremely well-organized groups, whose operations are intricate and complicated.

Monthly meetings are held, dues paid and the next year's procedure carefully planned. All members are individually responsible for their costumes. They may make them—most of them do—or have them made to order.

The regalia consists of a large and resplendent crown of feathers, a wig, an apron, a jacket, a shirt, tights, trousers and moccasins. They vie with each other and with other tribes as to richness and elaborateness. Materials used include satins, velvet, silver and gold lamé and various furs. The trimmings are sequins, crystal, colored and pearl beads, sparkling imitation jewels, rhinestones, spangles and gold clips put to extravagant use. Color is used without restraint. (Flame, scarlet and orange are possibly the preferred shades.)

Amazingly intricate designs are often worked out in beads and brilliants against the rich materials. A huge serpent of pearls may writhe on a gold lamé breast, an immense spider of silver beads appears to be crawling on a back of flame satin. Sometimes a chief will choose to appear in pure white. A regal crown of snowy feathers, rising from a base of crystal beads, will adorn his head, and all other parts of his costume will be of white velvet heavily encrusted with rhinestones and crystals. All costumes are worn with the arrogance expressed in such songs as

Oh, the Little Red, White and Blues,
Tu-way-pa-ka-way,
Bravest Indians in the land.
Tu-way-pa-ka-way.
They are on the march today.
Tu-way-pa-ka-way.
If you should get in their way,
Tu-way-pa-ka-way,
Be prepared to die.
Tu-way-pa-ka-way.
Oowa-a-a!
Oowa-a-a!

Ten years ago the various tribes actually fought when they met. Sometimes combatants were seriously injured. When two tribes sighted each other, they would immediately go into battle formation, headed by the first, second and third spy boys of each side. Then the two head chiefs would cast their spears —iron rods—into the ground, the first to do so crying, "Umba?", which was an inquiry if the other were willing to surrender. The second chief replied, "Me no umba!" There was never a surrender, never a retreat. There would follow a series of dances by the two chiefs, each around his spear, with pauses now and then to fling back and forth the exclamations, "Umba?" "Me no umba!" While this continued, sometimes for four or five minutes, the tribes stood expectantly poised, waiting for the inevitable break that would be an invitation for a free-for-all mêlée. Once a police officer was badly injured by an Indian's spear. After that occurrence a law was passed forbidding the tribes of maskers to carry weapons.

Today the tribes are all friendly. The following song is a warning against the tactics of other days.

Shootin' don't make it, no no no no.
Shootin' don't make it, no no no no.
Shootin' don't make it, no no no no.
If you see your man sittin' in the bush,
Knock him in the head and give him a push,
'Cause shootin' don't make it, no no.
Shootin' don't make it, no no no no.

The Golden Blades marched all day through main thoroughfares and narrow side streets. At the train tracks and Broadway came the news the spy boys had sighted the Little Red, White and Blues.

The tribes met on either side of a vacant space of ground, and with a whoop and loud cries.

"Me, Chief 'Happy Peanut.' My tribe Golden Blades."

The other replied: "Me, Chief Battle Brown. My tribe Little Red, White and Blues."

Palms still extended, they spoke as one, "Peace."

Then they met, put arms around each other's necks. Together they proceeded toward the nearest saloon, the two tribes behind them mingling and talking, the medicine men chanting a weird duet:

Shh-bam-hang the ham.
Follow me, follow me, follow me.
Wha-wha-wha-follow me.
Wha-wha-wha-follow me.
Shh-bam-hang the ham.
Wha-wha-wha-follow me.
Wha-wha-wha-follow me. . . .

NATCHEZ PILGRIMAGE [23]

The garden movement was spreading over the country; for the spring of 1931 the Mississippi State Federation of Garden Clubs arranged its annual meeting in Natchez. The exact order of the next occurrences is what may be termed, by way of understatement in Natchez, controversy. According to one side, Natchez suffered a blighting freeze on the eve of the meeting; there were no gardens to show, and suddenly they thought of the houses. By the other version, one or two far-sighted women realized that, in the bad times that had come, the plantation gardens were gone; the only things to show were the homes. In any case, it was a matter of houses, not plantings.

After some argument, owners of many big houses were persuaded to show them to the federation delegates. That year for the first time hundreds walked in groups through the echoing rooms, pausing in astonishment before the profusion, the expanses of drawing room and hallway, paneled ceilings and gold-bordered pier glasses. Polite eyes passed over a cracked wall, a slightly damaged sofa that had kept its lines. The meeting was a success; the delegates talked for months afterward, and so, too, did the town folks. Now enters a woman whose story is much the story of these later days—Katherine Grafton Miller, a dark-eyed, brunette young matron with something of the pent-up energy of a buzz-bomb.

*   *   *   *   *

. . . Katherine, says her faction, birthed the project, but others deny her the credit. She volunteers the information that many chortled at the thought of her as president of the garden club, or anything. But now it was the houses that had become Katherine Miller's new hobby; and though some may not have sensed it, Woman had met Career. With others, she was quickly pushing a scheme for a broader plan, a "pilgrimage of houses" the following spring, with an invitation to the whole country to come to Natchez. Why not charge admission, arrange a week or so of visits, and let the money be used to restore the houses themselves?

There was hesitation when she and her co-workers called on the home owners. Protests were tentative or firm. Complete strangers would be tracking in and out; and would they be interested, anyway? The advocates of the idea went about town, talking to everybody, business men, city officials. Negro congregations, urging them all to join the plan, grow flowers, help along. They worked the way white people aren't supposed to work in the South. Some of the hardest

[23] From *Natchez on the Mississippi*, by Harnett T. Kane, pp. 336-348. Copyright, 1947, by Harnett T. Kane. New York: William Morrow & Company.

arguments were with those in the big houses. They tried many presentations: Natchez had a story to tell the world, something to show that the nation would want to look at. It would assist the town, assist everybody; it was patriotic, wasn't it? They would only be doing what others did. American towns offered the country electric power, lake sites, facilities for paper making. Natchez had one asset, one natural resource—its past.

They won out, but then they began to worry. Suppose, after all, nobody did come? They organized the town, drafted volunteers, buttonholed bankers, doctors, storekeepers; they "borrowed" stenographers to type letters, they found the Natchez *Democrat* a strong ally. They circularized newspapers, addressed women's clubs and men's organizations. The business men proved dubious; how could a thing like this work? After appealing to these merchants in every way except by tears, the garden club obtained a concession of a few dollars, and worked away with that.

Toward the end, as April approached, they grew jittery. They had received many letters, but how could they tell what would happen? Finally they added a parade; that would at least draw the country people, and assure some crowd. The night before, they sat around trying to joke but listening to their knees shake. Early the next morning they went downtown, with a handful who had agreed to serve as guides, if necessary, and took places at the empty registration tables. Knees still quivered.

Suddenly it happened. From all directions, by car, bus, and train, people were pouring in—women alone, women in parties, women with husbands and children, young men with cameras, teachers with pupils, aged travelers with chauffeurs and laprobes, honeymooners, professors, architects; and more were coming every few minutes. Nobody had expected it to be quite this way; for a while everything went awry. Then hurried calls went out for help. Hopefully, they had arranged to have six or so automobiles for the first arrivals; now automobiles were appealed for, begged, almost commandeered. More guides were pressed into service, given a quick briefing, and sent forth.

Stores sent stenographers and clerks to help. Hotels stretched their space; owners of homes agreed to take in guests. Restaurants added extra waitresses, called in cooks to throw together sandwiches, pots of shrimp and rice, more coffee, more everything. Garage attendants scurried to take care of lines of cars such as they had never seen; piles of picture post-cards ran out in an hour. More long-distance calls were made from Natchez in two or three days than it had ever known. It was terrible, and wonderful too, said those who took aspirins and rubbed their feet and throats after full days of walking and talking. "We'd never had anything like this since the Federals took the town in the war."

Practically everybody shared in the prosperity—jobs, money at the drugstore, money at hastily improvised "tea-shops." The business men were either exultant or sheepish. "I'll be damned," said one, summing it up for his confreres. "I'll be *good* and damned." (Many, against it from the start, now discovered that they had expected this to happen, all along.) A matron, who ran a tea shop, told about her Negro girl helper, who stood there puzzled as she cleared a table. By a plate she found a fifty-cent piece. "Lawdy, somebody lef' 'is money!" She had to be persuaded that this was her tip. Few incidents better illustrate the effect of the pilgrimage.

When Natchez subsided limply, it was found that each home owner would receive some hundreds of dollars. To outsiders the amount might look small; but for some it meant a house saved, enough to live on, with care, for a year. "Now we can have two pints of milk this summer, instead of one," said an elderly woman, her hand trembling. Oddly, it was discovered that some of the last hold-outs, who had been sure they had not wanted outsiders prying about their houses, had had the best time of all. Several stood there talking so long about their families that they had to be prodded into letting the tour continue.

After that the matter was settled. The town wanted the pilgrimage and more of it; so, it would seem, did people from everywhere else. By word of mouth, the name of Natchez spread. Depression or no depression, new routes to Natchez were blazed. More were arriving by automobile than had ever visited in the steamboat days. The prosperity overflowed through following months, and people still kept coming. It became Natchez' event of the year, socially, financially, and in other ways. People talked about it, planned for it, thought about it. The men, forgetting any questions they had raised, presented Katherine Miller with a loving cup.

The events expanded by the year, in scope and scale. A Confederate ball was started, with tableaux ending always with the flying of the Stars and Bars, in rousing climaxes that found the No'th'ners, too, standing while the band played Dixie. Now and then it was noted that every Confederate man in the tableaux had the rank of General, but that didn't matter. Wasn't every girl a belle? More and more balls were held, with kings and queens. Why should New Orleans' Mardi Gras have a monopoly on make-believe royalty? Afterward came candle-light dances, a "ball of a thousand candles," barbecued chicken picnics. Even the Negroes, hardly to be counted among Natchez' privileged, were given a part—a pageant, "Heaven Bound," performed in a church, with Good Man, Sinner and Undecided acting out a morality play in the aisles and at the front. Everybody was getting into the act.

The ladies had started by dressing in hoopskirt style, in bright prints. As the affair took on more color, more dash, these were replaced by satins and taffetas. Women went up to their attics, to pull out ancient costumes, donned mitts and carried lace umbrellas that their ancestors had sported. They persuaded their Negro helpers to wear bandannas or livery and escort the "pilgrims" in and out. Some Negroes may have wondered at the quality's bowing this way to Northerners, who had freed their slaves back in reb-time; but they could enjoy it like anybody else.

This was only the beginning. The word Natchez became a kind of talismanic one. "Southern perfumes," sometimes manufactured in the Mid-West, were named for the place, and then wallpapers, wall draperies and other patterns. Natchez houses, doorways and galleries were copied in homes all over the country. Those who came to Natchez during the pilgrimage after some years of absence were startled at the way it was sprucing up. Out of the spreading interest, plans crystallized for restoring and beautifying parts of the town, the bluffs, old roadways, old public buildings. The pilgrimage had much to do with crystallizing the movement for the recreation of the Natchez Trace, between the town and Nashville.

Beyond this, the pilgrimage did much to revitalize the town, perk up its drooping spirits. The spring show had become one of the town's major industries, perhaps its most dependable. Natchez had tapped the American desire to travel and the country's nostalgia for the past. It is easy, of course, to snicker at much of this—the vapid tourist, the ever-smiling hostess. For a time everything became "ante-bellum." When a woman from Pennsylvania asked a Natchez child what kind of dog that was, she replied: "Oh, nothing special. Just a little old ante-bellum dog."

Yet by and large, both sides have held up well. A few have been of the supposedly standard type of uncomprehending gapers; some complaints arose that sightseers were indulging their American habit of filching ash trays and baby spoons for souvenirs. A little skill in arranging, and that was eliminated. On the other hand, a number of Natchezians spread Old South so thickly that it brought a bilious reaction in the listeners. For the most part, the Natchezians extended an easy, good-mannered welcome; the callers behaved with no less tact.

This also I know. The Natchezians met more new people and learned more about the rest of the world than most of them had ever done in their lives. That, along with the spread of a little more purchasing power among blacks as well as whites, didn't hurt anyone in Natchez. Town horizons lifted in more than one way. If it made the people, plantation or not plantation, want a little more —an indoor toilet, another store-bought dress—that wasn't to the bad.

As for the houses, pilgrimage money made it possible to paint some for the first time in decades. Sagging pillars were shored up, roofs put back; now and then it meant the saving of a doomed home. Others, that had been empty in decay, had new owners, or old ones back again, to rescue them from oblivion. So things went, higher, higher. Then, 1935, and high-pitched hell broke over Natchez, in what the town has ever afterward called "the split." It developed over personalities, individual rivalries, principles if you will, and also money —specifically, the take. Yearly the pilgrimage organization had expanded. But now various home owners were complaining that they were being outvoted by folks who didn't have even a flower pot. Also, they thought they should get more than two-thirds of the money that came in. The other side denied the charges about the voting and argued that this other third should go to pretty up the town.

The first thing you knew everybody was pink in the face. Doors slammed in heat; there were battles of proxies, talk of unladylike knifings, "misrepresentation" and so on. Katherine Miller went up the river for a time, to organize the "Descendants of the Participants in the Campaign, Battle and Siege of Vicksburg," with tableaux to match. Then, all at once Natchez had not one but two pilgrimages, Natchez Garden Club and Pilgrimage Garden Club. (The Millerites were the latter.) More houses were shown, and there were two Confederate balls, two kings, two queens, and so on down the line. At first matters didn't work out too badly. The events were stretched out twice as long; hotel, restaurant and other business men were not unpleased. Everything was so polite between the rival groups that it hurt the teeth to listen. Somebody called it "honey time"; all the ladies were telling their guests: "Glad to see you, come again, honey." As one wit put it, the slogan was: "Come see my house, not her house," but everything was genteel.

For a time Natchez had even a third pilgrimage. The Merrill murder case had broken, and Dick Dana was inviting the world to Come to Goat Castle, where another part of the New South lived. Slowly, however, the snakes were crawling about the pilgrimage gardens. Like everything else, hot feeling was doubling. Life-long friendships broke up; cousins on different sides stopped speaking. Families united by generations of friendship went in different directions. To be seen drinking coffee with the opposition was to invite ostracism; or you might come home and find your wife giving you the silent treatment. When one organization had its show, practically every house in the other group slammed shut, with "No Admittance" signs on the door. Only one or two people managed, or tried, to keep out of the depths of the fight. One salty Natchezian penned a famous ditty:

> I'm wild and woolly, and I'm full of fleas,
> But I'll show my house when I God-damned please.

Gradually the situation tightened. In this petticoat battle, this War of the Camellias, there could be no neutrals. You had to be one or the other, see? The whole town was drawn in. The amused Ernie Pyle came to Natchez, had such a fine time that he said he didn't know whether he was Jeff Davis or himself, but admitted that the hostilities had him whipped: "It's the AFL and CIO all over again." The ladies jockeyed for position, preferred time, use of the auditorium and so on.

The year 1941 brought the blow-off. Without attempting to give the details, it may be observed that the two pilgrimage dates overlapped. "Pilgrims" arrived one day to find both going full tilt. Rival headquarters operated a block or so apart. Negro musicians played loud and long, and old battle hymns and sweet Southern songs rent the air. A campaign of banners, placards and circulars ensued, "making the town look like a carnival show," as an official put it. Somehow Negro employes got mixed in the thing, handing out cards for the white folks. Inevitably bewildered tourists found themselves pulled in two directions. A few announced that this was altogether too much Dixie hospitality and stalked off. A florid Westerner stood as much as he could, and slumped over with a heart attack.

A contingent of Yankee soldiers from a nearby military camp unloaded on Natchez, to find two sets of hoopskirted ladies smiling at them, determination in their eyes. "Such popularity . . ." murmured a captain from Brooklyn. "Was the Civil War like this, ma'am?" A tactful officer hit on a solution. He split the soldier-tourists in half. You guys go to this one, you guys to that one. At ease! In the middle of it someone thought of the law. Into court went the Natchez

Garden club, demanding an injunction against the Pilgrimage Garden club. Two judges had their thumbs mashed in the mix-up. The first one gave the injunction, then took it back almost at once, saying he'd made a mistake. The ladies picked a judge in another town, and he agreed with them. Stern orders were handed down, forbidding the second club to keep up its performance.

Thick-fingered deputies started out, nailing notices to Georgian doors. One chatelaine, not knowing what was happening, saw the law coming up her walk and mistook it for a tourist. She dropped him a deep bow, "and then he handed me an injunction!" That, sir, was hardly the act of a gentleman. Certain ladies scurried about town, fleeing justice; one rode to the Devil's Punchbowl, where bandits of the Natchez Trace used to hide out when the law was tailing them. Town officials, pressed to "do something," stared at the ground. The mayor found he had business in New York and left for a week; many husbands wished they could follow him.

Two can play at the game of justice. The Pilgrimage Garden club turned around and sued the Natchez Garden club. Both sides asked damages, charging humiliation and many more things. The judge listened patiently, looked over their voluminous books, and cleared his throat to utter a few truths. The pilgrimages, he pointed out, were supposed to show the world "how the old South lived." This was hardly it, now was it? The success of the pilgrimage had been a Godsend, he observed, but he expressed his suspicion that this wrangling might be killing the goose that laid the golden eggs. He dismissed the whole matter and sent all the ladies packing, hoopskirts and all.

In one respect, the judge wasn't quite right. The fight, despite the snickerings, brought Natchez more attention than anything that had happened there. Thousands of Americans made up their mind to go there, to see the houses that all the fuss was about. They're still doing it.

World War II forced a suspension of pilgrimages, though thousands continued to visit the town. The year 1947 brought peace. The ladies sat around a council table and worked out a formula; the clubs remained separate but joined for a full month of pilgrimage, and all the houses were open. There was one Confederate ball, with King and Queen to be divided among the two groups. Things went as merrily as an old time candle-light dance. Mrs. Melchior Beltzhoover, president of the Pilgrimage Club, bowed on the stage to Mrs. Homer Whittington, president of the Garden Club, who bowed back in a swirl of skirts. They shook hands, and the audience broke into shouts of joy. It was, said a sniffling matron, a little like the fine climactic scene in which the Blue and the Gray clasped hands. A philosopher observed that since the ladies had shown they could do it, he had become more hopeful that the United Nations would work.

BEER AND "GEMÜTLICHKEIT" IN ST. LOUIS [24]

[Adolphus] Busch, who had come to St. Louis from Germany just before the [Civil] War, married a daughter of Eberhard Anheuser, the owner of a small brewery. He worked his way into control of the firm and began laying the groundwork for the Anheuser-Busch brewery, which is now the largest in the world. Busch made good beer, but his success proceeded primarily from his gift for salesmanship. Disdaining the cutthroat competition of the local market, he traveled the nation and the world, preaching the gospel of beer, particularly his own, and the glories of expansive living. Busch became internationally renowned, and so did his beer. He hobnobbed with German royalty and was unofficially dubbed "Prince Busch," by his friend, President Taft. At home he lived in splendor, in a chateau on the brewery grounds; in New York he entertained regally at the Plaza Hotel, and he had villas in Pasadena and in Langenschwalbach, Germany. A generous philanthropist and a good liver, Busch did much to enrich the natural *Gemütlichkeit* of St. Louis. His death, in 1913, was viewed as a calamity. On the day of the funeral not a wheel or spigot turned in his gigantic 142-acre plant. A hundred American flags flapped in the breeze and fifty salutes were fired from a brass cannon in the shipping yards. Twenty-five trucks carried floral offerings behind a funeral car draped in black, like Wellington's. Busch was buried in a German-made casket weighing 800 pounds.

The period from the end of the Civil War until well past the turn of the century might well be termed the Busch era. St. Louis ceased to be merely a growing city and settled down to becoming a civilization. The city had escaped physical damage during the war and its infant manufacturing facilities had grown to manhood with the help of an expenditure there of $180,000,000 by the Chief Quartermaster. Feeble talk about moving the national capital to St. Louis was lost in the happy clamor from proliferating beer gardens, Schmierkäse gardens, and wine caves; from the temples of German dramatics and opera and the halls of choral societies and *sängerbunds*.

The spirit of beer was contagious. "Formerly," a sober local historian wrote in 1878, "beer was regarded as a beverage almost exclusively indulged in by persons of German origin. This is not true. The consumption of beer is promoted by all classes—Americans, Irishmen, Swedes, Italians and Frenchmen —and women of all nationalities and in all classes of society drink more or less of the Teutonic beverage, lager beer. But," he added, "despite the almost universal practice of beer sipping indulged in by the inhabitants of St. Louis, it has been remarked that drunkenness is not extensively prevalent."

The virus of New England Puritanism, which was already infecting many parts of the West, never had a chance in St. Louis. Church-going was almost universal, but Sunday afternoon was a fiesta time. Picnics were held *en famille*

[24] From "The Cities of America: St. Louis," by Jack Alexander, *The Saturday Evening Post*, Vol. 219 (December 7, 1946), No. 23, p. 83. Copyright, 1946, by the Curtis Publishing Company. Philadelphia.

in the parks, and the roads leading to the country were dusty with carriage traffic headed for public groves and gardens. . . .

In the downtown district, where hard-liquor saloons held forth for the sporty steamboat trade, a certain moral problem arose. Ladies were brazenly ogled by street-corner sports, and ropers and steerers for glamorous gambling palaces harvested their suckers without interference from the police. But this side of the city's life was no more characteristic of it than the roughneck doings of a seaport's dockside section. St. Louis' solid citizens (the population was 350,000 by 1880) were simply intent on having a good time, and were pretty determined about it.

AK-SAR-BEN [25]

It all began with the [Nebraska] State Fair in 1894. Then, night after night, weary women stood about in the streets holding the moist hands of crying children with nowhere to go. Somebody who saw this forcefully pointed out that, unless the city provided evening entertainment for out-of-town patrons, Omaha would never see the State Fair again.

Stunned by this appalling prospect, the merchants formed their booster outfit. It was agreed that whatever was done must be spectacular, big, striking enough to blanket the shopping district—and absolutely *free*. The first plan was for a Harvest Festival topped off by a night parade. Conservative merchants protested, "That will take a lot of cash, publicity, and organization." But the boosters replied, "It will be worth it."

The next question was, "What shall we call the thing?"

Nobody had the answer until one member of the group spoke up: "Why not reverse the name of the state? Nebraska spelled backwards is Ak-Sar-Ben. We are to save the fair for Omaha, so we will be the Knights of Ak-Sar-Ben."

The order devoted itself to winning the good will—and the business—of the people of the state. In those days, the Missouri Valley was a joiners' paradise.

Some four hundred years ago the Spanish conquistador Coronado rode over the plains toward the Missouri, searching for the golden cities of the fabulous Kingdom of Quivera. This fact inspired the scribes who concocted the ritual of Ak-Sar-Ben. Their initiation ceremony is a unique free show combining the horseplay of a college fraternity hell-week and the solemnity of a dignified secret order, all written into the plot of a home-talent comic opera. The novices are assigned unrehearsed parts in the play. These and the spectators are brought by special train from all over the neighboring country on both sides of the river to share in the entertainment, which is held in the order's great "fun plant"—a huge auditorium known as the Madison Square Garden of the Middle West.

The great event is a stunning coronation ceremony at which some civic leader is crowned king of Quivera for the year, and one of the leading debutantes of the season is crowned queen.

[25] From *The Missouri*, by Stanley Vestal, pp. 136-137. Copyright, 1945, by Walter Stanley Campbell. New York: Rinehart & Company, Inc.

Since its organization, Ak-Sar-Ben has sponsored parades, flower shows, harvest festivals, horse racing, and livestock shows, changing its program to suit conditions as the years pass. Its leaders include many of the leading citizens and industrialists of the region, and its slogan is "Knights to the rescue!" Its purpose is to do whatever will make Nebraska "more prosperous, happier, and a better place in which to live." The Livestock Show attracts representatives of nearly a hundred thousand Four-H Club members and has brought into being the superior breeds of hogs and cattle common in all that country.

PROMENADE IN LAREDO [26]

It was a quarter to nine on a Sunday night in Laredo, Texas. The thermometer at the corner of the plaza said 82; the air was soft and a light breeze washed past. Stars twinkled, a brittle blue in the dark sky. All Laredo was bathed in a sweet odor of orange blossoms, which faded and came back as you walked along. The block-square plaza was thick with green trees, and there was a circular lighted bandstand in the middle. The sidewalks were crowded with walkers, all dark-skinned. Loungers, two by two, lay or sat on the grass. You heard no English spoken, for Laredo was eighty per cent Mexican, or Spanish American, as the transplanted Mexicans prefer to be called. Boys and girls, coatless and hatless, were everywhere. They strolled, and talked, and took their time. But it seemed more than mere strolling around the plaza. There was something different.

Gradually it came to you. The boys were all walking in one direction, and the girls in the other—in twos and sometimes threes, row after row, walking along rather rapidly, like an army on a broken-step march. They never paused—just kept going round and round the square. And then you noticed that the outer edge of the sidewalk, clear around the plaza, was lined with still more young men, standing in a solid row like a picket fence. They stood mostly in silence, watching the girls as they passed.

I asked questions, and I found it was a custom as old as Mexico, which the Mexicans brought over into the United States with them. They call it the "promenade." Every town and city in Mexico has its open block-square plaza with a bandstand in the middle, and cement or gravel walks leading inward from the four corners. Every Sunday night, and in some places every Thursday night too, the young people of the town turn out for the promenade around the plaza. All over Mexico that night girls were parading around plazas in one direction and boys in the other, looking at each other.

The purpose of the promenade is to let the young men see what likely-looking girls there are in town, and many a marriage has come out of the first shy glances in the plaza. In the old days the girls were always chaperoned. If a boy liked a girl's looks, he would turn and fall into step with her and walk along talking—properly chaperoned, of course. Now, even though there weren't

[26] From *Home Country*, by Ernie Pyle, pp. 27-28. Copyright, 1947, by William Sloane Associates, Inc. New York.

any chaperons, I noticed only a few boys joining the girls. The promenade had become more an excuse just to come downtown and stand around.

I stood for a long time watching the girls' faces, and never saw one that would launch a rowboat, let alone a battleship. They were nice faces, but not what we in our country consider beautiful. The girls were all in light summer dresses. Some were quite small, still in short skirts. Some ranged up close to the thirties. Most of them were slim, though now and then you would see a fat one. There must have been five hundred girls parading, and as many boys walking or standing along the walk.

Pretty soon a truck pulled up to the curb. It had loud-speakers on top, and it was tuned to a Mexican radio station, very loudly. The strollers strolled on, to the music, and the crowds stood or sat on the grass, and talked and listened. The parading went on for nearly two hours. Gradually the crowd thinned out. At ten o'clock the music stopped. By ten-fifteen the plaza was empty and dark. The boys had seen the girls and the girls had seen the boys, and they'd both had their walks, and it was all over for another week.

SANTA FE FIESTA [27]

Early in September, Santa Fe has its fiesta. It differs from the purely native fiestas in that it reenacts one of the most dramatic episodes in Spanish colonial history with the combination of Spanish folkways, Indian dances, and American carnival. With the exception of our Puritan Thanksgiving Day it is the oldest historical celebration in the United States, a focus of the romance interwoven by three races during the past three centuries.

The fiesta began in the year 1712 when the Marqués de la Peñuela issued a bando commanding the town to commemorate the reconquest of this province by Captain-General Diego de Vargas in 1692. The Marqués was the D.A.R. of his day, restoring the oldest church at his own expense and insisting even then that Santa Fe should take an active interest in her history. He saw that the reconquest of the Holy City, a perilous feat of only twenty years before, had all the essentials of a stirring drama. Such pageants, depicting the martial glories of the mother country, were highly popular in Spain. Here in this isolated province, a historical fiesta would inspire the colonists toward greater zeal in subduing the Indian country and give them that typical Spanish outlet for national feeling in drama. The Marqués set the stage with a de Vargas riding up to the city walls in resplendent armor, velvet cape, and plumed helmet, accompanied by his soldiers and brown-gowned padres. There was the tense moment of the captain-general entering the gate of the hostile pueblo, relieved when the cross and the scarlet and gold banners of Castilla were again planted before the Royal Palace.

After more than two centuries the same drama thrills us with its crisis. The fiesta begins with Sunday vespers in the Cathedral and a solemn march in the

[27] From *Caballeros*, by Ruth Laughlin, pp. 201-205. Copyright, 1931, by Ruth Laughlin. Caldwell, Idaho: The Caxton Printers, Ltd. 1945.

September twilight for a community service at the Cross of the Martyrs. The
way is marked with little bonfires burning along the road and a thousand
lighted candles held in the hands of men and women winding up and down
the hill in the dusk. Above, the milky way reflects the twinkling tapers, and
big stars burn in the quiet night-blue sky.

The next morning de Vargas once more rides in on his silver saddle to recon-
quer the Villa Real. The cross and royal banner are planted before the Palace
of the Governors as they were in 1692, and the Alcalde in his brocade satin
coat reads the ancient edict for the two hundredth time. The return of de
Vargas to his camp outside the city, followed by soldiers, padres, and war-
painted Indians, is a signal for the merrymaking to begin.

The fiesta needs no artificial scenery, for the Plaza and the Palace of the
Governors furnish an unequalled stage setting. The historic park, no longer a
battlefield, is gay with banners of all colors waving through the trees. Crowds
in costume throng through it in holiday saunterings, stopping now beside a
blind fiddler seated on a bench and then following gay troubadours and joining
in the chorus of the yard-long verses of "Adelita."

The Historical Pageant is followed the next day by the Hysterical Pageant
giving full reign to the artist colony's ingenuity in caricaturing every issue in
village life from Detour Buses to the Painters' Dream of selling pictures as fast
as oil stock. The native people enter into it with the zest of their happy Latin
temperament, dressed as buffalo hunters with raised spears, followed by high
wagons whose two solid wooden wheels creak loudly with every turn. Trailing
them are long lines of women in the gay flowered dresses their grandmothers
wore. The Hysterical Pageant is the highlight of the Pasatiempo, inviting every
one to pass their time in a merry carnival spirit.

The portal of the Palace with its scarlet and gold banners has become a

Spanish Market where everything from native herbs to syrupy Mexican punch is sold. Colorful Chimayo blankets fill one stall and quaint carvings, hand-woven carpets, and hooked rugs are displayed in the Spanish Colonial Arts Exhibit. Following the customs of earlier days, country people have driven their covered wagons up to the Plaza curb, vending red-cheeked peaches and vegetables, squawking hens and bright-hued flowers. Even the children have a part in the fiesta for the Pet Show is their special affair. They come to the Plaza not only with favorite dogs, cats, and ponies, but with such pets as caterpillars, turtles, snakes, monkeys, and horned toads, equally precious to a child's heart.

Inside the patio, Indian dances are going on, pueblos vying with each other in presenting the best dances and reviving many an old ceremony which might have been forgotten. There, too, is the Indian Fair with the finest examples of baskets, pottery, weaving, and turquoise jewelry offered as exhibits and awarded prizes to encourage these original arts. At the Art Museum paintings of Southwestern artists fill the galleries with the Annual Fiesta Show.

The feature which makes the fiesta unique and colorful is the whole-souled participation of the hundreds of native people who come in from tiny mountain hamlets to join with Spanish Santa Feans in making the Pasatiempo truly their own. Under the leadership of a large Spanish-American society they make the most of this opportunity to show their pride of racial heritage, and to enjoy their own type of good time. One year they represent Pancho Villa and his bandits with delightful buffoonery, another year they are the Ciboleros, the buffalo hunters who went forth from Santa Fe to search the plains for herds of buffalo, bringing back dried meat and skins. Their costumes, crude equipment, and solid wheeled wagons are authentic, for they are supervised by old men who hunted the buffalo sixty years ago. The buffalo hunt takes place on the College grounds, and the supper for the Ciboleros, served by laughing women in old-fashioned dresses, recalls that first dim memory of the cave man being fed by his woman when he came back from the hunt. In the evening they join in old songs and folk dances such as La Cuna, Paso Doble, and La Escoba with jokes and laughter, the bright-colored costumes flashing under the lights.

It reminds one of folk dances in Hungary or Russia, yet it is essentially a part of historic Santa Fe as the center of the Spanish Southwest. There is no exhibitionism about it but the spontaneous Latin gayety which is the delight of every native fiesta. As one breathless grandmother exclaimed, when she sank into her seat after the swift steps of the quadrilla, "Qué fun!"

One night is given over to the Conquistadores' Ball when grandees in velvet and lace dance with court ladies in rare shawls and mantillas. Another night offers a highly-colored Western melodrama presented by the Santa Fe Players. Zozobra, Old Father Gloom, is burned on a huge pyre and the Pasatiempo revelry reaches its height. The Conquistadores' Band plays for street dancing, confetti rains in a multicolored shower, and the youngsters do a serpentine around the venerable Plaza. Finally the luminarios, those old-time lanterns made of candles set in sand-filled paper bags, gutter out where they have outlined the Palace portal, and the fiesta is over for another year.

BUCKSKINS AND FRILLS [28]

. . . [In 1897] Cheyenne had its first Frontier Days with the help of
to pack all of its colorful history into its rough-stuff pageant. It was not planned
Buffalo Bill. Cheyenne, proud of its struggle in taming a remote outpost, tries
as a tourist trap, for in 1897, the automobile brigade out to see America first
was definitely a thing of the future. But Cheyenne welcomes the 6,000,000 to
7,000,000 travelers who pause there each year now and tries to put on a summer program that pleases.

Beginning in June, soon after the last snow, Cheyenne "camps" chuck wagons
at its main highway approaches and starts a long advance ballyhoo for its big
annual Frontier Days fiesta. Young men in the garb of buckaroos hand out
pamphlets telling of the approaching Wild West events. As part of the advance
celebrating, every Wednesday and Friday evening a block in midtown is lariated
off for street dancing. A band pours Western tunes into a loud-speaker system.
The first dozen out-of-state ladies who step forward, breaking down the you-
go-first complex, get corsages, and the evening frolic is under way. It's hard to
be shy in Cheyenne; people catch the spirit. One night last June there were
men and women from thirty-two states out there at the same time, kicking up
their heels. Appropriately costumed performers from the city's old-time dance
clubs instruct the first-time tenderfeet in the vigorous art of square dancing and
also put on dazzling exhibitions.

Civic enterprise works up to the roaring climax the last full week in July—
the week of Frontier Days. During this one week of playing cowboy, Indian
and stagecoach holdup, every tourist cabin within 100 miles is full, and all
roads lead to Old Cheyenne. But apparently there are folks who don't worry
about housing. One visitor was asked about his hotel, and he retorted, "Hotel!
I'm not signed up at any hotel; only going to be here three days."

For Frontier Days Cheyenne is transformed by false store fronts and wooden
galleries with leaning posts, and every relic of the past is hauled out for a
period parade. Indians by the tribe wander in and throw up their tepees. Since
Wyoming Indians dress like more recent American citizens, Cheyenne has had
to invest in a tremendous wardrobe of authentic costumes, so that its parading
braves will be fittingly feathered and blanketed.

A part of the program is an arena performance that is as rough as man can
think up, but the pageantry is far out of the class of a tinhorn rodeo. The celebration is a community event in which nearly every resident participates. For
instance, there is Federal District Judge T. Blake Kennedy, who years ago presided at some of the hearings of the Teapot Dome scandal. Ordinarily he dresses
sedately and on Sunday strolls into the First Presbyterian Church wearing
striped pants and morning coat, and carrying a cane. But during Frontier Days
he puts on full Western regalia and is a timekeeper for broncbusting and wild-

[28] From "The Cities of America: Cheyenne," by Lewis Nordyke, *The Saturday Evening
Post*, Vol. 223 (June 2, 1951), No. 49, p. 118. Copyright, 1951, by the Curtis Publishing
Company. Philadelphia.

mare-milking events. Profit from the show finances the year-round youth-recreation program—folk dancing, softball, tennis. It has built a dozen cement tennis courts and developed parks that are beauty spots and play places.

After the dust of the big show has settled, Cheyenners put away their buckskins and frills and get back to work, and you seldom come upon a character who looks as if he'd just drunk water out of a cow track. However, there remains a lingering atmosphere which suggests that something exciting might lurk just around the next corner. It is this intangible that makes Cheyenne— without enough scenery or natural attraction to make a traveler stop longer than it takes to get five gallons of gas—one of the popular tourist spots in the West.

It has also given Cheyenne an astonishing specialty retail business. Some years ago Sol Bernstein opened a Western goods store, and it went over with a bang. Now the city has a dozen such places, and all are flourishing. Bernstein's store has developed into a mail-order business that ships Western toggery all over the country. It is this store that stocks Texas-made cowboy boots and fills Texas orders by the score. Bernstein mails Philadelphia-made ten-gallon hats to customers in nearly all the states, although the buyers could get the same skypieces in their home-town men's stores. Tourists by the thousands, especially those on their way to dude ranches, buy their Western stuff in Cheyenne.

SAN DIEGO GRUNION DERBY [29]

[In San Diego] we have fish which come ashore here and can be gathered off the beach for eating. But I hesitate to mention them because such phenomena usually occur in the Southern Hemisphere, in the South Seas, in the interior of Africa, far away where only explorers are allowed to report on them.

* * * * *

These fish are grunion, built much after the order of fair-sized sardines. Grunion belong to the smelt family, yet grunion and smelt are not the same. Unfortunately for the grunion, their arrivals on the beach can be predicted with the accuracy of a time-table. The spring tides, which accompany the full and dark of the moon, are the time-tables by which the grunion runs can be predicted. And unless the grunion watch out they soon may be exterminated as punishment for their own regularity. Nothing on this earth should be as regular as grunion and still hope to survive.

The grunion arrive on the third or fourth nights following the full of the moon and the dark of the moon. For about an hour after the turn of the tide these little fish flop about on the beach. The female digs tail-first into the sand, depositing her eggs, which the male fertilizes. . . .

* * * * *

The succeeding tides bury the eggs more deeply into the sand where they lie until dug out two weeks later by the next series of high tides. At this time the

[29] From *I Cover the Waterfront*, by Max Miller, pp. 111-114. Copyright, 1932, by E. P. Dutton & Co., Inc. New York.

eggs hatch and the tiny fish are washed into the ocean. Their life has been going on like this for a good many fish-generations now, and their family tree was blackened by the scandal of many beach parties long before the coming of Cabrillo to this sunny coast. But the grunion never will learn to hunt new shorelines distant from the reach of automobiles of this city, and for this reason the grunion-run has turned into an entertainment which I no longer sit up to watch.

On grunion-run night the beach is not the lonely beach of most nights. Instead, the sands are illuminated by fires each few yards. People by the dozens have arrived to turn the ocean, my ocean, into theatricals. And if I had the power to call out to the grunion not to come ashore on these nights, I would do so. I would call as loudly as I could. And on some other night when the people were all gone, I would whisper to the grunion: "It's all right now. You may come in."

But of course the grunion do arrive, and they arrive on schedule. First a few arrive, and the people begin to scream in their excitement. They have not had fish come right up to them before like this, and in the heat of the chase the people forget about their shoes and their clothing. They follow the fish back into the surf. They capture the fish with their bare hands and with hand-nets and with common window-screen. They jab the screen down into the sand between the grunion and the sea. The ebbing surf rushes through the screen, but the grunion is caught by it and held for capture.

When the run is over, men walk away with grunion by the buckets. And when too many are caught for eating, the surplus is thrown away.

VI. Local Legends and Sagas

The voice of a city is heard not only in anecdotes, jests and witticisms, in rival cracks and slams, in local characters and regional customs, but also in local legends and sagas. These are part of the place lore that grows up in every locality about topographical features, landmarks, place names, local sayings, shibboleths, characters, customs—to celebrate them or account for their origin. Something less than history and something more than it, they are fables and symbols, reminding us of Lessing's dictum that "history begins with the fact and ends with the symbol."

Local legends range from apocryphal unhistorical "historical" traditions attached to historic personages and events to migratory legends which become localized in various times and places. Local sagas are biographical narratives relating and glorifying the achievements of founding fathers, industrialists, builders and dreamers, or the history of a particular institution or product.

Some legends and sagas are fragments of epics, like Brigham Young's prophetic vision of "This Is the Place," the curse pronounced by another Mormon, Orson Hyde, on the people of Carson and Washoe valleys, Nevada, or the Feliz curse, rumored to be responsible for the landslide in Elysian Park, Los Angeles. Others involve hoaxes, like the sawing off of Manhattan Island. Still others, combining rumors, hoaxes and hallucinations (such as plagued San Francisco during and after the fire) are uncanny stories of miracles, superstitions, ghosts, revenants, devils.

As hidden or buried history, legend interests the historian, who may use it for indirect historical evidence, as in the story of Mrs. O'Leary's cow, examining and sifting conflicting testimony and hearsay. As fables and inspiring examples of courage, individual ingenuity and vision, legends may also attract writers—bardic poets and storytellers like Longfellow and Irving, who recreate old wives' tales in literary ballads and legends. Thus, along the path of history or literature, legends and sagas may pass from local into national tradition.

From the test story of Boston's Faneuil Hall Grasshopper to the strange noises that haunted Portland's Mount Cleall Castle, the following tales represent well-known types, themes and motifs of the legend and folktale. They are presented here, however, as good stories and as documents that tell us something about the life of a community and the character of its people, as well as about cities and men in general.

THE FANEUIL HALL GRASSHOPPER TEST [1]

. . . Many changes and additions have been made to the original structure [of Faneuil Hall] during the past century and a half, but a grasshopper still visible as the weather vane was for a long time thought to be part of the Faneuil crest. It seems more probable, however, that it was executed by

[1] From *Boston and the Boston Legend*, by Lucius Beebe, pp. 286-287. Copyright, 1935, by D. Appleton-Century Company, Inc. New York: Appleton-Century-Crofts, Inc.

its designer, "that cunning artificer," Deacon Shem Drowne, in imitation of the celebrated grasshopper vane on the Royal Exchange at London. (Deacon Drowne also made the vane so famous atop the Province House—a poised Indian representing the arms of Massachusetts.) From time to time the grasshopper has received repairs, and on one such occasion a paper was taken from its innards with the following inscription:

> Shem Drowne made it, May 25, 1742. To my brethren and fellow grasshoppers. Fell in ye year 1753, Nov. 18, early in ye morning by a great earthquake by my Old Master above. . . . Again like to have met my utter ruin by fire, but hopping timely from my Public Scituation, came of with broken bones and much bruised. Cured and fixed. . . . Old Master's son Thomas Drowne, June 26, 1768, and though I promise to discharge my office, yet I shall vary as ye wind.

Faneuil Hall grasshopper is as much a symbol of Boston as the gilded dome of the State House or the lion and the unicorn of the Old State House, and Samuel Cooper, when he was American consul at Glasgow, reports that he once used it to test some sailors asking him for fare home to Boston, which they claimed as their native town. As proper Boston identification he asked each what was on Faneuil Hall vane. One said a fish, which wasn't so bad a guess, one a horse, and the third named the grasshopper. Mr. Cooper very justly threw the first two out as impostors and gave ear to the complaints of the third.

THE SAWING-OFF OF MANHATTAN ISLAND [2]

One of the most extraordinary hoaxes ever perpetrated in New York originated a little more than a hundred years ago in the fertile imagination of a little dried-up old man named Lozier, who had amassed a competence as a carpenter and contractor and had then retired to enjoy life. For almost two months during the summer of 1824 Lozier's fantastic activities, which he carried on with the enthusiastic assistance of John DeVoe, a retired butcher better known as Uncle John, kept a considerable portion of middle- and lower-class New York in a veritable frenzy of excitement. In later years Uncle John's nephew, Thomas F. DeVoe, an honored member of the New York Historical Society and himself a prosperous butcher of Civil War days, incorporated an account of the hoax in his two-volume work: *The Market Book, Containing a Historical Account of the Public Markets in the Cities of New York, Boston, Philadelphia, and Brooklyn, With a Brief Description of Every Article of Human Food Sold Therein, the Introduction of Cattle in America and Notices of Many Remarkable Specimens, et cetera, et cetera, et cetera.*

In those early days, when the present American metropolis was a comparatively small city of not more than 150,000 population, a favorite loafing-place was the old Centre Market at Grand, Baxter, and Centre Streets. A dozen long benches lined the Grand Street side of the Market, and every afternoon from

[2] From *All Around the Town*, by Herbert Asbury, pp. 102-113. Copyright, 1929, 1930, 1931, 1932, 1933, 1934, by Alfred A. Knopf, Inc. New York.

spring to winter they were filled with amateur statesmen, principally retired butchers and other such small business men, most of whom combined scant knowledge with excessive gullibility. Chief among them were Lozier and Uncle John DeVoe, and of these two venerable jokesters, Lozier was the leader. He did most of the talking at the daily forums in front of the Market and was invariably able to produce a definite and apparently practicable remedy for every conceivable financial, political, or economic ill. He was always listened to with enormous respect, for he was wealthy, he possessed more education than his fellows and was therefore better able to express himself, and he was a recognized traveler, having made several voyages to Europe as a ship's carpenter. There was no lack of subjects to talk about, for those were wondrous times. The first great wave of Irish immigration had begun to beat against American shores as a result of the potato famine of 1822; Brazil and Mexico had thrown off the shackles of Portugal and Spain; the first steamship had crossed the Atlantic only a few years before; President James Monroe had just promulgated the Monroe Doctrine; and Mrs. Monroe had almost precipitated a revolution in New York and Washington society by announcing that as the First Lady of the Land she would no longer return social calls. The gifted Lozier professed to know the inside stories of all these momentous events, and so convincing was he that there were many who believed that he was high in the confidence not only of the President, but of foreign potentates as well.

Early in July, 1824, Lozier was absent from his accustomed bench for several days, an unparalleled occurrence which aroused much comment. When he returned, he refused to join in the flow of conversation and even declined to settle arguments. He talked only to Uncle John DeVoe, and for the most part sat alone, brooding, obviously concerned with weighty matters. When his friends asked where he had been, and sought diligently to learn what mighty thoughts troubled his mind, he would at first divulge no information. At length, however, he admitted that he had been at City Hall in consultation with Mayor Stephen Allen. No one doubted the truth of this statement, which caused even more talk than had his absence. In those days the Mayor of New York was a personage of impressive dignity; he was not so approachable as now, and a man who had been summoned by His Honor automatically became a person of considerable importance. For almost a week Lozier kept his friends and admirers on tenterhooks of curiosity. Finally, on a day when all the market benches were occupied, and he was thus assured of an audience worthy of his talents, he made a full and complete explanation.

It appeared that Lozier and Mayor Allen had had a long conversation about Manhattan Island and had reached the conclusion that it was much too heavy on the Battery end, because of the many large buildings. The situation was rapidly becoming dangerous. Already the island had begun to sag, as was plain from the fact that it was all downhill from City Hall, and there were numerous and alarming indications that it might break off and sink into the sea, with appalling losses of life and property. Lozier and the Mayor had decided, therefore, that the island must be sawed off at Kingsbridge, at the northern end, and turned around, so that the Kingsbridge end would be where the Battery end had been for ages. The Battery end, of course, if it did not fall off in transit, would take the place of the Kingsbridge end. Once the turn had been made, the weaker end of the island would be anchored to the mainland, thus averting the danger of collapse.

When the conferences at City Hall began, it further appeared, Lozier and Mayor Allen were not in complete agreement as to the best method of accomplishing the mighty task. The Mayor thought that before Manhattan could be turned around it would be necessary to detach Long Island from its moorings and tow it out of the way, returning it later to its proper place. Lozier finally convinced him, however, that there was ample space in the harbor and the bay. It was at length decided, therefore, simply to saw Manhattan Island off, float it down past Governors and Ellis Islands, turn it around, and then float it back to its new position. For political reasons Mayor Allen wished the job to appear as a private undertaking and had turned the whole project over to Lozier, instructing him to employ the necessary labor and to superintend the work.

Such were the force of Lozier's personality, the power of his reputation, and the credulity of his generation that practically none who heard him thought of questioning the feasibility of the scheme. The few who were inclined to scoff were soon silenced, if not actually convinced, by his earnestness, and by the acclaim which had greeted the announcement of the project. Every one realized at once that it was truly a gigantic plan, but they had Lozier's word for it that it could be accomplished. Moreover, as Lozier pointed out, the construction of the famous Erie Canal, which was then nearing completion, had once been called impossible even by competent engineers, and much derision had greeted the prediction that steam ships would one day cross the ocean. If man could run a river through the very heart of a mountain, and if he could cause a simple steam engine to propel a gigantic boat, why couldn't he saw off an island? Nobody knew the answer, and Lozier's story was swallowed *in toto,* hook, line, and sinker.

Sawing Manhattan Island off soon became the principal subject of argument and conversation at Centre Market, and elsewhere as news of the great project spread. Neither then nor later, however, did the few newspapers of the period pay any attention to Lozier's activities. It is doubtful if the editors ever heard of him, for in those days the only way of transmitting intelligence was by word of mouth, or by letter, which was even more uncertain. Important happenings in one part of the city did not become generally known for weeks or months, and frequently not at all. And Grand Street then was as far uptown as the farthest reaches of the Bronx are to-day.

A few days after he had started the ball rolling, Lozier appeared at Centre Market with a huge ledger, in which he proposed to record the names of all applicants for jobs, pending an examination to determine their fitness. This and other clerical work which developed during the progress of the hoax was the special care of Uncle John DeVoe, who ceremoniously set down the names, ages, and places of residence of all who applied. Work was none too plentiful that year, and laborers, many of them recently-arrived Irishmen, answered

Lozier's call in such numbers that the big ledger soon bore the names of some three hundred men, all eager to begin the great work of sawing off Manhattan Island.

Lozier further aroused confidence in his scheme by notifying various butchers of his acquaintance to begin assembling the enormous herds of cattle, droves of hogs, and flocks of chickens which would be necessary to feed his army of workmen. He estimated that he would require at once five hundred head of cattle, an equal number of hogs, and at least three thousand chickens. He was especially anxious to obtain as many fowls as possible, for he had definitely promised that all who obtained jobs would have chicken dinners twice a week. There was great excitement among the butchers, the immediate effect of which was an increase in the prices of all sorts of meat. One enterprising butcher had in his pens fifty fat hogs awaiting slaughter, and to make certain of a sale to Lozier he drove them north and penned them near Kingsbridge, where he fed them for almost a month at considerable expense.

With his food supply assured, Lozier engaged a score of small contractors and carpenters to furnish lumber and to superintend, under his direction, the building of the great barracks which were to house the workmen during the sawing operations. A separate building, to be constructed of the best materials, was ordered for the convenience of the twenty or thirty women, wives of laborers, who had been employed to cook and wash for the entire crew. Several of these contractors let their enthusiasm get the better of their judgment and actually hauled a dozen loads of lumber to the northern end of the island and dumped them near Kingsbridge. They implored Lozier to let them begin building, but he said that actual construction must wait until he had engaged all the men he would need and had assembled all his materials. It was his intention, he announced, to muster his workmen at a central meeting-place when everything was ready and march them in a body to Kingsbridge. He assured the contractors that by using a new method of building which he had devised, but which he declined to disclose in advance, they could easily erect the necessary buildings within a few hours.

The excitement was now at fever heat, and Lozier added fuel to the flame by producing elaborate plans for the various appliances which were to be used in the project. First, there were the great saws with which Manhattan Island was to be cut loose from the mainland. Each was to be one hundred feet long, with teeth three feet high. Fifty men would be required to manipulate one of these giant tools, and Lozier estimated that he would need at least a score. Then there were twenty-four huge oars, each two hundred and fifty feet long; and twenty-four great cast-iron towers, or oar-locks, in which the oars were to be mounted, twelve on the Hudson River shore and twelve on the East River. A hundred men would bend their backs at each oar, and row Manhattan Island down the bay after the sawyers had finished their work, then sweep it around and row it back. Great chains and anchors were to be provided to keep the island from being carried out to sea in the event that a storm arose. Lozier gave the plans and specifications of these Gargantuan implements to a score of blacksmiths, carpenters, and mechanics, who retired forthwith to their shops and feverishly began to estimate the cost, and the quantities of material that must go into their manufacture.

Lozier now turned his attention to the unskilled laborers whose names Uncle John DeVoe had set down as potential sawyers and rowers. He sent word for them to report at Centre Market for examination and announced that he would pay triple wages to those who performed the hazardous work of sawing off that part of the island which lay under water. The longest-winded men would be awarded these dangerous but desirable jobs. Laborers swarmed to the market, and every day for a week Lozier sat enthroned on a bench while man after man stepped forward and held his breath. As each displayed his prowess, Uncle John DeVoe timed them and entered the result in his ledger.

Lozier kept delaying the commencement of actual work by professing dissatisfaction with the estimates on the oars and towers and by insisting that he had not hired nearly enough men to do the job properly. At last, however, "the numbers became so thick and pressing," as DeVoe put it in The Market Book, that Lozier was compelled to fix a date for the grand trek northward. He hurriedly awarded the contracts for manufacturing the saws, oars, and towers, and ordered them rushed to completion. He then instructed all who were to have a hand in the great work to report at the Bowery and Spring Street, where they would be met by a fife and drum corps which he had thoughtfully engaged to lead the march to Kingsbridge. The exact number who appeared at the rendezvous is unknown, of course, but DeVoe says that "great numbers presented themselves," and there were probably between five hundred and a thousand persons. Laborers were there by the score, many accompanied by their wives and children; the contractors and carpenters drove up in style, escorting wagons laden with lumber and tools; the butchers were on hand with cattle and hogs, and carts loaded with crated chickens. Practically every one who had ever heard of the project was there, in fact, excepting Lozier and Uncle John DeVoe. When several hours had elapsed and they still had failed to appear, a volunteer delegation went to Centre Market in search of them. They found a message that both Lozier and Uncle John had left town on account of their health.

The crowd at Bowery and Spring Street milled about uncertainly for another hour or two, while the hogs grunted, the cattle mooed, the chickens cackled, the children squalled, and the fife and drum corps industriously dispensed martial music. At length, for the first time in weeks, if not in years, some of the more intelligent of Lozier's victims began to think, and the more they thought, the less likely it appeared that Manhattan Island would ever be sawed off. Gradually this conviction spread, and after a while the crowd began shamefacedly to disperse. A few of the more hot-headed went looking for Lozier, vowing that if they couldn't saw Manhattan off they could at least saw Lozier off, but they never found him. Lozier and Uncle John DeVoe had fled to Brooklyn as soon as Lozier had issued his final instructions, and had sought refuge in the home of a friend. There was much talk of having them arrested, but no one seemed willing to make a complaint to the authorities and so admit that he had been duped, and both Lozier and Uncle John went scot-free. However, it was several months before they again appeared at Centre Market, and when they did, Lozier found himself an oracle without a temple. The Centre Market statesmen had had enough.

THE WONDERFUL RABBI OF RIVINGTON STREET [3]

The little Hungarian Jewish synagogue on Rivington Street is still famous for its wonderful red-headed Rabbi. It was not only his beard that was wonderful, for that was a rare beard indeed, being the color of rich salmon and the size of a small mattress, but it was the extraordinary miracles he performed in his unique career that made him so passionately admired. The ladies far and wide in the world around Rivington Street swore that his holy amulets never failed to bring children in barren households. There were few diseases indeed that he could not cure, for faith can vanquish all evil, as everybody knows. And he was the holiest of men. A blessing from the red-headed Rabbi of Rivington Street was no small matter. It always brought good health, good luck, and prosperity. And his miracles were the pride of the congregation and the neighborhood.

The real test of his power, however, was yet to come, was yet to startle the faithful as nothing had before. For the Rabbi could and did *stop Time itself in its tracks*, with the help of God, and this is how it came to pass:

One sunny Friday the Rabbi took his favorite disciple and went to visit a first cousin in the Bronx. They spent quite a while over herring and tea, and it was not early when they bestirred themselves for home. It is a far cry from the East Bronx to Rivington Street, and it happened that they were not too familiar with the subway, and took the slow asthmatic local. So that as they were riding home it became evident that they had started too late, that they would never reach home before sundown, and that the Sabbath would be upon them while they were en route. The sin of riding on the Sabbath was more than the disciple could bear.

"Rabbi," he cried, the tears starting in his eyes. "What shall we do? In a few minutes it will be the Sabbath, Rabbi. What shall we do?"

The Rabbi of Rivington Street puckered his lips and stroked his flaming beard. His mouth moved, but no sound came out. He looked carefully around him, at the miscellaneous fellow passengers, at the cold cream ads, the cereal ads, the nose drop ads. He stroked his beard while the disciple stared at him with great distraught eyes. "Rabbi," he began again.

But the Rabbi silenced him with one gesture of his pale hands. "Enough. God will not forsake us in this trial. Have faith. I will pray."

And he prayed there in the subway, while the astonished crowd looked on. The disciple later told of the look on his face. It was the look of an angel, he said—"only of an angel, I tell you."

[3] From *Manhattan Mythology*, Manuscripts of the Federal Writers' Project of the Works Progress Administration in New York City. Deposited Library of Congress, 1940.

"God will not forsake us," said the Rabbi calmly after he had prayed. "The will of God is all-powerful."

No sooner had he said these words than a faint gold mist, barely perceptible to the naked eye, surrounded both of them. It was sunlight. "Lo!" said the wonderful Rabbi. "For us it is still Friday!" And their hearts rejoiced. For Friday was with them until they were safely home, while for the rest of the passengers on all sides, nay, for the rest of the world, it was already the holy Sabbath.

The wonderful Rabbi of Rivington Street had once more performed a miracle, the greatest miracle of them all. Once more the faithful sang his praises and rejoiced. For what other synagogue could boast a Rabbi like theirs?

SARATOGA CHIP [4]

. . . The Saratoga chip . . . was to the Saratoga potato even more than the popover was to the Bar Harbor biscuit. First served almost exactly one hundred years ago, at Moon's Lake House in 1853, the development of the chip was the result of a cook's outburst of temper. The cook of the old Moon's was an irascible half-breed named George Crum, the son of a mulatto jockey and an Indian woman. No man to trifle with, he had no less than five wives, all of whom he apparently kept happy at once and all of whom served as waitresses in his establishment. When a fastidious diner sent back Crum's French fried potatoes with the comment that he wished them sliced thinner, Crum, in the time-honored manner of cooks, hit the ceiling. He shaved off some potato slices paper-thin, wrapped them in a napkin and plunged them into a tub of ice water. Then, after he had kept the diner waiting for a full half hour, he first dropped the chilled slices into a kettle of boiling grease, then ladled them out and salted them, and, finally, more or less as a practical joke, sent them in to the diner by one of his wife-waitresses. Instead of the commotion and indignation Crum expected, the diner promptly called for more. Then and there, the Saratoga chip was born. Moon's immediately saw in the discovery an excellent thirst-producer, one well calculated to increase liquor consumption, and that very day distributed the chips free to patrons in paper cornucopias; by the next day chips were placed in a huge bowl on the bar with a sign reading, Saratoga style: "HELP YOURSELF."

THE WISTAR PARTY OF PHILADELPHIA [5]

Among the most delightful of [Philadelphia's] clubs, and possessing even more than a usual degree of exclusiveness, is the Wistar Party. To belong to this very limited club, membership in the Philosophical Society is prerequisite, and even that is by no means a certain open sesame, a unanimous vote of the

[4] From *The Last Resorts*, by Cleveland Amory, pp. 411-412. Copyright, 1948, 1952, by Cleveland Amory; 1951, 1952, by the Curtis Publishing Company. New York: Harper & Brothers.
[5] From *The Book of Philadelphia*, by Robert Shackleton, pp. 206-208. Copyright, 1918, by the Penn Publishing Company. Philadelphia.

Wistar members being required. And it is a club such as could come to existence in no other city than this.

Doctor Caspar Wistar was one of the descendants of a Wistar who was one of the early settlers of Pennsylvania. There were, indeed, two Wistars, brothers, and in course of time the descendants of one spelled their name "Wister," while the others continued it as "Wistar"; or it may be doubtful which was actually the original spelling; but at any rate, by some freak, some whimsy, there came to be a social cleavage, and those of the Wistars with an "a" were gradually given, in general estimation, a higher social standing than the Wisters of the "e." And this long-ago distinction has continued so strongly in force, even up to present times, that you will find many prejudiced and precise people, if they chance to speak of Owen Wister, the distinguished author, consider, as much more important than his *Virginian,* the fact of whether his wife, also a descendant of the early Wistars, is of the present-day "e's" or "a's."

Doctor Caspar Wistar was a surgeon of high professional standing, and at the same time a man of highest social standing. He was also a man of most hospitable ways, and he gathered at his house, one evening in each week, numbers of his closest friends, with the understanding that any distinguished visitor from out of town was also to be brought by any of them. It was a gathering for men only, and the club still holds to that old-time rule. Wistar died in 1818, but so important had the parties become, as social features, that it was decided to continue them, and the club was formally organized, to meet in turn at the homes of the members. And evenings with the Wistar Party are among the most delightful experiences that this city can offer. The form of invitation, for visitors, is still the form of long ago; a card, headed "Wistar Party," bearing a little vignette of Doctor Wistar.

And the doctor is remembered in one of the most charming of all possible ways, for there is named after him a vine which clambers up the front of myriads of houses in this and other cities, in this and other countries, one of the most beautiful of all flowering vines, delicately tossing to the breeze the pale purple of its plumes; for the French botanist Michaux, who visited America and met Wistar and loved him, named in his honor the Wistaria.

The old Wistar House still stands, carefully tableted and preserved, and is one of the most interesting of early Philadelphia homes. . . .

THE GRACIOUS GHOSTS OF DOVER, DELAWARE [6]

The most famous of [Dover's] historic wraiths, perhaps, is the ghost of Chief Justice Samuel Chew, who died in his great house on the Green, but whose ghost, from some whim, would appear on moonless nights beneath a poplar tree beside a road leading into town. Judge Chew's ghost frightened so many tavern-bound rustics back to their firesides that evening business in Dover groggeries slumped severely. The tavernkeepers then had a grave dug beneath

[6] From "The Cities of America: Dover, Delaware," by Harold H. Martin, *The Saturday Evening Post,* Vol. 222 (August 20, 1949), No. 8, p. 80. Copyright, 1949, by the Curtis Publishing Company. Philadelphia.

the poplar and hired a preacher to read a burial service, committing Judge Chew's restless shade to the earth in which his body had been lying for some time. It seemed to work.

Several Doverites report, unperturbedly, that they have seen visitors from the other world or have felt their presence. Mrs. Lou Tilghman, secretary of the Chamber of Commerce and an extremely factual sort of person, distinctly remembers seeing what must have been the ghost of a little girl, wearing a quaint old-fashioned dress of red-checked gingham, standing by the pool in the garden at Woodburne. Mrs. Ridgely, who is known for her sound judgment, her wit and her keen, incisive mind, has also seen one. Late one afternoon, she says, in an upstairs room in her house, she saw, quite clearly in the summer gloom, a tall and beautiful lady dressed in clinging robes. She recognized her as a relative who had died in that room years before.

The only specter moving about in Dover at the moment is the one which is said to haunt the residence of Mr. and Mrs. Lee Layton, Jr., on State Street. This is the ghost of a tall, handsome, gray-eyed gentleman of mature years. Mrs. Layton first saw him the day they moved into the house. "He moved across the upper hall and bowed and smiled as if welcoming us there," Mrs. Layton says.

The Layton ghost ambles about the house quite freely, nodding and smiling amiably. He is now such a familiar figure that Michael, the Layton Chesapeake retriever, and Beatrice Perkins, the Layton cat, merely raise their heads and watch him as he passes. His one mildly exasperating trait seems to stem from his frugality. He drifts out onto the back porch after supper and turns off the light over the refrigerator. This disturbs the cook, who is afraid to go out and turn it on again. Finding that his presence made it difficult for her to keep servants in the house, Mrs. Layton once thought of asking a minister to conduct some sort of service of exorcism, such as that which laid to rest the ghost of Chief Justice Chew. After thinking the matter over, though, she decided not to. It would be a discourtesy, she felt, to such a friendly spook.

Dover's most famous haunted house is also one of its oldest and finest. Stately Woodburne, on the King's Highway north of the Green, was built about 1790, and in the years before the Civil War was a busy station on the Underground Railroad which aided escaping slaves in their journey to freedom in the North. Woodburne is supposedly haunted by a solemn-looking old gentleman in old-fashioned clothing, who doesn't seem to do much but stalk about the place, looking morose. This disembodied spirit, Dover says, once passed Lorenzo Dow, the famous backwoods evangelist, on the stairs at Woodburne as Dow went down to join his host and hostess at breakfast. When they asked Dow to say grace, he asked if they did not wish to wait for the other guest whom he had just met on the stairs. That wasn't a guest, they explained; it was a ghost—one of the lady's forefathers who habitually wandered about the place. The present owners of the house have never seen him, but he seems to be still around, for they have told friends that they have felt his presence and have turned aside to let him pass them on the stairs.

LEGEND OF THE WASHINGTON CATHEDRAL [7]

A great deal of legend had already grown up about the Washington Cathedral, though it wasn't even finished. One was about a laborer who had worked on the cathedral for years and become infused with its spirit and wanted to have his wife buried there. When he was refused, the story goes, he had her cremated, and then one day he dropped the ashes in a barrow of fresh cement, and his wife was forever entombed in the cathedral he loved. Nobody but the man himself, if there was one, knew whether the story was true or not. Bishop James E. Freeman said no such request was ever made of him. But it might have happened before he became bishop. Cathedral officials said it could easily be true, and they thought it probably was.

THE WHITE HOUSE GHOSTS [8]

When night settles over the White House, does the ghost of Lincoln roam the lonely corridors? Does the wraith of Andrew Jackson send bursts of eerie laughter echoing from the Great Beyond? Have the macabre shadows that are said to lurk in the moonbeams of the Oval Room a spectral leg to stand on? Or are these "phantoms"—which caused overnight guests to keel over in a faint and servants to flee—merely illusions created by curtains shimmering in the breeze, and ancient beams groaning under the weight of history?

The notion that our Executive Mansion might be haunted isn't just a wild pipe-dream of my own. The idea would seem preposterous had it not been dignified by a mention from President Harry S. Truman's own pen in the book, *Mr. President.* Tucked away in his diary entry for May 27, 1945, on page 116, is the following passage:

"My daughter and her two pals, Jane Lingo and Mrs. Wright—both lovely kids, are sleeping in Lincoln's bed tonight! If I were not afraid it would scare them too badly I would have Lincoln appear. The maids and butlers swear he has appeared on several occasions. It is said that even Mrs. Coolidge saw him."

Now here was an admission that no reporter could afford to disregard: an intimation by the President of the United States that he might be sharing the White House with a ghost—and a Republican President at that.

I decided this was one ghost story worth investigating.

My first hope was that Mr. Truman would write it himself. He agreed to discuss this possibility in Kansas City. When I arrived at his office the ex-President stepped briskly from behind his desk, shook my hand warmly and thanked me for making the long trip from New York. The Democratic leader struck me

[7] From *Home Country*, by Ernie Pyle, p. 21. Copyright, 1947, by William Sloane Associates, Inc. New York.

[8] From *The Legend of Ghosts in the White House*, by Leslie Lieber, *This Week Magazine*, April 25, 1954, pp. 7, 31, 45, 50. Copyright, 1954, by the United Newspapers Magazine Corporation.

as the sort of down-to-earth man who would have dealt firmly with any ghosts who happened to worm their way into his administration.

During our conversations, Mr. Truman demurred at actually doing the article himself. However, he did express himself openly on the subject.

It was true, he said, that people in the White House sometimes claimed to see ghosts. He had first heard about them from his barber in the White House. The main ghost, Truman learned, was allegedly the visible spirit of the Great Emancipator.

According to the legend, this wraith becomes especially troubled and restive on the eve of national calamities, such as war. At such times, Mr. Truman told me, White House staffers who are "attuned" to such things insist they can hear Lincoln's boots pacing worriedly back and forth on the second floor.

We asked Mr. Truman if he personally had ever sensed anything "spooky" during his tenancy. He prefaced his answer with a cautious reminder that many old houses creak at the seams like storm-tossed schooners. And prior to its face-lifting operation in 1947, the Executive Mansion was structurally 4-F—a nightmare of sagging ceilings, falling plaster, leaning walls, shaky chandeliers, cracked bricks and moldy pine planks—vintage 1814.

The ancient woodwork could account for most of the ghost alarms. But Mr. Truman cited at least one incident that might qualify as "creepy." In fact, he said, the same thing had happened to him twice during the war.

He had been awakened in the night by a rapping on his bedroom door. Each time he thought it was somebody notifying him that Winston Churchill was phoning from London. He got out of bed, hastened to the door, opened it—and stood aghast. Nobody was there.

I left Kansas City determined to peer deeper behind the gossamer curtain. Next stop: Eleanor Roosevelt. Frankly, I expected Mrs. Roosevelt to refuse to discuss the subject. I was wrong. The former First Lady, who had used Lincoln's bedroom as her sitting room, gave me more than I had bargained for.

"Ghost scare? Yes, you might say we had one shortly after we moved into the White House," said Mrs. Roosevelt. "It was in 1934. There was a member of the staff named Mary Eban. One afternoon she went to the second floor. She couldn't have been up there more than three minutes. But when she ran downstairs she was terribly wrought up. She gasped that she had just seen Abraham Lincoln seated on his bed pulling on his boots."

I asked Mrs. Roosevelt if she ever had any "contact" with the eerie side of the White House.

"It's the same thing in all creaky old houses," she declared. "If you're prowling around late at night you get a feeling that 'someone is there.' Old-timers in the White House are more conscious of Lincoln than of other Presidents because each room he used is marked by a plaque. My own sitting room had been his bedroom. Sometimes when I worked at my desk late at night I'd get a feeling that someone was standing behind me. I'd have to turn around and look."

Mrs. Roosevelt then volunteered another strange incident.

"One day, Carl Sandburg, a man steeped in Lincoln lore, dropped in to the

White House for a chat with Franklin. The poet and the President soon drifted to the subject of Lincoln, speculating as to which room he had used to compose certain letters. Mr. Sandburg said he had always felt the work had been done in the Oval Room—so they decided to go in there.

"While Franklin sat meditating in silence, Sandburg stood quietly at the window that faces the Potomac Flats—the very window where Lincoln often stood during the Civil War, gazing toward the front in Virginia. For fully ten minutes Mr. Sandburg looked out. No word broke the silence. Then, suddenly, he turned around and, with great finality, said: 'Mr. President, this is the room.' "

The story had an additional uncanny twist. In the past half century, several employees have reported seeing Lincoln's gaunt apparition standing at that very Oval Room window.

At this juncture I sent a letter to James C. Hagerty, press secretary to President Eisenhower, asking for the Republican viewpoint on ectoplasm. While awaiting an answer, I searched library shelves for reference to supernatural doings in the White House. There was evidence aplenty.

The memoirs of Ike Hoover, Chief Usher of the White House for over 40 years, abound with specters. The household of William Howard Taft, for instance, was shaken by a ghost scare. It was sparked by the most prolific ghost-glimpser in the Mansion's history, a janitor named Jerry Smith.

"Old Jerry," as he was called, had feather-dusted the premises since the days of Ulysses S. Grant. He swore the place was haunted not only by Lincoln but by Grant and William Henry Harrison (who died in the White House) as well.

The Taft administration evidently held an unusual attraction for the "other side."

For it was during this regime that employees began reporting daily sightings of their first woman ghost—Abigail Adams, wife of the second President. The first First Lady in the White House was known to have used the East Room to string out the family wash. Servants claimed to see Abigail walking at daybreak right through the closed doors of the East Room.

The Wilson administration also has a lady ghost to its credit. This one appeared following an order to the gardener from Mrs. Wilson to transplant some rosebushes from one spot to another.

A few hours later, pandemonium broke loose. From all sections of the White House came reports that dainty Dolly Madison was up and around. She had been spotted hovering dejectedly around the garden, sniffing for roses that weren't in their old familiar plot.

Sure enough, it was discovered that the original bushes had been planted by Dolly Madison. She was reputedly annoyed at their having been moved. But after a few days of earthly prowling she vanished from the garden and hasn't been seen since.

Brimming with such spine-tingling history, I was somewhat let down by my answer from James C. Hagerty. He had forwarded my letter to Howell G. Crim, inheritor of Ike Hoover's job as Chief Usher.

"After working around the clock for over twenty years," he wrote, "I have never seen, heard or felt it or them. Neither has any other employee presently on duty here."

I can sympathize with Mr. Crim's desire to stamp out ghost yarns. But a telephone call to old John Mays, White House doorman and greeter for over 40 years, put me back on the track of enough "ghosts" to last a lifetime and several hereafters.

"The man you want to see is the ex-valet of President Franklin D. Roosevelt," he said. "They say he ran out of here one night into the arms of a guard, shouting that he had just seen Lincoln."

We found the ex-valet at his home in Washington. He was reluctant to talk. "I don't think President Eisenhower would like it if he knew the White House was haunted," he said.

He finally opened up with the proviso that we disguise his name. So we'll call him "Mr. Camacho." He was FDR's valet and houseman for 11 years. He is now employed in the U.S. Post Office, where, incidentally, he has never spied a ghost, even in the dead-letter department.

But they were sure swarming thick as flies in the White House.

"Whenever someone close to the White House was going to die," he told me, "a painting would fall off the wall for no apparent reason. Once I was standing next to the President when one of his marine paintings fell to the floor in the next room. Each time someone in the White House died the same day or the following one.

"The night before FDR's mother died at Hyde Park, there was such a scuffle of footsteps in the Blue Room that Harry Hopkins got annoyed. He told me to see who was making all the noise. It wasn't anybody."

During the war, continued Camacho, a very famous woman was staying at the White House. She was accompanied by a secretary and a lady-in-waiting. [*Editor's note:* Possibly Queen Wilhelmina of Holland.] Her quarters were the Rose Room, which later housed the King and Queen of England.

"One evening the butler and I were serving cocktails to the guest and the President. The great lady turned to Mr. Roosevelt and made the startling announcement that she had fainted the night before. The President was shocked and asked what had happened. 'Someone knocked on my door in the middle of the night,' she said. 'I got up and opened it and—I know this sounds ridiculous —but I saw Abraham Lincoln standing there. Then everything went black and I came to on the floor.'"

One morning while making his rounds, Camacho came upon a well-known couple hurriedly packing their bags.

"Is anything wrong?" he asked.

"Wrong?" said the husband. "I'll say there is. We've just spent the most miserable night of our lives. Somebody—my wife insists it was a ghost—was trying to set fire to our beds all night long."

At one time Camacho was disturbed by a voice emanating from the ceiling of the Yellow Room.

"It repeated over and over again, 'I'm Mr. Burns, I'm Mr. Burns.' At first the only connection I made was with Mr. Byrnes, the Secretary of State. But one day, a year after I left the White House employ, I ran across an item in an old history book: in the 1790's the land for the White House was donated to the U.S. government by a man named Burns."

Katurah Brooks, a White House employee from 1931 to 1938, makes no bones about a strange experience she had.

"One night," she said, "I was working late in the Rose Room. There was no one else on the second floor. Suddenly a burst of laughter—loud and booming, like out of a cavern—came from what somebody told me was the old Andrew Jackson bed. I ran out of that room as fast as I could, and never wanted to go back."

Does this article prove that the White House is or has been haunted? You've read the evidence. You be the judge. But nobody can deny that over a long period of years, sincere people on the inside have reacted with various shades of horror and fascination to what they considered to be genuine visions.

Delvers into the supernatural say that a renovation, such as the White House underwent in 1950, would scatter any lingering specters to the four winds. So perhaps today Mr. Crim is right, and the ghosts have fled. The "Andrew Jackson bed" may have had its last laugh. The beams may have been silenced, and the curtains stilled.

But should I ever be invited to spend a night at the White House, I think I'd sleep with the lights turned on.

THE PAWNEE WAR AT RICHMOND [9]

One Sunday, soon after Virginia's succession, Richmond, now the Capital of the Confederacy, was startled by the ringing of the tocsin. Back and forth swung the great bell up in the tower on Capitol Square—back and forth, back and forth, loudly protesting—and the churches were emptied of their menfolk.

What had happened? every one was crying.

Then at last the news:

The Governor of Virginia had received official intelligence that the Yankee sloop of war *Pawnee* with 10-inch columbiads had passed City Point, sixty miles below, and was steaming up the James toward Richmond, which it meant to shell, burn, and raze.

But with the regular troops gone off to another front, who would defend the city?

The First Virginia Volunteers, to whom military tactics were still largely matters of theory, their sole experience being "dry land engagements with partridges and squirrels," lined up alongside Randolph's battery of light howitzers.

How equip them?

[9] From *Virginia Is a State of Mind,* by Virginia Moore, pp. 222-224. Copyright, 1942, by E. P. Dutton & Co., Inc. New York.

Men caught up rusty old fowling pieces and duck guns of prodigious bore, says Bagby (to whom I owe this story), falchions which had let fly at Cornwallis, pistols of odd calibre without caps, flintlocks without flints, and a blunderbuss so laden with verdigris it could pass for a "cucumber of precocious growth." Though it was Sunday, the gunsmith Sunderland did a rousing business. When he had sold all his guns, he offered bowie knives and old dirks.

Till some one thought of the Virginia Armory and a bevy of citizens rushed off to haul out the pair of magnificent, quaintly embellished bronze guns presented to Virginia in the name of the French Government half a century ago by the Count de Rochambeau. Hoisting them onto a dray, the strange cavalcade roared down Broad Street to the Custom House. But no ball or cartridge in the city would fit the guns. They had to abandon them on the street!

Meanwhile a motley host had marched off to the wharves with horse pistols, clasp knives, brandy flasks, and haversacks stuffed with cold ham and biscuit; and soon Church Hill, high above Rockett's, swarmed with onlookers ensconced in steeples and hanging out of windows.

But where was the *Pawnee?* Not a puff of smoke! At last the sun set in the west. Twilight deepened. The army had made a stand at Rockett's all right—had halted for fresh quids of tobacco!

That night the troops bivouacked on the James in the mild air, and the next morning called it a jolly frolic.

And, come to think of it, how could the *Pawnee* ascend the river as far as Richmond? At places the channel ran so close to the banks a single felled tree would serve as a barricade. Moreover, the *Pawnee* was a wooden ship, vulnerable to pot-shooting from the steep bluffs on the farms of Mr. Drewry and Mr. Chaffin. Why, the foolhardiest Annapolis midshipman would realize the madness of such a project!

"Extra! Extra!" shouted the newsboys, waving short slips of yellow Confederate paper.

Richmond held its sides.

One of the reports carried out of the city by self-appointed messengers was that the Pawnee Indians, surging down the Central Railroad, had taken possession of some Richmond suburbs and were tomahawking and scalping at a frightful rate.

THE BULL OF DURHAM

I [10]

When you approach Durham by road from any direction, you note that the landscape is dominated by the tall steel water tanks (American Byzantine) of its tobacco factories. These lend support to the hotly contested theory of some students that the Civil War conferred benefits upon the South other than

[10] From "Durham: The New South," by David L. Cohn, *The Atlantic Monthly,* Vol. 165 (May 1940), No. 5, p. 615. Copyright, 1940, by the Atlantic Monthly Company. Boston.

those contained in the book and motion picture called *Gone with the Wind.*
For example: the tobacco industry.

On a soft April day about seventy-five years ago, thousands of men wearing
uniforms of blue or gray were gathered at a little hamlet in North Carolina
called Durham's Station. They played games, swapped horses and stories, and
enjoyed the novelty of fraternizing with the enemy. What if they were soldiers
of the opposing armies of Generals Sherman and Johnston who were camped
near by awaiting battle? Durham's Station was a neutral area by mutual con-
sent, where Yank and Reb met to play. Here the men found a house full of
smoking tobacco that had been manufactured by John R. Green for Confederate
soldiers, but when the house was sacked the tobacco was equitably divided
between the Blue and the Gray. (The moral holiday of war is sometimes observed with punctiliousness.) Later the groups separated, fought the battle
demanded by the conventions of the military, Johnston surrendered to Sherman,
the Civil War receded into history, and the men scattered to their distant homes.

American boys were once taught at home and in school that, if you worked
hard, served your boss well, and saved your money, you might become rich.
Chance, according to these teachers, played no part in the rise of any man
worthy of the name; it was even deplored as slightly immoral; it flew in the
face of the early-to-rise, early-to-bed doctrine of success. Let's see the workings
of chance at Durham's Station, as the postmaster received letters from ex-soldiers
asking where they could buy tobacco—the same soldiers who had stolen it at
Durham's Station. The letters were turned over to John R. Green—the same
Green who had been the victim of the robbery. He now sacked some of his
tobacco and mailed it to his erstwhile despoilers whom peace had turned into
paying customers. The accident of war had given him at small cost the nucleus
of a national distribution of his product, and set him on the road to riches. Mr.
Green called his brand Bull Durham Smoking Tobacco. The Bull of Durham
was to go everywhere in the world, roll up great wealth for his owners, create an
industry, a town, and a giant source of revenue to the federal government.

At first Bull Durham went into pipes alone, but later in the nineteenth
century, and much of the twentieth, millions of coatless men walked the summer
streets of America with a sack of Bull attached to a shirt button, and cigarette
papers for making "coffin nails" in their pockets. The ability to roll one's own
deftly, with a minimum of saliva and under any conditions of wind, came to
be a badge of manhood which the unskilful envied and to which youth aspired.
America had become the greatest tobacco-producing and tobacco-consuming
country in the world, and Durham one of its most important provincial capitals.

II [11]

. . . An enormous bull, painted on paneled sheet iron, decorated the
front of the [Bull Durham factory] building and the steam whistle, by means of
a mechanical gadget, imitated the bellow of a bull. Each bellow, it was said, cost
six dollars and could be clearly heard thirteen miles away. The bull was the

[11] From *Tobacco Tycoon,* The Story of James Buchanan Duke, by John K. Winkler, p.
44. Copyright, 1942, by John K. Winkler. New York: Random House.

masterpiece of J. Gilmer Kerner, eccentric and temperamental artist, whose sign-painting nom de plume was "Reuben Rink." Raging and triumphant, Reuben Rink's bulls seemed to paw the ground and emit flame from their nostrils. Eventually they appeared on barns and boulders and billboards throughout the country, even in Europe and the Near East; and to Reuben Rink is credited the catch-phrase description of Durham as the "Town Renowned the World Around."

THE THIRSTY DEAD OF TRUMBO'S COURT [12]

Before Trumbo Street ran through the old Gardiner property from Trapman Street west [in Charleston], the dead-end roadway was known as Columbus Trumbo's Court. At the corner stood the building afterward known as the Trapman Street Hospital. This was not Dr. Ogier's hospital for colored folk in Wilson Street, where the Methodist church is now, but Dr. Chisholm's, afterward a soldiers' hospital during the Confederate War. It stood on the southwest corner of Trapman Street and Trumbo's Court, halfway between Broad and Queen Streets.

It was a long, low wooden building, quite unbeautiful. Its north wall abutted on the pavement in Trumbo's Court, so that a girl could chat with a friend in the street from the lower floor windows. There were piazzas along the south side of the house, low built, with boxed wooden columns painted white. The house itself was painted a dull slate blue or leaden gray, one cannot be sure just which; but it makes no difference. When the tenants in Trumbo's Court looked out of their windows at night, the hospital building was just the color of fog, only a little more solid. There were eighteen rooms in the building; and under them a basement for storage. It was into the basement they carried the dead, and set them in rows on stretchers.

The old house is gone now; a cyclone wrecked its roof, and an earthquake shook the chimneys down. A tenement took the place where the hospital had stood; and the people living in the tenement did not like to mention the subject.

Nothing ever grew where the hospital stood; not a green leaf or blade of grass; not even vetch grew there, though vetch will grow almost anywhere.

It was a private hospital until after the savage fight at Secessionville. Many young men from the town died there, or were brought back to town covered with wounds. The hospital was a shambles; for the young men were shot, cut with sabers, stabbed, torn and run through by bayonets, their faces were beaten in by gun butts, and their lips were often already black with mortification; all were white from loss of blood. There was time neither for mercy nor delay in that place: there were sixteen rooms full.

For lack of proper surgical instruments wounds were probed with straws snapped from the brooms which swept the hospital floors; there were no ano-dynes to ease their agony. There was no laudanum, no morphine, no opiates of

[12] From *The Doctor to the Dead*, Grotesque Legends & Folk Tales of Old Charleston, by John Bennett, pp. 123-127. Copyright, 1943, 1946, by John Bennett. New York: Rinehart & Company, Inc. [As told by Mary Simmons, cook and washerwoman.]

any sort; there was not even whisky: the blockade had prevented their entry. A little to ease the festering wounds the surgeons gathered the jelly bags of the ladies of the town, filled them with moss or cotton, soaked them in cool well water, and hung them so that the slow drip from their evaporating damp might fall upon the inflamed wounds and cool them if but a trifle. But the weather was intensely hot; gangrene is swift; the wounded died like flies. Death stood waiting in the piazza.

Afterward the house was sold. Nobody would move into it, until, long after, a poor colored washerwoman, attracted by the low rent, moved into a room on the upper floor with her lazy bitch of a daughter. There was nobody else lodged in the house but a colored harlot or two, who also had rooms on the upper floor.

At the end of the lower piazza a flight of wooden steps went down to the ground; and a few yards from the steps was an old well from which the household drew its supply of water. It was an old-time well, such as one may still find in old yards about the city, closed by a shield-shaped cast-iron lid, lifted by an iron ring. The lid was too heavy for a dead man to lift. So that the drinks of the dead were long between and their thirst very great.

One close, hot night in midsummer, the upper rooms were full of a choking heat and steam. The women were trying to finish a two weeks' wash in one, a wash already overdue. They were behind with the rent, also, and were working hard to be done. Thirsty with the heat, the steam, and the toil, the old woman said to her daughter, "Go fetch a bucket of water from the well, that we all may drink." The daughter, a perverse, bitchy girl, said, "No; I won't carry water for harlots or horses. . . . You may go get it yourself." So the woman herself took the bucket, and went down alone through the dark house and along the piazza to the well.

As she lifted the heavy iron lid and the cold, stagnant smell of the water puffed up into her face, something behind her heaved a long sigh. Startled, she looked behind her; but there was nobody. She let the bucket down into the well, gave a jerk, let it fill, drew it up brimming full, and started back to the house.

As she came to the piazza steps and lifted her arm before her, so that, by lifting the bucket, the water might not be spilled by the bucket striking the steps, something she could not see took the bucket out of her hand. The starlight was bright in the open, bright enough for her to have seen any one there. She saw nothing. But something took the bucket out of her hand.

She saw it go up the steps, one, two, three . . . and then, as she stared dumfounded, she saw it go along the piazza, lifting, tipping, and swinging along in scallops through the air, there was nothing but the empty wind, while she stood gasping at the piazza steps.

At the peak of each long scallop, the bucket paused, stood still, tipped sidewise; and then went swinging on again in the swooping scallops. After each pause she heard, there in the empty piazza, long-drawn breaths and deep, contented sighs, such as thirsty men heave when, after long hours of waiting, their thirst at last has been quenched. All the while not one drop of water was spilled from the bucket's rim.

Then the bucket came back, swinging, scalloping, rising and tipping, down the outer side of the piazza, turned itself in the air, with never a visible hand to hold it, and offered itself, handle-to, for her taking.

Knowing that the dead had taken it out of her hand to quench their thirst, she durst not touch the handle; but cried out, "Oh, Jesus! No. Take the bucket away!"

The women upstairs heard her cry out, and hurried down to see what had befallen. They found her crouched against the piazza steps on her knees; and, beside her, on the steps, the bucket, still wet, but without a drop of water in it.

The woman who had borne the bucket and drawn the water was taken by a long trembling which lasted three days.

If ever a woman told the truth, this is true; I was there, and saw it. I was the perverse bitch of a daughter. And the man from whom we rented those rooms was Henry Gardiner whom everybody knows.

THE FOUNTAIN OF YOUTH [18]

. . . Although Ponce de Leon is said to have sought for [the Fountain of Youth] in vain, it was actually "discovered" by a refugee from the Klondike named Louella Day McConnell. Mme. McConnell, who was none other than Robert W. Service's "Lady Who's Known as Lou," was an old harpy with a foghorn voice who had seen literally everything before she descended on St. Augustine. There she chose to support her declining years by erecting a concession on what she declared was the exact spot on which Ponce de Leon first set foot on American soil.

The fountain—or rather a slow-flowing spring—had apparently been under Ponce's feet, although he failed to recognize it for what it was. Lou did, though, and in return for the price of admission—then five cents—she offered tourists as much of its rejuvenating water as they could drink. Doubting Thomases who complained were told that the water was so full of iron it was worth a nickel whether it rejuvenated them or not.

When Lou was eventually requested by the municipal authorities to cease gulling the public, she is said to have replied indignantly, "But there is iron in that spring! I know, because I threw an old cookstove in it."

The same concession, prettied up, is operated today by Walter B. Fraser, many times St. Augustine's mayor, its state senator until Pope defeated him, and still the city's foremost politician and promoter. In addition to being president-manager of the Fountain of Youth Enterprises, Inc., Fraser, a native of Georgia, is also the proprietor of The Oldest Wooden Schoolhouse and The Oldest Orange Grove.

At The Fountain of Youth, attractive girls in Spanish-looking costumes herd visitors around the elaborate park—it is a really beautiful spot—that Fraser has developed on the site. The [1949] price of admission [was] eighty cents, includ-

[18] From "The Cities of America: St. Augustine," by Leigh White, *The Saturday Evening Post*, Vol. 221 (March 5, 1949), No. 36, p. 100. Copyright, 1949, by the Curtis Publishing Company. Philadelphia.

ing the Federal amusement tax. Among the wonders on display are some old Spanish water jars and a cemetery full of the skeletons of what are said to have been the first Indians to enjoy Christian burial in the United States. On the way out you are urged to inspect such wares for sale in ye olde Spanish gifte shoppe as a needle-point fire screen said to have been woven in the time of Mary Queen of Scots.

The Fountain of Youth? It's still there, just as in Lou McConnell's time, although Fraser has since built a Spanish-looking "ruin" around it. One of Fraser's *señoritas* stands near by to serve you a drink of its water in a sanitary paper cup.

"This is The Fountain of Youth," she intones, with a fixed, professional smile. "Drink a glass of this and you'll grow ten years younger."

I asked Fraser if the water was still full of iron, but he dismissed the subject with a wave of his hand and began to tell me about his plans for establishing a Pan-American university in St. Augustine. He inaugurated the project a few years ago by shipping half-gallon bottles of free water—"from The Fountain of Youth"—to every governor in the United States and to every president of the Latin-American republics. He has since pasted the polite but non-committal replies he received into the black leather scrapbooks which he offers as proof of the regard in which his effort to recreate American history is held.

Fraser is resigned to skepticism, however, for on the wall of the living room of his luxurious home is the following quotation from Elbert Hubbard: "Never explain. . . . Your friends don't need it, and your enemies wouldn't believe it anyway."

They don't, even though Fraser hands out folding business cards with a picture of The Fountain of Youth on one side and two choice testimonials on the other. One of the testimonials, dated October 3, 1931, is signed "Ruth Bryan Owen, Member of Congress." It reads, "Although Florida is a mine of historical treasure, it remained for your vision and artistry to create, of this birthplace of American history, a shrine of unforgetable [*sic*] beauty."

DUELS UNDER THE OAKS [14]

Within sight of the cemetery [on the old Metairie race track in New Orleans], a part of the same ridge of land, sinking into the same stretch of swamp, lies another relic of past time and civilization—the old dueling ground, now a park, a cemetery, too, in its way, although but one tomb stands there, that of its last owner, who, infatuated with love for his beautiful oaks, requested to be buried under the shadow of their branches. In the childish days of the city, when disputes were scarce, we hear of the officers drawing their swords and fighting for pastime in the moonlight on the levee; for other humors there were always quiet and retirement to be found anywhere outside of the city walls. When the *émigrés* from France and the islands arrived with their different times and different manners, and when the disbanded soldiers from Bonaparte's

[14] From *New Orleans, The Place and the People*, by Grace King, pp. 292-295. Copyright, 1895, by The Macmillan Company. New York.

armies dropped into the population, there was as great a renaissance in dueling, as in the other condiments of life, so to speak. Fencing masters flourished, and "salles d'escrime" were the places of fashionable culture for young men. In Paris, gentlemen would step out and fight *à l'impromptu* "sous le fanal de la comédie." Young blades, returning from Paris, sharpened by encounters over there with blades noted in the whole European world, must therefore fight also *à l'impromptu* "sous le fanal de l'opéra," otherwise the great lantern of the Orleans theater, whose circle of light on a broad, smooth pavement furnished as pretty conditions for the settlement of a question about a soprano's voice or a ballet dancer's steps as could be desired anywhere. The weather not permitting this, all adjourned to Ponton's, the fashionable fencing room, just below the theater. "When we fought at Ponton's." "Oh, he gave me a beautiful thrust at Ponton's." . . . This was the beginning of many a good friendship, and of many a good story of the fathers, uncles, cousins, and elder brothers of the young gentlemen at the Orleans college.

The stories of another generation take in the Oaks. What a trooping of ghosts under the old trees, if all the votaries of honor who had fought or assisted others to fight there could revisit the place in spirit! What a throng would mine host of the restaurant opposite have to welcome, if all who quaffed a glass, in a happy reprieve from death or wounds, at that bar could return again! And he was the man of all in the city, it was said, who could, if he would, tell as much as the old oaks. Everybody fought with everybody then; the score of duels was kept like the score of marriage offers of a belle. Individuals counted up eighteen, thirty, fifty of them. Mandeville Marigny fought with his brother-in-law. A father and a son fought duels the same day. On one Sunday in 1839 ten duels were fought. "Killed on the field of honor!" The legend is a common enough one in the old cemeteries.

Besides the great national differences between the Americans and Creoles, which were settled in a great national way, with shotguns and rifles, there was every other imaginable difference settled under those trees—politics, love, ballroom etiquette, legal points, even scientific questions. A learned scientist, an hydraulic engineer, permitting himself to say (in justice to him, it was to exaggerate the importance of some personal theory) that the Mississippi was a mere rill in comparison to rivers in Europe, a Creole answered him: "Sir, I will never allow the Mississippi to be disparaged in my presence by an arrogant pretender to knowledge." A challenge followed, and the mouth of the defamer was cut across from one cheek to another. In a ball-room a gentleman petitioned a belle: "Honor me with half this dance?" "Ask monsieur," she answered, "it belongs to him." "Never," spoke her cavalier, bearing her off in the waltz, and just catching the softly spoken, "Ah, vous êtes mal élevé." Not a word more was said. The next morning the critic received a challenge and in the afternoon a neat thrust. Almost every day for years the Gascon cowherds in the neighborhood would see pilgrims on foot or in carriages wending their way to the Oaks; and the inquisitive would peep, and in the cool green light under the trees, witness the reparation of honor as required by the code; a flashing, pretty sight from a distance, when the combatants were lithe and young and the coliche-mardes worthy of their art.

NEEDLE AND BLACK BOTTLE MEN [15]

"No, sir!" declared Mamie Smith emphatically, her eyes huge and white in her fat black face. "I sure don't go out much at this time of year. You takes a chance jest walkin' on the streets. Them Needle Mens is everywhere. They always comes round in the fall, and they's round to about March. You see, them Needle Mens is medical students from the Charity Hospital tryin' to git your body to work on. That's 'cause stiffs is very scarce at this time of the year. But them mens ain't workin' on my body. No, sir! If they ever sticks their needles in your arm you is jest a plain goner. All they gotta do is jest brush by you, and there you is; you is been stuck. 'Course I believes it!"

Hundreds of New Orleans Negroes believe it. Fear of the Needle Men, which dates back to early days, could possibly be traced to voodooism. Then epileptics were thought to have had a spell cast upon them. Sometimes such an individual would die in the streets during an attack, and when this occurred Negroes were certain the Needle Men had been at work. Mamie believes in protecting herself from these corpse-hunting "students."

"Sure, I carries my gun," she said. "I always got it with me. I don't fool around! Any of them Needle Mens come after me they gonna be makin' stiffs of theirselves. Oh, yes, I goes to church. I been on the board 'leven years now. I jest been 'pointed head of the toilet committee. My duties is to show the new members where the toilet is at."

Apparently, Needle Men have actually appeared on several occasions, though this is debatable. In 1924 there was a Needle Man scare in the Carrollton section of the city. It was reported that these "fiends" slunk about the darkest streets, sprang from behind trees or from vacant lots overgrown with weeds, jabbed women with their needles and fled. Cruel skeptics insinuated the "victims" were suffering from a combination of imagination and Prohibition gin, but indignant females, of all colors, swore to the existence of these particular Needle Men.

On a Sunday night in February, when good citizens were returning from church, the police managed to arrest a pair of Negroes, one armed with a twenty-six-inch bayonet. The man with the bayonet protested he packed the weapon to protect himself against the Needle Men, but the police were certain they had their man. Both prowlers were tried in night court, sentenced to thirty days, and the Needle Men vanished from Carrollton.

Only a few years ago Needle Men appeared, according to reports, and began stabbing young women while they were seated in moving-picture theatres, ren-

[15] From *Gumbo Ya-Ya*, A Collection of Louisiana Folk Tales, compiled by Lyle Saxon, State Director, Edward Dreyer, Assistant State Director, Robert Tallant, Special Writer, pp. 75-77. Material Gathered by Workers of the Works Progress Administration, Louisiana Writers' Project. Copyright, 1945, by the Louisiana Library Commission, Essae M. Culver, Executive Secretary. Boston: Houghton Mifflin Company.

dering them partially unconscious and carrying them off into white slavery and a fate "worse than death." For months in New Orleans downtown cinemas, women were screaming and fainting and crying out they had been jabbed with a needle. But so far as can be ascertained, the period offered no more disappearances than usual, nor is it known that any New Orleans women strayed down the primrose path via this particular route.

Similar to the Needle Men, at least in intent, are the Black Bottle Men. The Black Bottle is reputed to be a potent dose administered to the innocent and unknowing on entry to the Charity Hospital. Instant death is certain to follow, the body then to be rendered up to the students for carving.

The explanation for this is simple. Every person entering Charity Hospital is given a dose of cascara upon admission. Pure cascara is nearly black and when magnesia is added, as is the custom, it becomes a deep brown, the change in color causing Negroes to fear it is a death-dealing drug.

HENRY FORD AND THE TWELVE CLOCKS [16]

It was in the Baker Street Jewelry Shop that Henry Ford went to work when he was 16 years old. This is how it came about: Henry, ambitious to find a larger field for his talent for machinery, left the Dearborn farm and went to Detroit. He arranged for board and lodging at the home of Mrs. James S. Payton, 452 Baker street. The consideration was $3.50 a week. But his job at the James Flowers' Bros. Foundry & Machine Shop paid him only $2.50. Here was born the young mechanic's first major problem in finance, a subject in which he was years later to demonstrate himself as something of a wizard.

The extremity drove him to the Baker Street Jewelry Shop at Baker and Twentieth streets, where he renewed an agreeable acquaintance with one Robert Magill, a former Dearborn neighbor, who was now the proud proprietor of the shop. The two struck a bargain. For the sum of fifty cents a night, Henry was to sit in the workshop in back of the store and repair what clocks and watches found their way to the premises. It was a happy arrangement for both parties. Henry closed the deficit for board and room, with something to spare. Magill became possessed of the services of a young genius. But how was Magill to know that away back then?

Henry was kept tucked away at his workbench in the small back room, concealed from the prying eyes of Magill's canny clients. For Magill was shrewd enough to know that his customers would never entrust their treasured timepieces to the ministrations of a mere stripling. A man to handle watches had to know his way about the delicate mechanism. He couldn't be just an ordinary country lout!

So Henry had to use the side door and he had to be careful to keep well-hidden among the dials and pendulums. John S. Haggerty, another schoolboy pal, recounts the fiction of Henry's summary dismissal from Magill's employ because of a too great efficiency. Magill, it appears, went forth one evening to

[16] From In Old Detroit, by George W. Stark, pp. 56-57. Copyright, 1939, by Arnold-Powers, Inc. Detroit, Chicago, New York.

fulfill a social obligation. He enjoined on Henry the necessity of looking after the trade, but warned him not to do any actual labor within sight of the customers.

When Magill returned he found twelve clocks that had been sitting in silent gloom for several days, ticking right merrily. They were in full flight and fine fettle. In Magill's absence, Henry had fixed them all! The Haggerty version has it that Magill was so infuriated that he discharged the hapless Henry on the spot. That would be nice to believe, but it strays slightly from the truth. It is one of the small exaggerations of the legend. What really happened was that Magill first anxiously inquired if Henry had performed the miracle of the twelve clocks in the seclusion of his own small workshop, or if he had performed any of his magic in the presence of the trade. Henry assured his employer that it had all been done in the seclusion of his own private precinct. Magill was highly pleased. So was Henry Ford. It was his first triumph in mass production!

MRS. O'LEARY'S COW [17]

THE GREAT CALAMITY OF THE AGE!
CHICAGO IN ASHES!

The South, the North, and a Portion of the West
Divisions of the City in Ruins.

All the Hotels, Banks, Public Buildings, Newspaper
Offices, and Great Business
Blocks Swept Away.

THE CONFLAGRATION STILL IN PROGRESS

"Chicago is burning! Up to this hour of writing (1 o'clock P.M.) the best part of the city is already in ashes. . . . The entire South Division, from Harrison Street north to the river, almost the entire North Division, from the river to Lincoln Park, and several blocks in the West Division are burned."

So read the opening lines of *The Evening Journal-Extra*, Chicago, Monday, October 9, 1871—the only downtown paper issued in Chicago on that date.

*   *   *   *   *

"The fire broke out," says the *Journal-Extra*, "on the corner of De Koven and Twelfth [rather Jefferson] streets, at about nine o'clock on Sunday evening, being caused by a cow kicking over a lamp in a stable in which a woman was milking. An alarm was immediately given, but owing to the high southwest wind, the building was speedily consumed, and thence the fire spread rapidly. The firemen could not, with all their efforts, get the mastery of the flames."

This was, be it observed, the very first appearance of *The Cow*. How largely she has figured in the pages of history since then is known to all the world.

[17] From *Reminiscences of Chicago During the Great Fire*, by Mabel McIlvaine, pp. xiii-xviii. Chicago: The Lakeside Press, R. R. Donnelley & Sons Company. [N.d.]

The reader's attention is called to the fact that in this account the cow did the kicking in the presence of the lady, but that the latter's name had not yet been dragged into the affair.

After the lapse of nine days, in *The Chicago Times* of October 18, we read: "Flames were discovered in a small stable in the rear of a house on the corner of De Koven and Jefferson streets. Living at the place indicated was an old Irish woman. . . . On the morning of the fire she was found by a reporter for *The Times* sitting on the front steps of her own house. . . . At first she refused to speak one word about the fire, but only screamed at the top of her voice, 'My poor cow, my poor cow! She is gone and I have nothing left in the world.' Finally she was induced to talk, and this is what she said: It had been her regular nightly habit to visit the stable and see if her cow was all right. On Sunday night, about 9½ [*sic*] o'clock, she took a lamp in her hands and went out to have a look at her pet. Then she took a notion the cow must have some salt, and she set down the lamp and went in the house for some. In a moment the cow had accidentally kicked over the lamp, an explosion followed, and in an instant the structure was enveloped in flames."

**THE LEGENDARY START OF THE GREAT
CHICAGO FIRE**

The woman who lived at the place indicated was Mrs. Patrick O'Leary, 137 De Koven Street, about three doors from Jefferson Street.

The points to be noted in this *non verbatim* interview are, that the lady was not herself present at the moment of the kicking, and that in any case the cow did it *accidentally!*

Further light is shed upon the subject by a document which has recently been deposited at the Chicago Historical Society by Mr. S. H. Kimball, of Oak Park, Illinois, from which we are permitted to quote:

I saw the start of the fire from the roof of our house. . . . Tuesday morning Mr. Clarence Merriam, a young man with a remarkable talent for drawing, called at our house and asked my brother Arthur and myself to go with him to the location where the fire started, as he wanted to make some sketches. We reached the O'Leary house, and immediately proceeded to what was left of the shed where the fire started. As I recall the matter, the south wall of the shed was still standing, but the balance of the shed had been nearly destroyed by fire. My friend commenced to make a drawing, and I began looking for some memento, as I was at that time a relic collector. . . .

We had hardly been there but a few moments when Mrs. O'Leary came out with a broomstick in her hand and drove us away. . . . The three of us immediately went to a spot to the east and south of the house, where my friend started to make a sketch of the house. . . . I slipped back again to the shed. . . . As I was looking about, I noticed that one of the planks in the floor of the shed had been broken, forming a V-shaped space. This space was filled with burnt hay, and a glitter and sparkle caught my eye. Leaning down I picked up the bottom of a small glass lamp.

I slipped this into my pocket with the excited feeling that I had in my possession the bottom of the lamp which set Chicago on fire. I ran to my brother and friend and told them to follow me as fast as they could. . . . During the following months I gathered a fine bunch of Chicago Fire relics, which I put in a large cabinet. . . . Finally we hired an Irish cook. One day I was showing her these relics, and when I showed her the piece of lamp she was very much excited and told me that she could tell me how the Chicago Fire started, but that I must say nothing about it.

It seems she lived in the vicinity of the O'Leary house, and knew the O'Learys. She also had a family of friends living near the O'Leary's. She made the statement to me that a lot of young people were having a dance the evening the Fire started. They wanted to make a little punch but were out of milk, and someone suggested that they go over and milk Mrs. O'Leary's cow. They picked up a glass lamp which was in this house, and went to the shed, and, while attempting to milk the cow, the lamp was kicked over, and they fled.

I showed her the piece of lamp, and she said she was very positive that it was the style of lamp that they had in their house. She seemed greatly excited about the matter and got my promise that I would say nothing about it for fear these people should get into trouble. A very short time after that she left the house, without giving any warning, and we were never able to locate her. Soon after she left I found that this piece of lamp had disappeared.

The cow, the lamp, and the bowl of punch have been made much of in Chicago for reasons of our own. The fact that we had fifty-six miles of wooden-block pavement, and six hundred and fifty-one miles of wooden sidewalks might have seemed too much like "preparedness." And the other facts of our having but one pumping-station in the whole city, and that roofed with wood, together with our fourteen fire-engines among some three hundred thousand inhabitants —these things are too inconvenient to discuss. Then, too, our custom of allowing landlords to erect wooden cottages in the immediate vicinity of gas works, and at the approaches to bridges and tunnels—well, we knew better, but we did not like to appear militant.

THE CHRISTMAS TREE SHIP [18]

As long ago as 1887 the two Schuenemanns, Herman and August, had sailed down in a schooner from Manistique, Michigan, with a load of spruce and tied up beside the dock behind the old-red-brick commission houses at the Clark Street bridge. There Chicago found them and bought their stock, and called Herman captain and remembered to look for him the following year. When snow fell on Chicago's streets in December days, the father of the family would say, "Guess I'll have to go down to the Clark Street bridge to see if the captain is in and get us a tree."

Fifty years ago the work of providing trees for Christmas was not yet the mass-production business it has become in recent times. No dealer contracted for thousands of trees as a speculation and destroyed great numbers if he had guessed wrong on the demand. No man cut down whole hillsides to satisfy the whims of people who followed a custom but didn't know how to pray. There were plenty of trees for all. The Schuenemanns went into the woods behind Manistique and Thompson, Michigan, where young trees grew on land that had been cut over to make the lumber that went into midwestern houses a generation before. They chose the trees carefully, including some tall ones for which they had orders from churches and hotels. Sometimes they had to work in the snow and when the trees reached Chicago there was still snow on the branches. The brothers thought they had done well when they made a modest profit on a trip that occupied about six weeks of the wintry season, when it was hard to haul other cargoes.

The work was not easy, neither the cutting nor the sailing, for they always came when Lake Michigan kicked up a lot of rough sea. In 1898 August had just set sail with a load of trees when a storm arose and he and his ship were lost. Thereupon Herman determined to carry on alone. In 1899 he was back at the Clark Street dock with his boat, the *Rouse Simmons*, loaded with Christmas trees. He was a jovial man, with a very ruddy complexion and laughing wrinkles around his blue eyes, and everybody liked him.

For eleven years Herman arrived with his cargo and many people depended on him for a tree year after year. Then came the hard season of 1912, with storms and heavy seas on Lake Michigan. Late in November Herman cut his trees in the woods behind Manistique and started for Chicago in the *Rouse Simmons*, with a crew of seventeen men. There were head winds and heavy seas from the start, and soon the schooner was struggling in a raging snowstorm. What took place on board we can only guess. The *Rouse Simmons* sailed into the silence that covers all the fine ships that have fallen victim to the gales of Lake Michigan, which have taken the lives of so many, from the days of La Salle's *Griffon* until now.

[18] From *The Chicago*, by Harry Hansen, pp. 241-245. Copyright, 1942, by Harry Hansen. New York: Rinehart & Company, Inc.

Long before Chicago missed the *Rouse Simmons* at its dock reports began to come of the ship's distress. A schooner resembling it was said to have been sighted off Kewaunee, Wisconsin, flying distress signals. The steamer *George W. Orr* reported to the revenue cutter *Tuscarora* that she had seen the *Rouse Simmons* three miles offshore, but the captain later admitted that he might have been mistaken. But on December 5, 1912, fishermen off Two Rivers Point, seven miles north of Manitowoc, Wisconsin, found the tops of spruce trees entangled in their nets. Trees had been roped together on the deck of the *Rouse Simmons,* and how could they get into the lake at that point if not off a ship?

On December 13th a watcher on the beach at Sheboygan, Wisconsin, reported that he had picked up a bottle containing a message that came from the captain. It had been written on a page of the ship's log and read:

> Friday—everybody goodbye. I guess we are all through. Sea washed over our deckload Thursday. During the night the small boat was washed over. Leaking bad. Ingvald and Steve fell overboard Thursday. God help us.
>
> Herman Schuenemann

The men referred to were believed to have been Steve E. Nelson, mate, and Ingvald Nylons, seaman. But if there was such a message, it never reached the captain's wife, who was eagerly waiting for scraps of news in her Manistique home. She was a valiant little woman, with a great deal of stamina. When she realized that her three little girls, Elsie and the twins, Pearl and Hazel, were now dependent wholly on her efforts, she resolved to take up her husband's task.

There was no Christmas ship at the Clark Street dock in 1912. But when 1913 came, Chicago residents who looked over the railings of the bridge beheld another schooner, loaded with trees, as in the days when Captain Herman held forth there. On board was the plucky little wife of the captain. She had gone into the woods with the woodcutters and supervised the felling of the trees. With her, too, were her girls, as well as women to weave wreaths and garlands. Chicago was to become well acquainted with the Schuenemanns. They were to come season after season for twenty-two years after the *Rouse Simmons* went down.

For years Chicago friends would ask the captain's wife whether there had been any definite report on the *Rouse Simmons,* and she could only shake her head sorrowfully. Yet the sea, which guards its secrets well, reluctantly gave up tangible evidence fourteen years after the disaster. On April 23, 1924, the wallet of Captain Schuenemann was found at Two Rivers Point, where the spruce trees had been tangled in the fishermen's nets. It still had the original rubber band around it and the cards and clippings inside seemed to be made of plaster. Some of the clippings related to earlier voyages of the Christmas tree ship. Three years after this find a bottle with a note signed by Charles Nelson was picked up. It read:

> These lines were written at 10:30 P.M. Schooner R.S. ready to go down about 20 miles southeast Two Rivers Point, between fifteen or twenty miles off shore. All hands lashed to one line. Goodbye.

Eventually the family made its last voyage to the Chicago market with Christmas trees. The mother had grown gray; the girls were handsome young women. Forty-seven years had elapsed since Herman, as an 18-year-old lad, had steered his first cargo into the Chicago. The ship had become an institution.

Its fame grew. Today when the winds blow hard on the lake and the heavy surf pounds the frozen shore line, watchers in the lighthouses recall the *Rouse Simmons*. Long ago it inspired a ballad. When word of its loss reached Chicago newspapers Vincent Starrett, bibliophile and author of many books of fiction and belles-lettres, was a reporter on the *Daily News*. His editor was Henry Justin Smith. "It would make a fine ballad," said Starrett. "Why don't you write it?" replied Smith. So Starrett composed "The Ballad of the Christmas Ship," a poem of many, many quatrains, and Smith found room for it among the crowded columns of the day's news. It may never challenge the efforts of youthful orators as often as "The Wreck of the Hesperus," but the legend is just as moving and the intentions of the poet were as good as Longfellow's.

THE DEVIL BABY AT HULL HOUSE [19]

The knowledge of his existence burst upon the residents of Hull House one day when three Italian women, with an excited rush through the door, demanded that he be shown to them. No amount of denial convinced them that he was not there, for they knew exactly what he was like, with his cloven hoofs, his pointed ears and diminutive tail; the Devil Baby had, moreover, been able to speak as soon as he was born and was most shockingly profane.

The three women were but the forerunners of a veritable multitude; for six weeks, from every part of the city and suburbs, the streams of visitors to this mythical baby poured in all day long and so far into the night that the regular activities of the settlement were almost swamped.

The Italian version, with a hundred variations, dealt with a pious Italian girl married to an atheist. Her husband in a rage had torn a holy picture from the bedroom wall saying that he would quite as soon have a devil in the house as such a thing, whereupon the devil incarnated himself in her coming child. As soon as the Devil Baby was born, he ran about the table shaking his finger in deep reproach at his father, who finally caught him and, in fear and trembling, brought him to Hull House. When the residents there, in spite of the baby's shocking appearance, wishing to save his soul, took him to church for baptism, they found that the shawl was empty and the Devil Baby, fleeing from the holy water, was running lightly over the backs of the pews.

The Jewish version, again with variations, was to the effect that the father of six daughters had said before the birth of a seventh child that he would rather have a devil in the family than another girl, whereupon the Devil Baby promptly appeared.

Save for a red automobile which occasionally figured in the story and a stray

[19] From *The Long Road of Woman's Memory*, by Jane Addams, pp. 2-6. Copyright, 1926, by The Macmillan Company. New York.

cigar which, in some versions, the new-born child had snatched from his father's lips, the tale might have been fashioned a thousand years ago.

Although the visitors to the Devil Baby included persons of every degree of prosperity and education, even physicians and trained nurses, who assured us of their scientific interest, the story constantly demonstrated the power of an old wives' tale among thousands of men and women in modern society who are living in a corner of their own, their vision fixed, their intelligence held by some iron chain of silent habit. To such primitive people the metaphor is still the very "stuff of life," or rather no other form of statement reaches them; the tremendous tonnage of current writing for them has no existence. It was in keeping with their simple habits that the reputed presence of the Devil Baby should not reach the newspapers until the fifth week of his sojourn at Hull House—after thousands of people had already been informed of his whereabouts by the old method of passing news from mouth to mouth.

For six weeks as I went about the house, I would hear a voice at the telephone repeating for the hundredth time that day, "No, there is no such baby"; "No, we never had it here"; "No, he couldn't have seen it for fifty cents"; "We didn't send it anywhere, because we never had it"; "I don't mean to say that your sister-in-law lied, but there must be some mistake"; "There is no use getting up an excursion from Milwaukee, for there isn't any Devil Baby at Hull House"; "We can't give reduced rates, because we are not exhibiting anything"; and so on and on. As I came near the front door, I would catch snatches of arguments that were often acrimonious: "Why do you let so many people believe it, if it isn't here?" "We have taken three lines of cars to come and we have as much right to see it as anybody else"; "This is a pretty big place, of course you could hide it easy enough"; "What are you saying that for, are you going to raise the price of admission?"

THE RAILROAD COMES TO IOWA CITY [20]

The work of construction in Iowa had been delegated to the firm of Farnam and Durant. On June 30, 1855, the Davenport *Gazette* announced that the first iron rail had been laid in Iowa. In July the locomotive "Antoine Le Claire" was ferried across the Mississippi to Davenport. The work progressed so satisfactorily that on August 28th a special excursion train was run to Walcott. The press prophesied that the railroad would reach Iowa City by December 1st. It did actually arrive at midnight on December 31, 1855, just before the dawn of the New Year.

The citizens of Iowa City had done all within their power to bring about an early arrival of the railroad. Wm. Penn Clarke and LeGrand Byington had gone to Davenport to meet representatives of the Mississippi and Missouri Railroad. They went prepared to subscribe for stock in the enterprise and to offer a bonus of $50,000, provided a train of cars drawn by a steam locomotive should reach the depot at Iowa City on or before December 31, 1855. Resolved to meet

[20] From *The Old Stone Capitol Remembers*, by Benjamin F. Shambaugh, pp. 382-383. Copyright, 1939, by the State Historical Society of Iowa.

the offer, the management of the road urged the construction crews to do their utmost to reach Iowa City. Tradition illuminates the story.

By nine o'clock on the evening of December 31, 1855, the iron rails had been laid to a point within one thousand feet of the Iowa City depot. Could the goal be reached before midnight? Many citizens joined the regular track-layers in their effort to complete the work. The weather had turned to bitter cold, the thermometer registering many degrees below zero. Huge wood fires were kindled along the line to warm the men and light the way. At eleven o'clock the trackmen had reached an elevation that was not more than two hundred feet from the depot.

Exhausted and numb with cold, the workmen applied themselves in an heroic effort to complete "the last lap." At this critical moment the engine "froze up." With the assistance of officers and volunteers the remaining rails were hastily laid upon temporarily placed ties. Then workmen and volunteer citizens with pinch bars and outstretched arms pushed and pulled the frozen engine to the end of the track "just as the church bells began to welcome the incoming New Year." Rousing cheers went up from the crowd of workmen. Charles Strickles, the engineer, fell unconscious beside his frozen engine.

THE LINCOLN SALT BASIN LEGEND [21]

Lincoln, Nebraska, my home town, was selected in the mid-nineteenth century as the capital of the state chiefly because of the now-vanished salt basin a few miles to the west. In my youth, the basin proper, the "big basin," was about a mile long and half a mile wide. It was early a salt lick for Indians and buffalo. When my parents came to Lincoln, its large white expanse was the leading feature of Lancaster County. It attracted visitors of all types. In pioneer times settlers came from near and far to scrape up salt crystals or to trade with others for them if recent rains had flooded the basin.

The area was discovered by government officials in 1856 and it must have been much larger then, perhaps very large in still earlier times. In the 1890's there were salt basins extending six miles north of Lincoln along the west bank of Salt Creek, a stream flowing northeast into the Platte. The "big basin" was the southwestern one. It was thought that millions would be made from it. Horace Wesson of the Smith and Wesson firearm manufacturing firm expended some $50,000 in all, a large sum for that day, for the improvement of the basin. But the project was not successful: not a cent was realized by his or any other serious attempts to develop the basin. The salt springs in the southern part were active in producing brine; but the overflow of the near-by Salt Creek bottoms after the rains carried down the creek the vats damming the salt. Work was stopped, too, by disputes over the title to the region. Investigators finally reported that the production of salt from the brine, found at the depth of several hundred feet, could not be made profitable. When the railroads came, cheaper

[21] From "The Legend of the Lincoln Salt Basin," by Louise Pound, *Western Folklore*, Vol. X (April 1951), No. 2, pp. 109, 110-111, 115, 116. Copyright, 1951, by the California Folklore Society. Berkeley.

salt could be brought from Utah and Kansas and soon salt could also be had
from Michigan. The optimistic dreams of vast wealth to be derived from the
location of the capital city near the salt basin were not realized.

Salt Creek, which so hampered the development of the basin, has been
straightened at various times in later years and some of it has been drawn off.
It is now a far from impressive stream, whatever it may have been once. Apparently it was large enough in earlier times not to be overlooked. . . .

. . . In the second decade of the eighteenth century is the first mention of
the Platte and Salt Creek region, its supply of salt and the Indians' knowledge
of it. The narrative of Lewis and Clark, early in the nineteenth century, notes
that they reached the Saline River on July 21, 1804. On the river were Otoe
and other villages. Lewis and Clark did not ascend the stream as far as the salt
basin.

Late in the nineteenth century the water from Oak Creek, a stream from the
northwest, was turned into the salt basin and a small "lake," so called, was
formed, making mild boating possible for a time. The picturesque and historic
white expanse of basin disappeared for good. Newcomers to Lincoln know
nothing of it. "Capital Beach," which succeeded it, became an amusement park
and its salt-water swimming pool formed a chief attraction. By this time, the
mid-twentieth century, the main body of water from Oak Creek has been
diverted to form Oak Park Lake some distance northeast.

Though no traces of Indian villages or burial grounds have been found in
the salt basin area to indicate that Indian tribes ever stayed permanently in
the vicinity, their knowledge of it is unmistakable. W. W. Cox, historian of
Seward County, says that as late as 1862 a vast throng of Omaha Indians
camped at the head of the basin, adding that Indians often came there on their
way to their summer hunting grounds on the Republican River. The Omaha
Indian word or name for the salt basin is said to have been *niskithki*.

Apparently all over Nebraska in pioneer days names were given to conspicuous natural features by Indians and whites. Then the whites created some
legend, often originated or written up in a poem, to account for the name, and
the legend came to be ascribed to the Indians. That a legend should be associated with so striking a natural feature as the Lincoln salt basin was inevitable.
The legend is now all but forgotten by Lincoln people, like the basin itself,
and its origin is nearly forgotten too. . . .

*   *   *   *   *

Here is a version of the legend from the 1930's. . . . It was obtained from
Irene Courtenay Johnson of Atkinson, Nebraska, the granddaughter of a Lincoln pioneer. . . .

When John Irving, [1812-1906, nephew of Washington Irving] who
was searching for material for a new book, came to the unsettled land of
Nebraska in 1833, he heard of the salt basin which was located near the
present site of Lincoln. In answer to Mr. Irving's inquiries about the fertile
source of the salt the Indians related an old legend of the tribe.
The Otoe Indian tribe was living about thirty miles west of Omaha on

the present location of Ashland. A strong young chief of the tribe had taken for his bride a beautiful Indian maiden whom he loved. They had not lived together many moons when the dark-eyed girl became ill and died. Sorrow and grief overtook the young chief, and he became so sad and restless that he determined to leave the tribe.

From that time onward the brave was a wanderer; he often went on trips by himself from which he would not return for many weeks. It was while he was on such a trip down the Saline river that the unhappy Indian saw a vision—or was it a reality? As he was paddling down the stream by night the chief heard a cry from the shore. When he looked up he saw an old squaw with a club beating a younger woman. The brave went to the rescue but as he neared the two the hag pulled the maiden's hair so that her face was lighted by the moon. To the chief's horror he recognized the features as those of his buried bride. He raised his hand to strike the squaw but as he lowered it the two figures turned into a block of salt.

Thus the salt basin came into being.

*   *   *   *   *

. . . On the whole, the record of the Lincoln salt basin, gone now and forgotten like the Indians and buffalo that haunted it, seems to me a melancholy one. The [white, pseudo-Indian] legend is all that remains, and I do not see how it can outlast much longer the historic expanse of salt that it purported to explain.

HOW HENRY OVERHOLSER SAVED OKLAHOMA CITY [22]

. . . When the depression of 1893 struck the town [of Oklahoma City], the population shrank to 4000 people. . . . Two of the four banks had closed, and there was a run on another. [Henry] Overholser had no financial interest in this institution; indeed, it was controlled by rival interests. But he caught the first train for Guthrie and advised the territorial treasurer to place all public funds in the threatened bank at once.

Well, the territory didn't have much money either, and $5000 in silver and currency was the best that could be managed. But Overholser, it develops, had mastered the oblique art of public relations long before such experts as Ivy Lee and Eddie Bernays had mastered their alphabets. He wired ahead to have guards ready for the transfer of $25,000 from the railroad station to the bank. The silver was put in canvas bags—and also in canvas bags were placed all the available iron nuts and washers which could be bought, borrowed, or stolen from Guthrie's hardware stores. The bank notes were carefully wrapped in packages, and so were thousands of sheets of blank paper cut to a similar size.

When the train arrived, there were armed guards there to meet it. There were armed guards on the horse-drawn drays and armed guards at the bank entrance. There was also a line of depositors—or, more properly, withdrawers —who extended far down the street. Ostentatiously, the bags of money and

²² From "The Cities of America: Oklahoma City," by Milton MacKaye, *The Saturday Evening Post*, Vol. 220 (June 5, 1948), No. 49, p. 129. Copyright, 1948, by the Curtis Publishing Company. Philadelphia.

currency were carried into the bank. There every one could see the silver dollars and the bank notes as the packages were opened. The pieces of blank paper and the bags of nuts and washers provided a handsome background for the spectacle. Within a few minutes, the run on the First National Bank had vanished.

All this, of course, was highly illegal. Overholser had risked not only his own reputation but that of the territorial treasurer, who was, as a matter of fact, his own father-in-law. Both would have been ripe for prison sentences if the stratagem had not been successful. But it was successful and Oklahoma City saved.

THE SHAM BATTLE IN ALBUQUERQUE [23]

Colonel Sellers, President of the New Mexico Territorial Fair, decided to liven things up by staging a sham battle involving Indians, cowboys, and a real troop of US Cavalry. As the Colonel had lived on the Navajo Reservation and was a convincing cuss he readily assembled his cast. In San Juan County he recruited seventeen cowboys and two hundred Navajo men, women and children. Captain Clark at Ft. Wingate promised a troop of cavalry. The cowboys and the soldiers made their own way to Albuquerque. The Colonel and José Platero, an educated Navajo with perfect English, rode across with the Navajos—five days from San Juan County to Albuquerque.

The Navajo men were mounted and so were many women, riding a-stride as no white women did then, with ample calico skirts swinging free. On their backs rode babies tied to boards. Older women, swarms of children, supplies, and finery of velvet, calico, sateen, and silver came in covered wagons. Colonel Sellers had supplemented the Indians' own grub with plenty of bread and at Pueblo Bonito he bought two steers for them to butcher and barbecue. All went well as the Navajo who acted as chief maintained good order. He was Peshi Cli, a stern, rock-faced old man. The cavalcade camped at Alameda and rode on into Albuquerque west of the river because the road that is now Highway 85 was so sandy that animals could not haul loaded wagons through it. They reached Albuquerque the evening before their big performance on Thursday, *Albuquerque Day*.

Colonel Sellers' plan was good. He was to ride out onto the baseball diamond in the center of the half-mile race track, mounted on his big gray, and portraying a lone wanderer on the desert wastes. Indians were then to attack, dashing out of hiding, whooping and shooting. Enter cowboys, also whooping and shooting. They all had plenty of blank cartridges supplied by the US Army. Sham battle then with odds favoring the Indians until the arrival of the Cavalry, thirty mounted men, riding hard with pennons fluttering, guns smoking and cracking. Defeat of Indians. Rescue of the intrepid Colonel and his gray horse.

The show was scheduled for two o'clock. When Colonel Sellers reached the

[23] From *Erna Fergusson's Albuquerque*, pp. 69-70. Copyright, 1947, by Erna Fergusson. Albuquerque: Merle Armitage Editions.

Fair Grounds about one the Grand Stand was already filling up with people who had brought their lunches and spent the morning in the exhibit halls. A good clear day. Fat watering carts had laid the dust a little. Indians were ready with Peshi Cli in command. Cowboys resplendent beyond belief. Cavalry rested in the shade while their mounts cropped grass growing among the pigweed along the track. Street cars, loaded on platforms, steps and roofs, came creaking up behind pitifully straining and sweating half-starved horses. Everything was ready.

José Platero came up to Colonel Sellers and spoke low. "Colonel, you see Peshi Cli eating there with those men? They're all wearing their own six-shooters; not the ones the Army issued. I think there's trouble coming. That Peshi Cli got in trouble with Captain Clark last year out beyond Pueblo Bonito . . ."

Without waiting for the end of the story, Colonel Sellers moved. Silent as a cat he stepped up behind Peshi Cli, just reaching into the pot for a hunk of mutton. Deft and quick he grabbed the Indian's gun from its holster, broke it, and revealed live cartridges.

"Call McMillan," he said. "Dis-arm these other guys." With Peshi Cli's gun he was covering ten Indians. "José, you tell 'em to put up their hands. The first man that moves I'll kill him sure!"

In a matter of seconds Chief McMillan and his men were there and the disarmed Indians were packed into a buggy and hauled off to the New Town jail. A search revealed thirty guns, all loaded. Those Navajos were going to revenge their arrest a year before at Pueblo Bonito.

But the show must go on. People in the Grand Stand had seen nothing. Promptly at two o'clock Colonel Sellers rode onto the baseball diamond in the center of the half-mile track . . . The battle proceeded according to plan. There was plenty of whooping, but no shooting.

Years later Colonel Sellers met General Cook on a train and began to tell him the story of the sham battle that almost turned out to be no sham. "Yes," said the General, "I know all about it. The affair was reported to Washington and the Army issued orders that there should never again be a sham battle involving Indians."

DIVORCE CAPITAL LORE [24]

The usual divorce comes after six weeks' actual residence with the intention of becoming a citizen of Nevada. If the defendant will not sign a power of attorney to a local attorney and a waiver of property rights before the six weeks are up, the plaintiff must wait thirty days more. If the spouse must be advertised for legally (in county papers), because no one knows where he is, the delay is 58-60 days beyond the six weeks. Most applicants do not need to wait beyond the minimum time, and their hearing in the judge's chambers takes five minutes or less. In one classic instance, Mayor Roberts appeared be-

[24] From *Desert Challenge*, An Interpretation of Nevada, by Richard G. Lillard, pp. 354-358, 368, 373-374. Copyright, 1942, by Richard G. Lillard. New York: Alfred A. Knopf, Inc.

fore Judge Moran as attorney in seven cases that were settled with decrees inside of thirty minutes' total time. In another, anecdote reports, he appeared in a successful suit a day for twenty-seven consecutive court days.

One can sit in the corridor outside the chambers on the second floor of the courthouse and see the attorneys and plaintiffs hobnob as they wait their turns. They don't have long to wait. Meanwhile they gossip, talk about parties, compose telegrams, or even pitch pennies at the brass "gaboon" on the tiled floor. Associated and United Press reporters angle for news stories. The divorcees wait nervously (as if legal obstructions might come up at the last minute) and rehearse their answers to the lawyers' questions. In Las Vegas the hearing is likely to be private in the judge's chambers. In Reno it is as likely to be held in the courtroom, where an alert bailiff sternly represses any whisperers or candid photographers in the audience.

Wherever conducted, the hearing is likely to be perfunctory. Often judge and attorneys speak so low that listeners hear only a few vowel sounds and s's. The attorney for the plaintiff asks questions that quickly establish his client's name, Nevada address, and the date residence was established. This last is so closely figured that the judge checks the total of days and weeks on a scratch pad. The client must show forty-two days of residence somewhere in Nevada. If he has been out of the state for three days, he must show a total of forty-five days, and so on. The client's witness, landlady or garageman or employer—who will probably get $10 for the service—testifies to his presence daily in Nevada for the six-week period. The client swears to the integrity of his intention to become a resident of the state. On rare occasions there is a slip here, as illustrated by a stock story.

Lawyer: Where do you live?
Client: New York City.
Lawyer: You mean you *did* live in New York City! You now live in Nevada.
Client: Oh, yes!

The client verbally recognizes the name of his mate and explains the need for an unconditional separation. Usually the mate has been cruel and has affected health by causing worry and nervous breakdown. The attorney asks convenient leading questions:

Attorney: Did not your wife repeatedly drink to excess and have affairs at home while you were at work, and did not your employer tell you about this?
Client: Yes.

Since Nevada courts award no alimony or child custody, if there are such matters to settle, the lawyers refer to an Exhibit A, perhaps an Exhibit B, too, and insert them in the court record. These are legal contracts that the lawyers have arranged. The judge mumbles his decree. Attorneys, client, and witnesses depart.

This routine, unorthodox to old-style Americans, has produced its batch of anecdotes about striking exceptions. After many a decree a divorcee goes downstairs and remarries at once or wires the former mate to go ahead with his marriage in some other state. Several local citizens have adjusted their patterns of life to the inherent possibilities of the county courthouse. One schoolma'am divorced the same lawyer three times, remarried him, and is now suing for separate maintenance. The proprietor of a confectionery, varying spouses, has married and divorced four times.

In some of the stories time and space and circumstance are compressed as in a stage farce—or a one-act tragedy. One woman remarried eleven minutes after she was divorced and was on an eastbound train in fifteen minutes. In immediate sequence the wife of an Eastern banker and a well-known author obtained Reno divorces. One waited for the other and they went at once to the county clerk's office for a license and then upstairs to be married by the judge who had given them their divorces. Two divorcees from the same city met and formed an acquaintance. Mrs. A. said, "I'm divorcing the meanest man on earth." Mrs. B. said, "I'm marrying the dearest man in existence." Mrs. A. mentioned her brutal husband's full name. "My God!" exclaimed Mrs. B., "he's the man I'm going to marry!" The twice-married wife of a San Francisco psychiatrist divorced him in late December. Early in February a New York socialite divorced her husband. The next week the psychiatrist married her. She was his fifth.

Two women went to Reno together and got divorces. They returned home, where, by prearrangement, each married the other's former husband. A woman obtained a divorce, expecting to marry a popular tenor. As her suit was granted the tenor married a stage dancer, and the woman was left without the comfort of either her former husband or her intended replacement. A Philadelphia man sent another man's wife to Reno for a divorce, paying her expenses. While there she met some one who was interesting and handsome and married him. One wife came to Las Vegas for a divorce, bringing her lover along for company. Six weeks later her husband, their daughter, and his wife-to-be arrived. All attended the divorce ceremony and later got in a car and drove off together. "You come in with the tied and you go out with the tied"—so goes a Reno jest.

A lawyer brought suit for a woman on the ground of infidelity. He assured the court solemnly that she wanted her freedom because her husband was an infidel. A six-foot-three Negro was in court before Judge Bartlett. The counsel asked the perfunctory question, "What did your wife do to you?" The man replied, "She done say she goin' to put poison in mah soup! She say, too, she goin' cut out mah gizzuhd while I'se asleep." "What was the effect of your wife's treatment upon your health," asked Judge Bartlett, and the answer came, "Well, Judge, I jes nachelly lost mah appetite and I couldn't sleep."

"Lurid" newspaper anecdotes, taken at their surface value, have helped to fix several misconceptions about Nevada divorce that now lurk in the minds of many Americans. One is that most of the persons who go there to get a divorce already have another marriage lined up. The reverse is true. The very attorneys who tell the stories of immediate remarriage also estimate that fewer than one-fifth of their clients have another marriage in mind. The minority that do are likely to be persons long separated from their mates, finally determined on divorce only because another Right One has come along.

Another misconception is that divorce is always legally easy. Actually, there are contested cases, heard behind closed doors. There are cases in which divorce pleas are refused. For example, pleas have been denied a husband who claimed his wife was extremely cruel when there was evidence that he, too, was guilty of extreme cruelty; a husband who claimed cruelty when he himself provoked the violence and misconduct complained of; a party that claimed desertion when there was evidence to satisfy the court that his invitation to his mate to return and live with him was not in good faith.

* * * * *

While the divorce business has continued to publicize Las Vegas and Reno, a related legal service has developed to sizable proportions. This is quick marriage. As a county official once grinned, "We knot 'em as well as untie 'em."

* * * * *

Recently in Las Vegas a young "Mr. and Mrs." spent a night at an auto court that offered, in blue neon: "Marriages Completed in 30 Minutes with Minister or Judge. Wedding Chapel, Everything Arranged, including License. Open Day and Night." The next morning, ashamed to face their landlord, the couple drove down the street a block to get married at a similar place. The proprietor saw this and got mad. "The damn cheapskates. Why didn't they get married here? They saw our sign. Damn *them!*" It didn't occur to him that the couple would be embarrassed.

THE MORMON CURSE [25]

The curse was pronounced on Virginia City, Carson City, Silver City, and the rest, before Reno was born. The curse was pronounced in print by a Mormon, Orson Hyde.

When the Mormons were called back from Nevada to Salt Lake City, after having been the earliest settlers in this region of the Washoe, the property left by Orson Hyde and his Mormon partners included a sawmill.

On leaving the country, in answer to a summons by Brigham Young, they rented the sawmill but received for their rent only "one span of small indifferent mules, an old, worn-out harness, two yoke of oxen, and an old wagon."

The Mormons believed the property was worth at least twenty thousand dollars. The Mormons asked that this be paid, but the request was ignored, so the Mormons pronounced in print:

> . . . this demand of ours, remaining uncancelled, shall be to the people of Carson and Washoe valleys, as was the Ark of God among the Philistines. . . .

[25] From *Reno*, by Max Miller, pp. 18-19. Copyright, 1941, by Dodd, Mead and Company. New York.

You shall be visited by the Lord of Hosts with thunder and with earthquakes, with pestilence and with famine until your names are not known amongst men, for you have rejected the authority of God, trampled His laws and His ordinances, and given yourselves up to the God of this world. . . .

You have chuckled and gloried in taking the property of the Mormons and withholding from them the benefits thereof. You have despised rule and authority, and put God and man at defiance. If perchance, however, there should be an honest man amongst you, I would advise him to leave; but let him not go to California for safety, for he will not find it there. . . .

The hand of God is already beginning to be upon you for evil and not for good. The golden treasures are there to call together the worshippers of the God of this world, and you may there receive a common fate. . . .

This lengthy document, preserved in Nevada since 1862, has been entered into the Nevada histories so that even the school children of Nevada may know of it and can read it.

For pestilence and fire did come to Virginia City with its one-time population of forty thousand. And Carson City has been obliged to advertise itself as: "The smallest state capital in the United States." The sign has been erected over one of the entrances to Carson City much in the same manner as the famed arch of Reno, though not nearly so bright nor so big.

BRIGHAM YOUNG'S VISION [26]

The work party under Pratt and Snow entered the Salt Lake Valley on July 23 [1847]; and on July 24 the main body of the pioneer party, including the Mississippi Saints, arrived. Brigham Young had been sick with mountain fever for several days. He was riding on a bed in Apostle Woodruff's carriage. Concerning his first view of the valley, there is a legend that he raised himself up on his elbow and, after viewing the scene a moment, said: *"It is enough. This is the place. Drive on."*

What precisely Brigham Young did say may not be important, even though the Mormons have made "This is the place" the subject of a Utah song. Wilford Woodruff wrote later his own impressions of the scene and his report on the reactions of Young, who "expressed his entire satisfaction at the appearance of the valley as a resting place for the Saints. While lying on his bed in my carriage, gazing upon the scene before us, many things of the future concerning the valley were shown to him in a vision."

There are legends that President Young had seen the valley in a vision and that his expression "This is the place" was a confirmation of his vision. Even the skeptics were convinced. There was none to listen to Samuel Brannan.

Whatever Brigham Young may have said about "the place," coming into the valley was an occasion for dreaming dreams and seeing visions. Here was a haven found after seventeen years of wandering in Babylon. After four times failing to establish Zion in the midst of the Gentiles, they were now in a place

[26] From *Desert Saints*, The Mormon Frontier in Utah, by Nels Anderson, pp. 67-69. Copyright, 1942, by The University of Chicago Press. Chicago.

of safety. If they could not attain the perfect society in this isolated mountain haven, then perfection was not within mortal reach.

Here was "the place," where the city of Zion would be erected, where they would "dig in," as Prophet Joseph predicted, and the Devil would not again root them out. In this place they would build Zion by their own plan, live life by their own pattern, and no law of gentile design would be foisted on them.

In this mountain place at long last Zion would plant her feet to grow strong and mighty, never again to be driven by the black-face mob or thrown into the dust by the enemies of truth. This was "the place" where the weary trail emerged from the wilderness. Here were met in "the place" of God's selection, God's chosen people and his appointed time.

July 25, the second day in the Salt Lake Valley, was Sunday. All met to hear Orson Pratt, the pioneer of the pioneers, preach to the text: "How beautiful upon the mountains are the feet of him that bringeth good tidings," and so portrayed a vision of hosts of angels rejoicing at the deliverance of Zion.

Then Brigham Young rose to speak. He was still weak from illness. He was never more eloquent or ever more brief. He described the blessed society that would inhabit this new home.

No man can buy land here, for no one has any land to sell.
But every man shall have his land measured out to him, which he must cultivate in order to keep it.
Besides, there shall be no private ownership of the streams that come out of the canyons, nor the timber that grows on the hills.
These belong to the people: all the people.

It was verily true that no one had any land to sell, for all the area was being lost to Mexico and did not pass over to the United States until the treaty of Guadalupe Hidalgo on February 2, 1848, several months later. When the Mormon Battalion veterans, working at Sutters Mill, discovered gold on January 24, 1848, all of California was still Mexican territory.

When the conquered territory became a part of the United States, it was still true that no one had any land to sell, for the new land became Indian territory, not open for settlement. These legal technicalities did not greatly bother Brigham Young.

The location was surveyed for a city, and the land was divided into town lots, small farms, and larger farms. Each family head was given land of a type and in amount to meet his needs and circumstance. For example, mechanics and shopkeepers, who would be part-time farmers, were given small one- to five-acre lots near the center of the community. Men who lived by farming alone were given the larger lots, the ten- to eighty-acre tracts farther out.

The size of a man's farm was determined by the size of his family. A man with one wife and a few children would receive a few acres, perhaps up to fifteen. A man with two or more wives and many children would receive proportionately larger farms, even up to eighty acres. Once it was determined what acreage was due to the head of a family, the location of his farm would be settled by drawing lots.

RAMONA'S MARRIAGE PLACE [27]

The words "Ramona's Marriage Place" are painted in letters huge and black across the outside walls. The letters glare down the former main highway into San Diego from Los Angeles.

The highway still goes by there and by the sign, but the highway no longer is the main highway. Yet buses of today continue making "Ramona's Marriage Place" a definite point of call, allowing the passengers their half-hour or so for strolling through the well-kept patio, for dropping their dimes into the "wishing well," for buying their copies of *Ramona*, for hearing their theatrically illuminated lecture on old missions of California, for looking at an oxcart, for looking at a lot of things, including the desk and chair used (or, at least, so the visitors are told) by Helen Hunt Jackson in her writing of this novelized report back to Washington of Indian conditions in California.

For this ancient adobe structure, the former dwelling of the Estudillo family, is certainly one of the principal industries of Old Town today—and has been since 1909, when the San Diego streetcar company, to encourage patronage from the San Diego of today to the Old Town of the beginning, purchased the home from members of the Estudillo descendants and turned it into a museum, a permanent connecting link between the bygone and the present. And we who could be cynical about "Ramona's Marriage Place" are only so at first.

"Ramona's Marriage Place" is a game of make-believe that even the patrons enjoy playing, one can be sure. Besides, they receive more than the worth of their dimes. We know that. For the Estudillo home, patio and all, was built in 1827. And if it had not been preserved, what would it be now?

Nor should Helen Hunt Jackson be blamed if, out of a composite of persons around Old Town, she developed such a fictionized character that visitors want to believe that the character was real and that Ramona truly was married at the spot which this sign, huge and black, indicates. Most of us have stopped worrying, and most of us have stopped trying to correct the visitors who ask: "But isn't it really true?"

Yes, it is very true—as true as that editorial writer's answer to the little girl's letter about Santa Claus.

Nor could Tommy Getz, a former vaudeville trouper who helped recondition the old Estudillo home into "Ramona's Marriage Place"—nor could Tommy Getz really believe his luck when troops of visitors day after day solemnly paid their dimes to enter the establishment. He would confide to the visitors that Ramona and her Alessandro were, after all, the results of a novelist's poetic license. But the confidence was more resented than appreciated. The visitors preferred their dream.

Tommy Getz, a good friend and a good showman, is dead now. But the manner he used through the years in operating "Ramona's Marriage Place"

[27] From *Harbor of the Sun*, The Story of the Port of San Diego, by Max Miller, pp. 219-222, 224-229. Copyright, 1940, by Max Miller. Garden City, New York: Doubleday & Company, Inc.

continues much the same. And the place remains one of the harbor's everlasting institutions, the same as the navy, the climate, and the tip of Point Loma with its antique lighthouse.

Nobody is hurt, nobody is injured. Furthermore, the dimes of "Ramona's Marriage Place" have helped to keep in employment some of the descendants of the original Mexican and Spanish families who have clung to Old Town right up to now. And the best place in San Diego to buy tortillas is in Old Town, too, there by the river bed and surrounded by a few other adobe dwellings—some of them even older than the Estudillo place. Yes, we would have it so.

For the present San Diego, the San Diego of buildings and business streets and modern residences, was started as a separate town about three miles to the south of the original settlement around the presidio. The present city was the artificial result of an unconquerable realtor, Alonzo Erastus Horton. Horton specialized in selling climate and sometimes sold it as high as ten thousand dollars a lot. Anyway, the present San Diego has little of the original San Diego, Old Town, which like a cast-off grandparent has been allowed to sleep away its lingering days beside the junction of Mission Valley and the bay.

* * * * *

. . . Father Antonio D. Ubach [was one] of those Methuselahlike beings in whom all history could seem but a matter of his own personal memory. He was the Father Gaspara in the book *Ramona*. He was a friend of Mrs. Jackson during her stay in San Diego when she was preparing the novel. He was the working model from which she drew her composite picture of the priest who befriended both Ramona and her Alessandro and who finally married them.

* * * * *

Father Ubach supplied much information to Mrs. Jackson for the book, and in an interview two years before his death he emphasized once again that there was no real Ramona and no real Alessandro. But he did say he could name actual characters whom Mrs. Jackson had used in part for her heroine and hero. He said he could give the names but did not care to do so at the time because of the unfairness to others who deserved almost equal mention.

* * * * *

He was still much alive when "Ramona's Marriage Place" first started to get under way for business. And when asked constantly, as would be expected, if this was where he really had married Ramona and Alessandro, his reply remained:

"If you recall the novel, they were married in the Church. Why, Father Gaspara or any priest would not marry them outside of the Church. Catholics know that. Still, even they keep asking."

But already the tide was setting in; already the visitors from far and away were so desperately anxious to believe that the girl Ramona was real and that she was earnest that all this just naturally took its own course. And so "Ramona's Marriage Place" is the answer.

But one can miss the theatrical touch of Tommy Getz out there now. Perhaps all of us do. For he had entered show life in 1873 as boy soprano in the Kelly and Leon minstrels, which may explain a little why his twice-daily lectures on the missions of California were accompanied by the actual tinkling of bells—yes, and by the twinkling of lights. During his years of developing the fame of "Ramona's Marriage Place" he insisted on action in his show. If at all possible he no doubt would have liked to have at each performance an old mission Indian singing "Ramona" to the accompaniment of tom-toms.

There was the time, too, when a quarter of the wall was torn away from the old adobe kitchen. Being a showman, he had not objected to a rumor that a secret treasure had long been buried in the ancient place by Spaniards. He may not have started the rumor, but he certainly had done nothing to stop it. And he had been so convincing one morning that next day two men arrived from Los Angeles bearing a bag of radium material. The bag was supposed to swing when in the vicinity of precious treasures, and it swung towards the kitchen wall.

"We've found it," the men told Tommy.

With picks they went at the wall as if it were a tomb in need of filling. They worked tirelessly, the wall being a foot thick. At each inch of penetration the bag swung with increased tempo.

The last of the mortar was [full] of stones. When these were lifted out the bag stopped swinging, nor could any urging start it swinging again.

"Um," one of the men said. "There must be a little metal in the stones. Isn't that interesting!"

He was answered with other "ums," making in all about three "ums."

The men departed then, leaving Tommy to contemplate the hole his own convincing talk had caused.

"Cheer up," we said, for we felt obliged to say something to him. "Cheer up. Maybe now you can tell your customers that the hole was caused by cannon balls long ago. Maybe it was."

"Say, you know," he answered, thinking hard, "maybe it was."

The afternoon bus began unloading its flock at the gateway just then. Tommy left the kitchen hole to guide the flock into the lecture room, which had for its curtain a monstrous map of the old footpaths from San Diego to the Golden Gate.

"Stay around," he begged us. "I've a great act. Stay around and I'll show it to you."

Tagging behind him, we found a bench in the showroom, and he walked with an exaggerated wobble as he crossed the floor.

"I'm not drunk, friends," he told the visitors from off the bus. "I have to walk this way because of the old tiling on the floor. Look how uneven it is. Look how worn down in the center it is. This tile was made in 1770 and is the first work of civilized man in California. Furthermore . . ." The lecture had started.

If ever one wanted to be made sad—while Tommy was still alive—all one had to do was to sit on a bench in that dark, cool room, surrounded by darkened paintings and bars, and have him tell about the old friars being obliged to protect themselves by sprinkling broken wineglasses over the walls; or have him recite again the misery of the young Spanish courtiers of old who could not get inside the girl's house until they were engaged. . . .

"How'd you like my act?" he whispered to us, his friends, when it was all over and we were once more in the sunshine where friars did not sprinkle their walls with broken wineglasses. "Pretty good, eh?"

"Yes." We meant it, as every one meant it, once they heard him.

And his wishing well in the patio!

"Quaff ye the Waters of Ramona's Well," suggested (and still suggests) an inscription carved in wood. On the bottom of the well were abalone shells and pieces of what appeared to be broken tiling and dimes. During racing season at the former Tijuana track, fans from Los Angeles would stop at "Ramona's Marriage Place" on their way to the races. They would stop at the well, and the wishes they made concerned the galloping health of such mounts of that day as Hydromel, Ervast, and Golden Prince. But Tommy had a cheerful story about the well not concerned with commerce. One morning early he saw an old Spanish mother kneeling there. He asked her what could be the nature of her wish that she should be there so early. "I'm wishing," she answered, "that everybody in the world could be as happy as I am today."

"Ramona's Marriage Place" was in its greatest glory, perhaps, when the main highway from Los Angeles passed by there before the present cut-off was built. Those were the days when the original Tijuana track, and later the Agua Caliente track, and also Prohibition, caused a river of cars to flow constantly by the place en route to Mexico during week ends and holidays.

Tommy said that during that period the biggest record attendance at "Ramona's Marriage Place" was on a Labor Day when 1,632 persons dropped their dimes. This may help to indicate how Ramona and all thoughts about Ramona have become a San Diego institution. One cannot explain why the name still means so much to visitors from everywhere, but it does.

Tommy also said the worst day was the day of a cloudburst when only one woman succeeded in driving her car to the place. She insisted on going the entire rounds, including Tommy's full-length lecture on the missions of California. He delivered the full talk to her, along with the tinkling and the twinkling and his own exaggerated wobble across the floor tiles. And later, when he went to collect the day's receipts from the box at the door, there was none. She had picked up her dime as she went out.

ELYSIAN PARK [28]

Elysian Park is a large, quiet, brush and tree-covered hill off North Broadway [Los Angeles], offering from its crest an unobstructed view of the

---

[28] From *My L.A.*, by Matt Weinstock, pp. 166-167. Copyright, 1947, by Matt Weinstock. New York: Current Books, Inc., A. A. Wyn, Publisher.

Southern Pacific, Union Pacific, and Santa Fe railroad tracks, the trickle known as the Los Angeles River, and the haze-covered industrial section. Though only five minutes from the civic center, the park is somehow remote. It has become cut off, paradoxically, by recently constructed freeways which slash through it.

Early in November 1937, a three-inch crack appeared in the earth near the crest. Five days later the crack measured three feet.

Reporters, photographers, radio announcers, geologists, and engineers swarmed to the widening crevice. Policemen kept sight-seers out of the park. A fire siren was kept handy.

Two hundred feet below, several thousand persons stood by day and night, waiting for doom to strike. Shortly after 10 P.M. November 26, a million tons of earth and rock, approximately one hundred yards of hillside, slid away.

Geologists made clear that the slide was simply a matter of the law of gravity catching up with a batch of loose, rain-soaked earth that happened to be on the side of a cliff. The public would have no such nonsense. Mysterious forces having to do with earthquakes, witch doctors, sin, or radio static clearly were at work.

Eastern papers headlined LOS ANGELES SLIDING INTO OCEAN. Relatives in Nebraska and New Hampshire wired, as they had done after the 1933 quake: ARE YOU ALL RIGHT?

During the excitement, one paper printed a piece of folklore to the effect that a spell was cast over the acre seventy-five years before. Antonio Feliz, who died in 1863, willed his land to his niece, Petronella, went the story, but when she tried to take it over she found a new occupant there. Petronella, according to the paper, turned her face toward the Verdugo Hills and called down a curse on the old homestead. She invoked the wrath of heaven and hell to kill those who had cheated her and asked that fire and water destroy the rancho. So saying, went the story, she fell dead. All in all, it was a pretty good tale, but the Federal Writers' Project, checking history, found it didn't apply to Elysian Park but to Griffith Park, which was doing fine.

Reporters prodding about for news leads came upon a closed-up tunnel in the face of the sliding cliff and the more daring of them removed the barriers and went in. They were able to continue into the cliff some thousand feet, plodding through a muddy six-foot cavern. They found many subsidiary caves and what seemed walled-up rooms. They also found fragmentary evidence that the system of underground passages might have dated centuries back, to the days of the padres. The reporters formed a club, the Troglodytes, and planned further safaris inside the magic mountain. But suddenly their bubble burst. Kids in the neighborhood, it was disclosed, had been using the cave as a playhouse for years. In more recent years hoboes had used it for their private depression.

Now Elysian Park is very quiet. From a nine-day wonder, the landslide is just something geology professors tell their classes about.

THE BRODERICK-TERRY DUEL [29]

The Broderick-Terry duel [in 1859] was something more than just a duel between two men. It was a duel between two moral expediences. It was one of the side-shows in the great circus ring of politics. Behind a curtain of personal rancors lay the raw wounds of the slavery question. How evenly California was divided in the fifties on this matter may be indicated by the fact that one of its national senators was David C. Broderick, a free labor Democrat and a graduate from Tammany Hall, while the other was William Gwin, equally a Democrat but as ardent an advocate of slavery as ever drifted north of the Mason-Dixon line. These two men were at variance on practically every count. Broderick had sprung from obscurity, without prestige or background. Gwin was a man of family, an aristocrat.

David S. Terry, being a Southerner, was a supporter of pro-slavery policies. When he failed to be returned to his judgeship on the supreme bench, he blamed Broderick for his defeat. This led to an exchange of insults which, in turn, led to a challenge from Judge Terry for satisfaction. There are those who maintain that the whole thing was a frame-up on the part of the Southern contingent to rid the Democratic party in California of a man inhospitable to the extension of slavery. Which, in plain words, means that Terry plotted in cold blood to kill his man. But, even with all the bias in the world, this charge seems, at a safe distance, far-fetched.

Both were hot-headed men. Broderick had Irish blood in his veins. And, if he was not "agin everything" he was passionately "agin" enough things to maintain the Celtic tradition of violent opposition. Judge Terry was equally quick-tempered. Both of them had indulged in mud-slinging and to a less pretentious generation it would seem that if mud were the weapon chosen by both parties it might be a very good weapon for continuing a fight. But in those days, gentlemen resented being called dishonest, even when they knew that the charge against them was true. Broderick seemed to have high aims but devious methods of achieving them, and Judge Terry was by no means a civic angel. Perhaps the mud gave out. At all events, on the morning of September 13, 1859, these two fiery politicians met on the southern shore of the Laguna de la Merced with pistols in their hands.

There is always something impressive about a duel, even in the face of the empty bombast back of it. The Broderick-Terry duel had as much absurdity at its root as any, and yet a sense of purging tragedy sends a tingle down the spine as one reads the account. Here is how Theodore Hittell describes it:

> At the appointed time the parties and their friends . . . reached the ground. There were about eighty other persons present. Each principal was accompanied by his seconds and a group of friends. . . .
> A few matters, including the important one as to choice of weapons, had been left for determination on the ground; and they were now settled by

[29] From *San Francisco, A Pageant*, by Charles Caldwell Dobie, pp. 302-305. Copyright, 1933, by D. Appleton-Century Company, Inc. New York: Appleton-Century-Crofts, Inc.

tossing up a half dollar. Terry won the choice of weapons. . . . Broderick won the choice of ground and the giving of the word. The pistols were examined and the one intended for Broderick loaded by the armorer, and that intended for Terry by his friend, Samuel H. Brooks, while the principals were placed in position fronting each other. It was a raw cold morning. Both wore overcoats, which they now threw off, and appeared in full, black suits, their frock coats buttoned across the breast, and without shirt collars. Each had given over to one of his seconds the contents of his pockets; and each was then what was called examined, to see that he wore no armor, by a second of his adversary, and handed his pistol. Each stood erect; Broderick with his black, soft-wool hat drawn down over his eyes, while Terry had his hat of similar kind thrown over his forehead; and each, though firm and rigid, showed evident signs of suppressed excitement—Terry, however, being much cooler than Broderick. The word, as it was to be given by Colton (Broderick's second) was then plainly stated, or what in dueling phrase is called exemplified, by him and repeated by Benham (Terry's second). The seconds stepped back and the principals stood alone, each with his cocked pistol pointing down at his side.

By this time it was nearly seven o'clock. Colton in a clear voice asked, "Gentlemen, are you ready?" Terry replied at once, "Ready," but Broderick hesitated a moment, adjusting his weapon, and then answered, with a nod to Colton, "Ready." Then came the word, "Fire—one—two." At the word "one," as Broderick was raising his pistol, it went off and the ball struck the ground nine or ten feet from him but in direct line with his antagonist. Before the word "two," Terry fired. There was a slight show of dust upon the right lapel of Broderick's buttoned coat, indicating where Terry's ball had struck. In a moment Broderick involuntarily raised his arms; there was a visible shuddering of the body and then a contraction of the right hand, from which the pistol had dropped to the ground. A violent convulsion of his frame next took place; there was a turn toward the left; his body sank, his left knee gave way, then his right, and he fell half prostrate, his left arm supporting him from falling prone. His seconds and surgeons rushed to his aid. . . .

Terry . . . deliberately folded his arms and stood perfectly still.

Broderick died three days later. His friends said that he was deliberately murdered. They pointed out that the pistols had been supplied by Terry and that the one given to Broderick had a defect in it. This had caused it to discharge prematurely thus giving Terry an excuse for firing before the signal.

At all events, Terry was looked upon by many as "a man with the mark of Cain upon his brow," whereas Broderick became great in his martyrdom. His death made him the symbol of a cause. Without doubt it did much to crystallize public sentiment in California against slavery.

The homage paid Broderick at his death was only equal to the homage paid the memory of James King of William, his enemy, a few years before. The State legislature even appropriated money to put a monument over his grave. . . . As a child, passing this broken shaft in Laurel Hill cemetery, I used to feel a spasm of fear at what its shattered top implied—a life snuffed out by violence.

INCIDENTS OF THE SAN FRANCISCO EARTHQUAKE AND FIRE [30]

I. Rumors

Wild rumors of cruelty and greed and murder among the injured afterward got about; stories of men who begged to be killed, and others who cursed their mothers, of parents who left their wounded children unaided, while they, unheeding, made their selfish way to safety; stories, too, of friends who cut rings from the fingers of the dead, and of swift punishment by quick-shooting soldiers. But followed out to the end most of these stories have been proved mere rumors, the weird hallucinations of overstrained minds. To the eternal credit of mankind it is known that here uncountable deeds of bighearted, unselfish kindness were done; and that many who died beyond the reach of help closed their eyes without complaint—stoics to the end.

* * * * *

Of what was actually taking place there behind the smoke they knew nothing. No regular papers were distributed that morning; no extras were issued; no man knew what was happening beyond the range of his own vision. Oblivious to the stirring scenes around, the newspaper bulletin boards foolishly announced the trivial news of the day before—the doings of Congress and the President, and all the other commonplace matter that had seemed so important then. As to the real news of the day there was nothing anywhere; nothing as to the damage in other parts of the city, the number of fatalities, the fate of nearby cities—nothing but anxious speculation, and a chance word here and there. Disquieting rumors began to circulate—that the city's prisoners lay dead in the ruins of the jail; that hundreds had been crushed at the City Hall and thousands killed in various hotels south of Market street; that the Mechanics' Pavilion had burned before the injured and dying who had been taken to it could be removed to places of safety. None knew then how little truth there was in most of the rumors. Later wild stories that Chicago had slid into Lake Michigan, that Manhattan Island was submerged, that all the Pacific Coast cities were demolished by earthquake, or were burning, spread among the people; but they created only a mild surprise. They were thought probable enough, but of doubtful origin. Anyway it would be time to find out after the fire stopped and ordinary life had been resumed. . . .

II. Dago Red

All Friday morning the south and west slopes burned. On the heights the houses were hung with blankets saturated in casks of wine (real "Dago red")

---

[30] From *A History of the Earthquake and Fire in San Francisco*, An Account of the Disaster of April 18, 1906 and its Immediate Results, by Frank W. Aitken and Edward Hilton, pp. 21-22, 71-72, 120, 138, 140, 142, 144, 146, 159-160, 167-168, 181-182. Copyright, 1906, by The Edward Hilton Co. San Francisco.

and many were saved. By such primitive methods, also, were the flames stopped at Montgomery street just west of the precipice that forms the east face of the hill. A fringe of houses, lonely and desolate, tops the bluff—all that remains of San Francisco's "Little Italy."

III. TRAGEDIES

Down on the waterfront had stood a cheap restaurant conducted by two men who were old friends as well as business associates. Nelson cooked; Johnson served. With the shock of the earthquake the frail building collapsed and took fire. With utmost difficulty Johnson at last extricated himself from the ruins of the dining room. Nelson was nowhere to be seen; the roaring pillar of flame that had been the kitchen made a search for him impossible. For many days Johnson sought his old friend and partner, but in vain. At last he took up his search at the old place. Bricks from the walls of neighboring buildings lay in great piles where the little restaurant had been. For days he worked among the hot debris; at the bottom, pinned under the overturned stove at which he had been cooking, lay the charred body of him he sought.

Through the South of Market district there must have been many such cases. Scores, pinned in the wreckage, were burned to death in the fires which followed the caving in of hotels and lodging houses. Many there were who were nearly saved and in the end had to be left to their cruel fate, despite all that they and their heroic, stouthearted rescuers could do. One man who was taken out of such a wreck at the last minute tells of two others who were near him, and who, like him, were unable to free themselves. Even as the fire approached they cheered each other. "I'm not at all hurt," said one, "but there's a big beam across my back and I can't get out. I guess they'll have us soon, though." "I could get out all right myself," said the other, "only that my wrist is held tight in the timbers." And there they had to be left while the merciless fire burned those around, and, finally, themselves.

*   *   *   *   *

. . . There are stories of crazed men who could not tear themselves away from the horrid fascination of the fire; stories of men who in a moment's madness leaped into the flames. One such tale seems to touch the utmost depths of horror and grisly tragedy. A dealer at the Italian market, it seems, was so terrified, or so unbalanced, by the sudden falling of walls about his place (a number of men and horses, backed up beside the market for their morning supplies, were buried beneath its wall) that he ran into the great refrigerator and slammed the heavy door behind him. In the confusion and excitement his absence was not noticed; and in a few hours the building burned. The refrigerator, covered with fallen brick, remained unharmed, and in it the unwilling prisoner, ignorant of the fire, ignorant of the death or flight of his comrades, awaited the opening of his lonely cell. For eight days and eight nights he remained there, breathing the polluted air of the refrigerating chamber (but slightly renewed by its ventilators), drinking the water which came from the melting of the ice, tearing at the raw meat which hung within reach. At length those who came to clear up the market heard faint sounds from within the refrigerator. They opened it. On the floor lay their former companion, faint, weakened, scarcely living, a hopeless maniac. What he had suffered they never knew; for within the day he died.

IV. HALLUCINATIONS

. . . Others brought to the authorities stories so wild that it seemed certain their reason had left them; and even after the immediate excitement had ended, people were telling of sights that never could have existed at all. They seem strange now, but were believed readily enough when told by supposed eye-witnesses.

Thus one man was sure that he himself had seen the Cliff House floating on the sea; if he had, its return to its accustomed place must have been marvelous to behold. A woman fleeing frightened to Oakland told, hysterically, of her terrible trip down Market street, and of crossing great crevasses there on rickety planks which served as bridges; so terrified was she by her wholly imaginary experience that she could not be induced to return to San Francisco! No less startling are the stories told of the great buildings on this same street. As one man passed below it, the Call Building was inclined at an angle of fifteen degrees from the perpendicular; another passed it just before it fell into the street; yet it is still standing, as straight and sturdy as it was when first erected. Sincerely believed, there can be but one explanation for such stories—a very reasonable one, too, that many saw only what their fantastic fears told them was present, and for a while many minds were unstrung.

*　　*　　*　　*　　*

. . . During the fire a tremendous, hurried, frightened rush out of the city had taken place. At first the report that the ferry slips had burned had kept many away, but nevertheless large crowds crossed the bay Wednesday, and on Thursday, Friday and Saturday the great ferryboats, crossing the bay as rapidly as they could work in and out of the slips, were crowded to their utmost. The rush out of the city during these days had in it something, almost, of the feverish haste of delirium. It was not merely the burned-out who fled, but those also who were untouched by the fire. People fled from an expected visitation from on High; from a much-imagined tidal wave; from more terrible earthquakes which they feared were coming to destroy them utterly. Saturday and Sunday they fled from the dread fear that typhoid or smallpox was about to devastate the city. Many, of course, went out of the city because they knew of places where they would be better accommodated; but on the whole the exodus was frenzied, purposeless, unreasoning, mad. The current story, that the throngs pressing on the boats from the slip had crowded off into the bay those who had gone on in the lead, seemed almost possible, though of course unfounded. The fear of a smallpox epidemic, at any rate, seemed based on actual dementia. It resulted largely from warnings spread through the region near the Park, to the effect that the Park camps were infected with the disease, coupled with the admonition to flee at once, as a quarantine was imminent. Although there were a few isolated cases, the condition of the camps at the time, and the subsequent outcome, indicate that this was very probably only a hallucination of an over-sensitive mind.

V. Resumption

It was not a matter of hours, but in a short time people generally began to think of ordinary things again. Clerks and employees began to get in touch with their employers. Stenographers hurried across town on foot to take dictations, and letters innumerable were sent out by business men to tell their "customers" that it would not take long to have everything running smoothly, and that the customers had better send in their orders right away. Egotism sublime!

The first trade was in soda water. The city had "gone dry" by the Mayor's order on the morning of the earthquake, and to its eternal credit raised no objection when a similar edict kept it dry for weeks afterward. The lid was on and nailed down tight. This suggested a thirst-quencher to enterprising men, the need of which was further emphasized by the very limited supply of putrid, ill-smelling water that was doled out from the tail end of sprinkling carts. Facetious boys had threatened to go fishing in those carts, and even sedate old men called them aquariums. As soon as travel was resumed on Market street, as soon as Fillmore street was "discovered," they were lined with men and boys who made the neighborhood resound with the popping of stoppers, a nickel the pop.

At about the same time came those dispensing souvenirs of the fire for a consideration. It was remarkable how people who had been burned out and had scarcely any money at all went down town and spent a dime for a broken cup or twisted vase or other trifle from the ruins.

VI. Signs

The city at large was possessed with a cheery spirit of hopefulness. Men met on the street and congratulated each other that it was no worse. Even amid the inconveniences of cooking in the street and living in a tent, the people showed a brave humor. A sign on a tent in one of the camps bore the legend, "The Whole Dam Family." Another bid the curious to "Ring the Bell for Landlady." Still others announced that "Cars Stop Here," and that the "Elevator Is Not Running." Some of the kitchens were jokingly called after the city's most pretentious restaurants—Tait's, Techau's, Zinkand's. Others bore fantastic names—the "Outside Inn," the "Inside Out," the "Step Inn," the "Goodfellows' Grotto." One, not much larger than a dog kennel, displayed the crudely lettered sign, "Un-Fairmont Hotel. Open all night. Will exchange for country property." Another bore the motto, "Eat, drink, and be merry, for tomorrow we may have to go to Oakland." "Cheer up," said still another. "Have one on me. Come in and spend a quiet evening."

Even the ruins were made to play their part in the fun. A firm which had occupied salesrooms on the ground floor of one of the large buildings announced that it had moved because the elevator was not running; and another, "because of alterations in the building on the eighteenth of April."

PIGGOTT'S FOLLY [31]

There can be but few persons in Portland [Oregon] who can't point out the city's one haunted castle to you, and many of them have on tap a collection of romantic if very vague stories regarding its history; yet there are few, indeed, who really know anything about the place. The haunted castle, in case you just arrived in town yesterday and haven't seen it yet, is that Moorish pile of brick which stands out boldly on the hill south of the city's main business district. In case you wanted to write a letter to the castle, it should carry the somewhat royal address of 2591 Southwest Buckingham Avenue.

Mount Gleall castle, as the place was named by its builder, isn't a very ancient chateau, as time is considered by chateaux fanciers. It was built in 1892 by Charles H. Piggott, remembered by middle-aged Portlanders as an eccentric sort of gentleman. Eccentric or not, he managed to keep his feet on the ground long enough to have acquired, by the early '90's, what was a comfortable fortune, estimated variously from $75,000 to $200,000. He himself said in later life that he was worth $85,000 when he built Mount Gleall Castle.

Piggott owned and managed a brick yard on what was then Sandy Road. He operated a fuel concern and he also speculated in timber lands. He was admitted to the Oregon bar. But he liked best to appear as a writer, philosopher, iconoclast, and prophet. He wore his hair rather long and dressed in a manner affected by Elbert Hubbard. He knew he was considered a crank and gloried in living up to the reputation given him. In his collected writings, which he published himself, he admonished readers to become cranks; for, he said, all human progress was pioneered by cranks. His volume of prose and poetry was published in 1908 under the all-inclusive title, *Pearls at Random Strung, or Life's Tragedy from Wedding to Tomb, Including the Scientific Causes of All Diseases, Poverty, Premature Death and Longevity,* by C. H. Piggott, A.A.1.

Philosopher Piggott advocated birth control; moderate use of tobacco; whisky for snake bites and, with a little water added, to be taken in "extreme fatigue to prolong life"; thought every community should have a public fool-killer and listed a number of subjects to keep him busy; said there was no need of any one being "goggle-eyed" (i.e., wearing glasses); damned breakfast foods as tooth-rotters, and claimed he had devised an absolute cure for leprosy. In a paragraph of "Suggestions to Those Contemplating Marriage" he warned women that "no man ever hangs around a courthouse, doctor's office or dentist's office—he must be sympathetic and honest to be good."

[31] From "Castle of Mystery to Open to Public; Supposed Haunt of Spooks in Hands of Local Group; Open Rendezvous Plan; Strange Structure on Heights of Portland Repaired after Years of Neglect," by Stewart H. Holbrook, *The Sunday Oregonian,* August 19, 1934, Section V, page 1, column 1; page 2, columns 1, 2, 3.

Castle Holds First Open House Today. Today, for the first time in its long and weird history, Mount Gleall Castle, better known as Portland's "haunted" castle, will be thrown open to the public. Science has laid low the haunts which infested its high-domed halls and corridors; several thousand dollars have been spent in repairing the vandalism of two decades, and a modern road leads directly to the courtyard. The occasion is the first open house of Everyman's Castle, Inc., a group sponsored by prominent citizens, of which more is told in the accompanying article.—Ed.

Piggott married a Portland girl of good family. There were three children, Gladys, Earl, and Lloyd. From the first two letters of each name Piggott made Gleall, to christen the castle.

Piggott said he paid $2500, in 1891, for half a block of land on what was then known as Seventh Street Terrace. Expense of building the castle, he said, was $11,000. The brick came from his own yard and was hauled to the hilltop by four-horse teams. He wanted a dwelling in which no two rooms would be alike and in which there were no straight lines. He got the idea of building the castle, he said, from a picture he had seen of one which once stood on one of Rome's Seven Hills. A local architect was hired to draw the plans but gave up the job. Piggott himself drew them and turned the construction work over to the late Harry Smith, long a well-known builder of Portland.

There are two main doors to the three-floored castle. One on the road level leads directly into the huge cellar. Servants' quarters are on this floor, and the ground room of the tower makes a very pleasant alcove where a tired varlet or serf might sit and contemplate the city of Portland far below.

A flight of broad stone steps leads upward from the road to the main entrance, which is on the second floor. All the rooms are high-domed and well-lighted. The main hall is long and narrow. Kitchen, pantry, and dining room are neither large nor distinguished. The stairway, leading to the floor above, is circular and quite aristocratic, as is still another which leads to the roof. The upper floor has one large and two smaller rooms, a bathroom, and, of course, an alcove in the main tower. Entrance to the top room of the tower—of which more presently —is from the battlements of the roof only.

The building has few straight lines. There are many curves, alcoves, nooks, and towers. The top room in the main tower was Piggott's sanctum sanctorum. It is a very small room, hardly enough space for a table and chair. Here was the one room of the castle where, so long as Piggott owned the place, no woman ever trod. Not even his wife or daughter, he said, was allowed in the room. It was where he retired from the world to think and write. "There I thought my thoughts and dreamed my dreams," he was fond of saying. "On a moonlit night Mount Hood and Mount Saint Helena can be seen, wraithlike and dim against the purple background of the evening sky. Below are the lights of Portland, like the reflection of a starlit sky."

But the Piggotts were not to live long in the castle. Hard times hit the Piggott fortune and the castle went in the crash. It was about this time that the place first took on its various haunts. It was vacant for many years. Small boys broke the windows and larger boys stripped the interior. Locks, door knobs, pipe, even the very floors were removed by vandals, and grass and weeds grew tall and rank in the courtyard of Mount Gleall Castle. All long-deserted houses are susceptible to haunts, and an odd house, such as the castle, was sure to have its share. Curious people going through the vacant pile heard weird noises—hair-raising whisperings coming from nowhere and chilling echoes. "Piggott's Folly," as the castle was named by Portlanders, was in for its two decades of haunts.

Eleven years ago the original Piggott property was purchased by the present owner. He spent several thousand dollars in restoring the castle to something approaching its original appearance, except for the exterior, which he painted a cream color. The foundations and walls were found to be in perfect condition, as they are today, and the new owner set about to discover the source of the haunts.

"First thing I did," he told me the other day, as we sat in the middle room of the main tower, "was to take out the old speaking-tube system which had been installed when the place was built. Immediately the strange whisperings ceased. They had been caused by noises—chiefly those of switching engines in Albina, several miles away—which were wafted up the hill on a curious current of air and into the exterior part of the speaking tube. And they were certainly weird noises when transferred to the rooms from the various tube apertures.

"This place is so situated that until several of the higher downtown buildings were erected, a locomotive running on a certain stretch of track between Portland and Vancouver made a terrific noise in the house. But gradually it disappeared as the downtown buildings were built higher. Another thing that bothered was the generator at the old Portland Lumber Company, down on the south Portland waterfront. Whenever that was in operation, you could hardly hear yourself talk in the castle. After the lumber plant was dismantled the noise ceased.

"Another noise was made by the flickers which lived in that big tree across the road. They liked to get up on the castle tower and hammer on the sheet iron up there. Flickers like to make a lot of noise, and I guess this was as fine a sounding board as they ever had. They don't bother so much now."

There have been three or four tenants in the castle during the past decade or so, and it was recently leased to a group known as Everyman's Castle, Inc. The plan, according to Israel Park, president, is to provide a place where old people may come for a day's visit whenever they wish, meet others of their age, view Portland and its environs from the finest vantage point nature has provided. The group plans to install a telescope on the tower and to convert the cellar into a dining room. (The cellar is not underground, but is really the ground floor.) Mr. Park and his board of directors, all of whom are prominent citizens, are enthusiastic regarding the project. The group is to be financed by donations, is non-profit-making, and no charges of any kind will be made to guests. All races and creeds will be welcome, Mr. Park says. A fine electric range has already been donated and the long empty castle chambers are gradually being filled with furniture and pictures. Visitors are welcome at all times.

I enjoyed my visit to the castle immensely. It was a glorious day last week, and never before had I had such a sweeping view of all Portland and its surroundings. The long-neglected rooms and halls of the chateau have been done in landscape wall paper. New floors have been laid and new glass put in the staring sashes. Up on the battlements the sun shone brightly and I could hardly blame the flickers for wanting to make it their headquarters. In my time I've been quite a chateau addict myself, inspecting a number in England, France, and Germany; and although my tours took me through larger and older castles, I don't remember one which commanded a finer view than does Mount Gleall.

Mr. and Mrs. Piggott died several years ago. So did one of the sons. The other son and daughter are living in California. The haunts of the place have been laid low and the castle may now be entering on a new phase of its strange history. Mr. Piggott may have been an eccentric, but when it came to picking a site for a castle in Portland, he had no peers. It's a grand and a fascinating place.

VII. Way Back When

Writing lyrically (in Caroline Kirkland's *Chicago Yesterdays*) of "The Yesterday of the Horse," Hobart C. Chatfield-Taylor gives vent to the city-dweller's nostalgia for the good old days, which for most old-timers were the horse-and-buggy days.

The clicking of the hoofs upon the hard macadam, the rhythmical creaking of the harness, the merry rattle of the lead-bars are delectable sounds, I recall, as I sit before an autumn fire dreaming of those days long gone. I seem to see my old team of chestnuts before me and feel the weight of their reins upon my forearm. Sniffing their stable from afar, they spring into their collars with a will, while coach-lamps shed their glimmering rays upon the white roadway ahead. Pricking up their trim little ears, the leaders shy at a shadow; a wheel-horse starts to break, and as I speak a soothing word, the familiar notes of *Who'll Buy a Broom?* sound sweet and clear upon the night air.

Harking back to old times, the oldest inhabitants have much in common with city folk from small towns and rural areas who hark back to old scenes, back where they come from. Both remain essentially small-town folk at heart. And what both are seeking to recapture is what young city couples hope to recover by moving to the suburbs—the old neighborhood life. For in the old days the city neighborhood, like the region, was a living entity and a force—and not so much the neighborhood as the neighborhood spirit, characterized by neighborly feelings rather than mere proximity. Thus Al Smith in *Up to Now* recalls affectionately the East Side neighborhood where he was born and grew up in the Golden Age of the Eighties and Nineties—the volunteer firemen with their rivalries and parades, the old swimming hole in the East River, learning to swim in three feet of water in the fish cars back of the fish market, roller skating in the City Hall Park, open trolley rides to Central Park, boat trips to Coney Island, the building of Brooklyn Bridge, the shipping and warehousing at the tip of Manhattan (the "cradle of the city," where the "city was born"), the Tammany neighborhood clubs with their chowders and picnics.

Old pastimes, trades, songs, stories, street cries—these are the stuff of folklore in its anachronistic and nostalgic phases, with the Twenties now taking the place of the Nineties as the golden age for the middle generation of city folk. These sentimental and illuminating glimpses of the recent or remote past also throw light on the history of a city, its various stages and periods of growth, and on the process of change and resistance to change. But the ways of acceptance and resistance are as strange as the ways of change. "I made my mistake in the beginning," says Robert Casey's maker of wooden Indians, "when I thought this kind of art would go on lasting just because it's lasted a couple of hundred years. It ain't too late to correct the mistake. I'm going to do something permanent. . . . I'll be sitting right here carving out wooden horses for harness shops. Horses ain't goin' to change. . . ."

229

"THE SIDEWALKS OF NEW YORK" [1]

On January 14, 1933, James W. Blake, then seventy years old, checked out of the Penn View Hotel, a dollar-a-night hostelry near Pennsylvania Station in New York. With his blind brother, John D. Blake, and his sister, Mary F. Blake, they proceeded to the railway terminal. Then they checked their few belongings and went over to a sandwich counter. Jim Blake spent the last few pennies they had for coffee and rolls, and the three started up Seventh Avenue. At Fortieth Street, Jim looked west, noticed the building of the New York *Herald Tribune,* and recalled that some years previously that newspaper had printed an interview with him. Leaving his brother and sister to await, he went up to the city room and, as it happened, walked right into the *Herald Tribune's* front page the next day. For Jim Blake, with his friend, Charles B. Lawlor, a vaudeville singer, wrote the song that since 1894 has characterized the city and later became Governor Alfred E. Smith's Presidential campaign chant, "The Sidewalks of New York."

Jobless, penniless, and without food, he and his brother and sister had been dispossessed from their little flat in the Bronx. Blake had been a velour salesman. But velour and velvet were expensive materials that people found easy to forego during the depression, and the concern for which he worked no longer had need of his services. He explained his plight to a staff man of the *Herald Tribune,* and the newspaper speedily interceded. The Emergency Unemployed Relief Committee was notified, and presently charitable machinery began turning that ultimately re-established (with the personal attention of Al Smith) Jim Blake, his brother, and sister as housed, clothed, and fed citizens.

As Blake concluded his story in the *Herald Tribune* offices, he fetched out a decrepit wallet and extracted a mellowed cutting. It was a story a small-town paper had printed about him when he was on the road selling velour. The story detailed his career and closed with this comment: "His song has made Jimmy Blake the idol of New Yorkers, whose city he immortalized. He has but to ask and he has."

Blake folded the cutting back into his wallet. "That is rather ironic," he said. East side, west side, all around the town he had been, and there was no dancing in the streets. Blake, in 1894, was a salesman in the shop of John Golding, a hatter. One day Charlie Lawlor came in, hummed a melody, and asked Blake to write a lyric for it. "I want it to be something about New York," said Lawlor. And Blake, between customers, scribbled down these lines:

Down in front of Casey's old brown wooden stoop,
On a summer's evening we formed a merry group.
Boys and girls together, we would sing and waltz
While the Ginnie played the organ on the sidewalks of New York.

[1] From *Lost Chords,* The Diverting Story of American Popular Songs, by Douglas Gilbert, pp. 255-258. Copyright, 1942, by Douglas Gilbert. Garden City, New York: Doubleday & Company, Inc.

Chorus:

> East side, west side, all around the town,
> The tots sang Ring-a-Rosie, London bridge is falling down.
> Boys and girls together, me and Mamie O'Rourke,
> Tripped the light fantastic on the sidewalks of New York.

> That's where Johnny Casey and little Jimmy Crowe,
> With Jakey Krause, the baker, who always had the dough,
> Pretty Nellie Shannon, with a dude as light as cork,
> First picked up the waltz step on the sidewalks of New York.

> Things have changed since those times, some are up in G.
> Others they are on the hog, but they all feel just like me.
> They would part with all they've got could they but once more walk
> With their best girl and have a twirl on the sidewalks of New York.[2]

They are all originals in the song, all neighbors centering about the 312 East Eighteenth Street address that had been the Blake family's home for seventy-five years. They bought their bread from Jakey Krause, and a real Mamie O'Rourke had taught Jim to waltz. Nellie Shannon's beau *was* a dude—checkered weskit, pearl-gray bowler, and incredible trousers. He was probably James C. Shannon, a gallery-stooge singer for Lottie Gilson, for he married Nellie. The brown stoop actually fronted the house of a man named Higgins, but Jim thought Casey sounded better.

Lottie Gilson sang the "Sidewalks" song at the old London Theater in the Bowery, and it scored an immediate success. A little later, Blake and Lawlor sold their interest in the song outright for $5,000. Blake died in 1935. He left a tuneful characterization of the town and its times and its simple people that amounts to a historical footnote.

"THE BOWERY"[3]

["The Sidewalks of New York"] is a kindlier song than "The Bowery," although that satirical fling at New York's quaint avenue of derelicts and mulc-ters was of equal social significance. It accompanied virtually every reference in motion pictures and on the radio to the city's lower East Side. Like Jim Blake's casual classic, it pins the town to a tune now internationally known. It scored immediately when it was first sung by Harry Conor in Charles H. Hoyt's musical satire, *A Trip to Chinatown.* Soon its recognition became so pronounced that the furious shopkeepers of the Bowery protested—futilely, of course—its public presentation.

Hoyt, a Boston newspaperman and a prolific writer of farces, was the author of the words, and Percy Gaunt, musical director of *A Trip to Chinatown* (he had similarly served for Harrigan and Hart), put his name to the music. Its theme is fast, and the descriptive lyric, if commonplace, is authoritative. For the Bowery, when Hoyt produced his play on November 9, 1891, at the Madison Square

---

[2] Copyright, 1894, by James W. Blake and Charles B. Lawlor. Copyright, 1921, by James W. Blake and Charles B. Lawlor.

[3] *Ibid.,* pp. 258-260.

Oh! the night that I struck New York,

I went out for a qui - et walk;

Folks who are "on to" the ci - ty say,

Bet - ter by far that I took Broad - way;

But I was out to en - joy the sights,

There was the Bow- 'ry a - blaze with lights;

I had one of the dev - il's own nights! I'll

nev - er go there an - y more.___

The Bow - 'ry, the Bow - 'ry!

They say such things, and they do strange things On

the Bow - 'ry, the Bow - 'ry!

I'll nev - er go there an - y more!___

Theater, was no cloister—is not to-day, except that the dives and brothels have been supplanted by one-night flop joints and "smoke" joints ("smoke" is slightly non-poisonous alcohol and water sold at five or ten cents per glass). Here are the first, fourth, and sixth verses and the chorus of

THE BOWERY

Oh! the night that I struck New York,
I went out for a quiet walk.
Folks who are "on to" the city say
Better by far that I took Broadway.
But I was out to enjoy the sights,
There was the Bow'ry ablaze with lights—
I had one of the devil's own nights!
I'll never go there any more.

Chorus:

The Bow'ry, the Bow'ry!
They say such things, and they do strange things
On the Bow'ry, the Bow'ry!
I'll never go there any more!

I went into a concert hall,
I didn't have a good time at all.
Just the minute that I sat down,
Girls began singing, "New Coon in Town."
I got up mad and spoke out free,
"Somebody put that man out," said she.
A man called a bouncer attended to me—
I'll never go there any more!

I struck a place they called a dive,
I was in luck to get out alive.
When the policeman heard my woes,
Saw my black eyes and battered nose,
"You've been held up," said the copper, "fly!"
"No, sir, but I've been knocked down!" said I.
Then he laughed, though I couldn't see why!
I'll never go there any more!

Yes, the lines are clumsy. But Hoyt was writing for a specific characterization: that of a rustic on his first visit to New York. And Conor caught the spirit of the song and character admirably. Rube types were often portrayed in the vaudeville of the '90's. But Conor added a touch of the coster to his performance that not only made it outstanding, it virtually created a new style in pop-tune technique. Critical banter . . . was acceptable practice in the '90's. But the coster twist, seemingly foreign to Hoyt's song, actually assured its success. Many coster types followed: "My Pearl's a Bowery Girl," "My Pet Is a Chelsea Girl," "On the Proper Side of Broadway on a Saturday P.M." It was a curious, unintentional derivation.

THE OLD BOWERY THEATER [4]

It was well past the time of beginning when we returned to the Old Bowery Theater, and crossing the worn and broken tiles of the vestibule passed within the "warm precincts" of the auditorium, captured a fugacious usher, and were conducted to our allotted quarter. The action of the play already had begun to involve its characters in mysteries inexplicable by the unassisted intellect. Issuing forth in quest of a house-bill, I was informed that they were all distributed. Enquiring then what was the title and drift of the drama, the humorous usher replied that he was blest if he knew. By dint of close application and much analogy, we determined that we were witnessing a version of the stock Irish play, in which a virtuous peasant-girl and a high-minded patriot with knee-breeches and a brogue and an illicit whisky-still utterly expose and confound a number of designing dukes, lords, etc., who were assisted by a numerous family of murderers.

One feature of the play was the worn device of confounding the real action with imaginary action; the first act being of real life, and inducing the dream, which thereupon carried forward the story through complications and woeful horrors until a happy waking in the last scene of the fourth act rewarded the virtue that had never been tempted, and utterly blasted the plotting vice that never had existed. The incidents were many and exciting. The scene where the midnight murderers prepared a grave for their coming victim (an afflicted lady who is to be deserted by her husband at this spot), and are affrighted at their noisome task by anguishing groans of the patriot, mourning the lady's unfaithfulness to him, as he distils unlawful potheen among the rocks overhead, was chilling in its awful gloom; while nothing could be finer than the manner in which the patriot, disinterestedly suffering his pots to boil over, came flying to the rescue of innocence over frightful pasteboard precipices and down deep descents of lumber, engaging the whole band of felons at once. The combat deepens, thwack go the stuffed clubs, plunge the impossible daggers; the wounded ruffians reel and fall and struggle up again knee-high, discharging dreadful cuts at the legs of the deliverer. Those yet unhurt close in upon him, but only rip his machine-sewed shirt, receiving in return such fierce and telling blows that life departs from each in turn, till triumphant virtue takes one shuddering glance at success and faints in an agony of perspiration across the long-since-swooning body of the destined victim.

Summary of six corpses and quasi-corpses in painful attitudes—sudden effect of limelight, and apparition of constabulary and red-coats (too late, as usual), as "the great green curtain fell on all," amid deafening shouts of "Hi!" "That's too thin!" and "Cheese it!" from pit to fourth tier.

We missed many of the points of this great drama, for the house was a study more interesting than the stage. We idled about somewhat, behind the seats of the balcony, with audible steps among the thick-strewn peanut-shells.

[4] From *Reminiscences of New York by an Octogenarian* (1816 to 1860), by Chas. H. Haswell, pp. 360-365. Copyright, 1896, by Harper & Brothers. New York.
Entry of December 21, 1840.

In the front lobby we met a man whom somebody had just "gone through," the check-taker and usher calmly comparing guesses concerning the offender. Clambering to the mephitic fourth tier, we watched, as long as untrained lungs could last in that atmosphere, the crowd of rough youth there compacted. Plenty of native sharpness was noticeable in speech and looks among those skyward seats, which doubtless contained also much native good, some of which would work itself clear in time and do something of account in the world; but the main expression of that crowd was of nursing vulgarity and vice, with an indescribable air of sordid ignorance and brutal, fierce impatience of all lovely, graceful delicate things.

Though a promenade was worth making, the house could be best studied from our box. The whole effect was more interesting than any detached portions, and this was all before us—the pit and first tier below; the second tier meeting the box exactly at our level; overhead, the third tier, its thronging faces full in the flame of the gas; and, darkly above, the true Olympus of the gallery gods. There were no vacant seats. Steadily sloping upward from the footlights was lifted, row above row, the close-packed, stamping, shrieking, cat-calling, true Bowery crowd. The house contained a good number of women, rough-clad but of decent looks, some mothers of families with the families small and great together, and a few "children in arms," which the Bowery rules did not forbid. I saw but two gloved women in the audience; they, by force of their attire, I suppose, felt a certain application of the saying, *noblesse oblige*, since they went much out of their way to be agreeable to us, and were very courteous and hospitably minded indeed.

Beside the proper and prevailing peanut, the spectators refreshed themselves with a great variety of bodily nutriment. Ham sandwich and sausage seemed to have precedence, being both portable and nourishing, but pork chops also were prominent, receiving the undivided attention of a large family party in the second tier, the members of which consumed chops with a noble persistence through all the intermissions; holding the small end of the bone in the hand and working downward from the meaty portion. The denuded bones were most of them playfully shied at the heads of acquaintances in the pit; if you never have seen it done, you can hardly fancy how well you can telegraph with pork-bones when the aim is sure; and if you hit the wrong man, you have only to look innocent and unconscious.

The Bowery audience was by no means content with inarticulate noise; besides the time-honored, technical modes of encouraging the players, there was full and free communication in speech, sometimes a set colloquy with the actors —which the audience counted on, and waited for with great expectancy. This the actors well understood, and when the Irish patriot had a line of particularly overpowering moral import, his sure way to make a point with it was to come down to the front, declaim it vociferously, and end by saying, "Is that so, boys?" or "Don't you, boys?" or something of the kind, and then the acclaim and outcry were so loud and long that all babies in the house cried out the moment they could get a chance to be heard, which caused another terrible din, with uncomplimentary remarks about the infants, and "Cheese it!" again—always this cry, which, though it be, as I have learned, a highly plastic expression, yet, from the variety of its frequent application during the evening, must have come in sometimes with great irrelevance.

The second play was a burlesque of "Don Giovanni," with Leporello's part given to the clown, an amusing fellow and clever acrobat. The chief part of the story was preserved, though there were many cuts and not a few additions. The players earned their money. The orchestra never ceased its swift, lilting measures, as though for some endless, preternaturally quick quadrille, and the action of the stage was allowed no resting-place until the whole was done; so, notwithstanding great lack of appliances by way of machinery for transformations and the like, the thing went well by virtue of constant action and the utmost possible rapidity. Shipwreck gave the clown opportunity for an extravagant swimming-scene, and when the Don kicked him out of a two-story window, his descent, clinging to the top of a ladder, and describing a great arc that landed him down by the footlights, was very skilfully made. The cream of the play was thought to be in the banquet scene, where the clown and an absurd old Irishwoman wrangled over a wash-bowl full of macaroni. The by-play of this scene is not to be here reported, though it pleased the audience greatly. Scarce any of the humor was more relished by most of the spectators than the exquisite device of throwing the macaroni at the orchestra-players, and finally at the "pay-people" in the pit. It cannot be pleasant to be wiped across the face with a string of wet macaroni, and probably those who were thus distinguished did not enjoy it, but all the others did, and the upper tiers howled approbation like a great company of demoniacs. The statue came for the Don at last, and the clown was too well frightened to throw macaroni then, so the hero went for his waiting gin-and-water, with profuse accompaniment of red devils and penny fireworks. When we came away at a quarter before twelve, the third piece, "The Babes in the Wood," was just beginning, and the ridiculous heavy villains were just warming to their fiendish work.

Since that evening young men have grown old, but still I have a clear image of the old theater; the crowd, the air, the crackling peanuts underfoot, the strayed reveller with empty pocket, the chops and sandwiches, the courteous gloved young women, the raging fourth tier, and eager, bent looks of the rough faces; the ceaseless lilt and drone of the music sounds in my ears (a dab of macaroni on the neck of the contrabass). I hear the swish of the Don's rapier and the thump of the clown's posteriors on the stage; the amusing strifes and murders take place again, and the "very tragical mirth." Indeed the single sensation of strangeness that comes from the absence of all familiar faces from among so many of one's own townspeople was alone almost worth seeking.

SPIELERS [5]

The dance-hall is truly a passion with working-girls. The desire to waltz is bred in the feminine bone. It is a familiar thing to see little girls on

[5] From *Types from City Streets*, by Hutchins Hapgood, pp. 134-136. Copyright, 1910, by Funk & Wagnalls Company. New York and London.

the East Side dancing rhythmically on the street, to the music of some hand-organ, while heavy wagons roll by unheeded. When those little girls grow older and become shop-girls they often continue to indulge their passion for the waltz. Some of them dance every night, and are so confirmed in it that they are technically known as "spielers." Many a girl, nice girl, too, loves the art so much that she will dance with any man she meets, whatever his character or appearance. Often two girls will go to some dance-hall, which may or may not be entirely respectable, and deliberately look for men to dance with. On one occasion, at a Harlem dancing-place, where all kinds of working-girls go, I saw a girl compel her escort, a man who could not dance, to ask men she had never met, and whom she did not know, to dance with her. A girl of that character may never want to see her fellow waltzer again, but many of these girls get involved with undesirable men, simply through their uncontrollable passion for the waltz. When carried to an excess, it is as bad as drink or gambling.

Girls of the "spieler" class of society are of an extreme simplicity, too simple even to be practical. They lack the hardness of the swell department-store girls; but make up for it by their "toughness," which . . . is the conventional atmosphere of the Bowery. . . .

YIDDISH THEATER [6]

The Yiddish theater on the East Side was flourishing. Great actors from Europe were glad to perform before such an admiring and appreciative audience. Like the Synagogue and the Annual Ball, the theater served as a social function. There was no reserve among the audience, every one talked to every one else. During the intermission it was a common sight to see some well-cushioned ladies standing in the orchestra aisle waving their arms or making sounds like "pst, pst," to attract the attention of friends in the gallery and converse across the vast expanse of the theater. "How's Mama's feet?" or "Did you hear who died last week?" There would be voluble "tut-tuts" and sympathetic wagging of heads. Those who were near listened with undisguised interest, except when too busy talking among themselves. Others sociably and noisily drank soda water purchased from the ushers who marched up and down the aisles, shrilly calling, "Candy, soda water, candy, soda water!"

Some of the plays were classics, such as The Kreutzer Sonata, Gott, Mench und Teufel (God, Man, and the Devil), and works by Shakespeare. I remember a Shylock, played by the great tragedian, Jacob Adler, who gave me an unforgettable memory of that great role. Some years later, Adler played it on Broadway, in Yiddish, with an entire English-speaking cast. Adler was not the only great star of the Yiddish stage. There were still others like Madam Kalish, who, speaking both languages fluently, became an English-speaking star, after her success on the Yiddish stage. Although enormously successful on her tour through the States, she came back time and again to the audiences of the East

[6] From Horsecars and Cobblestones, by Sophie Ruskay, pp. 50-54. Copyright, 1918, by Sophie Ruskay. New York: The Beechhurst Press.

Side, playing again before "her *Yiddishe* volk" the roles which she had created.

But it was the simple drama of our own day which I preferred. To me, all plays were good, even the bad ones. Not understanding Yiddish too well, except for occasional words and the homely expressions which embroidered every one's speech, I relied almost entirely upon the acting, which was so natural and expressive I could grasp the meaning of the play.

There was one play which served as a pattern for many others. It was the story of a family that had come to America. The son, after a few years, had grown prosperous. He had discarded his religious practices as old-fashioned, and was embarrassed when his aged parents visited his now ultra-fashionable home. He felt he did his duty by providing for their material needs, but this, the father told him, had now become "gall and wormwood in their mouths."

In a scene bordering on the tragic, the mother, in ritual wig, dressed in old-world grandeur, tries in vain to ingratiate herself with her American-born daughter-in-law and her grandchildren. They look upon her as some one strange and alien. The father succeeds no better. He reminds his son, "Your Milton is past eleven years; it is time he was learning for *Bar Mitzvah.*"

"Please, father, spare me that," says the son, as he looks uncomfortably at his friends, who are at a table playing pinochle and are highly amused by such a suggestion.

Broken-hearted, the father dies. The grave yawns right before the audience; nothing is left to the imagination.

"I repent, I repent," says the son, as he tries to fling himself into the grave.

The aged mother restrains him, and there follows a tearful reconciliation. "You can perform a *mitzvah* [good deed] that will bring joy to your father in Paradise," she says. "Your great uncle's only child is an old maid; already she is twenty. If you, my son, will provide the wedding and the dowry for this penniless orphan, a husband can be found."

With the assistance of the *shadchen* (marriage broker), a comic but nostalgic figure to those who so recently came from Europe, but an object of ridicule to the American-born children, the match is made. The *chuppa* (wedding canopy) is brought on the stage, and after a ceremony in which tears flow freely, there are feasting and rejoicing. The *shammus* (sexton), his red bandana streaming from his coat-tails, starts a traditional dance in which the male guests solemnly join. Women stand in a circle and clap their hands as they beat out the rhythm. The music grows wilder and wilder. The curtain falls.

To Mama and to us it was all simply wonderful.

SINGING WAITERS [7]

     . . . Eddie [Cantor] and me had lots of fun [at Kerry Walsh's, Coney Island], the two of us. We seemed to match. If a guy would ask for a song, and we didn't know the song, we'd make one up on the spot. If a guy wanted "The Hills of Kentucky," which I didn't know or ever heard of, I'd fake a

[7] From *Schnozzola*, The Story of Jimmy Durante, by Gene Fowler, pp. 21-22. Copyright, 1951, by Gene Fowler. New York: The Viking Press, Inc.

melody and Eddie would sing, "The Hills of Kentucky are far, far away, and when you're from them hills, you're away from them hills, yes, away from them hills of Kentucky." So the guy who'd asked for the song and slipped us a couple of bucks for it, would object, "What the hell did you sing to me?" Then Eddie would say, "Why, 'The Hills of Kentucky.'" Then the guy would say, "What? That ain't the words." And Eddie would say, innocent like, "Are there *two* of them? Well, gee, I'll ask the piano player does he know the other one?" And then we'd go on from there, and we'd make a regular routine out of it, and Eddie would say to the man, "Oh," he'd say, "you must mean *this* one." And he'd sing the title right in the guy's kisser and turn to make double talk like he's singin' some lyrics, and I'd follow him on the piano: "Old Kentucky in the hills, which we love so dear. . . ." And the guy would yell his brains out, "Stop it! That's not it either." He'd say, "What are you guys? Wise guys?" Eddie, with his big brown eyes, would shed real tears and sob. "No," he'd cry, "and if you want the money back, we'll give you the money back!" But as he says this he's walkin' away from the guy. The money is in his shoe already, and the guy wants his money back; but Eddie walks away too fast. What a guy, that Eddie! He's tops.

"WOULDN'T THAT JAR YOU!" [8]

. . . "Cheese it, the cop" was the boys' warning of the approach of a policeman, not infrequently uttered by them to give themselves the feeling of being engaged in an illegal action which really did not exist.

"Cut behind" or "hitch behind" notified a driver that a boy was stealing a ride on the back of his vehicle, by hanging on to it or by attaching his bob-sled.

Throwing yourself on a sled to force it into a short run on even ground produced "belly-whoppers."

"Scizzors" were firecrackers that had not exploded, bent double so as to crack open, and lighted.

"Chokers" were the high straight collars worn especially by dudes.

A "dicer" was a stiff hat.

"Peek-a-boo waist" came in with the perforated blouse that afforded tiny dotted vistas of uncovered skin.

For a while after the publication of Du Maurier's *Trilby* ladies' feet were archly referred to as "trilbies."

To "skip the tralaloo" was to take French leave.

"How's that for high?" was a bid for commendation.

"Wouldn't that jar you?" is fairly clear for "Isn't that provoking?"

"Over the left" implied the reverse, as "He's a fine fellow—over the left."

"Gallus" meant something like "tip-top."

"He wouldn't tumble if a house fell down" was applied to unobservant people.

[8] From *Manhattan Kaleidoscope*, by Frank Weitenkampf, pp. 83-84. Copyright, 1947, by Charles Scribner's Sons. New York.

Some of these expressions are still somewhat in use, yet some have already aroused antiquarian interest.—F.W.

"His name is Denis" implied that one was a goner.

You were said to be "talking through your hat" when you appeared unfamiliar with your topic.

The "boarding house reach" at the dining-room table was supposed, in the popular idea of humor, to be necessary in order to overcome restrictions as to food in boarding-houses. (What a profitable subject the boarding-house mistress was for the comic artists!)

"Baggage smasher" was applied to the handler of baggage on railroads, jocularly supposed to play havoc even with the enormous iron-bound Saratoga trunks.

And passing counterfeit money was "shoving the queer."

OLD FIGURE SIGNS [9]

What might be called the plastic side of our subject [of pictorial signboards] is exemplified by the tangible representation of certain objects and figures bearing more or less relation to the business of the merchant who sets them up in front of his shop or over his door.

The mortar and pestle of the druggist, the gilt boots and hats of the shoemaker and hatter, and the giant eyeglasses of the optician are as familiar and as suggestive of the various trades they represent as are the three gilt balls of the pawnbroker shops, the cigar store Indian, and the barber pole.

Similarly, dealers in sporting goods indicate their calling by mammoth guns (to which a Murray Street dealer adds a huge cartridge), and locksmiths hang out keys and saws. Huge cigars, pens, pipes, and horseshoes pendant over doors also leave no doubt as to what can be had inside, while single umbrellas or perpendicular strings thereof remind us that we must be prepared for a rainy day. Many of these carved figures are gilt. Some chiropodists place big sawed-

[9] *Ibid.*, pp. 37-40.

off white feet before their doors, just as a large gloved hand shows us where to get gloves.

The conventional mortar of the druggist is occasionally varied by the addition of an eagle, or even of a cupid-like imp, and Gall and Lembke add to the usual opticians' spectacles an enormous pair of opera glasses. Huge gilt molars are still found pendant before some dentists' offices, William Demuth indicates his business by a huge meerschaum pipe, and more than one wine dealer sets up a finger post for thirsty humanity in the shape of an immense demijohn. A large pair of scissors indicates the business of some cutlery shops, and a wooden red-striped stocking emphasized the lettered-sign in front of a knitting establishment on Sixth Street, while a Bowery sausage-maker lures in the gourmand by a fine gilt wurst, and a gilt wheel steers you into the store of a Fourth Avenue firm dealing in yachting uniforms and furnishings. A palette is a not unfamiliar sign over artist materials stores, while the little pyramid of painted barrels is quite extensively used by dealers in painters' materials. Some photographers set up a dummy camera as a sign; Fischer, the music dealer, blows his own trumpet to attract bandmasters, and a manufacturer of musical instruments on Twenty-third Street, near Third Avenue, has long used a huge and weather-beaten French horn. Similarly Gemünder hangs up a gold "Strad" to make sure that you do not mistake your man, and a downtown gold beater has hung out a large gilt arm, grasping a hammer. The large lantern that hangs out over the "L," not far from Franklin Square, leaves no doubt as to what is manufactured in that building, and many probably remember the huge teapot that used to decorate the establishment of a well-known dealer in hardware. One saloon on Seventh Street has a swinging sign, into an open space of which is set the carved representation of a foaming glass of beer. An enormous bamboo cane, which stretches up along the front of the building, indicates the business of a firm of cane manufacturers on East Fourth Street, while cards are advertised a few doors further on by a sign shaped like a card with its left upper corner turned down.

We occasionally come across old figures, marked out on boards, cut out, and painted on both sides. Such flat figures are found in front of some old shooting galleries, and a Fourth Street carpenter glories in an "Equestrian statue" of Washington made in this way.

Stuffed bears hang on to poles in front of many furriers' establishments, and dealers in carriages and harness are supplied from Paris with life-size presentments of fiery dapple-gray steeds to set up in their windows or before their doors.

Some downtown streets are particularly rich in figure signs. One Warren Street dealer in cutlery has set up a huge knife and fork over his door on one side and an equally large razor on the other, while on Frankfort Street a rocket of enormous dimensions conjures up visions of the "glorious Fourth."

The gilt figure of an ostrich proclaims the business carried on at Sixth Avenue and Seventeenth Street, and it was B. Fitch of Fourth Avenue, I think, who for years advertised his business in feather beds by a stuffed goose reposing on a bed of down. Some undertakers still affect the wooden tombstone, a few dealers in leather and findings indicate their business by a large awl, and the beehive is occasionally found over the doors of savings banks.

Purely symbolic signs like the latter are not very common, however, although the wine merchant's bunch of grapes and the baker's sheaf of wheat are still met with.

One Broadway toydealer trades under the protective presence of Santa Claus, and a firm dealing in woolen rags has the figure of a ragman perched up on top of its building on West Street. The fireman on the Bowery, near Grand Street, and Gambrinus, about Thirty-fifth Street and Broadway, now somewhat dilapidated, are both old and familiar figures. Schirmer has now set up a bust of Beethoven, possibly to show that he wishes to keep music up to a classical standard, and another firm, near Steinway's, has decorated the front of its house with a number of busts of musicians.

The well-known group, "You Dirty Boy," has been reproduced and set up on the front of the soap establishment on Canal Street.

* * * * *

[Other] signs in plastic form [include]: a footrule (Grand Street, near the Bowery), a gilt spool of cotton thread (Franklin Street, near Broadway, 1907), a large carriage lamp (Broome Street, near Center), a gilt rat (used by a vermin destroyer on Center Street, 1903), a skate, a billowing gilt shirt mounted on a pole (Brooklyn, 1907), a gilt tie set in a frame (dealer in ready-made four-in-hands, Bowery, near Spring, 1897), half a trunk projecting from a signboard, a large gilt boar (over the door of the store, long gone, of the charcutier, Perceval, on Sixth Avenue, near Ninth Street)—all self-explanatory.

Not a few such objects could be seen well into the present century. Gilt horses' heads jutted out over the entrance of more than one livery stable; one of the latter, the Knickerbocker Stables at 238 West Fifty-fourth Street, had its front decorated with a figure of Father Knickerbocker. Watch and clock makers pointed the way to their establishment by erecting a tall post with a clock (sometimes a real one) at the top, at the curb. Such a one stood for years on Fifth Avenue just above Twenty third Street; it appeared in etchings by Robert F. Blum and F. H. Lungren. That was in the days of freer occupation of sidewalks by awning-poles and the like. Be it noted, too, that in the old days the barber pole, with red and white stripes, was a stationary affair of wood; today it turns in a case. And finally there was for some years a possibly unique sign, a huge elephant's tusk, on the south side of Fourteenth Street, a little East of Fourth Avenue, no doubt in front of the shop of F. Grote & Co., dealers in billiard ivories, at No. 114.

THE MAN WHO MADE WOODEN INDIANS [10]

Among my best friends when the old nineteenth century breathed its last was a very fine sculptor who carved wooden Indians for cigar stores. His name, as I remember it, was Walter Campbell, and he maintained an atelier in

[10] From *Chicago Medium Rare, When We Were Both Younger*, by Robert J. Casey, pp. 221-227. Copyright, 1949, 1950, by the Chicago Herald-American; 1952, by The Bobbs-Merrill Company, Inc. Indianapolis and New York.

the basement of one of those seagoing boarding houses just north of the old Rush Street bridge.

He was so old that he had to wear a jeweler's glass eye for his fine work— which didn't seem to me to be very fine—but in spite of that and other infirmities a lot of people, including me, rated him as the top wooden-Indian carver of North America.

* * * * * *

Nowadays, unless you are a frequenter of museums, you won't see many specimens of the work of Sculptor Campbell or the thousands of other unknown chiselers who went before him. But in the nineties there were more wooden Indians within a mile of the site of Old Fort Dearborn than there had been live Potawatomi at the time of the massacre.

Cigar store Indians now
eagerly sought for
by Collectors.

. . . [In] 1700 . . . the first of their wooden tribe displayed his bundle of nonsmokable cigars to the citizens of Boston. No tobacconist for the next 200 years would have thought of trying to do business without them any more than he would have thought of dispensing with materials for ignition, such as flint and steel and tinder, or a little charcoal brazier, or sputtering sulphur matches, or a glass gas torch swinging on a rubber base.

In Chicago the wooden Indians seemed like the only institution likely to remain unchanged tomorrow and the next day, until the end of time. . . .

It may be that their elimination was due not to any fault of their own, nor any lack of public appreciation, but to subtle changes that crept into the tobacco business almost unnoticed. As recently as 1900 nobody would have thought of going into a tobacco shop to bet on a horse or to buy neckties, soda water, whisky, fountain pens, lip rouge, stockings, candy or hundreds of other things for which an Indian could claim no responsibility. . . .

* * * * *

Inasmuch as Walter Campbell was an active part of what amounted to the country's most flourishing advertising business, it is not remarkable that he was quick to notice a restlessness in the trade he served. He would speak of it bitterly and for hours on end.

"When you are dealing in a specialized product, you can sell only to a specialized market," was the burden of his song. "And frills and furbelows in the tobacco business won't do a wooden Indian no good. I been at this sculpturing for maybe fifty years, man and boy, and I know what I'm a-talking about.

"I started out to be an innovator. Up in Canada I got the idea of making totems for the French fur shops. They wasn't Indians. They was what they called 'couriers du bois,' which means 'wooden couriers.'

"Them wooden couriers was the first trappers. So I made some. They didn't sell well. Not a-tall. An' that certainly showed me there was no place for novelty in business.

"But you can't tell these tobacco men that. I seen it coming, this nonsense. Once you could put out an Indian with one feather in his bonnet an' dress him up in leather pants. But seems like styles change. So pretty soon I'm workin' on full-size war-bonnet headdresses, an' the lowest priced chief you can turn out has to wear beaded war moccasins.

"That ain't all—you got to show every vein in the feathers and carve out every bead. You got to make the hair look like it's just come out of a wig shop. An' you've got to carve fingernails—good ones—an' give the Indian lines on his hand that a fortune-teller could read.

"These newfangled see-gars are comin' in with paper bands on 'em. An' the wooden-Indian buyers insist that you put bands in bas-relief on every doggoned smoke in the Indian's bundle.

"If you do an honest job on an Indian nowadays, it takes twice as much time as it did when I was starting out. Prices ain't improved much. An' besides that you got the cutthroat competition of crooks who make the delicate parts out of plaster an' paste 'em on."

Despite such difficulties, Old Walter did fairly well for several years before the last retreat of the cigar-store redskins really began.

* * * * *

In 1900 a finicky City Council passed an ordinance forbidding shopkeepers to clutter up the sidewalks with picturesque emblems of their business. The ruling affected not only wooden Indians but isolated barber's poles, the fascinating exterior showcases of pawnbrokers, whistling peanut roasters, the stuffed bears of furriers and other similar menaces to traffic. It was, indeed, a sad day.

"Well," said Old Walter, in his farewell to the Indians, "I've been getting ready for this. I made my mistake in the beginning when I thought this kind of art would go on lasting just because it's lasted a couple of hundred years. It ain't too late to correct the mistake. I'm going to do something permanent.

"Mark my words. In ten years all the cigar-store Indians in this town are going to be made out of plaster. But not by me.

"When that happens I'll be sitting right here carving out wooden horses for harness shops. Horses ain't goin' to change. An' we're always goin' to have thousands of them . . . thousands of them and thousands more as the city grows. . . ."

"Campbell?" queried the man who ran the magazine shop [next door]. "I dunno exactly what did happen to him. Went out of here all of a sudden. Beats all. Heard somebody say he was goin' to California. . . ."

He may have found out something that changed his mind about the permanency of horses.

HOTELS OF THE EARLY NINETIES [11]

We were still in the age when women were classed politically with criminals and idiots and our kindly attitude toward the gentler sex obliged to travel alone is a sweet and beautiful retrospect. After dark no first-class hotel would receive her unaccompanied by a male relative. Even then she was compelled to come and go through a dingy door on the side street, labeled "Ladies' Entrance." She might just as well have worn the scarlet letter as to walk through the main corridor. In order that she might not pollute the pure atmosphere created by the masculine guests, she was huddled into a dark room in an obscure and inaccessible part of the building ostentatiously labeled "Ladies' Parlor." No sunlight or cheerfulness was ever allowed to penetrate this padded cell and visitors were constantly under the supervision of a lynx-eyed chambermaid who dusted chairs ceaselessly and thus artlessly performed the duties of a chaperone. A generation was to elapse ere the town was electrified by the news that a woman traveler had peremptorily declined to leave the Waldorf upon the night clerk's refusal to provide her with accommodations. She had been guilty of arriving after sundown. The hotel capitulated and the whole country rang with the sensational tidings next morning.

The new attitude met with public approval. Mr. Boldt announced that thereafter a certain floor of the hotel would be open to provide for these strange wayfarers. Other hotels read the handwriting on the wall, and gradually this archaic restriction was finally removed. But it took time, and is nothing to brag about.

Before the days of the telephone, hotels had annunciator boards to indicate the room number of a guest calling up the office for service. Then, later, in the Eighties, some one invented a machine to do away with fifty per cent of the toil involved in a journey to find out what was wanted and a later journey in supplying it. This machine was in use in most of the hotels of the early Nineties.

In each room in the hotel was a dial with a movable arrow like a clock hand. On the dial was printed the names of everything a guest would be at all likely to want—all the drinks that were ever heard of, paper, envelopes, telegraph blanks, "help," a doctor, police, chambermaid, messenger boy, eggs, toast, milk, soup, oysters, breakfast, dinner, tea—in fact every eatable in common demand, a city directory, playing cards, cigars, cigarettes, chewing tobacco, a barber; in short, everything in a list of one hundred or one hundred and fifty necessaries. The guest pointed the arrow to the name of whatever he wanted

[11] From *Valentine's Manual of Old New York, 1926*, edited by Henry Collins Brown, pp. 96-98. Copyright, 1925, by Henry Collins Brown. New York: Valentine's Manual, Inc.

and by pressing a button registered his demand on the dial behind the clerk's desk.

It was discovered, however, that notwithstanding the wide compass of the dial there was always something a guest wanted that did not appear on its catalogue. Then again the dial was prone to get out of order and a guest calling for ice water was on occasion surprised with a service of hot tea. The dials were not long in use before they were superseded by the telephone.

COMPLAINT OF A CREOLE BOARDINGHOUSE-KEEPER [12]

O la canaille! la canaille! All time after dis I will make dem to pay in advance.

De first dat I have, say he vas a capitaine. I know not if he vas a capitaine; but he vas a misérable. After he have eat and sleep here six week and not pay me, I tell him, "Monsieur, I must money have."

He say: "Madame, you take me for tief?"

I say: "Monsieur, it is right dat you pay; I have wait long time assez."

He den say: "I learn you how to speak me in a manner so much insolent. Now, I not pay you till when I be ready, and I not hurry myself."

"Go out from my house!" I say.

"I go out, madame, from your dirty house when it me please"—dat how he speak me. And I could not force him to part till when I had take all de furniture out from his room. He owe me not more as seventy dollaire!

. . . After, I have one Frenchman, I tink him well elevated—le coco. He nail his valise on de floor for make me tink heavy; and he dispar one night—owing me forty-nine dollaire! I find noting in his valise only one *syringe*.

. . . After, I have two married. Dey pay me enough well, until when de woman run away wit some oder man. Her husban' stay till when he owe me eighty dollaire. After, he go too; and write me letter as dis:

"Madame, I cheat you of eighty dollaire; and I not wish only I could cheat you of eighty thousand dollaire. It was for cause of you dat my wife have run away."

After, I find out she not was his wife.

. . . Den I have a sick man. He fall on de banquette in face of my house, and I take him in to nurse. When dat he get well he tell me he vas one professor of langedge. He eat and sleep here four mont; and first he pay a little. He complain much from noise. He vas what you call nerveux—so like I was oblige for to make my daughter walk witout shoes in naked foots; and we to speak in dumb and deaf langedge by fear of make him trouble. He smoke in de bed and burn de cover; also he break de pot and de cradle-chair, and after, de window, an' de armoire an' de—vat you call de pendule;—he let fall ink on de carpet, and he spit tobacc' on de wall, and he vomit in de bed. But I

[12] From *Creole Sketches,* by Lafcadio Hearn, edited by Charles Woodward Hutson, *The Writings of Lafcadio Hearn,* Large-Paper Edition, Volume I, pp. 128-130. Copyright, 1887, by Roberts Brothers, and 1911 and 1922, by Houghton Mifflin Company. Boston.
Reprinted from the New Orleans *Item,* September 27, 1879.

noting say, as he not 'ave baggage;—ainsi, when he owe me forty dollaire I not want turn him out for dat I get my money more late. When at de end I tell him to go out, he tell me he have receive a checque and pay me on Monday. But I nevaire see him after. He owe me one hundred and sixty-seven dollaire— and seventy cent vat I lend him for medicine to buy.

. . . After, I have one woman, species of camel (espèce de chameau) and one doctor, her husband (tout ce qu'il y avait d'abominable). She pretend to be—and you call dat?—sage femme; and he is not so much doctor as my cat; but for all dey doctor me for two hundred and fifty dollaire, and I not ever obtain of it not one sou.

. . . After, I have tree familee—all vat vas of rough and ugly; for one mont I not receive of rent. So I serve to dem notice of quit. But dey tell me dey not me pay nevaire, and not quit until when I make law-suit. Eh bien, de rent of de house vas not more as fifty dollaire, and de law cost me perhaps one affair of more like one hundred dollaire. Ainsi, I quit de house, an' leave dem all dere to do like dey would please. But before dat I could leave, dey steal me two buckets, and one stove, and one broom, and one clock, and one iron, and one coffee-mill, and one hen, and one leetle cat vat I much vas fond of, and one plate, and some linen of womans vat to me not belong.

"ALL DRESSED UP LIKE A FIRE ENGINE" [13]

One of the most notable traits of the old-time volunteer fireman was the great affection, amounting almost to worship, in which he held his engine, hose cart, or hook and ladder truck. . . . Especially was this true of a member of an engine company, for more than any other type of fire-fighting apparatus an engine possessed a definite personality. Moreover, it was mechanically temperamental, and developed innumerable peculiarities which made it seem very human and alive. To a fireman an engine or a hose cart was always feminine; he invariably spoke of it as "the old gal" and often addressed it in endearing terms. It was not unusual to see a jubilant fire laddie publicly kiss his machine, and embrace as much of it as his arms would surround, after it had worsted a rival in fair contest, or had performed some other noteworthy feat.

. . . The more he loved the machine the greater was his desire to ornament it with brightly-colored pictures of his own selection. So insistent, indeed, were the firemen upon the right to paint their own engines and hose carts to suit themselves that it soon became customary for the city authorities, on delivering a new machine, to paint it a temporary dull gray or other neutral color, leaving the question of permanent decoration—and the task of paying for it—to the particular company to which the apparatus had been assigned. And to the firemen the matter was one of extraordinary importance. Special committees were appointed to consider various color combinations and to make arrangements with an artist, and their reports were subjected to almost endless debate. Sometimes months elapsed before obdurate firemen would abandon their personal

[13] From *Ye Olde Fire Laddies*, by Herbert Asbury, pp. 140-144, 150-153, 156, 165-171, 175. Copyright, 1930, by Herbert Asbury. New York: Alfred A. Knopf, Inc.

preferences, and the attitude assumed by a member of Engine Company No. 3, long cited as a classic example of the fireman's viewpoint, was not uncommon. Having received a new engine in the winter of 1820, the men of No. 3 held a special meeting at the Tea-Water Tavern, opposite the old Tea-Water Pump in Chatham Street, where the matter of decorating the machine was discussed over great bowls of steaming punch. The Tea-Water Pump had that day been given a new coat of pea-green, and one of the firemen was greatly impressed by the striking contrast between the white snow and the bright green of the paint. He listened to the reports of the various committees, meanwhile industriously imbibing punch, and finally he arose and said with great gravity:

"I don't care a damn, fellers, what color yer paint the old gal, if yer'll only listen to me and paint her green!"

He sank back in his chair and slumbered, rousing every few moments to shout, "Paint the old gal green!" His advice was not followed, but his phrase caught the fancy of the firemen, and thereafter when they extinguished a fire they boasted that they had painted it green, an expression which is still used occasionally by modern firemen. And the company poet, after much travail, composed a ditty which the men of No. 3 sang as they rolled home from a fire:

> We're coming back rejoicing,
> The liveliest boys you've seen;
> We've beat them other fellers,
> At the fire we painted green.

A few months later, however, three small fires occurred within twenty-four hours, and at all of them No. 3 was last on the scene. At two she even arrived too late to get into action. There was great rejoicing among the other companies, and some unknown genius produced a poem commemorating No. 3's failure to make good her boast, which was sung in every engine house in New York:

> There is an engine house,
> Not far away;
> Where they're last at fires,
> Three times a day.
>
> Oh, how the boys all scream,
> When they see Three's put on steam,
> For the fires they can't paint green,
> Three times a day.

Because of their construction the old engine and hose carts, with wide panels and backs and a considerable extent of surface, lent themselves admirably to decorative schemes, even when conceived on a grand scale; and until the formation of the paid fire department and the introduction of steam engines, which made fire-fighting more of a business and less of a romantic adventure, they were the gaudiest vehicles in Christendom. Many of the finest decorations were not painted upon the engine or hose cart proper, but were emblazoned on false backs, of various fine woods and very heavy, which were attached to the machines only for parades and other exhibitions. They were in great demand as souvenirs when the volunteer companies were disbanded, but most of them were retained by the veteran fireman organizations. In time it became the custom to present them to expectant fathers, who made them into cradles. The finest of all the ornamented backs is said to have been that of Columbian Engine No. 14, on which the artist J. Quidor, about 1850, painted the portrait of an Indian chieftain and his squaw, against an appropriate background of forest. It was of solid mahogany, and with the picture cost nearly one thousand dollars, all of which was subscribed by the members of the company. Peter Ottignon, better known as the Jolly Butcher, who was Foreman at the time, enjoyed a considerable renown as a fighter. Soon after the painting had been completed he led his men in an attack upon a rival company, and to punish No. 14 the Fire and Water Committee of the Common Council suspended the entire membership and ordered the engine removed to the Corporation Yard—the greatest disgrace that could befall a company. When a city truck arrived to haul away the machine, however, Quidor's masterpiece had vanished, and the firemen professed ignorance of its whereabouts. Detectives tried to find it, but while they searched New York the painting was travelling across the Atlantic Ocean on a packet of which Jim Lyons, a member of No. 14, was mate. By the time Lyons' ship returned to the United States the company had been reinstated, and the painting was again installed on the engine.

The practice of ornamenting fire engines and hose carts, from which came the common expression "all dressed up like a fire engine," was begun in 1796, when a wreath of roses was painted on the back and panels of No. 15, which was thereafter known as Old Wreath of Roses. Within the next fifty years the custom had become so popular that some of the foremost artists of the day were frequently called upon to exercise their talent upon the machines. . . .

Once an engine or a hose cart had been decorated to the satisfaction of the firemen it was hauled very ceremoniously to the company house under the supervision of a special committee, and there placed on exhibition for several hours, during which time all alarms of fire were ignored.

*   *   *   *   *

Whenever a fire company gave a dance or a chowder party, admission to which was by ticket of extraordinary ornamentation, the engine or hose cart was installed in the center of the floor, and the false mahogany back formed the central point, and determined the color scheme, of the decorations. The most elaborately painted machines were also displayed at the Firemen's Ball—an important annual social function for which Theodore Thomas and orchestra occasionally provided music—and were often sent to other cities for exhibition. On such tours the machines were escorted by their crews in full uniform and, when a company could afford the expense, by Dodworth's famous band. Frequently the companies had their apparatus specially decorated for the parades, and for the torch-light processions in which they particularly loved to march they added such appropriate and thrilling effects as calcium lights, rockets, colored lamps, reflectors, Roman candles, and wild animals. . . .

When a fire engine or a hose cart was assigned to a company and officially put in service, the men who ran with it held a special meeting and solemnly christened their new darling, usually with some such patriotic or historical name as Hudson, Washington, Lafayette, Clinton, Fulton, Columbian, Franklin, Rutgers, etc. However, there were exceptions to the rule, for sometimes the firemen named their machines in honor of famous fire heroes or other public figures, or to commemorate events of great interest. For example, when, on June 14, 1849, the celebrated racing mare Lady Suffolk trotted a mile in the then remarkable time of 2:26, the name of Atlantic Hose Company No. 14 was promptly changed to Lady Suffolk, and pictures of the trotter were painted on the panels of the cart, while a new weather vane, carved to resemble the mare in action, was erected atop the company house with suitable ceremonies. Fashion Hose Company No. 25 was also named for a famous race horse of about the same period. The lifters of Fashion's hose reel represented a horse's head, the jaws of which opened when the lids were raised. Croton Engine Company No. 16 was so designated in honor of the opening of the Croton Aqueduct; and Pocahontas Engine No. 49, which was organized in Harlem after the Great Fire of 1835, took its name, not from the Indian maiden who rescued Captain John Smith, but from the Pocahontas Dairy operated by Gouverneur Morris.

* * * * *

After a fire company had appeared at a few fires it usually received a sobriquet, either because of the peculiarities of the engine or hose cart, or those of the men who manned the machine, by which it was popularly known. Sometimes the nickname was applied to the apparatus alone, and sometimes to the company also. Empire Engine No. 42 was called Old Hay-Wagon and Man-Killer because of its ungainly appearance and the fact that strong men were required to operate it. . . .

* * * * *

By common usage among the old volunteer firemen the word engine became en-jine, and a man was never said to be a member of a fire company, but to "run with the masheen." An engine of unusual weight and power was called a bull en-jine, an expression which the Negroes who delighted to see the apparatus careening through the streets corrupted to bull-jine. . . .

No fireman would ever admit that his own engine was not a bull-jine, and if necessary he resorted to his fists to impress an appreciation of its worth upon scoffers. Out of this pride of possession, and the natural desire to be first, grew the feuds, jealousies, and brawls which kept the department in an uproar from the importation of the two original New York fire engines from London in 1731 to the disbanding of the volunteers in 1865. The rivalries of the firemen were at their height during the great riot era of 1830-1850, when New York was so torn by election and abolition disturbances, and outbreaks by the criminal gangs of the Bowery and the Five Points, that soldiers were frequently called upon to suppress the rioters, who dispersed only when they heard the rumble of artillery and saw the gleam of bayonets. Scarcely a fire occurred at which there were not several fights between rival companies, and there is no record of an alarm that was not enlivened by clashes between the runners.

Fierce combats began simply because an engine or a hose company had beaten another to the scene of action, or had usurped the only handy fire-plug. During the summer months, and occasionally even in winter, the firemen posted lines of sentinels from the nearest alarm stations to their company headquarters, and when an alarm came it was relayed down the line. Once the news of a fire and its location had reached a house, special groups of fighting men were rushed ahead to capture a fire hydrant or a cistern, and defend it against other companies until their machine arrived. One of the members of such an advance force wore no uniform, but carried a small barrel, which he popped over a

hydrant. He then sat nonchalantly upon it, while his mates lurked in nearby doorways ready to assist him, and scouts of rival companies scurried about searching for the fire plug. When the engine or hose cart arrived, the barrel was tipped over and the hose attached to the hydrant, and a great shout of victory arose as the water was played upon the fire, or, as often happened in the exuberance of the moment, upon the other firemen. Occasionally at night, when the city was not very well lighted, the hydrant hunters made ludicrous mistakes, and mistook all sorts of objects for fire-plugs. Once Lady Suffolk Hose Company No. 14 fought for two hours with another company for possession of what had seemed to be a hydrant, but which proved to be the end of a half-buried old cannon. Quite often the firemen devoted more time to fighting for fire-plugs than to extinguishing the flames.

The fire companies not only fought each other whenever an opportunity offered, but they were in almost constant conflict with the many clubs of desperate fighting men which infested New York for many years before the Civil War. Practically all of these bullies enjoyed the protection of Tammany politicians, who employed them as repeaters at elections, and to drive honest citizens away from the polls. . . .

*   *   *   *   *   *

The principal cause of warfare among the firemen themselves was the washing of one engine by another, which means that the first machine pumped so much water into the second that it overflowed the box, causing irreparable damage to the paint and decorations. Most of the washings occurred at fires, but contests of this sort, together with tests for height, force and distance of stream, were frequently held at the Liberty Poles which were scattered in great profusion about the city, and beneath which patriotic exercises were held on the Fourth of July and other holidays. The most important of these contests, and perhaps the only ones that were carried through in a good humor, took place each Thanksgiving afternoon at Riley's famous Pole at Franklin Street and West Broadway. The judges sat on the roof of Riley's Fifth Ward Hotel and Museum, on the southwest corner. Although the engine with the strongest men at the brakes could almost invariably wash another machine of the same type, for an engine to be washed was considered the acme of humiliation, and members of some of the companies whose machines had been so worsted wore mourning bands and flew streamers of crape from their apparatus until the disgrace had been washed out by daring deeds, or by washing other engines. Some took such a calamity even more to heart, as did a member of Black Joke

Black Joke Engine

Engine Company No. 33. This old fire-eater contracted tuberculosis from exposure, and the time came when he could no longer answer an alarm. Late one afternoon he heard the ringing of the fire bells, and when a friend, also a member of Black Joke, called a few hours later, he eagerly asked for information about the fire and, above all, about the conduct of No. 33. But for a few moments the friend vouchsafed no word, not even of greeting, but sat gloomily beside the bed. Finally he burst out:

"Oh, Jake! If I could but be in your place this moment, it would be happiness to what I now suffer!"

"What's happened to the en-jine?" demanded the sick man.

"Jake, the en-jine got washed today!"

With a supreme effort Jake raised himself on his pillows.

"Who washed her?" he asked, feebly.

"Twelve en-jine."

"Then let me die!" cried the invalid. "I envy not your hold on life!"

He sank back, and passed away with the honor of his engine.

Until a fire engine had been washed it was called a maiden, and a machine which retained its virginity year after year was finally invested with the honorable title of Old Maid, and to all intents and purposes was canonized by the firemen.

VOLUNTEER FIREMEN'S SONGS [14]

The majority of men in San Francisco, in the early Fifties, had had some experience of the sea, either having shipped before the mast or sailed as passengers on the long voyage from the Isthmus or around the Horn. Engine No. 8, in fact, was composed of so many sailors that it was never known otherwise than as Sailor Eight. It was the sailors who introduced the chantey into the Fire Department, to be sung especially at the laborious task of pumping water by hand.

. . . A chantey . . . sung by all the companies and . . . a favorite of Engine Ten and Engine Fourteen . . . illustrates admirably the sailors' influence upon San Francisco; it carries, as well, the impress of the War with Mexico (many of the pioneers made directly from that war for the gold fields); and it pictures the firemen's life.

> Santa Anna is dead and gone,
>   Hurrah, Santa Anna!
> Oh, we won our day at Monterrey,
>   All on the plains of Mexico.
>
> Oh, Mexico and Texas, too,
> I wouldn't be Santy's son, you know.
>
> Number One, she's always on the run,
> Number Two always had a bully crew.
>
> Number Three had a chowderie,
> Number Four is lying at the door.
>
> Number Five is always alive,
> Number Six is a bully set of bricks.
>
> Number Seven will never get to heaven,
> Number Eight is always late.
>
> Number Nine is never on time,
> Number Ten had a great set of men.
>
> Number Eleven was just like seven,
> Number Twelve is on the shelf.
>
> Number Thirteen was never to be seen,
> Number Fourteen was always a-courtin'.

*   *   *   *   *

Another song of the Fifties, beloved by all, and enchanting alike the firemen and the people, was "The Fireman's Bride." It is a key to the heart of the

[14] From *City of the Golden 'Fifties,* by Pauline Jacobson, pp. 85-89. Copyright, 1941, by the Regents of the University of California. Berkeley and Los Angeles: University of California Press.

fireman and to the glamour which surrounded him, and a glowing account, as well, of his glory and his deeds. Curly Jack was the first man to hear it in San Francisco. He had it from Felix Desmond, who brought it down from Sacramento. It was in this manner, in the old days, that songs were disseminated on this coast; a good singer had it from some stranger, or caught it from an actor on the stage.

> As I strolled out on a fine summer's evening,
>> The weather it was fine and clear,
> I overheard a tender mother
>> Conversing with her daughter dear,
> Saying, "Daughter, dear, I would like you to marry,
>> No longer lead a single life."
> "Yes, dear mother, I am going to marry,
>> I'm going to be a fireman's wife."

Chorus:

> "Who wouldn't be a fireman's darling?
> Who wouldn't be a fireman's bride?
>> I'm going to be a fireman's lover,
>> I'm going to be a fireman's wife."

> "Firemen they are young and foolish,
>> Firemen they are inclined to roam,
> Firemen they would leave you broken-hearted,
>> They would leave your heart forlorn."
> "Give me the lad with the red fire shirt on,
>> Give me my heart's delight,
> Give me the lad with the fire coat and hat on,
>> For I'm going to be a fireman's bride."

> Hark, don't you hear the Hall bell-a-ringing?
>> Hark, don't you hear the doomful sound?
> Hark, don't you hear the firemen a-running?
>> As they cry, "Pull on, brave boys, pull on!"
> "Number One, start your water!"
> "Light up!" "Pick up and play your water high!"
> Don't you see the ladder up against the building?
>> Out of the crowd steps a brave fire boy.

> Up, up the ladder, see how he's a-tripping,
>> Without dread and without fear.
> Into the flames see how he's a-going,
>> As he cries aloud, "Brave boys, we are here!"
> Down, down the ladder, see how he's a-coming,
>> Without dread and without fear.
> In his arm he carries a mother;
>> See how she clings to her baby dear.

> The fire's all out, and we can work no longer.
>> Take up! Reel up! And play your ladders high!
> Command your rope! And we'll clean her in the morning,
>> We are a bully good crew, and if we want to try.

THE FIRE HORSE [15]

. . . It was the Age of the Horse—and New York's firemen loved their horses with a passion that it is difficult for a motor age to appreciate.

They were extraordinary animals, too, these equine members of the Department, who understood their work as thoroughly as their human colleagues. They couldn't be retired from service, even when sold to other owners after they were too old to pull equipment. Fire Department records are full of instances in which apparatus arrived at a fire, accompanied by some driverless garbage truck or milk wagon, drawn by a snorting old *plug* who was greeted by the men with shouts of welcome. He would always turn out to be a retired fire horse who had recognized his old outfit en route to a blaze.

"Jim," of Engine 17, even knew the numbers of the alarm boxes to which his company was scheduled to respond. When the bell sounded, "Jim" would race to his place beside the fire-engine tongue and snap his pole-strap into place, counting the strokes meanwhile. If they indicated a box to which No. 17 responded, "Jim" would reach over and pull the bunk-room gong with his teeth, a task for which a regular fireman was assigned. Then he would neigh his delight as his comrades came sliding down the pole and ran to complete hitching him up.

Like another famous horse which belonged to Engine 8, he could not be kept in his stall unless he wanted to remain there, because he knew how to unstrap the barrier with his teeth. When either of these accomplished animals wanted to drink, he would let himself out of his stall, stroll across to the hydrant which filled the watering trough, and turn on the water. Each of them would turn the water off when he had finished and then returned to his place.

The harness was always kept suspended over the tongue or shafts, spread upon an automatic iron hanger and held in position by springs. The driver, leaping to his seat, merely grabbed the reins, thereby releasing the tension on the springs and the harness dropped into place. A watchman sprang to snap the collars fast, the work of a fraction of a second—and the apparatus roared away as the members of the crew sprang to their places, donning their hats and coats en route. Everything was automatic except the movement of the horses from their stall and the snapping of the collars.

Crack crews made amazing time. Drivers Lyell and Root of Patrol No. 3 repeatedly got their truck going within two seconds after the alarm sounded, and [Augustine E.] Costello [in *Our Firemen,* New York, 1887] tells how an exhibition was staged for the Grand Duke Alexis at which an engine was manned, driven four blocks, and had a stream going in two minutes and thirty-five seconds.

[15] From *History of the New York Fire Department,* by Lowell M. Limpus, pp. 301-302. Copyright, 1940, by E. P. Dutton & Co., Inc. New York.

"CARRIAGE?" [16]

For most people, the Old-Worldliness of the Plaza is best typified by the horse-drawn landaus, victorias, and cabs waiting along both sides of 59th Street between the statue and the fountain. Until 1907 the cabbies and their nags waited at the side and in front of the hotel; but the first taxicabs came to New York with the opening of the new building; and the hackies had to move across the street, where they have remained ever since, glaring—the old-timers at least—at the motorized land-loupers. Traditionally, the cabman's costume is a dark coat with an astrakhan collar and a high silk or beaver hat; some still cling to this garb, but the majority have discarded it in recent years. For the most part, they are a morose and bitter crew, as well they might be. Few jobs in the city pay so poorly for so long a workday (most of the men stay out twelve hours at a time). There are now only ninety-five men hacked up, as the drivers say, but the number that shows up for work each day varies with the number of hangovers from the night before, according to one habitué of the neighborhood. A red nose used to be almost as obligatory as a high hard hat. The Hack Bureau regulates the charge for hire, which currently is $3 for the first half hour and $1 for each additional half hour, or part thereof.

According to Wenzel Generowiscz, a thin, ruddy-faced man who somewhat resembles the old print called *The Cheerful Philosopher,* and who has four carriages hacked up at this stand, many people, particularly out-of-towners, are prone to complain that the hack charges are too high. "Tips? Huh!" Generowiscz grunted one day last autumn. "Right now it's a miserable business. People just don't seem to want to ride any more." The number of hackies has dropped off through the years for several reasons: lack of demand, poor pay, long hours, and, above all, the difficulty of getting carriages and the high price of boarding horses or renting them (some of the drivers own neither rigs nor steeds). The drivers get few calls, these days, for trips other than the usual drive around Central Park, but sometimes, late at night, a party of well-heeled revelers will reel out of one of the hotels and demand to be taken to their respective homes.

The cabbies and their rigs, although regarded as landmarks, are an occasional source of irritation to the doormen at the various hotels, depending upon the prevailing winds, which have an unkind and inconsiderate habit of wafting the ripe aroma of horses across the open expanse. . . .

"TWO BELLS AND AWAY WE GO" [17]

Eddie Mann taught me how to collect fares, how to pull the bell cord, how to handle the problem of children's ages—all the rudimentary

[16] From "The Plaza," by Richard B. Gehman, *Park East,* Vol. 12 (February 1952), No. 2, pp. 10-11. Copyright, 1952, by Park Magazine Company, Inc. New York.
[17] From *Another Day, Another Dollar,* by John T. Winterich, pp. 141-143. Copyright, 1942, 1945, 1946, 1947, by John T. Winterich. Philadelphia and New York: J. B. Lippincott Company.

essentials that the passenger thought he knew as much about as the conductor did. Therein the passenger erred.

In collecting fares, for example, the conductor depended largely on the automatic honesty of humanity. This was not a moral or ethical quality. It was merely a matter of habit. To present his nickel when the conductor extended his fare-collector was a normal and natural reaction on the part of the passenger. Conductors on regular runs were occasionally confronted with the phenomenon of the habitual would-be fare evader—it was always matter for debate whether he was trying to save money or merely playing a sort of game, as he was usually an old man with not many interests left in life. The policy was to make things miserable for him by jabbing the fare-collector at him every time one passed his seat.

Giving starting and stopping signals might appear to have been an elementary business, but actually there was an art to it. Nothing annoyed a motorman so much as "hard bells." The gong and its little brass clapper were only a couple of feet from his right ear, and hard bells repeated time after time wore down his nervous system. Many a time in later years, as a passenger, I have seen motormen face around savagely and look words they dared not utter in public at a clumsy, hard-bell conductor. When the pair were on the outs about something, a conductor would occasionally give a motorman hard bells deliberately. This made for good feeling all around.

The considerate, skilled conductor soon acquired a technique of signaling that produced a gentle but fully audible *ting* which was almost soothing to the ear. Eddie Mann's bells sounded like tiny carillons.

There was a little game we conductors used to play with the bell cord. An occasional passenger would regard himself as fully capable of ringing his own stop signal. In the case of a habitual offender our procedure was as follows: As the car approached the passenger's stop, the conductor, standing on the back platform, would put his hand to the bell cord and pull it gently taut. This brought the clapper up against the front-end bell without ringing it. When the passenger reached for the bell cord he would yank it, and yank it again, without result. The conductor would be looking somewhere else, and would not notice the passenger until the latter had been carried beyond his stop. The passenger seemed never to discover just what had been put over on him, but he suspected that something had, and thereafter he usually left the operation of the car to the conductor.

If the conductor suspected that a mother was trying to palm off an eight-year-old child on him as an under-fiver, he would keep his fare-collector aimed at her after he had taken her own nickel (the device looked startlingly like a clumsy forty-five). Frequently this would shame her into inserting a second nickel. If she held her ground, and if the conductor was pretty certain that his judgment was accurate, he would inquire, "How old is that child?" in a voice audible to every one aboard. Few mothers could stand up under that. There was always the chance that if she said, "Four and a half," the tot would cut in with "The hell you say" or something like that.

The running board of an open car had not then become the hazard into which it developed with the growing popularity of the automobile. I recall no near-disasters involving myself, but merely considerable inconvenience when the board was crowded, as it sometimes was, with passengers riding two deep. I once carried ninety-eight fares on a thirteen-bench bloomer capable of seating sixty-five—of the excess, ten or a dozen were squeezed on the back platform; the rest were on the running board. They tried to be helpful, and scrunched back as tightly as they could to let me by in the performance of my duties; even so every passage I made up and down the board involved throwing one arm around a cluster of humanity and groping blindly for the next handle before letting the first hand loose.

Except on a few long-distance runs, only one of which operated out of Olneyville, a trolley ride in Providence cost a nickel, with a free transfer if the passenger wanted it. Company executives had passes, and fellow-motormen and conductors rode on their hats. The longest local run, to Buttonwoods, down Narragansett Bay, operated out of the Broad Street carhouse. It employed a special type of closed car, with sidewise seats like a railroad coach, and for a good part of the distance it had its own right of way. To my unsophisticated eye the Buttonwoods car had all the pomp and splendor of the Gilt Edge Express from Boston to New York. You had to pay twenty cents to go from downtown Providence to Buttonwoods, but such a magnificent journey was worth every cent of it.

"STREETCAR RUNS RIGHT BY HER DOOR" [18]

In . . . 1885, Baltimore saw on its streets the first commercially operated electric cars in the United States. The line ran by way of Huntington Avenue to Hampden, a few miles outside the city limits. It replaced the horse-cars. In fact the same cars were used, being propelled by electric locomotives instead of drawn by horses. Power was conducted by a third rail except at street crossings, where an overhead trolley was used. The innovation inspired the popular song which advertised Baltimore through the East and whose words, set to the tune of "Ta-ra-ra-Boom-de-ay," were:

> I've got a girl in Baltimore,
> Streetcar runs right by her door.
> Brussels carpet on the floor,
> I've got a girl in Baltimore.

But the electric streetcars were ahead of their time. The line failed to pay and, after eighteen months, the horses were put back on the job.

[18] From *The Amiable Baltimoreans*, by Francis F. Beirne, p. 305. Copyright, 1951, by E. P. Dutton & Co., Inc. New York.

SAN FRANCISCO CABLE-CAR LORE

I [19]

. . . Cable car operators are not just motormen.[20] They are to San Francisco what gondoliers are to Venice—guides, gentlemen, musicians, and "characters." As we got part way up Russian Hill [on the Powell Street cable car] a male passenger's hat blew off. He jumped off to retrieve it, since cable cars proceed at only a fixed 9.5 miles per hour. "Don't hurry!" shouted the gripman. "I'll wait for you at the top of the hill." And he did. It was like a family picnic.

Cable grip-car and trailer on Clay Street, San Francisco, in 1873

. . . On the turns the gripman would shout "Hold on!" or something that sounded like " 'Koutferdakoive!" which, translated, means, "Look out for the curve!"

There have been famous gripmen on Powell, one of whom was the late Gertrude Stein's brother. He had the job early in the century and used to spend his leisure time giving away candy to children and cigars to gentlemen. Finally, he became too fat to stand between the narrow seats where gripmen stand, and thereupon became a conductor. In her autobiography Miss Stein tells how her brother eventually gave up this job, too, because he found it bothersome to tell the difference between a nickel and a five-dollar gold piece.

[19] From "Powell Street—The Spirit of San Francisco," by Paul Tunley, *The American Magazine*, Vol. 157 (February 1954), No. 2, pp. 83-84. Copyright, 1954, by the Crowell-Collier Publishing Company. New York.
[20] [Gripmen, as the operators are called] operate the "grip," a lever which grasps the ever-moving cable under the tracks.—R.T.

One of the delightful things about a cable car is the bell. It is musical in tone, and the gripmen learn to ring it rhythmically. The city encourages this by holding contests occasionally and awarding prizes to the top bell-ringers. It is especially interesting when two gripmen pass each other on the hills and sound off a musical greeting, sometimes with extraordinary skill. As we rolled along Powell that day, our Negro gripman tapped out a staccato syncopation that was straight out of Africa, or maybe New Orleans. I was reminded of the time John Ringgold, San Francisco pianist, told me he'd once heard two passing gripmen create a rhythm "every bit as exciting as Beethoven's Ninth."

II [21]

There has always been humor connected with the slightly comical cable cars. Back in the 1880's the whole town giggled about the Chinese cook named Ching Pon, who, upon seeing a Washington Street cable stalled at Polk, hurried over to the gripman and inquired: "Whatsa malla—sling bloke?" For a couple of decades after, delighted San Franciscans hurled that pidgin sentence whenever they spotted a cable car stalled in its tracks.

The children of that pre-automobile age had fun with the clacking cables too. A favorite sport of the roller-skating set was to drop a bent wire through the slot, hook onto the strand, and get themselves a free pull up a hill. Other inventive moppets conceived the fanciful idea of hitching empty boxes on a string and snagging them to the cable. It was no uncommon sight to see as many as thirty cartons galloping bravely over a hilltop, while the young gagsters stood cheering and yelling at the bottom.

And the gripmen, apparently, have always been as unique as their vehicles. Obligingly, they'd stop in the middle of a block to let a steady customer dismount directly in front of his home—a courtesy that was usually amply repaid. At Christmas time in the must-have-been-gay Nineties, every gripman from the California Cable Company would line up at Braunschweiger's Whisky House to get a gift bottle of rock and rye, as thanks for stopping daily in front of the Braunschweiger mansion at 2216 California Street.

* * * * *

. . . Of course practically every San Franciscan has his own gag about the cables. For instance, if you're a tourist, don't walk up to a San Francynic and ask him how the cars operate. A favorite, bored retort is: "Well, you see that gimmick there in the middle? It's got a gizmo on the end that hooks onto the dingbat in the slot—that's all there is to it."

* * * * *

. . . A Powell Street conductor one day explained to me why he's so crazy about the rickety ground grippers. "Look," he said. "I'm standing on the back platform, and my cap falls off. So do I get excited? Do I signal for a halt? Nyah. I jump off, pick up my cap, run back, and jump on again. What other kind of transportation moves so slow and easy-like these days?"

[21] From *Baghdad-by-the-Bay*, by Herb Caen, pp. 116-117, 118. Copyright, 1949, by Herb Caen. Garden City, New York: Doubleday & Company, Inc.

Another conductor I know is in the habit of jumping off his cable as it trundles past the Dunkit Donut Shop on Columbus Avenue near Chestnut. He runs inside, yells "Gimme six!" grabs the bag of doughnuts and catches up with his still-moving car without even a sprint. A third conductor holds up three fingers as he passes Bruno's Lunchroom at Columbus and Taylor, which is the signal for Bruno to get three hamburgers ready. Then, on the cable's return trip from the Bay-Taylor turntable, the conductor dashes in, picks up his 'burgers, and gallops back to his car.

WHEN THE RAILROAD MET MAIN STREET [22]

. . . For nearly a hundred years now [in 1935] . . . the main-line passenger tracks of the New York Central [went] right down the middle of one of [Syracuse's] important streets. To the country at large, most of which at one time or another has ridden upon the main-line trains of the Central, Syracuse is better known by this unique feature than by any other. Foreigners comment upon it, unfavorably, despite the fact that once I found the same sort of thing in the old French city of Nantes. Formerly this intimate dalliance between street and railroad was a feature of a good many of our important eastern towns. And [when it passes] out of existence in Syracuse, people there will hardly realize what it is not to have their everyday existence punctuated by the slow and dignified [six-mile-an-hour] passage of the *North Shore Limited* or the *Empire* up and down Main Street, with all the Syracuse folk staring at the passengers in the cars and the passengers in the cars staring, with equal unintelligence, at the Syracuse folk. [All this will be eliminated by the new union passenger station.] With it goes a grade-removal project, in a slightly different part of the town, and then the tearing up of the tracks through Washington Street. I think that Syracusans are going to miss the long, fine trains much more than the trains are going to miss Syracuse. They brought a curiously alien touch at all hours into the workaday life of the brisk town; a sort of daily, almost hourly, rubbing of its shoulders by New York and Chicago and St. Louis and Detroit.

THE LONGEST BAR [23]

In the days when drinking emporiums were known only as saloons, many, if not all, Western states liked to claim a saloon "with the longest bar in the world." . . .

We had one of those bars in the Northwest, and you should know that once upon a time the City of Portland, Oregon, was famed less for its gorgeous roses than for an institution commonly called Erickson's, a saloon patently designed

[22] From *Pathway of Empire*, by Edward Hungerford, pp. 122-123. Copyright, 1935, by Edward Hungerford. New York: The McBride Company, Inc.

[23] From *Far Corner*, A Personal View of the Pacific Northwest, by Stewart H. Holbrook, pp. 80-85. Copyright, 1952, by Stewart H. Holbrook. New York: The Macmillan Company.

for the refreshment of giants. It occupied the best part of a city block on Portland's Skidroad, which was, and is, Burnside Street, and its noble bar presented a total length of exactly 684 lineal feet. Men of Gath might have lifted their schooners here in comfort.

It was founded in the early eighties by August Erickson, an immigrant from Finland. . . .

Perhaps a score of Western cities staked claims to drinking places having "a mile-long bar." These turned out, I have discovered by no little research and occasionally by actual measurement, to have been bars of one hundred feet or less. Erickson's mighty total was no myth. It comprised five great bars that ran continuously around and across one gigantic room. Two of these ran from the Second Avenue side to Third Avenue. Two more connecting bars completed the vast quadrangle. And the other bar ran down the middle. Incidentally, the stretch of bar nearest the Second Avenue entrance was known, because Russians liked to congregate there, as the St. Petersburg.

Size alone probably would have brought fame to Erickson's, but the place offered much else. The bars, fixtures, and mirrors were the best money could buy. No tony twenty-five-cent place had better. There was a concert stage, on one side of which was "a $5,000 Grand Pipe Organ." Around the mezzanine were small booths where ladies were permitted, though no sirens of any sort were connected with the establishment. And no female was allowed on the hallowed main floor.

Art was not forgotten. Besides numerous elegant and allegedly classical nudes, there was a thumping great oil, "The Slave Market," which depicted an auction sale of Roman captives and was highly thought of by the connoisseurs of art who infested Erickson's. The late Edward (Spider) Johnson, onetime chief bouncer for Erickson, said it was common for these art lovers to weep into their schooners at the plight of the poor slaves.

Yet this was no place for tears. It was vital and throbbing with the surge of life, the place where men of the outdoors came to meet and to ease their tensions, a true club of working stiffs. Indeed, in time Erickson added an outside sign which designated his establishment as the Workingman's Club. Itinerants in funds made a beeline for the place. Five minutes after the swift *Telephone* or the graceful *Harvest Queen* docked, anywhere from fifty to five hundred wage slaves converged on Erickson's, like so many homing pigeons. Seven minutes after arrival of a Northern Pacific or a Southern Pacific train, in barged another crowd. It was said, and with some truth, that if you wanted to find a certain logger you went to Erickson's, and waited, he would be there soon or late. It was common, too, to address letters to footloose friends in care of Erickson's. The place often held hundreds of such missives waiting to be claimed.

Patrons of Erickson's discussed almost but not quite everything over their beverages. Jobs, wages, working conditions were popular subjects. Stupendous feats of work were bragged about; so, too, other foremen were praised or assassinated; but hot discussions of religion, economics, or politics were forbidden. The mildest form of discouragement from Erickson's corps of competent bouncers was a sharp word of admonition. This was followed, if not instantly heeded, by the bum's rush, performed by the finest practitioners procurable— of whom more later.

Men might forget the Erickson paintings, or even the $5,000 Grand Pipe Organ, but no man ever forgot the Erickson Free Lunch. This was really prodigious. On his business cards August Erickson described this feature of his place modestly as "A Dainty Lunch." The word was not quite exact. Erickson's free lunch centered around the roast quarter of a shorthorn steer, done to the right pink turn that permitted juices to flow as it was sliced. Bread for sand- wiches was cut precisely one and one-half inches thick. The Swedish hardtack bread, round and almost as large and hard as grindstones, stood in towering stacks. The mustard pots each held one quart. The mustard was homemade on the spot; it would remove the fur from any tongue. Round logs of sliced sausages filled platters. So did immense hunks of Scandinavian cheeses, including *gjetost* (of goat's milk) and *gammelost* (meaning "old"), the latter of monstrous strength; one whiff of it caused the weak to pale. "Gude ripe," Gus Erickson said of it, and he did not lie. Pickled herrings swam in big buckets of brine. At Christmas generous kettles of *lutefisk* were added to the dainty lunch.

Beer was five cents, and the local brew was served in schooners of thick glass yet of honest capacity. I possess two of these veritable glasses. They each hold sixteen fluid ounces. Strong men used both hands to lift a filled schooner. Genuine Dublin porter was a nickel a small glass. Imported German brews cost a dime. All hard liquor was two for a quarter. Lone drinkers were looked askance, but when one did appear it was taken for granted he would require not one but two glasses of whisky.

The regiment of bartenders needed to operate a saloon as large as Erickson's was carefully selected; the men ran to grenadier size. All wore beautifully roached hair. All had carefully tended mustaches. Across the broad white vest of each was a heavy watch chain. Below the vest was a spick-and-span apron. No coats were worn. There was no regulation in regard to neckties, but all bartenders' shirts were white. Arm elastics were an individual matter. Scandi- navian bartenders liked pink; all others had a weakness for purple. Trousers were held in place by distinctly he-man galluses, the Hercules brand, fit to stand the strain of lifting a keg and the torsion incident to heaving a bung starter. The bartenders were known for their courtesy, and were able to con- verse learnedly about prizefighters, bike champions, and such; to give sound advice in matters of love or business; to prescribe suitable eye-openers, pick-me- ups, and for lost manhood.

All of the Erickson beverages were sound. A handsome likeness of August Erickson himself appeared on the label of the house whisky. He was a good- looking, even a studious-appearing man, blue-eyed, blond, and had a neatly curled mustache. He wore, oddly enough for one of his occupation, pince-nez with gold chain. His broadcloth suits were tailored for him. He was a man who liked order, and this applied to his saloon.

Order in Gus Erickson's was kept, with rare recourse to the city police, by his own staff. My friend, the aforementioned Spider Johnson, was for a period chief of these bouncers. Spider was a tall, genial, and most courteous man, and of many intellectual interests. He handled men well too. But when stern necessity called, he was lightning-quick, and carried a punch that was rightly feared. One of his staff was a delightful person known as Jumbo Reilly. He was big, well over three hundred pounds, and though he really wasn't much of a fighter, his size and general aspect were so forbidding that he had no difficulty holding his job. "Jumbo," Spider recalled, "had the appearance of a gigantic and ill-natured orangutan. He also could emit a hideous laugh-snarl that cowed almost any one except the most stouthearted. His fighting tactics were to fall boldly upon his opponent. While not fatal, this was very discouraging. Jumbo's special ability lay in his version of the bum's rush. It was swift and expert."

A favorite story around Erickson's, which had five entrances from three streets, concerned a character called Halfpint Halverson, a troublesome Swede logger who liked to argue about the comparative abilities of different nationalities. On one such occasion, when he disregarded Jumbo Reilly's warning, the bouncer plucked Halverson by the collar and pants and threw him out the Second Avenue entrance. Halverson presently wandered in through one of the three Burnside Street doors. Out he went again in a heap. This continued until he had been ejected through four different doors. Working his way around to the Third Avenue side, Halverson made his entry through the fifth door. Just inside stood the mountainous Jumbo. Halverson stopped short. "Yesus!" he said, "vas yu bouncer en every place dis town?"

Loggers loved places as big as that.

Gus Erickson was a man who took things as they came. His place was but two short blocks from the waterfront, and when what is still referred to as the Flood of Ninety-four made much of downtown Portland something like Venice, and his own and most other saloons were inundated, Gus promptly chartered a big houseboat, stocked it complete, including the Dainty Lunch, and moored the craft plumb in the center of Burnside Street. Men in rowboats, homemade rafts, and catamarans, and single loggers riding big fir logs came paddling for succor to Erickson's floating saloon. Spider Johnson remembered that a score of customers never once left the place during the several days of flood.

The glory of Erickson's lasted for nearly forty years. Prohibition did not close it, nor did it become a bootlegging establishment. It simply carried on halfheartedly with near beer and added an out-and-out lunch counter, not free. The paintings of the pretty plump nudes, and even "The Slave Market," were sold. So was the $5,000 Grand Pipe Organ. The size of the place was cut in half. The bar when I first saw it ran to no more than two hundred feet, and this has been reduced again, to fit the new and dreary times. August Erickson himself died in 1925, in mid-Prohibition. Repeal did not bring a return to the great days; Oregon's liquor law permits the sale of beer over a bar, but not whisky.

Thus does Erickson's, still the Workingman's Club, survive as a shadow of its former immensity. The stuffed head of a deer, sad-eyed and disconsolate, is all that remains of the stupendous old wall *décor*.[24] Beer, tea, milk, and—God forbid—soda pop are the only beverages to pass over the mahogany. Yet the fame of Erickson's has not wholly evaporated. Every little while some old-timer, filled with nostalgia, stops off in Portland for no other reason than that of seeing if the longest bar in the world still retains its old-time polish. It does, but there is less than sixty feet of it left. Perhaps this is just as well, for within a block of the old saloon is now a manicure parlor that caters to lumberjacks and other now thoroughly tamed men. In such a civilization, there could be no place for the lusty joint that was Erickson's.

[24] The most typical relic of the saloon's heyday is a cherished fixture now in Tom Burns's Time Shop, just around the corner from the present single entrance to Erickson's. It is a cigar lighter, in the form of a bronze and charming female, from whose pretty mouth issued a steady bright flame of gas. It is well worth seeing.—S.H.H.

VIII. From This They Make a Living

Street lore is the heart of city folklore; and street cries were among the earliest occupational lore to be collected. In 1808, Samuel Wood printed and sold at the Juvenile Book Store on Pearl Street a little paperback book called *The Cries of New York*. As quaint and charming as the cries themselves and the accompanying woodcuts are the author's edifying comments, in which he preaches a "Poor Richard" tradesman's morality of honesty, industry, frugality, thrift, charity, temperance, health, cleanliness, resourcefulness and contentment. Thus the little radish girls ("Do you want any radishes?") teach the dignity of labor and useful employment: ". . . It is not to be doubted but that many, exclusive of the desire for radishes, are induced to purchase in order to encourage the little ones in their laudable examples of application and industry. We are born to labor; and it is not only an injunction laid upon but an honor to us to be found eating our bread by the sweat of our brows." But the youth selling gingerbread ("Hot, Spic'd Gin-ger-bread!") arouses compassion because the "sweets are the produce of cruel slavery."

On these "lower strata of commercialism" musical street cries have followed outmoded street trades into limbo, along with the organ-grinder and his monkey, the hurdy-gurdy and the German street band. But though the umbrella mender and the line-up man are no longer with us, the sales oratory of the sidewalk salesman and barker may still be heard above the hum and roar of traffic, practicing the "fine art of making a pitch," as described by Louie the Peeler to Maurice Zolotow:

There is, first, the opener, which is used to attract a tip [crowd]; the opener may have nothing to do with the spiel. Louie told of a flukum worker who starts by lighting a newspaper and waving a torch mysteriously around his head until a crowd collects. The body of the routine is the spiel, but in spieling it is important that your eyes do not watch what your fingers are doing. . . . Your eyes must be riveted on the tip. You stare now at one, now at another person. "You cannot ever let the tip get out of your control," Louie says, "you have got to have them watch you like a bird watches a snake. Then as you get ready to turn the tip and crack the price, you make a few jokes. As soon as you have them laughing, you know it will be easier to get that geedus out of their pokes. Usually, if you know your business, by the time you are ready to crack the price there will be somebody who is reaching into his poke, and then you work directly at him, and as you finish you reach for the merchandise and duke him, that is, you hand him the article and say thanks."

While the salesman, of whom the pitchman may be taken as the type and symbol, tends to steal the show, he is not the whole show in the city's occupational life and lore. In 1939 the Living Lore Unit of the Federal Writers' Project undertook to explore the folklore of New York City, and in particular to find out to what extent modern industrial workers are producing a folklore comparable to that of the sailor, the cowboy, the lumberjack and the farmer. Among the informants were workers in all types of construction, manufacturing, shipping, transportation, service and white-collar occupations—including sand hogs, ironworkers, needle-trade workers, shoe workers, hospital workers and taxi drivers. Their stories, jokes and sayings (sampled below) throw light on work processes and customs and on the attitudes of the worker toward his job, fellow workers, foreman and boss. Rich in gags, wisecracks, practical jokes and lingo, this hard-boiled, hard-hitting lore also reveals the superstitions, totems, taboos and other fantasies of urban occupations. The following selections have been chosen to illustrate all these values as well as some of the odd occupations in the city's complicated occupational structure, and the relation between cities and local and regional industries built around local resources and products—beer, tobacco, steel.

But first let us listen in on a few of these New York City workers talking about their job.

Here a night-club doorman on New York's "strip alley," West Fifty-second Street, explains the secrets of his spiel to an inquirer:

"Here's my opinion. Any man, any feller, that works around here—if he's lively, or if he has a nice personality, a nice smile—you have a lot of pep in you—in other words, you're willing to make friends with the average person that passes—understand me? So I feel by doing that and being lively, you have a good spiel. Yes, that's fifty percent of it. That encourages the average person in. You got to do something to attract a person's attention—sailor, serviceman, or even a civilian—you've got to do something to attract his attention. . . .

". . . You must be careful. Therefore you can say certain things that might insult him whereas a man that has his wife with him you must have respect for her to a certain extent. . . . We tell him: 'We have the most exciting show on the block.' You've got to clean it up a bit. 'We have music for your dancing and listening pleasure. Presenting the sensational and lovely amazon. . . .'

". . . All right, gentlemen, no waiting. Presenting six feet and four inches of extreme loveliness—the beautiful amazon. . . .'"

"A colored fellow told me a yarn one day," says one sand hog to another. " 'If you ever see a woman looking down in that hole I wouldn't go down, because as sure as I went down I would never come up again.' When they were sinking the shaft, if a woman looked down where they were working it was hard luck!" "You don't have to have a woman down there," says the other, "there will be plenty of hard luck anyway." "If there was a girl in the hole I wouldn't come out. I'm not superstitious. Do I look like a monkey?"

"When we come out," says a sand hog, "we drink coffee. It's supposed to help prevent the bends. Black coffee supplied by the company. Some of it is terrible." "When they get tired drinking it," says another, "they cut it in hunks and eat it."

"You know what they say," confides a taxi driver, "there's worms in apples and worms in radishes. Take the worm in a radish—he thinks the whole world is radishes."

Above the racket of his jackhammer, a street worker tearing up the pavement on Ninth Avenue tells an inquirer: "We always have a stock answer for people who ask questions. We say we lost a quarter here three years ago and we're looking for it. And when they ask, 'What are you digging?' I say 'I'm digging a hole.' "

MILWAUKEE BUCKET BOY [1]

The newspaper [*Germania*] on which father worked in 1908 was on the top floor of the Germania Building on West Water Street. One of its busiest employees, especially on hot summer days—and it used to get very hot in Milwaukee in July and August—was Heinz, the *Kesseljunge* [Bucket Boy].

The bucket boy was not a boy at all. He was a superannuated bookkeeper in a brewery. But at sixty he was let go because his eyesight failed.

Yet Heinz was lucky to get the job of *Kesseljunge* at the *Germania,* for it was an important post and his services were in great demand. He himself constructed the tools of his trade: two poles, each about five feet long and each artfully and deeply notched. The notches were designed firmly to hold the handles of one-quart beer pails, and Heinz had mastered the art of carrying six full buckets on each pole without spilling a drop.

Often I used to visit father at the newspaper plant. Heinz and I became friends, and the old man took such a fancy to me that he told me some of the secrets of his trade. He was proud of his post and he implied that if I applied myself assiduously and took his counsel to heart I might some day become a *Kesseljunge* and be held in high esteem by the gentlemen in the city room— even the *chef redakteur* himself, no less.

"There is one important thing to remember," he said, "and that is, never take the passenger elevator, even if you are in haste and the thirst of the gentlemen is great. For sometimes the passenger elevator is a bit crowded, and people jostle against me, and though I am careful as can be it happens that I may spill a little beer out of one of the twelve cans. This is not only a regrettable waste, but it is frequently followed by sad consequences. Is it not amazing, my boy, how some people can kick up a fuss over having a little beer spilled on their shoes—and good Gettelman brew, too, mind you!"

I told Heinz that such happenings were most disheartening and that the world was in a bad way. Heinz nodded solemnly, and he said:

"So that is why I always take the freight elevator in the back, even though it is a slow affair and it is a greater distance from this elevator to the saloon at the corner. This, too, has an added inconvenience because beer has a bad habit of shrinking in transit when the foam goes down in the can. That is why, when I enter the basement and before I ring the bell for the freight elevator, I give each can a good *Schwupptich.*"

I asked Heinz what a *Schwupptich* was, and he explained patiently:

"I take each can and twirl it a bit, round and round, but slowly—in this fashion. That is a *Schwupptich.* This causes a certain agitation in the beer, making the foam rise, and consequently again filling my buckets. Therefore a *Schwupptich* is highly essential, otherwise the gentlemen, seeing the buckets

[1] From *Bucket Boy, A Milwaukee Legend,* by Ernest L. Meyer, pp. 1-3. Copyright, 1947, by Ernest L. Meyer; 1933, 1942, by the American Mercury. New York: Hastings House Publishers, Inc.

only partially filled, might suspect that I had taken a private sip in the basement."

"Do you, Heinz?"

Heinz looked at me, astonished.

"But of course I do," he cried.

"THE FINER, THE LIGHTER, THE MILDER LEAF" [2]

Between the Civil War and 1910 Louisville was known as the greatest tobacco market in the world. There be those yet living who remember Main Street, the tobacco center, as it was in the '80's—the busiest street in the city; drays and great four-horse wagons, mostly with Negro drivers, clattering by, loaded with huge tobacco hogsheads, barrels of whisky, boxes, and bales; ambling little horse cars, carriages, and hacks threading their way through the commerce to deposit travelers at the portals of the Louisville Hotel or the Galt House (where Dickens had been so comfortable), the city's two finest hostelries, both on this broad street.

From Eighth Street to Twelfth there was almost a solid rank of tobacco warehouses, especially on the north side; the air was filled with the pleasant aroma of cured tobacco and the broad sidewalks were so cluttered with hogsheads that pedestrians could scarcely thread their way through. In one season 185,000,000 pounds of tobacco, mostly burley, were sold on the Main Street "breaks"—a curious term whose logic is cryptic. Much of the dark tobacco was being sold at Mayfield, Hopkinsville, Paducah, and other western towns.

One of the most picturesque features of the old hogshead marketing days was the Negro roustabout—"cooper," as he was called—who handled the hogsheads; a real man's job. An old cooper who had worked in warehouses both at Mayfield and Louisville told me that whereas the burley hogsheads, package and all, might weigh 1,000 to 1,500 pounds, the soggy dark stuff from western Kentucky might run from 1,600 to 2,500 pounds per hogshead. It took four men to roll a hogshead and six or seven to stand it on end—more, if it were one of the heavier of the dark product.

A Negro does everything rhythmically. Those coopers of yesterday had chanteys, most of which unfortunately have been lost. (I even had trouble in finding two of the old coopers in Louisville.) As they rolled a hogshead in the Main Street warehouses, they sometimes sang:

> Roll him! Roll him! Roll him!
> All I wants is my reg'lar rights;
> Three squah meals, an' my rest at nights.
> Roll! Roll him, boys! Roll!

Rolling the casks down the wide center aisle in the warehouse, they presently came to the spot where they must make a right-angle turn. Colonel Manton Davis tells me of seeing in the warehouses at Mayfield a man who was an

[2] From "Weep No More, My Lady," by Alvin F. Harlow, pp. 384-389. Copyright, 1942, by Alvin F. Harlow. New York and London: Whittlesey House, McGraw-Hill Book Company, Inc.

acknowledged star at this sort of thing hustle out in front of the hogshead, bearing a wedge nearly as long as your arm, wedge-shaped only at one end, a straight billet three or four inches thick the rest of the way. As the hogshead neared the precise spot where it must make the turn, he would, from a distance of 15 or 20 feet, throw the billet so that its wedge end stuck precisely under the center of the hogshead. As the big cask rode up on the billet, the men behind chanting, "Swing him, boys! Swing him around!" pivoted it on the wedge and started down the side passage as accurately as if machine directed. As it rolled off the wedge, one of those behind picked up the latter and hurled it over the hogshead, directly at the man in front. He, with the prideful technique of a true artist, waited until it seemed about to strike his face, then flipped his head aside and caught the missile magnificently with one hand as it passed over his shoulder. There was a real maestro!

"Set him on his end, boys! Set him on his end!" chanted the squad as they prepared to upend the better part of a ton; and with grunts and the creaking of staves, the mighty arms and loins heaved it to an upright position. Here the coopers removed the lower hoops, and seventy years ago the buyers drew out at three points ten pounds of samples (never paid for), hence the expression, the "breaks." If the owner refused a buyer's offer, another ten pounds might be taken, until at last, if continued, says a satirical commentator, the selling problem would solve itself; the hogshead would all go as samples.

This came to be a scandal, and a new system came into vogue. The hogshead was uncoopered and the Negroes lifted it off, leaving the cylinder of tobacco standing on end to be examined. An official inspector looked it over, took out three samples here and there and marked them with his seal. If the rest of the hogshead did not measure up to the samples, the buyer might look to the inspector for restitution. Then another improvement appeared—small hoists all around the warehouse which lifted the partly unhooped hogsheads and held them suspended above their tobacco until the sale was over.

When preparing for the winter auctions, which began in November, an extra force all around had to be on the job. A day's supply of hogsheads must be set on end, uncoopered, and hoisted off the tobacco. The sales began at 7 A.M. The auctioneer's lingo wasn't quite as daft as that of today, but it was lively enough. Prices per hundredweight rose by 25-cent stages. "Eleven—one—one—one—" meant $11.25; when it changed to "Eleven-two-two-toodle-oodle-oodle," etc., that meant $11.50; "thrrree—ree-ree-ree-ree" was $11.75. Bidding was done much as it is now—a nod, a wink, pressure against the auctioneer's body, the motion of a finger; sticking out the tip of a tongue meant 75 cents. As long as a buyer kept his eyes fixed on the auctioneer, the latter knew he was bidding; when he turned his glance away, he was through.

Auctioneers themselves and others about the warehouse often did a bit of "pinhooking," or private buying of tobacco from growers (this was finally banned by the warehouses, but secretly kept up). John Singhiser, a veteran auctioneer of Louisville, now retired, told me of buying a hogshead at 16 cents a pound; the samples drawn were poor—the unfortunate farmer's boy might have put in the bad hands, Singhiser thought—but the bulk of it was really fine tobacco; next day some better samples were distributed, and he sold it at 74 cents a pound. He saw tobacco sold even thirty years ago at 99 cents.

As soon as the big chunks of weed were sold, the Negroes began lowering the hogsheads over them, recoopering them, chanting as usual. "But didn't really need no singin'," said an old cooper. "De hatchets made music by dey-selves"—for of course the wielders played jigs with them. Then the hogsheads must be moved out, to make room for others. "Gwine to lay him down, boys," would come the warning, and the hogshead would be tilted on the chine. "Boy! Boy! Ev'ybody git right!" for the vast package musn't be dropped too hard. "Ev'ybody right?" asked a spokesman. "Yas, suh, ev'ybody right." *"Lay him down!"* Boom! The big cask hit the floor and was rolled away.

At the height of the season, nobody around the warehouse—officials, clerks, auctioneers, coopers—saw their homes from Monday morning to Saturday night. Closing up the day's sales and preparing for the next day might take until 3 A.M. As the night wore on, the singing of the Negroes ceased, and only a low-toned word or two was heard at intervals as, antlike, they wrestled with their heavy loads. "Boss, mah feet is gittin' so *round* on de bottom, Ah cain't hardly stand up," one complained to Singhiser. But those years seem so happy in retrospect that two old coopers to whom I talked had forgotten the weariness. Everybody slept on the job. The room for the Negroes, with benches all around for them to sleep on, and a glowing stove in the center, was jocularly called the "hothouse," but Mr. Singhiser thinks it might have been more aptly entitled the Black Hole of Calcutta.

On the doorstep of a pitiful tenement in Louisville's Harlem I talked to one old cooper whose massive barrel of a body testified to his giant strength once upon a time. The postman stopped and handed him a long envelope—his relief check. He peeped into the cover embarrassedly to see that the amount was right. "Yas, suh, got a little tiahed endurin' de night," he said as his faded eyes looked back longingly through the years, "but we had so much fun we didn't mind it. Dey'd give us a hot lunch an' some whisky at midnight, an' dat he'ped a lot. Hog-killin' time in de early winter, you know, an' maybe we'd git hot po'k ribs an' puzzle. You dunno what puzzle is?" He chuckled. "It's de hog backbone. Yas, suh, dem was great ol' days, an' I wish dey was back. Hard as we had to wo'k, I'd th'ow dis—" he held out the relief check—"away dis minute ef I could git back my ol' job in de warehouse."

Around 1900 and after, there were times when not only the sidewalks but the whole street would be so covered with hogsheads that police and street-car officials rallied to break the blockade, so that the trolley cars could get by. But trouble for Louisville was just around the corner. Buyers had long been complaining that after holding a hogshead a year or more, they found it to contain tobacco inferior to the samples. In 1907, a loose-leaf market was established at Lexington, and rapidly the vending of tobacco changed its character; instead of hogsheads, the loose hands were now stacked on big flat baskets. Whereas three auctioneers used to sell a thousand hogsheads in a day, now one may sell 3,000 baskets, with his "Fo'teen-a-lee-di-leen-a-lee-di-leen—" then "Qua-qua-qua-qua-qua-wa-wa-wa-" ($14.25), "Ha-ha-ha-ha-ha-ha-" ($14.50), "Three-di-lee-di-lee-" ($14.75), then "Fifteen!" and finally "Sold" to that company which bores its hearers pallid on the radio every week with its "Paid 28 per cent more per pound than all other companies at Richmond, Ky., 30 per cent more at Danville, Va., 32 per cent more at Willow Springs, N.C., yes, sir, 32 per cent more to get the *finer,* the *lighter,* the *milder* leaf . . ."

And so Lexington took the "Greatest-in-the-world" label away from Louisville, and Main Street fell into desuetude. Lingering in the old neighborhood the other day, I saw buildings that used to be warehouses; on two of them I could even trace the old signs, though they have now been painted over—"Central Tobacco Warehouse," "Green River Tobacco Warehouse." There are still some large warehouses at Louisville, but they are away out in the commons, south of town, where trucks can reach them without threading city traffic. Some tobacco brokers still have offices on Main, and in one of them is one of the most curious exhibits—a wall case full of hands or bunches of tobacco leaves from all over the world: Russia and Brazil, both tiny leaves five to eight inches long, Japan—very pale in color—Canada, the Caucasus, Siam, Herzegovina, Cuba, Haiti, Jamaica, Puerto Rico, Mexico, Colombia, Ecuador, Venezuela, Paraguay; queer cigars and cigarettes, some of the latter from Brazil only an inch and a half long.

TAMPA TABAQUERO [3]

"*Señor,*" said Alfonso Fernandez, of Ybor City in Tampa, "I do not like that name cigar maker. I am a *tabaquero.* I make cigars, yes, but I do not call it work. It is an art, as you shall see. I do not nail boards together like a carpenter. I do not watch a great noisy, oily machine grind and crush loads of cheap tobacco and turn out poor cigars by the hundreds of thousands. It is my privilege to combine the fine clear Havana tobacco with my own skilled craftsmanship in a way that only Latins can do. You shall see how a real *tabaquero* makes cigars."

On the way to the factory Alfonso told me that he had learned the art of cigar making from his father, who was born in Cuba, and from his grandfather, born in Spain. He, himself, is Tampa-born and is far more proud of his American nativity and citizenship than of his Cuban and Spanish descent. Far surpassing all this, however, is his pride in his skill, his ego of the artist.

The cigar factory was typical of others in Ybor City, known as "Little Havana": a rectangular brick building with a flat roof. It contains three floors and a basement, the latter being almost entirely above ground. Even outside the building the odor of tobacco was strong, and it increased as we passed through the lobby and climbed the two flights of boxed-in stairs to the *tabaqueros'* room.

The huge room covered the entire floor. Its ceiling was very high, and on all four sides were unusually tall windows spaced no more than eight feet apart. In a smaller room, or one not so well aired, the fumes of tobacco would have

[3] By Edmond Sharrock. Manuscripts of the Federal Writers' Project of the Works Progress Administration for the State of Florida. 1940.

been overpowering. There were literally tons of tobacco here, and more tons on the floor above, the floor below, and in the basement. No wonder that those who work in this building day after day find it impossible to rid their bodies and clothing of the all-pervading odor; for in such quantities even the finest Cuban tobacco gives off an odor rather than a fragrance.

Alfonso led the way through aisles between row after row of tables, some occupied and some vacant, until he reached his own *vapor*. A *vapor*, Spanish for ship, consists of six tables in two rows of three each, with broad aisles between them. In this room 120 *vapores* accommodate 720 *tabaqueros*. Each table, approximately four feet long and thirty inches wide, is encircled by a low rail on three sides, leaving the front open. The wood top of the rear rail is known as the dust guard, or *guardo polvo*; Alfonso tossed his hat on it. He wore no coat but was dressed in a soft blue shirt open at the throat, well-creased dark trousers, supported by a leather belt, and tan shoes. Exchanging greetings with others on his *vapor*, he donned a white crash apron that covered him from shoulder to knees and bore the name of the company stitched in red on the upper part.

At a series of bins in charge of a clerk, or *dependiente*, Alfonso received a supply of filler tobacco, known as *tripa*. This had been carefully selected for the grade of cigar Alfonso is working on. It had been sorted and cured on the floor above and had come down to the *dependiente's* bins through a series of wooden chutes or canals. In northern cigar factories *tripa* is carefully weighed and the cigar makers' output checked against the weight. Not so in Tampa. Alfonso and his fellow-workers would resent such surveillance.

Alfonso carried the *tripa* back to his *vapor* in his apron and placed it on the right hand upper corner of his table within easy reach. He then went to a railed-in enclosure in the center of the room where at *barrila*, half barrels set with open end up, the selectors, or *rezegadores*, pick the wrappers for the several grades of cigars. Seated upon backless stools that do not impede the movements of their arms, they hold the wrapper leaves in their aprons. Swiftly they finger each leaf and drape it over the edge of the *barril* in its proper group. They make thirty to thirty-five separate groups, according to quality, texture, and color. So well do their sensitive fingers know tobacco that the slightest differences in quality or texture are instantly detected. These wrapper leaves have been previously stripped by girls working in a basement room adjoining the warehouse. The entire center stem is removed so that each wrapper leaf makes two leaves or two wrappers.

Alfonso called out the name of the cigars he was about to roll and was given a pad of wrappers. These were charged to him and he had to turn in a cigar for each wrapper, except those he was permitted to make for himself. Returning to his *vapor*, he remarked to me, "Now, Señor, you will see us make cigars, and you will learn where Americans who build boats and automobiles and airplanes got their idea of streamlining. We who fashion handmade cigars were the first to use streamlining. Is it not so?"

Just then the coffee man appeared, arousing a Babel of talk in English, Spanish, and Italian. Every *tabaquero* bought coffee and rolls or cakes. Alfonso explained that cigar makers seldom ate breakfast at home, preferring to start the day with coffee at their *vapores*. So he drew his chair, called a *tabarette*, from under his table, and drew up one for me. I found it a most comfortable seat, slightly higher than an ordinary chair and with seat and back of tightly stretched cowhide, but without arms.

Coffee and rolls having been consumed, Alfonso was at last ready to begin his day's work. His table was furnished with a cutting board about twelve by eighteen inches, a small gauge and trimmer for measuring the thickness of the cigars and trimming them to the proper length, and a cigar maker's knife— a *chaveta*. No common knife, no *cuchillo* or *navajo*, may fashion a handmade cigar. It must be trimmed and shaped with a *chaveta*, which in Spanish means key but also carries the sense of judgment or reason—priceless ingredients in handmade cigars. The *chaveta* is like no other knife. It is an ovoid piece of metal about four inches long and one-half as wide. It has no corners but is rounded on all sides and every part of the edge is equally sharp; hence there is no lost motion in trimming either filler or wrapper.

Now for his after-breakfast cigar. It is an inviolate custom in Tampa handmade cigar factories that no real *tabaquero* would ever dream of making a cigar for his employer before he has made one for himself. Seated at his board, Alfonso selects the largest leaf in his pad of wrappers and with a few swift, deft movements of his *chaveta* quickly trims it to the proper size and shape. His long, slender fingers, slightly widened and flattened at the ends, reach into the pile of *tripa* and unerringly pick up the correct amount of filler for a good big cigar. The leaves are carefully placed with the veins upward and toward the left in such a way as to create a draft for the smoke, and each is trimmed to the same length. While he keeps up a running fire of talk, it is easy to see that Alfonso is vastly proud of his ability to arrange the filler by the "feel of the hand."

The cigar is bunched, then slipping a small rubber band over one end, he inserts it in the gauge. Both ends are trimmed, and starting at the "tuck," the end to be lighted, he rolls the wrapper on quickly and smoothly. As he gets to the "head," which is the end held in the smoker's mouth, he slips off the rubber band and fastens the wrapper with a tiny drop of tragacanth, a tasteless, vegetable adhesive gum brought from Asia.

The cigar is completed—an unusually large one—and he hands it to me. "Smoke it, *Señor*," he says. "There is a cigar fit for a king or for an American gentleman."

Again he selects a very large wrapper and almost before my cigar is burning he has rolled another for himself. By this time nearly every cigar maker is smoking, but their fingers have lost none of their speed. Slowly Alfonso's pile of finished cigars fills the hexagon-shaped holder on the upper left corner of his table, and each cigar seems as perfect as its mate.

In a continuous rhythm Alfonso selects, rejects or accepts, and bunches the tobacco he needs. He presses and smooths and seemingly caresses the bunch until his fingers tell him it is just right. Then he swiftly rolls it in the trimmed wrapper, and after a careful scrutiny places it on his pile. The foreman who comes through about noon will examine one or two cigars on each table. No more than that, or the *tabaquero* would take it as a personal affront and resent it deeply.

I asked Alfonso how long he had been making cigars.

"Fifteen years I have been in this factory. I came as *mochilla*. You know what *mochilla* is? In cigar making *mochilla* is a beginner. The Spanish word for apprentice is *apprendiz*, but in the cigar factories we say *mochilla*, which means knapsack for carrying supplies. When a young man starts in a cigar factory we say '*Hacer la mochilla*'—make the knapsack—that is, provide food for a journey, but in this case, provide for a career, for a journey through life.

"Yes, fifteen years since I was *mochilla*. Then we did not talk so much among ourselves, nor sing to while away the time. We had *lectores* to entertain us." He glanced at the other five *tabaqueros,* all of whom were listening. "Remember *lectores?*" All nodded, their faces lighted with the memory.

"I will tell you about *lectores,*" Alfonso said. "They were smart men. Actors. Readers. Elocutionists. Singers. The bosses did not pay them. We paid them ourselves. Each man chipped in at pay day and a good *lector* in a good factory like this would make as much as $75 a week. He was worth it, too. He sat on a platform in the middle of the room and read to us while we rolled cigars. Yes, we got all the news then and we were smarter than we are now, because we knew what was going on outside. The *lector* would read Spanish language newspapers and American newspapers. He would read history and stories and pieces from the magazines. He would read plays and often act them out. He had a strong, rich voice that never seemed to tire. He didn't need a loud speaker. Every one in the room could hear him well. Sometimes he told us stories of his own or would sing an old Cuban or Spanish song. I remember one song that we always liked. Come on, fellows, let us give the *Señor* 'A Lady from Nassau.'"

In low tones, then, all six started singing. Soon the song was taken up at other *vapores,* until the whole room swam with its soft cadences and the peculiar mixture of Spanish and "pidgin" English. Here is a very free translation:

> The boat from Cuba hardly tie the cable at Key West
> Before a Nassau maiden win my heart—and this no jest.
> "No savvy Cubano," says this girl; so softly in her ear
> I try Castillian; still she stand, as if she no can hear.
>
> That night she met me at the gate, and I, in much despair,
> Try English. "Likee me?" I say. "Come in and have a chair,"
> She tell me, so I take one seat and every effort bent
> To speaky English so this girl could savvy what I meant.
>
> "Well, what you want to tell me?" says the girl. "A Cuban swain
> Rates high, but an American gives me an awful pain.
> The dirty double-crossers. . . ." "Wait!" I interrupt her. "Stop!"
> Don't class me American. . . . I Cuban, feet to top.
>
> "No please don't think I try to shoot this—what you call it—bull,
> I want to marry—I not joke, no try to pull the wool.
> Don't think I 'take you for a ride,' for at your door I knock
> Tomorrow, and you see me here at seven by the clock.

"I speaky English not so good, but I am here to say,
The fire I have here for you will burn until that day
When I shall kiss that little mouth and press you to my heart,
For those red lips were made for me, and we must never part.

"I make seegars here, my dear, and closely hit the ball.
I makee only very best or makee none at all.
The strike is on, but I have cash in bank and pocket, too.
And I no have to work today, so speakee here with you."

* * * * *

As the impromptu concert ended I asked Alfonso what had happened to the *lectores*. "We don't have them now for seven or eight years," he said. "The bosses said they were making trouble about strikes and labor and trying to make cigar workers discontent and unhappy. So they had to go. We tried radio for a little while but it is not the same. So now we talk and laugh and sometimes sing. It is not too bad."

By this time it was almost noon. Alfonso made two more extra large cigars, one for himself and one for me.

"We must light these before we go out, or they will be charged against my day's allowance."

"Are you permitted so many each day?" I asked.

"Oh, yes," he said. "We can smoke all we want in the shop, but seldom do, except the after-breakfast smoke. Then we can smoke one going to lunch and have one for after lunch, too. At night we can take three for smoking in the evening. But these must not be hidden. They must be carried out in plain sight. You know now how to make cigars, yes?" Alfonso queried. "Maybe you like to come into factory and *hacer la mochilla*," he added, laughing.

HERRING AND ONIONS [4]

[Fish smells] were soaked into me from sweatshop days. Whenever the boss had wanted us to work late without pay, he treated the machine hands to herring and onions. Among themselves the girls grumbled as they bolted the bitter bribe. One night Sara Solomon flared up.

"I got my feller waiting for me on the corner. All I need yet, he should pick himself up another girl——"

"You got to meet your feller?" I said. "I got to go to night school. I'm going to be a stenographer——"

"*Nu?* So tell the boss to choke himself with his herring——"

"Sure I will!" I grabbed my shawl and stood up. "I don't care if the shop burns down. We sell him our days, but the nights are ours."

Their faces froze. I felt the boss's hand on my neck.

"Out you go! Out of my shop! I want no fresh-mouthed *Amerikanerins!* Greenhorns! The minute they learn a word English, they get flies in their noses and wanna be ladies. I don't want no ladies here!"

[4] From *Red Ribbon on a White Horse*, by Anzia Yezierska, p. 104. Copyright, 1950, by Anzia Yezierska. New York: Charles Scribner's Sons.

BY HIM WAS A REGULAR DEPARTMENT STORE [5]

I remind myself of a shop on East Broadway. At that time I was living on Henry Street, near the Henry Street *shul* [synagogue]. Naturally, there was a president of the *shul*. And the boss from this shop, he was also the president. Every one has to belong to a *shul*. So we also belong to his *shul*.

He practically didn't pay the people anything for their work. The cheapest labor he used to have. After we are working a couple of weeks, we come over and ask him, "How's about a raise?"

"Oh," he says, "times is bad. How can I raise you? I'm losing money. If you want the truth, I should lay you all off. But, after all, aren't you my *landsmen* [fellow-countrymen]? If we don't look out for our own, who else? I'll tell you what. Next Saturday, come to the *shul*, and I'll give you an *aleah!*" [6]

You think that's all he was? Don't ask! He was a regular department store. He was also an agent to sell tickets to bring over the wives. Or, let us say, some one was bringing over a family. So he was selling tickets for the boat.

The wages at that time for a cloakmaker was fifteen dollars a week. By him you used to work for seven, or five dollars.

After a few months, all shops are starting to unionize. The workers don't want no more *aleahs*. When he sees that, he calls me over. "How long are you here? Why don't you bring over your wife? By me it's no life if a family is in two pieces. You think it's right, Gold?"

"How can I? You think I can save from those wages?"

"All right. I'll tell you what I'll do. I'll give you a ticket. And I'll take out of the wages."

So already he had me tied to work another year.

Strikes used to be there at that time. And by him also. When he saw it's bad, he came over to us. First he got a telegram, made by himself to him. With a story that some one's daughter is sick. Or the *shul* in the old country burned up. Or something like that. He called us all together and told us what's happening.

"And I'm giving for this purpose $100—unless I'll have to give ten per cent more wages."

Well? We were involved. After all, in the old country is still our fathers, mothers, brothers. So we work again for him.

Always he had some craziness to keep us. But when we are no longer greeners, we used to say to him: "We have you in hell, with the *shul*, with the tickets, with your beard, with everything!"

---

[5] As told by Mr. Gold, of Max Wiesen & Sons, Dresses, to Sam Schwartz and Terry Roth, New York City, May 29, 1939. "Living Lore of New York City." Manuscripts of the Federal Writers' Project of the Works Progress Administration in New York City.

[6] The honor of being summoned to ascend the rostrum in the *shul* as the torah is read.

"SHOEMAKING, NOT TO SING"[7]

I. "Caruso," the Laster

I've been working in a shoe factory about 1913 or 1914, in the Gold Shoe Company. It was custom-made, very high-grade. Was working there about thirty to forty people. That's a true thing. So a shoemaker brought his brother from Italy to work in the shop as a laster. The very first day, you hear, the brother proposed to us that the new person could sing, that he's a great singer. So the first day the brother asked him to sing, but he couldn't. He didn't feel at home. On another day he start to sing. When he sang, we all listen. We think he's a real opera singer. And it happened, you know, just after Caruso died. We all thought this was the next Caruso. So every day he used to sing. We put away our tools and listened to him. And from the shoe factory developed a regular opera. Until one day the boss comes around and yells: "What's going on here? Is this the Metropolitan or a shoe factory?"

We thought after all that the boss is right. So we hold a meeting and we decide that this here shoemaker, the laster from Italy, shouldn't work no more to annoy the boss, that he should go to a music school. We hold a meeting and we decide each one of us should give one dollar a week to keep up the fellow. Then we took him to a tester of music. You know, to a tester on Flatbush Avenue. And it was a joke. The music tester said: "Let him better to go shoe-making, not to sing."

Finally we got used to him. We didn't care any more when the tester told us he's not so hot. We used to go on working. While he used to holler his lungs out, we kept on working. Still, we used to call him "Caruso." He always remained by us, "Caruso," the laster.

II. "Like Dopes in White"

I worked for a fellow, Goldstein. That was 1908. He used to make ballet shoes, the high-grade shoes for the millionaires. Each worker had to be dressed in white like a doctor because the shoes was satin, all white satin.

Before Christmas, he was very busy and he advertised for help. So a feller come along, an Italian feller, and he mentioned the name for whom he was working. The boss took him up to work and he give him a uniform in white and for no money does he want to wear that uniform. His excuse was this: For the last thirty years he's working on shoes, and he never work in white. But he needed that job and the boss insist that he wear the white uniform. So he trained his wife that she would bring him lunch every day. And then it came out why he really didn't want to wear the uniform. He said: "My wife will bring me dinner every day and then she will get scared when she sees me in white."

[7] From "To Shoe Making, Not to Sing," by Irving Nicholson. "Living Lore of New York City." Manuscripts of the Federal Writers' Project of the Works Progress Administration in New York City. 1939.

A younger man then played a trick on him. He knew that his wife was coming, so he called out the worker who kicked to meet his wife with that lunch before he could change out of the uniform. When she saw him she said: "What's the matter, Jimmy? You sick? They gonna take you to the hospital?"

The man got bashful and in the hall where you go into work, he took off his white uniform and he finished his dinner and he wants to leave the job. So the boss liked his work very much. And he begged him he should come to work and sit without a uniform as long as he should sit and work. When he finally sit down he sit like a hero because he sit like a real shoe maker and they sit like dopes in white.

A WHEELBARROWFUL OF MUD AND A SKINFUL OF SOOT [8]

[In Bouton, Pennsylvania] I stood behind the [open-hearth] furnace near the spout, which still spread a wave of heat about it, and Nick, the second-helper, beside me yelling things in Anglo-Serbian, into my face. He was a loose-limbed, sallow-faced Serbian, with black hair under a green-visored cap, always on the back of his head. His shirt was torn on both sleeves and open nearly to his waist, and in the uncertain lights of the mill his chest and abdomen shone with sweat.

"Goddam you, what you think. Get me"—a long blur of Serbian, here—"spout, quick mak a"—more Serbian with tremendous volume of voice—"furnace, see? You get that goddam mud!"

When a man says that to you with profound emotion, it seems insulting to say, "What" to it. But that was what I did.

"All right, all right," he said; "what the hell, me get myself, all the work"—blurred here—"son of a—third-helper—wheelbarrow, why don' you—— ——— *quick now when I say!*"

"All right, all right, I'll do it," I said, and went away. I was never in my life so much impressed with the necessity of *doing it*. His language and gesture had been profoundly expressive—of what? I tried to concentrate on the phrases that seeped through emotion and Serbian into English. "Wheelbarrow"—hang on to that; "mud"—that's easy: a wheelbarrow of mud. Good!

I got it at the other end of the mill—opposite Number 4.

"Hey! don't use that shovel for mud!" said the second-helper on Number 4. So I didn't.

I wheeled back to the gallery behind Seven, and found Nick coming out at me. When he saw that hard-won mud of mine, I thought he was going to snap the cords in his throat.

"Goddam it!" he said, when articulation returned. "I tell you, get wheelbarrow dolomite, and half-wheelbarrow clay, and pail of water, and look what you bring, goddam it!"

So that was it—he probably said pail of water with his feet.

[8] From *Steel*, The Diary of a Furnace Worker, by Charles Rumford Walker, pp. 38-43. Copyright, 1922, by Charles Rumford Walker. Boston: Atlantic Monthly Press.

"Oh, all right," I said, smiling like a skull; "I thought you said mud. I'll get it, I'll get it."

This is amusing enough on the first day; you can go off and laugh in a superior way to yourself about the queer words the foreigners use. But after seven days of it, fourteen hours each, it gets under the skin, it burns along the nerves, as the furnace heat burns along the arms when you make back-wall. It suddenly occurred to me one day, after some one had bawled me out picturesquely for not knowing where something was that I had never heard of, that this was what every immigrant Hunky endured; it was a matter of language largely, of understanding, of knowing the names of things, the uses of things, the language of the boss. Here was this Serbian second-helper bossing his third-helper largely in an unknown tongue, and the latter getting the full emotional experience of the immigrant. I thought of Bill, the pit boss, telling a Hunky to do a clean-up job for him; and when the Hunky said, "What?" he turned to me and said: "Lord! but these Hunkies are dumb."

Most of the false starts, waste motion, misunderstandings, fights, burnings, accidents, nerve-wrack, and desperation of soul would fall away if there were understanding—a common language, of mind as well as tongue.

But then, I thought, all this may be because I'm oversensitive. I had this qualm till one day I met Jack. He was an old regular-army sergeant, a man about thirty. He had come back from fixing a bad spout. They had sledged it out—sledged through the steel that had crept into the dolomite and closed the tap-hole.

"Do you ever feel low?" he said, sitting down on the back of a shovel. "Every once'n while I feel like telling 'em to take their job and go to hell with it; you strain your guts out, and then they swear at you."

"I sometimes feel like a worm," I said, "with no right to be living any way, or so mad I want to lick the bosses and the president."

"If you were first-helper, it wouldn't be so bad," he mused; "you wouldn't have to bring up that damn manganese in a wheelbarrow—and they wouldn't kick you round so much."

"Will I ever get that job?"

We were washing up at one end of the mill, near the Bessemers. There was plenty of hot water, and good broad sinks. I took off my shirt and threw it on top of a locker; the cinder on the front and sleeves had become mud.

Forty men stood up to the sinks, also with their shirts off, their arms and faces and bodies covered with soap, and saying: "Ah, ooh," and "ffu," with the other noises a man makes when getting clean. Every now and then somebody would look into a three-cornered fragment of looking-glass on one of the lockers, and return to apply soap and a scrubbing-brush to the bridge of his nose.

A group of Slovene boys, who worked on the Bessemer, picked on one of their number, and covered him with soap and American oaths. Somebody told an obscene story loudly in broken English.

The men who had had a long turn or a hard one washed up silently, except for excessive outbreaks if anybody took their soap. Some few hurried, and left grease or soot on their hands or under their eyes.

"I wash up a little here," said Fred, the American first-helper on Number 7, "and the rest at home. Once after a twenty-four hour shift, I fell asleep in the bathtub, and woke up to find the water cold. Of course, you can't really get this stuff off in one or two wash-ups. It gets under your skin. When the furnace used to get down for repairs, and we were laid off, I'd be clean at the end of a week." He laughed and went off.

I had scraped most of the soot from arms and chest, and was struggling desperately with the small of my back. A thick-chested workman at the next bowl, with fringes of gray hair, and a scar on his cheek, grabbed the brush out of my hand.

"Me show you how we do in coal-mine," he said; and proceeded vigorously to grind the bristles into my back, and get up a tremendous lather, that dripped down on my trousers to the floor.

"You wash your buddy's back, buddy wash yours," he said.

SOME GREEN SAND HOGS AND OTHERS [9]

We use a bar for handling heavy timbers. They call this bar the devil. The miner tells his helper to go out and get the devil, to raise the timber. So the fellow that was running the job was a very rough customer, very ugly looking. This helper didn't know who he was and he went up to him and said, "The miner wants to see you." So when he came back the fellow asked the miner, "What did you want with me?" The miner said, "I don't want you." So the miner says to the helper, "What did I send you after?" "You told me to get the devil and this is the nearest thing I could find."

We was working in a casing one time. A fellow got his finger cut off, caught between the bucket and the decking. One of the gang said, "If he kept his hands in his pockets, he wouldn't have got his finger cut off."

A man was holding his hands up and he didn't want anybody to bump into him. "Don't touch me. I got the measurement of a board." His hands were waving back and forth like an accordion.

A mule is a machine for taking the slack up on the holts. He told me to send the motor up to bring down the mule and two bags of sawdust. So this guy says, "What in the hell do you want with the motor? Put the sawdust on the mule's back and send it down."

There used to be a trick on greenhorns—send them up to the heading and explain that in the front of the shield they can see the fish swimming in the water. Of course, it's foolish because the shield is about twenty feet under the bed of the rivei.

[9] As told to Marion Charles Hatch by sand hogs in the "hoghouse" during the construction of the Queens Mid-town Tunnel, 42nd Street and the East River, New York City, February-April, 1939. "Living Lore of New York City." Manuscripts of the Federal Writers' Project of the Works Progress Administration in New York City.

On some of these jobs where you are long hours in the air, the lock tender sometimes makes tea. That's to warm the men up, it being kind of wet and damp down there. They all chip in a quarter a week to pay for this tea. It's all out of our own money. This greenhorn comes in and wants to know what was in the pot, with the cups. The motorman tells him that that's the compliments of the contractor and if he waits long enough the biscuits will be up as soon as the lock tender bakes them. The greenhorn sits down, making himself comfortable, confidently waiting for the hot biscuits and asking if they will have any butter on them.

A lock is a big iron door weighing possibly one thousand pounds. It can be closed only with air pressure. It is known as a lock. This is what we do whenever we get a greenhorn down into the heading. You ask him to go up and ask the lock tender for the key to open the lock. Of course there's no such thing. He gets sent around from place to place. So this particular fellow goes looking for this key. This is all actual facts. Now we do have a plate of iron in the tunnel that builds into the ring. That we call the "key"—weighing about seven hundred pounds. So what does this guy do but have it put on a flat car and have it brought all the way down to the heading. So he turns the joke on the other fellows, because they have to make it their business to get rid of it.

They make it a rule on these jobs to give the men hot coffee when they come out of the air to warm their stomachs. We was over in Brooklyn in the poor part of the neighborhood. These jobs are naturally in the poor part of the neighborhood. In strays a tramp. The coffee man, being a good-hearted old soul, gave him a cup of coffee free. The next day he found he had a coffee and bread line outside, which he, of course, had to chase, after getting much abuse from the bums.

A sand hog got drunk over in Jersey. He laid down on the sidewalk. Another Irish fellow came along and seen him, thought he recognized him. He read the badge [identification disk] and on the badge it says ["if this man is stricken on street"] rush him to the medical lock. So he took him down to the medical center in Jersey City. There's a medical lock there.

So the guy inside in the hospital thought that the two of them was sand hogs. Only the drunken guy was a sand hog. So the guy in the hospital put the two of them in the medical lock [under compressed air]. Neither one of them should have gotten under. So the guy that wasn't a sand hog he was jumping around in the air. He didn't know what to do. The doctor thought there was something fishy. You know, he could see through the little glass window. The man was jumping to beat hell, waving his hands.

If you raise your hand anywhere in the air, they will turn the air right off. If you get blocked, that is, and feel like your head is coming off your shoulders. This guy got blocked in the lock. So they let him out. When he came out, the doctor says, "What's the matter with you?" He said to the doctor: "There's nothing the matter with me. But from now on all the sand hogs in the world can be dead before I take one to the hospital again."

IRONWORKERS [10]

I. CONVERSATION

Popeye. An ironworker isn't a man. He's only a monk without a tail.

William Doyle. This fellow was up on a bridge and slipped and he held on to a cable. He was hangin' about 200 feet up. One of the fellows yelled to him. "Hold on! I'll be right there to get you!" He yelled back, "Don't worry! I have no intention of lettin' go!"

Popeye. What's the third end of a line? Put the two ends together and then you throw it. That's the third end.

S.B. Tell him about the time you fell up two floors!

Squarehead. I fell four floors on the Frick building in Pittsburgh. I had a pint of whiskey in my hip pocket. I almost broke my neck. I did break my hip. I broke both arms. But I didn't break the bottle of whiskey.

Johnny Goketchum. Another time the pint broke in his pocket. He took off his pants, squeezed his pocket and licked up the drops.

F. Kitilson. Here's how he happened to fall. He went to spit. His chewing tobacco happened to fall out and he went out after it.

W. Ruble. There was a man. He got his toes smashed. The toes were only hangin' by the skin. He went to the doctor. It was on 47th Street. He came to work the next morning. He had his foot wrapped up and had the leather toe of his shoe cut off. Somebody asked him, "Did you hurt yourself much?" He said, "Oh, no!" Then he pulled his toes out of his pocket and showed them to the gang.

Thomas F. Meagher. In Quebec, Canada, I happened to leave there three days before the bridge went down. I jumped into Pittsburgh. I was workin' in the Wabash. Got on a little toot and in the meantime that went down. Twenty-nine got killed. Both the bridges went down and I missed them both. The Lord was with me.

II. JOKES AND STORIES

How To Get into Heaven[11]

There was a fellow went to heaven one time. He was a millionaire. When he go up he wanted to sneak in, without answering questions.

Peter stopped him.

"What did you do when you was down below?"

[10] As told to Marion Charles Hatch by members of the International Association of Bridge, Structural, and Ornamental Iron Workers, Local 40, New York City, March 1939. "Living Lore of New York City." Manuscripts of the Federal Writers' Project of the Works Progress Administration in New York City.

[11] By Mike Ryan.

THE HEAVEN-REACHING SKYSCRAPER

THE AMALGAMATED ANGEL LABOR UNION OF 1910 AT WORK

"I was a millionaire!"

"Did you work for it?"

"No."

"Did you rob and steal from laborers to get that million?"

"Yes."

"Never done no work in your life?"

"No."

"You gotta do some work before you get in here. Go over there to that store-room and get a bucket. Come back and see me. You see that lake down there?"

"Yes."

"Fly down and bail out that lake and when you have done it come back and see me!"

Took him 200 years. Well, he come up and reported.

"Nothin' doin'; you can't get in yet! Hang on to the pail. Go over to the boy in the storeroom and get a pick and a shovel. Come back and see me! See that mountain down there?"

"Yes."

"Take that pick and shovel and pail and go and dig that mountain down. Throw it into the lake where you bailed the water out of it. Come back and see me."

That took him 500 years. That was seven hundred years. He went up.

"Go and put away your tools in the storeroom and come back and see me."

Peter looked down at the job he had done for seven hundred years and was very well satisfied with it. A good worker.

"You won't have to do any more hard work but you can't get in yet! Go down to the Labor Temple on 84th Street between Second and Third Avenue. There's a fellow named Fred Kitilson owns a saloon there and stand with your belly up against Kitilson's bar till that squarehead son-of-a-bitch buys you a drink and then I'll let you in!"

The First Time I Left the Ground [12]

The first time I left the ground I went up 205 feet. That wasn't real iron work. I was out in western Kansas. Goodland, Kansas. I been workin' at the round house so a party came in from Chicago puttin' up a smokestack.

So we picked up a bunch of fellows mostly farm boys. They couldn't get a steeple jack and so forth.

After they get the smokestack up it has to be painted. He was payin' us fellows about fifty cents an hour on the ground. He told us, "When I get ready to paint the stack I've got to get somebody to help me do it." So every-body wanted that job to begin with.

All these fellows wanted to go to work at paintin' it because they're sup-posed to get $1 an hour while they were paintin' it. That was a lot of money. Everybody wanted this job but I didn't mention it. I didn't want to go. Well when it come time to paint all of those fellows that wanted to go in the first place, refused.

The boss turned to me and says, "Ruble, you haven't mentioned anything about going up!"

I said, "I've never been off the ground. I'm scared to go up." This place was right on the prairie. You can see for miles and miles. He says, "Ruble, I'll make a steeple jack out of you." So I told him I'd take a chance!

They put me in a bosun's chair. I had a paint bucket hangin' onto the bosun's chair, with a brush hangin' onto the bucket, with a wire hook.

[12] By William Ruble.

When they started up with me I didn't look down till I got half way up. When I did look down I thought I was a mile high in the sky.

I almost froze to the ropes. I called to him and asked them to please let me down. The wind was blowin' so hard I was almost frightened to death. They couldn't hear me due to the wind blowing. I kicked the brush off the bucket with my foot. Naturally when the brush fell, they knew I couldn't work, so they had to let me down.

So the foreman told me to go back in there in the bosun's chair and to not look down and to go all the way to the top and don't look at anything except the stack direct in front of me and I would not be afraid.

Which after about ten minutes coaxing I got back in the bosun's chair. They pulled me to the top of the stack and then I made my half hitch over the hook and went to work. After working a few minutes I started to look off in the far distance, and then I began to get used to it but I was afraid to look down.

Before the day was over I had gotten over my nervous spell and haven't been frightened since. The boss told me that if I had not gone back the second time the same day while I was scared I would never have been able to went high again.

Since then I've been on eighteen, twenty stories, thirty-five stories high. The French Building, thirty stories. I worked on the Williamsburg, the Brooklyn and different bridges. Now I pay no attention to it. It just comes natural.

*　*　*　*　*

High Romance[13]

I was working on a job on 86th Street. I get talking to a pot walloper [maid]. I was working all morning. The girl hollered over, "I want to see you at 12 o'clock." I asked her where would she be. She said she'd be in the bathroom.

Between the building I'm on and the building she's in is fifteen feet. It was about fifteen stories high. I get ahold of a plank and put it over to the bathroom from the other building.

I sneaks over in the bathroom, and my boss sees me. He takes the plank away as a joke. I'm in the bathroom and giving this here pot walloper a good time.

When I'm all done I open up the window to go back on the job and the plank is gone. So I didn't know what the hell to do.

So the girl she wouldn't leave the bathroom because she'd get caught and she didn't know what to do.

So I go to the bathroom window and started hollering would they please put the plank back and they wouldn't. They were laughing at me. So they were all working. I was scared.

So I made up my mind I'm going out the door. So I ran into the girl's missus. She asked me what I was doing there. So I says that they threw a hot rivet into the bathroom and I went over to get it so the house wouldn't set afire. The plank fell to the basement fifteen floors. I got to get out some way. I can't jump down, so I came out this way.

She says, what was the girl doing there? I told her, "What would you do if there was a hot rivet in there? You'd try to cool it off wouldn't you?"

I go back on the job and I get fired that night at 4:30.

Who's down on the street but the same girl I had in the bathroom and she was fired too. So I asked her, "What did you get fired for?" And she said, "The same thing as you did. Having an affair in the bathroom."

How To Bring a Man To[14]

I was working at 132nd Street and North River on the pier. The needle —that's the beam that holds up the scaffold—broke and the scaffold went down. Three of us went down with it. One of the fellows goes into the North River. It was January ninth, cold. It was two below zero.

He falls down there. We had to try to fish him out. I jumped in the river and put the lines around him and they had to pull the two of us out. They fished us out and took us into the shanty and by that time they had a quart of whiskey in there for us. He was unconscious.

So they were rolling him on the barrel, to get the water out. He wouldn't come to. No life in him at all. The overalls frozen. Poured some whiskey into him and he wouldn't respond.

I say "I'll get him to."

I stuck my hand in his pocket, "I want to see how much money is in here!"

Soon as I reached in for his bank roll he said, "Take that hand out of there. You're trying to rob me."

HACKING NEW YORK[15]

I. Cops

—One of the boys goes in front of the judge and gets a dismissal. "What's the charge?" "Retardin' traffic." "Did you whistle or signal to him?" So Gilbright says, "I'm tired of all the time movin' my hand"—like that—"and blowin' my whistle." "You're a public servant. Case dismissed!"

—I run across a finagler last Monday. I was doin' a coolie over at the stand at Fortieth and Seventh. He pulls a thumb at me and says, "Get out of here quick and let this Packard in!" Luckily I seen him take a buck from the driver and stick it in his top pocket. So I says, "Nothin' doin', I'm stayin' right here. This is a public hackstand, ain't it?" So he gives me a ticket. "Okay," I says, "but you're goin' to the station with me right now." I tell my story to the Captain, and he makes out he don't believe me. "This is a very serious charge,"

[14] By F. Kitilson.
[15] Collected by Marion Charles Hatch, written by Herman Spector and Hyde Partnow. From "Living Lore of New York City." Manuscripts of the Federal Writers' Project of the Works Progress Administration in New York City. 1939.

he says. So I reach in the copper's pocket and pulls out the buck. Lemme tell you, that shut them up fast!

—Take one of these thick-headed coppers like Donovan. He's so dumb, if he found a dead horse on Kosciusko Street he'd have to drag it over to Gates so as he could spell it right on the ticket. Ain't that right? You know the guy.

—Talkin' about dumb cops. I got a friend Charlie, whenever they give him a ticket and they ask where he was born, he says "Czechoslovakia." So the flatfoot gets sore and says, "Keep movin', buddie, scram!"

II. Schmegeggies

—I been on one identical spot, pretty near, for sixteen years, and I never seen it so bad. The longer you're in it, the poorer you get. You keep sinkin' and sinkin', like Sleepy up the line there. The guy never gets a good sleep in his life. I ask him, "What's the matter, Sleepy? Can't you grab some shuteye at home? The kids runnin' round the apartment, or what?" "Nah," he says. "It's me mother-in-law. Since she come to live with us, I gotta sleep on the couch, so I'm all broken up." That's why he's always rollin' up at the wheel. You hear about the time he gets a three buck call up on the West Side and stops on a light, and falls asleep? The lights change. All the cars is passin' him by. He's right in the middle of traffic. A cop comes over, and he wakes up with a snap. He looks back in the cab, and don't you think that fare took a powder on him!

—Here's what he done last week. Two old ladies give him a hail under the viaduct. They want to go to Pennsy. He's just after takin' a nap, so he rolls down Madison, turns over to Thirty-fourth, and there's the stream goin' north to the theater district. So he tails them around until he winds up right back at the Central, right on the line. Then he falls asleep again.

—What happened to the dames?

—Well he wakes up again, you know the way he does, like a stinkin' sentry, and here's these hens sittin' in the cab. So he scrams around the corner, figures, "To hell with everything!" When he comes back, they're gone.

—He's what you call a *schmegeggie*.[16] But you got him trimmed a mile, aintcha, Barber? When a guy tells you "Tudor City," what do you do? You say, "What bridge do I take to get there?"

—Oh yeah? When they want to go to Canarsie, they always pick Maxie. All they gotta say is, "Waldorf Astoria," and he'll take them right out—to Astoria!

—So it happened once! There was lots of noise. I couldn't hear the guy. But how about the time you pulled in here with a yokel, a dame from out of town, and she asks you, "What's on the clock?" "Eighty-five, madame." Then she turns right around and says, "Why, driver, it's only thirty-five on the meter. Don't you think I can read? Ha, ha, ha!"

—"So what? What's funny about it?" I says. "If you knew it all the while, why did you ask me, lady? Tryin' to make a crook outa me for a lousy half a buck?"

—Trouble with you is, you're always ribbin' somebody. I won't even kid the shirt off a guy like Yonkel Stadium. What for? What's the sense?

—Somethin' screwy about Yonkel if you ask me. He's a fine feller but he ain't all there, if you know what I mean.

—That his right name, Maxie, or did you stick him with it?

—I don't rightly know what the hell his name is. He gets a call out to Yankee Stadium, the way I heared it, and the guy's green. He just don't know the joint from a hole in the wall, but he won't let on. So he keeps ridin' and trustin' to luck and lands up at Battery Park. So he breaks down and asks a cop, "Yonkel Stadium, where is it?" The copper has a good laugh, tells him how to get there, but by the time he makes it the game's over and there's eight bucks on the clock!

—Tie score! Yonkel didn't get there and the fare didn't pay.

III. DAMES

—Dames! They'll skunk you every time. Ride one for an ice-breaker and you won't book a thing all day.

—Say, did I ever tell you guys about the frail who says, "Call me a taxi"? So I says, "O.K., lady, you're a taxi." So she thanks me profusely and walks away. Ha ha ha!

—I happened to cruise by the Hipp once. It was rainin' cats and dogs, so the wheels spilled a little mud on a dame's dress. I'm Kid Galahad. I stops and offers to take her home, no charge. She steps in, and when I turns around, she says, "Mount Vernon." I could have spat in her eye.

—What did you say?

—I says, "Lady, take the train if you wish and just sue the company." That's all.

—A lady calls up the office, in Brooklyn. You know they got these stations out there. And they send him over. He rings the bell. The lady hollers she's comin' right down, so he starts cleanin' up the cab. While he's got the door open, a dog jumps in. So he chased it out and seen it run up the porch where there's another mutt. Just then the lady comes out, gets in the cab, and the

---

[16] *Schlemihl,* inept person.

two dogs jump in with her. He takes the fare to Bensonhurst, the lady pays him, and the dogs jump out and follow her. So he thinks nothin' of it. Next day the same lady phones the office she wants a cab again. "But don't send me the young man I had yesterday," she says. "What's the matter? Anything wrong with the guy?" "Oh," she says, "he's all right. I don't like the idea drivin' with a fellow who carries two dogs along when he's on the job." Can you beat it?

YOU CAN'T FIGURE ON A LIFETIME [17]

My boss, that nosey thing, he was always sitting on me with them over-developed muscles until I got sick and tired.

Where I got the incentive that day I don't know. Maybe it was because I was wearing white, I like white. I wear everything with a white collar. It makes me feel good.

The boss was in the front with a big customer. I was sitting there and typing like my heart would break. I was hankering for life. Rose, I said to myself, in this day and age you can't figure on a lifetime. Marriage is getting pushed further and further in the background. If you're single it's no stigma. I got up from my desk, I opened the boss's door and I yelled: "Look, Mr. Sternberg, you can wait a hundred years and you'll never get a typist like me. Look at my hair, my white blouse, my nails. I never look unruly, I'm never idle a minute, and I got artistic ability besides. Next payday I want twelve dollars."

He opened up his big mouth right away and pushed his muscles and he yelled: "Miss Rosenthal, see me in the back." The most terrible thing, you understand, see me in the back. I don't know, I wasn't even scared. I was in the mood of making money, nothing bothered me. Listen, don't you think they know if you're worth it to them? They got big mouths but they know if you're worth it, don't worry. You think he fired me?

I'm telling you from that day until he lost his business he was so nice to me—like my office boy, he used to bring me up milk shakes. He was at my beck and call.

Before he was sitting on me. In the future everything was in reverse. I was sitting on him.

"HOW ARE YOU FIXED FOR SOAP?" [18]

"Wake up! Wake up, you dreamers, and listen to me!"

The crowd which thronged the busy Denver street on that June day in the late 'eighties turned curious eyes toward the source of the stentorian tones.

"Wake up! The hour has come to face the problems of our country!"

Half a dozen cowhands, lazing in the sun, some visiting stockmen, a few

[17] By Hyde Partnow. From "Living Lore of New York City." Manuscripts of the Federal Writers' Project of the Works Progress Administration in New York City. 1939.
[18] From *The Reign of Soapy Smith*, Monarch of Misrule, in the Last Days of the Old West and the Klondike Gold Rush, by William Ross Collier and Edwin Victor Westrate, pp. 1-8. Copyright, 1935, by Doubleday, Doran & Company, Inc. Garden City, New York: Doubleday & Company, Inc.

horse wranglers, and a tourist or two, idly ready for any diversion, drifted toward the speaker.

"One question—the supreme question—before us today is vital to the welfare of the republic!"

Tall, lithe, he was an arresting figure, and the flashing eyes which gleamed from the youthful face belied the impression of greater age his jet-black beard obviously sought to create. He had taken his stand a few yards from a corner on Seventeenth Street, half a block from the old Elephant Corral in the Colorado capital. Before him, on a low tripod, was an open sample case of liberal dimensions, the typical "tripe" and "keister" of the street hawker.

As he continued his smooth-flowing oratory, a growing crowd pressed forward to gaze interestedly at the contents of the sample case, surprised to see only a stack of blue wrapping paper and a considerable number of two-inch cubes of some white substance.

"Gentlemen, the all-important question which I propound to you and for which I earnestly seek the answer is this: *How are you fixed for soap?*"

A quick smile flashed across the face of the speaker as he paused for the briefest moment, then went on:

"I hear no response. I fear I embarrass you. In all honesty, gentlemen, most of you look as though you needed soap, and your silence distresses me.

"But, seriously, though my message is that of soap, it is, likewise, a message of hope. For today, to meet that great need which is so apparent in you, I bring a new soap—a wonder soap." He held one of the white cubes aloft. "Here is the finest cleansing product ever brought forth by man's scientific ingenuity, the fruit of many weary months of patient research and experiment in my own laboratories.

"Use this soap upon your skin and it will shine like the moon, and your face will gleam with the radiance of the sun at noonday. Is that bald spot growing? Use this soap and patriarchal locks once more will adorn your brow. Is your hair turning gray? Wash your scalp with this soap and to the silver threads will return the pristine glory of youth. Does conscience keep you tossing, sleepless, in the silent watches of the night? Use this soap and wash your sins away.

"Perhaps this glorious chance to purify body and soul should be enough, but, gentlemen, I offer you far more than this. On this day of all days, to introduce this marvelous product, I am giving—yes, *giving*, my friends—enormous cash prizes to those upon whose shoulders the Goddess of Luck has taken her perch. Cleanliness, gentlemen, is next to godliness, but the feel of good, crisp greenbacks in the pocket is Paradise itself. Step up, my friends, and watch me closely."

From his wallet he extracted a bundle of greenbacks and dropped them into the sample case, their denominations impressively visible—a hundred, several fifties and twenties, numerous ones and twos.

"Through posterity, my friends, my fame will rest upon this soap—this boon to mankind which I am offering to you."

Swiftly, dexterously, he began wrapping the soap cubes in the blue paper. At intervals, with apparent nonchalance, he enclosed a cube in one of the greenbacks; then he wrapped the blue sheet tightly about money and soap and tossed the package carelessly into the growing pile.

"Now, gentlemen, I am offering this miracle-working soap at twenty-five cents—if you wish to buy the soap alone. If there be any such among you,"— this in a very deprecating voice—"I will accept your quarter and you will find it the best two-bit investment you ever made.

"*But*—if you have any sporting blood and wish to take a chance on winning one of those little green papers with the big numbers on them, ranging up to one hundred dollars, I will sell you a bar of soap from these I have already wrapped, for the ridiculous price of five dollars—and you will have the privilege of drawing your own package.

"If you have been watching me as closely as I hope, it should be simple to select a bar of soap wrapped in real money—and the first man up has the best chance." He lifted several of the intriguing, wrapped cubes and permitted them to drop back into the pile.

"Who will buy? Who will take a chance on winning a hundred-dollar bill, a fifty, or even such small change as a twenty—all for five dollars? Think of it, men, if you land the hundred, you make 2,000 per cent. profit on your investment!

"What? No answer from the great unwashed? Gentlemen, you amaze me. I am astounded. But, no. I understand. You want proof—proof that I am willing to give you something for nothing, in order to convince you of the miraculous properties of this soap. Very well. So be it. The customer is always right, and I aim to please. Now, listen carefully.

"If anyone in this crowd will show me ten dollars in gold, in silver, or in currency, I will give him a ten as a present—free—gratis—for nothing. Could anything be fairer than that? Is there a ten among you? Not one? Remember that the first man who shows me a ten gets a ten."

A rangy cowboy, in red shirt, chaps, sombrero, high heels, and clanking spurs, a bit unsteady after a session at the bar of the Elephant Corral, elbowed his way to the fore.

"I'm yore man," he drawled. "I call your bluff. Here's my ten, stranger. Take a good look at it." He dangled a bill high in the air, so all could see.

The bearded young soap dispenser smiled.

"Right you are, my friend," he said, "and here's my ten." He dipped his fingers into his vest pocket and brought forth a thin dime which he dropped into the horny palm of the cowpuncher. "There you are, you're welcome to it my man. You win. I lose and I ask for no sympathy. I'm game. I always keep my word and pay my debts. I said a ten for a peek at a ten and I've given it to you. So, now, we're all square."

The indignant howl of the discomfited cowboy was drowned in the roars of the crowd's laughter, and the ice was broken. An unkempt individual stepped forward, extended a five-dollar gold piece, and reached for one of the bars of soap.

"I been watchin' this one," he said, with a chuckle. While the crowd surged toward him, he unwrapped the soap cube and gave a shrill yip of triumph as he waved a fifty-dollar bill over his head. "Got you, stranger," he shouted, gleefully, pushed the money into his wallet, and vanished into the crowd.

Business came with a rush. Gold, silver, and bills in five-dollar amounts poured into the hands of the salesman. The wrathful cowpuncher forgot his indignation and was among the first to buy, grunting disappointment anew when he found he had drawn a blank, but immediately investing the other half of his ten-dollar bill for another draw, which was equally fruitless. An amazing number of the speculators found their packages to be blanks or, at best, containing no more than one- or two-dollar bills. Even when the wrapped cubes were practically sold out, not more than half a dozen bills of larger denomination had been retrieved of the apparently much greater number which the soap salesman had enclosed in the packages.

TOOTH POWDER HAWKER GIVING A
DEMONSTRATION

For two hours business went on briskly. At the end of that time the crowd had dwindled to a handful, and the salesman closed his sample case and folded his tripod. Then he walked rapidly down the street. Arrived at one of the typical hotels of the Denver of that day, he went up to a room, where he found half a dozen curiously assorted men awaiting him. A close observer at the soap stand would have recognized them as the only purchasers who had won more than two dollars. Now, with one accord, they extended their winnings to the salesman extraordinary.

"Here y'are, Soapy," they said, one adding, "Looked like a good haul today."

"Not so bad," he replied. He counted the bills carefully. "All present and accounted for. I thought for a while I had slipped, but I was pretty sure these were all I had left in the pile for you to pick up." He stowed the money away. "How about a drink?"

This then was Jefferson Randolph "Soapy" Smith—at the age of twenty-eight, just on the threshold of his career; for the next ten years to be unchallenged King of Bunco throughout the West; and already chief of a gang which for sheer cussedness was unrivaled.

Recognition of his supremacy already awaited him. From his corner soap stand in the streets of Denver he was destined to rise to absolute mastery of cities. During his reign, history was made on the last frontiers, and to that history the fruits of his wryly twisted soul was to contribute no little.

FOUNTAIN-PEN SALESMAN [19]

Now here is a pen that gives you any sort of line without changing the point. Now if you understand, realize, and appreciate a real good value, and if my physiognomy is not too conspicuous to be comprehended, I'm gonna clarify to such an extent that each and every individual standin' here at the present time can very well afford it. I'm gonna give you this Parker 51 type. Now don't forget. You can take my pen and bring it into any pawnshop, ask them for ten dollars, see how quick they'll chase you out. But you ask them for five dollars, they may give it to you. And to-day I'm not gonna charge you no dollar bills for the pens, but the first lady or gentleman gives me twenty-five cents gets the pen. And I think it's worth a quarter to anybody. Any one who understands and realizes and appreciates something real good.

You can go downtown, uptown, out of town, into town, in the summer time, in the winter time, all the way through, you'll never get a pen like this. By golly, that was a heavy quarter. Thank you. Every one gets the same chance. Here is another one like the last one. Look—not to discriminate, to make fish of one and flesh of another—you know, Saturday my wife says to me, "George, I want you to come home. I'm gonna give you something." I have a neighbor that's very nosey—he said to me, "What's she going to give you? What is the wife going to give you? Look at what my wife gave me Friday night. Fish."

Believe me, as long as you live, and may you live as long as you wish, and don't forget that all the money that you spend with me goes to a good cause —'cause my wife wants money—the butcher, the baker—everybody wants money.

Look at this. You can write Yiddish, you can write English, you can print,

[19] Recorded by Tony Schwartz, West Forty-second Street, between Sixth Avenue and Broadway, New York City, July 2, 1952. Transcribed by B. A. Botkin.

you can sketch, with this very same pen. You show me another pen, regardless how much you may spend for it, that will give you this service and this satisfaction. Now this being the last demonstration, you don't have to give me no dollar bills. But if you want a pen that makes writing easier for you and yours, a pen that improves your penmanship one hundred and one per cent, here is the pen right here.

Now believe you me, it is very hard to demonstrate, but this is the finest and best. Now every man, every woman, every child who needs a fountain pen shouldn't hesitate one minute in receiving a pen that's superior in quality, in texture, in writing ability, and at a price that can't be beat anywheres. It is by far the finest, the best, that money can buy.

Look at the way the pen writes. Here is a pen that slides and glides over your paper just the same as a ball or a marble over a sheet of glass. During this adver-tise-ment, you get this very same pen—*not a dollar and a quarter but a quarter of a dollar*. That's yours. Give me a hundred dollar bill, I'll run away faster than you. Make sure you give me the right amount, because I don't want too much. Four nickels and one is five. God bless your stingy soul!

Everybody who understands what I'm talking about—you know what I'm talking about—you want something that's really good. Why be confused? This is not something that will cure a headache, a earache and a toothache, remove any spots, stains, corns, calluses, ingrowing toe nails—won't make you richer, won't make you poorer. It will do only one thing for you. If you want a pen that will write any language, here is a pen writes English, Yiddish, Chinese, Japanese, Turkish, Scandinavian, upside down, printing, sketching, drawing. Believe you me, when you spend a quarter with me, you find five dollars in the street.

A red one? Right there. You take a green one and it'll turn red. You take a red one and it'll turn green. You have two different colors. Every man and woman who understands—no, I don't care if you're a man that was chased out of the bread line because you wanted to have toast. I don't care if you fell asleep the first night you were married—if that would make any difference—here it is right here. I got a cousin of mine that is the strongest man in the country—he lives out West and he holds up trains.

Believe me, this fellow Milton Berle—there's only one little difference between Milton Berle and myself: he gets a thousand dollars for one song and I get a dollar for a thousand songs. Here is the greatest value you ever anticipated in having in a long while. Now when you see a value of this kind, I guarantee you—look at this—can you show me anywheres a pen as good as this? I think I'll give this one here to the president of the Amalgamated Shoe Stores. Everybody gets one. Don't hesitate. Hesitation means you'll never get it. First time in the United States of America that you get a value like this. When you go uptown and out of town or anywheres at all, you never see a value like this. Now look at this. . . .

HOW HARRY REICHENBACH PUBLICIZED
"TARZAN OF THE APES" [20]

At the age of nine I could neither walk nor talk. I lay bound to my mattress by a muscleless inertia, speechless and limp, a hopeless and permanent invalid. If anybody had predicted then in 1893 that by 1915 I'd travel twice around the world as a magician's press agent, hiking a good part of the way, or that I'd talk so much eventually that people would have to make me toastmaster at every banquet I attended, that same prophet could have foretold prohibition, bobbed hair and the market of 1929. He could even have foretold that in future murder trials, they would always free the defendant and lock up the jury.

How I learned to walk and talk again was a secret that remained between providence and my mother. For nearly seven years, from the time I was two, she cared for me in my illness, and in spite of the increasing burdens of a growing family, she fed me and watched over me as if I were her only child. Children in the region of George's Creek were expected to shift for themselves like chicks as soon as the fuzz turned to feathers. Other boys at my age were already working in mines or mills. Maybe there wasn't enough inducement in a healthy mining life for me to get well too fast.

I found a far more absorbing existence in the boy magazines and books with which my mother stacked the little bed. While my body lay in a numbing apathy of energy, my mind grew alert and active fed by tales of the wildest romance and the most fantastic imagination. It was only the rhythm of the spectacular and unusual that found a response in me. The extravagant stories of Frank Reade, Jr. and Frank Merriwell formed the kernel of my later life.

I remember one story in particular about a human ape out of the African jungle, who mixed among the people of a civilized community and learned the language and the customs of men. He was devoted to his master who was in great trouble and then at a most exciting point in the story the installment ended. I worked up a feverish frenzy of impatience and suspense waiting for the next number of the boy's magazine in which the story ran. My mother couldn't afford to get me a regular subscription to any magazine and generally picked up old copies from neighbors, but when she saw the effect that reading had on me, she stopped my education abruptly and altogether. I never learned the end of that wonder tale until 1917, twenty-four years later, when it suddenly played a vital part in my life and the idea it inspired brought me more than fifty thousand dollars after earning a million and a half for another man, besides saving him from getting shot.

It was in the early winter of 1917 that I met "Smiling Billy" Parsons, a huge, genial Westerner who had wheedled the cowboys and ranchers of Wyoming and Montana into parting with their little coin bags so that he could produce

[20] From *Phantom Fame,* the Anatomy of Ballyhoo, by Harry Reichenbach, as told to David Freedman, pp. 24–29. Copyright, 1931, by Lucinda Reichenbach and David Freedman. New York: Simon and Schuster, Inc.

a picture that would lift the mortgage from every ranch in the two states. He produced the picture for a quarter of a million dollars, then a fabulous cost, but now a sum spent just for dinners to discuss mergers. He called the picture, "Tarzan of the Apes" because there were monkeys in it, but at the preview the wise ones christened it, "Tarzan of the Crepes." It was unanimously voted the worst mess of celluloid in moviedom. Even the cattle in Wyoming and Montana stampeded when they heard about it. It suddenly occurred to the cowboys that in view of Billy Parsons' size and bulk he would make an easy and tempting target. If he ever came back to the prairies they would give him a resounding welcome. The twenty-one gun salute would be a cork-pop to their loud and accurate reception.

Smiling Bill wore a sickly grin as he told me of the ovation that awaited him. He persuaded me to see the picture and decide if anything could be done to salvage it. For fifteen months he had kept it on a shelf, but his funds were down to gravel and even New York would soon be too small a place to hide in. As I sat in the private projection room watching "Tarzan" a curious feeling of excitement gripped me. As a rule I seldom looked at the pictures I had to publicize for fear they would disillusion me and destroy the honest enthusiasm with which I could write about a picture I hadn't seen. But this time I was stirred to deep memories that harked back to the early story I had read in my childhood. A long interrupted dream was suddenly being continued.

"Bill, you've got a great picture!" I exclaimed at the end of the showing.

"H'm-h'm!" he nodded dolefully.

"To show you how great it is, I'm willing to handle it on a commission basis instead of a flat salary."

"I can't take such advantage of you," he objected. "Let me tell you the whole truth. This picture has been turned down by every distributor. If I could sell out for $50,000, I'd be happy." There was something sad and wistful in his tone. I could see him with the $50,000 tucked into a satchel taking a boat to an island at the other end of the earth where the cowboys could never reach him.

"I'll accept fifteen per cent from all the money you make *over* fifty thousand! Does that reassure you?"

"You can have the fifteen per cent," he said pityingly. "But I insist on giving you a salary of a hundred a week besides, because I have a sneaking hunch that the salary is all you'll ever get out of it."

On that basis I set to work. As no standard producer would buy or rent the film I leased the Broadway Theatre from Carl Laemmle and handled the entire production of the picture myself. I had the jungle trees and foliage that were used in the picture sent on from California and dressed the lobby and the whole interior of the theatre to give the effect of an African wilderness. Between two palms loomed the shaggy mane of a ferocious, stuffed lion and in the boxes, chattering, gibbering monkeys were swinging from cocoanut trees. I turned loose another troupe of four live apes in the lobby forest. Then came the opening of "Tarzan of the Apes" and something strange and startling happened to complete for me a wonder story I had begun twenty-four years earlier.

On the front pages of all the newspapers ran a feature story that had every earmark of a Frank Reade, Jr. fairy tale. It answered to such headlines as, "Simian Royalty Steps Out" and "Jungle Prince Makes Society Debut." The story told of a certain Prince Charley, a giant ourang-outang, who, dressed in a neat-fitting tuxedo and high silk hat, entered the fashionable Knickerbocker Hotel on Saturday night while the lobby was aglitter with New York's élite. Prince Charley, timid and embarrassed, was about to introduce himself to this brilliant assemblage when he noticed a revolving door on the Forty-second Street side and began to spin wildly around in it. Exhilarated by this turn in social life, the big ape leaped back into the lobby with greater confidence and cordially screeched to the other high hats to try his new sport, but they had all made a clearance in record time.

The only way they could be persuaded to return was under cover of the police. A committee of twelve bluecoats surrounded the Prince at a respectful distance and cajoled him into driving down with them to see the sights. The jungle lord expressed his admiration for the city by screeches of wonder that rocked the elevated structure. When he arrived at the police station he began to enjoy his adventures and tried to show his appreciation to the sergeant by leaping over the desk and landing in his lap. The sergeant ducked this crushing welcome by an eyelash and when he finally managed to crawl out from under his desk, he ordered the foreigner taken to night court on a charge of disorderly conduct. Frederick Groehl, the presiding magistrate, tried to question the hairy prince, but all he could get out of him was static. He was inclined to fine him as a warning to all monkeys who paraded in tuxedos, but suspended sentence on condition that the Jungle Prince would stick to cocoanuts and keep out of hotels. Prince Charley nodded penitently and started to eat his high-hat. His day in society was over and he returned mournfully to his jungle in the lobby of the Broadway Theatre.

He was the ape who made the Tarzan picture a world-wide triumph yielding over a million and a half in receipts, saving Billy Parsons' life and bringing me more than $50,000 in commission. But to me he has always been the human ape of the early Frank Reade, Jr. stories, projected into real life by an odd trick of chance. The idea that it would be possible for a monkey dressed in natty clothes to crash into society was something unusual, unbelievable, and when it happened, it furnished front-page material. The fact that I had planted this episode and used it to promote the Tarzan picture established more firmly in my mind that the whole difference between the things one dreamed about and reality was simply a matter of projection. Many publicity stunts that occurred later on in my work took on this magic-lantern effect. An idea that would seem at first flush extravagant and impossible became, by the proper projection into life, a big item of commanding news value.

FRENZIED FINANCE [21]

. . . The genius who promoted a demonstration of dizzy finance in Los Angeles [in 1941] cut out all the middlemen. . . . His initial investment was about a dollar for a want ad in the *Times*: "This is your last chance to send your dollar to Peter Snockwatch, Somethingorother Hollywood Boulevard."

That's all there was to it. He didn't offer anything. He didn't set out any rules. He didn't require anything in exchange for anything. He didn't even ask for the dollar. He just opened the door of opportunity to those who might care to send one.

And eventually when he went out of business—which is to say when he withdrew his advertising—it was at the request, not the order, of the F.B.I.

Postal inspectors and government agents of one sort or another had begun to descend upon him four days after the first printing of his announcement. They found him sitting in his living room opening letters and piling up dollar bills in neat stacks. They were astounded—why, I don't know. After all it was their home town.

They asked him the nature of his business and they got a straight answer.

"I haven't got any business except the taking in of dollars that volunteer friends care to send me," he said. "I keep a careful record of these donations for the benefit of my income-tax return, which I assure you will be in good order. I offer nothing. I make no pretenses, false or otherwise. And what is illegal about that?"

The representative from the U.S. District Attorney's office shook his head.

"Nothing, I'm afraid," he decided, and the delegation walked out. The business went on vigorously for another week. Then the F.B.I. and postal men came back.

"Look here," said the spokesman. "We admit that you're in the clear. There is no law or regulation on which you could be prosecuted. But your eager customers are beginning to get the mail service all gummed up and we're asking you to quit."

So Mr. Snockwatch, or whatever his name was, quit. After all, he was getting into a bracket where the government would have taken most of his income anyway.

RACE-TRACK STOOPERS [22]

Of the thousands of new horse-players around town, some are pretty careless with their winning pari-mutuel tickets. At this writing, $193,871.35 worth of this season's winning stubs haven't been cashed. That is less than a tenth of one per cent of the amount handled in the tote, but it still seems a

[21] From *More Interesting People*, by Robert J. Casey, pp. 43-44. Copyright, 1947, by The Bobbs-Merrill Company, Inc. Indianapolis and New York.

[22] From "The Race Track: Of Stoopers," by Audax Minor, *The New Yorker*, Vol. 19 (October 23, 1943), No. 36, pp. 74-75. Copyright, 1943, by The F-R Publishing Corporation. New York.

sum worth mentioning. Chances are that most of the outs, as missing tickets are called in the industry, never will be turned in, because they were torn up by mistake or in an unreasoned rage, or were just lost. A few probably were tucked away in vest pockets for safekeeping and forgotten by their holders. Next April, in accordance with regulations, the racing associations will turn over to the state treasury all the money that hasn't been collected. If you find your lost ticket after that and want to collect, you can, but you'll have to struggle through miles of red tape.

There is no way of telling, naturally, how many of the tickets that are cashed were lost or thrown away by their purchasers and later found by stoopers. A stooper, not to mince words about it, is a fellow who spends his afternoons wandering around the grandstand and the betting ring, picking up discarded tote tickets off the floor in the hope he'll find a live one. There are a lot of amateur stoopers and some professional ones around the tracks. Several of the professionals, sometimes referred to as ground squirrels, don't do at all badly. In the course of a season, their pickings may average more than a hundred dollars a week. This, obviously, has it all over betting on favorites.

The most enterprising of these artists is E. R. Pyle, who has a post-office-box address in Baltimore and transacts all his business with racing associations by mail. Nobody seems to know much more than that about Mr. Pyle, or even whether there actually is a Mr. Pyle. The name may well be a nom de course. Some pari-mutuel men believe that he represents a syndicate of ground squirrels or that he handles, on a commission basis, tickets found by cleaners and trash men, because the tickets he sends in have been "stooped" at the New England and Jersey tracks as well as those in Maryland and New York. Then there is Carlos Alton, who lives in Jamaica during the summer so as to be near his work and follows it South in the winter. There's even a lady ground squirrel, but chivalrous pari-mutuel men won't tell anyone her name.

To be a good stooper, Mr. Alton says, requires concentration and long training. The sole trade secret Mr. Alton will give away is that he memorizes the code word and the winning numbers for every race. (A code word—five letters that usually don't make much sense—is printed on all tickets, and there is a different one for each race to make counterfeiting harder.) Then he just walks around with his eyes open. It's difficult enough to spot a live ticket that has merely been crumpled up or torn in two. To find all the pieces of one that's been reduced to confetti and put them together again seems like working a small miracle. In the batches Mr. Pyle and Mr. Alton send in to the cashiers at the end of a meeting, there are always a few tickets so deftly and lovingly patched up with Scotch tape that they are little gems of reconstruction. All torn tickets turned in for redemption are double-checked. They are inspected by New York State Tax Commission men after the track's experts have passed on them. The better ground squirrels, consequently, are quite proud that payment has never been refused on any reconstruction jobs they have turned in.

STRIP TEASE [23]

I. How It Started

It is quarter to twelve. . . . The last show is over at the Republic Theatre. The carpeted aisles are littered with cigarette butts, cigar stubs, candy wrappers, and newspapers. The performers, red-eyed and exhausted, are going home. You make your way backstage and introduce yourself to Beatrice Vivian. You want to talk to her about the beginnings of the strip tease. She ought to be able to tell you something; she's been producing burlesque shows for the Minskys since 1930.

"What started all this?" you ask her.

"An accident at the Gotham," she replies.

"Sounds like a mystery story," you say.

"In a way it is. It may not have been an accident, it probably wasn't the Gotham, no one's sure who the girl was."

Mrs. Vivian tells you that some one in the show was singing, or dancing, or maybe she was just in the chorus when her shoulder strap broke. The audience riotously approved. The girl liked the applause. At the next performance she broke the strap herself but not at the one after. She was in jail, the first of a long, long line.

"What year was that?" you ask.

"About 1927, I suppose."

"And that's all there was to it?"

"What more would there be? The girl went back to her show, wherever it was, and continued breaking her shoulder strap until she discovered a few snappers could be undone with less effort and more grace."

"But how did they get away with it, after the raid?"

"How do they get away with it now?" asks Mrs. V. "Besides," she points out, "it was no longer a stunt or an isolated instance. By the time the first stripper got back to her stage, every burlesque show in town had an imitator."

"It certainly spread fast enough," you say.

"It's like that with everything in burlesque," puts in the straight man who has stopped to listen to the conversation. "When an idea clicks for one show, all the rest have it before the next performance. If a Broadway musical opens with a few funny skits, versions of them are playing in every burlesque house the next day. The strippers steal each other's stuff. And the comedians? They have to rehearse a new bit in a corner so rivals in the same show won't cop it."

"Whether that's so or not," interrupts Mrs. V., "the strip was all over town the next day and the originator's identity was lost among dozens of claimants."

Mrs. V. can't give you any more time. You're not sorry about that. She was giving you legend, not lowdown. You have a notion that there was little of the accident about the use of the strip tease on a stage, but you'll put off theo-

[23] From *Strip Tease, The Vanished Art of Burlesque*, by H. M. Alexander, pp. 14-21, 33-38. Copyright, 1938, by Knight Publishers, Inc. New York.

rizing until you've spoken to Ed Garns. He's the stage manager. The publicity agent has asked him to wait around for you.

You find him sitting on a stool in front of the electrician's switchboard, eating a piece of pie and drinking milk out of a bottle. Garns looks like a milk drinker—a pleasant, sunburned little guy who parts his hair on the side and wears brown silk polo shirts. He's been an actor and a master of ceremonies in a night club. He seems like the much-bruited individual who is happy as long as he has something to do around a theatre.

"Do you know anything about how the strip started?" you ask him.

He still has a mouthful of pie. While he washes it down, you tell him in a few words what Mrs. V. has had to say. No use hearing the same thing twice.

"It's funny about that story," grins Garns, "but I don't think there's anything in it."

"That's more like it," you say. "I had an idea myself that the strip was related to a profession which may not be the oldest but certainly antedates 1927."

"I wouldn't know a thing about that," says Garns, "but girls were certainly doing shimmys, quivers, and grinds when your old man was a kid."

"On the stage?"

"At stag shows. Billy Minsky didn't invent the strip. He just brought it out from the back room."

"When was that?" you ask. You'd like to get the date more or less fixed.

"About 1925. The Broadway leg-shows forced him to do it."

You feel that's quite probable. You have no difficulty recalling that blackouts and nudity were first featured in the revues of the early twenties. You remember that the Shuberts were allowed to show chorines with nude busts as long as they made the poses "artistic" and did not require the girls to move. The courts felt that forms aesthetic in repose became erotic in motion.

"You see," says Garns, "the rough stuff was what made burly tick. It had never given them a Sunday-school show. When nudity hit Broadway, burlesque not only had to have it, it had to top it."

"The tease must've been a click the first time out," you say.

"Well," says Garns, "they didn't use it right away. At first they tried putting a nude chorus near the footlights instead of upstage as in the revues. It only drew yawns. Minsky knew why. The boys wanted to see a girl come out dressed and take her clothes off."

"So the strip started with dropping a shoulder strap . . ." you begin.

". . . and ended up in a G-string," finishes Garns.

"That's what I don't understand," you say. "How did the strip get so naked? Did the bosses give more money to the girls who took off more clothes?"

"The girls who drew the most customers got the most dough," says Garns. "It was pretty plain that the strip was the magnet, as soon as it appeared in burlesque. The girls knew the crowds came to see flesh. Little by little, they showed more."

"Then it was competition that was responsible for the peeling."

"Yeah," Garns laughs. "They tried to outstrip each other. The first teaser flashed a breast. A second topped her with a suggestive song. A third added the bump and the grind. The last showed her backside and the G-string. Put 'em all together and you've got the routine of the strip."

*   *   *   *   *

This leads you to a factor in the development of the strip tease which Garns overlooked. It paved the way, as it were, for the competition that arose among the strippers.

The first strip-women really teased. They didn't show much, but they were clever about it and held their audiences. Whatever "art" the strip may be said to have had centered around this early phase: a certain coquetry that ended in the dropping of a shoulder strap. The overlooked factor has to do with the part played by the audience in all this. The people who attend burlesque shows go in heavily for what has been called "audience participation." A visiting critic of the American theatre has observed this. You have seen for yourself that when they like something, they let out a yell. There is nothing silent about their disapproval. It is not difficult to imagine the impatience of this ruttish mob with the wiles of the first teasers and the trifling concession of a bared breast a second before the blackout. One day—if it is possible to infer the past from the present—some maddened individual let out the bellow: "TAKE IT OFF!" Delightedly—you imagine—the crowd took up the cry. You weren't there but you're willing to bet that after a second of stunned surprise, the teaser . . . stripped.

II. The Stripper's Art

A certain amount is done for the stripper.

She is given the stage, an expertly handled spot that will usually match the color of her costume, music that she considers appropriate, and an offstage singer who will croon a chorus or two of a sentimental ballad. The show will contribute one other item to the creation of "mood" in the form of an introduction over the amplifiers. The announcer will actually recite the adjectives by which the stripper wants to be described. "The sweet, the elusive, the dainty" . . . "the wild, the flaming, the dynamic." If any one in the audience can't find words to describe what he sees, he's got 'em.

The rest is up to herself.

Costume: She buys her own wardrobe and she has to have changes every week. Some go in for bedroomy things: stockings, garter belts, step-ins, negligees, pyjamas. Still others use picture hats, flounces, bodices, and what-nots to outrage conventions remembered only by people who don't go to burlesque shows. All the clothes are especially prepared with snappers. The G-string is another essential. Every stripper has dozens of them.

Hair: She must dye her hair a definite color. Red or yellow or black. The spot does funny things to the natural shades considered beautiful. Honey and ash blonde, for example. Red hair picks up wonderful highlights from a lavender spot.

Make-up: Burlesque theatres supply no make-up man. The stripper must learn what effects become her and obtain them herself.

Hands: Should be used gracefully and not too much. Most strippers don't know what to do with them. Their idea of grace is to stick out the little finger like a kid drinking a glass of water.

The walk: Should fix character. Only a few know how to walk on a stage. The rest either march to the music or try to glide, dipping and whirling on the turns with arms extended. Margie Hart is one of those who manages to get something from her trailers. Her walk is nonchalant. Dorothea Maye's is coquettish. Evelyn Myers, a little girl who takes exaggeratedly long steps, gets a sophisticated effect.

Pace: A definite pace must be created and sustained. This means the tempo of the stripper's movements from the time she appears until she exits. If she works fast, she has to keep her foot on the pedal. If she parades, she can't throw in a little *Suzy Q* or a truckin' step.

Timing: A sense of timing is important. The stripper has to know when to take off what. If the audience is cold, she has to get her stuff off early. If the audience is receptive, she may tease—if she can. The fundamental trick here is for the stripper to continually appear to be taking more off (for 3½ minutes, the length of the number) and really show nothing. By "nothing" the stripper's intimate person is meant. Bust and backside are somehow legal.

Sweet or hot, she mustn't fumble: If the girl is Margie Hart, she has to get out of her clothes smoothly. If the girl is Georgia Sothern, her clothes have to strip at a grab.

A bit of business helps: A stripper will often become famous for some little trick. Gypsy Rose Lee undoes herself with pins. The spot catches them as she throws them to the customers who save them and get in free the next time. Mary Sunde uses the same stunt with a champagne pop. Others will do a trailer right in the audience. The spot follows them as they kiss bald heads, give out apples and other rubbish. Only the real lookers, of which there are few, can leave the stage where the lights do so much for them.

Placing in the show: This counts for a lot. The feature spots are at the middle and before the finale. The two top-flighters on each bill get these places without question. Apart from this, all strippers like to follow a comic if the bit is funny. It puts the audience in a good humor, makes it easier for them to draw a response. They also like to have a comic follow them. After their number's over, the lights go up and the comics yell and holler to get attention. But the audience calls back the stripper. This flatters them; makes them look as though they were stopping the show.

These are the technical elements of the theatre strip. A few variations are practised in night clubs, none of any importance. The girl has to make her entrance from the middle of the floor instead of from a wing; one trailer is done among the tables where she introduces herself to the guests; the blackout is prolonged to give her a chance to cover herself before she takes a bow. The spirit of the act, however, is much different—more restrained, even a little humorous with itself.

MAIN STEM AND SLAVE MARKET [24]

Slim and I rode the "cushins" into Pittsburgh. It was during the [First] World War, and riding the "cushins" was the only safe course in the East, according to the bums we had consulted. There were a lot of soldiers guarding the railroad tunnels and bridges, prepared to take a crack at any 'bo seen on the trains. Besides, we had enough money to pay our fare.

It was late winter, and Pittsburgh was glacial. As we walked rapidly down the street which leads from the station, Slim and I loosed these arguments through chattering teeth:

"If you want to get a job, why in hell don't you stop at the next drug store, look up the classified ads in the telephone book, and find out where the employment agencies are?"

"You're a gay cat all right, all right. There are a lot of good reasons. First place, you look like a bum already, just as I do. You haven't shaved for a week; your nose is snotty with the cold; and your sleeve shows where you've wiped it off. Your face is dirty and your pants look like hell. They'd give you the bum's rush. Second place, it simply isn't done. No stiff ever got information about a job through a telephone book. The telephone book is a dispenser of information to the bourgeoisie; the working plug has his own channels. And it is to these channels of information that we must go. . . . Hey, Jack, d'ye know where a stiff can find a job?"

This last sentence Slim addressed to a tattered, purple-nosed fellow who was wearily walking in our direction.

"Dey got some purty good jobs on de windows down by Chicago Joe's saloon. I'm shippin' out fer a job meself dis evenin'. 'Leven hours' pay, ten hours' work, forty cents an hour. De flophouse is free and de chuck is tirty cents a trow. I axed a stiff dat's been dere wot it was like. He says de java's good and de flops ain't crummy [lousy]."

"Where is the place, Jack?"

" 'Sup aroun' Johnstown."

"And where is Chicago Joe's?"

"Ye go up dere about two blocks. Dat's de main stem. Den ye goes up like dat," and he waved to the right. "Wen ye gits near de river, ax any stiff, an' he'll tell yez."

As we parted, Slim looked at me triumphantly. "Do you see why a telephone directory is inadequate? We have already learned where the employment agencies are; we have heard of a job which has been recommended by a chap who's been there; and we've heard of Chicago Joe's. Why, man, the gestic words 'Chicago Joe' are alone reason enough to avoid a 'phone book."

In spite of this, Slim and I met, a few years later, a super-tramp who consulted the telephone directory. His name was Bozo, a name which fitted him

[24] From *The Main Stem*, by William Edge, pp. 16-21. Copyright, 1927, by Vanguard Press. New York.

superbly. He would call up the passenger station, find out the hour of an express departure, and would then lay his plans to "deck the cannon-ball on the fly."

Soon our feet were treading the main stem. As we slowed our pace, Slim said: "We are now on the 'stem' or 'main stem,' or 'main drag,' as you have just heard that worthy say. The main stem is the principal street from the hobo's point of view. It is not the main residential street; it is not the main business street; it is the hobo's street. On this street 'stemming' flourishes. 'Stemming' is hobohemian for panhandling. It is on this street that the homeless have put their stamp of approval. Here the bum finds friends; the drunk finds fellow drinkers; the red finds his comrades; the dope-fiend finds peddlers. Here it is that nickels and dimes can be coaxed from passers-by."

In a few minutes we were in the employment agency section. The place was striking because of the absence of women and children. The slave market of every city is the most masculine portion. Stiffs were standing on the curbs, deciphering the scrawly blackboards behind the windows of the employment agencies. A few drunks were entertaining a little group of job-hunters.

One of the drunks was being applauded with hearty laughs as he exhibited a hiding place for his razor. His ragged four-in-hand tie was open at the top and closed at the bottom. This formed a long pocket into which he could slip his razor. While we passed he acted as if he were about to be attacked; he wheeled on his imaginary antagonist, whipped his razor from its cloth scabbard, and performed murder. Then he wiped the blood from his razor, pointed critically to a nick in it, closed it carefully, and rammed Durandal back into its cloth sheath. This pantomine provoked much laughter from the shivering bums.

Another drunk was behind his cheap and battered straw suitcase, which stood on end. He acted as if he were selling something over a counter; and his sales speech was like this:

"Today I am selling this magic collar button for only five cents, half a dime. It will not tarnish, rust, break, bend, or color the skin. It was invented by his Nibs, the Right Honorable Prince of Wales, London, England. He couldn't wear the ties of the new mode without this button, which permits the scarf to be flat, and does not tear the fine silk of the most luxurious tie. Ye better buy it now. You've heard of Shakespeare, who said, 'Here today and gone tomorrow?' Well, I'm not that kind of a guy. I'm here today and gone *tonight*."

In the slave market, buddies on former jobs find each other again, much as American tourists meet their former fellow-passengers in Westminster Abbey, the Louvre, or at the American Express. They discuss possibilities as they see them. We met a laborer whom Slim had known in Cleveland. Since his departure from the Forest City, he had worked on two or three of the jobs advertised, and had informed himself thoroughly about two or three others. He warned us against them all.

"De flops is crummier'n hell. Dey feeds yer condensed horse manure. An' de pay ain't nuttin." This, with variations and repetitions, was his opinion of all the jobs.

One never accepts a job lightly. One walks about, reads every board, discusses the probabilities with other job-hunters. Much information is thus passed along.

A typical day for a stiff about to hire himself out might be like this: Shorty decides, for reasons of his own, that he wants to get a job. Perhaps he has been on a spree, and faces either work or panhandling—something the work-stiff is not clever enough to do permanently. Perhaps he is going to reform, and become a regular-working, patriotic citizen. This is not a joke. Migratory workers are forever waging a futile fight with respectability and a steady job. Shorty, convinced, then, that he must work, goes into the employment agency district. He reads on one of the boards:

GANDYDANCERS
Neer Elisabeth, New Jers.
35c an hour, 10 hours
Overtime after 8 hours.
Free camp   Meals 30c

This looks well; but no need to rush things. Shorty's neighbor on the sidewalk, a dark-skinned fellow, is also deciphering the sign. Shorty says: "Say, Blackey, y'ever been on that 'Lizabeth job?"

"Yeah, hell of a hole. De jamocha is rotten. De goddam chuck dey hands yer is rotten. . . . Ya got a butt on ya, Shorty?"

Shorty has a butt, and a friendship has begun. After a few hours' reading of boards, discussion of possibilities, avoidance of jobs which require a medical examination, Shorty and Blackey decide on a job at Hog Island. The employment agent has told them to report at four in the afternoon. It is now about twelve.

Blackey has long ago confessed that he is dead broke, or "clean," and Shorty has confessed that he has "a little jack," one "iron man." Frequently the Shortys have two iron men, but admit only one. When a friendship has been of long standing, such "holding out" is treason. But at the beginning it is both overlooked and easily kept secret.

The stiffs spend their dollar together according to their standards of consumption. Frequently tobacco and liquor are more imperative than food. Sometimes a migratory will spend his last dime on a stale, marbled chocolate bar. Sometimes he will get a shave or a haircut. At four they report for the job, perhaps sober, perhaps drunk. They are then conducted by the man catcher to the station, and shipped at the employer's expense to their destination. Here they go through the necessary employment routine, are fed, and are assigned beds in the camp.

The new job is usually as bad as the old one had been. There is a sardonic hobo poem which describes the futility of changing jobs:

Things are dull in San Francisco,
"On the bum" in New Orleans;
"Rawther punk" in cultured Boston,
Famed for codfish, pork and beans.
"On the hog" in Kansas City;
Out in Denver, things are jarred;

And they're "beefing" in Chicago
That the times are rather hard.

There's a howl from Cincinnati,
New York City, Brooklyn, too;
In Milwaukee's foamy limits
There is little work to do.
In the face of all such rumors
It seems not amiss to say
That no matter where you're going
You had better stay away.

IX. How the Other Half Lives

In 1881, Wallis Nash, in *Two Years in Oregon,* wrote that the word "hoodlum" originated twenty years before in the San Francisco water-front toughs' warning cry of "huddle-um" when the police appeared. The same water front in the Sixties was infested with boardinghouse crimps and runners engaged in the nefarious trade of shanghaiing (from making a "Shanghai voyage") and fleecing sailors. According to the underworld code of dog eat dog, the hoodlums preyed upon San Francisco's Chinese, who in turn, with their slave girls, Tong wars and underground passages, trafficked in vice and rackets.

The terminology of New York City's slums, underworld and demimonde keeps pace with the changes in the seamy side of the metropolis through the years. One of the oldest problems of the city was created by the homeless, vagrant children known as street Arabs, guttersnipes and waifs. According to George C. Needham in *Arabs of the City* (1883), the term "street Arab" was used to designate the young nomads of the streets, while "guttersnipe" was employed for a class of children "too utterly weak, both mentally and physically, to cope with the more sturdy Arab," and "waif" is the more comprehensive term for many types of young unfortunates.

Perhaps the most famous New York street type was the "Bowery b'hoy," who in the 1830s was an apprentice, generally to a butcher, and "ran with a machine" (or fire engine) and was distinguished by his dress and speech.

In *Reminiscences of an Octogenarian* (1896), Charles H. Haswell gives us a vivid picture of the type, which later became famous on the stage through Frank Chanfrau's impersonation of Big Mose in a cycle of plays beginning with *A Glance at New York in 1848.* On Sundays and holidays the B'hoy wore "a high beaver hat, with the nap divided and brushed in opposite directions, the hair on his head clipped close, while in front the temple locks were curled and greased (hence, the well known term of 'soap locks' applied to the wearer of them), a smooth face, a gaudy silk neckcloth, black frock-coat, full pantaloons turned up at the bottom over heavy boots designed for service in slaughter-houses and at fires; and when thus equipped, with his girl hanging on his arm, it would have been very injudicious to offer him any obstruction or to utter an offensive remark." A later version of the Bowery Boy was introduced by "Chuck" Connors, the Mayor of Chinatown, who derived his costume from the London costermonger and set the pattern for what is generally thought to be Bowery talk. Here is Chuck's description of a gent, a junk and a chump, as noted by Hutchins Hapgood in *Types from City Streets* (1910):

Wat's a gent, did yer say? A gent, wat you call a gentleman, is a bloke wat ain't a junk. A gent is a man wat shakes hands wid yer; wat don't wear no fence [collar] around his neck, wat don't wear no tall hat, wat don't call yer a bum. When a bloke wat ain't got a nickel asks a junk for a nickel, the junk [wat] ain't a gent calls him a bum. You can always tell a junk dat way. A junk ain't no gent, dat's all, see? A gent is a damned good man, a good man that ain't looking fer no good advice. A bloke wat takes good advice ain't no gent. I hate a man wat takes good advice. He's too good a feller, yer know. A chump is a good, good man. A chump is slang for a sucker. If you fetch him a jab in de wizard, he'll grin, feeble like, an' if you tell him you didn't mean it he'll shake yer hand as friendly as yer like. He's a good, good man, a chump is, which is slang fer a sucker, but he ain't no gent, though he is a lot better than a junk. A junk is de worst t'ing dere is. A chump is good to yer, but he's mean to himself. He does himself all the harm he does, and dat's why he is a sucker. But a junk is a down bad man, real bad, yer know, wid a fence around his neck.

The Bowery boys ran and fought in gangs, as well as in rival volunteer fire companies, and were the successors of the picturesquely named Five Points gangs of the 1820s—Roach Guards, Plug Uglies, Shirt Tails, Dead Rabbits.

A hotbed of crime, the Five Points was New York's "slum of slums" and the American slum to end all slums. In the Seventies and Eighties slumming was known as "hunting the elephant," a variant of seeing the elephant or having a disillusioning experience. And "hunting the elephant" or prowling the jungle of the city—the dens and dives of the Five Points, the Bowery and the water front—was a favorite sport of "Paul Prowler" (Samuel A. McKeever) in the *National Police Gazette.* Founded in 1845 as a reform sheet by a journalist, George Wilkes, and a journalist-turned-lawyer, Enoch Camp, the *Police Gazette* took its name from its avowed purpose of "serving as an instrument . . . to assist the operations of the police department, and to perform the species of service which does not lie within the scope of the present system." In 1876 it was taken over by Richard K. Fox, and the "pale pink periodical" became the precursor of the tabloids, devoted as much to titillating the senses and imaginations of its readers as to unveiling the mysteries of the gay and wicked city.

The *Police Gazette* was the crowning glory of the lurid gaslight school of documentary journalism, a sort of dime-novel social history of the lights and shades of life in New York, Chicago, Denver, etc., by "gaslight" or "after dark." "Whoever writes of New York truly," said Matthew Hale Smith in *Sunshine and Shadow in New York* (1896), "will do so in lines of light and gloom"—the extremes and contrasts of the city's low life and high life, poverty and wealth.

So in every era and city, vice and crime have developed their own words and ways. A product of the "Wild Seventies" in New York is "Tenderloin." According to H. L. Mencken, this term originated in a statement of Police Captain A. A. Williams when in 1876 he was transferred to the West Thirtieth Street precinct in the heart of the city's gay and wicked district bounded by Twenty-fourth and Fortieth streets and Fifth and Seventh avenues: "I've been having chuck steak ever since I've been on the force, and now I'm going to have a bit of tenderloin."

Among the signal contributions of the Chicago bullet barons to murder lore and lingo is "taking a man for a ride," a phrase derived from taxi talk. According to Stanley Walker, this was a more efficient method of bumping off a man than the Sicilian custom of inviting him to a banquet and lulling him with food and wine. The practice, however, was better suited to the geography of sprawling Chicago than to that of vertical New York—an example of regional adaptation in metropolitan crime.

As every town has its "wrong side of the tracks," so every city has its Skid Road (usually corrupted into "Skid Row"), the local variant of the Bowery. This is the street of broken men and hopes, with its saloons, cheap restaurants, pawnshops, employment agencies, flophouses, dead beats, drunks, mission stiffs, "professors" (including the Bowery's late Professor

Walter Edwin Peck) and smells. Skid Road, writes Herb Caen of San
Francisco's dozen blocks south of Market and between, roughly, Second
and Seventh streets, "has a smell of its own—of poverty and dirt, of
cheap wine and disinfectant, of frying grease and coffee that has been
boiled twice too often."

Every Skid Road has its characters and legends. San Francisco had its
"Hemstitch Nettie," nicknamed for her hypo-needle-punctured skin;
"Shammy Kid," who made watch "pockets" out of discarded chamois
skins; and "Tough Tessie," a prostitute who hated men and liked to throw
them downstairs into the street, naked. New Orleans' "Exchange Alley" had
its has-beens—"Sidney the Sage," one-time famous chef; "50-50 Charlie"
Quirk, one-time patent-medicine salesman and pitchman.

A local variant of Skid Road characters are the beachcombers of a port
like Galveston. George Sessions Perry tells of the two beachcombers who
"never went to bed at night without patrolling the shore to see what the
gulf had washed in to them: . . . a wooden bucket, a sodden mattress . . . a nice rocking chair. . . . Then, on one stormy night, there
came the sweetest surprise of all—a cozy frame house, into which, with
their previously collected articles, they moved [to live], unmolested, with
serenity and aplomb."

THE RISE AND FALL OF CANAL STREET, BUFFALO [1]

. . . Unbelievable wickedness and gaiety and heartbreak . . . at one
time made the Canal Street area of Buffalo as infamous as the Barbary Coast
of San Francisco. . . . The most roaring days of Canal Street were between
1826 and 1850, before the railroads and the Welland Canal had cut into the
traffic too much. Those were the days when the amount of human energy and
muscle that went into the problem of transporting people and freight, even by
the relatively easy method of canal boat on the Erie Canal, was tremendous.

*   *   *   *   *

Canal Street was more than a street. It was the name of a district, the heart
of a district, a small and sinful neighborhood. It was and is an irregular area,
bounded on the west by the harbor, on the south by Main Street, on the east
by the Terrace and on the north by Erie Street, roughly speaking. As late as the
1880's, there were ninety-three saloons there, among which were sprinkled
fifteen other dives known as concert halls plus sundry establishments designed
to separate the sucker from his money as swiftly as possible, painlessly by
preference, but painfully if necessary.

In the early days, almost the only legitimate businesses in the area were
blacksmith shops for shoeing the "Canawl" mules and horses, and the warehouses and offices of the Erie Canal and Great Lakes shipping interests. . . .

Canal Street was laid out in 1829 along the west bank of the newly dug
canal, as Cross Street, only fifty feet of cobblestones from sidewalk to sidewalk,
and only a quarter of a mile long. It was then the only street bisecting the
short streets running from the Terrace to the harbor. In the earliest days the

[1] From *Niagara Country*, by Lloyd Graham, pp. 196, 205-215. Copyright, 1949, by
Lloyd Graham. New York: Duell, Sloan & Pearce, Inc.

Great Lakes sailors looked upon the "canawl" men with contempt and derision. A hate developed that persisted until the end of the century. But the Erie Canal had not been in operation many years before the "canawlers" far out-numbered the Great Lakes sailors. At one time the situation was complicated by New England sailors coming into the Niagara country to get jobs on the Lakes. There were fights and riots and murders, involving the two groups.

The "canawlers" won a kind of victory in 1854 when they vociferously demanded and got the name Cross Street changed to Canal Street. Then there came a time after the turn of the century when it began to be respectable. Hard-working, decent Italian families began to move into the cheap quarters vacated by the underworld folk. A movement was led by Father J. V. Hennessey, pastor of the Church of Our Lady of Mount Carmel at Fly and LeCouteulx Streets to change the name. (The latter name, in honor of an early pioneer, was locally pronounced Lucky-Too Street.) In 1919, victory of a kind perched on the banner of the crusaders when the city fathers perhaps unwittingly, but appropriately, gave the street the name of the author of the *Inferno*—Dante Place.

Canal Street had a good start in the role of a giddy tart of a thoroughfare as early as 1835 when it was still called Cross Street. In that year a traveling Englishman, Thomas S. Woodcock, exploring the wilds of America, visited the Niagara country by Canal packet. In a book on his experiences, he referred to Cross Street as a "corrupt place, with its denizens in a melancholy state morally."

Down through the years, certain characters stand out. There was the notorious Mother Carey, . . . a thrifty if unprincipled soul who ran a "boarding house" and a saloon and a dance hall. The boarding house was operated chiefly for reasons one might expect, but she also specialized in furnishing from it "cooks" for lonely captains of canal barges—well, feminine companions politely termed "cooks" who were supposed to provide some lighter moments to make life a little more bearable for the "canawlers" in the long, lonesome stretches of the Big Ditch.

City directories of the period report an enormous number of women living in the Canal Street district—beside, behind, and above the saloons and dance halls. Generally they were listed as "laundresses, seamstresses, fortune tellers, or boarding house keepers"—about five hundred of them. Every now and then the law-enforcement agencies promised to clean up the place, but they never did. Even Sheriff Grover Cleveland of Erie County tried it in 1870 and failed. Finally, the city fathers resorted to segregation. The women "down there" were ordered not to go into the city north of the Liberty Pole on the Terrace, except for shopping purposes. On such excursions they had to show purchases to police on their return or were thrown in the jug. Thirty days in jail was the usual sentence for those who could not give a good, decent reason for going into the city above the Liberty Pole.

*   *   *   *   *

. . . Among the men, famous names include "Choppy Fix," who got his pseudonym when, in a white heat of fury, he took an ax and wrecked everything in his own saloon. We find the names of Jack Gaffney and Patrick Fahey, partners in crime, and "Shang" Draper and Billy Hope and Mike Morrison. Mike was an all-around bad guy, especially when in his cups. He and his mother lived in a little hut on the tow-path. He went home one night, got into an argument with her, and stabbed her through the heart with a long bread knife. They hanged him for it.

Jack Gaffney and Patrick Fahey came back to their usual haunts in Canal Street one night after doing a job down state. Gaffney had most of the money, more than his share, Fahey thought. There was an argument, and the two separated in a saloon. Finally, nursing a drink and a grudge, Fahey shouted to Gaffney at the other end of the bar.

"Jack, if you don't do the right thing by me, I'll turn up your toes."

He had scarcely uttered the words when Gaffney pulled a revolver out of his hip pocket and shot Fahey three times. Fahey spun away from the bar and staggered across the room in stunned surprise. He fetched up against a table and shouted: "Jack, I guess you finished me." With that, he made for the door, got as far as the cobblestones of Canal Street, and fell dead. Gaffney calmly sat down at a table until the police came. He gave up without a fight and was tried and hanged in the old Delaware Avenue jail yard in 1872.

*   *   *   *   *

John Ott was another character of note. Some say he was manager of an establishment egotistically named The Only Theater. Others say he was merely the bum bouncer. Over the years he had probably bounced more men than he could remember. He knew, or thought he knew, all of the angles of a precarious business in a sodden hole.

One night a stranger entered the place. With the uncanny knack which comes only from experience, the waiters and girls sized the guy up as looking like ready money. He wore a collar and the clothes of a gentleman. In the characteristic manner of the time and place, one of the women there gave him permission to buy her a drink. He was agreeable and ordered two beers. He laid a bill of large denomination on the table. The waiter brought a bottle of beer and two glasses and took the money. An argument arose over the change when the waiter returned. The customer loudly demanded the correct amount.

Just then the husky John Ott appeared on the scene and told the customer to shut up or get out. They did not permit loud arguments and unseemly scenes in this, a place of entertainment for ladies and gentlemen. The customer said he would not shut up, nor would he get out until he got the right change.

Ott made a lunge at the stranger and, somehow, failed to connect. Then he made his second mistake. The next time he lunged, the stranger pulled a big razor out of his vest pocket, flashed it open, and all but slashed John Ott's head off. John Ott was dead—deader than the Dickensian doornail. His life's blood poured out staining the sawdust on the floor. Police took the stranger in. Who was he? John Smith. At least that was all they could ever get out of him, even to the end of the term he did in Auburn Prison for manslaughter.

A lot of lies have been told about Canal Street. It has been said that in its most infamous days, it was the scene of a murder a day. As a matter of fact, the highest average was probably no more than a murder every other day.

Police used to be assigned to Canal Street in trios. And their beats were small. It was the custom for two policemen to patrol together while the third remained stationed at the patrol box in order to send for the wagon when the first hint of trouble arose. There was a period of several years when police warned strangers in respectable clothes, say those in white collars, to get out of the district and stay out if they knew what was good for them. Otherwise they proceeded at their own risk. The motto of the women and liquor dispensers was "collect and get it quick."

Sailors and "canawlers" were, of course, the chief victims. They came off their ships and canal boats with money burning holes in their pockets. The Canal Street "business people" knew just what to do for that. In order to understand the procedure, it is necessary to understand the customary layout of the places. Usually there would be a stage at the end of a long auditorium. There would be entertainment on the stage, comedy acts, singing and dancing, women with appropriate curves and scanty attire. They could neither sing nor dance and knew it was not really necessary. Invariably there was a piano with some one banging away. (It was figured out one time that there were more pianos in the Canal District than in the whole length of fashionable Delaware Avenue. But the tunes from the two neighborhoods of pianos were different. For example, the "Arkansas Traveler" is said to have been composed and first played and sung in Canal Street.)

Along the walls of the auditorium were chromos of ships and railroad trains and luscious-looking dames. Overhead were festoons of streamers and colored papers. Lights were bright. Waiters constantly yelled their orders above the entertainment. But nobody seemed to mind.

A sailor would spot a girl who appealed to him, and the waiter was always willing to escort him to the footlights and oblige with an introduction. The lady then invited the sailor backstage to a place of more privacy. He was invited to buy drinks. But this could only go on for a short time. Patience was short, and time was fleeting. There was work to be done. If the sailor was the kind who could stand a lot of liquor, his lady would soon get restless and along would come a drink for him with knock-out drops.

Next morning, he might wake up in the gutter or in a frowsy room, without money and valuables. Even this disposal of the sailor or "canawler" might be too bothersome. Places along the east side of Canal Street had their backs to the Erie Canal. Through a convenient trap door or back window, the customer could be dropped into the scum-covered water, but not before he had been robbed.

The canal was favored by some operators because the ducking would usually revive the victim but put him in a chastened mood so that he would not make trouble when he finally crawled out. If the plunge in the canal did not revive him—well, from Canal Street's point of view it did not much matter. Canal Street, long before P. T. Barnum, realized that a sucker was born every minute.

So often were the interruptions while a gentleman was drinking in a Canal

Street emporium that he might have to leave the bar or table and his drink to see the fun. It became customary to leave a note informing any it might concern that the drink was not abandoned but still awaited consumption by the man who had paid for it. Such notes of ownership were generally respected, but occasionally they led to amusing results. The story is told of one man who left a note pinned to his umbrella before his drink on a bar. The note read: "The man who owns this weighs 300 pounds and is a former prize fighter. He will be back."

When he returned he found his drink and umbrella gone and another note which read: "The man who took this weighs 85 pounds and can run like the devil. He won't be back."

*   *   *   *   *

By mid-twentieth century Canal Street was but a faded memory. Economics and changing times had taken care of that. Economics started to take a hand when sail began to go and steam came in, when horses and mules began to leave the towpath and steam tugs and then Diesel-powered barges intruded with a handful of men handling conveyance of relatively huge cargoes in the place of a great number of men, divided into many small crews, each crew handling a cargo tiny compared with those of the 1940's.

The scum-covered, mystery-hiding waters of the Erie Canal have long since gone, and the ditch has been filled in.

Even the name Dante Place has lost its significance. Parking lots and new business blocks have wiped the Canal Street area of yore off the map. . . .

THE LIFE AND DEATH OF LITTLE PETE [2]

The greatest and most successful of Chinatown's tong chieftains was Fung Jing Toy, better known as Little Pete, who was head of the Sum Yops and in control of other tongs with which the Sum Yops were allied. For nearly ten years he was the most powerful Chinaman on the Pacific Coast, and although it is doubtful if he ever swung a hatchet or fired a pistol, he was responsible for the deaths of no fewer than fifty men. He had a fair command of English, which he acquired at American night-schools, but if the stories told about him are true, he could neither read nor speak Chinese and employed an interpreter to assist him in communicating with many of his henchmen. He lived with his wife and two children on the third floor of a three-story building at Washington Street and Waverly Place, from the balcony of which, as a boy of ten, he had watched the great fight between the Suey Sings and the Kwong Docks in 1875. He slept in a windowless room behind a barred and bolted door, on either side of which was chained a vicious dog. During his waking hours he wore a coat of chain mail, and inside his hat was a thin sheet of steel curved to fit his head. He employed a bodyguard of three white men, and when he went abroad, one walked beside him, and another in front, while the third brought up the rear. And prowling within call were half a dozen of his own

[2] From *The Barbary Coast: An Informal History of the San Francisco Underworld*, by Herbert Asbury, pp. 191-197. Copyright, 1933, by Alfred A. Knopf, Inc. New York.

boo how doy [fighting men, hatchet men, highbinders], heavily armed. Also, wherever Little Pete went he was accompanied by a trusted servant bearing his jewel-case and toilet articles, for the tong leader was a great dandy, and much concerned about his appearance. He possessed many diamond rings, a dozen handsomely engraved gold watches, and half a score of gold and platinum match boxes set with diamonds and other precious stones. He changed his jewelry several times daily and never wore a suit—he had forty—two days in succession. Two hours each morning he spent combing, brushing, and oiling his long and glossy queue, of which he was inordinately proud. In his leisure time he played upon the zither, listened to the music of his crickets, or wrote comedies, which were translated into Chinese and performed at the Jackson Street Theatre. He owned the playhouse and never had any trouble getting his pieces produced.

Little Pete was five years old when his father, a merchant, brought him to San Francisco, from Canton. He began his career as an errand-boy for a Chinese shoe-manufacturer, and during his late teens peddled slippers from house to house in Chinatown. When he was about twenty-one years old, he embarked upon the only honest business venture of his adult life—a shoe-factory under the firm name of J. C. Peters & Company. Soon afterwards, attracted by the profits in vice, he became interested in gambling houses and opium dens and also entered the slave trade in partnership with Kwan Leung and the latter's wife, Fong Suey, a noted procuress. Backed by the Sum Yop tong, of which he gained complete control before his twenty-fifth birthday, he soon enlarged his activities. Instead of buying girls, he began to steal them, particularly from dealers and crib-owners who were members of the Sue Yop tong, one of the most powerful organizations in Chinatown. He also interfered in other Sue Yop enterprises, and the two tongs were soon engaged in one of the bitterest and bloodiest of all the wars of Chinatown. During the early stages of this conflict Little Pete overreached himself. He forgot that in the final analysis vice in Chinatown existed only upon the sufferance of the white authorities. When one of his killers was arrested and placed on trial for the murder of a Sue Yop man in 1887, Little Pete boldly tried to bribe the jurors, the District Attorney, and every one else connected with the prosecution. He was promptly clapped into jail, later convicted of attempted bribery, and sent to San Quentin Prison for five years.

When Little Pete was released, he again assumed his position as head of the Sum Yops and fanned into flame the embers of the war with the Sue Yops, which had subsided during his incarceration. He also strengthened his position by retaining as counsel for the Sum Yops an influential criminal lawyer, Thomas D. Riordan, and by forming an alliance with Christopher A. Buckley, the famous blind political boss of San Francisco, whom Little Pete called the Blind White Devil. With Buckley's support, Little Pete was soon the undisputed king of Chinatown. Every form of vice, and almost every form of legitimate business as well, paid him tribute. If the owners of gambling houses, opium dens, or brothels refused to pay, their establishments were immediately closed by the white police—and reopened a few days later with Little Pete's men in charge.

The girls in all of the cribs operated by Little Pete and his associates were supplied with counterfeit half-dollars, which they gave as change to drunken men.

Little Pete's income from his various enterprises must have been enormous, but he was not satisfied. He looked around for new sources of revenue and became greatly interested in the possibilities of horse racing. Early in the spring of 1896 he became a familiar figure in the betting rings of the Bay District and Ingleside tracks and soon attracted attention by the size of his bets. He regularly wagered eight thousand dollars a day, and he never lost. Within two months he had won a hundred thousand dollars, and the stewards of the Pacific Coast Jockey Club began to believe that there might be some connection between Little Pete's streak of luck and the sudden epidemic of sick horses and bungling rides by hitherto skilful jockeys. Private detectives followed several riders to the offices of J. C. Peters & Company, and further investigations disclosed the fact that Little Pete was not only paying the jockeys to lose races, but was bribing trainers and stablemen to poison horses against which he wished to wager. As a result of the inquiry Jockeys Jerry Chorn and Young Chevalier were ruled off the turf for life, while Jockey Arthur Hinrichs and Dow Williams, who had been Lucky Baldwin's trainer, were barred from the two tracks which Little Pete had honored with his operations. Nothing could be done to Little Pete, who retired to Chinatown with a substantial addition to his fortune.

Little Pete's star, however, was setting. He had become so rapacious that the Sue Yops determined, once and for all, to end his reign. They invited twelve other tongs, all of which had felt the weight of Little Pete's heavy hand, to join them in a war of extermination against the Sum Yops, and a formidable force of *boo how doy* took the field. A price of three thousand dollars was placed upon Little Pete's head, probably the largest sum that the tongs have ever offered for the death of an enemy. For weeks the hatchetmen of the allies kept close upon the trail of the chieftain of the Sum Yops, as did many free-lance professional killers, all eager to win the amount, which to them meant an old age of luxury in China. But none could pierce the wall of white bodyguards and *boo how doy* with which Little Pete had surrounded himself.

In January, 1897, there arrived in San Francisco two young Chinamen, Lem Jung and Chew Tin Gop, who had been prospecting in the mountains near Baker City, Oregon. They had accumulated a small fortune and had come to San Francisco to see the sights of Chinatown, after which they intended to return to China. They were members of the Suey Sing tong, now allied with the enemies of the Sum Yops, but they were men of peace. Neither had ever handled a hatchet or fired a pistol or participated in a tong fight. They knew nothing of Little Pete, and first learned of his villainies, and of the money that would be paid to his slayer, from their cousin, Lem Jok Lep, who represented the Suey Sings on the board of strategy that had been created by the allied tongs to devise means of eradicating the Sum Yops. With rising indignation Lem Jung and Chew Tin Gop listened to Lem Jok Lep's recital of the many indignities which Little Pete had heaped upon the heads of their tong brothers.

"There is no reason," said Lem Jung, "why we should not earn this money. I myself shall kill this man."

With no experience in fighting and with scarcely any plan of campaign, these young men rushed in where the bravest of hatchetmen had trodden with the utmost caution. On the evening of January 23, 1897, which was the Chinese New Year's Eve, Lem Jung and Chew Tin Gop walked calmly into a barber-shop on the ground floor of Little Pete's building at Waverly Place and Washington Street. There they found Little Pete bending over with his head under a faucet, while the barber wetted his hair preparatory to plaiting it into a queue. Every circumstance favored the assassins. Little Pete had left his apartment in a hurry, accompanied by only one of his bodyguard. And this man he had sent out to buy a paper only a few minutes before Lem Jung and Chew Tin Gop entered the shop. For the moment Little Pete was defenseless. Chew Tin Gop remained near the door on guard while Lem Jung quickly stepped forward, caught Little Pete by the hair, brushed the barber aside, and shoved the muzzle of a heavy revolver down the back of the tong leader's neck, inside the coat of mail. He pulled the trigger, and Little Pete fell to the floor dead, with five bullets in his spine. The murderers escaped, received their money, and fled to Portland, where they were received as heroes. Eventually they took ship to China. The police arrested four Chinese, Chin Poy, Wing Sing, Won Lung, and Won Chung, who had been found loitering near the barber-shop. On each were found revolvers, knives, and hatchets. Wing Sing and Chin Poy were brought to trial for the murder, but were acquitted.

The death of Little Pete demoralized the Sum Yops, and the *boo how doy* of the Sue Yops and their allies promptly began a slaughter, which ended only upon the intervention of the Emperor Kwang Hsu of China, to whom Thomas Riordan, attorney for Little Pete and the Sum Yops, cabled for help. The Emperor called into consultation the great Chinese statesman Li Hung Chang.

"The matter has been attended to," said Li Hung Chang. "I have cast into prison all relatives of the Sue Yops in China, and have cabled to California that their heads will be chopped off if another Sum Yop is killed in San Francisco."

And in far-away America the war ended with startling suddenness, and the Sue Yops and the Sum Yops signed a treaty of peace which has never been violated.

The spirit of Little Pete ascended to his ancestors in a blaze of magnificence . . . for his funeral was probably the most spectacular ever held in San Francisco. A cortege more than a mile long followed the body to the grave, and the air rang with the report of fire-crackers, the "windy chaos" created by three Chinese bands, and the crackling of rattles swung by black-gowned priests. Scores of hacks had been rented for the occasion, and a dozen express wagons hauled the baked meats and the rice and the cases of gin and tea which had been provided that the spirit of the tong chieftain might refresh itself before beginning the long flight to heaven. But at the cemetery a company of hoodlums fell upon the cortege, routed the mourners, and feasted upon the funeral viands.

"FRANKIE AND ALBERT"

I. The Story[3]

In the oldest versions of the song, the name of Frankie's man is Albert. *Frankie and Albert* hails from St. Louis, where a colored sporting woman and her gambling man lived out the legend [in 1899].

"You say, boy, of Frankie, she had dice in one hand and a gun in the other."

Frankie Baker of St. Louis and the sporting circuit, Omaha, Kansas City, Denver, San Francisco, Chicago, shot her man in her twenty-seventh year, having already gained notoriety by her open handedness, good looks, and her proud and racy bearing.

"For a long time I knew Frankie quite well and kept in touch with her for a number of years but lately (since marrying) have lost track of her although think she is in Portland. . . . I have talked with Frankie on different times concerning the shooting and never thought of asking her just why of the killing as it seemed to annoy her.

"She was a beautiful, light brown girl, who liked to make money and spend it. She dressed very richly, sat for company in magenta lady's cloth, diamonds as big as hen's eggs in her ears. There was a long razor scar down the side of her face she got in her teens from a girl who was jealous of her. She only weighed about a hundred and fifteen pounds, but she had the eye of one you couldn't monkey with. She was a queen sport."

She was a queen sport in a society which for flamboyant elegance and fast living ranks alone in the sporting west.

This society was built around the woman and her mack. It began in the period of restoration with the rivermen bringing girls to the levees and the railroad camps to fill the work gang's need for women.

New Orleans had already had her *maquereau*, a colored exquisite, who made his percentage out of the sporting white's weakness for black girls. But the *maquereau* was a hanger-on. His girls could get along without him. The river man was of a different stripe. He parlayed what his woman turned over, in games with the work hands. He was a card sharp, a finished gambler.

When their pockets were full of spikes, the pair would turn their faces to a live town. St. Louis was filling in with their like. Before long it was a sporting depot, with tracks running east to Chicago and west towards the coast. Macking had become a full-fledged business. The smartest macks touted the women who could take in the most, then gambled between themselves. The play was always for high stakes and a great deal of money changed hands.

St. Louis became known as the toughest town in the west. Boogie-joints and bucket-shops opened up on Twelfth, Carr, Targee, and Pine Streets. The fast colored men and women lived up to their necks. Stack-o-lee stepped out and made a legend of his Stetson hat. The girls wore red for Billy Lyons. Duncan

[3] From *Frankie and Johnny*, by John Huston, pp. 104-111. Copyright, 1930, by Albert and Charles Boni. New York.

killed Brady. The ten pimps that bore the dead were kept on parade between the infirmary and the graveyard.

The advent of the mack was something new in the American scene. His dress and his gamey affectations quickened the tempo of the life around him.

He invented styles that took the eye of the sporting world at large. . . . The St. Louis flats, heel-less and of extra length for the men off the steamboats who had gone barefooted so long they could not stand the cramp of regular shoes. Mirrors were set in the toes. Gaiters matched the velvet trouser cuff, the vest, and hat, the Stetson high roller, with nudes and racers inlaid with eyelets in the crown. The linens were of fine quality, with starched, embroidered bosoms and cuffs—the cuffs worn low so that the diamond solitaire on the little finger just showed. . . . And the wealth of jewelry, solvent diamonds—diamond suspender clasps, sleeve garters, diamond initials on the watch ribbon, diamonds in the teeth.

> Put a twenty-dollar gold piece on my watch chain
> To let the Lord know I'm standing pat.

The gold piece was the note of humility. No matter how high a man's fortune, he always wore his gold piece. So long as he had it he was not broke. At the tail-end of his luck the gold piece was always the last to go.

*   *   *   *   *

Frankie shot Allen Britt on October 15, 1899. Allen, or Albert, as he liked to be called, was a tall, slender, ginger boy, only seventeen years old. He first met Frankie at a ball in Stoles Hall, at 13th and Biddle Streets. Soon afterwards he went to live with her at 212 Targee Street, where Frankie sat for company.

Richard Clay, a St. Louis Negro, knew Albert very well. He was with him at the ball the night he met Frankie, and he talked with Albert when the boy was dying at the City Hospital.

"Frankie loved Albert all right. He was wise for his years but not old enough to be level with any woman. Frankie was ready money. She bought him everything he wanted, and kept his pockets full. Then while she was waiting on company he would be out playing around."

On the Sunday night of the shooting Frankie went out to look for Albert. She surprised him in the hallway of the old Phoenix hotel, making up to a girl named Alice Pryar. She called Albert outside and began quarreling with him. A crowd gathered and listened to the row. Albert would not go home with her. Finally she went on alone. It was nearly daylight when Albert followed. He found Frankie waiting up for him. There was more quarreling as he got ready for bed. He admitted to Frankie that he had been with Alice in her room at the hotel, and he warned her that he was ready to throw her over for good. She began to cry and said she was going to find Alice Pryar. Albert said he would kill her if she tried to go. She started for the door and Albert threw the lamp at her. In the darkness Frankie shot him as he came after her with a knife.

Albert made his way out of the house and down the street to the home of his parents at number 32. His mother heard him calling. She came out and found him lying on the front steps in his pajamas. He told her what had happened, and she began to scream, "Frankie's shot Allen! Frankie's shot Allen!"

Inside of a few minutes the word was all over that Frankie had gotten her man.

Albert was taken to the City Hospital. He died at 2:15 on the morning of the 19th with a bullet wound of the liver.

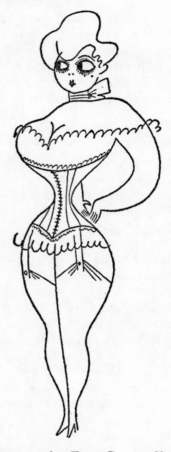

Frankie gave herself up at the Four Courts. She was released after the inquest on the coroner's decision of justifiable homicide.

Allen Britt, son of George and Nancy Britt, was buried in St. Peter's Cemetery, October 22, 1899.

On the 19th of October the St. Louis *Post-Dispatch* ran this account of the story:

AMID THE SUFFERING

Allen Britt's brief experience in the art of love cost him his life. He died at the City Hospital Wednesday night from knife wounds inflicted by Frankie Baker, an ebony hued cake-walker. Britt was also colored. He was seventeen years old. He met Frankie at the Orange Blossom's Ball and was smitten with her. Thereafter they were lovers.

In the rear of 212 Targee Street lived Britt. There his sweetheart wended her way a few nights ago and lectured Allen for his alleged duplicity. Allen's reply was not intended to cheer the dusky damsel and a glint of steel gleamed in the darkness. An instant later the boy fell to the floor mortally wounded.

Frankie Baker is locked up at the Four Courts.

Frankie Baker is still alive [in 1930]. She lives in Portland, Oregon, where she runs a shoe shining parlor. She is fifty-eight years old. The song has not been traced to any Frankie before her.

Frank-ie and Al - bert were lov-ers, O Lord-y, how_ they could love. Swore to be true_ to each oth- er, .true as the stars a- bove;_ He was_ her man, but he done her wrong.

II. The St. Louis Version[4]

Frankie and Albert were lovers, O Lordy, how they could love.
Swore to be true to each other, true as the stars above;
He was her man, but he done her wrong.

Frankie she was a good woman, just like every one knows.
She spent a hundred dollars for a suit of Albert's clothes.
He was her man, but he done her wrong.

Frankie and Albert went walking, Albert in a brand new suit.
"Oh, good Lord," says Frankie, "but don't my Albert look cute?"
He was her man, but he done her wrong.

Frankie went down to Memphis, she went on the evening train.
She paid one hundred dollars for Albert a watch and chain.
He was her man, but he done her wrong.

Frankie lived in the crib house, crib house had only two doors;
Gave all her money to Albert, he spent it on those call house whores.
He was her man, but he done her wrong.

Albert's mother told him, and she was mighty wise,
"Don't spend Frankie's money on that parlor Alice Pry.
You're Frankie's man, and you're doing her wrong."

Frankie and Albert were lovers, they had a quarrel one day,
Albert he up and told Frankie, "Bye-bye, babe, I'm going away.
I was your man, but I'm just gone."

[4] *Ibid.*, pp. 95-103. Tune from *The American Songbag*, by Carl Sandburg (New York: Harcourt, Brace and Company, 1928), p. 79.

Frankie went down to the corner to buy a glass of beer.
Says to the fat bartender, "Has my lovingest man been here?
He was my man, but he's doing me wrong."

"Ain't going to tell you no story, ain't going to tell you no lie,
I seen your man 'bout an hour ago with a girl named Alice Pry.
If he's your man, he's doing you wrong."

Frankie went down to the pawnshop, she didn't go there for fun;
She hocked all of her jewelry, bought a pearl-handled forty-four gun
For to get her man who was doing her wrong.

Frankie she went down Broadway, with her gun in her hand,
Sayin', "Stand back, all you livin' women, I'm a-looking for my gambolin' man.
For he's my man, won't treat me right."

Frankie went down to the hotel, looked in the window so high,
There she saw her loving Albert a-loving up Alice Pry.
Damn his soul, he was mining in coal.

Frankie went down to the hotel, she rang that hotel bell.
"Stand back, all of you chippies, or I'll blow you all to hell.
I want my man, who's doing me wrong."

Frankie threw back her kimono, she took out her forty-four,
Root-a-toot-toot three times she shot right through that hotel door.
She was after her man who was doing her wrong.

Albert grabbed off his Stetson, "Oh, good Lord, Frankie, don't shoot!"
But Frankie pulled the trigger and the gun went root-a-toot-toot.
He was her man, but she shot him down.

Albert he mounted the staircase, crying, "Oh, Frankie, don't you shoot!"
Three times she pulled that forty-four a-root-a-toot-toot-toot-toot.
She shot her man who threw her down.

First time she shot him he staggered, second time she shot him he fell.
Third time she shot him, O Lordy, there was a new man's face in hell.
She killed her man who had done her wrong.

"Roll me over easy, roll me over slow,
Roll me over on my left side for the bullet hurt me so.
I was her man, but I done her wrong."

"Oh my baby, kiss me, once before I go.
Turn me over on my right side, the bullet hurt me so.
I was your man, but I done you wrong."

Albert he was a gambler, he gambled for the gain,
The very last words that Albert said were, "High-low Jack and the game."
He was her man, but he done her wrong.

Frankie heard a rumbling away down in the ground.
Maybe it was Albert where she had shot him down.
He was her man and she done him wrong.

Bring out your long black coffin, bring out your funeral clothes,
Bring out Albert's mother, to the churchyard Albert goes.
He was her man, but he done her wrong.

Oh, bring on your rubber-tired hearses, bring on your rubber-tired hacks,
They're taking Albert to the cemetery and they ain't a-bringing him back.
He was her man, but he done her wrong.

Eleven macks a-riding to the graveyard, all in a rubber-tired hack,
Eleven macks a-riding to the graveyard, only ten a-coming back.
He was her man, but he done her wrong.

Frankie went to the coffin, she looked down on Albert's face,
She said, "Oh, Lord, have mercy on me, I wish I could take his place.
He was my man and I done him wrong."

Frankie went to Mrs. Halcomb, she fell down on her knees,
She said to Mrs. Halcomb, "Forgive me if you please.
I've killed my man for doing me wrong."

"Forgive you, Frankie darling, forgive you I never can.
Forgive you, Frankie darling, for killing your only man.
He was your man, though he done you wrong."

The judge said to the jury, "It's as plain as plain can be.
This woman shot her man, it's murder in the second degree.
He was her man, though he done her wrong."

Now it was not murder in the second degree, it was not murder in the third.
The woman simply dropped her man, like a hunter drops his bird.
He was her man and he done her wrong.

"Oh bring a thousand policemen, bring them around today,
Oh, lock me in that dungeon and throw the key away.
I killed my man 'cause he done me wrong."

"Oh, put me in that dungeon. Oh, put me in that cell,
Put me where the northeast wind blows from the southwest corner of hell.
I shot my man 'cause he done me wrong."

Frankie walked up the scaffold, as calm as a girl can be,
And turning her eyes to heaven she said, "Good Lord, I'm coming to thee.
He was my man, and I done him wrong."

BATHHOUSE JOHN AND HINKY DINK HOLD A WARD BALL [5]

I. THE BATHHOUSE

Favored spots of Joe [Coughlin] and his cronies, next to the saloons, were the city's bathhouses. To these emporiums of relaxation and cleanliness came prize fighters and jockeys, race-horse trainers and stew bums, politicians and prominent merchants. In them a man could scrub himself in an ample tin-lined tub, steam in a cabinet, take a quick shower and get a tingling rubdown with salt or sand. Some of the bathhouses were elaborate affairs, equipped with rooms and cots on which a customer could sleep off a cold or a drunk after an hour in the steam room. Finest bathhouse in Chicago was in the Palmer House

[5] From *Lords of the Levee*, The Story of Bathhouse John and Hinky Dink, by Lloyd Wendt and Herman Kogan, pp. 15-18, 26-27, 73-74, 75, 76-77, 79, 153, 154-156. Copyright, 1943, by The Bobbs-Merrill Company, Inc. Indianapolis and New York.

where, in addition to the wainscoted baths, was a tiny pool in which the clients could swim. The Palmer House baths were famous throughout the country, and drew the patronage of wealthy and powerful men as well as the sporting gentry. A scouring scrub at the Palmer House following a roaring night in the Levee was considered one of the grandest luxuries the nation afforded, and visiting dignitaries often availed themselves of this delightful, if enervating, experience.

The lesser bathhouses were equipped with concrete floors, makeshift showers, and crude bath cabinets, and some, unable to meet the competition of more favored places, were little more than brothels, where the customers if they so desired could receive the ministrations of female attendants.

Racing and fighting men provided the best clientele for the baths, and it was not difficult for Joe Coughlin and his friends to convince the owner of a bath-house at 205 Clark Street, in the heart of the First Ward, that the employment of Joe's [nineteen-year-old] brother [John] would bring him a healthy business.

Big John got the job and rushed home elated. "Kid," he shouted to Kate, "I got a real job! I'm a rubber in a Turkish bathhouse. Now ain't that a real job?"

In the Clark Street bathhouse, Coughlin first laid the foundations for the career he would follow in the next fifty years and more. He reveled in the racy talk of jockeys and touts and quickly developed a fantastic interest in horses. He spoke fervently of the day when he himself might own a horse and enter it at Washington Park. The politicians who patronized the place also impressed him mightily. Their pompous demeanor, their ready oratory, their dress, their glib talk of election plots, and their easy spending fascinated the young rubber. The patrons liked hearty Coughlin too, for he soon learned the art of laughing uproariously at every joke and greeting each customer as if he were the most important man in town. And in time young Coughlin learned that the most prominent citizen, shucked down to the skin, is much like every one else.

"I formed my philosophy," The Bath liked to say in later years, when he had learned the meaning of the word, "while watching and studying the types of people who patronized the bathhouses. Priests, ministers, brokers, politicians, and gamblers visited there. I watched, and learned never to quarrel, never to feud. I had the best schooling a young feller could have. I met 'em all, big and little, from La Salle Street to Armour Avenue. You could learn from every one. Ain't much difference between the big man and the little man. One's lucky, that's all."

A year later Coughlin got a job in the Palmer House baths, reaching the status of head rubber in a few months. Here came the big politicians and businessmen, the congressmen and senators traveling through from Washington, and, on rare occasions, a person as distinguished as Marshall Field. Coughlin was a favorite with these men; he learned their whims and how to please them. They were rich, and tips were good.

Through a friendship thus formed with John Morris, a popular First Ward saloonkeeper and politician, Coughlin was able to open his own place in 1882. Morris supplemented $800 which Coughlin had religiously saved, and the erstwhile rubber purchased a bathhouse at 143 East Madison Street. At the time it seemed to Coughlin that he had attained the ultimate goal of his own existence. Waving a receipt, he shouted to the Coughlin family, "I'm my own boss! I got my own bathhouse!" The next day he went to St. John's Church on Eighteenth Street and prayed. Kate lost six pounds hemming dozens of towels for the grand opening.

So successful was this venture that in a few months Coughlin had made enough money to open another bath several blocks west, in the basement of the fashionable, canary-tinted Brevoort Hotel. He was now able to hire a staff of rubbers and attendants, but each morning he appeared promptly at seven o'clock at one of his establishments or the other to greet, with a boisterous jest, those patrons who had slept off all-night jags in the little white cast-iron beds in the locker rooms, or to supervise the service and bustle about, proud and happy in the endless marvel of ownership.

Coughlin was becoming a man of property. He took on more poundage, grew a full mustache and lengthy sideburns and combed his hair in the high, fashionable pompadour of the time. To his patrons he became known as Bathhouse John and he delighted in the name, just as in his boyhood he felt that his nickname of Dusty John drew him more attention. He set out to get more business. On the walls of his bathhouses and in downtown barbershops he displayed signs reading:

GOOD HEALTH IS PRICELESS
CLEANLINESS GIVES HEALTH
HEALTH IS RICHES—HEALTH IS LIFE
THERE'S HEALTH IN COUGHLIN'S BATHS!

II. THE LEVEE AND THE FIRST WARD

The Levee included not only South State Street but Clark Street and Plymouth Court as well. On these streets were the hop joints, concert saloons, and brothels, from the twenty-five-cent bagnios to the more expensive houses operated by Carrie Watson, Mae Clark, Ike Bloom, Freddie Train, and others. Off Dearborn Street, in the heart of the city, was Gamblers' Alley and near by, on Randolph Street, from Clark to State Streets, was the infamous Hairtrigger Block, lined with gambling houses of every description. And at Clark and Monroe Streets stood The Store, the extensive establishment of Michael Cassius (King Mike) McDonald, the city's gambling and political boss.

Throughout the [First] Ward [of whose Democratic Club John was four times elected President] were endless stretches of lesser saloons and dice and faro houses from which by night issued the pimps, piffers, and pickpockets to prey upon citizens and visitors. Dime museums and concert halls, peep shows and bucket shops were interspersed among the newly built wholesale houses and commission offices. To the north and west, along the river, were great shipping wharves, on which the lake boats discharged their limestone, coal, and lumber, and the grain boats from Europe loaded their bins. Near them were the railroad freight houses and huge red and yellow elevators. To the east, in the center of the ward, were the office buildings and the great department stores, the finest hotels and splendid restaurants and theaters, surrounding a solemn, marble-pillared city hall.

The population of this polyglot district got on well together. The businessmen who lived clear of the ruck, on the fringes of the ward or out of it altogether, cared little how it was governed so long as the price of privilege was not too high. The bums and foreign laboring element were equally unconcerned. It was the saloon men, the keepers of brothels, the gamblers and the numerous denizens of the underworld who took the most practical interest in the ward's politics for they were at the constant mercy of the police and they had to elect, buy, and hire politicians to protect them.

III. HINKY DINK

Michael Kenna, like Bathhouse John, was another noble product of the First Ward. . . .

All formal education came to an end for young Michael when he was ten. His mind was nimble enough, but he could not relish the schoolroom regimen. He found his way eastward to State Street where he took to hawking newspapers. A fellow salesman was the future Republican boss, Billy Lorimer, who was a playmate of young Coughlin's. But swimming and play and boyish sports were not to the liking of this midget of a boy with an old man's face. He darted in and out of saloons and restaurants, selling his newspapers, running errands for saloonkeepers and porters, striking up valued friendships with saloon hostesses and brothel madams and their charges. At twelve he felt the need for greater profits, and with fifty dollars loaned him by a bartender he purchased from an older boy the rights to a newsstand at Monroe and Dearborn Streets, just outside the old *Tribune* building. So rapidly did he prosper that he repaid the loan in less than a month.

It was then, according to insistent First Ward legend, that Kenna got his nickname, from none other than Joseph Medill, august *Tribune* editor, who liked to discover what his newsboys thought of the way the dispatches of the night were being handled.

"What's your name, boy?" Medill is said to have asked of the newsie.

"Kenna's my name," the lad replied. "Michael Kenna, from over on Polk Street."

"That's a good Irish name," Medill replied, "but I'm going to call you Hinky Dink because you are such a little fellow."

*   *   *   *   *

By 1882, when he was only twenty-four, Kenna had become a successful saloonkeeper and political underling, aiding Chesterfield Joe Mackin and the First Ward Democrats thereafter in the frequent elections. . . . [After his appointment as captain of his saloon precinct, in the vicinity of Clark and Van Buren Streets] Kenna's political activities brought him close to the ward's other political neophyte, Bathhouse John. . . .

. . . The gambling raids and the rising importance of detested [Billy] Ska-kel in the ward prompted Hinky Dink to consider an alliance with Coughlin. . . . Kenna saw not only a chance to save his own stake in the ward, but to gather under a Coughlin-Kenna protectorate the gambling house owners whose establishments were beset by the raiders. He needed a council spokesman, and certainly Bathhouse John Coughlin needed him.

* * * * *

Kenna began . . . to lay the groundwork for an extensive benefit system that would attract supporters and knit his organization together. He proposed the establishment of a defense fund in which a percentage of the protection money paid by the brothel keepers and the gamblers should be pooled for the assistance of all Kenna-Coughlin followers who got into trouble. . . .

IV. The First Ward Ball

The subject of cash was continuously in [Alderman Coughlin's] mind. A few months hence a new aldermanic election was scheduled, and while the First Ward organization was strong in its friends on the central committee, neither Coughlin nor Kenna wanted to be caught again with insufficient funds. The stream of graft was thin. The gamblers, harried by drives which the reformers pressed upon Mayor Swift, were making less money, and they either paid less for protection or chased the Coughlin-Kenna collectors from their establishments.

The big man and the little man had surveyed the possibilities for raising revenue. The solution came to them in an inspired moment one day in Hinky Dink's saloon, shortly before the approach of the Christmas season. They were bewailing the fact that this year, unlike the fifteen years preceding, there would not be the annual party for Lame Jimmy the crippled pianist and fiddler at Carrie Watson's parlor house. . . .

. . . At the 1895 party a drunken Harrison Street detective, braving the high indignation of other guests at his lapse in Levee decorum, grew boisterous and shot and critically wounded a fellow officer. This evoked a great civic outcry, demands were made upon the high police command for immediate action, and not even the intervention of Bathhouse John, who had attended many of the affairs, could save Lame Jimmy from the order: No more balls.

As he lamented the passing of the Lame Jimmy festivities, Bathhouse Cough-lin came suddenly to the realization that the little brothel professor's misfortune was a great opportunity for the First Ward Democratic organization. Lame Jimmy's parties had been held in a small hall; tickets sold for one dollar each; three hundred attended. Why, if a ball—a real ball, a lavish ball, a gigantic ball in a gigantic hall—were to be held, who would know how much its sponsors might make? Coughlin and Kenna had friends willing to contribute wines and liquors, the madams and their girls would come. . . .

* * * * *

Word spread swiftly through the First Ward of the ball to be held under the auspices of Bathhouse John and Hinky Dink, and for the benefit of persons then unknown. The place: Seventh Regiment Armory. The time: eight o'clock till—?

Aldermanic couriers carried the information to the First Ward faithful. They visited saloons and cigar stores and dropped into every parlor house with blocks of tickets and a glowing verbal prospectus. They met few objections.

The saloonkeepers and brothel owners and purveyors to the pleasures of the Levee either genuinely welcomed the projected frolic, or possibly saw its deeper significance. Whatever the stimuli, they bought tickets, lots of tickets. Waiters, apprised of what they might expect in tips, eagerly shucked out five dollars each for the right to serve at the fete. Brewers and wine merchants and whisky distillers knew without being told that it was to their benefit to provide stocks of liquors at moderate prices and at unlimited credit. One could always be certain there might come a day when a favor from the First Ward overlords might be needed.

Tickets sold speedily. All the prospective participants in the festivities were allotted places in the general floor plan. The tavern owners and madams and wine sellers were to be allowed to decorate their boxes—at their own expense—and the brewers were assigned wide sections in the corridors and basement. The Bath subdivided the armory with the sagacity of a real-estate broker and the money rolled in. Throughout the ward it was considered wise to be co-operative and enthusiastic. No parlor house was too grand, no ten-cent crib too lowly to be represented.

This first of the First Ward balls was to be like nothing ever before seen in the Levee. It captured the imagination of the *souteneurs* and the *filles de joie,* and when they heard that Alderman Coughlin was preparing a special costume for the event, they rushed out to do likewise.

It was clear at the very beginning that the First Ward ball surpassed Lame Jimmy's parties as completely as Carrie Watson's house eclipsed a Clark Street crib. The Bath's love of garish pomp had found amazing expression. The bizarre decorations were like freshly painted nightmares from Tommy Wong's hop house. But these were exceeded by the alderman's startling personal splendor. Even the girls from the expensive brothels, some of whom had spent as much as $200 for their costume gowns, bemoaned the poverty of their ingenuity when Coughlin stepped from his personal box at midnight to lead the Grand March.

His tail coat was a crisp billiard-cloth green, his vest a delicate mauve. His trousers were lavender, as was his glowing cravat, and his kid gloves a pale pink. His pumps shone a gleaming yellow, and perched on his glistening pompadour was a silken top hat that sparkled like the plate-glass windows of Marshall Field's department store.

This sartorial elegance, even more than the ball itself, was the attraction of the evening. The glowing descriptions recounted the next morning by wide-eyed reporters were reprinted in newspapers of other cities and editorials sneered at the Chicago council not only for its reputation for boodle and graft but as the stamping grounds of a statesman in green coat and lavender pants. The effete East saw in this outfit the supreme symbol of wickedness in the Chicago government. The reformers at home were aghast at this "open display of vice and debauchery," as they read of the gambols of the frisky brothel girls, the number-less drunken assaults in the armory basement, the almost unanimous attendance of the residents of such choice districts as the Black Hole, the Bad Lands, Bed Bug Row, and Hell's Half Acre, the mingling of pimps and pickpockets with political leaders, policemen with burglars and confidence men.

Churchmen raised their hands to heaven and wailed that organized vice, at which all the city winked and whispered, had gone on public display. "It has," they said, "pushed beyond all bounds of decency and offered insolent challenge to the rest of the community." They hurled colorful epithets, "a Saturnalian orgy," a "vile, dissolute affair," a "bawdy Dionysian festival," "a black stain on the name of Chicago."

But Hinky Dink called it a lalapalooza and spent a day totaling the $25,000 in profits. . . .

THE ORIGINAL SKID ROAD [6]

[The] region south of Yesler Way [Seattle], has been known by many names. For a time it was called Maynardtown, after Doc Maynard; later, when Yesler's Mill had been running long enough for its debris to fill the tidal inlets, the area was known simply as Down on the Sawdust. After its character became established during the seventies it was called variously the Lava Beds, the Tenderloin, White Chapel, and the Great Restricted District. For a while it was referred to as Wappyville, in honor of a chief of police who distinguished himself by the amount of graft he collected there. But the first name, the functional name, has outlasted all the others. When the pioneers rolled logs by hand down to the waterfront, when the ox-teams plodded over the hill dragging logs for Yesler's steam mill, this was the skid road, and it is the Skid Road today. This district south of Yesler Way, this land below the Deadline, has helped fix the word on the American language. The Skid Road: the place of dead dreams.

You see here the things you see on other skid roads in America: men sitting on curbs and sleeping in doorways, doors padlocked for non-payment of rent, condemned buildings, signs that read: "Beds, twenty cents." "Oatmeal, five cents. With sugar, seven cents. With cream, nine cents." "Be Saved by Sister Faye." "A charge of three cents will be made for packages stored more than two days." "Indians who want wine must show documents they are not wards of the government." The *People's World* is sold on the street corners, and second-hand nudist magazines are on sale in cigar stores. There are missions and taverns and wine shops and stores where you can buy a suit for $3.75.

And there are things peculiar to Seattle: a totem pole; cafés with Indian names; a manifesto posted on the wall, which recalls the day when this was a stronghold of the IWW and the One Big Union promised an eight-hour day. "Fellow Workers! Unite for the 4-hour day and the 4-day week. No cut in pay."

[6] From *Skid Road*, An Informal Portrait of Seattle, by Murray Morgan, pp. 9-10. Copyright, 1951, by Murray Morgan. New York: The Viking Press, Inc.

THE BALL OF THE TWO WELL-KNOWN GENTLEMEN [7]

In the old days of Basin Street the girls who inhabited it had their own carnival ball, which was sponsored by two men who were powers in the neighborhood, and were known simply as the "Two Well-Known Gentlemen." At the Ball of the Two Well-Known Gentlemen there was more abandon and less formality than at the society affairs, but the balls were nonetheless elegant and expensive affairs, and were attended not only by the whores and their men, but by many political and police officials. The whole thing was a burlesque of the balls outside the sporting world, with some prominent madam reigning as queen and a court of maids who were proudly advertised as "the best whores in the world."

But, and not strangely, many persons outside of Basin Street became jealous and in time invitations to a Ball of the Two Well-Known Gentlemen became possibly even more valuable than those to Comus. It was, of course, usually men who sought them, but some sophisticated women attended, too, although well escorted and often wearing masks. It was this kind of snobbery that infuriated the prostitutes, and one year Josie Arlington, a notorious madam of the era, along with Tom Anderson, powerful king of the New Orleans red-light district, prevailed upon the police to raid the affair. Prostitution was legal in those days, so only the females present who could not produce licenses to practice the profession were carried off to jail. These were, of course, all the respectable women present. Having rid themselves of undesirable guests, the residents of Basin Street resumed their ball. There are all kinds of snobbery.

BROTHEL BOOKKEEPING [8]

Bookkeeping in Houston brothels in the early 1900's was an uncomplicated system of towels, one being given to each customer. At the end of the night's work the madam counted the towels, and paid the girls accordingly. Which is the basis of a story, possibly apocryphal, about the brothel near the downtown area that burned in those days. The girls and their patrons fled as best they could while the madam galumphed out the back door. A minute later she saw the porter jump from a second-floor window, his arms loaded with towels.

"Thank God!" she said. "He saved the books."

[7] From *The Romantic New Orleanians*, by Robert Tallant, p. 148. Copyright, 1950, by Robert Tallant. New York: E. P. Dutton & Co., Inc.

[8] From *Houston: Land of the Big Rich*, by George Fuermann, p. 160. Copyright, 1951, by George Fuermann. Garden City, New York· Doubleday & Company, Inc.

HURDY-GURDY HOUSE [9]

. . . The hurdy-gurdy . . . was the standard musical instrument of the pioneer gambling and amusement centers, which were invariably called hurdy-gurdy houses. . . .

The hurdy-gurdy was the basis for a famous law case in Montana's capital city, Helena, located atop the Continental Divide. At the turn of the century hurdy-gurdy houses flourished, to the great distress of a number of puritanically inclined citizens. Eventually this group succeeded in electing to office an official with whom they achieved a meeting of the minds, and he at once clamped down on the hurdy-gurdy establishments with especial emphasis on one run by a female character known throughout the Northwest as "Chicago Joe."

Chicago Joe, an enormously corpulent woman, whose body required a special casket when she died, went to court with the evidence seized in her hurdy-gurdy house—her bevy of girls, gamblers, and the other accouterments of pleasure. A rising, and smart, young lawyer accompanied her. Her accusers read the charge: "Keeping a hurdy-gurdy house."

Thereupon her lawyer rose to his feet with a Webster's dictionary in his hand. "I'd like to read the definition of a hurdy-gurdy," he said, and quoted Webster: "A stringed musical instrument."

"We're accused of operating a hurdy-gurdy house," he said, closing the book. "A hurdy-gurdy house, I maintain, is a place where a hurdy-gurdy is played or found. I challenge the prosecution to submit as evidence a single hurdy-gurdy they have been able to find in my client's establishment!"

The judge . . . released Chicago Joe and the anti-vice campaign fizzled. . . .

IZZIE AND MOE [10]

In a $14-a-month flat on Ridge Street, in New York's lower East Side, lived a bulbous little man named Isadore Einstein, whom everyone called Izzy. He had been a salesman, both inside and on the road, but was now a minor clerk at Station K of the New York Post Office. It required very shrewd management to feed, house, and clothe his family—his wife and four children and his father—on the meager salary of a postal employee. He was looking for something better, and decided that he had found it when he read in his newspaper about the government's plans to pay enforcement agents up to $2,500 a year.

But James Shevlin, Chief Enforcement Agent for the Southern District of New York, was not enthusiastic about Izzy. "I must say, Mr. Einstein," he said, "you don't look much like a detective." And that was the truth. Probably no one ever looked less like a detective than Izzy Einstein. He was forty years

[9] From *The Majestic Land*, Peaks, Parks & Prevaricators of the Rockies & Highlands of the Northwest, by Eric Thane, pp. 22-23. Copyright, 1950, by The Bobbs-Merrill Company, Inc. Indianapolis and New York.

[10] From "The Noble Experiment of Izzie and Moe," by Herbert Asbury, in *The Aspirin Age, 1919-1941*, edited by Isabel Leighton, pp. 35-49. Copyright, 1949, by Simon and Schuster, Inc. New York.

old, almost bald, five feet and five inches tall, and weighed 225 pounds. Most of this poundage was around his middle, so that when he walked, his noble paunch, gently wobbling, moved majestically ahead like the breast of an overfed pouter pigeon.

But Izzy was accomplished. Besides English and Yiddish, he spoke German, Polish, and Hungarian fluently, and could make headway, though haltingly, in French, Italian, and Russian. He had even picked up a few words and phrases of Chinese. Moreover, Izzy had a knack of getting along with people and inspiring confidence. No one, looking at his round, jolly face and twinkling black eyes, could believe that he was a government snooper. Down on the lower East Side in New York he was the neighborhood cutup; whenever he dropped into the corner cigar stores and the coffee houses his witticisms and high spirits never failed to draw an appreciative crowd.

"I guess Mr. Shevlin never saw a type like me," Izzy said afterward. "Maybe I fascinated him or something. Anyhow, I sold him on the idea that this prohibition business needed a new type of people that couldn't be spotted so easy."

Whatever the reason, Izzy got the job.

"But I must warn you," said Shevlin, "that hunting down liquor sellers isn't exactly a safe line of work. Some law violator might get mad and try to crack a bottle over your head."

"Bottles," said Izzy, "I can dodge."

Izzy's first assignment was to clean up a place in Brooklyn which the enforcement authorities shrewdly suspected housed a speakeasy, since drunken men had been seen staggering from the building, and the air for half a block around was redolent with the fumes of beer and whisky. Several agents had snooped and slunk around the house; one had watched all one afternoon from a roof across the street, and another had hidden for hours in an adjoining doorway, obtaining an accurate count of the number of men who entered and left. But none had been able to get inside. Izzy knew nothing of sleuthing procedures; he simply walked up to the joint and knocked on the door. A peephole was opened, and a hoarse voice demanded to know who was there.

"Izzy Einstein," said Izzy. "I want a drink."

"Oh, yeah? Who sent you here, bud? What's your business?"

"My boss sent me," Izzy explained. "I'm a prohibition agent. I just got appointed."

The door swung open and the doorman slapped Izzy jovially on the back.

"Ho! ho!" he cried. "Come right in, bud. That's the best gag I've heard yet."

Izzy stepped into a room where half a dozen men were drinking at a small makeshift bar.

"Hey, boss!" the doorman yelled. "Here's a prohibition agent wants a drink! You got a badge, too, bud?"

"Sure I have," said Izzy, and produced it.

"Well, I'll be damned," said the man behind the bar. "Looks just like the real thing."

He poured a slug of whisky, and Izzy downed it. That was a mistake, for

when the time came to make the pinch Izzy had no evidence. He tried to grab
the bottle but the bartender ran out the back door with it.

"I learned right there," said Izzy, "that a slug of hooch in an agent's belly
might feel good, but it ain't evidence."

So when he went home that night he rigged up an evidence-collector. He
put a small funnel in the upper left-hand pocket of his vest, and connected it,
by means of a rubber tube, with a flat bottle concealed in the lining of the
garment. Thereafter, when a drink was served to him, Izzy took a small sip,
then poured the remainder into the funnel while the bartender was making
change. The bottle wouldn't hold much, but there was always enough for
analysis and to offer in evidence. "I'd have died if it hadn't been for that little
funnel and the bottle," said Izzy. "And most of the stuff I got in those places
was terrible."

Izzy used his original device of giving his real name, with some variation,
more than twenty times during the next five years. It was successful even
after he became so well known, and so greatly feared, that his picture hung
behind the bar in many speakeasies, that all might see and be warned. Occasionally Izzy would prance into a gin-mill with his badge pinned to his lapel,
in plain sight, and shout jovially, "How about a drink for a hard-working
prohibition agent?" Seeing the round little man trying so hard to be funny,
everyone in the place would rush forward to hand him something alcoholic, and
Izzy would arrest them and close the joint.

Once he went into a gin-mill where three huge portraits of himself, framed
in what he described as "black, creepy crape," ornamented the back bar. He
asked for a drink, and the bartender refused to serve it.

"I don't know you," he said.

"Why," said Izzy, laughing. "I'm Izzy Epstein, the famous prohibition detective."

"Get the name right, bud," growled the bartender. "The bum's name is
Einstein."

"Epstein," said Izzy. "Don't I know my own name?"

"Maybe you do, but the low-life you're trying to act like is named Einstein.
E-i-n-s-t-e-i-n."

"Brother," said Izzy, "I ain't never wrong about a name. It's Epstein."

"Einstein!" roared the bartender.

"Epstein!" shouted Izzy.

"You're nuts!" yelled the bartender, furiously. "I'll bet you anything you want
it's Einstein!"

"Okay," said Izzy. "I'll bet you the drinks."

The bartender called his other customers, and after much argument and
pointing to Izzy's pictures, they agreed that the name was Einstein. So Izzy—
or rather the government—had to buy nine drinks, and the bartender served
them, and shortly after went to jail.

After Izzy had been an enforcement agent for a few weeks, he began to miss
his old friend Moe Smith, with whom he had spent many pleasant evenings in

the East Side coffee houses. Like Izzy, Moe was a natural comedian, and, also like Izzy, he was corpulent. He tipped the scales at about 235 pounds, but he was a couple of inches taller than Izzy and didn't look quite so roly-poly. Moe had been a cigar salesman, and manager of a small fight club at Orchard and Grand Streets, New York City, and had invested his savings in a little cigar store, where he was doing well. Izzy persuaded him to put a relative in charge of the store, and to apply for a job as enforcement agent.

Moe could probably have got on the enforcement staff by his own efforts, for his background and experience were at least as good as those of nine-tenths of the agents who were hired, but he obtained the post a little quicker through Izzy's recommendation. As soon as he was sworn in as an agent, he and Izzy teamed up together, and most of the time thereafter worked as a pair. Their first assignment took them to Rockaway Beach, near New York, where they confiscated a still and arrested the operator. This man apparently took a great liking to Izzy, for after he got out of jail he made several trips to New York especially to urge Izzy to go on a fishing trip with him.

"I'll take you three miles out to sea," he said. "You'll have quite a time."

But Izzy firmly declined the invitation. "Sure he'll take me out to sea," he said, "but will he bring me back? He could leave me with the fishes."

In those early days of the noble experiment everything that happened in connection with prohibition was news, and some of New York's best reporters covered enforcement headquarters. Casting about for a way to enliven their stories and provide exercise for their imaginations, they seized upon the exploits of Izzy and Moe. The two fat and indefatigable agents supplied human-interest material by the yard; moreover, they were extraordinarily co-operative. They frequently scheduled their raids to suit the convenience of the reporters and the newspaper photographers, and soon learned that there was more room in the papers on Monday morning than on any other day of the week.

*   *   *   *   *

Hundreds of stories, a great many of them truthful, were written about Izzy and Moe and their grotesque adventures, and they probably made the front pages oftener than any other personages of their time except the President and the Prince of Wales.

*   *   *   *   *

What the newspapers enjoyed most about Izzy and Moe was their ingenuity. Once they went after a speakeasy where half a dozen dry agents had tried without success to buy a drink. The bartender positively wouldn't sell to anyone he didn't know. So on a cold winter night Izzy stood in front of the gin-mill, in his shirt sleeves, until he was red and shivering and his teeth were chattering. Then Moe half-carried him into the speakeasy, shouting excitedly:

"Give this man a drink! He's just been bitten by a frost!"

The kindhearted bartender, startled by Moe's excitement and upset by Izzy's miserable appearance, rushed forward with a bottle of whisky. Moe promptly snatched the bottle and put him under arrest.

One of Izzy's most brilliant ideas was always to carry something on his raids, the nature of the burden depending upon the character of the neighborhood and of a particular speakeasy's clientele. When he wanted to get into a place frequented by musicians, for example, he carried a violin or a trombone, and if, as sometimes happened, he was asked to play the instrument, he could do it. He usually played "How Dry I Am." On the East Side and in the poorer sections of the Bronx, if the weather permitted, Izzy went around in his shirt sleeves carrying a pitcher of milk, the very pattern of an honest man on his way home from the grocery. Once in Brooklyn he was admitted to half a dozen gin-mills because he was lugging a big pail of dill pickles. "A fat man with pickles!" said Izzy. "Who'd ever think a fat man with pickles was an agent?"

When Izzy operated on the beaches around New York he always carried a fishing rod or a bathing suit; he had great success one day at Sheepshead Bay with a string of fish slung over his shoulder. The doorman of the Assembly, a café in Brooklyn which catered to judges and lawyers, let him in without question because he wore a frock coat and carried a huge tome bound in sheepskin. Once inside, Izzy opened his book and adjusted a pair of horn-rimmed spectacles and, with lips moving and brow furrowed, marched with stately tread across the room and barged into the bar. Without lifting his eyes from the book, he called sonorously for "a beverage, please," and the fascinated bartender poured a slug of whisky before he realized what he was doing. When Izzy and Moe visited Reisenweber's, a famous and expensive resort on Broadway, they carried two lovely blondes and wore "full-dress tuxedoes," with rings on their fingers, sweet-smelling pomade on their hair, and huge imitation-pearl studs in their shirt fronts. The headwaiter asked them for references when they ordered liquor, and Izzy searched his pockets and pulled out the first card he found. It happened to be the card of a rabbi, with which Izzy planned to ensnare a sacramental-wine store. But the headwaiter, a man of scant perception, bowed deferentially and sold them a bottle of whisky. "He deserved to be arrested," said Izzy, indignantly. "Imagine! A rabbi with a blonde and no beard!"

Up in Van Cortlandt Park, in New York City, near the public playing fields, was a soft-drink establishment which was suspected of being one of the retail outlets of a big rum ring. Many complaints were made to enforcement headquarters that customers had become tipsy after a few shots of the soda water sold in the place; one woman wrote that by mistake her milk shake had been filled with gin. Bad gin, too, she added. The job of getting the evidence was given to Izzy. It proved a difficult task, for the owner of the joint would sell liquor to no one he didn't know personally. So on a Saturday afternoon in November Izzy assembled a group of half a dozen dry agents, clad them in football uniforms, and smeared their arms and faces with fresh dirt. Then Izzy tucked a football under his arm, hung a helmet over his ears, and led them whooping and rah-rahing into the suspected speakeasy, where they shouted that they had just won the last game of the season and wanted to break training in a big way. The speakeasy owner, pleased at such a rush of business, sold each agent a pint of whisky. "Have fun, boys," he said. "The same to you," said Izzy, handing him a summons.

Flushed with this striking success, which showed that at heart he was a college boy, Izzy went to Ithaca, N.Y., to investigate a complaint by officials of Cornell University that some soda fountains near the campus were not confining their sales to pop. Izzy disguised himself as an undergraduate by putting on a little cap and a pair of white linen knickers, not so little, and for several days strolled about the campus. He hummed snatches of Cornell songs which he had learned, and played safe by addressing every one with a mustache as "Professor," and every one with a beard as "Dean." Having located the soda fountains which sold liquor, he dashed into them one by one, establishing himself as a student by shouting, "Sizzle Boom! Sizzle Boom! Rah! Rah! Rah!" The speakeasy boys thought he was a comedian, which indeed he was, and they gladly sold him all the booze he wanted, after which he went from place to place distributing "diplomas," or summonses.

*   *   *   *   *

For more than five years the whole country laughed at the antics of Izzy and Moe, with the exception of the ardent drys, who thought the boys were wonderful, and the bootleggers and speakeasy proprietors, who thought they were crazy and feared them mightily. And their fear was justified, for in their comparatively brief career Izzy and Moe confiscated 5,000,000 bottles of booze, worth $15,000,000, besides thousands of gallons in kegs and barrels and hundreds of stills and breweries. They smashed an enormous quantity of saloon fixtures and equipment, and made 4,392 arrests, of which more than 95 per cent resulted in convictions. No other two agents even approached this record.

Nearly all of their victims were small-fry bootleggers and speakeasy operators, although they raided and confiscated a considerable number of large stills and breweries. Their largest single haul was 2,000 cases of bottled whisky and 365 barrels of whisky and brandy, which they found in a Bronx garage. And they made one terrifying swoop up and down Broadway which put the finishing touches to such celebrated night-life resorts as Jack's, the Ted Lewis Club, Shanley's, the Beaux Arts, and Reisenweber's.

Neither Izzy nor Moe molested hip-flask toters, nor, unlike other agents who made themselves obnoxious to the general public, did they go barging into restaurants sniffing at glasses and snatching bottles off tables. "Personally," wrote Izzy, "I never saw any call for such tactics. I did my work quietly, and extended courtesy to any law violator I had to deal with. If it was a high class place I was pinching, I'd sometimes even let the manager collect his dinner checks so he wouldn't be stuck for the food he'd served. Even in tough places I never abused my power. I used the name of the law and not blackjacks."

Izzy and Moe made many spectacular raids in Chicago, Detroit, and other cities ruled by the gangsters and the beer barons, but they never encountered Al Capone, Johnny Torrio, Frankie Yale, or any of the other great hoodlums who were the real beneficiaries of the Eighteenth Amendment. If they had, there is little doubt that they would have taken the triggermen in their stride, for neither Izzy nor Moe lacked courage. Izzy didn't approve of guns, and never carried one. Moe lugged a revolver around occasionally, but in five years fired it only twice. Once he shot out a lock that had resisted his efforts, and another time he shot a hole in a keg of whisky. Izzy said later that guns were pulled on him only twice. The first time was on Dock Street, in Yonkers, N.Y., where he had spent a pleasant and profitable evening with raids on five speakeasies. To make it an even half dozen, he stepped into a sixth place that looked suspicious, bought a slug of whisky for sixty cents, and poured it into the funnel in his vest pocket. While he was arresting the bartender, the owner of the joint came into the bar from another part of the house.

"He pulled an automatic from behind the bar," wrote Izzy. "She clicked but the trigger jammed. It was aimed right at my heart. I didn't like that. I grabbed his arm and he and I had a fierce fight all over the bar, till finally I got the pistol. I don't mind telling you I was afraid, particularly when I found the gun was loaded."

On another occasion an angry bartender shoved a revolver against Izzy's stomach. But Izzy didn't bat an eye; he calmly shoved the gun aside.

"Put that up, son," he said, soothingly. "Murdering me won't help your family."

Fortunately, the bartender had a family, and Izzy's warning brought to his mind a vision of his fatherless children weeping at the knee of their widowed mother, who was also weeping. He stopped to think. While he was thinking, Moe knocked him cold.

On one of his swings around the so-called enforcement circuit, Izzy made up a sort of schedule showing the length of time it took him to get a drink in various cities. New Orleans won first prize, a four-star hiss from the Anti-Saloon League. When Izzy arrived in the Crescent City he climbed into an ancient taxicab, and as the machine got under way he asked the driver where he could get a drink.

"Right here, suh," said the driver, and pulled out a bottle. "Fo' bits."

Time—thirty-five seconds.

In Pittsburgh, disguised as a Polish mill worker, Izzy bought a drink of terrible whisky in eleven minutes. Just seventeen minutes after he got off the train in Atlanta, he walked into a confectionery shop on Peachtree Street, bought a drink, and arrested the proprietor. In Chicago he bought a drink in twenty-one minutes without leaving the railroad station, and duplicated this feat in St. Louis. In Cleveland it took twenty-nine minutes, but that was because an usher in a vaudeville theater, who had offered to take him to a speakeasy, couldn't leave his job right away. In Baltimore, Izzy got on a trolley car and asked the conductor where he could find a speakeasy. "In the next block," the conductor replied. Time, fifteen minutes. It took longer in Washington than anywhere else; Izzy roamed the city for a whole hour before he could locate a gin-mill. He finally had to ask a policeman, who provided him with the necessary directions.

During the summer of 1925 the almost continual stories about Izzy and Moe in the newspapers got on the nerves of high prohibition enforcement officials in Washington, few of whom ever got mentioned in the papers at all. National headquarters announced that any agent whose name appeared in print in connection with his work would be suspended, and perhaps otherwise punished, on the ground that publicity brought discredit to the service. At the same time a high official called Izzy to Washington and spoke to him rather severely. "You get your name in the newspaper all the time, and in the headlines, too," he complained, "whereas mine is hardly ever mentioned. I must ask you to remember that you are merely a subordinate, not the whole show." For a while Izzy really tried to keep away from the reporters and out of the papers, but both he and Moe had become public personages, and it was impossible to keep the newspapermen from writing about them. When they refused to tell what they had done, the reporters invented stories about them, so a stream of angry denials and protests continued to come from Washington.

Finally, on November 13, 1925, it was announced that Izzy and Moe had turned in their gold badges and were no longer prohibition agents. Izzy's story was that he had been told he was to be transferred to Chicago. He had lived in New York since he was fifteen years old, and had no intention of ever living anywhere else, so he refused to go, and "thereby fired myself." Government officials, however, said that Izzy and Moe had been dismissed "for the good of the service." Off the record they added, "The service must be dignified. Izzy and Moe belong on the vaudeville stage." Most of the newspapers took the position that the whole problem of enforcement belonged on the vaudeville stage. The New York *Herald Tribune* said, "They [Izzy and Moe] never made prohibition much more of a joke than it has been made by some of the serious-minded prohibition officers."

Both Izzy and Moe went into the insurance business, and did well. They dropped out of the public eye, and remained out except for an occasional Sunday feature story, and a brief flurry of publicity in 1928, when Izzy went to Europe and returned with some entertaining accounts of his adventures. Izzy died in New York on February 17, 1938, by which time his four sons had all become successful lawyers.

THE CHICAGO BULLET BARONS [11]

The fantastic '20's in all truth were fantastic enough. The show that they put on will never be reproduced—not with the original cast. It was a convincing exemplification of the Alger story. The boys who made good in the gin-and-gun business were nobody you'd ever heard about before. Prohibition's first Chicago victim, Jim Colosimo, a restaurant operator who had prospered in the old red-light district and had miraculously survived the local Black Hand, might have given a capitalistic tinge to the early days of the industry. But he didn't last long enough. He got shot so soon after the passage of the Eighteenth Amendment that the cause of his removal was never quite clear. In one way, though, Jim established the motif for the prohibition racket. He mixed his hooch in the basement while decrying its effects upstairs.

Less than one week before they gathered up his body, he had dropped into

[11] From "The Bullet Barons," by Robert J. Casey, *Holiday*, Vol. 10 (October 1951), No. 4, pp. 91-95, 97, 136, 139, 141-144. Copyright, 1951, by the Curtis Publishing Company. Philadelphia.

a chair at the table of three or four reporters in his restaurant and had sounded his warning. "There ain't no good in this new whisky," he said. "They put you in jail if you sell it. And, damn it, they ought to."

The rocky gangsters of 1920 and 1921 had little resemblance to the quick-triggered, sure-shot pistol experts the movies have kept alive for us. All most of them knew about pistols was that you could raise three bucks on one in a hock shop. There were a few experienced thugs—euphemistically called body-guards—around the South Side. "Scar-Face" Al Brown, ne Capone, was one. John Torrio, who had come to Chicago to protect the person of Colosimo, and apparently had looked the wrong way at the wrong time, was another.

Such civic organizations as the Maffia never had much trouble hiring assassins. The price of a good knife job at Milton and Oak Streets was generally about fifty dollars. But in the main the pioneers mobilized to promote the hooch trade came to gun warfare unprepared.

Nobody has given much thought to the manner in which they were armed or trained, but as markets expanded and business became more profitable, a few professional gun toters began to drift into the ranks. These, like the pickpockets, panders and second-story men they came to assist, were simple people trying to get along—newspaper-circulation sluggers and so-called union organizers. Up to 1920 none of them had made a fortune out of murder, but they had con-tributed a lot of incident to the legend that Chicago was the last outpost on the old frontier. Whether or not they were the drillmasters for the mob, they should have been. They knew how to shoot and they lived wisely according to the first law of self-preservation: Never give a sucker an even break.

So the gunmen of the '20's never used a pistol unless they had to, and a sawed-off shotgun only when they couldn't get a machine gun. They never attacked unless they had numerical superiority and their best jobs were done from ambush. Except when cornered, they never stood up to the police.

All things considered, there is little of the heroic pattern about them. Save one or two, their names are now completely forgotten and it is difficult to see how their goings on could have given Chicago an international reputation—difficult, that is, for anybody unacquainted with the newspaper files of the period.

Chicago's rewrite men apparently had never heard of people being shot in the back before 1920. In their sheltered world, any victim of a murder was a fine upstanding citizen, criminals were always caught and killers were always hanged. When the first of the Taylor Street alcohol cookers—his name now escapes me—was tied up, shot, and dumped on a garbage pile on the banks of the drainage canal, much of Cook County was shocked into speechlessness. But the indignation of a rewrite man is something that can't be pent up.

"Fiends loose in Chicago," howled the headlines. And so began the era of roaring rhetoric.

There were more murders and presently everybody, even the newspapers, began to know what it was all about. The mob directors began to improve their condition with semantics. Bootleggers in the daily prints became "Rum Runners." Any clown who could distill the formaldehyde out of rubbing alcohol

was classified as a "Member of the Illicit Alcohol Ring." The lads who conducted negotiations with the City Hall—and habitually kept out of harm's
way—were "Gang Chiefs."

A pleasing folklore grew up about them. They were Robin Hoodlums who
ran soup kitchens for the needy, loved their mothers, spoiled their children and
carried photographs of their wives next to their hearts in solid gold cigarette
cases. They were really jolly fellows who followed a dangerous calling just for
the fun of it. But they were brave men, all of them, willing to die at the drop
of a hat—or anyway that was the legend. And when they died, they got nice
obituaries. A confused reading public might possibly have been led to believe
that their passing was somehow important.

"Gang guns blazed again last night on Death Corner, and Tony Acrophobia,
beloved leader of the Rigor Mortis gang, coughed out his lungs and his life
on the threshold of Smoky Sam Spiegel's palatially furnished soft-drink
dive. . . ."

"Out of the purple shadows of twelve long months in the alcohol distribution
business, the grim vengeance of Three Gun Bilotti leaped up last night to tear
the heart of One Eyed Jack Schmaltz, the West Side mob's perfectly tailored
psalm-singing mystery man. . . ."

No wonder Chicago began to get a reputation.

Along about 1923, there was no longer any secret about the make-up and
direction of the gangs. There never was any doubt about who killed whom
and why. That nobody ever went to jail for violation of the Volstead Act or got
himself hanged for shooting off firearms inside the city limits detracts nothing
from the essential frankness and honesty of those halcyon days. Life was un-
regimented, open, carefree, eventful and short.

It serves no purpose now to go into the ramifications of the alcohol business
in Cook County. John Torrio, thanks to his heritage from Colosimo, started
out with an organization, money and connections that gave him virtual control
of the First Ward. One of the henchmen he had brought from New York was
the dubious Al Brown Capone, who spent most of his days as a roustabout in
a dive called the Four Deuces at 2222 South Wabash Avenue. Torrio didn't
figure that Al was likely to get far. He was lazy and not very bright. But of
course he was loyal.

A more important lieutenant of the early organization was Dion O'Banion,
a circulation promoter and safe blower who had no sense of obligation to Torrio
and no detectable scruples about anything else. O'Banion had two features that
gave him some prominence in the early mob: he was intelligent and he knew
how to shoot a pistol.

Back around 1904, he was an altar boy at the cathedral where gang-war
bullet holes still scar the cornerstone. He also carried newspapers and was a
pleasant lad with interesting ambitions.

"Me," he said one day as we sat in a silent, empty street waiting for the
morning papers, "Me, I figure there's a lot of ways to make plenty of money
if you do something nobody else is doing. There's no dough in being a printer
or anything like that."

So, ten or eleven years later, he was a circulation hand and an accomplished yegg. In 1921, apparently unconcerned about the competition, he became a sort of tactician and master at arms for the hooch runners.

In 1923, O'Banion declared his independence and founded the North Side mob. Torrio raised no immediate objections. The business of the West Side was divided between the Genna Brothers, two unrelated sets of O'Donnells and some isolated groups of *braumeisters* and alcohol cookers.

Virtually all of the Big Shots who took part in this division of territory have been gathered to their fathers. Spike O'Donnell, of the South Side O'Donnells —as distinguished from the West Side O'Donnells—is still with us, a fine figure of a man and living proof of the theory that if you're born to be drowned you'll never be hanged, or vice versa. Spike, whose beer-running activities must have been something of an annoyance to Al Capone, was frequently a target in those days of promiscuous musketry. Inasmuch as he is over six feet tall and proportionately broad, his miraculous escapes caused some comment. Spike himself would never permit anybody to disparage the marksmanship of the Italian opposition. He preferred to think he had some special gift for leaping out of the way of bullets.

Spike never looked for cover in the daytime. He circulated freely and openly in the town, smiling cheerfully and clapping his friends on the back. Every day, after he had checked off the day's business, he would wander downtown to take up his stand in front of a Randolph Street hotel. There, at his ease, he held a sort of court.

George Stone, of the Chicago *Daily News,* and I ran into him one noon, three blocks away from his hotel.

"Hello, Spike," said George, "what are you doing over on this corner?"

"Well," said Spike, "I like it pretty good here. Pretty good." He adjusted his hat and flicked a little dust off the lapel of his three-hundred-dollar suit.

"I been thinking," he said, "that maybe I got something you boys could make a story out of. I'll tell it to you. Listen.

"I was over at Twenty-fifth and Wentworth Avenue this morning. Didn't have no reason to be there. No reason at all. I was just looking around and figuring what a swell day it was. All over the place there's the sun. And of course it's spring. And the little buds is just a-busting. Then all of a sudden I get it. And I says to myself, 'Gee, I feel it's great to be alive.' "

This would probably have been confusing to almost anyone who ever looked at the drab desolation of Twenty-fifth and Wentworth in those days. The pastoral loveliness of the scene he reported could be found only under O'Donnell's twenty-five-dollar derby hat.

"I'm standing right in front of a drugstore window, just wondering what I'll be doing next," Spike went on. "There's a little kid on a tricycle playing around on the sidewalk—a cute little kid. He's trying to run over my feet, I guess. But I keep moving 'em.

"And then I don't know what makes me turn my head, but I do. And here is this long, low car coming up from the south with the top up and the curtains on. And while I'm lookin' at it a guy sticks his head out the front and says, 'Hello, Spike, glad to see you.'

"Well, I takes a dive and I knocks the kid off the tricycle, and they turn on a Tommy gun. And, boys, they're pretty good. They make the front of that drugstore look like a sewing machine's been run over it. I can hardly believe my eyes when I get up and look.

"The kid and me, we're all right. The kid is crying a little because his nose is skinned. But I can't get no candy or nothing to fix it up because there ain't nobody left in the drugstore, and——"

"Wait a minute," interrupted George. "When did all this happen?"

"Well," Spike said, "it generally takes twenty minutes for me to get down here from Twenty-fifth Street and Wentworth. So's, let's say, it was about twenty minutes ago."

We both bowed deeply and went away.

"Take care of yourself, Spike," George murmured as we went.

And apparently Spike did.

It is difficult to give John Torrio his proper place in Chicago's hooch racket. Certainly his moral code was simple: Anything that would turn a quick dollar was right. Although he could handle a gun pretty well himself, Torrio set no store by it as a piece of business equipment. He was the sort of operator who was willing to take his losses when he had to and to sacrifice much to insure a peaceful market.

"There is no need for all this killing," he used to say. "This is a good big business and it ought to be run right—like the shoe business or the soap business. There's enough here for all of us."

It was to further this theory that he called a meeting of the principal figures in the local alcohol market to discuss territories and trade agreements. The Big Shots met at the Sieben brewery on May 19, 1924, were caught in a police raid, turned over to the Federal authorities and indicted. Despite the fact that Torrio was still the most influential hoodlum in Chicago and probably the most important hooch merchant in the country, he was brought to trial and found guilty. It was while he was out on bail pending action on his appeal that somebody ruined his hope for harmony by murdering Dion O'Banion.

A lot of people, it appears, were stirring up trouble just at the time when Johnny Torrio wasn't wanting any. His protégé and handyman, the sullen, unemotional Al Capone, killed a customer of the Four Deuces named Joseph Howard because Mr. Howard had been unkind to a waiter named Jake Guzick. (It may be added that a lot of people have died since that day just because they were unkind to Jake Guzick.) Capone established a precedent by getting turned loose after questioning. The South Side looked at him with new interest.

O'Banion, who had seen other oafs with delusions of grandeur, possibly should have recognized this menace. But he didn't. By hard work and advertising he had built up a considerable trade north of the river. With touching sentiment he installed himself in a flowershop opposite Holy Name Cathedral where, as a boy, he had sung in the choir. From this perfumed environment he peddled homemade alcohol at five dollars a gallon. And he was doing quite well until a progressive little West Side family known as the Genna brothers found out that you could make a profit on recooked canned heat at two dollars a gallon. O'Banion, who stood in high regard among his associates as a killer, served a cease-and-desist notice. The Gennas, who had basked in the favor of the now busy Torrio, carried their appeal to Capone.

So, on November 10, 1924, Dion O'Banion got a fifteen-column obituary in the local press.

The story seems a bit stale now, but it was an exciting piece of folklore at the time. O'Banion was busy in his flowershop preparing mortuary bouquets and wreaths for the funeral of Mike Merlo, late head of the Sicilian Union. He had plenty to do, for one of these floral exhibits was a life-size replica of the departed, artfully done in roses and lilies.

O'Banion was carrying a gun in each hip pocket and a pair of scissors in his hand when three men who acted like old acquaintances came into the shop. He extended his right hand in greeting to one of them, and the smiling visitor returned the grip and shot him six times.

Well, O'Banion had a fine funeral, perhaps the gaudiest the town will ever know. The silver-trimmed coffin cost $10,000, f.o.b. New York, and was brought to Chicago in a special baggage car. There were truckloads of flowers, including a handsome piece from Capone. Well-dressed judges and highly paid city officials took part in a wake that should properly have been held in the stadium. Brass bands and mourning thousands followed the corpse to the cemetery behind a motorcycle escort furnished by the Stickney (Cook County) police. Up to that time people who had made a study of such things thought that the send-off given Colosimo had been pretty grand. But they never would speak of it again except as something out of a bargain basement.

The prohibition mob, treated as a special breed by the newspapers and showered with gold by the fast-growing drinking populace, took itself seriously. In public, the mobsters tried hard to live up to their portraits as drawn by their press agents. There was a hint of ripe ham about them—ham and confusion and the sort of social obtuseness that produces three-ring funerals.

If we may believe the contemporary biographers, they were just overgrown boys at heart—and they resembled other men of the period in that they enjoyed getting drunk on their own versions of embalming fluid. But aside from that, they lived in a world of their own.

The shooting of Johnny Torrio, just before he withdrew his appeal in the Sieben brewery case, took his sentence and departed from Chicago for good, had features that stemmed directly from some witch's kitchen in Sicily. When the police picked up the half-dead Johnny, he was filled with brass bullets and shreds of garlic. That's why detectives in the case began to look suspiciously at Torrio's friend, Capone, for the deadliness of brass bullets treated with garlic was something Capone was likely to know about.

A gangster called Nails Morton—when he wasn't running hooch—loved to go cantering along the bridle paths of Lincoln Park. The horse, apparently, had no enthusiasm for these outings. One day Nails got pitched onto his head and broke his neck.

He was given a suitable funeral, although possibly not one of the first order. And he got a demonstration of loyalty that he probably would have appreciated had he been alive to look at it. His bereft associates located the horse that had thrown him and shot it dead.

There are other pictures that attest the gang world's utter unreality:

Sam Hunt, trying to look like a sportsman as he lugged a machine gun from one job to another in a golf bag.

Capone in a towering rage because some reporter, in accusing him of murder, misspelled his name Caponi.

Dion O'Banion leisurely munching a waffle in a North Side tearoom while six armed muscle men guarded the doors front and rear.

Samoots Amatuna, in a fur-trimmed summer suit and one of his hundred and fifty silk shirts, shooting at a milkman who had rattled bottles on his back porch.

Hymie Weiss, dousing himself with Christmas Night or Chanel #5 before riding into a fatal ambush in front of Holy Name Cathedral.

Big Tim Murphy charged with taking part in one mail robbery to raise funds for his defense in another.

And, of course, the classic case of John Daugherty, alias Duffy.

Daugherty, or Duffy—or whatever his name was—came to Chicago from Philadelphia in 1924, presumably at the call of the Genna Brothers. He was a gunman whose face was absolutely unknown west of Altoona—which made him an ideal choice for the job of murdering Dion O'Banion.

Duffy apparently wasn't a very engaging character. He was pig-headed, he was stupid, he was insolent, he valued his talents overhighly, and he talked too much. He bragged that he would erase this O'Banion as soon as he wanted to. But first, he said, he would take a little advantage of his expense account.

Pursuing his assignment, he managed to strike up a drinking acquaintance with one or two characters on the fringe of the O'Banion mob. Potatoes Kauffman, the wayward offspring of an honest commission merchant, was one. Then Duffy took up with a girl named Mabel Exley, recently arrived from Louisville, and established a love nest in Rogers Park. Mabel was a naive and hopeful dancer in a fifth-rate night club when she met the boastful Duffy. She gained wisdom after listening for a month to his boastful and unprofitable conversation and notified him that she was leaving. In a drunken rage, he shot her dead.

After that he was in a quandary. His assets were nil; his relations with his employers were strained; and he hadn't a friend this side of the Alleghenies. In his emergency he called Potatoes Kauffman and asked him to arrange a meeting with Dion O'Banion. This was about 11 P.M., February 22, 1924. He must have been persuasive because the date was made with top priority. At one o'clock in the morning of February 23, Kauffman saw Duffy getting into a blue coupé at South Wabash Avenue and Twenty-second Street. O'Banion was at the wheel. Louie Alterie, who had alighted to inspect Kauffman and frisk his friend, held the door open. Duffy was sitting between O'Banion and Alterie as the car headed south.

What happened then was one of the most preposterous things in the history of a preposterous era. Both O'Banion and Alterie knew that Duffy had come to Chicago to assassinate O'Banion. Kauffman had told them of Mabel Exley's murder. But some of the reasons for the present rendezvous seemed to be beyond belief.

"You're in a jam," said O'Banion. "But what's the idea of coming to me about it?"

"I know what you're thinking," whined the dim-witted Duffy. "But it ain't so. I never did anything to you. I crossed up the Gennas. And I need some sugar to get out of town."

"He's just a rat, any way you take him," observed Alterie to O'Banion. "We ought to give him the works."

Duffy, not much more sober than he had been two hours before, half turned toward Alterie, and said: "Keep out of this, you grease-ball so-and-so."

So Alterie killed him. The bullet narrowly missed O'Banion.

There was much speculation the next day when Exley's body was discovered in the Carmen Avenue flat and a few hours later somebody was stumbling over what was left of Daugherty-Duffy in the Clearing railroad yards. It took a little time to discover the connection between them and even longer to figure out what had happened. Potatoes Kauffman supplied a few details. Loose talk among the gangsters eventually gave credit for the kill to Alterie. And long afterward, in an expansive mood, Alterie himself told the story as it is set down here.

It is so totally in character that it deserves to be credited. A killer appeals to the man he had contracted to murder. An outraged lieutenant slaughters him not because he has admitted being a contemptible and lethal traitor but because he uses foul and abusive language. The moral codes of gangland may have been fearful. But they were also pretty wonderful.

The gross annual business of Al Capone in 1929 was estimated by Government investigators at a possible $200,000,000; Al had come a long way from the Four Deuces. Like Torrio, he was looking toward control of alcohol, gambling and prostitution in the Greater Chicago area. But he had none of Torrio's hope that such blessings could be obtained by simple conversation. No longer did anybody try to keep track of the toll in the beer wars. The men who died were mostly unknown and as they piled up in the alleys at the rate of from twenty-five to forty a year their names had no more news value than entries in a thick telephone book.

Capone—the Big Fellow, as he liked to be called—was presently to be put in his place by the Federal income-tax experts, and his trial was to show him to be only a false face—a stupid oaf who had seized the hooch-distributing machinery by force and held it by threat. But on February 14, 1929, when he reached the climax of his career as impresario of the slaughter generally known as the "St. Valentine's Day Massacre," he was an ogre of heroic stature.

The North Side mob, currently led by George "Bugs" Moran, had refused to listen to Capone's proposals for an amalgamation. On the morning of February fourteenth, the boys had gathered at their headquarters in a garage at 2122 North Clark Street for a briefing on the night's work. At the briefing were John May, Frank and Pete Gusenberg, James Clark and Adam Hyer, working mobsters; Reinhart Schwimmer, an optometrist who had an adolescent's admiration for gangsters; and Alfred Weinshank, a strong-arm man who had simply dropped in for a social call.

At eleven o'clock there were more callers—four men, two in police uniforms, who lined up the seven along the side wall of the garage and chopped them down with machine guns. "Bugs" Moran arrived as the butchery was in progress. He heard the machine guns and rapidly departed.

Al Capone was in Miami at the time. At eleven o'clock, Central Time, he was in conference with the district attorney of Dade County, Fla.—about the only sensible thing he did during his years of grandeur. His timing was perfect. There certainly was no sanity in the plan of the St. Valentine's slaughter, or in the "victory dinner" Capone gave a few months later.

The dinner was given for John Scalise, Albert Anselmi and Joe Guinta, murderers who had recently been released from jail by a sort of legal miracle, and it was attended by the usual imposing assortment of gangsters, panders, police and public officials. During the course of the festivities, Capone began to suspect the loyalty of the guests of honor. He mentioned afterward that he had been warned they intended to kill him. So, after the last toast had been drunk, he ordered them removed to a South Side basement and trussed up to the rafters with baling wire. There, some time later, the Big Fellow beat out their brains with a baseball bat.

Big as he was, the Big Fellow had to get out of town after that. He went to Philadelphia and contrived to get himself arrested and sentenced to a year in jail for carrying concealed weapons. He didn't show himself in Chicago much between that time and October 6, 1931, when he went on trial before Federal Judge James H. Wilkerson.

Capone's Chicago trial (where it was finally proved that he had cheated on his income tax) was surprising in that it showed the Big Fellow's wits to have been virtually nil. With bribery and terrorism he had come a long way, but when he came up against a force that he could neither intimidate nor buy he was without resource.

*   *   *   *   *

. . . As you remember, the Big Fellow eventually landed in Alcatraz. He died a natural death in January, 1947, and was buried in Chicago with no fanfare whatever.

Capone's "syndicate" made brave attempts to carry on after the repeal of the Prohibition Act. In the beginning it made forceful use of the racket technique, trying to force saloonkeepers to buy only syndicate beer and syndicate soda pop and to install syndicate juke boxes. But there was a difference. There was no reason why, in this new order, a threatened saloonkeeper couldn't ask the law for protection, and no reason—for the past several years, at any rate—why he couldn't figure on getting it. And the competition in the manufacture and sale of legal beer is pretty tough.

The old mob, in mellow age, still prospers to some extent in rackets outside the law—such as gambling and, from time to time, prostitution. But its activities nowadays seldom get north of Page 26.

THE DIP [12]

Maxie the Goniff is a professional. Practically all cannons are. He is not very bright. His body is slight and springy; his fingers are long, tapering, and nervous. His face resembles a parrot's, the beak long and hooked downward. His eyes are furtive. He decided over fifty years ago that picking "pokes" was a fine way of making a living. He apprenticed himself to a master, studied hard, graduated with honors, and went on his own. He wouldn't tell me how old he was at the time we spoke, but my guess is that he was at least sixty-five.

"I'm slowing up a little," was the most he would say. "My fingers got a little rheumatism."

Like most of his kind, Maxie has a long criminal record. He has been arrested seventy-one times in twenty-two states.

"Doesn't speak so well for you, Maxie," I goaded him. "A good thief doesn't get caught, you know."

He flushed angrily. "Every one of them pinches came after a whole season's work. In fifty years I done six years' time. I'm living good—well, pretty good —for forty-four years and it cost me six years! You should have it so good!"

He claims that both his parents were alcoholics, that they put him out of the house when he was twelve, and that he has been on his own ever since. For a time he was a petty thief, then a shoplifter, and finally, while still a kid, he met a man who took him on as an apprentice dip and taught him the business.

Picking pockets *is* a business, Maxie insists. "You've got to figure a certain amount of risk in any business. Suppose I open a saloon. I'm taking a chance, no? I might go broke, I might have to pay too much protection—it's all business."

Like all commercial enterprise, Maxie's has its seasons. "Summers we work the resorts, like Coney Island, and the buses and subways going to and from. Beaches are good too. Certain holidays is season for us. Before Easter and Christmas. There's lots of shopping. That's when I hit department stores. In the elevators or even on the floor."

When he has had a run of bad luck he will depart from his more accustomed beat and cover a church wedding. "You don't often find much dough on the guys, but, brother! are they easy to take! They don't expect a thief in a church."

Occasional gravy is a convention or parade. Maxie plays the crowds. He loves American Legion groups because "half the time they don't even know the next morning whether they've been hooked or just spent the dough."

"Most fun I had was in a hotel where there was a convention of these private

[12] From *Parole Chief*, by David Dressler, pp. 243-247. Copyright, 1948, 1950, 1951, by David Dressler. New York: The Viking Press, Inc.

dicks—you know, going over transoms to find the wife in bed with a man? They drink considerable and they like a good time. I hit one after the other, with my—er—associates. Mostly we scored off them in the men's rooms. And they're so ashamed they was taken that not a one makes a squeal!"

Maxie takes pride in his technique. He has little use for the lone operator, although he admits there are some good ones. He considers they take too many risks. Only his dire need for an immediate stake had led him to try for my wallet alone.

He likes to work in a mob of two to four people. Say you're on a subway or elevator. "You pick your mark and try to figure where he keeps his wallet. It ain't hard to find out. You just jostle the sucker and move off. Right away he puts his hand where he's got the wallet to see if it's there. He tips you off.

"Of course, if he don't fall for that, you've got to *fan* him. You feel around, very easy, until you locate the poke.

"Then comes pratting. You prat the guy around. That means you push him around, edge him around, not hard, gentle, just enough to distract his attention. Also to get him into position—the position you want him in for the score."

The man who does the pushing is the "stall." When the victim is in position, the "duke" (hand) of one thief extracts the poke. This man is called, variously, a "hook," "tool," "wire," or "instrument." He is the most skilful member of the team. The victim's attention is directed to the stall as the hook takes the wallet. Maxie is a hook.

"Funny thing," he said, chuckling. "Some guys look for a poke in a hip pocket. They like to take it from there. I'd rather score out of the breast pocket. Why? Because the sucker thinks he's cute, see? No offense meant to you, Mr. Dressler. He thinks if he carries it in the breast pocket it's tough to take. It is, but a good thief likes that kind of meat. I always do." (I doubt it. Professional cannons are awful liars. Chances are, Maxie, good businessman that he is, will always go for the easier score when possible.)

While taking from the inside pocket, the wire "shades" the duke—covers his hand so the victim won't see it, perhaps with a newspaper. "What I do," says Maxie, "is 'put a throw' in his face. I shade my duke with a paper and annoy the guy by flappin' it under his nose. That makes 'im mad. He's concentratin' on the throw while I'm 'takin' off the score.'

"In a good crowd, on a hip job, the 'push grift' works. No shadin' the duke, nothin'. Everybody's pushing, so you push all you want, and the guy don't even see or feel your hand."

In digging for the wallet the "straight hoist" is commonly employed. The cannon puts the first two fingers, held stiffly, into the pocket. He stiffens his body, lifts up on his toes, and out comes the wallet.

The next step is "cleaning." "The stall distracts attention, say. Now the wire's got the poke. He has to get clean right away. Because why? If the sucker 'blows' (discovers his loss) he's gonna figure right away it's the wire, because the wire was closest to him. So I pass the wallet on right away to one of my stalls—the one who will be first off the car or elevator. If the guy grabs me I'm clean. I beef like hell. If he goes for the stall, he drops the poke and he's clean. Or better yet, he plants it on some bystander and we take it back later."

Maxie is proudest of the fact that he is a specialist among specialists, "a left-breech hook." That's a man who can draw a score out of a left pants pocket. "There ain't many can do that. It's hard. Try it!"

I asked him how much he earned a year by grifting. He became very evasive, even apologetic. "Oh, I had my ups and downs. Why talk about it? You do all right, year in, year out, if you're good. Some years I run five, ten thousand. Other times not so good, maybe a couple of Gs."

"Where did your money go? In the ten years I used to run into you off and on, you were always broke."

"Well, the horses got a lot of it. Craps. Cards. Women. And I had to eat too." He forgot to mention that he has a wife and two children who are dependent upon him for their support.

I have never known an affluent pickpocket. I don't believe they make as much as Maxie claims, and their money seems to go fast. They live riotously. Some are drug addicts at times in their lives. Many have wives and children. I've never known one who wasn't a confirmed gambler or who wasn't fresh out of money every time I inquired.

* * * * *

"Maxie," I asked, "if you had it to do over again, what would you be instead of a pickpocket?"

"What's wrong," he snapped, "with this racket?"

HARLEM CULTS AND RACKETS [13]

. . . Under the economic stress, hundreds of cultists—fakirs and charlatans of every brand—swept into the Negro communities, set up shop, and began to flourish in a big way. Usually housed in dimly lit, smelly railroad flats in sections where they would not be hounded by the police, these men and women drew their "clients" and "members" from that army of bewildered and discouraged Negroes, caught in the economic maelstrom. The cultists were augmented by a number of herb doctors, clairvoyants, and "jackleg" preachers, who operated in places like the Triumph Church, the Metaphysical Church of the Divine Investigation, Saints of Christ, Pentecostal Pilgrims, and the Sixth Mt. Zion Church. At the last place a sermon was once delivered entitled "A Big Man Sleeps on a Little Woman's Lap."

Along the streets, to the accompaniment of much mumbo-jumbo, mystics hawked—as they do today—all manner of products to the credulous, including the "number" at a charge of twenty-five cents to win at the policy game. High John the Conqueror was Harlem's best known of the love-potion purveyors. The vendors were of many races: American Indians in feathered headdress and buckskin chaps sold snake oil, and roots, herbs, and maize for backyard plant-

[13] From "*New World A-Coming*," Inside Black America, by Roi Ottley, pp. 86-87. Copyright, 1943, by Roi Ottley. Boston: Houghton Mifflin Company.

ing. Native Africans, their faces marked by tribal identifications, offered teak-wood idols, hand-carved ivory bric-a-brac, and good-luck charms. Hindus sold perfume; East Indian Moslems peddled incense, oils, and teas; and gypsies told fortunes. Chinese in mandarin robes offered hand-wrought jade, boxes, and rugs; West Indians vended pamphlets explaining the mysteries of voodooism. Of the home-grown varieties, there were fire-eating Rajah Rabo, dream-book author, and the voluptuous, slant-eyed Madam Fu Futtam, a seeress of Negro-Chinese parentage.

The cultists—those jackals of the city jungles—appeared to have the right of way. Nearly two hundred places in Harlem were operating as "spiritualist churches," where the "spirits" needed little inducement to come knocking at the door. The Holy Star Spiritual Church, housed in the second-floor apartment of a tenement, was a typical outfit. In a small room a greenish light cast an eerie glow on a picture of Christ, which hung over a gold-and-white altar. A slick-haired black boy played rhythmic hymns on an old beaten upright piano, as the customers filed in to communicate with the spirit world. The "spiritual adviser," in this case the Reverend Mme. V.D.S. Armistead, a skinny woman in a lace-covered black cassock and jaunty priest's biretta, trailed into the room as sanctuary bells were tinkled by a black-robed altar boy. "Before I begin to transmit messages from the Spirit World," she would announce, "I want to tell you 'bout our Prosperity Oil." The product—"good to awaken slumbering souls" —sold for ten cents a bottle and proved to be a profitable item. Once that little matter was concluded, the business of bringing in the spirits got under way at twenty-five cents a head. Twenty to thirty persons were usually accommo-dated at one sitting.

Sometimes closed motion-picture houses, empty stores, and lodge halls were converted into "temples," with announcements plastered on the buildings that were cheap and alluring, calling the citizenry to find out what trouble was brewing. The operators of these places turned neat profits from the sale of dream books, policy pamphlets, love potions, and incense to destroy evil spirits. Two questions they unfailingly answered in the affirmative: "Am I going to find work?" and "Am I going to hit the numbers?" Harlem's *Amsterdam-Star News,* after investigations as late as 1940, estimated the "take" from these rackets as approximately a million dollars annually.

THE MECCA [14]

The Mecca Building is U-shaped. The dirt courtyard is littered with newspapers and tin cans, milk cartons and broken glass. Pigeons roost on a car on blocks. A skinny white dog huddles in a doorway. Iron fire escapes run up the building's face and ladders reach from them to the roof. There are four main entrances, two on Dearborn and two on State Street. At each is a gray

[14] From "The Strangest Place in Chicago," by John Bartlow Martin, *Harper's Magazine,* Vol. 201 (December 1950), No. 1207, pp. 87-90, 93-94, 96-97. Copyright, 1950, by Harper & Brothers. New York.
Drawing by Ben Shahn.

stone threshold and over each is carved "The Mecca." The Mecca was constructed as an apartment building in 1891, a splendid palace, a showplace of Chicago. Today it is still an apartment building and a showplace but of a very different sort. It has become one of the most remarkable Negro slum exhibits in the world. . . .

Inside, a powerful odor assails the visitor at once, musty, heavy, a smell compounded of urine and stale cooking and of age, not necessarily an unpleasant odor but a close powerful one, which, like that of marijuana, once smelled is never forgotten. The stone slab step is hollowed. The lower part of the walls of the vestibule once was covered with marble but now the marble has been stripped away in ragged patches, revealing naked brick and mortar. It is dark here. Ahead stretches a corridor; it is like a tunnel, it seems endless and it is indeed a block long, running all the way to the Dearborn Street entrance; down its whole length hang only five light bulbs, glowing feebly in the gloom. Tan paint is peeling from the wall, the doors of apartments open into the corridor. This is the base of the U in the U-shaped building.

The arms of the U are identical. They are great halls, each lit by a skylight four stories overhead which, because of the dirt that has accumulated on the glass through years of neglect, admits the kind of unreal light found underseas. This light slants down in great long angling shafts filled with floating dust, shifting as the sun moves across the sky, falling in fitful patches on the floor.

Around the walls run three balconies guarded by ornate wrought-iron grillwork, and off these balconies open the doors to the apartments, like tiers of cells in a prison cellblock. The floor in the center of the well is of hardwood, splintered now, and beneath the balconies it is of tile, broken in many places. A janitor with a wheelbarrow is slowly patching the tile with concrete; his shovel makes a rasping, scraping sound. From somewhere in the building comes always the sound of distant human voices—women talking, a baby squalling, children screaming, men muttering, no words distinguishable. Spittle splats flatly on the tile floor, falling from a great height, spat by a man or a woman standing on an upper balcony. All day long people stand at the balconies, leaning on the wrought-iron railings with hands clasped out over them, gazing out at other people facing them across the well in silence, gazing down at the floor far below, spitting, small human figures in a vast place, two or three on each of the four floors, occasionally calling back and forth to one another but most of the time just standing silent. The building is never entirely quiet, not even very late at night, since so many people live here; but it is so vast that it seems quiet, even amid uproar.

In the center on the ground floor is a long narrow bank of mailboxes, tarnished brass, 176 of them. One has thirteen names on it, including seven different family names, indicating that thirteen adults expecting mail occupy that particular apartment. Late in the morning the postman comes, a man in blue. Three tenants wait respectfully at the side while he distributes the mail. On the balcony above, two men leaning on the railing watch him critically: "He'll never get it all done doing it one at a time," and, "He's a new man." At last he finishes, and tenants emerge from their apartments to get their mail. From a high balcony a toddler throws a chuck of broken tile; it bounces on the floor by the mailboxes. A stooped old woman wearing a black sweater and black shawl, only her hair and her eyeballs white, moves slowly and painfully in the shadows beneath the balcony, keeping close to the wall as long as possible, touching it with bony fingers, and only leaving it when she must to venture across the open floor to the mailbox; gets her mail, then retreats along the wall to the stairs, where a man steps aside, saying kindly, "You come down to see what you got, didn't you?" and she says, in a gasping voice, "I'm going take my good time," then begins to ascend, pulling herself up by the railing, first her right foot up one step, then the left slowly after it, her body bent so low that her face almost touches the next step, stopping at the landing to rest and stare at the peeling walls with watery, half-blind eyes. Near the mailboxes three children are jumping rope, using a doubled rope, two boys swinging the two long strands in sweeping arcs while a girl rocks to and fro at one side to get into the rhythm before jumping in. Children ride battered tricycles across the floor, safe here from the traffic of the streets. On a balcony children are playing store, using a cardboard box. One of them throws a fistful of paper over the railing and it flutters down: policy slips, there must be a policy station here.

The wind blows in off Dearborn Street and a young woman neat in black enters, walking a leashed dog and humming a hymn. Somewhere a child is crying over and over, "Mummy, Mummy." In the long dark corridor a dog is nosing at garbage from an upset garbage can. From somewhere comes a clatter, perhaps of a falling garbage-can lid, and the high mad cackling laughter of an old man. A very young child standing on the third floor balcony urinates through the ornate iron grillwork and the urine falls to the ground floor far below and a woman calls to him, "Don't you do that, you got no right to do that, I'm going to tell your mother." The ice man comes wearing a leather protector on his shoulder and back, carrying a cake of ice that gleams whitely against his black face and hat. A woman calls from the third floor, "Bring fifty pounds to 304½," and he plods to the stairs.

In the shadows against a pillar marked with match-strikes leans a man, his shirt-collar buttoned but without a necktie, his hat-brim slanting low over his scarred face, a cigarette slanting from his mouth; he is just standing there watching. How many people live here? He laughs. "I don't know." Two thousand? "Oh, more than that. There's 176 apartments and some of 'em's got seven rooms and they're all full." A heavy round-faced man in a long white apron holding a ball-peen hammer approaches: "You are visiting some of the historic sites of the city? You found one all right. If it don't fall in on you while you're lookin'." How many people live here? "That," he says, "is a mystery. You'll find them sleeping in bathtubs, sleeping in the kitchen under the sink, anywhere they can sleep." Nobody, in truth, knows how many people inhabit the Mecca Building. The janitor, Jimmy Sanders, estimates 2,300; the Democratic precinct captain, William Patrick Fitzgerald, who has lived here eighteen years, estimates 1,400; the owner doesn't know. All the inhabitants except one woman are Negroes. The Mecca Building contains more people than most Chicago precincts; indeed, it constitutes a precinct in itself, the 27th Precinct of the 2nd Ward.

On the third floor an old woman stands by the railing, a towel wound round her head, a big gold ring on her finger. Watching dispassionately as children run in from school for lunch, their screams ringing piercingly through the building, she says judiciously, "That size runs to roller skates," and then, "When I first came here they used to control the children. White people hadn't been gone so long, 1917 it was. They used to have a policeman here nights, you could hear a needle drop. Now they's shooting here five times a night. Them young men and the young girls is the worst. I'd move out tonight if they'd find me a house. I moved out for a while once but I came back to have company, my daughter lives here and my granddaughter was born here," and she turns and shuffles into her flat.

In the flat, wallpaper hangs from the walls in great sheets. Clean newspapers are spread on the floor. Over the dresser are some artificial flowers, and a transparent plastic wrapper covers the bed. The sideboard, radio, and table are cluttered with family photographs. Mottoes and pictures hang on the walls, a picture of Jesus Christ and a crucifix put out by a liquor store, a plaque, "My Help cometh from the Lord," and also secular shrines: a large frame holding the pictures of Abraham Lincoln and Frederick Douglass flanked by Booker T. Washington, Paul Laurence Dunbar, W. E. B. DuBois, and other race leaders.

And a framed faded campaign picture of Franklin D. Roosevelt. She calls Lincoln "Abraham." She was born in Alabama. She is bent and stooped, aged. She says, "I live here all by myself, me and my Lord," and then, as her visitor departs, she touches his arm and says gently, "Do you know anything about that man we call Jesus, do you know him personally, you ought to get in touch with him." Outside her door a teen-age boy is standing at the balcony railing, trying to spit clear across to the other side.

In the long first-floor corridor the janitor passes, Jimmy, a short squat man in a leather cap and jacket, ambling along with a Yankee drill in his hand. "I'm the maintenance man," he says. "I do a little of everything—work a little, fight a little, sleep a little, play a little." Right now he is accompanying the rent collector, a white man, a wiry Scot named John. "I go around with him," Jimmy says, shifting the stub of his dead cigar to the other corner of his mouth, "because the young fellas in the building think he's got money with him." About a year ago the young fellows robbed an insurance collector of $17. The rent collector, John, says, "I lost all my hair fighting with these people," and laughs. Actually, he has little trouble collecting rents, which are cheap. His troubles are of a different sort: he and Jimmy fight a hopeless rearguard action against decay and vandalism. "Last night they shot out the light bulbs," says Jimmy. "And the windows—in the last year I bet I put in over two hundred windows. They break 'em fast as you put 'em in." Who does it? "Outsiders, most of it. And the kids here. The kids gets to playin' and throwin' at one another and first thing you know they break the glass. There's nothin' you can do about it. You can't kill one 'cause he broke the glass."

As the rent collector walks along, a woman calls from the third-floor balcony, "Hold your head up, John, John, hold your head up, I want to talk to you," but John plods on, grinning secretly. A sign by the basement stairs reads, "Put All Complaints in Mail Box." Near the State Street entrance another janitor has temporarily left his job of cementing a broken place in the floor and is stooping over at an apartment door, digging with a knife at something in the door. He gets it out: a bullet. "That's a thirty-eight," he says, turning it over in his hand, shiny and twisted. Then, to a woman who has come to the door, "They try to shoot you out last night?" She laughs. "Yeh, try to kill me. Like shootin' rabbits in a swamp down yonder." He says, "They was really shootin' here last night. Some of 'em shootin' for fun, some of 'em fightin'. That's every night around here. Couple of 'em got shot the other night." Any ever killed? "Oh, yes, one got killed summer before last up there in that corner," pointing upward. Why? "I don't know."

Down the stairs comes a man on crutches, his left leg off above the knee, his pants leg pinned up, coming down the steps, the crutch and his good leg visible first, then the man, thin, wearing white pants and a brown coat and hat; he walks diagonally past the mailboxes to the grocery, pausing to adjust his pipe.

High on the fourth west gallery, close up under the skylight, the balcony seems narrow. Two boys wrestle on it, and one falls heavily against the iron railing, which trembles but holds firm. It is four stories down to the ground floor; nobody ever heard of a child falling. An old woman is sweeping the floor. High up here at the north end a dozen young men and women are congregated, well-dressed, two of the men off to one side leaning idle on the railing and peering sullenly down, the others close together, laughing, fooling around with each other, the girls in tight white sweaters, the young men in snap-brim hats and suitcoats over sweaters.

* * * * *

Now near dusk, the fourth-floor balcony is wrapped in gloom, and young men congregate, lounging, smoking cigarettes, they are not talking; and down on the ground floor beneath the balcony a wiry girl of twelve wrestles with a smaller, prettier girl in a new blue snowsuit, throwing her to the floor, rolling over and over with her in the dirt by the fresh cement the janitor poured. And whooping from the darkness in the far recess of the well comes a rushing crowd of boys and girls, flowing past the iceman, who is still at work, and the din grows louder, screams and cries, loud thumps and thunderous footsteps as the crowd swirls on around the corner into the dark then back, ten children, perhaps ten or twelve years old, armed with spears and bows and arrows, running, screaming, whooping. A man says, "That's all day. And all night too." They are dark leaning shadows racing around a pillar; they have upset and plundered a garbage can and now they throw applecores and onions at each other across the well, the air is filled with flying applecores and onions, and a boy of sixteen armed with a whiskey bottle chases a girl on roller skates, at whom another boy shoots an arrow.

In a corner a small child sits on the floor, playing a mouth organ, and a boy about ten with a long-bladed knife lurks behind a post. Near the doorway two boys of nine or ten detach themselves from the rest and fight, fight in earnest, biting, kicking, hitting, swearing, then silently fighting, not talking, just breathing heavily, until a man comes in off the street and stops them, a tenant with a briefcase home from the office, taking one boy with him as he ascends into the upper reaches of the building.

When the Mecca Building was constructed it was considered one of the largest and finest apartment buildings in Chicago if not in America. It catered (almost needless to say) to a white clientele. But after 1900 the Negro migration to Chicago forced the black belt to expand, and by 1912 the Mecca Building was the home of the Negro elite—doctors, lawyers, business men.

A woman who lives there still, Mrs. Florence Clayton, arrived in 1916, and she remembers, "There were carpets on the stairs and halls. There were goldfish in the fountain. On the first floor there were lounge chairs and outdoors we had a flower garden and beautiful trees and green grass, you could go out there, oh, it was lovely. The courtyard was all fenced in and there was a lovely walk through the flowers."

The building started to deteriorate during the 1917-18 war. So did the whole neighborhood. Booming war industries pulled thousands of Negroes to Chicago. The luckier ones abandoned the region of 35th and State to the poor and the wicked. The black-and-tans where Chicago jazz flowered were right here. Jimmy, the janitor, recalls, "There were lots of fights and cuttings. Building was full of prostitutes. I saw a man throw a prostitute over the third floor railing—from the third floor to the first floor. Didn't hurt her much. She only weighed ninety pounds, kind of light. Finally one of the pimps killed the building watchman. Did it over a woman. And she wasn't even living with him." Jimmy pushes his leather cap back off his forehead. "That about ended it, though. They got a new watchman and he was a killer. He was just a little man but he had great big eyes and he'd shoot you with either hand. He had a cemetery of his own before he died. He only killed nine people—between the basement here and that wire fence. The building got kind of decent after that—families, working people."

And then the Depression came along, and the wicked left, and almost none but the poor remained. The Depression was awful in the black belt. About 1932 the bottom fell out. One woman who lived here then recalls, "The building was partly empty. One lady told me she was sitting down on the curb and the police passed and it was cold and they asked her what was the matter and she said she'd been set out and they told her to come on in here and the first flat she'd find, sit down. They carried her to court later but they didn't make her get out, they couldn't, people had no work to do then. It was always warm and nice in here during the Depression."

The Depression accounts for the presence today of the building's only white tenant, a heavy, soft-faced, white-haired woman of sixty-six. "I'd been a house-keeper at a hotel and one of my maids, a colored girl, she was married to a white doctor and they lived here in the Mecca Building. I couldn't find a job, I just got stuck, I couldn't make it, and they took me in." Some of the Mecca inhabitants who moved in while they were on relief are now earning good money in the steel mills or on Pullman cars and one or two earn upward of $5,000 a year, but they are imprisoned here by the scarcity of dwellings for Negroes. A few of the long-time tenants remain by choice, oddly proud of the building. A few earn money by living there—they sublet rooms in their apartments for as much as $12 a week. The janitor Jimmy says, "Every day people come in, many as ten or twelve a day, lookin' for a place, they been walkin' the street, lookin' for some place to go, say, 'Janitor, if you can get me an apartment in here I'll give you $100,' but there ain't none."

* * * * *

Until 1941 the Mecca Building was owned by a New York estate. The janitor Jimmy only once saw a representative of the estate. In 1941 the estate sold the Mecca to its next-door neighbor, the Illinois Institute of Technology. The Institute bought the building for only one purpose: to tear it down. The Institute was expanding its campus in accordance with a neat plan integrated with the neat plans of numerous other agencies for clearing the South Side slums. It wanted to replace the Mecca Building with a laboratory. But its plans ran head-on into an important need of the people who dwelt in the Mecca Building, the need for a place to live.

For nine years it has tried to evict them, taking them to court and warning them the Mecca is a firetrap. Thus far the tenants have managed to generate enough political pressure to stay. Recently, when the Institute again started eviction proceedings, State Senator C. C. Wimbish, a lawyer who has represented the tenants in court, said, "If they try to put these people out, they'll have a race riot down there on State Street and I intend to make it as tense as possible. Any roof is better than no roof."

It is quiet in the building on a summer morning, quiet as a tomb. Spit falls flatly on the ground floor, spat by a silent watcher high on the balcony, and in a dark corner recess on the topmost floor a young girl, pretty, wearing a tight white sweater, strains against a young man leaning on the wall. An old man in blue pajamas, his eyes wild and staring, his body very thin, totters along, clutching at the railing, saying in a high, cracked voice, to a visitor, "Call me a telephone number please, mister, will you call me a telephone number," but a large woman steps from a doorway and shakes her head at the visitor, making circling motions beside her temple, and moves to take the old man's arm, and seeing her he starts, as though to run, then weeps, and she leads him away. A puff of blue smoke hangs in the dead air on the second balcony where a man is leaning on the railing, smoking. A janitor collects garbage in a cart that rumbles on the broken tile like a tumbril. Everything echoes in the halls, voices are hard to comprehend, are confused with distant sounds.

A visitor twists the bell on Mrs. Griffin's apartment and she calls, "Who is it?" then unfastens the chain. Her mother is sitting by the window in the sun, as always. Mrs. Griffin says that when she got the most recent notice to vacate, she went house-hunting: "I found a place to buy at a real estate office way up on the North Side but no other colored people live right there, and I don't want to get bombed on," as indeed many Chicago Negroes have been when they tried to leave the black belt. She goes over beside her mother, who is rocking. "I think this housing situation is terrible, it's all politics, that's all. I'm not mad at the school. It's their property, we know that. I'm mad 'cause all this politics. Put 'em in office and they didn't did nothin'. They build streets and superhighways and recreation—not houses. They should turn that money loose and stop it—people has got to have some place to live. They gonna do *anything* if they don't."

She laughs, but does not sound amused: "They say they gonna place us somewhere. *Place* us! I don't wanta be placed anywhere myself. They might place me in some mudhole somewhere and I never did live in that," and she laughs again. Her mother mutters something. "I don't know what they going to do with us. After all, there's no use in pushing us around from one place to another, that's no way to live." And then, after a pause, "It's all so mean."

Her mother, rocking, has started muttering steadily; she is looking out the window, her head in its white lace cap bobbing gently up and down. What is Mrs. Griffin going to do?

"I don't know. I'll have to have a place for my mother. I couldn't tell you what I'm going to do, to save my neck." Her mother, rocking, begins to mutter louder, but her words are not intelligible, it is just a human voice, muttering, and it is impossible to tell whether in anger or in joy, it is only sound.

PACHUCOS AND SQUARES [15]

. . . Out of the estimated four hundred thousand persons of Mexican ancestry living in Los Angeles County, there [was in the Forties] a small group of teen-age boys and girls who by virtue of certain characteristics of dress and behavior [had] become a group apart from the normal Mexican population.

*   *   *   *   *

They have created their own lauguage, Pachucano talk; their own style of dress; their own folklore and behavior patterns. They have developed a neighborhood group spirit that has resulted in the establishment of a few-score areas and territories of influence for the groups of boys living in those areas—thus creating the so-called gangs.

The anxieties and maladjustments of these children have started in early childhood, for they are not Mexican by citizenship, nationality, or culture. They are Americans, but to the fifth generation they are known as "Mexicans," if their skin is dark and they bear a Spanish name. They seldom get the opportunity to meet the better representatives of either the Mexican or American cultures, and the "Americans" they do meet do not, as a rule, endear themselves to the inquiring mind and sensitive heart of a child. Unsympathetic teachers, superior "American" kids in school, the discriminating police and sheriff's deputies, the neighborhood merchants—most of these make clear their membership in the majority group. . . .

In the opinion of many Americans, well-to-do Mexicans, and most of the Los Angeles police force, all Pachucos are delinquent Mexican zootsuiters. Few realize that among the many thousands of youths of Mexican ancestry in Los Angeles County, only a small percentage, less than five per cent, are classified as delinquents. On the other hand, fully two-thirds of the underprivileged Mexican-American youth between 1940 and 1945 wore one form or another of the so-called zootsuit, a style of garment which classified them in the minds of many as troublemakers. The origin of the word "Pachuco" is not completely known. Around Los Angeles the term seems to have been applied colloquially to Mexican-American youths and their families coming from El Paso on the crest of one of the great migratory waves to California in the early twenties. The newcomers were proud of the name, as people from Los Angeles are proud of being called Angelinos. Settling as they did mostly in groups where living quarters were cheapest, they gradually made their influence felt among the teen-age children of earlier Mexican settlers. They had brought with them a jargon, a kind of special speech, attractive to the local youth, and a sartorial style—ducktail haircuts and flared bell-bottom trousers—that made them distinctive. They were clannish and often distinctly anti-social. To the adult local

[15] From *American Me*, by Beatrice Griffith, pp. 44-54. Copyright, 1947 and 1948, by Beatrice Winston Griffith. Boston: Houghton Mifflin Company.

Mexicans they were an irritant. To the younger ones they were a curiosity, and as rebels against authority something of a fascination. Words unfamiliar to their older friends and parents cropped up in the speech of local boys and girls. "You talk Pachuco," came to be a slightly derisive but more and more frequent comment.

The economic depression in the thirties had brought about problems of unemployment, hunger, broken homes, irregular crop work, and state or county "relief." Consequently the decade produced many maladjusted second-generation youth. Their sense of inferiority was augmented by their lack of opportunity to compete in industry with skilled "American" youth. At this time of social unrest and disorganization the Pachucos on Bunker Hill became the catalyst to precipitate rebellions among Mexican-American youngsters. This was true not so much because of leadership, since leadership in any Mexican neighborhood group changes from day to day. Their dress, speech, and behavior patterns were attractive to these particular adolescents who were in rebellion against the accepted customs of the cultures of their parents, teachers, and police.

Later, in the forties, zootsuits rode into fashion along with jitterbug dancing. They set the style for many underprivileged youths, often the children of Negro or foreign-born parents, between the ages of fifteen and twenty-five. Zootsuits provided the familiar costume in which to dress the social phenomenon known as "Pachuco," a group that had existed before the zootsuit came into style.

During the period from 1940 to 1945, the dress of the Pachuco boys was, with little variation, a version of the zootsuit, though their own triple-sole shoes and ducktail haircuts were not widely adopted by zootsuiters in other areas. Tattooing and the wearing of chin hairs by some boys were also distinguishing marks. The tattooing, made with a common pin and india ink, seldom consisted of more than gang names, names of friends, or certain other marks having a cabalistic appearance which were usually a variation of the sign of the cross.

The girls wore their own style of dress, consisting of a long finger-tip coat or letterman's sweater, draped slacks or a short, full skirt above or just to their brown knees, high bobby socks, and huaraches or "Zombie" slippers. They usually made up heavily with mascara and lipstick, and the favorite hair style was a high pompadour with flowers and earrings. As important as the costume itself was the manner in which it was worn. A bravado and swagger accentuated the dark beauty of these girls. They had an impudence attractive to all males, light or dark. Many of these Pachuquitas were "little tornadoes of sexual stimuli, swishing and flouncing down the streets."

Law-enforcement officials have frequently mistaken the result for the cause in dealing with Pachucos. In 1943, after the zootsuit riots had temporarily welded all the neighborhood groups together and caused hundreds of youths who had never previously worn zootsuits to adopt them, the City Council passed a civic ordinance against the wearing of the costume. The action was as futile as was the earlier and more drastic action of a few police who had their own ideas on how to "get rid of those zootsuits." A sister of one of the boys who was "de-zooted" by the police, said, "You know, the cops ran in two wagons of boys from the dance hall last Saturday night. They were dancing in a hall with their girls. Well, one big old cop went upstairs and sent all the boys down the long steps. When they got to the bottom there were two more cops, one on each side of the door—they cut the drapes and finger-tip coats of the boys. They cut them and said, 'Well, it'll be a long time before you wear these again, you Mexican son-of-a-bitch.' "

                                    *   *   *   *   *

It is not difficult to understand why this type of dress came to mean to many boys and girls the difference between having or not having status in life. Their psychology was characteristically that of individuals who need to compensate for a tormenting sense of inferiority. And although to many the name "Pachuco" has come to be a term of scorn, it is a mark of distinction to the comparatively few *real* Pachucos, and they are proud of it.

In Los Angeles and in the neighboring settlements, there are many districts swarming with Mexican-American children who live in overcrowded shacks and tenements. These lively youngsters find their social life where they can make it. The hangout of a Pachuco group may be Mona's malt shop, the garage where Joe's Ford is jacked up, the grocery store where old Maria hands out neighborhood gossip, with pop and beer, or one of numerous liquor shops and beer joints and small restaurants in the neighborhood. Few Pachucos have anywhere but the street to go for their fun, unless it is to a movie or dance hall.

Other underprivileged boys and girls in the neighborhood tend to gravitate to this rather noisy and rebellious core. For, although the number of seriously maladjusted Pachuco youth is small, they associate with many hundreds of Mexican-American youth who are not delinquents, and most of them during 1944-45 chose to dress in Pachuco dress. It is a mistake, however, to speak of these neighborhood groups as gangs in the accepted sense of the term. The Pachuco groups have a loosely organized, amorphous, and highly individualistic membership. There is little of the group spirit of loyalty to a given leader that is commonly associated with gangs, and no one boy or girl can be *jefe* [chief] for long. The ganging process is in continuous flux, and though Bimbo may capture the volatile imaginations of the group for the evening, his leadership may well be superseded by that of Torro or Chuey the following night. The loose, unorganized character of these groups allows the leadership to change without otherwise disturbing their tight-knit intimacy. In the mercurial flow of neighborhood gang life in Los Angeles there are some fifty Mexican-American groups usually active. Their activity may be anything from athletic participation with other gangs from nearby districts to intensive feuding.

Why do Pachucos feud among themselves, often with violence, resulting in serious injuries and death? As one older boy explained it, "These kids are all full of animal mad. That's why they fight each other. They can't fight the cops or the *gabachos* [Americans], their enemies, so to get the mad from their blood they fight each other. Mad . . . mad . . . it's black and falling down that makes 'em hate the other guys. They got to fight something, you know how it is."

* * * * *

The results of gang fights are often very bloody. But considering the weapons at hand, it is doubtful that Mexican-American youth are more cruel than any other underprivileged and neglected youths under similar conditions. Most people are latently cruel, but are inhibited by education, public opinion, or religion. When these inhibitions are not present there are often brutal results.

In considering the life of the members of the Pachuco gangs it is important to recognize machismo. In any group of Pachucos the respect individual members have for each other is commensurate with the ability to "take it" and not "chicken out." For machismo represents the large male ego that every Mexican-American, young or old, is endowed with. Machismo makes a boy swear big round oaths as a youngster, join the paratroopers or marines when he is older, seek dangerous positions in battle, "drop" his girl on the dance floor if he has sufficient provocation, and take any and all dares.

In any hangout, or on school lawns, wherever you see a group of Mexican-American boys sitting or standing, sooner or later you will see evidence of trials of machismo. They will throw punches at one another, or whale each other up. They keep this up until the first boy drops, then he may get it by the whole group. All the boys then have the right to beat him up. If he "takes it," he is proving machismo; if he doesn't, it's just too bad. Cruelty of the group toward the weaker member or opponent is reinforced by their own inbred sense of personal honor and fearlessness in challenging any one who insults them.

The fraternity of gang spirit among underprivileged youngsters has the broad base of bad housing, poverty, economic and social discrimination, upon which to build. And so it is natural that boys and girls of other ancestry than Mexican are occasionally absorbed into Pachuco gangs. You find youths of Scotch-Irish Protestant, Jewish or Italian, Russian or Negro backgrounds who have learned to speak Spanish with Pachuco emphasis, wear the traditional Pachuco clothes and haircuts, and otherwise become lost in the group. For the natural play group of the neighborhood became maladjusted and these youngsters with it.

* * * * *

Counselors and group-recreation leaders of the Los Angeles Probation Department estimate that for every ten boys who are members of a neighborhood gang group, there are about three girls who are members. That is, three girls who are closely associated with them. The few girl gangs that sprang up at the time of the zootsuit riots were short-lived, however, and were never the problems the local newspapers tried to make them out to be. During the short time they were active these groups followed the patterns of the boy gangs in general.

There are a few groups of girls who hang around together now, but do not follow the patterns of even the most casual gang, except in that they seek each other's companionship, and lend clothes or money when necessary.

As for those *few* Pachuquitas who are in the core of the boys' gangs, their demoralization is often worse than that of the boys. But the majority, the hundreds of girls who dressed in the Pachuco style (when it was "hep" to do so) affected the dress in a spirit of adventure. They wanted to be considered "slick chicks . . . fine chicks," who were up to date and not old-fashioned. Occasionally they criticized the behavior of some of the delinquent Pachuquitas, saying, "They're tough. They're a real disgrace to the Pachuca style."

The question is often asked: what of those Mexican-American youngsters who did not wear the zootsuits even though they were in style? How were they accepted, and how did they react to the Pachuco youth? Those youngsters who were distinguished by their normal dress and behavior are as a rule better adjusted to the cultural conflict between their home and school. They are the ones who most frequently finish high school, and a few of them go to college. During the zootsuit fad they were called "Squares" by those who were considered "hep."

Many Squares looked down on Pachucos for the same reasons that the "Americans" and "upper class" Mexicans looked down on them: "They should be ashamed to be like that, they're a disgrace to the race." Since the Squares seldom made any pretense of hiding their superior attitude, the Pachucos came to resent and hate their "big shot" manner. "They think they're *gabachos* [Americans], such big shots!"

For the most part the Pachucos left the Squares alone, but sometimes the latter got "messed up" by talking about them in school, commenting on their drapes or giving them dirty looks. It is often difficult, however, for the Squares to resist the remarks of the Pachucos with equanimity. For those youngsters who did not make the grade, whose home life is a broken one, whose school record has been spotty (with increasingly longer periods of work absences and truancies), the sight of a boy going to school with books under his arm is sometimes too much to take.

"Look at the little boy going to school," or calls of "Teacher's pet!" will dog his heels. Unless he is smart, diplomatic, and has a "good attitude," coupled with a strong desire for education, he may not have sufficient courage to endure the taunts of the neighborhood. That's why the fellows say, "It's hard for a Square to live in a Pachuco neighborhood. But a Square doesn't have much trouble if he lives where he's not so alone if he's dressing as a Square and going to school."

Some of the Pachucos have delighted in persecuting the Squares unjustly. They also have taken real pleasure in breaking up parties given by these youths to which they were not invited. One boy who was determined to have a college education became, in the course of his school career, a community leader at a local recreation center. He was so persecuted by the Pachucos who nagged him, followed and beat him up, that he eventually had a nervous collapse: "The kids were all having a party for the club that won in basketball. Pretty soon some

Pachuco guys came and stood around the porch in the dark, blew smoke in the windows to be smart. A couple of the boys went outside to talk to the Pachucos, cause Squares aren't sissies, they can fight good too. But they got dropped quick. The Pachucos moved in real quick . . . one, two . . . punch or knife a guy, and they were gone in the dark. When Johnnie realized those Pachucos were after him he just fainted. Just for that, he was so scared. I don't know what he did to get them to hate him so much, but they wouldn't leave him alone . . . never. Finally he went nuts. Those Pachucos did it . . . they were to blame."

THE PREACHER OF VESEY STREET [16]

He came along Vesey Street, hatless, a rather young man walking rapidly with a Bible held open in his hands. Halfway down the block he halted abruptly, cast his eyes about him at the moving crowd, and then, with his back against the palings of the iron fence that shuts off St. Paul's churchyard from the clamor of the thoroughfare, he began to recite from the open book:

"Our text today, brethern, is from the sixtieth verse of the eighth chapter of First Kings:

"That all the people of the Earth may know that the Lord is God, and that there is none else. Let your heart therefore be perfect with the Lord our God, to walk in his statutes and to keep his commandments, as at this day.

*   *   *   *   *

"What are you doing to prepare for the day of Judgment? What are you doing to make yourself ready for that awful day when all bodies will be rendered unto dust and all souls stand bare before the searching eyes of God? I want to tell you, brothers. I want to tell you how to make ready for that day, to cleanse your souls against the final judgment so that when you face God at last in all his awful majesty you need not hang your heads. Come unto me—" He gave a sweeping, embracing gesture. "Come unto me and hear the Word! Pause in your pursuit of earthly pleasures and think for a moment of your immortal souls, black with sin. Halt one moment in your busy ways and think of all eternity, the endless future that lies before you. Are you ready to begin it now?"

. . . Holding the book still open, he delved into his pocket and brought out a stubby bit of chalk and bent to the pavement.

His arm swung in a great arc, and the chalk left a white circle. He drew a line bisecting the circle, and along this line he wrote the one word, "Death." Then well toward the top of the circle he wrote "God" and immediately under it "Salvation." In the bottom of the circle he printed, very carefully, "Devil," and under it, "Eternal Torture."

*   *   *   *   *

"Now, my friends—" He closed the Bible and thrust it into his pocket. "Now, my good friends, I want to have a little talk with you about the most important

[16] From *That's New York!* by Morris Markey and Johan Bull, pp. 126-132. Copyright, 1927, by Macy-Masius, Publishers. New York: Vanguard Press.

thing on earth: your immortal souls. You know, we sometimes forget about our souls, rushing around the way we do, thinking about that job we want, and that girl we think is pretty, and that fellow who is trying to get the best of us. I know. Just because I am a minister of God, just because I have heard the divine call to come out and spread the Gospel of Salvation, is no reason why I should be different from everybody else. I have had temptations, too, to forget about God and go dollar-chasing.

"Do you think I am doing this just to earn my living? No! I could be a millionaire, if I wanted to. I could be rich, if I wanted to forget God and spend my days toiling after money. But God is more important to me than worldly riches and worldly pleasures. God is life! And the Devil is death!

"Listen to me!" His voice suddenly grew violent and more than a little angry. "Listen to me, I say! There is no halfway measures about this business. You are either going to God or you are going to the Devil. You have got to go to one or the other, and you had better make up your minds now. Go on like you have been doing. Go on chasing dollars. Go on running after worldly pleasures. And you'll go to the Devil just as sure as you are living this moment.

"Turn away from me now. Deafen your ears to me and walk on down the street. It will seem that you are just walking down to Broadway there. But you are walking somewhere else, too. You are walking into the arms of the Devil, who is waiting to receive you with fire and horrible torture.

"I don't see anybody leaving! No, you are awake now, aren't you? You don't want to walk down to Broadway and have the Devil touch you on the shoulder, do you?

*   *   *   *   *

"Listen to me! You can't get to heaven by just sitting around and patting yourself on the shoulder and saying, 'I'm a good fellow.' The Devil is looking for good fellows, and there are a lot of them burning in hell right this minute. No, that isn't the way. The only way to get into heaven is to work every foot of the journey, with no other thought in your mind but the destiny of your eternal soul.

"You must think of God the moment that you rise up in the morning. You must think of God all day, every minute of every day. And you must pray often for God's pity upon your sinful soul. Live with God, my friends! It is the only way to save yourselves from tortures that are so terrible that you can't even imagine them.

"Do you ever think about hell?" He leaned down with a sudden movement and in the lower half of his circle wrote the word "Fire." "There is fire in hell, fire that will be burning when this old wicked world is blown to dust, when all the stars have stopped shining and all the universe is just one black space. It will burn your bodies, and never destroy them, and you will wail for help, but no help will come. God forgets the man who goes to hell!"

He wrote another word in the circle: "Thirst." "There never has been a drop of water in hell, and there never will be. You will roll in the endless flames and moan for water, just one drop of water. And nobody will hear you.

Your tongue will hang out, black and dry as a cinder. And the Devil will come around and ladle out melted lead to pour over it."

. . . He reached down with his chalk and wrote again: "Torture."

"Yes!" he shouted. "Torture! A thousand devils driving red-hot irons into your screaming flesh! And never getting tired of it. Every day—day after day—with never an end. That is hell! That is where you are headed, every one of you, because you are too busy to take a little time off for God.

"But God loves you, even if you are not worth it. 'After whom is the King of Israel come out? After whom dost thou pursue? After a dead dog, after a flea.'

"You are fleas and dead dogs in the sight of God, but he loves you still. And he comes out after you. He sends me out after you, to tell you the way to heaven. Give up your sinfulness. Come into the fold, where God will smile on you and you will shine in his great light.

"Ah, it is a wicked world, a foul world that is a stench in the nose of God. Join with me, my friends, and make it a better place. Make it give up its devilish ways and think only of God. And you will be happier than you ever knew. As happy as I am. And nobody is happier than I am. I know. . . . My clothes are not in the latest style. I don't wear silk shirts. . . . I haven't got a big bank account. But I am the happiest man on earth because I live in the glory of God.

"You can be happy too, happy as I am. But you must work with all your souls to do it."

He opened the Bible, and thrust it out under the faces of those who were closest to him.

"If there are any who would like to contribute to the spreading of God's word, it will be gratefully received," he said.

X. Bright Lights

As the rise of the city coincided with and stimulated the growth of the amusement industry, cities became the nation's amusement centers. In rapid succession and in competition with one another, new forms of entertainment came into being to provide new outlets for the city dweller's increased leisure as well as new antidotes for his increased nervous tension, resulting from monotonous routine and the accelerated pace and "rat race" of city living.

The demand was not only for more outdoor recreation (in the form of spectator sports like racing and baseball and of participation sports like bicycling and roller skating) but also for cheaper indoor diversions. Here new scientific discoveries and inventions came to the aid of the tired businessman, bored belles and beaux and also the common man in quest of inexpensive pleasure for the whole family.

Thus in 1848 laughing-gas entertainments were held with great success for a week in a St. Louis church, according to the *Missouri Republican* and Robert B. Weaver's *Amusements and Sports in American Life.*

Twenty or thirty ladies and gentlemen inhaled the gas each evening, and the entertainment was such that the audience was kept in an uproar of laughter during the entire exhibition. Sixty gallons of gas were prepared for each evening, and it was declared that it did not contain a particle of ether and could be respired frequently with great advantage to the general health.

But laughing gas was not destined to have as widespread an entertainment use as other laugh-and-thrill-producing innovations of science and technology. In April 1896 the first showing of Edison's vitascope was held at Koster & Bial's Music Hall at Thirty-fourth Street and Herald Square, New York. Burgeoning and spreading over the land in nickelodeons, the "world of motion" revolutionized the entertainment field. The first moving-picture theaters were makeshift arrangements in the back of penny arcades. The penny arcade ("Admission Free") was an earlier purveyor of mechanical entertainment in the form of coin machines, including the kinetoscope (a predecessor of the vitascope) and the mutoscope, or drop-picture machine, with its naughty views of artists' models in various stages of deshabille. Besides its peep shows and gramophones (with earplugs at the end of long tubes) and mechanical gypsy fortunetellers, the penny arcade also contained muscle-testing devices such as punching bags and weight-lifting machines, which catered to the new vogue for physical culture.

While the humble store nickelodeon has given way to the movie palace, the penny arcade, with the addition of the pinball machine, still lingers in the amusement parks and amusement centers of the cities. Along with shooting galleries, soft-drink, hot-dog and popcorn stands, the arcade has even invaded Forty-second Street and Broadway since Times Square has gone honky-tonk.

The Coney Island atmosphere of city amusement centers has its origin in the Bowery, which was the gay and wicked big city's first street of pleasure. Alongside the more raffish dens and dives, the dime museum (which with the circus and the minstrel show was one of the progenitors of variety and vaudeville) had its original home on the Bowery. This is how Roy L. McCardell remembers the fakes and freaks of the Bowery dime museums—"When the Bowery Was in Bloom":

They were all arranged alike, with three floors of attractions and entertainments. The patrons paid their dimes and went up to the top floor, or curio hall, first. Here were mummy mermaids, stuffed alligators, doubtful antiques, crude waxwork figures of celebrities and famous murderers, tableaux of a condemned man in the electric chair, the Downward Path or How Girls Go Wrong, and the like.

Here the lecture began on the even hour, every hour. The crowd followed the lecturer to the floor below—the Hall of Human Curiosities. Here on platforms would be Madame Rosa, the bearded lady; Big Hannah, the fat woman; Billy Wells, the iron-skull man; George, the turtle boy; Jonathan Bass, the petrified man; Laloo, the Hindu Marvel; the Murray Midget Triplets; Eli Bowen, the armless wonder; the India-Rubber Boy; Jo-Jo, the Dog-faced Man; Zip, the What Is It, and so on.

There might also be glass spinners, making and selling their brittle souvenirs; exhibitionists such as Swipes the Newsboy; Steve Brodie, the Bridge Jumper Daredevil; and Bosco, the Snake Eater. All these, the lecturer announced repeatedly, would answer all proper questions, and had, he believed, their photographs for sale. Why this was only a matter of belief it is hard to say, for at the feet of each was a dozen or more of their graphic likenesses.

The lecturer would make his spiel before each living exhibit in turn, and like Silas Wegg, he would invariably close with this lyrical epilogue:

> Now you've seen our wonder wares,
> Next is the big show given downstairs.
> You'll see a drama most intense,
> The seats they'll cost you but five cents.
> Our star has long been known to fame;
> Fanny Herring is her name!
> Yes, Fanny Herring gives below
> A drama laid in O-hi-O.
> As the heroine she'll thwart her foes,
> Shoot the villain and goodness knows
> She'll prove her lover guiltless of crime—
> Remember, a seat costs but half a dime!

From the beginning the amusement industry ran afoul of Sunday closing and other Blue Laws and censorship. Though the saloon and the dance hall were the chief targets of crusaders and vice hunters, spicy vaudeville and bawdy burlesque also made work for the censors. The pre-eminence of New York as an amusement center and its attraction for tourists and sightseers had an equal and opposite reaction in what Benjamin de Casseres calls the "National New York complex"—the Puritanic and provincial resentment of the metropolis as a modern Babylon.

New York has always been the playground of the nation. The submerged Rabelais of the small town has always come to New York to get the air. Rural deacons and school teachers have visited the city for what William James called a "moral holiday." Every day is a Philadelphia Sunday in the Middle West and South. In New York every day used to be a Saturday night.

Sub rosa, rural America always wanted New York "wide open," no matter what happened "back ter home." . . .

Those who were fortunate enough "to take a flyer" in the life of gay New York went back home with radiant faces and tales of delectable pleasures. Those who listened to them grew sea-green with envy and malice. New York ought to be closed—it was a crying iniquity! It was a place where people really "lived"—therefore it was a scarlet sin and a magenta shame.

With the coming of Prohibition, the Jazz Age and the post-war boom, cities went on a new binge, hell-bent for pleasure and excitement, plus the added thrill of the illicit. On the eve of the stock-market crash, Walter Donaldson's "Making Whoopee" (1928) became the theme song of the Twenties. "A visitor spending freely in a night club, a farmer on a 'tear' in the city, a husband on the loose, a politician starting an insurgent movement, a banker banking recklessly, a businessman imprudently expanding —all were 'makin' whoopee.' " An earlier song, "The Big Butter and Egg Man" (1924), made the "big butter and egg man from the West," synonymous with the sucker or free spender—the inspiration of another catchword of the night club era, Texas Guinan's "Hello, Sucker!"

"Anything that concerns Greenwich Village also tickles the [National New York] complex," writes Benjamin de Casseres. In its first phase, 1910-1917, the Village attracted provincial youth and talent in revolt against social and artistic conventions and became the mecca of the Bohemian and the radical, in pursuit of happiness, the arts and social justice. With Prohibition the Village was invaded by out-of-town and "Uptown swillage" in search of "thrillage" and "distillage." Free spending and free drinking, "ginmills and love nests," inflating real estate values, dealt a death blow to the Bohemia of free speech and free thinking. And although it continued to attract talent, the Village became a tourist spot with the usual tourist bait of quaint shops and tea rooms, "atmosphere" and "interesting" characters. In thus cultivating and exploiting its Bohemian myth, the Village imitated the provincial cities (usually accused of imitating New York), which, combining business profit and tourist pleasure, have exploited their own local myths in the form of local color and local festivals.

As it accelerated, syncopated and jazzed up the tempo of modern living (New York to Jimmy Durante was "like a big band playin' all the time"), the city naturally fell into step with the music of the twentieth century— ragtime and jazz. The city was the birthplace and home of jazz. And the term *jazz*, implying what Sigmund Spaeth calls the "unnatural excitement and deliberate distortion characteristic of the jazz treatment in general and by no means limited to music itself," became, by the same token, the rhythm of the city—a synonym for its sin and pleasure and an epithet to describe modern metropolitan architecture and the urban way of life.

"GOING ON ALL THE TIME" [1]

"W-e-l-l, *well*, good peepul, there's *plenty* of time, plenty of time, before the large show is open. While you have time, money and oppahtunity, pass on the inside and see the wondahful monstrosities therein contained.

[1] From *Here We Are Again,* Recollections of an Old Circus Clown, by Robert Edmund Sherwood, pp. 139-140. Copyright, 1926, by The Bobbs-Merrill Company, Inc. Indianapolis and New York.

They're a-l-l heah: the long peepul, the short peepul, the fat peepul and the lean peepul for one dime—ten cents, if you wish to see them. Going on all the time; continuous performance—nevah out, nevah ovah. See what the world contains beside yourself—see it all to-day. Recollect this canvas will be torn down, packed up and carried away to the cyahs, long before the show in the large top is ovah—see it all now. Everything on the inside *ex-act-ly* as represented on the outside. Come *o-n*, good peepul, the small sum of a dime—ten cents, the tenth part of a dollah."

SCOLLAY SQUARE [2]

They say that Scollay Square is known all over the world.

They say that when two ships pass each other in the middle of the Atlantic they signal across the intervening water, and the wigwags, decoded, read "How are things on Scollay Square?"

They say that American Marines, fighting Japs and jungle and malaria and flies and more Japs on a stinking island in the Pacific, set up a signpost in their bivouac, "Scollay Square."

They say. . . .

The Boston mother, watching her little girl grow up, develop breasts, put on lipstick, waggle her hips, cries distractedly, "Do you want to end up on Scollay Square?"

The high school boy, playing hooky with his pal, grins self-consciously and whispers, "Want to go down to Scollay Square?"

And the Harvard boy, arriving from the Middle West for his first college semester with the legend of the Square ringing in his ears, strolls along thinking, "So this is Scollay Square," and feels vaguely cheated. . . .

Scollay Square is one short block in the twisted maze of Boston streets. But it is an important block. Think of it as the center point on a compass. The needle points east toward Tremont Street, gateway to the narrow, crowded "downtown" district. Now the needle swings southward across the historic green of Boston Common up to the crumbling brick and crumbling tradition of Beacon Hill, home of the Boston legend, the broad "a," the Harvard accent. The needle continues to circle toward the west down through the lower Beacon Hill, disputed no man's land, neither genteel nor slum, where renovated high-rental apartment buildings lean up against unheated, cold-water tenements, sharing rats and roaches indiscriminately. Old Yankee names are scribbled next to Irish, Jewish, and Polish names above the doorbells.

The needle journeys downward across the traffic of Cambridge Street into the West End, where all signs of old Boston end. Kosher butcher shops do a thriving business next to equally thriving Italian groceries. Children are everywhere, spilling out of doorways, dodging from behind ice trucks. Baby carriages crowd pedestrians off the narrow sidewalks. Here and there a house is boarded up—condemned—too rickety, unsanitary, vermin infested for even its lax standards. Schools stand empty, abandoned; schoolyards are padlocked. The parochial schools are taking over.

The needle points north now, almost completing the circle. Unlike the West End with its heterogeneous population, the North End is undisputedly Italian. Pizza palaces, spaghetti houses, and pastry shops. Overcrowded tenements, hall toilets, and garlic. Boys of all ages play the popular finger games, cries of "Uno . . . Cinque . . . Sette" crackling through their lips with pistol-like rapidity. And in the midst of it, the market district, with Faneuil Hall now just some brick and a spire above the market stalls. On Saturday afternoons the streets present a double row of horses, their wagons backed against the sidewalks, whence fruit and vegetables can be bought at bargain prices. Meats, cooked delicacies, pickles and olives are on display on outside counters along the store fronts.

And then the needle completes its circuit through the financial district back to Tremont Street. Downtown, Beacon Hill, West End, North End—all are but a few minutes walk from Scollay Square.

But Scollay Square is more than a geographical location.

There are very few buildings which actually comprise the Square. A tavern, two movie houses, a sandwich bar, a liquor store, a penny arcade, a cafeteria, a drugstore. . . . And across the street some more of the same, plus a few cafés where you can order a drink and see the floor show.

But Scollay Square is more than a row of buildings. It extends beyond its physical boundaries. How about the cafés on adjoining streets and side streets? How about Joe and Nemo's, whose address, strictly speaking, is Cambridge Street? To deny that they are actually part of Scollay Square is to deny them existence.

What, then, is Scollay Square? Ask any sailor whose ship lays up in the Boston Navy Yard. Ask the girls who gravitate toward it night after night. Ask the rum-dum, the bookie, the horse player, the whore. Ask the Shore Patrol and the police officers of Station 3.

Scollay Square is a mood, a rhythm. It builds up gradually through the day, from the slow shuffling tempo of the broken down drunk, the lazy talk of the horse fans studying the racing forms, the bookies with their Armstrongs, noting odds, jotting down figures, to the first provocative wiggle of the first hopeful girl emerging from the subway stairs at dusk. From there on the tempo takes on momentum. More girls spill out of the subway. Sailors converge on the Square on foot, by subway, by taxi. Music blares out and is silenced as doors open and close. The Shore Patrol lounges against buildings, arms crossed, wary, watchful. Policemen patrol the street. Groups mingle, exchange words and break up again, this time in twos. Fights break out and are quickly ended. Obscenities punctuate conversations, sometimes in a derisive male voice, sometimes a shrill female voice. Couples press up against buildings, getting acquainted tactually, mouths, hands and thighs making quick contact. A girl cries suddenly, unexpectedly, unexplainedly. A sailor sways through a swinging door and pukes over the curbstone. A heavily rouged, slack-breasted frump offers her wares.

The rhythm builds up to the grand finale at midnight when the doors open wide, spitting their customers into the street. That's when the Shore Patrol gets busy. That's when the real fights start. All that went before is preliminary to this, the main business of the evening, the final shuffling and reshuffling of man and girl so it all comes out even. Two girls fight over a sailor. Two sailors fight over a girl. Taxis pull up and pull away, carrying couples and foursomes and sixsomes, the girls laughing and shrieking as hands reach for them and draw them close.

Slowly the Square settles down to early morning quiet. Here and there the murmur of voices or a giggle from a doorway where two people strain toward each other, pressing harder against the walls, shutting out the passers-by, shutting out the street lights by the intensity of their need.

And the rest of those who met and drank and bantered and swore and kissed and rubbed bodies on Scollay Square? Where have they gone? Off in taxis to crummy hotels. Around this corner or that, to cheap rooming houses on dark streets. Or around to the Common where the ground is hard but free, and recumbent figures blend into the shadows of the trees. For there are no "houses" on Scollay Square. It is not a bordello. Rather it is the pimp, the procurer, the go-between. It brings the girls to the men and the men to the girls. The rest is up to them. Scollay has done its part. They take it from there.

"DOWN IN DEAR OLD GREENWICH VILLAGE" [3]

Bobby Edwards was "King of Greenwich Village" (reign: 1913-1918) and self-appointed president of the Crazy Cat Club. Through his extemporaneous songs Bobby got most of the things he wanted. He sang for his supper on many an occasion, sang for his wine and his women, sang himself onto the stage and the lecture platform, sang himself into the editorship of a Village magazine.

The first home of the Crazy Cat Club was with Enrico and Paglieri's on West Eleventh Street. "I talked to the proprietor about using his joint," Bobby relates, "but he was a tough egg. So I hauls out my uke, and I gives him a song right there on the pavement. He claps his hands. . . . 'Come on in! Bring 'em all in!' The fella knew what was good for his business. Later on, when we had the Black Cat, we made dough for that outfit too. The socialites from uptown and the stage people from Broadway flocked to our hangout to watch us cut up, and of course it never hurt the cash register any. . . ."

Why Bobby chose New York's Greenwich Village for his stamping ground after leaving Harvard in 1911 is something he can't quite explain to himself. Perhaps it was the same urge that prompted others whom he found there and whose names soon invaded the art and literary columns of the Press from Maine to California: Sinclair Lewis, Hendrick Willem Van Loon, Theodore Dreiser, Eugene O'Neill, Floyd Dell, Susan Glaspell, Ruth St. Denis, Mary Heaton Vorse, Rose O'Neill, Edna St. Vincent Millay, Harry Kemp, John Reed, and many others.

[3] From "Last of the Minstrels," by May Swenson. Manuscripts of the Federal Writers' Project of the Works Progress Administration in New York City, 1938. Deposited in the Village Folklore Section, Library of Congress, Washington, D.C.

The Crazy Cats experimented with everything—with dress, life, art, and even food. They tried to break all conventions at once. Many of them came from cruel small towns where no one had any freedom, and their pent-up souls busted loose. The women wore togas made of portieres and the men discarded stockings and neckties.

"Don't make the mistake," Bobby says, on this score, "of thinking that all these people came to the Village because they *wanted* to be writers or painters—a good many of them were already on their way—most of them came to the Village because they wanted to be free. Rose O'Neill and Mary Vorse had formed, or been instrumental in forming, a sort of colony of free-thinkers, and the guys and gals who had talent or a brain or two in their heads naturally found their way to the one place outside of Paris where they could forget convention—or so they thought—and concentrate on what they called 'creation.'

" 'Course, Red Lewis came expressly because he wanted to become a writer—and he did. Floyd Dell and Bodenheim hadn't either of them done anything yet to make the world sit up when they settled in the Village. Then when Paris closed down on account of the War, many of the Arty Set from there began drifting over, 'cause there was no place else for an exhibitionist to go. It was the Provincetown Players that were responsible for O'Neill's getting a leg up. He was in the Village at the time the Players organized, and they produced one of his first short plays."

Anyway, Bobby tells us, when he and his ukelele hit New York after four years at Harvard, he discovered that he was lonely. So he decided to form a club. He elected himself president, then sent out post cards to friends in art circles and to people whom he knew only by name, but wanted to meet as fellow artists. The purpose of the Crazy Cat Club was "to admire the President," and those who answered the invitations and collected at the appointed cafe (Enrico and Paglieri's) made their salaams to the tall, shy-looking young man seated on a table top, cradling a ukelele, heard him sing and play—and somehow they stayed.

"All the so-called Bohemians were glad any time for a chance and a place to peddle their 'ideas'—sit around a table and talk. No one ever listened to anybody else, of course. Everybody talked and nobody listened except to himself. It was great! My first songs I wrote in the Village were to annoy people, shock them into listening to me sing. And, you know, I discovered people liked being shocked. I became the fashion. I'd try out my rhymes on friends at cafe tables. If they didn't go over, I improvised till I got a laugh, and then rewrote. As I said, no Villager ever really listened to me, so I never got what you'd call real criticism. But then a snort can express much.

"Another thing. I always tried to make my songs as difficult as possible. I used up all the rhymes, so that they couldn't be added to or be improved upon. So you see, I deliberately frustrated what might have become a field for a genuine growth of folk songs. Sometimes, though, Harry Kemp or somebody would add a verse or two and burst out with it when I got through, and, well, if it was good enough, I'd keep it and use it. But most of the time what the others wanted to add was *too* good, and would have to be deleted out when we sang for the public."

Down in Greenwich Village was a product of the mass Bohemian mind, however, Bobby admits. And this ballad became one of the most popular among outsiders who frequented Village night clubs, as well as the Villagers themselves. Its many stanzas were pieced together after numerous improvisations at Polly's and The Black Cat.

Way down South in Greenwich Village,
That's the field for culture's tillage.
There they have artistic ravings,
Tea and other awful cravings.
But there the inspiration stops
And they start silly little shops.
You'll find them anywhere
Round Washington Square.

Down in dear old Greenwich Village,
There they wear no fancy frillage,
For the ladies of the Square
All wear smocks and bob their hair.
There they do not think it shocking
To wear stencils for a stocking.
That saves laundry bills
In Washington Square.

Tune notated by Helen Ramsey, in *More Pious Friends and Drunken Companions*, collected by Frank Shay (New York, The Macaulay Co., 1928), pp. 37-38.

Way down South in Greenwich Village
Where the spinsters come for thrillage,
There they practise sex relations
With the sordid Slavic nations.
'Neath the guise of feminism,
Dodging social ostracism,
They get away with much
In Washington Square.

Way down South in Greenwich Village
Where they all consume distillage,
Where the fashion illustrators
Flirt with interior decorators,
There the cheap Bohemian fakirs
And the boys from Wanamaker's
Gather "atmosphere"
In Washington Square.

Way down South in Greenwich Village
Where the brains amount to nillage
Where the girls are unconventional
And the men are unintentional,
There the girls are self-supporting,
There the ladies do the courting,
The ladies buy the "eats"
In Washington Square.

Way down South in Greenwich Village
Comes a bunch of Uptown Swillage.
Folks from Lenox Subway Stations
Come with lurid expectations.
There the Village informalities
Are construed as abnormalities
By the boobs that visit
Sheridan Square.

The "Uptown Swillage" which Edwards took such delight in satirizing in his songs were not the least of those instrumental in the development of his career, for many of them boasted bank accounts and social prestige. Their influence was indirect, inasmuch, as Bobby maintains, and his close acquaintances bear him up in this, as he consistently refused to stoop to retrieve their ten dollar and twenty dollar greenbacks, which in those inflated years during and immediately after the War would flutter at his feet at the end of an extemporaneous performance with his ukelele in the Village clubs. But contact with the "boobs from Uptown" got him a name as an illustrator when he had a studio on Fifty-fifth Street, and earned him many an appointment with fair and wealthy socialites, as portrait artist, when later he established himself as photographer at 46 Washington Square, calling his place Studio of Bobby Edwards. Before and after coming to New York, Edwards had, however, already a name as artist in his own right, having done illustrations for the *Saturday Evening Post* for ten years. Later, when his songs were collected and published with scores, he illustrated them all with engaging and appropriate cartoons.

A man with an amazing variety of skills, he soon began designing and constructing string instruments, and his oddly shaped ukeleles, whimsically painted and decorated by himself, found a wide sale.

It was through personal diligence therefore, and not by any means wholly through the minstrel's knack of wheedling money and favors from his audience, that Bobby acquired the reputation (it was after all largely reputation) of being the only artist with money in the Village.

He did own an apartment and studio with that rare luxury, a bathroom, and it was this distinction, rather than his tall good looks or his "wealth" which was responsible for his Monarchy in the Village.

"Everybody used to come up to my place to use the bathroom," he relates. "Especially the women. I don't know why, but my studio was always full of women. They'd be piled knee-deep on the landing when I'd get home— waiting for me to unlock the door. It was not one, but dozens of these lady bums who finally drove me to retaliate with the song about Lizzy Mossbasket, 'The Peril of Sheridan Square.'

"Those creatures were funny but awful, if you had to put up with them. I guess there are plenty of the type still chiseling around the Village. If you once let 'em get one foot in the door, you'd have to bed 'em and board 'em, or else——Those charming little leeches would do anything to get at your pocket book. After 'Lizzy Mossbasket' became popular, eight of them turned up and presented charges of slander. Each took the ditty as a personal insult.

"Lizzy wasn't invented, nor was she drawn from a single model. There were plenty of Lizzies—she's a type, not a person. We used to have fun choosing names to characterize some of the girlies—Tessie Hipflicker, Annie Bedmusser, Lena Bustimensa—and then we'd build a song or verse around them, or later on when I had *The Quill,* include them, with their antics, in the society columns."

> I know a girl I'd like to hurl
>   Into the river one day.
> You may think me crude when I allude
>   To any lady this way.
> But she's a pest. We get no rest
>   From her nagging for lodging and food,
> And when I resist, then she'll insist
>   That my reluctance is rude.

Chorus:

> For she's the belle of Hubert's Cafeteria,
> Down in Sheridan Square
> Where the nuts and the bums with their sex hysteria
> Patiently give her the air.
> She hasn't a home, no place of her own.
>   She domiciles anywhere.
> And her name, if you ask it, is Lizzie Mossbasket,
>   The Peril of Sheridan Square.

> This Village Queen—Lizzie, I mean—
>   Went into Hubert's to feed.
> But there she found, hanging around,

Others in desperate need.
She hoped to mash some bird with cash,
To pay for the food that she'd et,
But somehow I guess, she had little success
For the poor thing is sitting there yet.

The Peril of Sheridan Square

Words & music by Robert Edwards

Copyright 1933 by Robert Edwards

THE "MAYOR" OF BROADWAY [4]

To most people, Broadway is the name of New York's brilliantly illuminated main drag, one of the longest and most glamorous streets in the world, a symbol of the entertainment business. But to a relatively small, well-heeled, wisecracking, highly publicized group of men and women, Broadway is more than a street. It is a state of mind and a way of life. The group is made up of columnists, actors and actresses, singers, dancers, athletes, bookmakers, politicians and gangsters, and, inevitably, hangers-on, and it comprises a society that would dumbfound an anthropologist, who conceivably might go crazy trying to define its customs, moral structure, and standards for admission.

. . . Its headquarters are a group of restaurants—the twentieth-century counterparts of seventeenth-century grog shops—most of which, oddly enough, are not even located on Broadway proper. Its "mayor" is a man named George Solotaire . . . known to his friends as "Gentleman George," a nickname bestowed upon him by Earl Wilson. . . . He is not a celebrity in the usual sense, but many near-celebrities would pay handsome sums to get their names in the columns as frequently as his appears. He is as much a part of the Broadway scene as the nude man and woman who flank the waterfall on the huge Bond Clothes sign, although he antedates them by more than a quarter-century.

. . . He is one of the most prosperous ticket brokers in the business, a man who generally can be depended upon to dig up a pair to the current big hit when nobody else can. [And] he has a well-nigh perfect record as a prognosticator of the commercial success of Broadway shows.

There is [another] reason for Solotaire's fame in his natural habitat. The Broadway mob prizes an ability to kiss off any situation with an apt, funny remark second only to an ability to make a fast comeback to same. It also has a high regard for murderers of the mother tongue. Solotaire is a past master at repartee and word-coinage. Walter Winchell has called him a modern Wilson Mizner, referring, of course, to the japester of a generation ago who, upon hearing that Calvin Coolidge was dead, inquired, "How do they know?"

Winchell likes to tell of the time that he, Solotaire, and Oscar Levant were vacationing at the Saxony Hotel in Miami. William Saxon, the owner, told them that he'd received complaints from patrons who had been annoyed by Levant's practicing the piano in his room.

"Isn't that ridiculous?" Solotaire demanded. "There're people in this hotel who make more noise when they eat!"

*   *   *   *   *

One night when Solotaire was sitting with Levant, the latter, undisputed unhappiness champion of the Broadway crowd, talked for nearly an hour

[4] From "The Mayor of Broadway," by Richard B. Gehman, *Park East, The Magazine of New York,* Vol. 12 (September, 1952), No. 9, pp. 18-20. Copyright, 1952, by Park Magazine, Inc. New York.

about his physical and emotional complaints. Later a friend asked Solotaire how he managed to put up with such a recital of agony.

"Easy," he said, "I just keep him faded with grunts."

Leonard Lyons once asked Solotaire's opinion of a certain girl. "She looks like frayed curtains and she's got a profile like a bunch of keys," Solotaire said. On another occasion he described a gossipy woman thus: "She's got a long playing tongue."

*   *   *   *   *

Solotaire is physiologically incapable of uttering a simple declarative in ordinary English. He would never describe himself as being at dinner; instead, he would say, "I'm caught right in the middle of the food-way." When an acquaintance utters an unkind word about another, Solotaire says, "He's going to Knockville." Similarly, when a man and wife separate, he declares them "in Splitsville." A bad play is a "real rank stiff." A man alone is "single-o." A restaurant check is "the map."

If a sustained speech by Solotaire ever were written down and placed in a time capsule, it would keep linguists of the future busy for decades trying to determine what manner of dialect he used. One night Louis Sobol joined Solotaire and some friends and was asked how he felt. "Not bad, not bad at all," he replied. Solotaire gazed at him speculatively for several seconds, then began to speak.

"I'm glad to hear it," he said. "I wouldn't say you look it, chum, but you must be close to Radio City. Me, I'm still with blood—just about past Dinty Moore's, but I feel like when I was around the Flatiron. Feel that arm," he urged, extending it across the table. "Well, we all get to Oldsville sooner or later. I said to DiMag—I call him Doughmag now—you ain't gettin' any younger, chum—stash the etchings away. But no one has to tell Doughmag nothin' about hideaways for his Madisons, Clevelands, and Franklins, and don't think I mean he's got glue on his palms. When it comes to pickin' up the duke, he's a fast man on the draw—no fumblin', and what I like about it, he don't squint the tab and become a mathematical genius." Solotaire paused. "Well, excuse me, I gotta rustle up a couple shovels for The Gold Mine. Then I thought I'd check in at the Bird and see if W.W. or O.L. showed up yet. O.L. was in Nicky's with the graums last night, and I thought I'd hit him with the laugh-way."

Incomprehensible though this speech might have been to an outsider, or even to Dr. David W. Maurer, the University of Louisville's eminent slang-hunter, it was perfectly clear to Sobol and the others. In translation, all Solotaire was saying was:

"You must be close to fifty (*Radio City is at 50th Street in New York*). Me, I'm still young—just past forty-six (*Dinty Moore's restaurant is at 46th Street*), but feel like I was twenty-three (*Flatiron Building is at 23rd*). Well, we're all getting older. I said to Joe DiMaggio, you aren't getting any younger, so save your money. But nobody has to tell him about saving his $5,000, $1,000, and $100 bills, although he isn't stingy. When it comes to picking up the check, he reaches first, and he doesn't scrutinize the figures and add them. Well, excuse me, I've got to see if I can locate a pair of tickets for *South Pacific*. Then I thought I would go to the Stork Club and see if Walter Winchell or Oscar Levant are around. Oscar was in Blair House last night feeling blue, and I thought I might try to cheer him up."

HARLEM HOUSE-RENT PARTIES [5]

Negroes mostly sought their entertainment at house-rent parties, a distinctly Harlem innovation that became the vogue in other Black Belts of the country. Saturday night was the big night. Thursday night also was a favorite—"sleep-in" domestic workers usually had time off and were free to pitch and carry-on but found their small salaries inadequate for cabarets. Usually admission to house-rent parties was fifteen cents. What was spent once inside was another matter. A small bare room with a red glow for light served as the "ballroom," where the strenuous business of rug-cuttin' was performed. The only furniture was a piano from which a "box-beater" extracted close harmonies and "jump rhythms," or "gut-bucket," which is now called boogie-woogie. In the kitchen pots of chitterlings and pigs' feet stood ready for the hungry revelers. A jug of corn was a staple for such affairs, sold at a makeshift bar in the hallway in half-of-a-half-pint portions—called "shorties." Then there would be goings-on until daybreak, and rent next day for the landlord.

House-rent parties attracted a large transient trade, such as Pullman porters, interstate truck drivers, servants of footloose white folks, and innocent Negro tourists to the Black Metropolis. Additional business was promoted among that army of people who crowded the streets at night, seeking adventure and companionship in preference to remaining in dingy and ill-ventilated rooms. They found their way to these get-togethers through little business cards which were distributed by the "madams" to drum up trade. Only colored people were handed these "invitations," for during Prohibition any white face might be that of an enforcement agent; and moreover, the local police appeared more diligent in raiding these places, sometimes called "Buffet Flats," than known gin mills, or speakeasies, which flourished on almost every street corner. Here is a typical bit of doggerel sales talk:

> There'll be brownskin mamas,
>   High yallers too,
> And if you ain't got nothin' to do
>   Come on up to Mary Lou's.
>
> There'll be plenty of pig feet
>   And lots of gin;
> Jus' ring the bell
>   An' come on in.

[5] From *"New World A-Coming,"* Inside Black America, by Roi Ottley, pp. 63-64. Copyright, 1943, by Roi Ottley. Boston: Houghton Mifflin Company.

"TRY YOUR SKILL, FOLKS!" [6]

Since more than half of the five hundred separate business establishments in the resort part of modern Coney Island served food or drink in some form, visitors usually propitiated the inner man, woman or child before trying anything else. Concessionaires believed firmly that no visitor became pliable, and playful, until he had absorbed at least a hot dog and a glass of beer. Then for the first time he seemed to respond to the barker who had been yelling right along: "Try your skill, folks. Step right up. Here y'ar, folks. Three balls for a dime. Try your skill, folks, step right up."

After preliminary munches and gulps, the crowd proceeded to waste millions of nickels and dimes on more or less trashy diversions—ranging from weight-guessing to fortune-telling—which might be classed together as games. Generally they wanted to show off or to win something. Any game, therefore, that managed to combine both exhibitionism and gambling had a good chance of success.

As in the case of rides, shows and even refreshments, games changed from year to year according to the public taste and standard of expenditure. Weight-guessing once was quite hazardous. A comely woman approaching a scale back in the sporting days of the resort got touched on areas then considered rather intimate, but she could hardly object to scientific appraisal. Some hussies were suspected of using the scales for personal advertising. A prosperous-looking man would be tapped first on the hip, then on the breast, and finally on the sides. A signal from the guesser to a thief lurking nearby would indicate the location of the wallet, which could be removed after the man returned to

[6] From *Sodom by the Sea*, An Affectionate History of Coney Island, by Oliver Pilat and Jo Ranson, pp. 256-261. Copyright, 1941, by Oliver Pilat and Jo Ranson. Garden City, New York: Doubleday & Company, Inc.

the crowd. From their tip-off share of such proceeds some of Coney's more expert tappers earned as much as $7,000 a season.

Tapping went out of style when detectives began to stalk pickpockets at the seaside scales. Use of the hands was never really necessary. After a little practice, almost anybody could guess weight by eye alone. Modern guessers kept away from the bodies of customers but reached for their minds with a banal but shrewd sort of persiflage.

Dowdy matrons were addressed as "young lady." Adolescents on the fringe of the crowd were hailed as "that young fellow with the broad shoulders" or "the pretty girl with the green dress." Any unusually heavy or slim individual with an easy-going manner served for ballyhoo. "You must have a good boardinghouse," was the opening remark to Heavy, or "You drink plenty of beer, all right," or "No depression in your home, I see." With Slim, conversational gambits might be: "Don't you eat?" or "Say, does your wife eat first?"

Sometimes a guesser would underestimate a heavyweight and correct himself, to draw a scowling: "Why don't you stick to your first guess?" The crowd would whoop at his retort: "My dear sir, my first guess was only half of you!" Where such tactics failed, the guesser could select an egoist, whose face would shine with such satisfaction over winning a cane or a cheap box of candy (after the guesser had missed deliberately) that others would step forward.

One weight-guesser might make $20 a week, and another $40 in adjoining locations on the Coney Island Bowery, so greatly did revenue depend on effectiveness of patter. Lured into showing off or hoping for a prize, thousands of visitors paid dimes daily at the scales to be told what they already knew, whereas women on a reducing diet, or men trying to regain weight after liver trouble—who genuinely needed the information—would pay no more than a penny on any scale.

The most modern type of guesser at Coney Island dealt in years rather than in pounds. Unlike the weight-guesser, who bellowed loud enough for fishermen off Cholera Bank to hear, the guess-your-age expert glanced quietly at eyes and hands, then wrote a number on a piece of paper shown only to the customer. Such silent procedure gave no encouragement to exhibitionism. Then why should any one pay a dime to learn his own age? Apparently many persons thought they had an unusually good chance to fool the guesser. They were wrong; no more prizes were distributed at this game than any other.

Show-offs always flocked to the high-strikers and the shooting galleries. Where else could a man prove his muscle more magnificently than at the high-striker? Each time the weight of a well-swung sledge hammer sent a holed metal disk whizzing up the fifty-foot wire, a new hero was born. When the disk rang the bell at the very top of the scale, there used to be a pay-off in cigars, but cigars were replaced gradually by kewpie dolls and small boxes of chocolates, which enabled the hero to make an additional grandstand play by passing them on to a female companion.

Comparatively small or weak men with a good sense of timing could give a creditable performance on the high-striker. They were pretty sure to surpass the girls, for girls were tactful in such matters. Even the sting of a poor showing vanished quickly amid the laughter stirred by the whimsical measurements of strength on the scale. Down low would be Cake eater and Crooner, and toward the top, Aviator, Boilermaker, and Champ. In between—though no two high-strikers could agree on the time of day—there might be Office Boy, Pants Presser, He Works in a Bank, Pen Pusher, Crap Shooter, In Love, Hot-dog Eater, Taxi Driver, Beer Drinker, Piano Mover, Soldier, Sailor, Marine, and in recent years, WPA Worker. The standard price was two wallops for a nickel, five for a dime.

Operators of shooting galleries at Coney Island knew very well that their chief attraction for men was the chance to pose as a hunter or warrior. Customers enjoyed noise and smoke; the last thing they wanted was smokeless powder; the louder the report of the gun, the better. At some galleries large birds fell against a steel plate with such clatter that marksmen believed blissfully that they had smashed them to smithereens. This happened not to be true; the birds crashed all over again for the next customer. There was an element of skill involved in shooting, but skill wasn't essential to enjoyment of the range. A man could pretend to himself that he was J. Edgar Hoover sighting a public enemy or a soldier winning a cross for bravery. What though the gunload emptied without a ping on a pendulum? His girl still thrilled over his warlike stance.

International events always added a few newsworthy items to such normal targets as ducks, whales, bears, tigers, deer, lions, rabbits, elephants, Indians in canoes, submarines, torpedo boats and battleships. During the Spanish-American War stay-at-homes gloried in the opportunity to shoot General Weyler and other Spanish leaders—from the safety of a shooting-gallery counter. As for the soldiers, they were persuaded to buy buttons on which their pictures were pasted. "Your last chance," the barker would yell, shoving a sample into the face of the wearer of the blue. "You're going to Cuba and you'll probably get shot. It is only ten cents, and it is something your girl will have to remember you by, when you're gone." Surprisingly enough, many soldiers made the investment. They and the civilians in the clutch of the war fever cheered raucously when Coney Island's only Japanese female juggler drew a Spanish flag from a box, trampled it underfoot and then waved a Cuban flag.

During the First World War noncombatants gave the Kaiser an awful showering of lead in the Coney Island shooting galleries. Soldiers and sailors on leave considered it their patriotic duty to join in the symbolic warfare at the shooting galleries. Coney Island's contribution to the Second World War was the perfection of machine guns for gallery shooting—including one called Mow 'Em Down, devised by Charles Feltman, grandson of the inventor of the hot dog—and the use of German parachute troops as targets. The parachutists proved quite popular.

"Come and shoot down your enemy," the barkers yelled, very well aware that the United States was giving all-out aid to Britain. "Nail the Nazi before he lands!"

"COME CLOSER, MEN!" [7]

The Loop ends at Van Buren Street. State Street south of that is the sweet asylum of burlesque shows, pawn shops, flop-houses, chili parlors, and saloons where you can get a stein of beer for a nickel and a deadly glass of gin for a dime. This is the Bowery of Chicago—flashy, bawdy, vulgar, and only two blocks from the cool, clean sweep of the skyline on Michigan Boulevard and the Lake. The sidewalks are sprinkled with cigarette butts on South State Street, the air heavy with sweaty smells. The commoners who ramble up and down the impolite stretch are what is known as down-at-the-heelers—misfits, outcasts, bums.

. . . It is like walking through a particularly cheap carnival. Values have gone haywire here. A pair of socks sells for eight cents, a tie for nine, under-shirts for eleven. You can buy razor blades for a penny apiece, and fifty cents will get you tattooed for all time by the Tattoo King. Rooms run up as high as thirty cents a night, with free breakfast, and you can have *tattooing* removed (no needles used) for a pittance. . . .

On the cultural side, South State Street is right up there fighting. The artery is clogged with gimcrack movie houses. "Wages of Sin" ("Deceived and Deserted She Shot Her Lascivious BETRAYER") can be seen for ten cents in the coin of the realm. "Marihuana—Weed with Roots in Hell" runs up into more money—fifteen. If neither of these parables intrigue you, there is always good old "White Slave Racket Exposed!"—or "Abyss of Shame," showing "Pure Maidens Devoured by the Vulturous Passions of Men!" . . .

. . . I surrendered to the evil eye of a place called "Continuous Show—Special Today—5¢." This was a really miserable dive with drawings of nude women all over its open foyer. Tantalizing signs sent my metabolism way up by proclaiming: "Daring!" "Sensational!" "Reveals ALL!" "Straight from Paris Exposition!" [8] Over the ticket booth was this placard: "Nickel-Odium." There's no telling *what* the mind that thought that up might do next, so I paid my five cents and went inside, never to be heard of again.

The interior was bare and dirty. Some ten men were crowded before a plat-form and they all looked guilty. They were a strange cross-section of American manhood. There were two out-and-out bums, a man in freshly pressed tweeds, several minors who apparently held to the theory that hats cause baldness (all the others wore hats), a hollow-eyed young man in a raincoat, and an elderly gentleman who looked like *"My* loved ones are cared for!" in the insurance ads. They all seemed ill at ease, as if apprehended in some shameful act. They avoided each other's eyes, and no one spoke.

*   *   *   *   *

Suddenly a man appeared from behind a curtain and raised his hand. He was a man you wouldn't want to meet on a sunny day. His face was hard,

[7] From *The Strangest Places*, by Leonard Q. Ross [Leo Calvin Rosten], pp. 36-50. Copyright, 1939, by Harcourt, Brace and Company. New York.
[8] It didn't say which year.—L.Q.R.

sleek, refractory. Your glance bounded back off that face. He cried: . . . "Now, men. Behind this curtain is somethin' no live, red-blooded, he-man would ever want to miss! Three dancin' beauties, right in the flesh! No mor'n twelve inches from your very eyes!" He dropped his voice confidentially. "You men know why we can't show our real show out here in front. I don't hafta go into details. I ain't sayin' nothin' about police regulations. . . . All right, all right! But behind that curtain is the real thing! A work of art, in the flesh. When you see this, *you've seen everything!* Only twenny-five cents, men. . . ."

The two bums promptly pushed forward, paid their quarters, and went behind the curtain. (If those gents weren't decoys, then all my years of haunting phony auction sales have been a profligate waste of time.) Four or five art-lovers paid their quarters. The minors consulted hastily, growled in disgust, and left. I paid my quarter and went behind the curtain.

I was facing a tiny stage that was no more than four feet long, two feet deep, and about a foot off the floor. The backdrop seemed to be composed of an assortment of cheap sarongs, sewn together by a paralytic.

"All right, men," the Man announced. "First is our hot little Spanish dancer! Okay, Kenosha!" A victrola record began to croak and out came the hot little Spanish dancer, Kenosha. She was neither hot, little, Spanish, nor a dancer. She was a mammal with insensitive features and the expression of a paper-clip. She wore a feathery brassière, feathery tights, and pair of old street shoes. . . . Her "dance" consisted of shuffling each big foot cautiously and snapping two fingers. The feathers on the brassière were the only things that seemed to move. I was grateful for this. After a moment Kenosha stopped without any warning whatsoever and disappeared behind the outraged sarongs.

"Next," the Man cried fervently, "that sizzlin' ball of *fire*—Ginger!"

Out came the sizzling ball of *fire,* Ginger. The fire had been extinguished long, long ago. Ginger was a blonde—older and huskier than Kenosha, who was no sylph. She had even less expression. She was chewing gum. She wore an opaque brassière, sensible tights (as such things go), and a pair of house slippers. Her dance can only be described as a slight drooping of the shoulders relieved by an occasional nervous twitch. Once she raised a hand—then, exhausted, fell back into the twitching. She chewed her gum, indulged in a final half-hearted "bump," and went away.

"And now, the girl the whole town's talking about!" cried the Man loudly, but without conviction. "The one and only—Frenchy!"

Out came the one and only Frenchy—a tallow-skinned brunette who worked up a rather good sweat by throwing her elbows around pointlessly while she tried to fling her abdomen out of the front entrance. Her eyes seemed to be fixed on a distant star. She went through all the historic variations of rolling, grinding, shimmying, and champing at the bit. Then she stopped dead in her tracks, hitched her brassière up, and walked off. The performance for real, red-blooded he-men was over.

"Now, men!" the Man cried, with the air of one about to pull a giraffe out of thin air. "That was only a weak sample. Back here"—he pointed to yet another curtain—"there's a certain booth where the girls go to town. Dancin' on mirrors!" His voice became sedulous. "No need to go into details. Any you men here been to Paris know what I'm talkin' about!" His voice became brave, exultant. "When you see this, men, there's *no more to see!* Only twenny-five cents. . . ."

The two bums promptly pressed forward again, waving quarters. The other men hesitated. Then a rabbity little gent with glasses stepped forward nervously and went behind the curtain. The man in the business suit snickered and paid his admission. A fellow with a sour expression forked over. "*My* loved ones are cared for" went behind the curtain. I paid my quarter. No price is too high to pay for Art.

I saw a big square black booth, about eight feet high and four feet wide. On each of the four sides, at eye-level, were narrow observation slits. The other men had taken up their posts expectantly; the shills betrayed their function by hanging back. I went to a free space, put my eyes against the hole, and saw the moist, beady stare of all the other men's eyes. I hastily lowered my glance, and discovered that the booth had a large round mirror in the center of the floor. On benches around the sides sat none other than our old friends, Kenosha, Ginger, and Frenchy. They were in the same unforgettable costumes. Kenosha was yawning. Ginger still chewed gum. Frenchy was scratching her back.

The victrola began to play. Kenosha got up, stepped on the mirror, and began to imitate a dying Gaul. It was the same weary, dreary dance she had risen to a moment ago. The eye peering through the slits dropped to the mirror with a unanimity rare in the democratic state. There was nothing special to see.

Ginger followed Kenosha and Frenchy followed Ginger.

Frenchy stopped. The victrola stopped. The exhibition stopped. The men left the peep-holes. The businessman looked annoyed. Br'er Rabbit blinked his eyes. "*My* loved ones are cared for" didn't blink his eyes. The fellow with the sour look seemed curdled. We started to leave. Suddenly a man called to us from a flight of stairs I noticed for the first time: "Up here, men! This is where the real thing goes on. It's free. Just follow me." He gave us a finger-wiggling come-hither gesture.

We trooped up the long flight of stairs as one man. On the second floor we entered a room with red walls, lit by several dim red lights. It seemed very erotic. In the center of this lusty chamber was another peep-hole booth. It was the same size as the one downstairs, but it was octagonal and it had a top. Instead of open slits, this box had binocular peep-holes. Next to each aperture was a coin slot and a succinct sign: "Look Up," "Look Down," "Look Straight Ahead."

The man who had trapped us said softly, "Come closer, men, where I can talk to you private." He led us to a corner. "Come closer, men."

The men wouldn't come too close, and I don't blame them. Our guide can be visualized (vaguely) as the sort of creature you would expect to see if you picked up a rock. He had long, uncombed hair, long sideburns, pale eyes, and a pornographic look. His skin was the color of floor wax, and his teeth had the rich patina of cigarette smoke. When he smiled I sort of waited for a hyena to howl nearby.

"Men," he whispered. "This booth's been here eight years, which gives you an idea how popular it is with the real *man* public in Chi. It's run by the girl in there and the management don't get a cent from this special show. . . . I'm just here for your convenience, to make change." He eyed each of us in turn. "I ain't gonna give you a speech, men. I got only one thing to say. When you see this, men, you'll see the *end of the road!*" Some one coughed. "The one and only Fifi, doin' her famous Parisian dance. I advise you not to take your eyes off her for a single minute! Pick your favorite view, men—bird's view, worm's view, close-up. The *end of the road,* men! I got plenty nickels here. . . ."

There was a minor crush as the lords of creation got coins and hurried to their favorite views. By the time I changed a dollar, only "Look Straight Ahead" was left. There was a little tin plate behind the slot, so that I could see nothing. A victrola began to play. The ape-man cried, "Drop your nickels, men! let 'em have it, Fifi!" There was a cannonade of metallic clicks. The tin plates flipped up. From my post, I saw the face, neck, and philanthropic bosom of Fifi. She wasn't the sort of girl you'd bring home to meet Mother. She looked more like a Trixie than a Fifi. Her eyes were grotesquely mascaraed and she wore a black brassière. She was, I suppose, dancing. The only part of the action I could see was a frenetic oscillation of her shoulders; the rest of her responded solely through that phenomenon physicists have called sympathetic vibration. In twenty fleeing seconds the tin plate dropped. I inserted another nickel. The tin plate flipped up. Fifi was still oscillating. The tin plate dropped down and I inserted another nickel. This piquant process continued for several minutes, until the men began to desert the peep-holes in annoyance. The change-maker watched us like a hawk. Just at the strategic moment, when we were beginning to look for the exit, he yelled, "Fifi! Show them Fuzzy-Wuzzy!"

The men rushed back to the peep-holes in a frenzy and there was a downpour of nickels. This time I got "Look Down." Fifi's slightly animated legs were revealed to me. She was dancing on a mirror. She had on a pair of orchid tights and high-heeled boudoir slippers. What her dance was supposed to be I have never succeeded in figuring out. (In idle moods I think of it simply as "Diana and the Oil-Burner.") The tin plates kept dropping, nickels poured into the slots greedily, and the tin plates kept flipping up.

The sour young man came over to me and said, "Nuts!" After this *bon mot* he added, "If you see anything, let me know." I saw nothing and I let him know. He stood right next to me, waiting for bulletins. All was quiet on the libidinal front.

Again the men began to leave the peep-holes. The rabbity little mortal with the mustache looked bewildered. The businessman sneered quite openly now. "*My* loved ones are cared for" kept his dignity. The man suddenly yelled, "Give 'em sixty-six!" [9] and there was a stampede. This time I got "Look Up."

* I don't know what it meant either.—L.Q.R.

Looking up revealed a mirror in which I saw the reflection of Fifi from head to waist, a bodily zone which was clearly *hors de combat*.

In a few moments the men retreated from their posts, silent but annoyed. Now the son of Cain played his trump card. "Just a minute, fellows! I'm gonna ask Fifi if she won't put on the dance she did at Spider Kelly's in Juarez."

He rapped on the door to the booth; it half-opened. "Fifi," he said earnestly, "I was just wonderin' if you wouldn't put on the number you did down at Spider Kelly's. Just for this special group of men."

We heard a nasal feminine organ say, "Naw. I do not put that number on for nickels."

"Aw, come on," our provider cooed. "Just this once."

"I do not think I ought to, Joe."

"Aw, go on. These men would appreciate it."

They discussed this moot point for a few breathless moments, just loud enough for us to hear. Then Joe cried triumphantly, "Okay, men! She's gonna do it!"

The men beat their heads against the booth grabbing views. I got "Look Straight Ahead."

The victrola sang nostalgically of "Sweet Sue." The nickels dropped, the tin plates clicked, and we saw Fifi, the girl of no man's dreams, in the dance she had done at Spider Kelly's. I have never been in Juarez, but I got a pretty good idea as to why Fifi was working in Chicago. The alleged dance was the same demonstration of semi-static vegetation she had been doing all along, a nickel a peek.

Two or three views per man was enough. The sweet sound of nickels dropping stopped, for good. The hollow-eyed fellow in the raincoat went up to Joe and said coldly, "What a gyp."

Joe smiled.

"Is that all?" asked Hollow-eyes bitterly.

Joe said, "Yeh." He began to count the money he had taken in. "Exit straight ahead."

We left the Red Room *en masse*, went through a corridor modeled after the Black Hole of Calcutta, and took a long flight of stairs which let us out at the front of the building on South State Street, away from the entrance. The men who run the "Nickel-Odium" are no fools.

JOOK JOINT [10]

There's something about jooking that gets in your blood—the soothing smell of spilled beer, the whine of boogie-woogie from the resplendent jook organ, the sight of superwomen catering to lusty men. No cocktail lounge can equal it. Of course, there may be some degree of lust, hunger, and thirst in the cocktail lounge, but it is usually expressed according to the dictates of

[10] From *Palmetto Country*, by Stetson Kennedy, pp. 183-191. Copyright, 1942, by Stetson Kennedy. New York: Duell, Sloan & Pearce, Inc.

Emily Post, and not instinctively, as in the jook. In a cocktail lounge, events and conversation can be predicted with dreadful certainty; but in a jook anything can happen, and often does.

The vital importance of jooks in America's [Second World] war effort has been widely recognized. Although the Army's southeastern morale officer has said that servicemen prefer wholesome recreation to jooking, the Army and Navy have found it necessary to blacklist hundreds of jooks all over the South. As a private from New York City stationed at Florida's Camp Blanding said, "These jooks are tough joints. They'll murder you, caress you, and bless you. Not long ago I was in one and just because I'm a Yankee a cracker pulled a knife on me. He reached around my ribs and I was in the hospital three weeks."

*   *   *   *   *

As Southern as jazz, fried chicken, corn bread, channel cats, chewing tobacco, and lynching, the jook has a universal appeal which has carried it far beyond the Mason-Dixon Line. Also like jazz, it is a Negro contribution to Americana. Fittingly enough, Florida, "The Nation's Playground," is the home of the jook. Some years ago, when they made their phenomenal appearance throughout the Deep South, a Florida newspaper made an abortive attempt to explain them. Said the editorial:

> Back yonder a jook was a shack somewhere off the road where a Negro could go for a snort of moonshine or maybe a bottle of bootleg beer. After repeal of prohibition, many jooks for white folks appeared along the main highways, and plenty of them are a far cry from the Negro shacks which gave them their name. From a beer joint with a skimpy place for dancing, they range to establishments which put on country-club dog.

An insight into the original nature of the jook is given by the following editorial from the *Savannah Journal and Courier*, September 29, 1855:

> By reference to the recent homicide of a Negro, in another column, some facts will be seen suggestive of a state of things, in this part of our population, which should not exist, and which cannot endure, without danger, both to them and to us. The collision, which terminated thus fatally, occurred at an hour past midnight—a time when none but the evil-disposed are stirring.
>
> To the impunity thus given the Negroes by the darkness of midnight was added the incitement to crime drawn from the abuse of liquor. They had just left one of those resorts where the Negro is supplied with the most villainously-poisonous compounds, fit only to excite him to deeds of blood and violence. Indeed, we have the declaration of the slayer that the blow, by which he was exasperated so as to return it by the fatal stab, was inflicted by a bottle of brandy.

The derivation of the word "jook" is still obscure. In "A Note on Jook," Will McGuire has reported that nothing like it is to be found in the English language as far back as Chaucer. He believes "jook" to be a corruption of "dzug," a word in the African Wolof dialect meaning "to lead a disorderly life."

A different explanation is offered by Henry "Britches" Young, a century-old

Negro resident of Lake Butler, Florida. Says centenarian Young: A long time ago Negroes danced the jubilee, the predecessor to jitterbugging. The jubilee consisted of two steps, the Walkin Jawbone and the Jumpin Jim Josey. The men and women lined up opposite each other, and the two at the head of the lines approached each other, with jaws extended, in cakewalk fashion; then when they met they cut the lively Jumpin Jim Josey, a buck-wing step. At this point the other dancers shouted, "Go on, jubilee!" As time went on, says Young, this cry was shortened to "Go on, jube!" and then to "Jook it!"

Another idea is advanced by Webster's *International Dictionary*. It spells the word "juke" or "juck," and says that it came to be a designation for joints because of the notoriety given the Juke family as an example of the inheritance of criminal and immoral tendencies. Still another source maintains that jook is an Irish word which was first applied to San Francisco bawdy houses many years ago.

The spelling of the word (which is usually pronounced to rhyme with "took") once posed a problem for the Florida Supreme Court, as related in the following news story:

> Tallahassee, Nov. 3. (AP)—A case involving the so-called "jook" tax law caused a Supreme Court discussion today on the spelling of the word. Justice Rivers Buford, who spent his boyhood in the Apalachicola timberlands, suggested "j-o-o-k" and explained: "Before white folks started using the word, there were Negro jook joints as far back as I can remember."

The Court was hearing a case in which Bessie Pellicer of Jacksonville protested having to pay the $150 annual jook license on her small hotel. Attorney John E. Mathews, representing her, pointed out that large hotels are not required to pay the tax, and said the law "taxes this woman's jook and lets go free those other jooks with 300 rooms."

But it should never be said that a jook is worthy of the name if it lacks any of the following characteristics. A jook is an establishment that is usually crude but sometimes sumptuous; it is commonly equipped with tables or booths and space for dancing; beer, wine, and perhaps liquor are sold; edibles if any are apt to be barbecued ribs or sandwiches; music is provided by a jook organ (called a piccolo by Negroes) or jook band (ensemble of rhythm instruments); girls, as waitresses or hangers-around, are available for dancing without charge.

Most jooks are called somebody's Place, although some have more imaginative names like The Golden Slipper (Hotel Upstairs), The Ship Ahoy (on the fish docks), and Black Bottom (a white jook in Negro town). Black Bottom, incidentally, is graced by a work of art showing a debonair "darky" in checked trousers and derby hat emerging from an outhouse, and is also noted for a large black goat that wanders about under the tables eating lighted cigarettes, etc.

The major role of the jook is catering to the great masses of common people who can ill afford to pay admission, cover, or minimum charges. Offering a maximum of attractions at minimum cost, the jook is the answer to their problem of nocturnal entertainment; even the most underpaid wage-slave can go jooking on Saturday night (opponents of jooks, please note). Beer is ten cents per bottle, wine ten cents per glass, and a shot of whisky costs fifteen cents. Mixed drinks are considered to be unfit for human consumption, besides being wasteful of time and money. In addition to their cash customers, jooks attract many "look customers," as a jook girl has called them; "all they do is look in to see what they can see."

It is not to be denied that the jook has its less wholesome aspects, particularly that of serving as a clearing house for prostitution, both mercenary and eleemosynary. This may be accomplished either independently or by arrangement with the management. In the former case, the jook merely serves as a meeting- or market-place, and the couples depart on foot or in a taxi or automobile. But in the latter case the jooks maintain adjoining rooms or "Cabins for Tourists" (Innerspring Mattresses, Running Ice-water). This leads respectable tourist camps to erect signs which read "Out-of-State Travelers Only."

*   *   *   *   *

. . . There are also signs like this one, posted in the company-owned jook of a turpentine camp near Lakeland, Florida:

TO WHOM IT MAY CONCERN

Effective this date any one shooting a gun in these quarters will be charged $5 and required to forfeit the gun or go to JAIL. I will pay $2.50 for proof of any one shooting a gun.

The notice bears the signature of a company official.

At Benny's Place near Brooksville, Florida, this warning appears over the bar:

YOU CAN DRINK IN HEAR
BUT GO OUTSIDE TO GET DRUNK

Some signs are characteristic of cracker modes of expression, like the laconic pronouncement at Don's Place, Billygoat Hill, Jacksonville:

WE TAKE NO ADVISE FROM NOBODY

This spirit of pronounced individualism again crops up ferociously in an Alabama jook:

DON'T ASK US, NEITHER
BECAUSE WE DON'T KNOW, NEITHER
AND IF WE DID WE WOULDN'T TELL YOU, NEITHER

In the same jook, painted in red on the ceiling, is the question: WHAT IN HELL ARE YOU LOOKING UP HERE FOR?

In Baker Bryan's, on U.S. 1 just south of the Florida border, this cryptic notice hangs over the gambling room door:

NO WEMEN ALOUD IN HEAR
THIS DON'T MEAN BOB;
IT MEANS YOU

At nearby Mabel's Place, however, girls operate the gambling tables. One table is equipped with a novel rig: an ordinary scrubboard stands on a slant at one end, and dice are rolled down it to display their spots on the table. The girl whines interminably:

> The more you put down the more you pick up!
> Watch your pile grow like a Georgia pine!

Popular demand requires that the music provided by jook organs be corn and jazz. Much of the corn is produced in Jacksonville, Tampa, and other Southern cities, usually by a vocalist with a guitar. Two of the best-liked singers among Negroes are Tampa Red and Tampa Slim, and favorite titles include: "I Wonder Who's Booging My Woogie Now," "Rattlesnake Daddy," "Mistreatin' Mama," "No-Good Woman," "Teenincie Mama," "Jësse James Blues," "Bad Blood Blues," "B & O Busline Blues," and "Drinkin' My Blues Away."

One remarkable lament declares:

> From the ankles up you sho is sweet,
> But from the ankles down, you's too much meat!
> Oh, your feet too big, feet too big,
> Papa can't love you cause your feet too big!

Another hit sings praises of:

> Lou-u-ise,
>   Sweetest gal I know,
> She made me walk from Chicago,
>   To the Gulf of Mexico.
>
> I had a dozen women,
>   I had 'em big and small;
> But when I met this Mama,
>   Right then I quit 'em all.
>
> Somebody's been a-fishin'
>   Where I fished before;
> If I can ever catch 'em,
>   They ain't gonna fish no more.

Jook girls are deeply moved by jook music, and it is not the least of the attractions that lure them away from home. They seem perfectly contented while their favorite records are playing. Sometimes there is a mercenary reason for this: the management allots certain records to each girl, and pays them a percentage of all the nickels they can cajole out of customers to play their "favorite." Jook organs are seldom quiet; bleary-eyed customers who take a fancy to a particular tune have been known to keep it playing continuously until dawn—to the apparent enjoyment of all listeners.

Often the recorded songs become integrated with the lore of the region, and when this happens there are usually some changes made, like when a jook girl paraphrased "Blue Eyes"; "I'm thinking tonight of my brew-eyes—I wonder if he's thinking of me. . . ."

RUMBA IN MIAMI [11]

In many Latin countries the rumba is a dance, a graceful, even formal measure with a nice tradition. In Miami and The Beach it is the second coming of Saint Vitus on a commercial basis.

Night clubs and hotels feature rumba. Nearly every hotel has a rumba instructor who, in turn, keeps a battery of instructors and instructresses. Lessons are sold like any other commodity, but, in many cases, on the principle of *caveat emptor*.

Contests, generally sponsored by hotels or clubs, and entered, for the most part, by students of various rumba classes, are held night after night. In fact, the dance has more partisans than the Latin politicians who sit around the general area plotting new airline or administrative coups.

But for every one of its addicts who do the rumba well, there are hundreds who risk dislocations hour after hour. Age is no barrier. There is little difference between the hale and the halt when the palpitations set in.

Good rumba instructors are said to do well financially. According to local gossip, however, not all of their enterprise is confined to dance instruction. They get blamed for numerous scandals; if any one phrase describes their general conversational standing, they are the "automatically accused." If a straying blonde blights some characteristic Beach romance, the wags cry, "Cherchez le rumba." If some pillar of a community totters under the impact of the perennial carnival spirit to find new interests at age fifty or better, the comment is likely to be "Ah, them rumba lessons!" It doesn't matter if the accusation proves false.

If an errant wife drops a bundle at the races and seeks to recoup her cash through a phony jewel robbery for insurance, her rumba lessons are looked into. If the fat-and-fifty damsel with the pale green hair is escorted to a night club by anything darkly sleek and reasonably young, they credit the rumba industry. Even though the publicity folders put out by the press agents of the area *do* point out the effects of sunshine on the libido.

CONVENTION CITY [12]

. . . [In] Biloxi . . . no week passes winter or summer without a convention. Here is the cool, rambling Buena Vista, its bars and floor shows and banquet halls directed to the celebrating delegate; the great dignified Edgewater Gulf, an estate in itself and winter host to many hundreds, particularly from the Midwest; the Tivoli, with its kitchenette apartments for family holiday makers; the Biloxi with tall pillars; the exotic Broadwater Beach; the Riviera; the stately White House, and, back from the beach, hidden among the rolling

[11] From "Miami and the Beach," by Carl Biemiller, *Holiday*, Vol. 1 (December 1946), No. 10, pp. 45-46. Copyright, 1946, by the Curtis Publishing Company. Philadelphia.
[12] From *Gulf Coast Country*, by Hodding Carter and Anthony Ragusin, pp. 145-147. Copyright, 1951, by Hodding Carter and Anthony Ragusin. New York: Duell, Sloan & Pearce, Inc.

hills and bayous, Gulf Hills with its dude ranch and hazardous golf course and quiet swimming waters. . . .

Something doing every minute. . . .

The American Beekeeping Federation down from the Midwest's bleak January weather. The National Audio-Visual Association. Automobile dealers, dairymen, bottlers who show preference for other than soft drinks during their three-day stay. The thirteen hundred delegates of the Association of Southern Agricultural Workers; Masons and oil executives, grocers, safety-razor salesmen, farm-bureau presidents, National Guardsmen, and out-of-state industrialists. Mostly they look and behave alike, uniformly American, eternally small boys hastening to get their business over so that they may be Gulf Coast conventioneers; lumber dealers, master plumbers, sociologists, and insurance agents; bankers and reserve officers, funeral directors, Greek-letter fraternity brothers, dentists and cotton manufacturers, Lions and Elks, Rotarians, Kiwanians, Pilots, and chiropractors, druggists, teamsters, post-office clerks, theater owners, hardware men, and carpenters; American businessmen, and more than a few with their wives, on a mild American spree. A drink or two or three at the bar, a plunge or an excursion by water, the inevitable banquet with the speeches that seem even longer than they are; a fling at the gaming table, a drink with the boys in the room early in the morning, and then a call for the ten o'clock meeting which the faithful will attend. Mayors, governor's colonels, chain-store managers, veterans, and cottonseed crushers, editors, business women. I move we adjourn, second the motion, is there any unfinished business. . . . Nurses and Baptists, librarians, chancery clerks, and hospital directors. Resolved by the Brewers' Foundation that. . . . Fifty thousand conventioneers a year. Extolling tung oil, demanding bonuses, swapping stories, jockeying for office, eating, drinking, playing.

Fifty thousand of them a year.

And behind and beside them, the waiters, the chambermaids, the clerks, the managers and chefs and bartenders, the insignia manufacturers and souvenir dispensers, the boat captains and fishermen, florists and advertising salesmen and printers; the old-timers who wish that the outside world would leave them alone here, and the youngsters, the go-getters who become furious at the underhanded tactics that the state capital is using to lure the next year's convention away; speech-making city officials, Chamber of Commerce greeters, bored policemen, party girls and girls who would like to be, lifeguards and tour guides, wise taxi drivers and furtive peddlers. Big business, little business, monkey business. . . . Something doing every minute.

LADY LUCK IN THE SAGEBRUSH CASINOS [13]

How any given individual will react to the process of risking his money by pitting his skill or luck against that of the house can never be pre-

[13] From *Sagebrush Casinos, The Story of Legal Gambling in Nevada,* by Oscar Lewis, pp. 63-68. Copyright, 1953, by Oscar Lewis. Garden City, New York: Doubleday & Company, Inc.

dicted with certainty. It affects different people in quite different ways. It is no uncommon occurrence for normally quiet, unassertive players, once they fall under the strains and tensions of the games, to shunt off their mild, easygoing manner and become arrogant and contentious. On the other hand, noisy extroverts frequently grow silent and morose the minute they approach the tables and throughout their play exhibit all the qualities of confirmed misanthropes. This phenomenon has long interested and puzzled the Nevadans, both in and outside the profession. One veteran dealer at a Reno club puts the matter this way: "You can never tell in advance how any player's going to behave once he sits down at your table. I've been trying for twenty years and the one thing I've learned is that you can't expect even the unexpected."

However, although individual reactions are rarely predictable, certain patterns of behavior repeat themselves again and again. One of the most frequent is that of the casual tourist who, with little or no previous experience at gambling, visits a casino out of curiosity—that being one of the things to do when in Nevada—and makes a tentative wager or two, usually on the slot machines. It is no uncommon occurrence for the amateur, with the traditional beginner's luck, to hit a jackpot in the course of his—or her—first few tries. When that happens, the aftermath is almost always the same. The winner promptly catches the fever and, in a sort of happy trance, continues playing until his cash is exhausted or he is led away by commiserating friends.

Familiar, too, to all Nevadans are stories of summer tourists passing through the state who drop in at one or another of the clubs, intending to place only a bet or two, and end up hours later with funds so depleted as to require drastic changes in their vacation plans. In extreme cases, the luckless ones, in order to finance their journeys home, must hock their valuables at one of the town's many pawnshops or else telegraph appeals for funds to family or friends. Curiously, few of those who send such wires can bring themselves to admit the real cause of their plight. The stories they concoct show a singular lack of inventiveness. Almost unanimously, they mention having been relieved of their wallets, either by pickpockets or at the hands of armed footpads—thereby spreading abroad the impression that Nevada towns are infested with swarms of stick-up men. So many of the messages state that the senders are holdup victims that Western Union offices all over the state have become known to natives as "I Was Robbed Clubs."

There is, of course, a brighter side to the picture. Gamblers win as well as lose, and it is by no means rare for lucky players to parlay a modest initial wager into a sizable sum—and to have the good judgment to quit while it is still in their possession. Some clubs receive from time to time—and post on their bulletin boards—letters from customers thanking them for what their winnings have brought: more extended vacation trips, new tires for their cars, even, on occasion, such expensive items as fur coats or diamond rings.

However, comparatively few of the lucky ones put their windfalls to such prudent uses. The majority bear out the axiom of easy come, easy go by returning their winnings to circulation without delay, either by continuing to play and so giving it back to the house, or by blowing it in at the town's restaurants, night clubs, or cocktail bars. It is largely for their accommodation that the well-stocked jewelry shops in Reno and Las Vegas remain open far later than is customary elsewhere. One Reno jeweler states that the hours between 9 P.M. and midnight are the time when his business is liveliest. He adds that the objects most frequently in demand then are items of feminine adornment: pins or rings or wrist watches that the buyer carries home to present to his lady as visible evidence of his skill at the games.

This merchant has a valued San Francisco customer who regularly visits Reno once a month, buys $250 worth of chips at his favorite club, and shoots craps until he either loses it all or doubles his investment. When this last happens (which it does on an average of once every two or three months), he visits the store and invests his winnings in unset diamonds. Since this has been going on for more than ten years, the jeweler estimates that his customer's collection must by now be an uncommonly big and valuable one.

With players who quit while they are ahead, the temptation is always strong to return for one more session, the theory being that when one is having a run of luck it should be exploited to the full. More often than not, of course, the law of averages reasserts itself and the gambler sees his earlier profit go down the drain and with it a good deal more. Some players realize that pitfall and to guard against it they resort to a number of expedients. One favorite dodge is to slip one's winnings in an envelope, write one's name and address on the outside, and drop it into the nearest postbox. Others buy postal money orders, or telegraph their money home, or if they chance to be local residents, make use of the slots provided by the town's banks for the convenience of patrons who wish to make deposits after regular business hours.

Patrons who resort to such expedients are, however, comparatively rare. Of the throngs that daily and nightly crowd the more popular clubs, all but a few play primarily because they enjoy the excitement of the games, and these take the realistic view that the probabilities are they will be required to pay for their fun. Although the hope of making a killing is always present, they seldom become so deeply involved as to risk more than they can afford to lose. Each week end throughout the year, the highways and trains and airplanes leading to Reno and Las Vegas are crowded with Californians of this stamp—men and women who look on the trip as a pleasant outing and have put aside a certain fixed amount to cover its expenses. Most of these have several ends in view: to spend a few hours at the gaming tables, to put up overnight at one of the town's hotels or motor courts, and perhaps take in the show at one or another of the excellent—and inexpensive—supper clubs. A common procedure is for the prudent week-ender first of all to pay for his night's lodging, then to salt away enough to cover the cost of his meals and transportation home. Thus fortified against possible adversity, he blithely proceeds to his favorite club and hazards whatever remains of his hoard.

These are the bread-and-butter players to whom the casinos look to provide their steadiest and most dependable revenue. For they return again and again, and while the majority play conservatively, seldom losing sizable amounts on any one visit, over long periods the total mounts up. To be sure, the trade of transients is not scorned, whether these be cautious souls who limit their play to a few nickels or dimes or quarters on the slot machines, or the occasional plunger whose losses may run into the thousands. These, however, are at best supplementary sources of revenue in the big, popular resorts; for their steady, day-by-day profit they look to their thousands of regular customers who, having chosen a particular club, are likely to return to it year after year.

Casino owners regard these as favorite customers, notwithstanding the fact that it is members of this very group who most frequently win. This is partly because, as experienced players, they choose the games in which the house percentages are the most favorable and because they customarily place their bets or, in card games, play their hands with more than average skill. Moveover, the player who, as most of the regulars do, limits himself to a certain fixed sum —and who quits when he loses it—presents more of a risk to the owners than the general run of players. For the most the house can hope to gain is the amount the prudent player has decided to risk—whether it be five or ten or twenty-five dollars—whereas, granted a bit of luck, he stands a chance of running his winnings up to many times that figure.

HAM AND EGGS: FOLKLORE OF THE BREAKFAST CLUB [14]

The Breakfast Club meets once a week at nine o'clock in the morning. The most important professional and business men of the city [of Los Angeles] are members. The purpose of the club is to foster friendship and good will among its members and to entertain visiting celebrities.

The weekly meeting is held at the Riding Club, at long wooden tables laid under the trees in the garden. At our table, directly in front of the speakers' table, was a stone column three feet high, with a bronze tablet set in the top. On it was inscribed: "Founder Francis DeLong, Presented by his Pals." Painted on a board hung over the speaker's chair was the motto of the club: "The Man who is too busy to serve God and Humanity is *Too Busy*."

The Founder and Chairman of the Breakfast Club was a short man, rather solid and chunky, with a dark face, chocolate-colored eyes, and an expression of kindness and good will that looked as if it had been stamped on his features with a die. He wore a dark brown suit of extreme cut, beige waistcoat, and beige spats.

One of my neighbors drew my attention to a young woman in riding habit who had entered and sat down at another table.

"That's Miss ———, she's a devotee."

"A devotee of what?"

"Why, just a devotee. She rides horses before the Breakfast Club meets."

I stared at the devotee, trying to connect her with the Breakfast Club and one of its queer mottoes; "Friendship, Hospitality, Humanity, and Horses."

White-jacketed waiters brought us melon. While we ate, my neighbor expatiated on the Founder and Chairman.

[14] By Isabel Campbell. From *Space*, edited by B. A. Botkin, Vol. I (May 1934), No. 1, pp. 9-11. Copyright, 1934, by B. A. Botkin. Norman, Oklahoma.

"He's a wonderful man, Mr. DeLong. He's an idealistic."

"A *what?*"

"An idealistic—you know—a semi-religious. I don't mean that—it sounds funny, doesn't it? I mean he is really very religious, only kind of semi, you know. He's a wonderful man. Wait until you hear him read the Creed of the Club. He reads it every week and I always cry, he reads it so nice. He's an inspiration. I always go away feeling better. This is only for the sake of friendship, you know. No business is done here at all, and no advertising. I thought you would like to know I publish two magazines, 'Contentment' and 'Seeing California.' I always like to know who my neighbors are, don't you?"

After the melon was finished, Mr. DeLong arose and announced that we must now do some exercises. Would all the men please rise? The ladies did not have to. So we ladies kept our seats and the men climbed over the long benches. A man on a high platform began putting the men through vigorous calisthenics. As the guests went through the exercises, there was a great deal of laughing and pushing, accompanied by such witticisms as: "That makes room for the ham and eggs. Good old ham and eggs."

After that we settled down to ham and eggs and coffee, which had been hustled in during the setting-up exercises. Singing was next in order. Encouraged by the host (the host is changed every week and bears all the expense of the breakfast, which averages three hundred dollars), we laid our arms over the shoulders of our neighbors, swayed back and forth, and sang to the tune of *Tammany* a song printed on a blue card lying beside each plate:

> "Ham and Eggs! Ham and Eggs!
> I like mine fried good and brown,
> I like mine fried upside-down!
> "Ham and Eggs! Ham and Eggs!
> [*Shout*] "Flip 'em,
> Flop 'em
> Flop 'em
> Flip 'em.
> "HAM AND EGGS!"

Mr. DeLong arose again and urged us all to have a good time. "This is an opportunity," he said, "to meet big people. I want everybody to shake hands with everybody he can reach. Shake hands with everybody near you. That's right. Shake hands, everybody. And when you do it, say, Hello, Ham, and the other fellow says, Hello, Egg."

Then we sang:

> "Sea! Sea! Sea! Oh-oh, why are you angry with me?
> Ever since I left Dover,
> I've thought the boat would go over.
> Dear! Oh, dear! I've a queer sort of feeling on me.
> If I once reach the shore,
> I shall say au revoir
> To the Sea! Sea! Sea!"
> [*Repeat*]

We embraced and swayed once more.

Suddenly we were startled by a loud banging on the table farther down the garden and a burst of crowing from the men sitting there. They crowed and crowed and banged the tables again and again with their spoons. The crowd shouted with laughter, shouted and shouted and seemed unable to control its merriment. It seems that the older men, who dub themselves the "old roosters," sit together at one table, and after their ham and eggs begin to circulate, they feel like proving to the young cocks present that they (the old roosters) still have a kick in them. So they crow and bang on the table. If there has been any stiffness in the party up to this time, it is now immediately melted.

After the crowing, we ate pancakes and maple syrup and drank more coffee, and chanted a song printed on a yellow card:

"Oh! you Ham,
Oh! you Eggs.
We'll tell the world that we all like ham,
But ham without eggs isn't worth a damn.
All night long
We drink what should be in kegs.
But when day is dawning,
Our yappers are yawning
For 'Oh! you ham and eggs.'

"Ta, da, da, da, da.

"Oh! you Ham,
Oh! you Eggs.
We'll tell the world that we all like ham.
But ham without eggs isn't worth a damn.
All night long
We drink what should be in kegs.
It may not be kosher,
But so is your grocer.
So we'll eat ham with you eggs."

We were now fed and ready to listen to the speeches.

Mr. DeLong arranged the microphone and began to talk. He told the club that he was glad to see so many present, that he hoped we would walk about the club before we went away and once again read the signs on the fence recalling to us the objects of the club. "Don't forget," he said, "we stand for the Democracy of Ham and Eggs. If you have an enemy, bring him to the Breakfast Club. We will make him your friend. Don't forget that our symbol is the little golden hatchet which digs days into the clay of human friendship and that the club flower is the pansy."

There followed an awarding of prizes for horsemanship, donated by a gentleman designated as the "Beau Brummel of the Chamber of Commerce whose other duty is to meet everybody at the train."

We were now ready for the celebrities. The first and evidently the most important was the Governor.

Mr. DeLong introduced him to the club with appropriate words, and the Governor responded properly. Mr. DeLong then presented the Governor with a gold card, which, he announced, was a permanent card of membership in the

Breakfast Club. "If there was a Breakfast Club in every city in the world," he stated, "there would never be another war."

Then the Governor was initiated. Mr. DeLong presented his hand, saying: "Hello, Ham."

Governor, taking hand: "Hello, Egg."

Mr. DeLong: "And now we turn the egg over."

Clasped hands were turned over.

The Governor was now a member of the Breakfast Club. Loud crows from the Roosters.

The Famous Publicity Man was now introduced. He made an appropriate speech, warmly praising the purpose and ideals, to say nothing of the good food, of the Breakfast Club and finished with anecdotes of his career.

Last on the program of celebrities was the Famous Lady Novelist, who was so little and feminine she must stand on tiptoe and stretch her neck to talk into the microphone. (Business of masculine aid for the Famous Lady Novelist.)

"I must announce first of all," she screamed, "that this is my second visit to the Breakfast Club. My first visit to the Breakfast Club was last year, when I first partook of your delicious ham and eggs. I want to state to the members of the Breakfast Club that never have I tasted such ham and eggs anywhere else in the country. I have traveled all over the country since I was a guest here last year, eating ham and eggs in every sort of place, but never have I eaten such ham and eggs as I have eaten in the Breakfast Club. And now before I end I want to show you just what ham and eggs can do for a woman."

To our astonishment, this Famous Lady Novelist lifted her arms in what she thought was the manner of a cock's wings, raised her voice, and deliberately crowed into the microphone.

We all laughed heartily. "Women are gradually taking over all of men's prerogatives," said Mr. DeLong indulgently.

After music by the orchestra, Mr. DeLong ended the formal program by reading the Creed of the Breakfast Club, which was a poem in ten stanzas. As he read, the crowd quieted down, soft music accompanied him, once or twice his voice trembled with sincerity, and the sun shone from behind a cloud.

When all was over, Mr. DeLong urged us to make ourselves at home, to walk about and see everything. We wandered about, reading the signs painted on boards hung on the high fence:

"If you have an enemy, bring him here for breakfast. We will make him your friend."

"True happiness and genuine joy come only from doing something for someone else."

"We stand for the Democracy of Ham and Eggs."

"If you enter here with a frown, you will depart with a smile. We change sadness for gladness."

"Any ole ham can stay up all night, but it takes a thoroughbred to get up in the morning."

"I would rather have made a circle of friendship than to have taken a city."

"Four planks of our platform: Friendship, Hospitality, Humanity, Horses."

BEER AND BASEBALL [15]

. . . Chris von der Ahe, a saloonkeeper, . . . had a beer emporium near the [St. Louis] ballpark. Perceiving, from the rush of the fans to his bar before and after games, that thirst had an affinity for baseball, Von der Ahe bought the Browns, installed a chute-the-chutes in deep center field and created a circus atmosphere generally. Crowds packed the park and consumed more barrels of beer at Von der Ahe's than ever before. Von der Ahe, who proudly identified himself as "der poss bresident of der Prowns," saw his team win four American Association pennants in the late 1880's (they were the last pennants the town saw until the Cardinals broke a protracted pennant drought in 1926).

Before his death, der poss bresident, who had a sense of historical importance, had himself immortalized in a life-size granite statue depicting him in a statesmanlike pose wearing a frock coat. The statue marks his grave in Bellefontaine Cemetery; many other civic giants are buried there, but none in such rich splendor.

DODGER FANS [16]

Brooklyn's fans are the most loyal in the country. The team invariably is [near the top] in home attendance, being exceeded only [at times] by New York and Chicago. . . .

It has been said that the Dodger rooters are fans by instinct. Even in the dead of winter, some of the more hardy may be seen pushing perambulators around Ebbets Field and looking longingly at the closed park, as a homing pigeon might gaze at a cote which he found locked at the end of his return journey. A New York newspaper [once] conducted a contest to select a new name for the Dodgers. . . . It drew sacks of mail, but no likely nickname to succeed the Dodgers, which originally was Trolley Dodgers, by the way, because of the profusion of surface cars. The Brooklyn team has been known as the Superbas—named after a pantomime variety acrobatic act—the Bridegrooms, and the Robins. To the Brooklyn fan, however, the team is always "The Brooklyns" [or "dem bums"].

The highlight in the life of any Brooklyn fan is to defeat the hated Giants. Never was this done under such joyous circumstances as in the last two days of 1934, when the Dodgers won at the Polo Grounds, and enabled St. Louis to beat out the Giants for the pennant. Bill Terry that spring, in answer to a query as to what he thought of the Dodgers, had answered rather contemptuously, "Brooklyn—are they still in the League?"

Terry got plenty of assurance Brooklyn was still in the league on those last

[15] From "The Cities of America: St. Louis," by Jack Alexander, *The Saturday Evening Post*, Vol. 219 (December 7, 1946), No. 23, p. 84. Copyright, 1946, by the Curtis Publishing Company. Philadelphia.

[16] From "Once a Dodger—," by Tom Meany and Bill McCullough. *The Saturday Evening Post*, Vol. 209 (March 6, 1937), No. 36, pp. 13, 38. Copyright, 1937, by the Curtis Publishing Company. Philadelphia.

two days, as the Flatbush rooters stomped on the roof of the New York dugout and thrust homemade placards into the faces of the Giants' players bearing the following simple inscription: "YEP! WE'RE STILL IN THE LEAGUE!"

When the second game was won and the Giants had lost the pennant, excited fans carried Manager Stengel and Al Lopez from the field on their shoulders. They waited outside the Harlem clubhouse for Stengel that night, got on the subway with him, and refused to allow him to leave at his station. He twice rode to the end of the line before he escaped. There was some talk of hiring an armory for a gigantic celebration, but Casey escaped by leaving town.

Any Brooklyn wife will tell you of promises of a Sunday night at the movies with the family which are savagely canceled by Friend Hubby should the Dodgers lose that afternoon—as they frequently do. Uncle Wilbert Robinson, Max Carey, . . . Casey Stengel, [Leo Durocher,] as managers, have, time and again, been publicly called by irate cab drivers to explain their strategy. And all . . . have argued back, much to the confusion of vehicular traffic in Brooklyn, since the arguments invariably were carried on from one cab to another while proceeding at moderate speed through the streets of Flatbush.

Circulation managers of the two Brooklyn evening papers are the authority for the statement that the sale of sporting extras drops from 25 to 40 per cent on days when the Dodgers lose, and takes a corresponding jump on those . . . days when the Dodgers win. The fan doesn't want the harrowing details of any defeat, but he'll read every word of every line of each triumph.

There once was a Brooklyn fan who hurled a pop bottle at Umpire Cy Rigler. He was promptly detected, summarily ejected and haled before a magistrate. "Will you promise not to throw at Mr. Rigler again, if I suspend sentence?" asked the magistrate. "I'll hit him the next time!" promised the irate missile-heaver, who forthwith went to the detention pen to cool off.

"Wait till next year!" is the perennial slogan of the Brooklyn fans, who, like Micawber, are sure that everything will be taken care of through some unexplained necromancy.

Though Brooklyn rooters are colorful enough en masse, Ebbets Field has seen its share of spectacular individuals among its vocal adherents also. Such men as Big Abe Bettan, a large Jewish peddler who always sat in the same seat behind third base and cheered the visitors, deriding the Dodgers. Robbie met Big Abe after a game at the Polo Grounds and promised him a pass if he would throw his support to the Dodgers. Big Abe accepted, but after a few weeks returned the pass and thereafter paid his way in, so he would be able to direct his scorn, unsubsidized, at the Dodgers.

There was a woman who sat in the upper tier near first base and staunchly rooted for Brooklyn. In fact, she once descended to the old open press box and threatened to belabor one of the writers with an umbrella because she didn't like the tone of his articles. This woman, known to players and writers as Apple Mary, because of her round rosy cheeks and not because she was a vendor, didn't attend the games very often [after] Robbie was released. In the spring of 1933, however, she showed up on the sidewalk at a parade in honor of Hans Wagner's return to baseball.

Patiently, Apple Mary watched the procession of shiny touring cars pass by. The tops were down and the various baseball personages were bowing to the cheers of the populace. As the car containing Johnny Evers neared her position, Apple Mary stepped from the curb, edged to where the fiery Trojan was sitting, and said, "You crab!"—after which she disappeared in the crowd. It had been nearly twenty years since Evers had yowled back at the Brooklyn fans, but apparently Apple Mary hadn't forgotten.

There was a fan, called by the late Sid Mercer "The Spirit of Brooklyn," who sat in the same seat behind home plate daily. He was on a direct line with the plate; the better to umpire, no doubt. The Spirit of Brooklyn made a sandwich of all his epithets by placing a pronoun before and after, viz.: "You bum, you!" One day the entire Dodger team so disgusted him that he went plural and cried, "Youse bums, youse!" He never was seen at the park again.

* * * * *

Brooklyn also boasts, or at least numbers, among its followers the only "fall-and-hit" fan in history. When there were no high stands in left field, some of the fans used to roost in the trees, there to follow the fortunes or misfortunes of their idols. A small boy, Milton Hermann, was climbing into one of these trees one day in 1930 when his ascent was arrested by the fact that a 200-pound adult fell out of the same tree and crashed to the ground. Milton went to Kings County Hospital with a concussion, and the 200-pounder left under his own power and at high speed, the only recorded hit-and-run case of its kind in history.

WHEN THE BAND "WENT CRAZY" AFTER THE FUNERAL [17]

. . . New Orleans could always find an excuse for a parade, not only during Carnival, but for every national holiday, Jackson Day, Emancipation Day, and election campaigns. The most unusual of all were the funeral processions, under the auspices of the lodges, clubs, and societies. Everyone in New Orleans belonged to some secret order or society. When the member died, he had to have a band. "He was nothin' if he didn't have a band!" The societies used one side of their aprons for parades and the other for funerals. When the church bells tolled out mournfully, a couple of the brethren down on Rampart Street paused to remark:

"What's that I hear, twelve o'clock in the daytime—church bells ringin'?"

"Man, you don' hear no church bells ringin' twelve o'clock in the day!"

"Yes, indeed, somebody must be dead."

"Ain' nobody dead. Somebody must be dead drunk."

"No, I think there's a funeral."

"Why, looky here, I see there is a funeral."

"I b'lieve I hear that trambone moan."

[17] From "Bunk Johnson and the Eagle Band," by William Russell and Stephen W. Smith, in *Jazzmen*, edited by Frederic Ramsey, Jr., and Charles Edward Smith, pp. 26-28. Copyright, 1939, by Harcourt, Brace and Company. New York.

With a slow pausing tread, the procession marched to the graveyard. With the exception of a few older downtown cemeteries that had their whitewashed tombs above ground, graveyards were usually a couple of miles "up or back o' town." Most of the cemeteries, such as Cypress Grove, St. Joseph's, and Lafayette, had plots for the burial of Negroes. On the way out to the graveyard, the band played in dead-march time, with muffled drums, soft and somber dirges, including *Free As a Bird, When the Saints Go Marching On, Nearer My God to Thee,* and real funeral marches. But Zutty Singleton says that once the body was interred: "The mourning got over quick. Right out of the graveyard, the drummer would throw on the snares, roll the drums, get the cats together and light out. The cornet would give a few notes, and then about three blocks from the graveyard they would cut loose."

They came back playing *High Society* and *King Porter Stomp,* but first of all they swung out on *Didn't He Ramble, He Rambled Round the Town till the Butcher Cut Him Down.*

The funerals and parades always had a "second line" which consisted of the kids who danced along behind. The bands had a way of swinging their bodies, and of turning corners in spectacular fashion, and the boys who marched along on the sidewalk with them mimicked every action. When the big band "went crazy" after the funeral, the kids cut up with their primitive version of the "Susie Q" and danced the "shudders." With their leader, the boys joined in the general tumult as they shimmied along, and sang, yelled, and clapped. Many had tin flageolets or home-made whistles cut from stalks of reed on which they played the tune. Only the tough kids joined the second line. Their mothers did not approve; if they ever caught the kids, they jerked them out of the parade. A few of these future jazzmen were actually helpful. These were the water boys, who carried buckets of water to refresh the tired marchers whose lips were parched after a hot march under the boiling sun.

BEBOP FROM HARLEM TO THE LOOP [18]

. . . Bebop has precipitated the greatest jazz controversy since the Dixieland school was revived over a decade ago. Generally speaking, you can't sing it and you can't dance it. It is, to use the expression of a bewildered jazz man, "head music." These abstract and intellectual qualities make bebop squalling anarchy in dance-hall circles. "These birds," said one dance-hall manager, "are killing the goose that laid the golden egg." . . . The anti-bop school says it's a fad; the boppers say it is the music of the future.

*   *   *   *   *

. . . All of jazz is divided today into two countries. One of these is the land of bebop, and the other is the land of moldy figs. The bebops, or bops as they are known in the jazz mills, call themselves progressive musicians, by which

[18] From "And Now We Go Bebop!" by Harry Henderson and Sam Shaw, *Collier's,* Vol. 121 (March 20, 1948), No. 12, pp. 16-17, 88. Copyright, 1948, by the Crowell-Collier Publishing Company. New York.

they mean they believe music styles change, and that while the past jazz masters were great, that was yesterday.

On the other hand, the moldy figs, while decrying the sirupy outfits, are certain that the greatest jazz ever played was New Orleans-style jazz, out of which came Chicago style and a later development, Benny Goodman's swing. The bops lump them all together as "Dixieland," but the purists want their jazz played the way it was played in New Orleans in 1915. Hence the name "moldy figs." (Even when you discuss it, you go bebop.)

Bebop represents a revolt, not only from the monumental corn of big band arrangements but from the rigidity of tradition. Consequently, the boppers have cast aside many traditional jazz ideas and forms and introduced new effects. The melody, for example, doesn't linger on. It's gone—or is only occasionally perceptible. Instead the boppers strive for dissonance, or as many boppers put it, "new interesting sounds." There are swift changes of key and the simple danceable rhythms are gone. You have to be an extremely accomplished musician to attempt bop. It helps too if you happen to be more than slightly neurotic.

You can get a pretty fair idea of the difference between bop and Dixie by listening to Mr. Louis Zuccaro, who is major-domo of the pantry of Jazz, Limited, a swank Dixie palace in Chicago. Louis used to play a trumpet years ago and he says, "I dug that bebop for two months and I broke my back. The truth of the matter is that bebop is incoherent. Now that's no way to write a letter. When Louis Armstrong plays, he writes a letter. It says, 'Dear Joe, I am now in St. Louis. It is a sad city but I like it here. There is lots of night life and lots of fun, though sometimes things get blue. I wish you were here with me because we might have some fun together. Yours truly, Louis Armstrong.' See, you understand everything he says when he plays.

"But," adds Zuccaro, shaking his head, "when Gillespie plays, you don't understand anything. It begins, 'Yours truly, Dizzy Gillespie, sad mad fun Dear Joe St. Louis.' See, it's incoherent. Doesn't make a bit of sense."

*   *   *   *   *

. . . Bop isn't played just anywhere and most boppers, except its leading exponents, are unemployed. . . . They survive by playing reactionary music for meals and playing bop for kicks in jam sessions.

Some boppers carry their idealism to the starvation point. One musician . . . wouldn't tell us in the presence of other bops where he played. Later he confessed he was taking moldy-fig money—$150 a week. What brought him to this lowly state, he confessed, was that he had formed a bop combo—a small band— played a solid four weeks on Fifty-second Street. "But after that, we couldn't get any engagements. It's too advanced for the public. So I hadda go back to my fig job. But don't tell anyone."

This has been the fate of innumerable bops. . . . [One] combo was formed because a bop knew a hotel manager who needed a small band for his dining room. "But," said the idealistic bops, "we want no interference. We're progressive and we wanna play the way we like." The manager shrugged. "Sure," he said, "play the way you like. What I want is music." It was the open door. The boys crawled on the stand that night, happy as larks, and bopped off. The flight of the frightened patrons was so prompt that within ten minutes the bops had been canned. "But you said we could play our own style," they protested. "Yah-yah," screamed the distraught manager, "but I said, *music!*"

It is music, the boppers are insisting, and they now claim to have won over the majority of young musicians and young jazz fans. Its nonplaying addicts follow it chiefly through records and concerts. . . . These concerts have now reached such a peak of popularity that Variety, theatrical trade paper, speaks of them as "Wham Coin for Jazz Long-hairs."

. . . Chicago . . . has become the biggest bop-playing city in the country, although bop originated in Harlem. . . . Chicago . . . has long had a tradition of "live music," as Mr. Petrillo calls it. There is hardly a bar worthy of the name that doesn't have at least three musicians. In some of these establishments, chiefly broken-down gin mills and strip joints, the customers' interest is either in hooch or the gyrations of the strip-teasers. Virtually any kind of music is just so much noise to this type of clientele and consequently the dissonances and ear-bending chords of bop pass without the customers screaming. . . . Fights are common, customers are clipped and occasionally clubbed. This neither interests nor disturbs the musicians so long as they can bop.

Things are not on such a low level in the strip joints. For one thing the musicians get paid. For another, fights are rare. But the trouble is that some of the strip-teasers can't follow a bop beat. Obviously, this creates some agonizing moments for a man like Mickey Scrima, who used to play drums for Harry James, Gene Krupa and other big-name bands, and quit because "I gotta play a bop drum." Generally, he makes a concession and follows the girls. "The worst of it all," he says, "is the end. They never know when the thing is finished. So what I do is give 'em a big military flare. Then they know they're supposed to get off."

*   *   *   *   *

Many of the cafés and clubs within the Loop are controlled by a syndicate. According to Gipsy Silvers, a hefty bop saxophonist who would rather starve than play that fig music, some bops went to the syndicate's top men, showed them trade-paper clippings on the bop-versus-fig controversy, and suggested that bop be put into several of their spots. The syndicate's boss men agreed to consider it. They toured several bop joints, and came to a quick decision against it.

"It wasn't," says Gipsy sadly, "that they didn't like bop. They just said it attracts a beer-drinking crowd and they don't want it in the Loop because there's not enough in it for them."

The closest bop joint to the Loop is a dimly lighted café which is part of a South State Street block of movie grind houses, bedraggled burlesque shows, numerous gin mills and strip joints. The sole feature of the club is a continuous bop jam session, and most of the patrons are indifferent to it. Musicians, however, come from all over the city to bop and to listen. Some of them stay for days.

The only time the musicians in the audience really come to life is when another leaves the stand and then they all want to blow their tops in bop. This desire to get in the act—please remember, there's not a nickel in it for them—is so great that the management has had to post a sign saying: "Please get the piano player's permission to sit in."

Bebop was born in a place called Minton's Playhouse. A Harlem late spot on One Hundred and Eighteenth Street, it has long been a favorite hangout for musicians because its jam sessions permit them to have some musical fun, to experiment and to feel like individuals. This last element is important. A great deal of the drive behind bebop today comes from the pent-up, frustrated feelings of skilled musicians. Gypsy Silvers put it this way: "Here I have all this technique and I gotta play um-pah, um-pah, um-pah. Bop is more expressive. It lets you think and feel musically, more than any other style."

Though many musicians would disagree about this, they all praise Gillespie and Parker as two of the greatest jazz instrumentalists who ever lived. The boppers look upon them as living gods. But, even as jazz gods they are rather young. John Birks Gillespie was born in Cheraw, South Carolina, thirty years ago, while Charles Parker was born in Kansas City, Missouri, twenty-nine years ago. Both played in their school bands. By 1940 they were both in New York, trying to break into the big time. They were then barely of legal age and acknowledged masters of their instruments. Individually, they have played in enough big-name bands to fill out this column. Neither Parker nor Gillespie claims credit as the inventor of bebop. Parker had been experimenting along bebop lines for some time and Gillespie says that the first time he heard him at a jam session, he cried, "Man, this is it."

But somehow, even though they played together in Earl Hines' band, they never got together musically. They left the Hines band, and each became famous in his own right. Meanwhile Gillespie had been going to Minton's Playhouse to jam and with another brilliant young musician, Thelonious Monk, who played piano, he began working out chord changes. Parker began showing up to jam with them. One night a musical phrase by Monk caught the imaginations of Gillespie and Parker and they began to see what they could do, musically, with it. Soon they had developed the rudiments of what is known as bop.

For a while they played together in a small combo under Gillespie's name. Bookings were slim. A cross-country tour was a dismal affair, despite the fact that musicians were proclaiming them the top performers in jazz. But meanwhile they had made some records—collectors' items today and hard to find— and people getting a chance to hear a piece again and again began to understand. The name bebop was tagged onto their style of playing because, Gillespie explains, "we used to hum a little refrain when we began. It went 'bobba doodle dee, be-bop.' The song, Hey, Bobba-re-bop, which was a hit some months ago, grew out of this." (This is the place to tell you: Never, never call bebop rebop: it shows you're "square.")

*   *   *   *   *

The name bebop has come to haunt Parker and Gillespie, though in the beginning it helped to set them apart the way any trade-mark does. But today they hate the name. They wish people would just call it "music."

XI. Social Register

In every city fashionable society has its hierarchy of sets and grades, each with its own particular brand of snobbery. Place of residence is the most obvious criterion. Thus in Boston, Beacon Hill has been the traditional site of social supremacy, with Back Bay finding out that it "cannot buy with gold the old associations." In New York the descendants of old colonial families clung to Stuyvesant Square in spite of the fashionable trend toward Fifth Avenue.

In New York the first real break with the old aristocracy based on family came in 1883, when the new millionaire operagoers, tired of being sneered at by the nabobs in the old Academy of Music, built the Metropolitan Opera House. Here the "Diamond Horseshoe" and the "Golden Horseshoe" provided an adequate setting for their bejeweled splendor. Their motto might well have been the saying attributed to both "Diamond Jim" Brady and William J. ("Fingy") Conners, the Buffalo ex-longshoreman boss and magnate. When rebuked for wearing diamond studs, the latter replied: "Them as has 'em wears 'em."

"It used to be said," writes Cleveland Amory in *The Proper Bostonians,* "that, socially speaking, Philadelphia asked who a person is, New York how much is he worth, and Boston what does he know." Along with its first families Boston had its Brahmin intellectual aristocracy; and along with its nabobs of Nob Hill, San Francisco had its Bohemian Club. So New York in the Fifties and Sixties had its literary soirées—Mrs. Botta's Saturday nights and the Carey Sisters' Sunday receptions.

That the smart set was going to have to stress brains as well as wealth and family is indicated in a Gibson drawing in *Life,* 1890, which divided New York into "the Bohemian set, all brains and no style, Society proper, with a fair amount of each, and the Four Hundred, all style and no brains."

A second break with the old Fifth Avenue-Newport axis came in the 1920s when the third generation of Whitneys and their friends became bored and sought amusement in the direction of Broadway. They found it in the famous Round Table at the Algonquin Hotel on West Forty-fourth Street. This new mixture of family, wealth and wit came to be known as Café Society—a term coined by Maury Paul ("Cholly Knickerbocker") at the Ritz-Carlton in 1919 when he observed: "Society isn't staying home any more. Society is going out to dinner, out to night life, and letting down the barriers."

There were other reasons for letting down the barriers, as pointed out by a writer in *Fortune* for December 1937, such as benefit balls for Belgian and other war relief, which brought old families and new money together; Hollywood; the automobile and radio industries, which made new fortunes; prohibition, which pulled socialites into speak-easies; rising real-estate values, which led them to give up brownstone fronts for apartments; Greenwich Village, which lowered their sex standards; and the Depression, which shrank inherited incomes.

That the Boston aristocracy still resisted change is demonstrated by the fact that the "New York type gossip column is nonexistent in any Boston paper." Some of the most Proper Bostonians even refused to be listed in the Social Register and, according to Cleveland Amory, a Somerset Club bachelor "always referred to the [Social] Register as a 'damned telephone book' and regularly protested its size by making it a practice, upon receiving his annual copy, to tear it in half and return it to its New York headquarters."

Next to "grandfather on the brain," protocol has been the most magnificent obsession of fashionable society. This is especially true in a city like Washington, where society is mainly political. Perhaps the most famous example of Washington social protocol is the Longworth-Gann feud. When Vice-President Charles Curtis came into office with President Hoover, he, as widower, brought with him his sister, Mrs. Dolly Gann, as his official companion. In his dual capacity as Vice-President and president of the Senate, Mr. Curtis outranked by one seat at any official dinner table the speaker of the House, Nicholas Longworth. But the latter and Mrs. Longworth insisted that there was no such thing as a substitute wife and Mrs. Longworth would not be humiliated by having a seat below Mrs. Gann. As a result there was a crisis in Washington society, with Mrs. Gann accepting invitations to dinners and Mrs. Longworth declining them—until it came the turn of the Egyptian minister, Sesostris Sidarous Pasha, to give a state dinner in the winter of 1930-1931, to which he invited forty-eight guests, among them both Mrs. Longworth and Mrs. Gann. During cocktails before dinner there was one question on every one's mind: Which would go home? Then, as Charles Hurd tells the story in *Washington Cavalcade*—

> Then a footman opened the doors to the dining room of the legation. The male guests, all so schooled in protocol that they automatically started toward the ladies who would go in with them, were stopped by the host. He stepped in front of the doors, himself announced that dinner was served, then smiled broadly, and added:
> "Kindly sit where you please."
> The guests found the dining room dressed, not with the conventional long table, but a cluster of small tables seating four each. Consequently there was no head of the table and no foot of the table.

As one moved West fashionable society became more fluid if not actually chaotic. Thus the Pittsburgh saying that it is only three generations from shirt sleeves to shirt sleeves was interpreted by a British visitor, Harold Brydges, (in *Uncle Sam at Home*, 1888) to mean that the grade next to the top was "formed by those whose fathers had ceased to work in shirtsleeves," while the top level was reserved for those who could afford a blast furnace. The same traveler found the society of "Porkopolis" (Cincinnati) divided into Stick-'ems and Stuck-'ems—the wealthy butchers and the retired pork packers.

And so on, with new antics drawing new laughter. While the British laughed at the Eastern socialites for aping the British aristocracy, New York's Ward McAllister attempted to lay down the law to Chicago society, only to be laughed at for his pains.

In our own day fabulous Texas oil millionaires have found a new criterion of social prestige in the Neiman-Marcus trademark, as in the story of the Highland Park, Dallas, lady who reproved that fabulous department store's deliveryman for using an old black truck without lettering on the outside: "I'll have you know I expect my packages to be delivered in a Neiman-Marcus truck. I want to be sure that the neighbors know where I buy my things."

No less eccentric, if less famous, than Denver's "Unsinkable" Mrs. Brown is Houston's Mrs. Wille, who always carried two sets of false teeth with her—one for eating and one for talking—with a special nail file for sharpening the former.

SOCIETY IN EARLY DENVER

I. KATIE'S PETTICOATS[1]

[The period of the gold and silver rushes of 1859-1870] was a time of social anarchy [in Denver]. George Tillinghast Clark, a descendant of Governor Stephen Hopkins of Rhode Island, came to Colorado in 1860 in a buckboard to try his luck. He married an aristocratic young lady from New York, and to do their cooking and washing hired an Irish girl named Katie. The maid, innocently proud of her mistress' fine lace petticoats from Stewart's in New York City, used to hang them to dry on the highest hilltop of the mining camp. Later she became the wife of an Irish flour-miller, who made millions, and upon being introduced to her former mistress by the proprietor of the department store of Daniels & Fisher, cut her dead with a swish of her own lace petticoats. Today her daughters live in magnificent houses. . . .

II. TABOR'S OPERA HOUSE[2]

. . . Denver . . . was given its Tabor Opera House, which was to be as impressive as money could make it. With Frank Edbrooke, local architect, Tabor journeyed through the East making notes on all larger and handsomer theaters. Edbrooke was sent on to Europe to continue his studies there. In the end, however, Tabor was "practically his own architect" in designing "that matchless specimen of modern architecture, with its perfect plan and arrangement of detail, the auditorium with its graceful curves, its grand columns, exquisite carvings, and luxurious appointments, the stores opening on the streets, and the furnace, pumps, and artesian wells in the basement."

A five-storied office building of red pressed brick, with white stone trim, "an oddity of architectural originality," the general style of the Opera House was perhaps most aptly described as "modified Egyptian Moresque," a phrase coined for it by Eugene Field, who would never be more amused than by Tabor during the next few years.

The theater proper, so Tabor announced, was "designed upon the selected features of the Covent Garden Theater, London, and the Academy of Music, Paris, and combines the beauties and excellencies of both." Italian marble was imported for pilasters, wainscoting, and lintels. Throughout, the theater was finished in red cherry from Japan, and the woodwork everywhere was richly carved and upholstered. Heavy silk fabrics from the looms of France lined the boxes rising in three tiers, with a rare Italian tapestry stretched as a canopy over each.

[1] From *The Saga of American Society*, A Record of Social Aspiration, 1607-1937, by Dixon Wecter, p. 150. Copyright, 1937, by Charles Scribner's Sons. New York.
[2] From *Here They Dug the Gold*, by George F. Willison, pp. 250-252. Copyright, 1946, by George F. Willison. New York: Reynal & Hitchcock.

In the beamed ceiling was a large dome of cathedral glass, from the center of which hung an immense chandelier of cut crystals partially concealing many hundreds of gas jets. Two massive cherry columns supported the proscenium arch. Above, was a mural depicting Hector in the act of comforting Andromache as he sallied forth to battle.

The stage itself was large and well equipped, with an elaborately invested Green Room and many large dressing rooms below. Tabor spent a "small fortune on the curtain alone," giving the commission to a Robert Hopkin of Detroit, recommended to him as "essentially an artist in temperament and as an executant especially strong and effective in marine compositions." But the curtain of the Tabor Grand, famed in the West from that day to this, did not present a seascape but the ruins of an old Roman city, its former grandeur departed, with great marble buildings tumbling to the ground on every hand— a scene of melancholy desolation.

As the opening night approached, a heated and acrimonious debate raged on the question of whether it was to be a "full-dress, swallow-tail affair" or not. Both the *News* and the *Tribune* devoted many long editorials to the issue. Tabor insisted upon the proper formality and was roundly abused.

This, as the *Tribune* (Eugene Field) protested, "does not furnish good grounds for an assault. The wearing of a dress coat has never been regarded as a crime, even in Colorado. A man who will not wear a dress coat on a dress occasion is a snob. . . . When Tabor is before the public as a politician, he is legitimate subject for criticism. When he is before it as an enterprising citizen, he is not."

Tabor had installed Bill Bush as manager of the theater, and for the opening the latter secured the Emma Abbott English Grand Opera Company, which explains Miss Abbott's visit to Leadville. Programs for the occasion were printed on gorgeous white silk. The railways offered low excursion rates from all points within several hundred miles.

On September 5, 1881, an evening long remembered, the Tabor Grand celebrated its opening. A drizzle was falling, unfortunately, as the fashionable and the curious departed for the theater. There was an annoying scarcity of hacks. Disregarding the rain, a large crowd had collected in the street to see the more eminent drive smartly up in their own carriages and alight under the bright marquee. A red plush carpet ran across the sidewalk and up the steps and into the lobby. Here, to one side, was a luxurious reception room where the women doffed their "cloaks of snowy plush" and arranged their jewels and costly gowns —"heavily embroidered silken crapes and exquisite combinations of cashmere and swan's down, satin-lined."

The men improved the interval in the large and highly-polished saloon opening off the other side of the lobby.

Cheers went up in the streets as Tabor drove up and pushed his way into the bright and animated lobby. He was delighted with all he saw there—all but a portrait on the wall. Calling Bill Bush aside, he pointed at the portrait and, so the story goes, inquired:

"Who's that?"

"That's Shakespeare."

"Who the hell is he?"

"Why, the greatest author of plays who ever lived."

"Well, what has he ever done for Colorado? Take it down and put my picture up there!"

HOW SYRACUSE WELCOMED THE CROWN PRINCE OF SIAM [3]

One of the memorable events of the early '90's was the visit to Syracuse of the then Crown Prince of Siam, who stopped over in our town to inspect the [L. C.] Smith typewriter factory. The royal visitor was met at the depot by Mr. Lyman C. Smith and a party of local notables with a brass band and a four-horse chariot known as a tallyho. The prince, a shy, sallow little man, was ensconced on the box between his portly host and the driver from Cronin's livery stable, who was an expert tobacco spitter. The onlookers cheered and the band played. But the bandsmen, being unfamiliar with the Siamese national anthem, chose what they deemed the next most appropriate air with which to salute the future ruler of the Land of the White Elephant:

> Oh, the elephant he goes round,
> And the band begins to play,
> And the boys around the monkey's cage
> Had better keep away!

DOVER PROTOCOL [4]

Dover clings to many old customs which are based not on law but on habit and long tradition. Many of the town's most successful doctors and lawyers prefer to maintain their offices in a one-story wing of their two-story homes instead of clustering together in downtown office buildings. . . .

* * * * *

Newcomers can easily violate some cherished old Dover custom unwittingly. When William K. Paton came down [to Dover] from New Jersey to serve as president of the rich, venerable, and conservative Farmers Bank of the State of Delaware, he knew, of course, that twice a year he must be host to his directors at a dinner. Eager that everything should go off well, he had planned to serve particularly large and juicy steaks and had taken steps to obtain same. Vice-President Gordon Willis, who had been in Dover two years and had learned to move about sure-footedly, set him straight. Since 1807, Willis explained, the president of the Farmers Bank had served his directors Delaware diamondback terrapin and pheasant at the January meeting. At the July meeting the gentlemen must be fed on Lewes lobster and guinea hen.

[3] From *Gone Are the Days*, by E. Alexander Powell, pp. 286-287. Copyright, 1938, by E. Alexander Powell. Boston: Little, Brown and Company.

[4] From "The Cities of America: Dover, Delaware," by Harold H. Martin, *The Saturday Evening Post*, Vol. 222 (August 20, 1949), No. 8, p. 80. Copyright, 1949, by the Curtis Publishing Company. Philadelphia.

HOSPITALITY AT WHITEMARSH HALL [5]

. . . [Whitemarsh Hall] has been turned into a research laboratory by the Pennsylvania Salt Manufacturing Company. The place lies somewhat north of the Main Line proper, but in its heyday it represented all the lavishness and splendor that the Main Line stood for.

The estate was [the] property of Edward T. Stotesbury, partner of Drexel & Company. The mansion, which cost some $10,000,000 to build and furnish, was a white-marble masterpiece. A system of folding walls turned the spacious foyer and the ballroom into one vast dining hall. At its peak the estate kept a staff of 165 busy, and most of them lived in. Seven miles of paved roads wandered over the 310-acre property. At one time the garages sheltered four Rolls Royces and twenty-two lesser automobiles, some of which operated between the Hall and neighboring railroad stations on a round-the-clock schedule.

Queen of this empire was Mrs. Stotesbury, a handsome woman with gray hair upon which she often wore a tiara. She was a gracious hostess, much given to flowing gowns and pearls. She kept a social register of her own. It contained the names of about 300 families. Each January these were carefully weeded and a few new ones added.

Mrs. Stotesbury was one of America's most persistent hostesses and one of the last to make entertaining a spacious occupation. She particularly enjoyed having distinguished house guests and provided them with lavish quarters. A separate living room and perhaps two bedrooms constituted average accommodations. Bathrooms were of marble; the plumbing fixtures were plated with gold. She was one of the first hostesses to stock each guest's bathroom with a complete supply of brand-new toothbrushes, combs and other implements of toiletry.

A feature of the hospitality of Whitemarsh Hall was the questionnaire offered each guest. It contained some fifty questions, such as:

> At what hour do you wish to be awakened?
> At what hour do you wish breakfast?
> Please list your preferred breakfast menu. Lunch. Dinner.
> Shall your food be prepared in accordance with any dietary restrictions?
> Shall any idiosyncrasies of sleep be accommodated? Allergies? Noises?
> Resilience of mattress? Color scheme of sleeping room?
> Is the exposure of the room satisfactory?
> What games do you enjoy? What games do you not enjoy?

The first floor was larger than many a railroad station. Guests had at their disposal a superb billiard room, a library, a conservatory and a music room. They could take in a first-run movie at the private theater. They could wander through the Great Hall, or, outside, among the fountains. The Hall was kept filled with calla lilies, Mrs. Stotesbury's favorite flower. "She loves them," a gardener told me. "Why, sometimes she even comes to the greenhouse herself, in person." The fountains were replicas of those at Versailles. The water was delicately

[5] From "The Main Line," by James A. Michener, *Holiday*, Vol. 7 (April 1950), No. 4, pp. 55, 57. Copyright, 1950, by the Curtis Publishing Company. Philadelphia.

tinted by means of electric lights. About the fountains spread many impeccable gardens and lawns, where Mrs. Stotesbury gave her famous alfresco entertainments, at which she served imported wines and delicacies. Her dinners sometimes included 500 guests, and once, when she was feting a Russian duke, she fed 800.

In many respects Whitemarsh Hall was the perfect symbol of its age. There was only one off-key note. When the parties were over, a dignified, trim-looking man of moderate build would wander unobtrusively from one marbled room to another, turning out the lights. This was Mr. Stotesbury himself.

THE MUNNIKHUYSEN BALL [6]

Generally speaking, Baltimore society is sedate and astonishingly well behaved. Scandals are few and far between. But on the rare occasions when they occur society assumes a tolerant attitude. In one such instance this attitude was well illustrated by a comment made about the lady in the case: "Well, after all, she is just a poor Southern gentlewoman in very seduced circumstances."

In the whole of its long history nothing shocked Baltimore society so much as the incidents associated with the Munnikhuysen Ball. This event took place at the handsome brownstone-front residence of Mrs. William Munnikhuysen on North Charles Street in the early 1900's. The basement was transformed for the evening into "Hell" with demons running about in scarlet tights. Through an unfortunate error in judgment the champagne was allowed to flow too freely and the party got out of hand. Every one said it was too bad it had happened at Mrs. Munnikhuysen's because she was such a dear soul and hadn't planned it that way.

For weeks the town rang with gossip over what had gone on. Children cocked an ear and listened to the whispered conversations of the grownups. Before long the teen-age boys and girls in the private schools were chanting the limerick:

> There was a young lady named Nance
> Who attended the Munnikhuysen dance.
> She went down the cellar
> With a handsome young feller
> And now all her sisters are aunts.

WASHINGTON CAVE DWELLERS [7]

[Among] "the Little Innermost Circle of [Washington's] select residents and intense exclusives" [are those who] have long been called the Cave-Dwellers. Some of them live in shabby old relics of former genteel elegance; others occupy particularly handsome caves, if we may judge by their exteriors,

[6] From *The Amiable Baltimoreans*, by Francis F. Beirne, p. 297. Copyright, 1951, by E. P. Dutton & Co., Inc. New York.
[7] From *Washington, the Cinderella City*, by William Oliver Stevens, pp. 305-306. Copyright, 1943, by Dodd, Mead and Company. New York.

which is all the rest of us are likely to see. Rich or poor, however, their mental attitude is the same.

The daughter of one of these Dwellers returned from her visit to Europe with a number of souvenirs for her mother. One of these was a fine reproduction of a famous Whistler painting in the Luxembourg.

"Whistler's mother?" The lady's nose went aloft. "What on earth did you buy that for? Don't you know she was only a McNeill from North Carolina?"

THE GREAT OASIS [8]

During Prohibition [Washington] was fairly dry, yet blessed with unique islands within itself. In the beginning of the drouth, those parts of Washington that were legally "foreign soil" (that is, the ambassadorial establishments) loomed as a veritable mirage in the eyes of many Americans. Suddenly even a hitherto unnoticed bush-league-legation attaché found he had hundreds of bosom friends—all thirsty.

The smart embassies and legations—smart both ways—avoided the onslaught of thirsty hordes on the diplomatic hostesses' open days at home by blandly serving nothing stronger than tea or coffee, reserving alcoholic bounty for the invitational parties they gave on other days than the traditional Friday, when they could tell exactly who was coming and know how they would behave. Some of the minor diplomats, however, were taken for the most intoxicated "rides" in Washington history. For one thing, they didn't have the strict and capable social secretaries the other diplomats did; and for another, supposedly disinterested American "friends" probably sold them the idea that Prohibition was their priceless opportunity to cement American friendship for their countries.

Perhaps the climax of the whole thing came when rotund Samy Pasha, the Egyptian Minister at the time, who was as stubborn as he was rich, insisted on giving an "open" tea dance every week (set for Tuesday afternoon instead of the sacred Friday, thus antagonizing both the diplomats and the Congressional set, whose "day" it was) featuring a bar whose flow seemed inexhaustible as the Nile. Naturally word got around town that the Egyptian Legation was the Great Oasis; and poor Samy was hurt and bewildered when the "important" people he had expected to attract were crowded out and repelled by numbers of uncouth and disreputable people no one had known existed in Washington, who utterly overran the Legation, to sweet Mme. Samy's consternation.

The Minister, nevertheless, insisted on keeping up his parties; until it was discovered that they were actually included in "What's Going On in Washington This Week," the throwaway given out at all the cigar stands in town; and then even he had to admit defeat.

[8] From *There's No Place like Washington,* by Vera Bloom, pp. 39-40. Copyright, 1944, by Vera Bloom. New York: G. P. Putnam's Sons.

"LIKE MRS. ASTOR'S . . . HORSE"[9]

In the grand old days the real queen of Newport was Mrs. William Astor, widow of the grandson of the first John Jacob Astor. She was known simply as "Mrs. Astor" and was the dominant figure in New York and Newport society until her death in 1908. Her annual ball in her home at 842 Fifth Avenue was, as they say at the Madison bar, something. It was in the late nineteenth century that the gilded, overstuffed magnificence of Mrs. Astor led the peasants to say of any one who was rather ostentatiously dolled up: "She is dressed up like Mrs. Astor's plush horse." Sometimes the phrase was "Mrs. Astor's pet horse."

THE FOUR HUNDRED [10]

. . . Ward McAllister [was] "The Autocrat of Drawing Rooms," as he rejoiced to be known, though "ringmaster" might have been more accurate. . . .

*   *   *   *   *

In New York McAllister saw that Society was divided into the "nobs," old crustacean families who had position without fashion, and the "swells," who had to entertain and be smart in order to win their way. By a skilful mixture of both, he decided, Society might be given that solidity needed to resist invasion of the flashiest profiteers. As a matter of fact, McAllister was the only man of his time willing to give his days and nights to the study of heraldry, books of court etiquette, genealogy, and cookery, to getting up balls and banquets, to the making of guestlists and the interviewing of ambitious mothers with débutante daughters. These things he came to love as a miser his gold. It did not occur to him until near his death in 1895, when Society had dropped him after the publication of his fatuous book [*Society as I Have Found It*], that perhaps he had really been the glorified butler of the Four Hundred rather than its master. But meanwhile—set off against the coruscations of Mrs. Astor's jewels, and the pedigrees of his friends the Riveses, Kanes, and Livingstons— McAllister cut a very imperial figure, and his fame was borne so far by newspapers that, upon his rare travels through the hinterland, yokels would walk miles to catch a glimpse of "the world's greatest dude." In sober truth he was not an imposing sight, with his paunch, a weedy little Van Dyke, rapidly thinning hair, and expensive clothes which he wore so badly that they looked as if they had been thrust upon him. The secret of his success was the immense seriousness with which he took himself and his part as Grand Patriarch. "Fashion," he wrote, "selects its own votaries. You will see certain members of a family born to it, as it were, others of the same family with none of its

[9] From *Mrs. Astor's Horse*, by Stanley Walker, p. 8. Copyright, 1935, by Stanley Walker. Philadelphia and New York: J. B. Lippincott Company.
[10] From *The Saga of American Society*, A Record of Social Aspiration, 1607-1937, by Dixon Wecter, pp. 210, 212-213, 214, 215-216. Copyright, 1937, by Charles Scribner's Sons. New York.

attributes. You can give no explanation of this; 'One is taken, the other left.'
Such and such a man or woman is cited as having been always fashionable.
The talent of and for Society develops itself as does the talent for art." With
his Huguenot blood, it came to seem to McAllister much like the dogma of
predestination.

The means for organizing Society, he saw, lay in a revival of the old
assemblies. The New York Dancing Assembly, coeval with the Philadelphia
Assembly, had flourished in the eighteenth century; John Jay was one of its
ablest managers. In the early nineteenth century the Bachelor Balls had over-
shadowed all else. . . .

*　*　*　*　*

In 1866-67, shortly before Archibald Gracie King brought the début to
Delmonico's, Ward McAllister got up a series of cotillion suppers there—where
he sat among *grandes dames* at the head of the table and whispered confidential
forecasts about the social fate of newcomers. Encouraged by these successes,
and mindful of the great London tradition of Almack's, McAllister in the
winter of 1872-73 organized the Patriarchs, a committee of twenty-five men
"who had the right to create and lead Society" by inviting to each ball four
ladies and five gentlemen on their individual responsibility, which McAllister
stressed as a sacred trust. . . .

*　*　*　*　*

McAllister's flowering time was in the 1880's at the threshold of a new
social extravagance, when because of national economics gold replaced silver
plate, the orchid dwarfed the rose, music was played between the courses of
private dinners, butlers' wages rose from $40 a month to $75, and canvasbacks
formerly $2.50 a pair went up to $8 within a decade. McAllister's own vulgar
materialism and snobbery—"the mean admiration of mean things," as Thackeray
defined it—blended with real knowledge of wines and cooking, and interlarded
with anecdotes about the Grand Duke of Tuscany's receptions, suited to perfection the taste of this era. Also, in common with his age, he prided himself
upon belonging to the smallest possible groups but giving the largest possible
parties: the climax of his book is the New Year's Ball of 1890, given at the
Metropolitan Opera House for 1200, which he staged with the assistance of
300 servants in livery. He also encouraged a passing whim in New York—"to
build an addition to one's house, to be used but for one night, and to be made
large enough to comfortably hold, with the house, one thousand or twelve hundred people."

Yet to the newspapers his greatest fame lay in frequent statements like this
to a reporter from the Tribune on March 25, 1888: "Why, there are only
about 400 people in fashionable New York Society. If you go outside that
number you strike people who are either not at ease in a ballroom or else
make other people not at ease. See the point? . . . When we give a large ball
like the last New Year's ball for 800 guests, we go outside of the exclusive
fashionable set, and invite professional men, doctors, lawyers, editors, artists and

the like." The Four Hundred caught the fancy of the time. There were endless speculations about its membership, reports that it had been whittled to 150, and the contrary announcement of *Life* in 1890 that it had risen to 1500 because Wall Street had got control and watered the stock. The same magazine proposed to run Ward McAllister and Albert Wettin of Wales on a Society ticket for President and Vice-President, and published a Gibson drawing whose caption divided New York into "the Bohemian set, all brains and no style, Society proper with a fair amount of each, and the Four Hundred, all style and no brains." Gibson caricatured McAllister as a goose-girl rounding up the flock, and as a marshal on a hobbyhorse leading the parade of 400 marchers bearing 'scutcheons blazoned with "fur," "lumber," "groceries," and the like. When McAllister's memoirs, *Society as I Have Found It,* appeared, *Life* showed a patrolman who had just collared two drunks in white ties:

> *Captain.* What's that you've got, O'Hara?
> *Roundsman O'Hara.* Society as Oi have found it, sorr.

After tantalizing the public for years McAllister finally gave the official list of his Four Hundred to the New York *Times* on the occasion of Mrs. Astor's great ball, February 1, 1892—for, according to popular report, the dimensions of her ballroom coincided exactly with the limitations of gilt-edged Society. His list, it will be seen, comprises just over 300 names; perhaps, as has been suggested, the rest were abroad, had retired from social activity on account of age or mourning, or else belonged to the unstable fringe which fluctuated from season to season. As a matter of fact, his commitment to "Four Hundred" was probably the whim of a moment, under that genial intoxication which a press-reporter always evoked in McAllister; the list he had in mind was simply the roll-call of Patriarch Balls with its 250 requisite names, and a sprinkling of eligible visitors from other cities and abroad. . . .

KING LEHR

I. His Sayings[11]

"I don't suppose you have any idea of the way I live. . . . Well, I shall have to enlighten you. I live not on my wits, but on my wit. I make a career of being popular. [Wetzel makes all my clothes free.] He has an idea, which I naturally encourage, that it is a privilege to dress the man who, according to newspapers, 'sets' the fashion for American manhood. . . . He never even suggests anything so vulgar as payment for his suits. . . . I never pay for one single thing I wear, not even a tie or a handkerchief. . . . Now you are probably thinking that clothes are only a small part of a man's yearly expenditure, and that other things must cost far more. They don't. I get everything else in the same way. . . . It is quite easy to do it once you become the fashion."

[11] From *"King Lehr" and the Gilded Age,* with Extracts from the Locked Diary of Harry Lehr, by Elizabeth Drexel Lehr, pp. 38-40, 48, 53, 54-55, 59-60, 112-113, 154. Copyright, 1935, by Elizabeth Drexel Lehr. Philadelphia and New York: J. B. Lippincott Company.

"I never confide in any one. . . . Explaining oneself is the refuge of the weak; it always puts you at a disadvantage."

*   *   *   *   *

"Other men have to sweat in offices. I made up my mind I never would. I had only to be amusing to get a living, much better than working for one. . . ."

*   *   *   *   *

"I went to Wetzel's and had my clothes fitted on. I did the very best I could to hide how it bored me. Oh, if only I could wear ladies' clothes; all silks and dainty petticoats and laces, how I should love to choose them. I love shopping even for my wife."

*   *   *   *   *

"There are three ways of taking an insult. . . . You can resent it and walk out of the room, in which case you have committed yourself to a quarrel you may later regret; you can pretend not to hear, or you can laugh and turn it into a joke. I always choose the last, for I find it the most disarming. No one can quarrel with a man who laughs like an idiot."

*   *   *   *   *

[Advice to a woman on how to succeed at Newport.] "First, Be modest. Go quietly at the start; don't try to be original in your entertaining or your equipages. . . . Follow the lead of the others instead of striking out your own trail. Second, Never try to take any other woman's man, whether husband, lover, or well-wisher. Third, Never try to out-dress or out-jewel the other women."

*   *   *   *   *

"Samson's strength lay in his hair. . . . Mine lies in the favor of women. . . . All I have to do is to keep in their good graces and everything comes to me. . . ."

II. The Monkey Dinner[12]

Mrs. Stuyvesant Fish might have attained to the most coveted position in American society had it not been for the "Monkey Dinner," which created an enormous sensation.

I came in from driving one afternoon and met Harry Lehr in the hall.

"Joseph Leiter has just rung up," he told me. "He wanted to know whether he might bring a friend to our dinner party tomorrow night. I told him I was sure you would not mind as it is not to be a big, formal affair."

"Who is the friend?" I asked.

"Prince del Drago, who is staying on the yacht with him. Joe says he is a charming fellow, and comes from Corsica. I asked him whether he was any relation of the del Dragos whom we met in Rome, and he said that certainly he was. They all belong to the same family, only the Prince's is a distant

---

[12] Ibid., pp. 150-151.

branch. Joe thinks we shall like him immensely, but he warned me that he is a little inclined to be wild. He doesn't want us to give him too much to drink, because he is not used to it. Anything goes to his head, and then apparently he is apt to behave rather badly."

"Of course I shall be delighted to see him," I replied, "and I will tell the butler not to fill up his glass too often."

The story of our aristocratic guest spread like wildfire. Every one wanted to meet the charming Prince from Corsica.

A CHIMPANZEE IN AN ANCESTRAL TREE

The next evening, all the guests were assembled eagerly expecting a thrill, and they got one, but not the sort they were looking for. . . . Promptly at eight o'clock the doors were flung open and in walked Joe Leiter holding by the hand a small monkey correctly attired in full evening dress.

Of course, as the Prince was to be the guest of honor, there was nothing to be done except to treat him with befitting dignity. He was given the seat on my right with Mrs. Fish, who, like Harry Lehr, had been in the secret all the time, on his other side, and throughout dinner he behaved admirably. I hardly like to write that his manners compared favourably with those of some princes I have met, but it would be no less than the truth.

The dinner party was a great success, but somehow the story, absurdly exaggerated, got into the hands of the newspaper reporters and the result was a deluge of sarcastic comments. Harry and Mrs. Fish were stated to have "held up American society to ridicule. . . ."

"OLD BILLY" TRAVERS: RESORT WIT [18]

. . . The greatest of all the old-time resort wits . . . was William R. Travers. Newporter and Saratogian, lawyer and *bon vivant*, Travers had two town houses, three resort cottages and belonged to twenty-seven clubs; he was founder of the Racquet Club, predecessor of today's Racquet & Tennis Club, and the Travers Stakes at Saratoga, oldest horse race in the country, was named for him. A genial man with a port wine complexion, "Old Billy," as he was affectionately called, had a wit which was heightened by the fact that he stammered. Once accused by a friend of stammering worse in New York than he had in his native Baltimore, Travers replied, "This is a d-d-damned sight b-b-bigger city."

Back in Baltimore, Travers' first home was furnished in the early Victorian manner with a sign in worsted work hanging on the dining room wall; the sign read, of course, "God Bless Our Home." One day, after a prolonged period of servant trouble in the home, Mrs. Travers, who was nearsighted, noted a sign which, painstakingly made to parallel the old, had been placed on the opposite wall. Adjusting her glasses, she read, "God Damn Our Cook." One night Travers arrived home late and tiptoed upstairs. "Is that you, Bill?" his wife called out. "Y-y-yes," called back Travers. "Wh-wh-whom did y-y-you expect?" After the Travers family had bought a small farm in New Jersey, a large landowner from upstate New York became engaged to Travers' daughter and, on visiting the Travers farm, was surprised to find only a row of box stables, some gamecock walks and a few paddocks. "What do you raise here?" he asked Travers sharply. Travers sighed. "H-h-hell," he said.

Travers' most famous resort observation was undoubtedly the one which he made at Newport after being shown a vista of beautiful yachts, almost all of which, upon inquiry, he discovered belonged to Wall Street brokers. "Wh-wh-where," he asked, "are the c-c-customers' yachts?"

In New York one day, passing the Union Club, Travers was asked if all of the men who could be seen in their chairs from the street outside were actually habitués of the club. "N-n-no," said Travers, "s-s-some are s-s-sons of h-h-habit-ués." A Democrat in politics at a time when such feeling in resort circles was as akin to heresy as it is today, Travers particularly enjoyed taking the measure of a rising group of Republican millionaires. On one occasion A. T. Stewart, owner of Saratoga's Grand Union Hotel, took over a meeting, pulled

[18] From *The Last Resorts,* by Cleveland Amory, pp. 62-64. Copyright, 1948, 1952, by Cleveland Amory; 1951, 1952, by the Curtis Publishing Company. New York: Harper & Brothers.

a gold pencil case from his pocket and rapped for order. Cried Travers sharply, "C-c-cash." On another occasion seeing Newporter Henry Clews, who always boasted of being a self-made man, pompously enter a room, Travers stopped him. "I say, Cl-cl-clews," he said, "s-s-since you are a s-s-self-made man, why the d-d-devil didn't you put more h-h-hair on your h-h-head?"

Unlike most wits, Travers was haunted by the fear of repeating himself; with his wife and children he worked out a special arrangement of signals. If he began on a story which they knew the company present had heard him tell before, they would discreetly hold up one finger if he had told it once before, two fingers if twice before, and so forth. Unlike most wits also, Travers was funny to the end. He spent his last winter, at the age of sixty-eight, in Bermuda, in the hope that the climate might affect his diabetes. Unfortunately it did not. On his deathbed a friend called on him and mentioned what a nice resort Bermuda was for rest and change. "Y-y-yes," replied Travers wearily, "the w-w-waiters get the ch-ch-change and the h-h-hotel the r-r-rest."

THE COOGAN LEGEND [14]

As Newporters look back over their long history, they are impressed by the many ups and downs the resort has witnessed. Many families, notably Philadelphia's Wideners and Drexels, have made successes at Newport before they made them in their own home towns, and, conversely, other families who have made successes in their home towns have failed to duplicate these at Newport. The most curious case in Newport history concerned New York's Coogan family. Early in the 1900's the late James J. Coogan, former Manhattan Borough President and inheritor of large real estate holdings including the Polo Grounds, home of the New York Giants, decided to invade Newport. He bought on Catherine Street one of Newport's most beautiful cottages, called "Whitehall." This cottage boasted a handsome pillared portico, an enormous ballroom and music room, and solid mahogany doors with silver doorbells; Stanford White, who designed it, considered it his best Georgian work. In short order, "Whitehall" became a Newport legend.

This legend, as Newporters tell it, began in 1910 when, they say, the Coogans gave a housewarming to their cottage and to it invited all Newport's best. A retinue of servants readied grounds and groceries, and all manner of feasting and festivities were planned. On the night of the party the Coogans descended into their drawing room and waited. Not one guest appeared. Mrs. Fish, the legend goes, disliked the Coogans and she sent out invitations for a party of her own on the same night; as an additional insurance that no one would go to the Coogans she had announced that Paderewski would play. That very night the Coogans paid off their servants, took just one piece of luggage containing Mrs. Coogan's jewels and went back to New York. Then the Coogans took revenge. For the next thirty-five years they allowed "Whitehall" to stand just the way it was that fateful night—in its first days, with dishes and even food still on the table. As time went by, windows were smashed, the

[14] *Ibid.,* pp. 232-234.

cottage broken into, and everything of value stolen, including an enormous revolving statue of the son of William Tell, complete with arrow, apple and tree—a statue which took five men to lift. Outside, the once velvety lawns of the Coogans became hayfields, but each year the Coogans paid their taxes and not until 1945 did they decide that thirty-five years of revenge was enough and permit the town to tear down the dilapidated eyesore.

Actually this legend is false. The Coogans were in Newport for several seasons before the alleged housewarming took place. Mrs. Fish who was no enemy of the Coogans, did not either have Paderewski play or indeed give any party in opposition to theirs—in fact, the Coogans that year gave no party themselves. The winter before the alleged party took place, a severe fire had gutted "Whitehall" and the Coogans, believing that the cottage was totally destroyed, had not bothered to salvage what remained of their linen, clothes, silver, and china; this, of course, gave rise to the legend about the dishes and food still on the table. As for the strange idea of leaving "Whitehall" to stand as an eyesore for thirty-five years, this too is explained. Mrs. Coogan, an extremely independent woman, lived in virtual seclusion for many years in New York. She remembered liking "Whitehall" and determined that she would never tear it down; not until just two years before her death was her son able to persuade her to do so.

In spite of the lack of truth in the legend and the damage its currency did to the Coogan family, the legend is basic for an understanding of Newport Society. Far from attempting to hush the affair Coogan, Newporters enjoyed pointing out the ghost cottage on Catherine Street as a definite sight to see and a thing to know. Always sensitive to the charge that making good in Newport was primarily a matter of money, the Coogan legend was to Newport a visible example that the charge was false, and the fact that the legend too was false was to them just an unimportant technicality.

WARD McALLISTER AND CHICAGO SOCIETY [15]

There were other preparations to be made for the [World's] fair [of 1893]. It was time for a municipal election and the choice of a mayor to represent Chicago before the world. The Democrats named Carter H. Harrison—"Our Carter"—to run for a fifth term. . . . Harrison was elected by a narrow margin and his victory was taken as a sign that Chicago would be a wide-open town during his administration (except for those gamblers who had been so unwise as to oppose his candidacy). Mayor Harrison was quick to assure prospective visitors from over the country a genuine Chicago welcome. He promised the latchstring would always be out at the mayor's house. The city's hospitality might be rough, he said, but it would be genuine. He announced that he had purchased a supply of two hundred barrels of whisky for official entertaining—adding a discretionary warning that Chicago whisky could kill "at the distance of a mile."

[15] From *Fabulous Chicago,* by Emmett Dedmon, pp. 222-225. Copyright, 1953, by Emmett Dedmon. New York: Random House.

In New York, Ward McAllister, counselor and chamberlain to Mrs. William Astor, whose edicts were the supreme law of New York society, was alarmed at the prospect of New Yorkers being treated with such boisterous informality. Through the columns of the New York *World*, he suggested to Mayor Harrison that "it is not quantity but quality that the society here want. Hospitality which includes the whole human race is not desirable." He also conveyed some suggestions to Chicago hostesses. In New York, he explained, it was the custom to keep abreast of the times when entertaining. He recommended that Chicago women follow the practice of the East where "society supplies itself with a résumé of everything that is going on" before attending a dinner party. This, he said, explains the fact that "when you go into fashionable houses you will find a good deal of intellect."

Dining, McAllister explained, was a matter of great importance. "I would suggest that Chicago society import a number of fine French chefs," he said. "I should also advise that they do not frappé their wine too much. Let them put the bottle in the tub and be careful to keep the neck free from ice. For, the quantity of wine in the neck of the bottle being small, it will be acted upon by the ice first. In twenty-five minutes from the time of being placed in the tub it will be in perfect condition to be served immediately. What I mean by a perfect condition is that when the wine is poured from the bottle it should contain little flakes of ice. That is a real frappé." The *Journal*, reporting a dinner which the mayor was giving for sixty foreign naval officers, assured McAllister that "the mayor will not frappé his wine too much. He will frappé it just enough so the guests can blow the foam off the tops of the glasses without a vulgar exhibition of lung and lip power. His ham sandwiches, sinkers and Irish quail, better known in the Bridgeport vernacular as pigs' feet, will be triumphs of the gastronomic art."

Not wishing New Yorkers to become excessively alarmed, McAllister assured them that "the women of Chicago are well-dressed and cultivated. They will do their best to entertain New York society and they will have plenty of money to do it with." He disclosed that "a number of our young men are already beginning to make their investigations as to the wealth and beauty of Chicago women with the result that they are now more anxious to go to the fair than ever." These matrimonial investigations were somewhat aided by the *Journal* which ran a story of "Eligible Maidens [who] Abound in This Fair City"; but, the paper warned, though many of the girls have wealth, "fortune hunters find them possessed of a keen instinct and plenty of common sense."

Chicago's replies to McAllister's views were rapid in coming. He was addressed by the local papers in such terms of disaffection as Singular Personage, Head Butler, New York Flunky, A Mouse Colored Ass, A Popinjay, A Delightful Duffer, and by the *Times*, traditionally supreme in epithetical exchange, as The Premier of Cadsville. Gussie Gander, a columnist for the *Times*, submitted a list of questions which she thought applicants for high social position might be required to answer. One of them was: "Do you consider Ward McAllister a great man, a simple poseur, or an ordinary every day matter-of-fact damn fool?" To this McAllister replied haughtily, "I require no Chicago indorsement."

The uproar over McAllister's etiquette suggestions offended the New York *World*, which tried to explain with more condescension than good will that McAllister had only spoken "in a kindly spirit as one who is anxious to see the society of the West elevate itself by observing the society of the East." McAllister was almost pedantic in his detachment. "I never intended to convey the impression that any New Yorker as a man is necessarily superior to a native of Chicago," he said. "We in New York are familiar with the sharp character of Chicago magnates and many of us have learned to our cost that the Almighty Dollar is the trail they are following." But he did not think "these Chicagoans should pretend to rival the East and Old World in matters of refinement. Their growth has been too rapid for them to acquire both wealth and culture. . . . The leaders of society are the successful Stock Yards magnates, cottolene manufacturers, soapmakers, Chicago gas trust speculators, and dry goods princes. These gentlemen are undoubtedly great in business but perhaps in some cases unfamiliar with the niceties of life and difficult points of etiquette which constitute the society man or woman. For several years, for example, society persons have always hired a man to lead their Germans. He gets $25. That, to a New Yorker, appears extraordinary. It is a little out of line. Again, Chicago's most famous millionaires have a ballroom in the attic which is approached by an elevator. This seems to be an incongruity. Here, in the East, the opinion is that the approach should be as artistically effective as the ballroom itself."

Chicago was particularly vulnerable to the thrust about the third-floor ballrooms. Putting these seldom-used party rooms on the third floor was the accepted practice in almost every Chicago mansion. The city's press defended its finest houses and their unusual features only to incur more of McAllister's disapprobation. Denying that he had ever said anything unfavorable about "ladies sitting on the doorsteps in summer," he repeated that his sole criticism had been about "the novel idea of putting a ballroom in a man's attic. In this city we don't go to balls in private houses by climbing a ladder or going up in an elevator. . . . A bowling alley," he added for the benefit of those who had cited these appointments as an indication of the luxurious quality of the dwellings of Chicago millionaires, "is also an objectionable feature in any house. Why not have a shooting gallery?" In hopes of terminating the dispute, he turned to a philosophical approach. "It takes nearly a lifetime to educate a man how to live," he said. "Therefore Chicagoans can't expect to attain social knowledge without experience and contact with those who have made such things the study of their lives. In these modern days, society cannot get along without French chefs. The man who has been accustomed to delicate fillets of beef, terrapin, pâté de foie gras, truffled turkey, and things of that sort would not care to sit down to a boiled leg of mutton dinner with turnips. . . . One paper says it is evidently my opinion that cultivated society is one in which the entertainment of the stomach is perfectly understood. That is a sound maxim."

THE MET [16]

[The Met] had come into being in 1883 because of the jealousies between the old New York aristocracy and a new rising group of millionaires. The old aristocracy had, for thirty years before the advent of the Met, attended operas at the old Academy of Music, at Fourteenth Street and Irving Place. Here there had been enough boxes so that the elect of society could see one another and be seen by the multitude of ordinary opera-goers who, poor souls, attended the opera merely to hear the music. There they could come, these proud families, to sneer down at the members of the new aristocracy of mere wealth, sitting in their seats in the orchestra. Of course the latter could sneer back. But a sneer going down is far more effective than a sneer going up. The newcomers offered many thousands of dollars for the privilege of sitting in the boxes, but they were haughtily rejected.

Eventually, the rich occupants of the orchestra stalls at the Academy of Music got tired of the sneers of the nabobs seated above them and, unable to endure their sufferings any longer, purchased a plot of ground at Broadway and Thirty-ninth Street, where they proceeded to build an opera house which would be bigger and better in every way than the old Academy of Music. On its completion, their hopes were realized. Here was an opera house with more boxes and bigger boxes than had ever been seen before. These, in fact, over-shadowed every other feature of the building, including the stage.

On October 22, 1883 . . . the beginning of New York's 1883-1884 opera season was marked by *two* opening performances. At the Academy of Music, Colonel Mapleson, its veteran manager, put on Bellini's *Sonnambula,* with Etelka Gerster, an extremely popular diva, in the star role. At Broadway and Thirty-ninth Street, Manager Henry E. Abbey produced Gounod's *Faust* with Christine Nilsson, also a tremendously admired prima donna, as the principal star. "My audience is the Faubourg Saint-Germain," boasted the Colonel. "My rival is supported, I understand, by a number of rich persons who want a new way of spending money." And he sneeringly called the new Metropolitan Opera House "the new yellow brewery on Broadway."

At the end of that season the Mapleson-Abbey fight looked like a draw. Abbey . . . was badly shaken (the season had cost his backers around $600,-000), but he still held his lines. Mapleson, though his losses were less, was pro-portionately as badly shaken. But . . . he did not retreat. Instead, he prepared defiantly for the season of 1884-1885 with the renowned Adelina Patti as his most formidable asset.

The new opera house opened its second season under the aegis of Dr. Leopold Damrosch, who was not only its executive director but one of the leaders of its orchestra. One of the most ardent disciples of Richard Wagner, Damrosch wanted to introduce the Wagnerian operas in New York in proper fashion (up to that time they had been performed there only occasionally and

[16] From *Caruso,* The Man of Naples and the Voice of Gold, by T. R. Ybarra, pp. 109-113. Copyright, 1953, by T. R. Ybarra. New York: Harcourt, Brace and Company.

in an unsatisfactory manner). The directors of the Met voted in favor of the Damrosch proposal. The musical dictatorship of Wagner in New York had begun. It received what might have been a serious setback when Damrosch died early in 1885, with his first season in full swing. But the Wagnerites put in his place as musical director the famous Anton Seidl, one of the greatest of German Wagnerian conductors.

At the close of this season, the Academy of Music struck its flag. "I cannot fight Wall Street," sneered Colonel Mapleson. For its 1886-1887 season New York had only one opening night instead of two—and that one was at the "yellow brewery on Broadway."

For several seasons thereafter Anton Seidl labored mightily to add the conquest of America to the triumphs already achieved by Wagner in Europe. Filled with a fanatical zeal, Seidl met for a while with sweeping success.

But during this Wagner period there was rising discontent among the grand tier box-holders. How could they assert their importance adequately against the crashing orchestral opposition supplied by the master of Bayreuth? How much easier it had been to do so in competition with the music of the average Italian or French opera! Thus they grumbled, while Wagner rumbled. In their disgruntlement they began to undermine Richard Wagner and Anton Seidl, his prophet. Their efforts were successful. Soon Henry Abbey was put at the helm of the Met again.

In August, 1892, there was a fire that almost ended the opera house's career. Much of the orchestra floor and many of the boxes were devastated. But the restorers of the building reasserted the tremendous importance of the boxes in relation to everything else. At the brilliant reopening of the opera house on November 27, 1893, the year after the fire, the Diamond Horseshoe burst on the metropolis in all its gorgeousness and for many years it was to glow and shine and sparkle in its matchless glory. Prominent and prodigiously rich families and individuals figured all through that Golden Age of Opera among the Met's box-holders. They drove up to the portals of the opera house in costly carriages; and after they had seated themselves, the rest of the audience gazed in awe at the splendor of their apparel or the magnificence of their jewels. From 1893 onward the members of the audience found printed on their programs, to add to their enjoyment of each performance, a plan of the boxes with their numbers and the names of those holding them. From then onward the grand tier parterre boxes came to be known as the Diamond Horseshoe and the tier above as the Golden Horseshoe.

CAFÉ SOCIETY [17]

It was a bitter cold, windy, sleeting night in February of 1919. . . . In the downstairs dining room of the swank Ritz-Carlton in midtown Manhattan, the fat little society writer was as warm as toast, as comfortable as a marshmallow on a cushion and as delightfully nosy as ever. . . .

[17] From *Champagne Cholly, The Life and Times of Maury Paul,* by Eve Brown, pp. 277, 278-280. Copyright, 1947, by E. P. Dutton & Co., Inc. New York.

"This place!" he murmured to himself. "Society isn't staying home and entertaining any more. Society is going out to dinner, out to night life, and letting down the barriers. Heavens—that I should see a Widener, a Goelet, a Corrigan and a Warren all together. It's like a sea-food cocktail, with everything from eels to striped bass!"

The next morning, history, to coin a phrase, was made. For Maury Paul had given this new order of things a name. The name was: "Café Society." In the years to come that tag was to become more and more widely known; it was the title of a movie in which Madeleine Carroll played a headstrong débutante the way Hollywood heroines always play headstrong débutantes (with overtones of Jimmy Durante); it became the name of not one but *two* New York night-clubs (one of which first labeled itself "The Right Place to Meet the Wrong People," and had a ten-cent cover charge, but later degenerated into a standard cellar joint); it became the qualifying phrase for all murders involving any one who wore a white collar; and it even turned up as the title of a directory unsuccessfully designed to supplant the *Social Register* and known as *Café Society Register*. It became, as we say, a household word, as accepted as Walter Winchell's "blessed event" or "reno-vated," and as casually used as "glamor girl," also coined by Maury. It came into being simply because The Man sat in the Ritz one night and saw some Goelets sitting with a Widener and a Corrigan.

The popularity of the term, it must be admitted, is due in a great part to Lucius Beebe who started using it often in writing his weekly pillar in the *Herald Tribune* on cooking, drinking, and the best place to buy mauve garters. This was one instance where Mr. Beebe, ordinarily astute but never as shrewd as Maury by far, beat Mr. Paul to the draw. For when, in 1938, Paramount Pictures set about making their epic called *Café Society*, that organization paid $5,000 merely for the use of the title, but not to Maury Paul. They paid it to Lucius Beebe. This sent Maury into what amounted to a purple rage, but early in 1939 justice was done. As he explained it: "I was pretty m-a-d! Not because Beebe got the $5,000 (or was it $50,000?). No, indeed! I realize he's a struggling reporter without a New York penthouse, a Connecticut country estate, a Rolls Royce [ed. note—Maury had all these] or any of the other luxuries of life except a few eye-compelling habiliments. And I was glad to know he had put it over in such slick style on the usually alert Hollywoodians. It was being robbed of the 'honor'—not the money that gave me high blood pressure. Now at long last, that 'honor' has been returned to me by none other than Lucius Beebe (I'm wondering if he still has that $5,000 or was it $50,000?) and my blood pressure can return to normal. In last Sunday's *Herald Tribune*, writing from Hollywood, Lucius, who weaves words in such a natty way, even if he didn't weave 'Café Society,' says: 'A deafening tumult has raged in the public prints for the last two or three years over the origin of "Café Society." The eloquent Cholly Knickerbocker, without any contradiction from any source whatever, has asserted and reasserted he first coined the phrase back in the dim, forgotten era of the livery stable and Mrs. Stuyvesant Fish. . . . Any award which Paramount may be bestowing *pour le mérite* in the interests of "Café Society" should be bestowed upon Cholly Knickerbocker.'"

CHOLLY KNICKERBOCKER'S ENGLISH [18]

In describing his city of little jewels and their didoes, Maury [H. B. Paul] came up with the damnedest set of expressions in the history of civilized self-expression. The beginning writer always has a fanatic determination to steer clear of clear, simple prose, just as Harvard students, as Alexander Woollcott once wrote, "fastidiously avoid anything so simple as a simple declarative." Maury, who never professed to be a genius of the pen, was no exception. Furthermore, he fell deeply in love with the purple phrase and the lush simile, so that his expressions and phrases were wondrous to behold. It is likely that greater corn never has seen or ever will see the light of day.

If you were in Maury's embrace, you never heeded the calls of your screaming glands by falling in love. You "succumbed to the darts of that greatest of sharpshooters, Dan Cupid." If Mrs. Vanderbilt made a gaudy entrance into the Plaza, people didn't merely look at her. All Optics Turned In Her Direction. If it were a sunny day, Old Sol Reigned Supreme. Some of these are pure Maury Paul and could have been chiseled or turned by no one else; others are recognizable to authors and newspapermen as celebrated clichés which always are used by writers between their seventeenth and eighteenth years and then discarded with a shudder.

Let us look at a brief lexicon:

Dee-lighted: happy
Doughty Dowagers: rich women
Grand Old Provider, or *G.O.P.:* sugar-daddy
Hoity-toity: snobbish
Longuyland: Long Island
Oodles of ducats: money
Social Sultana: Mrs. O. H. P. Belmont
Soury Sours: nasty people
Staid and Steadies, or *Stout and Steadies:* ladies of the old guard
Sweetie Sweets: lovely people
Those Who Should Know Whereof They Speak: the well-informed
The Torrid Months: summer
The Turreted Tiara Set: opera first-nighters

And *ad nauseam.* A girl was never simply beautiful; she was beauteous. Women with black hair always were raven-hued or raven-tressed. Dollars, of course, were $$$$$$$. When a girl married, it was really a production—she "embraced holy matrimony" or "took a dip in the matrimonial seas." Similarly, a social climber "donned her Annette Kellermans" for a "dip in the turbulent social seas." Maury outdid himself on marriage break-ups, which always came out "the marital barque foundered in the matrimonial seas."

[18] *Ibid.,* pp. 61-63.

Society, in those dark moments when Maury was feeling petulant about some recent snub, wasn't going to the dogs; it was headed for the bow-wows. There was a flash of genius in his frequent descriptions of matrons as "afflicted with embonpoint." Photographers were Knights of the Camera, and the stuffier ones within the Cholly Knickerbocker orbit were the Tar and Mothball set. The *Social Register,* logically, was Society's Bible, and the café society people, who were beginning to rear their heads—Mona Williams, Elsa Maxwell and Company—were T-H-A-T Set.

BRENDA FRAZIER'S "ROMANCE" [19]

If all the men Brenda Frazier has been on the point of marrying—according to the gossips—could be gathered together in one place it would have saved all the trouble and expense of the draft. Most of these "romances" were the inventions of cameramen who wanted to get back the cost of their negatives. There is no doubt that she has had many proposals from everyone from college boys to counts. But the only men who were consistently linked with her name were Billy Livingston; Peter Arno, whose hair is always in such need of a trim that he qualifies among the ten best-tressed men in America; Howard Hughes, that intrepid flyer, film producer, and millionaire; and a man-about-town who, for some reason I have been unable to discover, is known almost nationally as Shipwreck Kelly.

It was during a hot and dull August when a new Frazier romance was breaking with every edition of the afternoon papers that Brenda, assisted by my wife and me, organized the Treadeasy hoax.

Brenda was tired of all this gossip. She realized that the only way to stop it was to begin going "regular" with one man. But there wasn't anyone to qualify for that position. And so Brenda decided to invent one.

She decided to call him Philo Treadeasy. Dixie Tighe decided that he was slim, and redheaded (doubtless, because I am large and dark-haired) with a weakness for rubber plants and watchdogs. And I decided that he was an heir to some cantaloupe millions. On the appointed day Dixie Tighe began her column in the *New York Post* with this:

> Brenda Frazier admits that her constant escort is Philo Treadeasy. Since their meeting in the Adirondacks, Treadeasy has been like her shadow. Not many of her friends have met him, but her house guest, Honey B. Dart, said of Mr. T., "I think this is the first time Brenda has ever been serious about one of her beaux."

At the Stork Club that evening Chick Farmer didn't buh-buh-be-be-buh when he sat down at our table. After hinting for a few moments, he came right out and asked: "Know anything about this guy Treadeasy?"

Two days later this paragraph appeared in the *New York Post:*

> Howard Hughes comes to town Wednesday; Philo Treadeasy, Brenda's new beau, says he absolutely refuses to get out of the picture for him.

[19] From *Trousers Will Be Worn,* by C. V. R. Thompson, pp. 103-105. Copyright, 1941, by C. V. R. Thompson. New York: G. P. Putnam's Sons.

Several cameramen telephoned Miss Frazier's home that day, asking where they might obtain photographs of Mr. Treadeasy.

There was another paragraph next day. It said:

> Good for you, Philo Treadeasy. You've already chased one of Brenda's beaux out of town. And, as a Frazier student, I must say I've never seen Brenda look as happy as when you're with her.

On that day a rival columnist talked about the new romance, and Cholly Knickerbocker, after going through all his social registers, index cards and telephone books, was reported to have put out careful inquiries in an attempt to explain the mystery of how Brenda Frazier had fallen in love with someone he had never even heard of.

At a conference we decided that now was the time to tell all. Brenda insisted that it should be reported her mother was coming down from the Adirondacks to find out what this engagement talk was about. Dixie was inspired with the suggestion that Philo had come to New York to enlist Brenda's services in doing for the melon business what she had done for doughnuts and shrimps by occasionally taking a fruit cocktail, and had fallen so much in love with her at first sight that he began eating shrimps too. My contribution was that he refused to go to Twenty-One because he thought it was a card club. By three o'clock in the morning a full column was on its way down to the *New York Post*.

There was an urgent call from the city editor just after dawn. "This is a front-page story," he said, excitedly. "Where can we get a picture of this guy, Treadeasy? How can we get Brenda's mother on the 'phone? How about his parents? And can't you get some quotes from Brenda?" Dixie lost her nerve. She confessed. The city editor was not amused, but he ran the story, even if he did explain in a footnote that Mr. Treadeasy was a creation from Brenda Frazier's pretty little head. And so died that romantic young melon salesman.

PRINCELY SHOPPERS [20]

The staff of Neiman-Marcus[21] prizes the story of the customer who bought three vicuña coats at one swoop. The vicuña coat, which is made from

---

[20] From "Tales of Neiman-Marcus," by James Howard, in *Folk Travelers*, Ballads, Tales, and Talk, edited by Mody C. Boatright, Wilson M. Hudson, Allen Maxwell, pp. 161-165, 168-169. Copyright, 1953, by the Texas Folklore Society, Austin. Publication of the Texas Folklore Society, No. XXV. Austin: The Texas Folklore Society. Dallas: Southern Methodist University Press.

[21] Neiman-Marcus is the name of a specialty store in Dallas, Texas. More accurately, it is a series of specialty shops collected under one management and administered with a single set of policies. The principal store is at Ervay and Main streets in downtown Dallas; a suburban branch, Preston Center, was opened in October, 1951, on Preston Road, at Northwest Highway. The company maintains buying offices in New York, London, Paris, and Florence. Neiman's sells clothing for women, children, and men, together with a number of related articles such as jewelry, luggage, and gifts. One of its major characteristics is its emphasis on fashion merchandise.

The Neiman-Marcus Company was founded in 1907 by Mr. Herbert Marcus, his sister Mrs. Carrie Neiman, and her husband Mr. Al Neiman. Mr. Neiman withdrew from the firm in 1928. Mrs. Carrie Neiman, on the other hand, continued her association with, the extremely soft fleece of a small South American animal, is often priced at from five to six hundred dollars, since in the hierarchy of woolens, vicuña ranks as high above cashmere as cashmere does above top-grade sheep's wool. The incident involving the shopper for these coats started to take shape when a salesman on the first floor of Neiman's telephoned upstairs to the president, Mr. Stanley Marcus, and reported, "A gentleman is down here who speaks with a foreign accent, looks very distinguished, has a swarthy complexion, and wears good clothes. The feeling around the floor is that he either owns the Iranian oil fields or is an actor. We think you ought to come down and meet him."

Stanley Marcus did come down. He was introduced to a tall, slightly balding gentleman, to his wife, and to their nineteen-year-old daughter. They were from French Morocco. The name of the family seemed to ring a bell in Mr. Marcus's memory.

"You have a house in Paris, don't you?" he asked.

"Yes, how did you know?" replied the visitor, his face lighting up.

"I had it pointed out to me when I was in France last year," the Dallas merchant said.

The world having been shrunk to manageable proportions, the conversation proceeded. "If you don't mind my asking," Stanley Marcus inquired, "what has brought you to Dallas?"

"We have come to shop," was the answer. "You see, my wife, my daughter, and I arrived in New York. We desired to have three vicuña coats, one for each of us, all of them alike. Yesterday we started out at New York to obtain the coats.

"At one store on Fifth Avenue," he continued, "they had coats for my wife and daughter, but none for me. At another store near by we found a fine man's coat, none for my wife and daughter. 'Where,' I asked the salesman, 'might we find three identical vicuña coats?'

" 'Oh,' he said, 'at Neiman-Marcus.'

" 'On what street is that?' I asked.

"The salesman laughed. 'It's not on any street. It's in Dallas, Texas.'

" 'Where is Dallas, Texas?' I wanted to know. He told me it was about six hours from New York by plane. 'We will fly down to Dallas,' I said."

---

and active participation in, the store until her death in 1953. Since the death of Mr. Herbert Marcus, in 1950, his four sons have taken over the management, the eldest son, Stanley Marcus, having succeeded to the presidency. The other three sons are executive officers in the company. Despite the fact that Neiman-Marcus is a corporation and has issued stock for public sale, it has remained to a marked extent a family enterprise, both in ownership and operation. One noteworthy trait of the Marcuses is their habit of leaving their offices and going out on the floor from time to time to aid a customer with his shopping.

The adjective "fabulous" is applied to this store with considerable frequency. If it is a fabled store, then it seems befitting to ask, what are some of the fables told about Neiman's? With that question in mind, I have collected a group of stories dealing with this Dallas institution. Many of these episodes are drawn from that rich mine of folklore, the Dallas *Morning News,* but, more specifically, my chief source has been the column headed "Neiman-Marcus Point of View," which since June, 1950, has twice a week formed part of the firm's advertisement in the Dallas *News.* This column, signed "Wales," is the work of Warren Leslie, assistant to the president of Neiman-Marcus and previously a reporter on the Dallas *News.*—J.H.

The store in Dallas was able to supply the three matching coats, and in two days of shopping the North African visitor purchased seventy-five thousand dollars' worth of clothing, linens, and furnishings.[22]

The figure of the princely shopper appears in other guises. In one story, emanating from the children's department of the store, he is cast as an expectant father. One day, the story goes, a man entered the infants' shop to inform a saleswoman, "I'll take the things in the window out there."

"I beg your pardon?" said the saleswoman, giving herself the opportunity to collect her wits.

"I want to buy everything in that window, if I may," the man repeated.

A hurried conference was held, the conclusion of which was that no good reason existed for not allowing the customer to have the contents of the window. The sale was accordingly completed.

Further talk with the young man revealed that he and his wife were looking forward to the birth of their first child within a couple of months. Since nothing had yet been bought for the child-to-come, the husband was simply trying to acquire a full set of the necessary gear for an infant, all in one package. "Otherwise I might forget something," he explained.[23]

In another episode the lordly shopper becomes an elderly gentleman who felt a compelling attraction toward one of the store's wax mannequins. This particular mannequin represented a small child. The white-haired gentleman saw a striking resemblance between the mannequin and his little granddaughter, to whom he was devoted. Consequently he came by to see the mannequin every time he was in the store. Invariably he ended these visits by buying all of the clothes on the wax figure, to give to his grandchild, who, it happened, was exactly the same size. This Hawthorne-like situation lasted until the mannequin's dresses were no longer large enough to fit the growing girl.[24]

At Christmas a Texas oilman selected a mink coat from Neiman-Marcus for a present to his wife. He was eager to have his gift placed in a proper setting. Somehow it didn't seem entirely appropriate to confine the mink coat within a mere box. He consulted Stanley Marcus: was there some way of adding the suitable flourish? A day or two before Christmas Mr. Marcus borrowed one of the spare rooms in the oilman's house. There he reproduced faithfully, down to the last detail, a Neiman-Marcus display window centered on a mannequin garbed in the mink coat.[25]

Back in 1939, the story goes, a customer from Houston flew the two-hundred fifty-odd miles to Dallas once a week in her own plane to have her hair done at Neiman's beauty salon. Several years later a woman airplane passenger phoned ahead to the store at Dallas that she would like to buy a fur coat during her brief stopover in Dallas. A detachment of salespeople moved on Love Field, the

[22] Dallas *Morning News*, June 30, 1950; John William Rogers, *The Lusty Texans of Dallas* (New York, 1951), pp. 322-323.—J.H.

[23] Dallas *Morning News*, December 1, 1950.—J.H.

[24] *Ibid.*

[25] Selma Robinson, "Texas Tells 'Em," *Colliers*, Vol. CIV (September 16, 1939), pp. 18-19.—J.H.

municipal airport, established a temporary outpost of the store at the terminal. There in a makeshift dressing room they sold the woman a mink coat in the twenty minutes that she had between planes.[26] These stories of princely shoppers form the most numerous group of Neiman-Marcus "fables."

* * * * *

[A variant of the princely shopper is the princely shopper in reverse.] Along in 1947 [Miss Marihelen McDuff] records, Neiman's ran an advertisement of an imposing diamond ring in the *Dallas News*. The advertisement did not make any mention of the ring's price; instead, it described the weight of the stone: 23.08 carats, abbreviating the word carats "cts." A woman from Lubbock, Texas, mailed in a post card ordering the ring. The credit office at Neiman's checked with a bank in Lubbock, to be informed that the woman, though she lived on a modest scale, was sufficiently wealthy to be able to buy the ring. The Lubbock banker, on the other hand, doubted that she had ever put out as much as $35,000, the cost of the diamond, on anything that was not loaded with cotton, saturated in oil, or liberally dotted with cattle. The next move was to call the woman herself long-distance, saying that the store customarily delivered merchandise of such value by personal messenger. Would she indicate a time that would be convenient for the messenger to bring out the package? She was unmistakably surprised at the request. How much was this ring that had to be guarded so carefully, anyway? When the figure of $35,000 reached her ears, she exclaimed, "My God, I thought it was twenty-three dollars and eight cents." She had misread the size of the ring for its price.[27]

THE GREAT WINNETKA FOX HUNT [28]

George Wharton, the champion story-teller of Chicago's Loop, was always especially interested in the North Shore, that suburban area in which the socially elect and the Blue Book aspirants make their homes.

George maintained you can stand in the Northwestern depot any day and tell where each woman passenger, as she arrived, had boarded the train. If she wore an evening gown, she came from Evanston; if she wore sports clothes, Lake Forest; a maternity gown, Winnetka.

He said all the males in Lake Forest sniffed at Winnetkans as culture-climbing tradesmen, while Winnetkans said Lake Foresters were nothing but remittance men.

Wharton said that for years Winnetkans made fun of the Onwentsia Club Fox-Hunt, the big event of the Lake Forest social season, describing how the gilded nobles went bouncing and jumping all over Lake County with dogs

[26] *Ibid.*; also Dallas *Morning News*, February 6, 1951.—J.H.
[27] Letter from Marihelen McDuff to Peter H. Wyden, July 14, 1950, Neiman-Marcus files.—J.H.
[28] From *It Takes All Kinds*, by Lloyd Lewis, pp. 208-210. Copyright, 1928, 1929, 1930, 1931, 1932, 1934, 1935, 1936, 1940, 1945, 1946, 1947, by Lloyd Lewis. New York: Harcourt, Brace and Company.
Reprinted from the *Chicago Sun*, September 2, 1945.

howling, terrified cows running blind into fences, farmers tearing for their cellars, and sirens screaming, as ambulances rushed to pick unhorsed riders with cracked collarbones out of ditches.

Wharton said he was naturally surprised one day to learn that Winnetka had organized a hunt of its own. He guessed Winnetka simply couldn't stand it any longer to have Lake Forest hog the society columns, so its more social burghers met in the school auditorium and voted, by Robert's Rules of Order, to buy horses, saddles, derbies, and pink coats. They chose a member to go down to Lyon & Healy's, get a horn, and take lessons till he learned it. Two members who had recently moved here from New York taught the others how to shout "View Halloo," and they ordered a fox from Sears, Roebuck, but they couldn't find a pack of hounds for sale.

So they put their pride in their pocket and named one of the younger members, whose sister had married into the Lake Forest set, to go ask the Onwentsia Hunt to please lend them their pack for the day. Onwentsia said all right, and on the day when the Winnetka Hunt was all assembled on horseback and waiting at the town hall, up rolled a station wagon and out got one dog— Little Ada was her name. The chauffeur said, sorry but all the other Onwentsia dogs had distemper.

Some riders wanted to call off the Winnetka Hunt, but others said it would make them a laughingstock to back out now, so they put a leash around Little Ada's neck, the Master of the Hounds blew the horn, and the procession clattered out through town toward the Skokie meadows where the fox had already been taken in a hencoop.

Wharton said it was a gay sight, those pink coats against the white picket fences, and everybody at the doorways waving handkerchiefs or copies of the *Yale Review*.

And out from every house, too, came a dog, to fall in behind the procession, for Little Ada had romance in her eye. She'd roll her eyes to the right and then to the left and then her eyelids would droop coquettishly, and by the time the parade hit the Skokie meadows, the Winnetka Hunt had a pack, all right— setters, police dogs, mastiffs, Doberman pinschers, Airedales, bulldogs, terriers, dachshunds—200 at least—with half of them Scotties.

Everybody was happy by now, talking about how good things like this were for the community.

Out into the meadow they came; the Master of the Hounds opened the hencoop door, the fox went like a shadow, Little Ada was unleashed, and followed. The pack took out after Little Ada. The horn blew and everybody let off a "View Halloo" that scared some of the horses.

The chase, however, started slowly, for fear the horses would step on the cloud of Pekingese who, at the tail of the pack, were slowed up by the long grass.

But things straightened out pretty soon on that score, for Little Ada, with one eye over her shoulder, got to watching the pack rather than the fox and instead of following Bold Reynard to the north, she went off on a triumphant circle of her own to the south, with the pack yipping at her heels. And no amount of horn-blowing could get her back on the track. The hunt milled, horses bumped, and several matrons fell off. At length eight men on foot caught Little Ada, put the leash on her, and everybody trailed home, muttering dark words about those Lake Foresters' sense of humor. Behind came the pack, setters ahead, Pekingese in the rear.

Wharton said the dogs knew they'd never see Little Ada again. It was over. They'd had a pretty good day, at that; and as each dog came to his home gate, he turned in, so that by the time the crestfallen Hunt reached the town hall where the station wagon was waiting, Little Ada hadn't a single admirer in sight.

WHEN THE KING OF BELGIUM VISITED PASADENA [29]

The millionaires of Pasadena have exhibited heat and passion only once. That was when the King of Belgium visited the town shortly after the [First World] War. That was a great day. An official half-holiday was declared. Covers were laid for a thousand luncheon guests at the Maryland Hotel—the King was coming for lunch. A triumphal rose-covered arch, paid for with the nickels and dimes of school-children, was erected on the main street. Thousands of people lined the sidewalks. For once the plutocrats came out of their shells *en masse*, resplendent and hot in morning clothes, to welcome the King. But the King was late.

And lo and behold, when he did arrive, the royal automobile shot through the town—on a side street at fifty miles an hour—to a siding where the royal train was parked, and a moment later the King was gone. He passed up Pasadena like a pay-car passing a tramp. A few cops and railroad switch-men got a fleeting glimpse of His Majesty; that was all. It was explained that the movie folk in Hollywood had kept him two hours past his schedule, and consequently he was forced to deprive himself of the pleasure of Pasadena's hospitality. He also passed up the monster afternoon reception which Mrs. Anita Baldwin had been planning for three weeks. Mrs. Baldwin had not only spent fifty thousand dollars; she had also invited every prominent person in California to meet the King.

Alas and alack-a-day. Before the sun went down behind the purple mountains, the hot, pathetic herd of outraged millionaires announced publicly that the movie magnates in Hollywood were a gang of unspeakable yahoos, and that, furthermore, they put no faith whatever in the ridiculous and utterly absurd stories of German atrocities in Belgium!

[29] From *Los Angeles,* by Morrow Mayo, pp. 218-219. Copyright, 1932, 1933, by Morrow Mayo. New York: Alfred A. Knopf, Inc.

XII. Go Fight City Hall

The classic story of fighting City Hall is perhaps the story of the citizens of St. Louis who complained to Mayor Ziegenhein about the prolonged black-out of their streets while the street lamps were being changed from arc lights to gas mantles. "We got a moon yet, ain't it?" replied "Uncle Henry."

Fighting City Hall is an urban sport ranging all the way from gripes to organized protests, demonstrations and political action. It is also a necessary evil inherent in the complexity and interdependence of city life. In the intricate structure of the city's services and occupations, the slightest interruption or delay in the daily and hourly round—a missing mail delivery, a traffic tie-up, a storm or a strike—may cause an annoying dislocation or a serious emergency.

On the level of personal liberty the individual finds his freedom of behavior hedged about by all kinds of restrictions in the interest of his own protection and the public welfare, as well as of efficiency. Young and old are also beset with fears and inconveniences occasioned by overcrowding, noise, dirt, smog and ever-present dangers. As the city grows, it grows more uncomfortable and inconvenient, putting a strain on facilities, funds and tempers. The picture is complicated by lawlessness, laxity, graft and corruption. In all this "the people are not innocent," as Lincoln Steffens pointed out in *The Shame of the Cities*. "Politics is business," and the people should make it their business, he goes on to say. They should make politics pay for all concerned by asking the practical politician for good politics, punishing him when he gives bad and rewarding him when he gives good. So if cities are "still corrupt," they are "still content"—in the sense that politicians and citizens alike "don't care."

"Still 'corrupt and content'" is the theme of Robert S. Allen's symposium, *Our Fair City* (1947), which attempts to bring *The Shame of the Cities* up to date. A glance at its pages reveals some of the reasons why city folk fight City Hall and why they lose. It also points up some common city problems, from Philadelphia's drinking water ("chlorine cocktails") to Detroit race riots and the growing nationwide problem of parasitic suburbs and satellite communities.

Less well known are the problems of city employees. In New York City the recent revival of the police "shoo-fly" (dating from Theodore Roosevelt's time) intensified the patrolman's "heaving" tactics. New York hospital workers are plagued with budget troubles and gripe about false ambulance calls, like the call to pick up a kid on West End Avenue. The ambulance arrived to find the kid perfectly well, with his mother pointing to him and saying, "There! I told you I'd call the ambulance if you wouldn't eat your cereal!"

In his column, "New York Day by Day," November 4, 1938, C. B. Driscoll reported that the Depression was seeping down into children's games—an example of fighting City Hall on the play level.

> Little girls in the lower East Side do not play house, as do other children, a social worker assures me. Their favorite game is called "Going on Relief." One girl represents a relief worker of some sort; the others

are mamas or just housewives. The investigator asks all kinds of questions about their family, and the girls show their dolls, telling fabulous tales of how many children they have to support.

The youngsters find this great fun. Sometimes they go to a neighboring stoop and pretend it is the relief office. Sometimes the one who plays investigator comes to the stoop where the little housewife is waiting. But always the fun seems to be in thinking up innumerable questions about private family matters and giving comprehensive answers. The ills attributed to the dolls are formidable and without number, in the verbal reports of the little mothers.

"Picketing" is a favorite game among the little boys, with girls sometimes joining "if they behave themselves." This game has taken the place of the old favorite, "Cops and Robbers," in many neighborhoods, and is just as rough.

The boys make banners and carry them. They shout such slogans as "Stay away from Sammie; he's a bum!" There are strike-breakers who try to rush through the picket line, and this phase furnishes the real rough-and-tumble that gives the game its zest.

THE TOWN FATHERS AND THE TEAMSTERS [1]

. . . Off State Street [Boston] we find Damnation Alley. As the story comes down to us, it seems that teamsters in the early days, meeting on this street and not being able to get by, said things to each other as they do today, for that matter, and this swearing gave the name to the street. The Town Fathers, we are told, got angry about it after a while and issued an order something like this: "Teamsters when they meet on these narrow streets must behave like good citizens, jump right down, and flip a coin to see who is to back out!"

POLITICS IN MIDDLEBURY [2]

There is some truth in the charge that Vermont has more than its share of Republicans. But there is no such thing as a Republican solid Vermont comparable to the Democratic solid South. There is certainly nothing solid about politics in Middlebury. . . .

* * * * *

. . . [Take] my old friend George Galvin, who happens to live in the near-by town of Salisbury, but who is sensible enough to spend a certain amount of time in Middlebury.

Some years ago, on one of the numerous occasions when Roosevelt was running for President, I happened to meet George at Caswell's filling station— or maybe it was Cartmell's, or Buddy Butterfield's, or Mit Brown's, or Gregory

[1] From *Hear Ye! Hear Ye! The New England Squeak and Other Stories*, Being the Strange Adventures of Heroic yet Primitive People, by James O. Fagan, pp. 24-25. Copyright, 1931, by James O. Fagan, Visitors Guide in the Old South Meeting House, Boston.
[2] From "The Cities of America: Middlebury, Vermont," by William Hazlett Upson, *The Saturday Evening Post*, Vol. 219 (March 22, 1947), No. 38, p. 130. Copyright, 1947, by the Curtis Publishing Company. Philadelphia.

and Johnson's, or Ferland's, or Brush's, or Provoncha's, or Persons and Foster's, or one of the others.

George told me he was supporting Roosevelt, and that he was also the Republican candidate for town representative from Salisbury in the state legislature.

"Wait a minute," I said. "In national affairs you are working for the Democrats?"

"Yes."

"In local affairs you are running on the Republican ticket?"

"Sure. You have to run as a Republican to get elected in Salisbury."

"Then just what are you anyway?"

"That's easy," said George. "I am a politician."

HOW BARNUM SALTED THE ALDERMEN [8]

The first man who ever publicly stated that he bribed the Aldermen of New York was not himself a politician or a contractor, but a showman, the renowned Phineas T. Barnum, "author of the woolly horse," as he sometimes called himself; and, somewhat funny to state, the object of the first confessed bribe was not a franchise, or a contract, or an office, but a fish! Still, the story is not at all "fishy," but true in every point, according to Barnum, who gave the particulars as follows:

Among the early attractions of his museum, which stood on the site of the present twenty-six-storied St. Paul Building (with one exception the highest of the high buildings of the metropolis) on the corner of Broadway and Ann street, Barnum had secured a couple of whales. There was no humbug about these whales; they were Simon-pure, although small, and proved a drawing card. Comparatively small as the whales were, they were really big fish, needing a lot of water, which it was found more and more difficult to supply.

Immense quantities of salt were put into the fresh-water tank, which held the whales; but somehow they did not thrive on this artificial sea-water. The cetaceans were no fools; they detected the cheat at once, pined for the original article, and it soon became evident that either they must be taken back to the sea or they must die unless somehow or other the sea be brought to them in their present location. The last of the horns of the dilemma was the one which Barnum determined to take. With the aid of a master plumber, he worked out the idea of having a pipe connection between his museum and the Hudson River, at the foot of Vesey Street.

Simple enough in itself and feasible, the work would cost about three thousand dollars—more money than the whales had originally cost. But Barnum was not the sort of man to higgle over the cost of a good thing; so that was settled. But suddenly he was notified officially that he could not lay his pipes without a permit from the Board of Aldermen. He placed his petition for the pipe before the Board, and to his surprise it was rejected. It took about a week to get the Board of Aldermen to reconsider its vote on this pipe matter and

[8] From *Thirty Years of New York Politics Up-to-Date*, by Matthew P. Breen, pp. 103-105. Copyright, 1899, by Matthew P. Breen. Published by the author. New York.

finally pass on it formally. The only argument meantime presented by the irrepressible Barnum was one thousand dollars, which, he alleged, was divided, in sums of fifty and one hundred dollars, among the members of the Board. The Aldermen put their little fifty or one hundred dollars apiece in their pockets; and then, on free passes, went to the museum to see the whales disport in the salt water, which had already "salted" the Aldermen.

THE LITTLE FLOWER

I. The Little Flower and the Pontiacs[4]

A good example of how ask-and-ye-shall-receive children can help in humanizing [the politician] occurred in New York City in July, 1934. The Pontiacs, a baseball team made up of twelve-year-old boys of the Borough of the Bronx, were in the midst of a battle with the Tigers on an enclosure in the Bronx when a policeman came along, drove the boys from the field and confiscated their League ball. The Pontiacs cogitated about this oppression, and their captain decided to write to the Mayor. What are Mayors for? Mr. La Guardia received the following letter:

My dear Mayor:
What would you do if you were a boy like us and a cop took a ball away in the park? The ball is an American League ball. We will greatly appreciate it if you would take this matter in your hands. Please answer our letter.

Your loving admirers—
The Pontiacs,
Saul Norflus, Captain

In this appeal were combined two great elements to which all American politicians must give heed—baseball and childhood. And in this appeal the child element was heightened because it was childhood oppressed, aggrieved. A keen member of the Mayor's secretariat read the letter and turned it over to Mr. La Guardia. The Mayor dictated the following to Captain Norflus:

I have your letter and thank you for writing me. I am sure that when the police officer asked you not to play ball, you obeyed. You must always obey a police officer. I am very sorry that he took your ball away from you. I know how badly I would feel if any one would have taken a ball away from me when I was a boy.
So what do you think I have for you? Well, I have asked Col Ruppert of the American League if he would give me an American League baseball and he was good enough to do so. Come down to see me at City Hall Monday, July 16, and I will give you this brand-new American League ball and then we can talk over your troubles.

That was well done by the Mayor. Note, first, that he seized the opportunity offered; second, that he handled the matter himself; third, that he did not send a ball but invited the boys to come to see him.

[4] From *The Politician*, His Habits, Outcries and Protective Coloring . . . , by J. H. Wallis, pp. 198-199. Copyright, 1935, by Frederick A. Stokes Company. New York.

Nearly all of the Pontiacs came at the appointed time. They were greeted by the flashlights of newspaper photographers and listened to by reporters. The Mayor put his arm around Captain Norflus. Then he autographed the new ball and presented it to the captain, insisting (perhaps vainly) that the boys play with the ball and not preserve it as a souvenir.

II. The Little Flower as Magistrate[5]

. . . As mayor, under Section 6 of the New York City Charter, [La Guardia] was also a magistrate and he occasionally presided in police court. One wintry day during the Depression a trembling old man charged with stealing a loaf of bread stood before him. He extenuated his act on the ground that his family was starving. "I've got to punish you," said La Guardia. "The law requires me to do that. I sentence you to a fine of $10," reaching into his pocket. "Here is $10 to pay your fine. Now I remit the fine," tossing the ten into his wide-brimmed hat, "and furthermore I hereby fine every person in this room fifty cents apiece, except the prisoner, for living in a town where a man has to steal in order to eat." The old man walked out of the police court with $47.50— according to one reporter, "with the light of Heaven in his eyes."

READING FROM RIGHT TO LEFT [6]

. . . Boss Platt, the Republican chief, after elections one autumn sent down to the East Side to learn what in hell had become of four hundred Jewish votes for which he had paid. But in Yiddish you read from right to left, and so those voters, having been told to make their marks in the "first column" on the ballot, had marked the first column *from the right* and cast their votes for Prohibition, the smallest party at that time! The joyous Prohibitionists had got drunk on ginger ale that night!

POLICE "HEAVING" TACTICS [7]

. . . A citizen on the way home from a highly respectable, but very late, meeting, saw a policeman stealthily letting himself out of a funeral parlor. The cop looked up and down the street furtively, then walked briskly off to a police telephone box on the corner. All this stuck in the citizen's mind. It seemed a little ghoulish, and a little foolish too. Who'd want anything in an undertaker's establishment? he asked himself. He went home to sleep, not realizing that he had stumbled upon an example of the real cause of the uproar in the Police Department over "shoo-flies."

The funeral home was this cop's "heaving hole." And policemen don't want

[5] From *A Nation of Nations,* by Louis Adamic, p. 30. Copyright, 1944, 1945, by Louis Adamic. New York: Harper & Brothers.

[6] From *The Bridge,* My Own Story, by Ernest Poole, p. 86. Copyright, 1940, by Ernest Poole. New York: The Macmillan Company.

[7] From "Heave-Hole Tactics Lull Cops to Sleep," by Allan Keller, the New York *World-Telegram and Sun,* February 15, 1954. Copyright, 1954, by the New York World-Telegram Corp.

anyone interfering with their ancient privilege of "heaving" on the late tours. Ever since cops wore hard helmets and soup-strainer mustaches they have ducked into all-night bakeries, cheap hotels, dentists' offices and other such spots to catch forty winks on the sly, although they are supposed to be out on the pavement protecting life and property.

The advent of the automobile changed nothing. It even made "heaving" easier. The prowl car became a built-in heaving hole. One man can sleep while the other drives. The squawk box alerts them to danger. One time a borough president, returning home with his wife, stepped off a ferry boat and found four prowl cars neatly lined up, one man awake and listening to the department broadcasts and his seven companions fast asleep.

This sort of heaving is complicated by the fact that motionless prowl cars do not run up mileage on the tachometers. But nothing like that defeats a cop who wants to sleep at night—on duty. He just jacks the car up in a garage and lets the wheels turn merrily.

Foot patrolmen have only to hide themselves, but the men in the mounted division have also shown considerable ingenuity in hiding their horses—a not inconsiderable task. When milk wagons and bakery carts were drawn by horses New York had many stables and it was a brave owner indeed who dared object to having a police mount or two stashed away for a few hours at night. The riding academies that maintained stables just off Central Park were also favorite "holes" of the cop cavalry.

One bitter winter night four mounted men rode their nags into one of these stables in the upper W. 60s and went to sleep, telling the stable boy when to call them. An hour or so later the boy shook them awake, whispering that "shooflies" were outside. The cops were on a spot. Horses cannot be tucked into desk drawers or behind books on the shelf. Then one of the four heaving riders had a brainstorm and told his pals. A minute later they had mounted, covered their heads with their raincoats and stood lined up abreast just inside the door. At a signal the stable boy threw open the door and the cops thundered out past the inspector's men before they could make a move to identify them.

Brooklyn is famous for good beer and you couldn't blame the boys of the Prospect Park mounted detachment from enjoying a stein or two. In the middle of the day, when things were quiet, several of them used to ride into a German beer garden, tie their mounts behind the wall and hoist a few. The captain missed them but couldn't find their heaving hole. One day one of the group remained home on sick call. It was a break for the poor harassed captain. He led the absent trooper's horse down the avenue, dropped the reins, and gave the nag a cut across the flank with his glove. The horse galloped off, straight for the beer garden, the captain trailing him hell-for-leather. Behind the wall were the other horses, and in the bar were the three mounted men, all bending their elbows. Each man got a five day "rip"—or cut in pay.

A cop on foot soon learns where the best heaving holes are on his beat. Furniture stores that employ night watchmen, schools with custodians and similar establishments have always been prime favorites. In the winter a small basement bakery of the family type combines the pleasant warmth from the ovens with the wonderful aroma of fresh bread to lull a weary cop to sleep.

Many cops like funeral homes because they are so quiet and because the windows and door are flush with the sidewalk. Any passing car with a siren will wake them up and they can be out and running before the sergeant becomes suspicious.

REVOLT IN CITY HOSPITAL [8]

When I was working at City Hospital we used to have an annual ceremony called running short on the budget. Then the chief would start cutting down on the wonderful meals the patients and doctors had been having all along and announce that the last few weeks of the fiscal year would be celebrated by the eating of a stew.

This time he decided to give out an order that everybody was to get no more than half a pint of milk daily, including that for cereal and coffee. Well, I boiled up at that. I promptly sat down and wrote out a hundred slips for a special increase in the allowance. So they sent down a special investigating committee and took away half the allowances and I got a bawling out. Just the thing to get me still hotter. When the patients asked me about the milk I didn't mince my words. I told them just why they weren't getting any milk. So they got sore as hell and began demanding proper rations. Then I went to the chief and told him I was having a lot of trouble convincing the patients that half a pint of milk was a perfect diet for them. He looked at me kind of funny as though he wanted to bust me in the nose. Then he began to roar, "If any of those people think they can behave like agitators here, send them up to see me," and so forth, and so forth.

That was all I needed. You know the Beggars' Opera. Well, I got the oldest crooks together, everybody who hadn't been out of bed for the last seven hundred years, and I explained the situation to them. I told them it was the only way. They caught on beautifully. In ten minutes the whole ward was empty and the halls were full of old men and women on crutches, in wheel chairs, staggering down to the big chief's office.

In half an hour I get a call from the office. Slimy Bill is yelling, "What the hell are those people from your ward doing here? They're disgracing my office. This has never happened before in the history of the hospital." I told him, "I only did exactly what you told me to do. If you can't take it, give them their milk back."

"All right, but for Chrissake get them the hell out of my office." So I went down and told them, "Let's go, boys and girls, you got your milk." Boy, did they let out a cheer for me!

[8] As told by a New York hospital doctor to Clarence Weinstock, June 14, 1939, New York City. Manuscripts of the Federal Writers' Project of the Works Progress Administration in New York City. Deposited in the Folklore Section, Library of Congress, Washington, D.C.

A SOUTHERN VIEW OF GENERAL SHERMAN'S STATUE [9]

Southerners have their own way of looking at things. It was so after the "War between the States." And it was so later at the turn of the century, when the statue of General Sherman was erected at the south front of the Treasury [in Washington]. General Sherman rode a horse, and the horse and rider were set upon a high pedestal, as you see them today, where Pennsylvania Avenue, after a straight sweep from the Capitol, bends an elbow to get around the Treasury. In those days Lyman J. Gage was Secretary of the Treasury. He presided at the unveiling of the monument to Sherman on horseback. He knew, of course, that Sherman was the man who had devastated Georgia from Atlanta to the sea, and who was hated by all true Southerners. So he timidly asked a Southern newspaper correspondent, who was present at the unveiling, what he thought of the monument. The Southerner hesitated, then slowly replied, "Well, Mr. Secretary, from the north side, where we stand, you see General Sherman as a soldier and gentleman, but from the south side all you can see is a horse's hind end."

HOW THE MAYOR OF RICHMOND WAS "DONE" [10]

In old times the municipality [of Richmond, Virginia], consisting of Mayor, Aldermen and Common Council, met as one body, and there being no City Hall for their sessions, they convened in an apartment rented for that purpose, in the square southwest of the market bridge, and commanding a view of Manchester on the opposite side of the river.

On one warm summer day the city fathers had met in council, and their labors for the public weal had rendered them droughty. In those primitive days the practice adopted in New York of eating, drinking and smoking at the expense of many thousands to their constituents had not been thought of by our unpaid commonalty; and in order to assuage their thirst with some pleasant beverage, Michael Ryan, one of the members (an author whose works are extinct), proposed a wager for a flowing bowl, and in deference to the Mayor he offered to make it with him. The Mayor replied that Mr. Ryan had already played him one trick, and he should not catch him again. "But," said Ryan, "if you are sure of winning this time, you'll take me up—and so to give you a chance, I will bet you that I can prove from your own admission, you are on the other side of the river." "I'll take that bet," said his honor. The wag, pointing to Manchester, asked if that was not one side of the river. "Certainly," replied the mayor. "And is not Richmond on the other side?" "Yes." "Are you not in Rich-

---

[9] From *Washington Is Like That*, by W. M. Kiplinger, p. 431. Copyright, 1942, by W. M. Kiplinger. New York: Harper & Brothers.

[10] From *Richmond in By-Gone Days*, by Samuel Mordecai, pp. 147-149. Copyright, 1946, by The Dietz Press, Inc., Richmond, Virginia. Republished from the Second Edition of 1860, *Virginia, Especially Richmond, in By-Gone Days, with a Glance at the Present; Being Reminiscences and Last Words of an Old Citizen . . .* , Richmond: West & Johnston, Publishers.

mond, and consequently on the other side?" The mayor was stumped, and ordered the beverage, but swore he would never make another bet. "I'll take you a dozen of porter on that," said Ryan. "Done!" cried the excited Mayor, and no sooner said than *done* he was.

RIGHT OF PETITION [11]

Coleman Livingston Blease's liberality in the pardon business while he was Governor of South Carolina taught him a lesson. It seems that one day when he was in the Senate one of his colleagues was talking to him about a petition that had been received regarding a certain measure. There were so many signatures showing that the people of the United States were obviously in favor of this measure and that the Senators owed it to the dignity of the Senate to pass this measure that so many people were advocating. "Well," Coley said, "I'll tell you. On that subject this reminds me of an experience I had back down in South Carolina when I was governor. There was a fellow from up in my home town in Newberry County. He had been sent up for murder and he got life. And he'd been in there about five years when in come a petition—in the middle of my second term—signed by 500 citizens of Newberry County, including several members of the jury that had convicted him, asking for clemency for him. So I showed the petition to my secretary and he said, 'Well, Governor, what are you going to do about it?' So I said to him, 'There are 500 signatures from Newberry County telling me to turn him loose. I guess I ought to do that.' He said, 'Now, Governor, it's all right if you turn him loose, but if you're paying any attention to signatures on petitions, have you ever thought of the fact that I could go out on the streets of Columbia and in two hours I could get 5,000 signatures for a petition to have you hung?' "

JUSTICE IN ATLANTA [12]

[At the federal court in Atlanta] unless the evidence was indisputable we freed the [moonshiners]. We [jurors] felt—I think the court held a similar view—that most of the offenders were ignorant and poor, and were tools of men higher up who reaped the profit and evaded the risk.

. . . One young fellow, on receiving a short sentence, addressed the court:

"Jedge, yo' honor," he said, "I'd like to go home and git in some plowin' befo' I start sentence. We've had a powerful lot of rain and the grass has got us. I'd sho like to get shet of it."

"All right," the court agreed with surprising willingness. "I think that can be arranged. I will talk with the probation officer."

. . . A middle-aged man in overalls was given a nine-month jail sentence. It did not seem to worry him; doubtless he had expected a longer term.

[11] As told by Raven I. McDavid, University of Colorado, Boulder, Colorado, July 18, 1950. Recorded and transcribed by B. A. Botkin.
[12] From *Georgia: Unfinished State*, by Hal Steed, pp. 228-229. Copyright, 1942, by Hal Steed. New York: Alfred A. Knopf, Inc.

"Judge," he suggested casually, "if you'd jes as lieve, I'd like to be sent to the jail at Gainesville. That's up in my diggin's, as the fella says, and me'n the sheriff's sort o' buddies. . . ."

"Why, yes," the court agreed, with equal casualness, "I will be glad to do that for you."

THE BATTLE OF THE SAVANNAH SQUARES [13]

The squares of Savannah are so arranged that they must all be circumnavigated by traffic, a situation that those who have to deal with the city's ever-increasing traffic find more than a moderate nuisance. It takes a brave man, however, to breathe much as a whisper about getting rid of them. When . . . a plan was afoot to do away with the squares that are spaced along a thoroughfare called Habersham Street, the discovery of a plot to poison the city's drinking water by a gang of Vermont Yankees could hardly have produced more excitement. The battle of the squares was fought over breakfast, lunch and dinner; letters were penned to the editor; petitions were drafted and signed; a determined phalanx of Savannahians moved on to Atlanta to face down the State Legislature; and the Habersham squares were finally saved. "Progress!" snorted a venerable gentleman of my grandfather's generation. "Sir, I say to hell with progress! We've had these squares since our city was founded and we intend to keep them!"

MR. HANDY AND MR. CRUMP ON BEALE STREET [14]

. . . As a band leader, W. C. Handy spent much of his time and made most of his money by playing for whites. And they usually found an excuse to hire a Negro orchestra for their banquets, conventions, dances, store-openings, and auctions. Southern politics, long on vaudeville, was no exception. In 1909 Memphis was enjoying a raucous mayor's race. For each of the three candidates a Negro band rode in a wagon around the city playing to street-corner crowds. Handy's band was to blare away for E. H. Crump, the reform candidate. For this job Handy gave his boys a new sort of tune, the first *blues composition*. He didn't know what it was. It had no title, no words. But when people gave it a big hand, he knew it was a hit. To give his boys some words to sing, he wrote out a one-stanza lyric for his tune on the old cigar stand at Pee Wee's:[15]

[13] From "Savannah and the Golden Isles," by Hamilton Basso, *Holiday*, Vol. 10 (December 1951), No. 5, pp. 46, 48. Copyright, 1951, by the Curtis Publishing Company. Philadelphia.

[14] From *Memphis, Down in Dixie*, by Shields McIlwaine, pp. 345-346. Copyright, 1948, by Shields McIlwaine. New York: E. P. Dutton & Co., Inc.

Drawing by David Stone Martin, from *Mister Jelly Roll*, by Alan Lomax (New York. Duell, Sloan & Pearce, Inc., 1950).

[15] Then musicians hung out at Pee Wee's, at 317 Beale, in the midst of the street's high life. They kept the check room full of horns, bull fiddles, violins, guitars and banjos. Pee Wee let them use his telephone to line up jobs. While loafing they could roll dice, play cards, or shoot pool, or try the policy game upstairs. . . . Pee Wee, the owner of the

Mister Crump won't 'low no easyriders here,
Mister Crump won't 'low no easyriders here,
I don't care what Mr. Crump don't 'low,
I'm gwine to barrel-house anyhow—
Mister Crump can go catch hisself some air!

joint, was a tiny Italian of incredible brawn and recklessness in gambling who had settled
on Beale over a decade before Handy came to make his place immortal in the history of
American music. On the old cigar stand Handy [also] wrote . . . the orchestration of "St.
Louis Blues" (1914).—S.M., p. 340.

This was Handy's sly joking. The words said in Beale Street lingo that folks didn't believe Mr. Crump, the fiery young redhead, could or would reform a good-time town like Memphis; folks would go on barrel housin' and guzzling liquor, just the same. The words also had funny double meanings: to Beale, *easyriders* meant pimps; to Main Street, political grafters and protected vice lords. Who in America has ever pulled off a slyer practical joke? Here was Mr. Crump with a campaign song telling him that his promises of reform and a business administration were hot air. And Handy knew that white folks wouldn't mind a coon song or make a political issue of it. They didn't. Many years later, he admitted playing "Mr. Crump" for another candidate in the same campaign! Br'er Rabbit, the Negro's ideal trickster, never had better reason than Handy to throw his cap on the ground and dance a jig.

. . . With a new title and with words by George Norton [the song] became the world-famous "Memphis Blues." . . .

HOW MAYOR TOM JOHNSON OF CLEVELAND WON FRIENDS AND INFLUENCED PEOPLE [16]

I. THE CLEVELAND INVESTIGATION BILL

. . . When the Ohio legislature was providing for one of its periodic investigations of the city government of Cincinnati, a hostile member introduced a bill calling for a similar investigation of Cleveland. On the very heels of this action Mayor Johnson sent a message to Representative (now Senator) John N. Stockwell of the Cleveland delegation telling him that he would arrive in Columbus late that night and asking him to arrange for an immediate interview with the member who had introduced the Cleveland investigation bill.

"I wondered what in the world Mr. Johnson could want of G—," says Senator Stockwell in relating this incident, "but I hunted him up and arranged for the interview. G— supposed, of course, the mayor was coming to take him to task for his bill. The mayor came, saw G—, told him what he wanted was his support of some important street railway legislation, explained the measure, convinced G— of the justice of it, and infused him with so much of his own enthusiasm that that man hustled around the whole night seeing other members in the interests of Mr. Johnson's bill, and supported it upon the floor of the house the next day. Mr. Johnson went back to Cleveland without ever referring to G—'s bill to have Cleveland investigated. . . ."

II. TENT MEETING CAMPAIGNING

Chance was responsible for my tent meeting campaigning. Once in one of my early Congressional campaigns when I wanted to have a meeting in the eighteenth ward in Cleveland there was no hall to be had. A traveling showman had a small tent pitched on a vacant lot and someone suggested that

[16] From *My Story*, by Tom L. Johnson, pp. xiv, 82-84. Copyright, 1911, by Columbia Sterling Publishing Co.; 1911, by B. W. Huebsch. New York, 1913.

it might be utilized. It had no chairs but there were a few boxes which could be used as seats. Very doubtful of the result, we made the experiment. It cost me eighteen dollars, I remember. After that I rented tents from a tent man and finally bought one and then several.

The tent meeting has many advantages over the hall meeting. Both sides, I should say all sides, will go to tent meetings—while as a rule only partisans go to halls. Women did not go to political meetings in halls in those days unless some especially distinguished person was advertised to speak, but they showed no reluctance about coming to tent meetings. In a tent there is a freedom from restraint that is seldom present in halls. The audience seems to feel that it has been invited there for the purpose of finding out the position of the various speakers. There is greater freedom in asking questions too, and this heckling is the most valuable form of political education. Tent meetings can be held in all parts of the city—in short the meetings are literally taken to the people. It was not long after I got into municipal politics in Cleveland before the custom of tent meetings was employed in behalf of ward councilmen as well as for candidates on the general ticket, and they too were heckled and made to put themselves on record. The custom of heckling is the most healthy influence in politics. It makes candidates respect pre-election pledges, forces them to meet not only the opposition candidates but their constituents.

But the greatest benefit of the tent meeting, the one which cannot be measured, is the educational influence on the people who compose the audience. It makes them take an interest as nothing else could do, and educates them on local questions as no amount of reading, even of the fairest newspaper accounts, could do. I do not believe there is a city in the country where the electorate is so well informed upon local political questions, nor upon the rights of the people as opposed to the privileges of corporations, as it is in Cleveland. Detroit and Toledo probably come next. The tent meeting is largely responsible for this public enlightenment of the people of Cleveland.

The one disadvantage of the tent is that it is not weather-proof. And yet it was seldom indeed that a meeting had to be abandoned on account of rain. Great audiences came even on rainy nights and our speakers have frequently spoken from under dripping umbrellas to good-natured crowds, a few individuals among them protected by umbrellas, but many sitting in the wet with strange indifference to physical discomfort.

At first my enemies called my tent a "circus menagerie" and no part of my political work has been so persistently cartooned; but when they employed tents somewhat later they called theirs "canvas auditoriums." The adoption of the tent meeting by these same enemies or their successors may not have been intended either as an endorsement of the method or as a compliment to my personal taste, but I can't help considering it a little of both.

WICHITA WATCH-AND-WARD [17]

It is against the law in Wichita [Kansas] to dress or undress a mannequin in any store window, unless curtains are drawn to shut out the public view. This law, sponsored by former Commissioner Henry J. Roetzel, retired wheat farmer and battler for righteousness, has been on the books in force so long that it has been forgotten by the police department, and nowadays one may occasionally see a half-draped figure in a department-store window. It is to be observed, however, that the lady models, whether wood or plastic, always are provided with discreet undergarments—out of respect, I suppose, to the memory of the late Mr. Roetzel and his supporters.

THE KANSAS CITY "RABBITS" AND "GOATS" [18]

The depth of the difference between the two principal Democratic factions in Jackson County was something an outsider could not readily appreciate, but it was suggested by the names of the rival groups—Rabbits and Goats. These popular designations were coined in the early days when the majority of the Pendergast following were Irish folk from the old sod who lived on the West Bluff [of Kansas City] in the laboring class neighborhood that grew up around the residential quarter of the Quality Hill nabobs. Many of these Irish families kept goats, which had no respect for private property or class distinctions and made themselves a public nuisance. The Shannon workers lived over the Hill, in what was then the southeast part of the town and is now near the center of the downtown business section. Their homes were close to the wooded bottoms in the valley of O. K. Creek, where rabbits and other small game frolicked.

In the heat of a campaign an opposition orator called the Pendergast partisans Goats, after their numerous animal pets. Jim Pendergast liked goats, and happily accepted them as a symbol of his faction's devotion to freedom and other liberal ideals. Leading his delegation on a march to a convention for a battle with the Shannon boys, he roared: "When we come over the hill like goats, they'll run like rabbits." When the contest was over, the Goats had seized control of the City Hall, ousting the Shannon men from their easy jobs. It was a cold April day when winter lingered into spring and snow covered the ground. "What will become of the poor fellows who are losing their jobs?" some tenderhearted citizen asked. "They'll eat snow, like the rabbits," said a Goat.

The names were appropriate in many ways. The Pendergast Goats were rugged, combative, clannish, and always hungry. The Shannon Rabbits were fleet, deceptive, and prolific. The Rabbits also had large appetites. They ate snow no oftener than the Goats were compelled to subsist on tin cans.

[17] From "The Cities of America: Wichita," by Charles B. Driscoll, *The Saturday Evening Post*, Vol. 220 (February 21, 1948), No. 34, p. 128. Copyright, 1948, by the Curtis Publishing Company. Philadelphia.

[18] From *Tom's Town*, Kansas City and the Pendergast Legend, by William M. Reddig, p. 34. Copyright, 1947, by William M. Reddig. Philadelphia and New York: J. B. Lippincott Company.

THE OMAHA "LOTTERY KING" [19]

James Monroe Pattee, the "Lottery King," as he was called, was a native of New Hampshire, having been born in Grafton county, and he was one of the shrewdest and biggest grafters that ever turned a trick in Omaha. Prior to his anchoring in this city he operated a lottery in California, the legislature of that state having legalized "gift concerts" for the benefit of charitable institutions. Pattee, under this act, worked his game very profitably and "got from under" by paying off the debt of the public schools of Nevada City. It was in 1871 that this cunning schemer turned up in Omaha and, "squaring" himself with the authorities and some of the influential citizens, inaugurated "a grand legal enterprise," alias lottery, giving employment to a large number of clerks, ticket sellers, and boosters. The newspapers here and elsewhere were liberally paid for big advertisements. Drawings were held monthly and some small prizes were given here and there to lead people to believe that the lottery was on the square. The big prizes were advertised as being drawn, but the winners were in collusion with the game.

Early in the life of this scheme Pattee made a donation of a few hundred books to the Omaha public library, which had recently been started in a small way and was under the control of a board of directors appointed by the city council. A publication of that period said: "For this beneficent gift our children and our children's children will call James M. Pattee blessed forever."

He next made a donation to Mercy hospital, for which he received more praise. He knew how to keep the people from kicking. "Such an act of generosity on the part of Mr. Pattee," said the same publication, "will certainly hand his name down to posterity as a philanthropist."

Having purchased Redick's opera house, he advertised it far and wide as the capital prize—worth $50,000—in his "grand legal enterprise." The drawing took place in the opera house, the affair being under the supervision of several distinguished citizens. When the numbers were announced through the press, a man from St. Louis bobbed up with the lucky ticket. Pattee organized a procession of boosters with the St. Louis ticket holder at the head, and visited all the principal booze joints in the city where the drinks were set up by the gentleman from Missouri. A few weeks later Pattee "bought back" the famous opera house, the deed being made to his wife. This was the end of Pattee's lottery owing to the vigorous protests of the people against allowing a barefaced fraud to continue to bleed the suckers and injure the fair name of Omaha. Pattee had accumulated a fortune out of this lottery and invested a large sum in Omaha real estate. These investments were to some extent forced upon him by persons whose good will he preferred to their enmity, and he was occasionally compelled to "divvy" with men who threatened to "close up his shop" if they were not properly "taken care of."

[19] From *The Story of Omaha from the Pioneer Days to the Present Time,* by Alfred Sorenson, pp. 487-489. Copyright, 1923, by Alfred Sorenson. Omaha: The National Printing Company.

Among several suits brought against Pattee was one by Dr. Childs and H. K. Smith, who were connected with his lotteries. They claimed they had sold tickets to the value of $50,000 and that Pattee had pocketed the money without paying them for their services. They also sued for $4,000 for money loaned to the lottery shark. Strickland & Webster were their attorneys. They attached all his property, he being in Europe at the time. Mr. Webster fails to remember just how the matter was settled, as it was in the hands of Strickland. After leaving Omaha Pattee made his home in St. Louis, where he resided until his death.

WORMS AND NICKELS [20]

[Oscar Ameringer of Milwaukee and Oklahoma City] was a stocky German of extraordinary energy. He had a wonderful gift of English words flavored with a thick, delicious German accent. On the platform he acted the details of a story with a drollery that convulsed his listeners. No comedian in our theater could approach Ameringer in putting an audience in a state of utter exhaustion from laughter. In illustrating the common occurrence of want in the face of plenty in our economic lunacy, he would tell of a worm eating its way into a large, red juicy apple, curling up in its middle and dying with the exclamation, "I give up. There is too much apple around me." To illustrate the theory of economic determinism Oscar would tell of a fight among boys of different religious creeds. The father of one of the boys tried to drag his son out of the fight. "Leave me alone, Pop," said the boy, "I've got my foot on a nickel." "Yes," said Oscar, "religious factors, moral issues, national aspirations and other influences may enter into the determination of wars. Some or more of these may be at work, but comrades, please keep your eye on the nickel under the foot."

BUSINESSMAN'S TOWN [21]

From the first, Oklahoma City was known as a "businessman's town." Some of the old-timers still tell the story of the cleric who, back in '89, mixed piety with commercial acumen. A Rev. Mr. Shaw, apparently of doubtful denominational persuasion, conducted the first Sunday school in a pasture. A few days later several men appeared, to claim the property as their own. The cleric told them he had taken the lots for church purposes, and with considerable graciousness they withdrew. The dominie put up a large sign which read: "Dedicated to the Lord." But a little later, when some Baptist brethren came looking for a church site—or so the story goes—he came out from behind the sign and sold the lots for $400. The original owners demanded an explanation.

[20] From *Didn't We Have Fun!* Stories out of a Long, Fruitful and Merry Life, by August Claessens, pp. 58-59. Copyright, 1953, by Rand School Press. New York.
[21] From "The Cities of America: Oklahoma City," by Milton MacKaye, *The Saturday Evening Post*, Vol. 220 (June 5, 1948), No. 49, p. 21. Copyright, 1948, by the Curtis Publishing Company. Philadelphia.

" 'Dedicated to the Lord,' " Mr. Shaw is reported to have said with finality, "does not mean 'donated to the Lord.' "

"MR. FORT WORTH" AND THE TRINITY CANAL PROJECT [22]

. . . Amon Carter is Mr. Fort Worth. He has been its dynamo for so long that he has come to resemble the town and it to resemble him. For years Amon Carter has given visiting firemen big Western hats as a token of Fort Worth hospitality—in two sizes: three-inch brims to medium shots, and five-inch brims to thoroughgoing big shots. His newspaper, the Star-Telegram, is a highly vocal spokesman for the Fort Worth cause, and when Mr. Carter has to go to Dallas on business, he carries his own lunch, in order to avoid making even so small a purchase as a hamburger from the Philistines.

*   *   *   *   *

. . . If these municipal Kilkenny cats [of Dallas and Fort Worth] make the fur fly on every other problem, there is one at least upon which harmony has, in the nature of things, had to prevail. And that is with regard to the proposed canalization of the Trinity River, which runs through both cities and which Boyce House, Fort Worth humorist, says is the only river in the world where the catfish have to swim backward to keep the mud out of their eyes.

Both cities are dedicated to the job of making the hundreds of intervening miles of the river navigable to the sea, and are supporters of the Trinity Improvement Association. . . . Amon Carter has virtually got a shovel in his hand most of the time. In fact, before his friend Will Rogers died, Mr. Carter spoke so lyrically and with such confidence in the outcome of [the Trinity Canal] project that Will closed his eyes, leaned back in his chair and said, "Amon, I can see the sea gulls now."

*   *   *   *   *

To open the river to barge traffic from the Gulf to Dallas and Fort Worth would require a system of locks that would lift the vessels 670 feet, would cost a good many millions, plus the political effort necessary to shout down the railroads, who, understandably, do not want their freight rates imperiled by barge competition. . . .

*   *   *   *   *

One of the most colorful figures in the canal project, or any other, for that matter, was the late great Commodore Basil Hatfield, to use only two of his eighteen names. He was a man with Buffalo Bill whiskers, a brave, round belly, and a dancing eye. He'd made and spent three fortunes, run guns to South America, organized the first standing Chinese army, once had a whole floor of Fort Worth's Neal P. Anderson Building for his oil company, from

[22] From "The Cities of America: Dallas and Fort Worth," by George Sessions Perry, *The Saturday Evening Post*, Vol. 218 (March 30, 1946), No. 39, pp. 43, 46. Copyright, 1946, by the Curtis Publishing Company. Philadelphia.

which he went, at the behest of the Federal Government, to tend the roses in Leavenworth's gardens. But the commodore was not a man to be disheartened by an occasional sojourn in the pokey. Eventually he built a scow and navigated it down the river from Fort Worth to the Gulf and back up again. He named his scow the "Amen" Carter, and when Mr. Carter complained of the misspelling, the commodore said he knew what he was about. "In Fort Worth," said the commodore, "you are the first word and also the last word. Therefore I have named my vessel the Amen Carter."

ART VS. BUSINESS IN SANTA FE [23]

The inevitable conflict between Art and Business in Santa Fe only simmers now. The Chamber of Commerce agitates the idea that the city deserves a more truly industrial foundation than the cabinetmaking of furniture to match the Santa Fe style, Indian handicrafts and the hand-weaving of neckties. The art colony jeers, comfortable in the knowledge that the city's [lack of direct] rail facilities continue to insure the absence of any extensive— and disfiguring—industrial enterprise. Back in the '20's and '30's, however, fierce controversy was the general rule. Its rather surprising outcome was that Business at last became the enthusiastic partner of Art in the apparently very unbusinesslike obsession with Santa Fe history and its preservation in the Santa Fe style.

Actually the central issue at the time was the matter of Santa Fe streets. In the business district they were old and narrow and winding, as if they had been laid out—in the words of the city's authentically colorful old newspaperman, Brian Boru (B.B.) Dunn—"By a tequila-drunk Indian riding a loco burro." Business wanted them made fit for the growing number of customers' automobiles. Art yelled that to impair by one iota the city's picturesque Spanish Colonial beauty would be grossly criminal. To their everlasting amazement, the artists discovered that their strongest support was coming from a most unexpected quarter—from those pillars of convention and sternest critics of the art colony's Bohemian ways, the members of the socially sacrosanct Women's Board of Trade.

It was probably not any appeal to their aesthetic sensibilities which persuaded the business interests to yield, but rather a solid economic fact—then just becoming apparent—which today is of ruling importance in Santa Fe life. During the late '20's, in multiplying numbers, that free-spending species, the American Tourist, was appearing in Santa Fe. Obviously he came in search of that same picturesque Spanish Colonial charm which the artists and the Women's Board of Trade were so vociferously defending. Curio shops crammed with Indian baskets, Indian blankets and textiles, Indian jewelry of silver and turquoise, are as crowded as the antique shops of New England summer resorts. The tolerance of Santa Fe business for narrow, inadequate

[23] From "The Cities of America: Santa Fe," by John Bishop, *The Saturday Evening Post*, Vol. 221 (September 18, 1948), No. 12, pp. 130-132. Copyright, 1948, by the Curtis Publishing Company. Philadelphia.

streets and its loyal adherence to the Santa Fe style of architecture are not
without a keen awareness that in them lie splendid profits.

TAOS FEUD [24]

It is at the [Taos] Pueblo . . . that the impact of modern ways
has had perhaps the most striking and, in some ways, the most disturbing
effect. Encouraged by the artists, the Indians have maintained their old form
of communal life and preserved many of their pagan ceremonies and traditions, as well as the Christian rites introduced by the early Spanish priests.
Their local government still consists of a council of thirty-odd men which
each year elects a governor and other officers. The councilmen remain in
office for life, admit new members only after long indoctrination and pass
the elective jobs around among themselves in a kind of closed-shop political
racket.

The dignified friendliness of the Indians and their colorful, uncomplicated
mode of life appealed from the first to many of the artists, who have worried
over and worked in behalf of the Pueblo ever since. Like everybody else, however, the Indians found isolation impossible and in the last half century they
have developed a sort of synthetic *rapprochement* with the white man's civilization.

The old-timers of the tribe still spurn the white man's ways, but they have
erected a large sign at the Pueblo entrance informing tourists that they must
pay a two-bit parking fee and that anyone taking photographs must pay additional fees, ranging up to five dollars for movie-camera addicts. They refuse to
permit running water or gas stoves in the Pueblo, but they have acquired a
collection of Grand Rapids furniture, wind-up phonographs and portable
radios. They send their children—about 200 of them—to the fine Federal
school adjacent to the Pueblo, but every so often the principal is informed
that one or more of the boys will be missing for a year because he is under-
going special training in the kivas. The boys and girls wear crew haircuts
and bobbed hair, natty sports suits and nylon stockings while in their teens,
but the majority revert to blankets and long braids by the time they reach mar-
riageable age.

In other words, the elders have encouraged the attitude that, while the
Pueblo can't entirely escape contact with civilization, it should delay entan-
glement as much as possible. The council has, for instance, forbidden the
Indians to take advantage of their right to vote in state and Federal elections,
because voting might lead to various obligations and would certainly infest
the Pueblo with vote-seeking politicians. It has also opposed the introduction
of electricity in the Pueblo because that would mean the advent of monthly
bills, and then a desire for electric refrigerators and the introduction of installment payments and thus, gradually, all the problems of modern civilization.

[24] From "The Cities of America: Taos, New Mexico," by Joe Alex Morris, *The Saturday Evening Post*, Vol. 223 (July 22, 1950), No. 4, pp. 64, 66. Copyright, 1950, by the
Curtis Publishing Company. Philadelphia.

In support of this attitude, it can be pointed out that life is relatively secure in the Indian village, and there is no record of either nervous breakdowns or ulcers among its residents. "We are not against progress," the council explained in a formal letter to El Crepusculo not long ago, "but we have our own kind of progress, and there are some things that might interfere with us and make our people look as unhappy as the people in the big cities."

Since the war, however, a considerable percentage of the young veterans and some of the older men, including a few members of the council, have raised objections to the static and dictatorial methods of tribal government, which they felt was not being conducted according to progressive or democratic principles. Some of their wives also wanted running water and electricity in the kitchen. This uprising was somewhat clouded by personal feuds and old grudges at the Pueblo, but it led early in 1949 to a series of protest meetings and formulation by the veterans' group of demands for a written charter, the right to a voice in choosing the council, more progressive management of Pueblo affairs and a periodic audit of community funds.

In former days, the controversy might well have been settled within the confines of the Pueblo, but on this occasion there were a number of eager outsiders ready to volunteer for battle, the local newspapers took opposing sides in the dispute, and the trouble soon emerged as a community issue.

Any attempt to weigh the merits of the controversy would involve a reckless plunge into the ramifications of the whole Indian problem, but a few incidents suggest that both sides rallied strong support and that the logical solution lay somewhere in between. On one occasion the rebels arranged a mass meeting at which Eric T. Hagberg, superintendent of the United Pueblos, was to listen to their complaints on behalf of the Bureau of Indian Affairs. Hagberg arrived at a Taos hotel shortly before the meeting, only to be advised by Seferino Martinez, who is regarded as the strong man of the Pueblo old guard, that he should keep out of Pueblo affairs and go back to Albuquerque immediately. When the superintendent ignored the warning, a human roadblock of council supporters barred his automobile en route to the meeting, forcing him to turn back.

News of this incident in the newspapers provided an opportunity that was too good for many townspeople to miss, and a long debate was carried on in the public prints, with El Crepusculo defending the council, and the Star spurring on the rebels. Mrs. Luhan, who has frequently had difficulty deciding just where she stands on Pueblo questions, but has never wavered in her distrust of commercialized America, wrote a letter to El Crepusculo. In the first paragraph, she pointed out that outsiders can't know or understand the mysteries of Indian life. In the next 1500 words, she explained to the Indian war veterans why deep down in their hearts they didn't really want the modern conveniences that some of them had been demanding. The letter said:

> Oh, yes, now they (the veterans) are imbued with the stupid methods of the logical world, the unhappy world. . . . This will be called Progress by some . . . (But) will it be any more FUN or will it just be faster? Should the veterans succeed in accomplishing their wishes for a copy of

our not-very-successful so-called civilization, it will be the end of the Pueblo, its life, its beauty, its success as a *modus vivendi*. I believe the council will prove stronger than the dismal accretion of cars, stoves, sinks *et al*. These young men know what I am saying is true. They will return to their fathers. The blood of their forerunners is still truly stronger in them than new needs for THINGS. Sure it is.

The following week the Taos Star published a letter from one of the rebellious war veterans, J. R. Martinez. He addressed himself to Mrs. Luhan, who was just getting herself settled in a new house, where the bedrooms are soundproof, the bathrooms are numerous and the kitchen is a gleaming red-white-and-black display. He wrote:

> *Dear Mrs. Luhan:* How would you like to exchange places? Say I live at your house, you live at mine. You can have all the horse and buggies you want and I'll have your nice new cars. You drink muddy water from the mountains and my five children will drink nice clean water from your faucets. . . . You have to understand that we want to live like humans and not like animals. By animals I mean monkey. Yes, we are tired of being fed by you writers and artists with peanuts. . . . Mrs. Luhan, take your peanuts someplace else.

JUSTICE IN EARLY TUCSON [25]

The most famous justice of the peace that Tucson had in the early days was Charles H. Meyer. His name is written imperishably in the annals of Tucson. He was a German by birth, and a druggist by profession. He was a man of conviction and loved justice, but knew little law. It was said that his law library consisted of only two books: A volume on *MATERIA MEDICA* and one on *FRACTURED BONES*. In a case of great perplexity he diligently consulted these two books. His vigorous and straightforward decisions were so much in the interest of honesty and good order that the worthier members of the legal profession used all their ingenuity to interpret the law in such a manner as to fit the decisions of the judge; though sometimes even very able lawyers found it hard to do this. Of course, to the crooked and pettifogging members of the legal profession Judge Meyer was a terror.

It was Judge Meyer who instituted the chain-gang system in Tucson. Every person convicted in his court was given an opportunity to work for the city for a period long or short. Meyer's salty sentences pleased the law-abiding citizens of Tucson very much, for never before had the streets been kept so clean, and never had the departure of vagrants and thieves been so prompt. Some of the lawyers protested when their clients were summarily committed to the chain-gang, and declared that this was contrary to the Constitution of the United States. To all these complaints Judge Meyer turned a deaf ear.

. . . One cold December evening five dirty and ragged, but healthy looking tramps were brought before him. They were without blankets or other baggage, and money was a thing unknown to them. He welcomed them to the

[25] By Frank C. Lockwood. From *Tucson—The Old Pueblo*, by Dean Frank C. Lockwood and Captain Donald W. Page, pp. 58-59, 60-61. Copyright, [1937?], by Frank C. Lockwood. Phoenix: Manufacturing Stationers, Inc.

city in a very affable manner, inquired about their health and asked whence they came and whither they were faring. One said he was an electrician.

"Dis city," said the justice with geniality, "has in darkness long avaited your coming."

Two said they were machinists and were skilled in the use of tools.

"Goot," said His Honor, "our picks and shovels vill now no longer vaste mit rust."

A fourth was a fireman.

"Most velcome," beamed the magistrate. "You are a man after mine own heart. These mornings are shilly and de great stove in de yard is seldom varm on my arrival to hold court, but now it vill glow mit consuming fuel and vill radiate through tier and cell."

The fifth was a traveler seeking adventure. The hospitable official promised to help him secure it. He smiled benignantly upon them all, assured them that the city was glad that they had come and would keep them.

"I vill order board and lodging for you within the city palace for the night," said he, "and vill promise you that tomorrow you shall have embloyment on the streets of our ancient town."

* * * * *

The ———— Saloon was the most unsavory resort in Tucson. It was a gambling hell and the rendezvous of all the toughs and criminals in the Old Pueblo. One night, rather late, Meyer heard a knocking at the door of his house. He had plenty of enemies, as he well knew, and had been threatened with assassination if he remained in town and continued to act as justice of the peace. He was, therefore, cautious about admitting anyone to his house. He went to the front door and opened the little look-out with which all the doors in Tucson were then provided.

"Who is it comes der?" he inquired.

"A friend," was the reply.

"Vat is it you vant?" asked the judge, cautiously.

"I want to give myself up," said the stranger. "I just killed a man down at the ———— Saloon."

"You killed a man?"

"Yes, I killed him. He called me a liar, and you know, Judge, there are things a gentleman can't stand, so I pulled my gun and killed him, and now I want to give myself up."

"You say you killed him at the ———— Saloon? Den, mine frient, you go back der and kill anoder von!" And, forthwith, he went back to bed.

The next morning a dead man was picked up on the street, but the murderer was not to be found.

MAYOR WILL ROGERS [26]

Beverly Hills became an incorporated city in 1914, after employing the tactics of María Rita who borrowed cattle in order to qualify for the original land grant. Beverly Hills expanded its city limits a little and thereby gained the necessary five hundred population for incorporation. Its first mayor was Will Rogers who set the precedent for all the mayors who have followed—they and the councilmen serve without pay. The only elective officer of the city who receives a salary is the treasurer, and he gets a dollar a year. The highest paid city employee is the city clerk, who is the active business manager of the city.

Will Rogers datelined many of his columns Beverly Hills and those who can remember them may recall how he frequently poked fun at the local real estate boom. "Real estate agents are as thick as bootleggers," he said once. ". . . After buying a lot you put it back in the hands of a real estate agent, for don't you think you're going to get away with that lot! It has to be sold three or four times that day. Why, every lot out here has its own individual agent. . . . If an agent has two lots he open a branch office." . . . And another time: "Your having no money don't worry the agents . . . if they can just get an old overcoat or shotgun as first payment."

The city prospered and Will Rogers, the lovable humorist and gum-chewing philosopher, probably did more than any one to promote it. Perhaps his greatest service was in 1929, after Beverly Hills had been turned down by the Treasury Department on a request for a stylish post office building commensurate with a very stylish town. Will Rogers sat down and wrote this letter to Secretary of the Treasury Andrew Mellon:

"We are getting an awful lot of mail out here, now, and they are handling it in a tent. It's mostly circulars from Washington with speeches on prosperity, but it makes awful good reading while you are waiting for the foreclosure.

"It seems that you owe us $250,000 to build a post office and they can't get the dough out of you, and I told them that I knew you and that you wasn't that kind of a fellow at heart. . . ."

Beverly Hills got its stylish post office.

SEATTLE SOAPBOXERS [27]

I. "NOTHING, JUST NOTHING!"

In pre-war days, from about 1900 on, soap-boxing reached a high stage of development in the Socialist Party. Very effective educational work was thus done, but many humorous incidents occurred. There was the case, for

[26] From *Fabulous Boulevard*, by Ralph Hancock, pp. 173-174. Copyright, 1949, by Funk & Wagnalls Company. New York.
[27] From *Pages from a Worker's Life*, by William Z. Foster, pp. 269-271. Copyright, 1939, by International Publishers, Inc. New York.

example, of Callaham, a printer in Seattle in 1906, who deeply cherished the usual ambition to become a soap-boxer. Finally, those of us in charge of this work locally agreed to give him a chance. He would begin in the usual manner by opening one of our Sunday evening meetings and introducing the principal speaker.

Callaham was intelligent and well-posted but badly afflicted with stage fright, and as his first trial at facing a street crowd approached, his heart sank. But he carefully memorized his five minute speech. When the long-feared time came, Callaham, with many quakings, mounted the platform.

"Fellow workers," he began, "tonight in the two hundred churches of Seattle two hundred preachers are at this moment entering their pulpits to preach. And what have they to say to the people? Nothing, just nothing!"

As Callaham went on, his stage fright visibly increased, and when he reached the point, "Nothing, just nothing," it quite overcame him. He became speechless; not another word could he utter, and he slid down from the box unable even to introduce the next speaker. He, too, it appeared, like his preachers, had "just nothing" to say. The crowd, catching the point, laughed good-naturedly and Callaham retired in confusion.

II. The Sick Society Dog

. . . Floyd Hyde, a well-known S.P. street speaker in Seattle during this period . . . was a Southern mountaineer, and he had an inveterate habit of "drawing the long bow," which often led him into fantastic exaggeration.

Typical was his description of a rich New York woman and her sick poodle dog. The original story, as it appeared in the daily newspapers, was to the effect that the dog of a society leader fell sick, and she took him to Florida for his health.

Now Floyd waxed plenty wrath over this outrageous solicitude for a dog while thousands of babies were dying in New York tenements for want of milk and other necessities. He told the story night after night, and under the combined effects of his just indignation and fertile imagination it grew in the repeated telling until it became almost unrecognizable.

Monday night Floyd told the story substantially as it appeared in the morning papers. Tuesday night, however, it began to develop: the woman, according to Floyd, had taken with her to Florida also a trained nurse to care for the indisposed poodle. Wednesday night Floyd indignantly had not only the owner and a nurse but a doctor as well, accompanying the sick dog to balmy Florida, all in special Pullman compartments. Thursday night Floyd introduced some additional medical members into the dog's entourage and had the whole outfit traveling in the aristocratic lady's private railroad car.

By Saturday night Floyd had so developed his dog story that the canine invalid had for its voyage South a special train with several doctors and a battery of nurses and maids. Each time he told the elastic story with added trimmings, the outraged Hyde seemed, if anything, to believe it the more implicitly. Nor did our amused protests that perhaps his nightly street corner crowds might remember his previous, more modest, versions have any effect in checking the growth of this fabulous tale. I often wondered what it would have eventually grown into had not its evolution been stopped abruptly on Saturday night by some big strike developments which distracted Floyd's attention from the adventures of the sick society dog.

XIII. They Have a Word for It

The history of city naming in the United States is a hodgepodge of the old and the new, the pedantic and the extemporaneous, the felicitous and the barbarous. Commemorative names were transferred from the Old World to the New and from older Eastern states to new Western territories. Thus Boston, a familiar example of the Colonial importation, narrowly escaped being transplanted to the Pacific Northwest when Portland, by the flip of a coin, won out as the name of the Oregon city. Minneapolis barely missed being "Minnehahapolis," and "Wau-ka-ru-sa" was rejected in favor of Lawrence when the settlers learned that the Indian name for the near-by river meant, inelegantly, "hip-deep" in water.

City nicknames were more often boosting (Lexington, the "Belle City of the Blue Grass Region"; Cincinnati, the "Queen City of the West"; Kansas City, the "Heart of America") than accurate (the "City of the Saints" for Salt Lake City; "Porkopolis" for Cincinnati). When, as in the latter city, an industry languished and the nickname became outmoded, a new one was sometimes found. Rochester switched from "Flour City" to "Flower City" when the flour mills moved west and nurseries took their place.

Street names often show more clearly how towns grew through various periods of colonization—Dutch and English in New York, as in the Bowery and Wall Street; French and American in New Orleans, as when the first American directory maker in that city erroneously translated Bernard de Marigny's "Bagatelle" (a game of chance) as Trifle Street. The hand of the censor is seen in some street-name changes, as in Rampart Street for New Orleans' Love Street, though many residents still continued to call it Love. For the folk always prefer their own names to official ones—Cow Alley instead of Philadelphia Street in Charleston and Sixth Avenue instead of Avenue of the Americas in New York.

Nicknames of neighborhoods are as poetic (Bughouse Square for Chicago's open-air soapbox forum) as official names are functional (Back Bay for the made land on the Charles to distinguish it from Front Bay or Boston Harbor). Negro Harlem's Strivers' Row and Sugar Hill express the social aspirations of groups within a group, just as the popular names of cities within a city—the Loop, the Barbary Coast—picturesquely delineate a business or a water-front district. Some neighborhoods are proverbial for an ethnic group—the East Side, Harlem—or for an era—Greenwich Village.

Where non-Anglo-Saxon strains are strong, their effect is noticeable in local speech and names, as in the German influence in Milwaukee or the Frenchifying of German family names in New Orleans—Sweig becoming La Branche and Jake Schneider, Schexnayrdre. Local preference for certain classes of given names as well as local peculiarities of pronunciation may give rise to a local witticism like the Bostonian's remark (regarding the succession of Josiahs in the Quincy family) that the line did not run from sire to son but from 'Siar to 'Siar.

A cosmopolitan city like New York contributes foreign words (usually humorous)—Jimmy Durante's *Umbriago,* Yiddishisms and "Yinglish" like

463

schlemihl, shmo, shmus, bagel, I should worry, so what, already (as in "Go already"), *Borscht Belt.* Single-industry cities like Hollywood and Washington have their pet words and pat phrases—Hollywoodese and red tape-ese—which often filter into general usage through radio and gossip columns. In metropolitan vernacular "-ese" (ad-ese, **Winchellese, Cholly Knickerbockerese,** New Yorkese), with its slang and humorous coinages and nonce-words, tends to outstrip "isms" or true localisms, which are more common in provincial cities like Charleston.

Cities have contributed names for occupations: e.g., "white wings" for street cleaners, originating in New York Street Cleaning Commissioner Colonel George F. Waring's order to his employees to wear white ducks because they would look cleaner and also, by their conspicuousness, discourage loafing on the job. Or names for vehicles—Concord Coach; Black Maria, the latter traditionally traced to Maria Lee, a Negro lodging-house keeper for sailors in Boston's North End. Powerful Maria was so successful in subduing obstreperous offenders that the police often enlisted her aid in getting them to the station house.

Local business firms are immortalized and advertised in brand names which become product names—San Francisco's Levi's—or in emblems—Macy's Red Star, which, legend has it, originated in the star by which founder Captain Macy, of Nantucket, once steered his ship safely to shore through the fog. In New York, "nobody, but nobody," spells Gimbel's. In Chicago "Give the lady what she wants" is synonymous with Marshall Field's, and "No orchestral din" with Henrici's restaurant in the Loop. A New York dance studio inspired a song whose title has proved worth millions in publicity—"Arthur Murray taught me dancing in a hurry."

In countless ways urban vernacular and word lore contribute both to the nation's language and to its merriment. To traveling salesmen the three Pennsylvania towns—Pottsville, Pottstown and Potts Grove are known as the "chamber-pot circuit." And to the world "dem bums" spells not only the Dodgers but much-maligned Brooklyn.

BANGOR—"NAMED AT A PINCH"[1]

In 1781 the citizens of a small community in Maine petitioned for incorporation, and sent their minister, the Reverend Seth Noble, to Boston on this errand. As the clerk was filling out the papers, Mr. Noble stood by, in true Yankee fashion, quietly humming a tune to himself. When the clerk suddenly asked him, "What's the name?" he absent-mindedly thought of the tune, not the town, and replied "Bangor." The naming from a hymn-tune became a repeated folk-tale. Even one of the greatest of New Englanders gave it circulation: "named at a pinch from a psalm tune," as Mr. Emerson wrote, disparagingly.

[1] From *Names on the Land*, A Historical Account of Place-Naming in the United States, by George R. Stewart, pp. 206-207. Copyright, 1945, by George R. Stewart. New York: Random House.

FROM "FLOUR CITY" TO "FLOWER CITY" [2]

In 1823 Rochester held a celebration to mark the opening of its section of the Erie Canal and the completion of the aqueduct which carried the canal across the Genesee River. . . . One great contribution of the canal to western New York was a drastic reduction in freight rates. Before its day, the high cost of transportation had limited the market of the Genesee farmer, who let his excess grain rot or turned it into whiskey. The canal enabled him to undersell his eastern competitors along the Hudson and the Mohawk. Genesee land values rose; settlers flocked to settle in the valley; more mills sawed lumber and ground flour; additional land was cleared and planted to wheat. The soil of the Genesee Valley bore rich harvests, and Rochester became the "Flour City." . . .

*   *   *   *   *

. . . As the western wheat fields were developed the milling industry began to move west and in the end Rochester was unable to sustain the competition in that field. . . . As flour-milling reached a plateau in its development and began to decline, other manufacturing processes made use of the city's water-power and transportation facilities: machine shops, cotton factories, breweries, boat-yards, coach and carriage, boot and shoe, and furniture factories. But the successor to milling in economic importance and repute was the nursery industry. . . . Rochester became the "Flower City," and assumed leadership in the growing and distributing of nursery stock and garden and farm seeds. An important contribution to the success of the industry was made by German gardeners, who came with the large German immigration after 1848, and transplanted their skill to the banks of the Genesee. . . . The industry reached its height in the Seventies and Eighties; the city was almost completely surrounded by vegetable, flower, and tree nurseries.

Aside from its economic importance, the nursery industry exerted a definite influence upon the physical development of the city. It inspired and encouraged the growth of the system of parks which is today one of the prides of Rochester. . . .

THE NAMING OF BUFFALO [3]

[Buffalo] is almost like a foster child in that it is not sure of its own name. Historians have tried for years to get an historically accurate reason for the name, and they have failed. There is one school of thought that it is a corruption of the exclamation of an enthusiastic Frenchman when he came out of the woods at what later became known as Buffalo River at the Niagara

[2] From *Rochester and Monroe County*, by the Federal Writers' Project of the Works Progress Administration for the State of New York, pp. 54-55, 59-61. Copyright, 1937, by the Genesee Book Club of Rochester. Rochester: Scrantom's.

[3] From *Niagara Country*, by Lloyd Graham, pp. 263-264. Copyright, 1949, by Lloyd Graham. New York: Duell, Sloan & Pearce, Inc.

and raved about "la belle fleuve." If you try hard you can make his phrase sound like Buffalo. There is also the mistaken belief that it was named for the American Bison. The plains "buffalo" never did roam Niagara Country, although the woods bison may have at one time.

Joncaire and the French of his time merely called the spot "la Rivière aux Chevaux," but that name did not last. Sometime between the French and American periods, the reservation settlement of Indians came to be known as Buffalo Creek. One story has it that a surveyor from down Pennsylvania way, where there is a Buffalo Creek, named the stream after his home community for lack of a real name.

People were careless about those things in the early days. When Joseph Ellicott came along and tried to tag the locality New Amsterdam in honor of his employers in Holland, it simply would not stick. The term Buffalo Creek was too well established by usage. And, as the community grew, the "Creek" part of the name was naturally dropped. But it is embarrassing to Buffalonians not to be able to utter their city's name with a ring of pride in an honored derivation of the name.

PORKOPOLIS [4]

It is difficult to discover when the first pork was packed in Cincinnati for other than local use. The business was being pretty rigidly regulated in 1809, as proven by notices inserted in the papers by Peter Mills, "Inspector of Hamilton County," who warned that the packing of Beef, Pork, or Lard for shipment must be done under the eye of city supervisors or not at all.

There being no form of transportation in early days for hogs unless the grower lived near a river, pioneer porkers walked to market on their own four feet. Ohio hogs crossed the Alleghenies thus to New York and Baltimore, with great loss in weight, despite many rest periods, and from eastern Ohio they continued to do so, even after Cincinnati became a market. But western and southern Ohio, as well as Indiana and Kentucky farmers found a new and welcome outlet in Queen City.

*   *   *   *   *

. . . In the 1820's, George W. Jones, president of the local branch of the Bank of the United States, and popularly known as "Bank" Jones, was so proud of the city's pork industry that he boosted it far and wide. In his letters to the bank's Liverpool correspondent, he seldom failed to mention the fact that from 25,000 to 30,000 hogs were being processed annually, and to predict Cincinnati's future supremacy as a provision market. At length the Liverpool man had two little papier-maché hogs made, branded "George W. Jones, as the Worthy Representative of Porkopolis," and sent them to the Cincinnatian. Jones was delighted with them, and the city's new pseudonym was soon known to all the world.

[4] From *The Serene Cincinnatians*, by Alvin F. Harlow, pp. 78-80, 91. Copyright, 1950, by Alvin F. Harlow. New York: E. P. Dutton & Co., Inc.

At first salt pork—mess pork, it was called by the trade; the principal and staple ingredient of the sailor's diet, which made scurvy the curse of the seven seas—was the packer's only product. The British Government began buying Cincinnati mess pork for its navy, and presently transferred nearly all its business from Dublin, then the world's greatest pork-packing center, to the Queen City, to become its biggest customer. In the meantime the industry had ramified rapidly—smokehouses to cure hams and bacon; then renderers of lard, and then factors of candles, lard oil, soap, chemical and other by-products. In 1840 two of the nation's greatest soap manufactories were being developed—that of Michel Werk and what all Cincinnati now calls P & G. It was told with awe in '59 that the latter had 80 employees and sold a million dollars' worth of soap and candles annually. Wholesalers and brokers of pork products became big business.

The industry soon localized itself. Slaughtering would not have been permitted, of course, in the downtown area, so two arenas of immolation were developed. Tinkling among moss-covered rocks down a wooded ravine from springs near the top of the plateau as you went to Walnut Hills came a pretty little stream called Deer Creek. One of Cincinnati's pioneer beer gardens was up that vale, centering around a fine spring, with much "ornamental" rock-work and an aviary of woodland birds. But now the pork-butchers chose this as one of their fields of operation because of the creek, which would carry away their sewage. The beer garden vanished and the once beautiful glen became a place of horror, the creek nicknamed Bloody Run or Bloody River—it literally ran red—and citizens weren't any too happy at seeing it entering the Ohio so close below the waterworks intake. The glen became the "Valley of the Shadow of Death," and as various odorous by-product plants were erected in it, "Valley of Desolation" was one of the least offensive of its sobriquets.

The other place of execution was Brighton, a suburb at the northwest corner of the Basin, as it were, where Mill Creek entered it. Down that stream's valley from up-country came great droves of hogs and herds of cattle and sheep, as the city's needs and the meat industry expanded. In the smokehouse and wholesale area, where the canal turned down along Deer Creek towards the river, two- and four-horse wagons, some loaded with barreled pork, some stacked high with whole or half carcasses, singed and drawn, threaded thoroughfares almost blocked by the barrels of pork which overflowed the sidewalks, into the streets. Mrs. Houstoun, a British visitor of the late '40's, was nauseated by it all. Cincinnati, she said, "is, literally speaking, a *city of pigs* . . . a monster piggery. . . . Alive and dead, whole and divided into portions, their outsides and their insides, their grunts and their squeals, meet you at every moment."

When she and some friends went for a drive in the suburbs, they encountered a great multitude of "the unclean beasts, grunting along under the very wheels of our carriage"—on their way to their deaths, of course.

. . . After 1859 American kerosene (not to mention gas) rapidly displaced candles and lard oil as illuminants. Candles for certain purposes persist even unto this day, however, and they are made in quantity in Cincinnati. But the Great Plains, now being threaded by steel rails, became a vast empire of grass and corn and wheat, and thereby a nursery for food animals, and packing plants naturally moved nearer to the source of supply. As Chicago became the nation's and the world's greatest railroad center, it currently became the chief producer of America's fresh and cured meats—ably seconded . . . by other plains cities, eventually including Kansas City and Omaha. Gradually, the packing houses of Cincinnati liquidated or moved away. A few are left —some very good ones, too; but the old predominance is gone.

LA SALLE'S PROPHECY [5]

. . . [Chicago's] strenuous future was forseen by the Chevalier de la Salle, almost the first white man to breathe its invigorating air. In a letter written upon the banks of the Chicago River nearly [three] hundred years ago, he made this amazing prophecy:

> This is the lowest point on the divide between the two great valleys of the St. Lawrence and the Mississippi. The boundless regions of the West must send their products to the East through this point. This will be the gate of empire, this the seat of commerce. Everything invites to action. The typical man who will grow up here must be an enterprising man. Each day as he rises he will exclaim, "I act, I move, I push," and there will be spread before him a boundless horizon, an illimitable field of activity. A limitless expanse of plain is here—to the east, water and at all other points, land. If I were to give this place a name I would derive it from the nature of the place and the nature of the man who will occupy this place —*ago*, I act; *circum*, all around: "Circago."

THE NAMING OF MINNEAPOLIS [6]

The Greek equivalent of City was *-polis,* and it had been used occasionally ever since Jamestown, perhaps humorously, had been called Jacobopolis in 1607. As Annapolis it became a state capital, and this tradition passed on to Indianapolis and Arkopolis. The last, however, lost in a local squabble, yielded to the more native Little Rock.

The town-kiters of the fifties used *-polis* occasionally, but the magnificently platted Kansopolis fizzled out. By and large, that suffix with its suggestion of metropolis was a little too grandiose even for the city-dreamers.

In 1852 the citizens of a little settlement not far from St. Paul were in need of a name. As with many great inventions, partisans have hotly pressed

[5] From *Chicago,* by H. C. Chatfield-Taylor, pp. 118-119. Copyright, 1917, by Hobart C. Chatfield-Taylor and Lester G. Hornby. Boston: Houghton Mifflin Company.
[6] From *Names on the Land,* A Historical Account of Place-Naming in the United States, by George R. Stewart, pp. 290-291. Copyright, 1945, by George R. Stewart. New York: Random House.

the claims of two rivals, Mr. Hoag and Mr. Bowman. The supporters of the latter at least tell a more circumstantial story.

Mr. Bowman was editor of the local paper. As such, he became familiar with the many names suggested for the town, but he felt them all lacking in something. One day he set off on horseback to visit friends in a village some thirty miles distant. The way was long, the horse jogged steadily, the editor's mind was active. To pass the time, he began to conjure up names. He invented many, and rejected them. Still jogging along, he began to consider -*polis*, and to make combinations with it. At last he began to work upon a pleasing idea.

Near his town was a beautiful waterfall. In the language of the Sioux, a waterfall was *haha*; water itself was *minne*. White men by a misunderstanding had coupled the two words, and produced Minnehaha Falls, a name thus meaning "water-waterfalls-falls." By complete though natural misrendering of *haha*, the name had been romantically translated as Laughing Water.

Like Shakespeare and other vigorous makers of language, the frontier American had no prejudice against the marriage of Greek and barbarian. Mr. Bowman's active mind worked quickly through Minnehahapolis and produced Minnehapolis, which he thought appropriate and expressive enough, but lacking in euphony. He decided it would sound better, if the *h* should be silent. All this inspiration occurred to him near a place on the road called Halfway House.

On his return, Mr. Bowman and his friend Mr. Hoag advocated the name, and finally presented it at a meeting of citizens. The meeting, with excellent sense, decided that a silent *h* might as well be dropped completely, and so adopted the name with the spelling Minneapolis.

"WAUKARUSA" [7]

. . . One night in 1849, when this [Kansas region] was unknown Indian territory, a party of overland emigrants for California chanced to camp near the Kansas River. One, Charles Robinson of Massachusetts, was deeply impressed with the beauty of the spot. The next morning the emigrants pressed on. They made scores of camps thereafter, on prairie slopes, in green valleys, among mountain glens, and by singing streams. . . .

When the goal was reached, Robinson took part in the most stirring scenes of California. Among other experiences he was shot in a Sacramento riot arising from a conflict about real estate titles. The ball passed through his body, entering the stomach and coming out at his back; but he seemed bullet-proof and soon recovered. Speculators had laid out a city, and held property at high figures. But it was upon Government land to which they had no perfected title. So other settlers "squatted" upon the lots, built houses, and claimed ownership; hence the Sacramento war. The courts sustained the speculators,

[7] From *Beyond the Mississippi: From the Great River to the Great Ocean, Life and Adventure on the Prairies, Mountains, and Pacific Coast . . . 1857-1867*, by Albert D. Richardson, pp. 36-37. Hartford, Connecticut: American Publishing Company.

and Robinson was imprisoned as a ringleader in the riots. But the squatters, who were largely in the majority, elected him to the legislature while he was still in bonds: so the governor pardoned him out, and he left his cell among the law-breakers, to take his seat as one of the law-makers.

Robinson returned to his New England home: but that shirt of Nessus, the restlessness born of border life, made him one of the earliest emigrants to Kansas. Through all the years, that green prairie by the softly flowing river, had been photographed in his memory. Thither he led his company of pioneers, and there they founded the first town in Kansas.

Five miles south ran the little Waukarusa. Pleased with the name, they gave it to their nascent city. Their first *Herald of Freedom*—for a newspaper is mother's milk to an infant town—bears date "Waukarusa, Kansas Territory, October 21, 1854."

'WAU-KA-RU-SA.'

But the settlers soon learned this unromantic legend of the origin and significance of the name:—Many moons ago, before white men ever saw these prairies, there was a great freshet. While the waters were rising, an Indian girl on horseback came to the stream and began fording it. Her steed went in deeper and deeper, until as she sat upon him she was half immersed. Surprised and affrighted she ejaculated "Wau-ka-ru-sa!" (hip-deep.) She finally crossed in safety, but after the invariable custom of the savages, they commemorated her adventure by re-naming both her and the stream, "Waukarusa." On reflection, the settlers decided not to perpetuate the story, and changed the name of their town to Lawrence, in honor of one of its most generous patrons, Amos Lawrence of Boston.

HOW PHOENIX ROSE FROM THE ASHES OF THE PAST [8]

. . . The first white American to pitch a tent there was John Y. T. Smith, who, in 1864, established a hay camp and contracted to supply

[8] From "The Cities of America: Phoenix," by Milton MacKaye, *The Saturday Evening Post*, Vol. 220 (October 18, 1947), No. 16, pp. 88-89. Copyright, 1947, by the Curtis Publishing Company. Philadelphia.

forage to Fort McDowell, an Army outpost thirty miles away. Three years later a man named Jack Swilling spent a few days at the hay camp and conceived another idea—farming on a big scale.

Jack Swilling had been a prospector for gold around Wickenburg, but he grasped the irrigation possibilities of the Salt River area. For one thing, he saw the remains of ancient canals. On the site of the present Phoenix, many centuries ago, a prehistoric race known to the Indians as the Hohokam, "the people who have gone," had managed a complicated agriculture by irrigation processes with which we have only caught up in present years. The Hohokam built buildings now crumbled, made a fertile area in a dry land, and vanished, leaving nothing for history except their pottery and their bones. Swilling brought with him $10,000 in capital and, as one of his partners in canal building, "Lord" Darrel Duppa, a scholarly and—by legend—inebriate Englishman.

Duppa was apparently a remittance man, but to this day little is known about his antecedents. To a nearby town where the present Arizona State College is located he gave the name "Tempe," because of the likeness of the location to the Vale of Tempe between Mount Olympus and Ossa in Thessaly. And looking at the area of prehistoric mounds and canals where Swilling proposed to make a settlement, he suggested that the new village be named for the mythical bird of the Greeks which was consumed by fire every 500 years and rose immediately from the ashes. Duppa is reported to have said that "a city will rise Phoenixlike, new and more beautiful, from the ashes of the past." The name became official when an election precinct was created.

HOW BERKELEY WAS CHRISTENED [9]

The morning was beautiful and clear. The men gathered on a slope of the Contra Costa hills one day in May, 1866, could see ships outward bound through the Golden Gate. Trustees of the College of California, they stood or sat at their ease around a rock where, six years earlier, they had dedicated a quarter-section of new land to the cause of learning. One of them, watching the ships, thoughtfully quoted the final stanza of a prophetic poem:

> Westward the course of empire takes its way;
> The four first acts already past,
> A fifth shall close the drama of the day;
> Time's noblest offspring is the last.

"Who wrote that poem, Billings?" asked one of his hearers. "Wasn't it Berkeley?"

Trustee Frederick Billings nodded; then, turning, asked suddenly: "Why wouldn't Berkeley be a good name for the college town?"

Others agreed. The discussion continued over luncheon in the new home of Dr. Samuel H. Willey, acting president of the college, near the campus site.

[9] From *Berkeley, The First Seventy-Five Years*, compiled by Workers of the Writers' Program of the Work Projects Administration in Northern California, pp. 5-6. Copyright, 1941, by Berkeley Festival Association. Berkeley: The Gillick Press.

And at their regular meeting, held in San Francisco, on May 24, 1866, the trustees unanimously adopted the name.

Thus, according to the most reliable accounts, the city of learning opposite the Golden Gate was christened. Much of the story sounds apocryphal, and it is probable that the scene by Founders' Rock has been embellished in the seventy-five years that have since passed. But parts of it, at least, are verified by official records and first-hand accounts: the name was suggested by Frederick Billings,[10] President of the Board of Trustees of the College of California, in honor of George Berkeley, Bishop of Cloyne, and was formally adopted at the meeting of the board on May 24, 1866.

TOSSING A COIN FOR "PORTLAND" [11]

. . . [Portland] came into being not only because of geography— which helped—but was made probable if not inevitable by a weather-beaten deep-sea skipper who wore thumping great earrings and was a man of no half-hearted opinions.

"To this very point," declared Captain John H. Couch, "to this exact point I can bring any ship that can get into the mouth of the Columbia river. And not, sir, a rod further."

The doughty captain was speaking of a site on the west bank of the Willamette in which, for the sum of 25 cents, Asa Lawrence Lovejoy from Massachusetts had just bought a one-half interest. The implications of the mariner's statement, delivered by a noted and forceful character of the time and place, were of the utmost importance.

Lovejoy's investment of a quarter of a dollar—it was for a filing fee—was something of a bargain. His partner in the enterprise, who was Francis Pettygrove from Maine, had to pay "$50 in store goods" for his half. A year later these two optimists had platted four streets and were prepared to name the metropolis. Pettygrove won the toss of a coin and forthwith called the Place Portland for the principal city of his native state. It might have been even worse; Lovejoy, who possessed no more of soaring imagination than his partner, was set on making it Boston.

[10] . . . Did Billings misquote the verse which served as his inspiration? Probably he did, if he read the same version that the eminent historian, George Bancroft, had used in his *History of the United States*—"Westward the star of empire takes its way"—a misquotation ascribed originally to John Quincy Adams in his "Oration at Plymouth" in 1802. Evidence that Billings did make this error is found in a letter from Dr. Willey to President Gilman on January 2, 1873, in which he says: "Berkeley's couplet about the 'Star of Empire' determined the choice."—*Ibid.*, p. 8.

[11] From *The Portland Story*, Written in Observance of Lipman's One Hundredth Anniversary, 1850-1950, by Stewart H. Holbrook, pp. 5-6. Copyright, 1950, by Lipman Wolfe & Co. Portland.

BRIMSTONE CORNER [12]

This site [of the Park Street Church, corner Tremont and Park Streets, Boston] is known as "Brimstone Corner," because in the War of 1812 gunpowder was stored in the basement. When Henry Ward Beecher, a believer in a literal Hell, preached vigorous guest sermons there, the Unitarians slyly said that the corner was well named.

MAIDEN LANE [13]

The origin of Maiden Lane's picturesque and romantic title is, like many another historical inheritance, lost in conflicting traditions. . . . There existed in the old days a rippling little stream that pursued its merry course along the curving path that has ever since marked the line of our thoroughfare. Directly or indirectly it was this very stream that led the old Dutch settlers of Manhattan Island to bestow on the locality, which was then but a short distance beyond the northern limit of the town, the name of *I Maagde Paatje*, the Maiden's path. According to one tradition, the housewives and their daughters congregated along the banks of the flowing water to wash the family linen, a custom, by the way, that was continued for a number of years during the early English period. Another and more romantic tale pictured the grassy slope with its murmuring rivulet as a favorite retreat for lovesick maidens and their favorite swains; hence, the picturesque designation.

TIN PAN ALLEY

These were fecund days, the 1900's, for the popular-music publishers. New houses sprang up, older companies consolidated for expansion, and most of them holed up in the brownstone-front warrens of Twenty-eighth Street between Broadway and Sixth Avenue, where the pounding of myriad pianos led to the sobriquet—Tin Pan Alley—bestowed by some unknown dubber.[14]

* * * * *

. . . It is probably in his [Harry Von Tilzer's] office, early in the 1900s, that Tin Pan Alley received its name. Here is the story as I received it from Harry himself.

It was Von Tilzer's custom, when playing the piano in his office, to achieve

[12] From *Massachusetts, A Guide to Its Places and People*, Written and Compiled by the Federal Writers' Project of the Works Progress Administration for the State of Massachusetts, p. 154. Copyright, 1937, by George M. Nutting, Director of Publicity, Commonwealth of Massachusetts. Boston: Houghton Mifflin Company.

[13] From *Maiden Lane*, The Story of a Single Street, by Albert Ulmann, p. 2. Copyright, 1931, by Albert Ulmann. New York: The Maiden Lane Historical Society.

[14] From *Lost Chords*, The Diverting Story of American Popular Songs, by Douglas Gilbert, p. 287. Copyright, 1942, by Douglas Gilbert. Garden City, New York: Doubleday & Company, Inc.

a queer effect by weaving strips of newspaper through the strings of his upright piano. It is not a musical effect; it is wispy, sometimes mandolin-like, and blurs the music just enough to accentuate the rhythms. Monroe H. Rosenfeld was a frequent visitor, not only as a composer and jingle-man, but as a newspaper writer in quest of material. He had just finished an article upon the music business—perhaps for the *Herald,* on which he worked for a number of years—and was casting about for a title. Harry happened to sit down and strum a tune, when Rosenfeld, catching the thin, "panny" effect, bounced up with the exclamation "I have it!" It was another "Eureka!"

"There's my name!" exclaimed Rosenfeld. "Your Kindler and Collins sounds exactly like a Tin Pan. I'll call the article Tin Pan Alley!"

There are those who doubt Rosenfeld's invention. The pianos of the professional parlors in those days, they will assure you, sounded so unmistakably like tin pans that the metaphor must have occurred to hundreds of listeners simultaneously. Yet, to those whose curiosity has extended to Rosenfeld's articles and verses, and to inferences as to his peculiar personality, it is easily credible that he was just the kind of man to name Tin Pan Alley.[15]

THE LITTLE CHURCH AROUND THE CORNER [16]

The famous Little Church around the Corner lies just off [Fifth] Avenue in Twenty-ninth Street. We are forgetting, I find, how the Church of the Transfiguration got that popular name. George Holland, actor, was dead; loved and lamented by his profession. Joseph Jefferson, in charge of arrangements, decided to give him a church funeral. Jefferson tried two or three churches along this stretch of Fifth Avenue. They would have none of him. As one pastor explained, Holland was an actor; therefore he had died in sin. Enter suddenly a friend of Holland, who said: "There is a little church around the corner which says it will take poor George in." "Then," said Jefferson, "God bless the little church around the corner!" And the stage, which loves tradition, still regards the Church of the Transfiguration as its very own.

CHARLESTON STREET NAMES AND NICKNAMES [17]

. . . Charleston's general history is pretty well told by street names. The town was always partial to religions, as Church Street and Meeting bear evidence. Long loyal to the Crown, she has a King, a Queen, and a Princess Street, and Nassau and Hanover by which to remember dynasties. Never unreservedly a part of the United States, she took care in the early part of the nineteenth century to change the name of Union Street to State, even though

[15] From *Tin Pan Alley,* A Chronicle of the American Popular Music Racket, by Isaac Goldberg, pp. 173-174. Copyright, 1930, by Isaac Goldberg. New York: The John Day Company.

[16] From *Highlights of Manhattan,* by Will Irwin, pp. 178-179. Copyright, 1926-1927, by New York Herald Tribune, Inc.; 1927, by the Century Co. New York and London.

[17] By Samuel Gaillard Stoney. From *Charleston: Azaleas and Old Bricks,* by Bayard Wooten and Samuel G. Stoney, pp. 18-19. Copyright, 1937, by Bayard Wooten and Samuel G. Stoney. Boston: Houghton Mifflin Company.

it had borne the older title for nearly a hundred years to commemorate the union of Scotland and England.

Unfortunately, old maps will show that such changes have not always had either such logical reasons or such comparatively harmless results. As with coinage, the names of the streets of Charleston seem to have followed the sad rule that bad should cast out good. So Friend Street has been swallowed up by Legaré for nothing but a snobbish excuse. Mazyck Street has been lost in Logan; Lamboll Street has overlaid Smith's Lane; and Atlantic Street, prevailing over Lightwood, has forced it to retreat around a corner and (with no right or reason) take over the very properly named Zig Zag Alley.

Even so, the town is rich in such functional names as Lodge Alley and Vendue Range. She keeps such light touches as Crab and Chinquapin Streets, and she glories above all in an infinity of nicknames. Low-Country Negroes believing that cunjuh, or bad-mouth, will go harder for a child if addressed by its true title, will make that name a mystery known only to its nearest and dearest and call it by a basket name until it grows up. In the process the real name is often forgotten and the person involved may hardly remember it himself. Whether or not Charleston was infected with something of the same spirit by her Negro citizens, the town seems to delight in using something like basket names in place of official ones for a number of localities. You will, for instance, get much better guidance to Marion Square if you will ask your way to the Citadel Green. You will hardly find your way to Washington Square by that name, but anyone can show you how to go to the City Hall Park. And if by any remarkable chain of circumstances you should want to see Philadelphia Street, ask for Cow Alley. It is almost a sign of a proper Charlestonian you will find, too, to speak of Rutledge Street Pond instead of Colonial Lake, and the Battery instead of White Point Garden.

Groups of names now give the best clues as to the way the town grew. Except as parts of such titles as St. Paul's Church, Radcliffeborough, or St. John's, Hampstead, the old boroughs and villages that succumbed to growing Charleston have lost all other identity than that which comes to them from the naming of their streets. But you can still trace the general outline of the village of Charleston by the names on its streets of the men who were governing the empire and the province at the time they were projected. George Street and Anson Street still mark Ansonboro, though it is unfortunate that Admiral Lord Anson's names for the other streets which he had run through a bit of land, won at cards (it is said) from a local worthy, should have perished, for as they were taken from famous ships commanded by the great circumnavigator, they had a topical interest of their own, and apart from that, Squirrel, Centurion, and Scarborough Streets should have had innate rights to go on existing. Another loss has been the extinction of the nomenclature of the village of Middlesex with such beautiful Wilksite allusions as Hand-in-Hand Corner and Corsican Walk. But, on the other hand, to make up for these losses, the adventurer into Wraggsboro will find himself walking, as it were, through a family party of Wragg children, passing in review John and Elizabeth and Judith and all the rest of their generation. And the pious gift of a glebe to St. Philip's Parish by

Mrs. Affra Coming can still be worked out in the neighborhood of Glebe Street, St. Philip, and Coming.

If there are, however, no *de facto* boroughs left in Charleston, you will find one section that is a borough *de jure*. Rotten Borough, spreading over the railroad tracks between East Bay and the Cooper, has a double claim to its title. The first is self-evident every day in the year, the other most notably on election days. Aside from merit the Borough seems to have got its name by a left-handed corruption of an inherited nickname. The filled-in marsh land it covers was, during the Revolution, said to have been occupied by a camp of Tory refugees come into Charleston to be under the protection of Lord Rawdon's red-coats. Thence the section was called contemptuously Rawdon's Borough, from whence it slipped into the present name. But do not hunt there now for Tories, for it is in these days the city's stronghold of democracy, veritably a borough that takes care of itself.

PEACHTREE STREET [18]

. . . Atlanta's famed Peachtree Street was an Indian trail that followed the highest ridge in town on its way through the Cherokee Nation toward Chattanooga. There's some difference of opinion as to the derivation of its name. Old Indian maps show that it crossed the Chattahoochee River near a landmark called "Standing Peachtree," which could have given the street its name. Others say the trail crossed a creek at a place where there was a big tree at which friends gathered to pass the time of day and toss knives at a mark on its side, that it was called "the pitch tree," which later became rearticulated as "Peachtree," and was retained in that form as the name of both the creek and the street. . . .

BRONZEVILLE [19]

. . . Most of the ordinary people in [Chicago's] Black Belt refer to their community as "the South Side," but everybody else is also familiar with another name for the area—Bronzeville. This name seems to have been used originally by an editor of the Chicago *Bee*, who, in 1930, sponsored a contest to elect a "Mayor of Bronzeville." A year or two later, when this newspaperman joined the *Defender* staff, he took his brain-child with him. The annual election of the "Mayor of Bronzeville" grew into a community event with a significance far beyond that of a circulation stunt. Each year a Board of Directors composed of outstanding citizens of the Black Belt takes charge of the mock-election. Ballots are cast at corner stores and in barbershops and poolrooms. The "Mayor," usually a businessman, is inaugurated with a colorful ceremony and a ball.

[18] From "The Cities of America: Atlanta," by George Sessions Perry, *The Saturday Evening Post*, Vol. 218 (September 22, 1945), No. 12, p. 27. Copyright, 1945, by the Curtis Publishing Company. Philadelphia.
[19] From *Black Metropolis*: A Study of Negro Life in a Northern City, by St. Clair Drake and Horace R. Cayton, p. 383. Copyright, 1945, by St. Clair Drake and Horace R. Cayton. New York: Harcourt, Brace and Company.

Throughout his tenure he is expected to serve as a symbol of the community's aspirations. He visits churches, files protests with the Mayor of the City, and acts as official greeter of visits to Bronzeville. Tens of thousands of people participate in the annual election of the "Mayor." . . .

CHARLESTONISMS [20]

Mention Charleston to some one who is fairly familiar with the city and the chances are ten to one that he will make some sort of joke about "the Bott'ry." The inhabitants of this Athens of the South are somewhat sensitive on this point; they deny vigorously that they say anything like "bott'ry" when they mean the Battery. However, it is undeniable that their short *a* is a very broad sound, shading over into a close approximation of *ah*. The natives just don't hear it.

Charleston speech is really unusual. For the person whose notion of Southern pronunciation is limited to the nasal grunting and groaning and the caterwauling you hear from inhabitants of some portions of God's country (I refrain from specifying), Charleston speech is likely to be a shock. . . . I know of one lady, who had never been off the Eastern seaboard and had not even any Irish ancestry, but who was sometimes taken for an Irishwoman.

. . . Some element of the original settlers' speech, plus the influence of the Huguenots, the Scotch, the Irish, the Santo Domingans, and certainly not least, that of the Negroes, has given to the people of the Low Country and its metropolis a pronunciation not to be duplicated, as far as I know, on this side of the Atlantic. There are elements of resemblance in the speech of the college-bred West Indian Negro but only elements. Call it Scotch without the burr and Irish without the harsh corners and still you haven't quite characterized it. Other Southerners have a way (envious, of course) of putting the matter. They say that Charleston people talk as if they had salt in their mouths.

To go into particulars, Charleston speech at its best is clear, rapid, and smooth. It may drop its g's here and there, but usually all the syllables are enunciated. The *r*, of course, is unrolled at the end of words, but so is the *r* of standard English, and you will never hear a Charleston native say "river" with the particularly repulsive second syllable that a Brooklynite brings out. It is a lip-speech; none of the hideous garglings of New York and Philadelphia afflict it, although catarrh is not unknown in the Low Country. In general the consonants are clear—not only by the standards of midwestern speech, but fairly crisp.

The vowels of good Charleston pronunciation are pure continental vowels without the diphthongal quality associated with most English. Where the average American, and the Englishman, make diphthongs of long *a* and long *o*, the Charlestonian produces a single sound without any further movement of the lips. He says "day" in a manner which, to foreign ears, sounds rather like "dee"; he says "go" in such a way that it almost sounds like "goo." More peculiarly still,

[20] From *Charleston*, A Gracious Heritage, by Robert Molloy, pp. 239-243. Copyright, 1947, by Robert Molloy. New York: Appleton-Century-Crofts, Inc.

he sometimes makes his short *i* so short that in such words as "fish" and "milk" he appears to have been on the point of saying "fush" and "mulk" and to have changed his mind at the last moment. This may sound grotesque, but good Charlestonese is not grotesque (a native speaking). Of course, to describe vowel sounds and inflections in the silence of print is rather like trying to describe accurately the difference between the tone color of an oboe and a clarinet to a person who has never heard either. So, if you think of the short *a* so pronounced as to make "battery" sound like "bott'ry," you are exaggerating, and no more can be said. Not that *some* Charleston speakers don't make it sound that way, but that is another story. There are degrees of Negroid influence which produce infinite differences of shading. It can generally be said, however, that if you hear somebody say "bettery" or "hend" you just know he isn't a native.

Some of the old-timers used to say "cyart" and "gyarden" and "gyirl" and "cyards" and doubtless a few of the younger generation still do, if English teachers haven't made them self-conscious about the matter. This is simply, I suppose, an exaggeration of the liquid sound of *g* and *c* as in "c(y)arry," "c(y)andy," "g(y)et," characteristic of all educated English that I ever heard. If you say "khabbage" with that guttural sound of the "k" you are a barbarian. So why not "cyart" and "gyarden"? And, anyway, they are not limited to Charleston.

As for the letter *o* as in "got," "pot," and "hot," it must be admitted that the Charlestonian says something very like "gawt" and "pawt" and "hawt," English fashion. Who hasn't heard affected speakers deliberately practise this? Some natives shorten the double *o* as in "book" to make a sound like "buck," but I have heard an Anglo-Indian do so too, and I have certainly heard "roof" and "food" made to rhyme with "good," and you can't hang these distortions on Charleston. And if the Charlestonians want to call it the "Cooper River," pronouncing the *oo* as in "book," well, it's their river, isn't it? Let them call it what they like and go on, by analogy, calling a chicken house a "coop" with the same shortened sound.

And nobody can deny that they have a very pretty way of saying such words as "church," "hurt," "pearl," or a soft pronunciation of short *e* as in "bed," "very," "America." You never hear a Charlestonian, however humble, say "Amurrica" or "vurry" or "bid."

Undeniably there are peculiarities in their way of choosing to pronounce some words. A good many of them say "ex*qui*site," but you could probably justify that if you traced it back sufficiently far. Their way of saying "dear," "fear," and "ear" has been traced back to Chaucer. "Buoy" is "boo-ey" instead of "boy"; a good deal of attention has been paid to the fact that top-grade Charlestonians pronounce the title, Mrs., "mistress."

They call a pier a wharf and a stone a rock and a spot a place. In fact, they rather abuse the word "place." It crops up in every description of Charleston— "the spirit of the place," "one of the characteristics of the place," until it becomes almost unbearable. You'd think they might use "locality" or "vicinity" once in a while for variety's sake, but they very rarely if ever do.

When it comes to "bough" and "house," I concur wholeheartedly with the

Charleston vocalization, which, instead of rhyming with the German *frau* and *haus* is midway between that sound and what might be indicated as "boo" and "hoose" but is neither. And if the folk of the Low Country make a long *o* in "glory" and "story" and "store," that sounds better than "glawry" and "stawry" and the like.

Naturally the people of the old city never say "you all" in the singular. If a native asks, "How are you all"? he delicately accents the "all," and he is asking about your family; he would not be so impolite as to ask just about yourself.

Some say "under the doctor," which is just old-fashioned, and "sick" for "ill," and they call white potatoes "Irish potatoes" and grits "hominy" and lunch "dinner" and dinner "supper."

Their speech, in general, is rich in racial idiom, and this gives it a liveliness it might not otherwise possess, for it is rather homespun in its choice of words. "Down in the mouth," "don't care a continental," "red cent" (some of the old-timers referred to "a copper"), "poor mouth" (probably Negro) are just a few of the elements in a firm decisive way of looking at things and speaking one's mind. . . .

YIDDISH PROVERBS IN ST. LOUIS [21]

It is interesting to know what the Russian Jewish immigrant thinks of this country. Many times he is disappointed in the land of his dreams, especially at first, when he has to live and work in unpleasant surroundings, and when he earns little money for the comforts of life. The most common expression of his disillusionment is, "Woe to Columbus!" The saying that he has heard in Russia about America is, "America is a golden land." He repeats this after he has been here a little time, but he says it with a shrug of the shoulder and a contemptuous purse of the lips. An expression that may surprise the descendants of the May-flower Pilgrims is, "There is no family pride in America."

America is a goldene medina.
America is a golden country.

Eich mir a medina!
Not much of a country!

A klog zu Columbus'n.
Woe to Columbus!

Es is dein America!
It is your America! [said to a person who is successful].

Er lebt zach op in America!
He's having a jolly time in America [said of one who is prosperous].

In America is nitto kein yichess.
There is no family pride in America.

[21] "Yiddish Proverbs, Sayings, etc., in St. Louis, Mo.," by Leah Rachel Yoffie, *The Journal of American Folk-Lore,* Vol. 33 (April-June 1920), No. 128, pp. 164-165. Lancaster, Pennsylvania, and New York: American Folk-Lore Society.

In der heim is er geven a schuster,
In der heim is er geven a schneider,
In der heim is er geven a ganef.
At home [in Russia] he was a shoemaker, tailor, thief [implying that here he has become a person of importance].

Er arbet far der city.
He works for the city [said of a person unemployed . . . walking the streets, looking for work, and counting the bricks in the sidewalk for the city. It may be a local St. Louis expression.]

"IT MAKES ME NO DIFFERENCE" [22]

Without disrespect to either Cincinnati or St. Louis, it may be asserted that Milwaukee's speech has been colored more by the German influence than any other city's in America. Native Milwaukeeans, even after being exposed to the cultural refinements of Eastern schools, often cling to phrases and inflections that give them away on the instant. It may be nothing short of a calamity at Vassar or Princeton, but it is still amusing at home.

The German *"ja"* for "yes" is a habit quickly and all but incurably acquired. *"Ach!"* makes an exclamation far more serviceable than "Oh." *"Aina?"* is deemed less clumsy than "Isn't it so?" It is not true that the thicker phrases of German origin are employed by more than a small fraction of the population, but a stranger making a tour of the town is certain to be startled and perplexed by certain remarks. For example:

"He inquired *after* you."

"The *schnapps* is *all*, but the beer is *yet*," meaning that whisky has disappeared but that still, *Gott sei dank*, there is enough beer.

"Where can I *become* a glass of May wine?" does not seek a miracle, merely a well-stocked tavern.

"*By* Vliet Street, where the car *bends*," means, "on Vliet Street where the streetcar turns."

"*Bring* it in the paper," meaning to print it there.

"Do you want some *butter bread?*"—otherwise, bread and butter.

"Button up your *neck*," sage advice in a Milwaukee winter, counsels keeping the collar buttoned and the neck warm.

"Did you see all the bargains *ever?*"

"I *first* got up at eight this morning *already.*"

"I had to laugh *from* her."

"I got a *invite* to the wedding."

"It *makes me* no difference."

"*Make* my apron shut," which means to tie it.

"Come *once*, just look at this *once*."

The untranslatable word, *gemütlichkeit*, which roughly means good will and good living, is generously employed in Milwaukee, more often than sometimes

[22] From "Milwaukee: Old Lady Thrift," by Richard S. Davis, in *Our Fair City*, edited by Robert S. Allen, pp. 201-202. Copyright, 1947, by Vanguard Press. New York.

seems warranted. Politicos, also, are very fond of the phrase, "He won't get schneider," a term borrowed from the favorite card games, skat and *schafskopf* (sheep's head), which are played in the old taverns. Not to "get schneider" means to make a poor showing.

JOKE TOWN: U.S.A.

The joke town belongs to the folklore of popular reproaches and local witticisms. Local cracks and slams[23] are part of the "geography of culture" and the universal tendency of the people of one village, country, region, or nation to distrust and dislike their neighbors. Some joke towns are expressive of local rivalry (the product of actual economic and political competition, trade wars and sectional feuds); others are laughed at for no particular reason except that they have come to be regarded as funny.

Certain states have similarly become butts of ridicule. Arkansas is perhaps the most sinned against in this respect. But there are also Iowa and Missouri. "Why is it that when I mention the name of my home state [Iowa] to an insular and sometimes insolent Easterner, I draw a laugh nine times out of ten? 'The state where the tall corn grows.' . . ."[24] "I'm a Missourian. Now, darn you, don't laugh."[25]

As a maligned spot, the joke town is to be distinguished from its close relative, the fool town, whose inhabitants are regarded as the proverbial embodiment of stupidity. The Gothamite tale has become the type and symbol of the noodle story told about egregious fools ironically known as "wise men" or "sages."[26]

Although Washington Irving nicknamed New York "Gotham" to call attention to its follies, Brooklyn and not Manhattan eventually became the joke town of the five boroughs. New York, however, still remains a town about which New Yorkers themselves as well as people outside of New York continue to jest, often bitterly. Perhaps the most famous crack about New York is the one attributed to the out-of-town visitor, with its several variants: "I like to visit New York, but I wouldn't live there if you gave it to me." "It's a great place to visit, but I wouldn't live in it for anything." This bromide sums up the attack on New York for being "too big" ("New York has too much of everything"), too "European" or "alien" ("New York is not America"), and "too everything," especially too "smug," "provincial," and "arrogant" ("After you leave New York," says the typical New Yorker, "every town is a Bridgeport").

The typical joke town, however, is not a big town but a small town, a hick town. The two traits most commonly associated with the hick town—rusticity and remoteness—are reflected in fictitious joke-town names—Goose Hill,

[23] See *A Treasury of American Folklore* (1944), pp. 317-323; also *Standard Dictionary of Folklore, Mythology, and Legend* (1949), I, pp. 258-259, where I have treated other phases of the subject.—B.A.B.
[24] Harriet Lahr, *American Notes and Queries* (1944), Vol. 4, p. 4.
[25] Ethelbert Talbot, *My People of the Plains* (1906), p. 160.
[26] Cf. W. A. Clouston, *The Book of Noodles* (1888), p. 17 ff., for a list of fool towns in ancient and medieval times. Perhaps the most famous, next to Gotham, are Chelm and Schildburg. In *New York: The World's Capital* (1948), Cleveland Rodgers and Rebecca B. Rankin indicate some of the Abderian "absurdities" of the city (pp. 344-345).

Skunk Center, Rabbit Ridge, Gobbler's Knob, Hog Heaven, Hog Eye, Cottonwood Crossing, Hayseed Center, Sagebrush Center, where the derogatory allusions to flora and fauna are obvious.[27] Similar uncomplimentary or grotesque names, suggestive of uncouthness and backwardness, were actually applied to backwoods settlements in the Appalachians (Dry Tripe and Jerk 'em Tight, in Virginia; Shabby Room and Stretch Yer Neck, in West Virginia; Frog Level and Shake a Rag, in North Carolina; No Time and No Business Knob, in eastern Tennessee; and Dug Down and Turkey Trot, in Georgia[28]) and to California mining camps (Jackass Gulch, Gouge Eye, Wild Cat Bar, Wild Goose Flat, Hen-Roots Camp, Lousy Ravine, Poverty Hill, Hog's Diggings, Ragtown[29]).

Many actual towns with odd-sounding names ("as though they were grotesque creations of fancy") owe much of their reputation as joke and hick towns to the "humorous connotation of certain Indian names" in which the letter k is prominent—Hohokus, Hoboken, Kalamazoo, Keokuk, Oshkosh, Skaneateles, Podunk.[30] Other k towns—Kokomo, Kankakee, along with Kalamazoo and Keokuk —are fabled and defamed in folk and popular rhymes and sayings:

> Joe, Joe, broke his toe
> On his way to Kokomo.[31]
>
> Joe Blow from Kankakee.[32]
>
> In Kokomo they laugh in glee
> About the name of Kankakee,
> And Kankakeeites pass the buck
> By poking fun at Keokuk.[33]
>
> O Kalamozozle—mazizzle—
>   Mazazzle, mazeezle-mazoo!
> The liquid, harmonious, easy euphonious
>   Name known as Kalamazoo.[34]
>
> I've got a gal in Kalamazoo,
> She eats ice cream and it runs right through.[35]
>
> 'Way down yander in Kalamzine
> Bullfrog sewed on a sewing machine;
> He sewed so hard and he sewed so fast,
> He sewed nine stitches in his a——.

[27] See H. L. Mencken, *The American Language* (1936), pp. 553-554.

[28] Horace Kephart, *Our Southern Highlanders* (1913), p. 302.

[29] *Put's Golden Songster* (1858), pp. 63-64.

[30] George Philip Krapp, *The English Language in America* (1925), I, p. 176. Mencken (*The American Language*, p. 553) calls attention to the letter k. For the humorous appeal of k in advertising, where it is commonly substituted for c in trade names and slogans, see Louise Pound, "The Kraze for 'K,'" in *Selected Writings of Louise Pound* (1949), pp. 321-323. For Podunk, see her article, "The Locus of Podunk," *American Speech*, Vol. IX (February 1934), p. 80.

[31] Children's rhyme.

[32] As told to me by Professor Bayard Still of New York University, who heard it among students at the University of Wisconsin.

[33] Evan Esar, *The Humor of Humor* (1952), p. 99.

[34] H. L. Mencken (*The American Language*, p. 553 n) gives this as the refrain of a newspaper poem popular about 1890 and credited to the Denver *News*.

[35] Reported by George Milburn from Oklahoma.

I've got a gal in Kalamazoo,
She don't wear no—yes, she do.
I've got a girl on the under square,
She don't wear no underwear.[36]

The joke town is commonly the neighbor of a Big Town, for which it serves as a convenient scapegoat and foil. Thus New York has its Hoboken, San Francisco has its Oakland, Los Angeles its Pasadena. "Yesterday's comedians would always get a big yak at the old Orpheum by asking the audience suddenly: 'Say, which'd ya rather be—a fried egg, or live in Oakland?' . . . Your reaction to Oakland should always be friendly but tinged with deliberate humor like 'After all, the Bay Bridge had to end somewhere.' . . ."[37] "Pasadena—that's a town where you can't mix an alka-seltzer after eight-thirty in the evening, and if you want to burp you have to go to Glendale."[38]

More often than not, the maligned town bears no resemblance to the legendary reputation pinned on it by the jokesters and the hoaxsters—a reputation that may, in fact, be the very opposite of the truth. Thus James Gray comes to the defense of Peoria, showing that the joke is not on the town but on its detractors: "Its very name has been used to suggest all that is parochial in American society. Nothing could more clearly betray the parochial attitude in the mind of the satirist. For Peoria's history is peculiarly free from the usual evidence in small-city life of prejudice, bigotry, and narrowness." In fact, Peoria was the home of the great agnostic and orator, Colonel Bob Ingersoll, who established a law firm there at the age of twenty-seven, and "prospered greatly and was loved for his generosity and goodwill," though his name became a "synonym, for some, of blasphemy and corruption."[39]

Not the least of these ironies of joke towns is the fact that the town may eventually live down its reputation, as, for example, when it is absorbed by the neighboring Big Town (as Watt was by Los Angeles and Highlandtown by Baltimore) or when, as happened to Hoboken during Prohibition, it "won its way to metropolitan envy and respect."[40]

NEW YORKESE [41]

Most New Yorkers speak English, but an understanding of the following expressions, while not essential to a pleasant visit to New York, will equip the visitor to deal with most of the ordinary situations encountered in the city. Ignorance of them may result in giving unnecessary offense, becoming involved with gendarmes, or even starving to death.

Fithavnya. An important thoroughfare running from Washington Square to 142nd Street in Manhattan.

[36] Reported by Josiah H. Combs from Knott County, Kentucky.
[37] Herb Caen, *Baghdad: 1951* (1950), p. 31, and *Baghdad-by-the-Bay* (1949), p. 146.
[38] Bob Hope, on his CBS radio program.
[39] *The Illinois* (1940), pp. 287, 289.
[40] H. L. Mencken, *The American Language*, p. 553.
[41] From *Almanac for New Yorkers 1937*, Compiled by Workers of the Federal Writers' Project of the Works Progress Administration in New York City, p. 122. Copyright, 1936, by Simon and Schuster, Inc. New York.

Freshegginit? Wistful inquiry made by soda counterman when a milkshake is ordered. The expected answer is "No."

Gimmyaringforwensdy. "Call me by telephone before next Wednesday."

Giverair! Mass chant shouted over a woman who has fainted.

Howzigohinbud? "Good day, friend. Are your affairs progressing favorably?"

Jeezisshot! Midsummer observation. Example of the slurred aspirate.

Juhearutased? Traditional second question policemen ask loiterers. Actions, not words, are indicated. See *Whyntchagoferawawk?*

Keepyurnozeouttathgutta. Advising temperance; "remember not to get too intoxicated."

Lawn Gyland. An insular appendix of New York State surrounding Amityville.

Lemawf! Lemawf! Subway guard's plea to allow passengers to leave the train.

Lezgehgohinbabe. "I suggest that we leave, Gwendolyn."

Maymineasame. Commonly spoken over a polished mahogany bar.

Phewkinfixzitlemmyknow. "In the event that you are able to make the desired arrangements, please inform me."

Sawlawf. "The suggested arrangement is not satisfactory" or "It is finished, over, done, ended."

Seeinya. Farewell, usually spoken in chorus; vaguely implies future meetings.

Sheeaingottafren, itzasista. What it costs a sailor two nickels to learn in a telephone booth.

Slovlyonyamodom. Salesgirl's inevitable reaction to any gown on any customer.

Smatterthya? Expression of solicitude for the state of another's health, or implying misgivings concerning his mental capacity.

Smosamonryethlessenogrease. Drugstore counterman's verification of an order for a smoked salmon sandwich on rye bread with lettuce, but without butter or mayonnaise.

Taykadeezy, Taykadeezy. Redundant expression intended to calm the emotions.

Thisunsonnahouse. Obsolete bar expression; now heard only when an old-time bartender forgets himself.

Washastep! Subway guard's version of "Take care in alighting from the train, ladies and gentlemen."

Whyntchagoferawawk? Traditional first question policemen ask loiterers. No answer is required.

Yessirollaypape! Newspaper vendor's cry; means nothing, intended to draw the customer near enough to be asked—

Yessirwaddyaread? "Which paper do you wish to purchase?"

"PEANUTS! THE PICKLE DEALERS" [42]

Are you a *muscler?* a *steam-pipe?* a *B. B.* or a *Sprinkler?* Do schoolboys at their play speak of you as a *Hawkeye,* a *Hercules,* or a *Chucker?* Do they refer to you as *Buttercup* or as a *Big Noise* or a *crabturtle?* Do they say

[42] From "Peanuts! The Pickle Dealers," by Julius G. Rothenberg, *American Speech,* Vol. 16 (October 1941), No. 3, pp. 187-191.

Moose in speaking of your daughter; or *fagocite, broadcaster,* or *ham on rye* of your son?

Ten years ago, in my professional contacts with adolescent boys of New York City, I first became attracted to the subject of their jargon while at play. Since that time, aided by my high-school students from four of the five boroughs, I have gathered specimens of this lingo. The specimens, many already dated and forgotten, are defined in the glossary that follows.

Vehicular Nuisances

Flash. A very slow-moving vehicle, especially when it interrupts a game: "Look out, boys! Flash's breeze'll knock you down."

Put a nickel in it! Get a horse! Yelled in contempt at the driver of a *flash.*

Big Noise. A person who honks his horn excessively.

Muscler. A person who interrupts the game, especially by stopping or parking or unnecessarily maneuvering on the field of play.

Butcher Wagon. Ambulance.

Child-Pests

Stoolie. A child who informs, one who tells the police just which boys were playing.

Moose. A sister, notably a kid-sister, who informs her mother when her brother is playing stick-ball, shooting dice, etc.

Women-Pests

Sour Face, Crab-Turtle. A grouchy woman who complains whenever boys play.

Squawker. A crab-turtle, especially one who phones the police.

Screwy. A crab-turtle, known for what the boys regard as erratic behavior.

Streamlined. A *crab-turtle* distinguished by excess poundage.

Mop-chaser. A *crab-turtle* who charges at the boys with a mop.

Steam-pipe. A *crab-turtle* with the voice of a calliope.

Sprinkler. A woman who tries to discourage youth at play by pouring water on them from above.

Ma's Waterflow. A *sprinkler,* or the water itself; often used in a warning context: "Look out! Here comes Ma's Waterflow!"

The Pot. Used exactly as *Ma's Waterflow,* though usually with the "sprinkler" herself less in mind than the impending deluge.

Cleanser. A ball that just barely touches a person; often used to mean that it has hit a pedestrian but hardly hurt him.

Men-Pests

Big Noise. A blustering man who yells and threatens when he catches boys playing in front of his house or store.

The Gorilla. A man who uses his physical superiority and beats or chases boys to break up a game.

Chicken-runner. A man who runs peculiarly while chasing the boys.

Janitors

Old Man Millionaire, Handlebars, My Friend. Nicknames applied to specific janitors.

Old Eagle-Eye. A janitor who throws coal at the boys with deadly accuracy.

Whiz. A janitor noted for his speed in pursuit.

Hawkeye. A janitor who uses a B-B gun on the boys.

Hotcakes. A certain colored superintendent who charges five cents for each ball retrieved.

Here's Elmer. Here comes Si. Cant warnings of the approach of the superintendent.

Chickee! Schnitzel! Cant warning of the approach of the janitor's dog.

Park and Playground Employees

Buttercup. The artificially sweet, gushing woman-librarian at the community center.

Park Commissioner, Pennywhistle. A park department employee or watchman who blows his whistle and chases the boys.

Parky, Johnny Greenleaf. A park attendant.

Police

Hercules, Slappy, Machine-gun Butch. A cop who gratuitously beats up the boys.

Ruby-lips. Nickname disparagingly applied to a specific policeman.

Sneaky Aloysius. A specific policeman who "gumshoes" to catch the boys at play.

B. B. (probably from "Brass Buttons," as in the jingle). A policeman.

Tin Badge, Flatty, Snake, Black and Blue, My Hero, Fagin. A policeman, used disparagingly.

C. O. D. Cop on duty.

Chucker. A policeman who destroys and throws away the boys' playing equipment.

Joe Fiddlesticks. A policeman who invariably breaks the stick-ball stick.

Ace-flat Copper. A decent, fair-minded, considerate policeman.

Nest of Snakes. A squad of policemen; more than two.

Two Worms in a Green Apple. Two cops in an all-green police car.

Pickle Dealers (from P. D.). *Pair of Monkeys, Sardines in a Can.* Policemen on duty in a police car.

Park Ave. Roadster, Doll Carriage, Ghost Patrol. A police car.

La Guardia's Diaper Service. A police car, the white and green kind.

Pie Wagon, Milk Wagon, Black Maria, Paddy Wagon. A police patrol or lock-up wagon.

To string a person up (probably from the euphemism for hanging people). To beat him up.

To invite a person to the ball (said of a policeman). To give a person a summons.

Merry-go-round. A chase by the police.
Green Light Hotel. Police station.

Expressions Patterned after or Borrowed from the Underworld

Stoolie. A stool pigeon (see under "Child-Pests" for specific application).
Broadcaster, Grapevine. Boys, generally small boys, standing at strategic spots, like corners, to warn the players of the approach of police.
To lay pootz, To lay bootz. To keep watch; to be a grapevine; to *lay chickee.*
Mouthpiece. The boy who tries to talk for all the boys and appease the police when the boys are caught playing.
Lam (used imperatively). Run (to elude police).
Lam. To be or to take it on the *lam;* to flee or to be in hiding from the police.
Twister. A police raid; as *"Lam! A twister!"*
To swallow the cud. To take the rap; said of the boy or boys taking the blame for all.
To pull a blow harbor, To take a powder. To flee from the police; to go away.
To eat the apple. To hide the ball, which is proof that a game was on.
To ditch the pole. To hide the stick used in stick-ball; often used with the previous expression, for the *apple* and the *pole* constitute evidence when the police come.
Duck it! (imperative). Hide the incriminating stick or ball!
Pootso! Knocko! Bootz! Pootz! These four and the next two are warnings, corresponding to the obsolescent *Chickee!* and *Cheese it!*
33! Probably from the cant of the shoe-salesman.
Peanuts! Used exclusively by pre-adolescents.

Expressions of Skepticism, Boredom, Etc.

Move over, will yuh? I bat left-handed. This and the next five are addressed to the disbelieved speaker.
Get me a pillow. Also often addressed to the other listeners.
Stop slicing it. The *it* probably refers to *bologna,* or to an improbable statement.
I wish you were on the radio (so I could turn you off).
I got a weak heart. Often accompanied by holding the heart and letting the knees buckle.
Have a heart; I got a family.
Shoot him! Said to the other listeners.
Over the hill. Go away, "scram."
To give somebody a tin ear. To talk boringly.
Turn out the lights. Oh, liver! The joke is no good.

Expressions Applied to Effeminate, Sissified, or Unathletic Boys

Fagocite. A *fag,* or effeminate boy.
Three-letter Man—F-A-G. See above.
Tender Lily, Sugar Sweet. A mollycoddle.
Ham on Rye. A *ham,* a tyro at athletics.

MISCELLANEOUS EXPRESSIONS

Short Beer. A Coca-Cola.
Drip, Droop, Schloomp. A stupid, mopy person.
To feel like an apple. To feel embarrassed.
To rip someone in the horn. To hit somebody on the head.
Ripped up. Angry.

A study of the expressions presented in the glossary reveals a number of curious and significant facts. For one thing, adolescents are critical listeners; numerous expressions attest to their boredom and skepticism. In the second place, the principles of slang in general are exemplified, as is to be expected, in boys' slang. For instance, their expressions often lack wide currency, so that the boys who live in one district and who speak of a *tin badge* will not know the meaning of *snake,* a synonymous term used in another district. Moreover, while the adolescents use *Pootso!* the smaller fry say, *Peanuts!* Also, the expressions are often short-lived, so that the adolescents of today are unfamiliar with the cant of the youth of five years ago; thus, *I got a weak heart,* an expression current in one year, lost vogue and yielded to *I got a family,* an expression used in a subsequent year to convey the same meaning.

Another interesting fact is that in their search for the novel or striking phrase, boys resort to the same devices as their elders do. For example, there is the use of abbreviations; as, *B. B.* (probably from "Brass Buttons") for *policeman,* and *C. O. D.* for *Cop on Duty.* Or again, boys may take common abbreviations and wrongly expand them for humorous effect; as, *Pickle Dealers* for *P. D.* Another type of expanding is illustrated by converting *ham,* which to boys denotes a tyro at sports, to *ham on rye.*

Another aspect of boys' slang is their cant. Thus, *swallow the cud, eat the apple,* and *knocko* are all designed to prevent the "authorities" from divining the boys' meaning. For example, to be able to speak of *Buttercup* within the hearing of recreation center employees gives the term piquancy.

The ebullience and imagination of the boys are often manifested in the figurative locutions. Boys don't steal; euphemistically, they *stitch* what they need. A ball, if need arises, becomes an *apple.* Bullying policemen are colorfully nicknamed *Hercules, Machine-Gun Butch,* and the like. Boys' contempt and irreverence often come out in such expressions as *big noise* for a driver who honks excessively, *Park Commissioner* for an officious park watchman, *a nest of snakes* for a squad of policemen, and *doll carriage* or *La Guardia's Diaper Service* for police car. Perhaps the most cleverly ironical expressions of all are *Flash* or *Put a nickel in it,* both used when a vehicle goes at a snail's pace and thus delays the game, and the double-barreled *three-letter man.* Normally, of course, the latter term is applied to the versatile college athlete who has earned three major awards for excellence in sports. Here, however, the expression is applied to a highly effeminate, unathletic person, the three letters being f-a-g, as previously defined.

The glossary, then, throws significant light upon the attitude of adolescents toward the many restrictions on their play life. Adolescent boys refuse to admit that the city was not meant for children; their slang is a form of revolt. The gushing community-center librarian, the overbearing policeman or park employee, the bullying janitor, the cranky housewife, and the tale-bearing child —all become the targets of merciless slang.

AD AGENCY-ESE

I. Madison Avenue[48]

. . . On Madison Avenue, when tackling a problem, a man never says: "Well, we're getting somewhere." That's much too easy. You have to trick it up a little. Recently, an ad agency executive . . . ended a conference with the words: "Well, the oars are in the water and we're headed upstream." That may easily be my favorite sentence since another genius over there let fly with: "Let's up periscope and look around." The metaphors are all sprouting water-wings.

On Madison Avenue, ideas are inspected, sniffed at, mulled over and tormented more than anywhere else and naturally this has brought forth language of unique beauty. One ad man, sniffing away at a program idea, turned to his colleagues and remarked: "Let's drop this down the well and see how big a splash it makes."

Then there was the network executive who, when confronted with an idea which demanded some cogitation, declared: "Let me take a temperature reading on this and I'll get it back to you." And another network executive, trying not to commit himself too deeply on one of his own ideas, qualified it with: "Mind you, I'm only giving a side-saddle opinion."

One crazy mixed-up ad agency man, nosing around a projected program, murmured: "Let's guinea pig that for size." Meaning, I guess, let's try it out on a small scale before getting stuck with it on a large one. As I say, I guess that's what it means. Sometimes this stuff comes in badly translated.

Then there was the case of one ad agency man trying to talk down the ideas of another one. Snarled the second one to the first one: "Don't low bridge me."

* * * * *

There is generally, in some of the later Madison Ave. patter, a note of pessimism, if not downright cynicism in their gropings with the spoken word. Take this one, for example, which is a very real example of Madison Ave.: "Let's roll some rocks and see what crawls out." Obviously the boys are not expecting much. In the old days, they used to "mother hen" an idea, or they'd say "let's incubate this and see what hatches," and this, with its intimations of maternity, was kind of sweet and touching. Now, they're rolling rocks and you know what crawls out from under those.

Of course, candor is something to be avoided at all costs in the advertising

[48] From "Radio and Television: A Stroll on Madison Avenue" and "The Ad Agency Language," by John Crosby, New York *Herald Tribune*, March 1, 1954, p. 15; April 3, 1954, p. 21.

dodge, which brought forth this remark from one of the boys, seeking guidance: "How shall we handle this. Do you want to keep anything back or do you want to make it an open-door policy?" I don't know what the decision was here, but I rather imagine that the "open-door policy" didn't make it. I have here one other example of Madison Ave. prose. I haven't any idea what it means: "I don't think we'll baby that agency any more. We'll just force-feed them." As I say, I don't know what it means but I like the idea of an agency being force-fed. It's high time.

II. HOLLYWOOD AND CHICAGO[44]

In my researches on the curiously inventive (and, in some cases, remarkably expressive) language of the advertising industry, I have confined myself pretty well to Madison Ave. But, of course, Madison Ave. isn't the whole story. You can find ad men all over the place—Chicago, Milwaukee and, naturally, Hollywood—and, while the general tenor of metaphor is the same, there are certain regional differences which I'm sure you students of language will find interesting.

In Hollywood, for instance, you will encounter the expression: "We were blown out of the tub," which means simply that the agency has lost a client or an account. When you want a junior account executive to handle detail work, you tell the personnel department: "Get a boy to carry the grips." There is a slightly larcenous practice out there (and elsewhere) concealing added charges in production fees which increases the agency take above the ordinary 15 per cent. This is known as "honking a live one." (The "live one" is a client with a fat wallet.) And when a guy fails to make a sale or land a new account, he is said to have "burnt off."

Out in Chicago they have an expression: "Keep your pores open on this one," which means don't do anything hasty. (And that, of course, is the general direction of almost all ad agency talk. The idea is for heaven's sake, be careful. Don't go rushing into anything.) And when you have finally decided the idea is definitely lousy, you "pull the chain on that one."

*   *   *   *   *

From one of my spies in Chicago comes word that ad agency-ese is developing what he calls the triple-redundancy. This is the technique of saying the same thing over and over to make it sound more impressive. He swears he heard an account executive tell a client: "We'll send this letter to all physicians, doctors and M. D.s." The same man was overheard to get up at a meeting, thump the table and say: "We'll put our front foot forward."

WASHINGTON RED TAPE-ESE [45]

Confidential work: We're so ashamed of what we're doing that we don't want any one to know about it.

[44] From "Radio and Television, The Ad Agency Language," by John Crosby, ibid., April 3, 1954, p. 21.
[45] From "The Federal Diary," by Jerry Klutz, the Washington Post, May 28, June 2, 1943.

Expedite: Stop everything. Put my case through at once. To hell with the others.

File this: Lose, if possible. If any one calls, we never heard of the case.

For your approval: You sign this, too, so if the boss kicks you can share the blame.

Have you any remarks? Can you give me an idea of what this is all about?

I approach the subject with an open mind: Completely ignorant on the subject.

In due course: Never.

Prepare this for my signature: You do the work, I'll take the credit, but if anything goes wrong, you take the blame.

Rush job: You do something about this quickly. I haven't done a thing about it in three months and the boss is mad.

Submitted for information: This means nothing to us. It may to you.

This will be borne in mind: No further action will be taken till you remind me.

Washington thinking on this: According to what official is doing the thinking.

With reference to: Whether it has or has not reference, this letter must begin somehow.

HOLLYWOODESE

I [46]

. . . Hollywood uses "dear" and "darling" with a sanguine disregard of sex. The theatrical tradition has long encouraged the wholesale use of affectionate lingo—but "dear," "sweetheart," "darling," and "honey" are bandied about in Hollywood with a frequency which confirms the suspicion that jealousies are often cloaked in the phrases of flattery.

Hollywood talks and thinks in superlatives. Movie people do not "like" things; they are "mad about" them. They do not dislike things; they loathe or detest them. All phenomena, from filigree brooches to tidal earthquakes, can be marvelous, terrific, colossal, or stupendous—or, in reverse English, cute, cunning, or chic. In its language, as in its behavior, Hollywood reveals a strenuous effort to deny doubt, by self-induced elation. The excessive use of adjectives such as "terrific" or "sensational" sets a Gresham's Law to work as inexorably in vocabulary as it does in money—superlatives drive sobriety out of circulation. The revealing story is told of two movie producers meeting on the street; "How's your picture doing?" asked the first. "Excellent." "Only excellent? That's too bad!"

Hollywood has a vocabulary of its own, and the argot is rich and expressive. *Flesh peddlers* and *ten percenters* are agents; *juicers* are electricians and *grips* are property men. *Switcheroo* denotes a change (switch) in plot structure; *double take* refers to the facial expressions which accompany delayed comprehension (a pleased smile, a pause, a sudden look of consternation). The

[46] From *Hollywood: The Movie Colony, The Movie Makers,* by Leo C. Rosten, pp. 47-48. Copyright, 1941, by Harcourt, Brace and Company. New York.

vernacular of the trade journals is equally rich in abbreviation and ingenuity. B.O. means box-office; *biz* means business, and *pix* is shorthand for pictures. *Meggers* (from "megaphone") are directors. *Stinkeroo* refers to a flop and *smasheroo* to a hit. The classic headline, "Stix Nix Hix Pix," from *Variety* some years ago, announced, in its own way, that rural audiences were disinclined to patronize pictures of the unsophisticated genre.

II [47]

. . . The proper expressions to use to an actor or producer just after you've seen his picture (we'll assume that it's a real stinker) . . . are: "This picture needs special handling" or: "The kids will love it." For soothing an actor who's just committed a horrible clinker: "You looked great in the rushes." For soothing a producer whose latest picture has got terrible notices: "Nobody likes it but the people."

One of the best ways to handle the situation at a preview is to rush up to the producer, grab his hand and ejaculate: "Bob, you've done it again!" This can mean anything. If you want to give it the real kiss of death, call it a "prestige-type" picture. Of course, it's just possible you might *like* the picture, in which case you say: "It's a great little picture." The use of the word "little" is very curious out here. Even "Quo Vadis" is referred to as a "great *little* picture." If you're talking about a bad picture among yourselves when no one involved is around, the proper expression is: "Don't miss it if you can."

Hollywood abounds in real weird characters and, naturally, expressions have sprung up to cope with these people. One line, guaranteed to wither the stoutest hide, is to turn to your companion and remark: "Get a stick and I'll help you kill it." Another one: "Follow him and see what he eats." . . .

Not all of these things are confined to Hollywood, of course. Some have seeped through to Broadway. One, which is common on both coasts, is the "nothing but" gambit. "He's got nothing but talent." "That picture will make nothing but money." Or: "He's got nothing but money." Money is on every one's lips and the proper line for a tight-fisted actor—hardly a new one but one you hear in Hollywood more often than anywhere else—"He's got the first dollar he ever earned."

Hollywood has always had a number of interesting words to call its women. Current at the moment to designate a doll who has passed through quite a few hands: "passion lips." For a girl, just any girl, the cats now say Mabel. Every girl is Mabel or a Mabel or, if plural, some Mabels.

One expression that has overflowed Hollywood but probably originated here and is still in wide usage: "Be my guest." This can be used almost anywhere. If you want to use a man's phone or sit down at his table at a nightclub or just hitch a lift in his car, it's "Be my guest"—usually with a faintly exasperated inflection. Every one has heard the brushoff line: "Don't call us. We'll call you." Out here, though, it's "Call you tomorrow." Tomorrow never comes.

Table hopping is practiced everywhere. But in Hollywood there's a practice

---

[47] From "Radio and Television," by John Crosby, New York *Herald Tribune*, October 29, 1952. Copyright, 1952, by New York Herald Tribune, Inc.

referred to as "people-hopping." A man who at a party or a bar jumps from person to person, always in quest of, never finding, the perfect companion, is a "people-hopper." Then there's a two-line play you hear quite a lot of. An agent, let us say, is trying to peddle a client to a producer. The dialogue goes like this:

AGENT: I think he's a great actor.
PRODUCER: When will you know definitely?

An expression for the star who has blossomed into the big time overnight: "Two years ago she couldn't get arrested." One catch phrase which you hear all over now but especially here is the girl or boy gambit. "Jane Doe, girl idiot," you say. Or "John Doe, boy slob." Frequently, these insults are meant as rough terms of endearment. Another expression which, through Martin and Lewis, has gone coast to coast is: "That's my boy!" or "That's my girl!" usually meaning that you'll go along all the way with him or her.

The two most overworked words in the Hollywood lexicon are "this" and "great." "This" prefaces almost every sentence. "This—I've got to see." Or "This has got to go." Or "This, I refuse to believe"—with the emphasis always on "this." As for the "great," the proper usage is the deprecatory "great" or "just great," a contradiction that disturbs nobody.

Then there's the situation when an actor tells you he's just been signed for another twelve pictures—or maybe for just one more. "Well, *bully* for you!"—with faintly mocking overtones. That'll cut him down to size.

THE TUXEDO [48]

. . . Located forty miles northwest of New York City in the rugged but picturesque Ramapo Hills overlooking Tuxedo Lake, Tuxedo [Park or, as it became more familiarly called, Tuxedo] was incorporated in 1886, originally as a hunting and fishing resort—in the words of its founder, a "short season place between New York and Newport." Gradually Tuxedo, which was between New York and Newport seasonally but not geographically, became not a resort at all; old-timer resorters deserted it because they found it too hot in the summer and too cold in the winter and, in between times, neither one thing nor the other. Nowadays, though still clubbable, it is nothing more or less than a year-round community outside of New York which, like the ancient resort of Nahant outside of Boston, still clings to its age-old reputation but which, in the final analysis, is really one more on the list of social ghost towns.

* * * * *

. . . It was at the first Autumn Ball in October, 1886, that young Griswold Lorillard, son of Pierre V, wore the tailless dress coat to which the resort gave its name. Today all Tuxedoites agree that, once having seen the coat, "every one wanted one like Grizzy's," but how the coat came to be worn in the first place, or even whether it was first worn at Tuxedo, can still start an

[48] From *The Last Resorts*, by Cleveland Amory, pp. 79, 89. Copyright, 1948, 1952, by Cleveland Amory; 1951, 1952, by the Curtis Publishing Company. New York: Harper & Brothers.

argument in any resort Society. Some resorters trace the origin of the coat to James Brown Potter's visit to the Prince of Wales, who wore a somewhat similar smoking jacket, some to the late E. Berry Wall, King of the Dudes, who was put off the dance floor of the Grand Union Hotel in Saratoga for wearing such a coat, and some to an anonymous leader of Irish Society who sported the coat at a dance at one of the Bowery's Chowder and Marching Clubs. Perhaps the simplest explanation is that given by Newport's young Louis Lorillard, great-great-grandson of Pierre V. "I've always heard," he says, "they just got tired of sitting around on their tails, so they cut them off." Two things are certain. One is that the coat which Griswold Lorillard wore was designed by his father and was a scarlet satin-lapelled affair which was tailored, if not tailed, along the lines of the pink coats worn by hunters riding to hounds. The other is that the coat was not an instant success. The Society journal *Town Topics* claimed that Griswold Lorillard looked "for all the world like a royal footman" and that he and his friends who wore the coats "ought to have been put in strait jackets long ago." Even today it is an ironical fact that in Society the word "tuxedo" is itself considered taboo, the use of "dinner jacket" in its stead being as mandatory as the Society patois which insists on "to-mah-to" for "to-may-to" and "my-onnaise" for "may-onnaise."

PHILADELPHIA LAWYER [49]

The saying, "sharp as a Philadelphia lawyer," dates from the trial, in August, 1735, of John Peter Zenger for libeling the British governor, William Cosby. Zenger's two attorneys, William Smith and James Alexander, leaders of the New York bar, had been arbitrarily disbarred on a technicality, and the defendant was unable to retain other counsel in New York. The aged Andrew Hamilton (then over 80) volunteered his services and came from Philadelphia at his own expense to defend Zenger. He won the case by his eloquence and audacity, supported by a rising popular sentiment against tyrants. After the trial the Friends of Liberty in New York gave Hamilton a public banquet and ovation. The fame of the exploit carried round the world the legend of the superiority of Schuylkill-bred legal talent.

MICKEY FINN [50]

The loathsome Mickey, in case you never heard of it, is an odorless, colorless, tasteless liquid that is dropped into a drink to "cure" an obstreperous drunk, gain cowardly revenge on an enemy, or make a particular point with an unreasonable columnist. Its effects are almost immediate, and so violent that they have caused countless fatalities. In the State of California, it is a felony to administer a Mickey. It is also a felony to commit murder, but people are

[49] By G.S.S. From *American Notes & Queries,* A Journal for the Curious, Vol. I (February 1942), No. 1, p. 175. New York.
[50] From *Don't Call It Frisco,* by Herb Caen, pp. 251-254. Copyright, 1953, by Herb Caen. Garden City, New York: Doubleday & Company, Inc.

still being murdered. And the Mickey is still being handed out by bartenders who would be surprised to learn that they are potential murderers. Or perhaps actual ones.

The archives contain remarkably little information on the history of the Mickey Finn, but historians generously concede it to be one of San Francisco's less notable contributions to the world of culture and gracious living. Besides, no other city has stepped forward to claim the honor. And so we are stuck with it.

Attorney Vincent J. Mullins, another serious student of the Mickey (but one without my first-hand experience), has unearthed the legend that the poison—for it is—was invented on the Barbary Coast, circa 1870, by a discredited Scotch chemist named Michael Finn. Finn, supposedly a fugitive from justice in Scotland, worked as a bartender on the Coast, and soon became known as a fine source of manpower for ship captains whose crews had deserted to the gold fields.

Under Mr. Finn's tender ministrations, sailors drinking in his bar became suddenly and surprisingly easy to handle, and could be Shanghaied aboard ship with no signs of protest. And, in most cases, very few signs of life.

And so Mickey Finn—"Miguelito" to the Mexican populace, "Mickola Finnola" to the wags, and just plain "Poison" to the toxicologists—became part of the San Francisco language.

If you are interested in recipes, there are several ways of concocting a Mickey. Sometimes it involves the use of Glauber's salts, a horse laxative. Sometimes it is made from chloral hydrate. But the true, historic Mickey is a preparation of antimony and potassium tartrate known as "tartar emetic."

Fortunately for the recipients of a Mickey, the poison has an unique reverse quality. That is, the greater the dose, the greater the chances for recovery—for the victim throws off the poison so fast that it has no time to get in its deadliest work. However, it does accomplish its purpose: sapping its victim of all physical and mental powers of resistance in a matter of minutes.

Toxicologists are convinced that hundreds of deaths attributed to other ailments have been caused by Mickeys. Given the proper dosage, a person with tuberculosis of the lungs, for example, would hemorrhage massively and probably die. A pregnant woman would abort spontaneously. And a person with a weak heart would suffer an immediate attack due to the violent pressures. A ruptured artery would not be unlikely, even in a person in good physical condition.

And yet the Mickey lives on, administered with impunity by bartenders and others who avoid murder only because they unwittingly give too large a dose.

Prosecution is next to impossible because of the difficulty of proof. And yet it is common knowledge in San Francisco that an Army officer was killed in a widely-known restaurant after getting a Mickey. Third-rate saloons, where B-girls and owners rob helpless drunks, slip the sucker a Mickey after his pockets have been emptied, and throw him into an alley to die a thousand deaths.

Bartenders have been known to play their own version of the fantastic game known as "Russian Roulette," involving several drinks—one of which contains a Mickey. The glasses, one to a player, are revolved several times on the bar, and then at a signal, each one grabs a glass and drinks. Good fun for all. Except one.

Despite the prevalence of the Mickey, there has been only one prosecution in the last thirty years for using the poison in San Francisco. The victims in this case were the members of an orchestra in a night club on Fisherman's Wharf. Apparently their music had been a source of no pleasure to the staff of the club, for on their closing night, the musicians were handed a large "Loving Cup" of brandy and all were invited to take a sip.

They became violently ill. The bandleader, who, as befitted his station, took the largest sip, was in bed for weeks. The aforementioned Vincent J. Mullins, then on the District Attorney's staff, prosecuted four members of the night club staff, and convicted all of them in what became celebrated in the headlines as "The Mickey Finn Case."

"NO TICKEE, NO WASHEE!" [51]

The emperor [Norton], having decided to pay his annual visit to the state Capital at Sacramento and discuss the problems of his empire with the worthy dignitaries under his rule, discovered his only clean shirt to be in Wan Leong's wash-house, on Kearny Street, a few doors from his rooming-house. Therefore, he betook himself to Leong's establishment, but unfortunately the great Emperor had lost the one and only laundry ticket which would identify his sole remaining shirt. But to such a dignitary a lost Chinese laundry ticket was an insignificant matter, but not to the Mongolian. When Emperor Norton strutted into the wash-house and demanded his clean shirt without having the required red ticket, Leong's English vocabulary consisted of the few words: "No sabbie, no tickee, no washee!" The emperor swore, fumed, fretted, and threatened the little Celestial without results other than "No sabbie. No tickee, no washee!" The emperor's proclamations and edicts, which heretofore had obtained his daily needs, were of no avail. Even a threat to have the stubborn washman deported had no effect. And in the mêlée that ensued, the enraged Chinaman hurled his saucepan smoothing iron at the august head of the great man, as he stamped his way out the door with threats to take the matter up with the Imperial Court of China.

It seems that the Chinaman's stubborn refusal to give the great emperor his shirt was not wholly because he had lost his laundry ticket, but hinged partially on a transaction of prior days when Norton was a most influential businessman in San Francisco. He had at one time tried with a grand effort to get a corner on the rice market, which staple [of rice] was a favorite article for speculation in those days. He purchased all that was in the city and all that he

[51] From *Pigtails and Gold Dust*, A Panorama of Chinese Life in Early California, by Alexander McLeod, pp. 121-122. Copyright, 1947, by the Caxton Printers, Ltd. Caldwell, Idaho.

could ascertain was in transit, paying high prices, with a view to controlling the market. Rice being the Celestial's favorite food, Leong had never forgotten the days he had to go hungry for the want of a few grains of high-priced rice, nor had he forgiven the great emperor. Unfortunately Norton had guessed wrong, as many others do today; the market went "flat" and he lost his fortune, and the mania that he was an emperor became manifest.

Whether this *Norton vs. Leong* affair was responsible for putting a curse upon the person who lost his Chinese laundry ticket, there seems to be no record; but from then onward until the rumble of the Troy steam laundry apparatus became louder and spelled the doom of a picturesque chapter in California's social history, forty-five thousand Chinese who were apprenticed at coast washboards remembered the slogan, "No tickee, no washee!"

"FINKS" AND "GOONS" [52]

[On the San Francisco water front] The small number of registered, or "Blue Book," longshoremen could not resist the mounting numbers of casual workmen—[Harry] Bridges among them—who drifted toward the ships moored there. Small knots of men gathered in front of the docks. Disgruntled, hungry, and troublesome, they began hooting and shouting at the "Blue Book" men who made up the "star gangs"—longshore gangs which always worked the best cargo holds and submitted to practically any employer demand in order to hold their jobs. Sometimes a "Blue Book" man who had a family to feed and would do anything rather than let his family go hungry would answer the hoots and derisive statements of bystanders with a heavy fist, a cargo hook, or a curse. Fights became common, and all along the 'front trouble began to develop between the employed and the idle, the "Blue Book" men and the casuals.

In the sailor's vocabulary the lowest possible kind of a prostitute has for many years been called a "fink." In 1923, when the sailors' strike was lost in San Pedro, Andrew Furuseth described the employers' new hiring hall as "Fink Hall," and thereafter the word began to be heard all up and down the Pacific Coast. To the growing mobs of idle workmen who hung around the waterfront during those first few months of the depression, members of the "Blue Book" union came to be known as "finks."

"A fink will prostitute himself in any way before the employer in order to get a few hours' work," was the way one man described them. "Nothing is lower than a fink—not even a whale's belly, and that's at the bottom of the sea!"

At about that time the nationally syndicated newspaper comic strip of Popeye the Sailor began to introduce a new type of character called a "goon." A goon was a long-armed, hairy creature with a pin-sized head who preyed upon sailors. Out on the Bird Islands, from which agricultural fertilizer companies gathered guano, lived a species of oversized, stupid birds of lazy, filthy habits, known to Pacific sailors as "goonie birds." The name "goon"

[52] From *San Francisco, Port of Gold,* by William Martin Camp, pp. 450-451. Copyright, 1947, by William Martin Camp. Garden City, New York: Doubleday & Company, Inc.

appeared particularly suitable for the racketeering, grafting gang bosses known all along the waterfront, and for a time they became known to longshoremen everywhere by that name. Later, however, when the strong-arm gangs which policed the ranks of the "Blue Book" union began to retaliate against mobs of idle casual workers on the docks, these squads of fink strong-arm men came to be known as "goon squads."

THE LIFE OF RILEY

I [53]

. . . [Some] speculate upon the possibility . . . that the phrase was engendered of the happy rural lyrics of James Whitcomb Riley. But there are those . . . who would like to believe that a popular song of the '90's begat the usage. The pertinent lines of this song, as we remember them, . . . are simply these:

> Is this Mister Riley they speak of so highly?
> Is this Mister Riley that keeps the hotel?
> God bless my soul, Riley! You're looking dom well!

II [54]

Touching upon the origin of the phrase, "the life of Riley," E. R. Budd, who used to be superintendent of the Ilwaco Railroad & Navigation Company, the line from Megler to Nahcotta, on the Washington side, wrote in the other day to propose an identification. Mr. Budd, who now is by way himself of living the life of Riley—he has retired from railroad supervision—vows that the editors of the *Butte Miner* will substantiate the suggested solution, which is this:

In 1897, a time which lately did not seem so very long ago, there was a man in Butte by the name of Riley. Of course there was. There were undoubtedly several of him, all with the bog brogue in their truculent, humorous larynges, every last Riley of them, and enough freckles on any one of them to answer for all. But this particular Riley, the Riley who was destined to tug at the heartstrings of a people, was a bookmaker at the Butte racetrack, among maybe two or three dozen of caterers to chance. This Riley, *the* Riley, had been giving better odds than any of his rivals. They put their heads together in a sure-fire plot and conspired with crooked race horse owners to break him.

Now this Riley was nowise downcast when he learned of it, as he did, and he continued to lay better odds, and to boast about it, declaring at every bet, "The horses will all run for Riley today, and when this race is over Riley will live at ease the rest of his life." And Riley knew what he was talking about, the spalpeen, for just before the last race was over he took all the money, most of which the conspirators had wagered, and called a hack,

[53] Editorial by Ben Hur Lampman, the Portland (Oregon) *Oregonian*, April 17, 1940.
[54] *Ibid.*, April 21, 1940.

and away to the depot—the daypo—and over into Utah. And then they couldn't do anything about it.

III [55]

In regards to the gentleman, Riley, and his world-envied life, he did win his pile at the Butte race track and the year was 1897. Only Riley wasn't a betting man except for one glorious occasion. He was a hard rock miner in Butte, listed on the payroll of the Anaconda mine as Patrick Jerome Riley.

Here is the story as told to me by my father, the late Mike Burke, who carried a dinner-pail up and down the Butte hill for fifty years and who worked partners with Riley at the famous Anaconda mine, and who enjoyed Riley's hospitality during the period of the latter's prosperity.

It was the pleasure of Marcus Daly, the noted copper tycoon of that period, to give his Butte miners a day off during the racing season that they might join him in the sport of kings.

It was on such a day that Riley, an ardent admirer of Daly, took his modest monthly paycheck to the mile track on the Butte flat. Riley, who, it was reported, did not know one end of a horse from the other, won all seven races and a roll of $30,000.

From that moment on, it was indeed the "life of Riley," as Riley had always wished to live it. His first official act after counting his winnings and thoroughly slacking his thirst at the racetrack bar, was to hire Barney Shannahan's hack, a famed and luxurious equipage of the day, on a 24-hour-daily basis at $5 per hour.

Riley then directed Barney to drive him to the Anaconda mine yard, where before the assembled night shift miners, he directed the night foreman in lusty and expressful if inelegant terms as to the proper disposal of his former job.

For thirty days each night saw Riley along with several of his favored cronies assembled and making wassail at the various roadhouses on Butte's famous "flat," always, of course, with Barney Shannahan, in faithful attendance at five bucks per hour.

For a glorious month Riley was the toast of the town and his exploits grew with each passing day.

At the end of the eventful month Riley was broke. That is with the exception of $1500 which the benevolent Lou Harpell had saved for him from the fortune. With this money Riley purchased a one-way ticket to Fairhaven, County Cork, Ireland, and is reported to have died there, undoubtedly never suspecting the much quoted expression his month of gay living had contributed to Americana.

Any old-time Butte miner can testify to the authenticity of the tale.

[55] Letter to the editor of the Portland (Oregon) *Oregonian* by William A. Burke, S.P.S. Railway, Vancouver, Washington, August 9, 1940.

XIV. Cracker Barrel

Urban stories like "The Man in the Middle" and "The White Satin Dress" are right out of the American cracker barrel. Contrary to the general belief, this rurally named institution of oral, native and vernacular storytelling, wit and humor is not restricted to the sticks but also has its place in the folklore of cities. The fact that these traveling and travelers' tales have been retold and rewritten by city slickers, including sophisticated raconteurs like Alexander Woollcott and Bennett Cerf, should not obscure their basis and vigorous life in oral tradition. They are the city relatives of yarns and tall tales that have been swapped for generations in country stores, in small-town barbershops, drugstores and saloons, and in smoke-filled hotel rooms and smoking cars across the country.

A favorite genre is the mystery, incredible but told as true, according to Alexander Woollcott's note on "The Vanishing Lady":

> For such a story to travel round the world by word of mouth, it is necessary that each teller of it must believe it true, and it is a common practice for the artless teller to seek to impart that belief to his listeners by affecting kinship, or at least a lifelong intimacy, with the protagonist of the adventure related. In my entertaining, desultory, and (with some exceptions) fruitless researches into the origin of twenty such world-girdling tales, I have often challenged one of these strawman authorities, only to have it vanish as utterly as did the ailing lady from the Place de la Concorde.

Many of these urban folk tales have an ancient lineage, like the story of the old couple who murdered their own son for his gold when they failed to recognize him on his return to what was to have been a happy and prosperous family reunion. Newspapermen like Robert J. Casey and Mark Hellinger have published variants of these "apparently indestructible anecdotes" that are constantly turning up in newspaper and magazine offices as "originals" and as having "happened" to, say, "Aunt Mabel's housekeeper." And veteran journalists are constantly being taken in by the "deceptive freshness" of what prove to be old chestnuts "in which nothing changes but the names of the characters." Meanwhile, the deathless stories continue to furnish entertainment to bored editors and copyreaders and copy for many a columnist, "especially if it is late and he has space to fill."

Their themes run the gamut from the gruesome to the hoaxing. On the morbid and sordid side is the one that Mark Hellinger tells as a "favorite around town whenever a new movie cathedral opens." It is also reminiscent of the mysteries of the great city that were first unveiled in the gaslight era.

In this one, the pretty little girlie is sitting next to the old lady. The girl suddenly becomes ill, and the dear old woman helps her up the aisle and into the street.

There are some who suggest a doctor, but the old woman will have none of it. She will see that the pretty child arrives home in perfect safety. So she summons a cab, places the now unconscious girl in the rear—and is driven away.

Invariably, in this type of fable the "old lady is a white slaver (remember them?); a man in woman's clothes and a wig. It was he who jabbed a hypodermic needle into the girl's arm as she sat next to him in the movie palace, and who has now dragged her off into a life that is worse than death, as the funny saying goes.

What happens to the beautiful young girl, I have never found out. The story always ends as do most stories. Right at the most interesting part. . . .

The strong element of hoax, victimizing both the reader and a character in the story, suggest a parallel with rural tall tales to prank tenderfeet. Fragments of older tall tales and "funny stories" are found in talking horse and other shaggy-dog stories, which belong to both contemporary and city folklore, being localized in individual cities and told by and about city folk. Just as certain dirty stories are switched from one person to another who happens to be in the public eye—Mae West, "Wally" Simpson, Eleanor Roosevelt—so the perennial humor of the wise and the foolish, absurd ignorance and mistakes, is constantly being brought up to date, with "Little Audrey" and "Little Moron" superseded by the "crazy" bopsters of the bop jokes.

A close relative of the shaggy-dog and "moron" genre is found in the boners and howlers attributed to Samuel Goldwyn, in imitation of true "Goldwynisms" or plain sayings with a new twist. Obvious "switches," invented by Hollywood wits, these apocryphal "Goldwynisms" have an equally obvious publicity value, of which the Goldwyn publicity office has not been unmindful or neglectful.

Similar mythical and hoaxing howlers have gone the rounds of the Emergency Relief Administration, the War Risk Insurance Bureau, the Veterans' Bureau and the Home Owners Loan Corporation, as "floating" paper literature (that is, circulated in typewritten form), with little more change than the substitution of one agency for another. These howlers capitalize on the illiteracy and ignorance of rural correspondents and so have an irresistible appeal for Washington bureaucrats and clerks in particular and for city folk in general.

The vogue of rural or quasi-rural humor in the cracker barrel and "cracker-box philosopher" tradition has seeped into radio and television in the repertoire of comedians like Herb Shriner and disc jockeys like John Henry Faulk, on whom the mantle of Will Rogers has fallen. In the Southern sector belongs the following fable reported from the North Carolina mountains by Jerry Klutz in his "Federal Diary" in the *Washington Post*, back in the days of World War II, when it used to be handed to officials who claimed that they couldn't find a replacement for one of their men for whom draft deferment was being sought:

Once there was a King and he hired a prophet to prophet him the weather. And one evening the King aimed to go fishing and the likeliest place was right close to his best girl's house, so the King notioned to wear his best clothes. So he asked his prophet was it liable to rain before sundown. And then the prophet says: "No, King, hit ain't a-comin' on, not even a sizzle-sazzle."

So the King he put on his best clothes and started toward the fishing place. And along came a farmer riding a jackass and the farmer he says: "King, if you ain't aimin' to get them clothes wetted, you'd best go back home, because hit's a-comin' on to rain a trash-mover and a gully-washer."

And the King says, "I hired a high-waged prophet to prophet me **my** weather, and he allows hit ain't a-comin' on, not even a sizzle-sazzle." So the King, he went ahead and it come on a trash-mover and a gully-washer, and the King's clothes were wetted, and his best girl, she seen him and laughed. And the King went back home and throwed out his prophet and he says: "Fetch me that there farmer," and they fetched him. And the King says: "Farmer, I throwed out my prophet, and I aim to hire you to prophet me my weather from this [day] onwards."

And the farmer says: "King, I ain't no prophet. All I done this evening was to look at my jackass, because if hit's a-comin' on to rain, his ears lop down, and the lower they lops, the harder hit's a-comin' on to rain, and this evenin' they was a-layin' and a-loppin'." So the King says: "Go home, farmer, and I'll hire me a jackass."

And that's how it started, and the jackasses have been holdin' all the high-waged gov'ment jobs ever since.

If stories like the Jackass Story served as a kind of escape literature as well as a fable for harried government officials, then the publicist and man-about-town heroes invented as gags by publicity and advertising men—the mythical Drew Berkowitz and Byron Keating, Henry Cullip and Sam Mitnik—may be described as a busman's holiday. In New York, wrote "Odd" McIntyre of the well-known gullibility of urban easy marks and suckers, "Reuben does not come to town; he lives there." Just as the city booster is the lineal descendant of the backwoods boaster, so the urban prankster is the heir of the village wag and practical joker from whom P. T. Barnum took his first lessons in hoaxing.

The fine art of ballyhoo has fathered many a zany stunt in the annals of press-agentry, like the announcement (recalled by Bruce Bliven, Jr., in "Ballyhoo Was No Lady") that the Statue of Liberty was to be given a bath with a popular brand of soap. Because "it was before the soap's brand name had become a household word . . . the omission of capitals in mentioning its trade name got it past the editors' blue pencils."

A brother-under-the-skin of the modern press agent was the traveling salesman of yesterday. In *The Country Store* Gerald Carson recalls the story of the D.A.R. celebration in Montpelier, Vermont, on the occasion of the unveiling of a plaque on the Pavilion Hotel to commemorate Lafayette's visit there. That morning a whisky salesman staying at the hotel looked the situation over and had an inspiration. In the afternoon, when the crowd had assembled and the band had finished playing, the orator of the day got up to speak. Winding up his spiel, he pointed to the flag that covered the plaque and cried: "When the American flag is lifted, you will see words to be read by generations unborn." Whereupon the flag was lifted, unveiling a large card with the words: "Wilson's Whisky—That's All."

BUBBLE BUSTER [1]

. . . [A] professional bubble buster [was] Brian G. Hughes, New York paper-box manufacturer and founder of that city's Dollar Savings Bank, who died in 1924 at the age of seventy-five years. Wealthy, Mr. Hughes enjoyed spending his money in no way better than by exposing inflated egos.

The owner of numerous pieces of property, he erected "Not for Sale" signs

[1] From *Hoaxes*, by Curtis D. MacDougall, pp. 281-282. Copyright, 1940, by The Macmillan Company. New York.

on all of them. Instead, he posed as a public benefactor by offering supposedly valuable gifts of real estate to official and semi-official bodies. On one occasion he appeared before the Board of Aldermen to announce he wished to donate a plot of ground in Brooklyn as a public park. After accepting the offer and extending gracious thanks, the board appointed a committee to inspect its acquisition. It turned out to be a two-by-eight-foot rectangle which Hughes had purchased for thirty-five dollars near Sixth Avenue and Sixty-third Street. Several historical societies accepted from Hughes a mansion which Lafayette was supposed to have occupied during the Revolutionary War, actually a dilapidated shack at 147th Street and Concord Avenue in the Bronx, tenanted by tramps.

Hughes is credited with having been the first to drop a package of imitation jewels in front of Tiffany's. He also distributed tickets to banquets and other functions which never were held. Once he caused a frantic search of the Metropolitan Museum of Art by leaving a set of burglar tools and some empty picture frames on its doorstep. Disguised ornately as the Prince of Amsdam, Cyprus and Aragon, he presented an old policeman's badge to the actress, Lavina Queen, who sat on an improvised throne in the old Waldorf-Astoria in the belief she was being made a Princess of the Order of St. Catherine of Mount Sinai.

All of Hughes' vans bore the mysterious letters, L.P.B.M.I.T.W., which stood for "Largest Paper Box Manufacturer in the World." Hughes delighted in hanging expensive umbrellas in public places and then watching their thieves, upon opening them, become showered with signs reading, "Stolen from Brian G. Hughes."

Best remembered of Hughes' pranks were those involving animals. For an entire year, through newspaper publicity, he kept alive interest in the South American Reetsa expedition which he said he had financed. Finally word came that one rare reetsa had been captured; quidnuncs lined North River to watch its arrival. Down the gangplank came an ordinary steer. Spell "reetsa" backwards.

Purchasing an alley cat for ten cents, Hughes belittled the ability of some of the world's leading cat judges by entering it in an important animal show as of the famous Dublin Brindle breed named Nicodemus by Broomstick out of Dustpan by Sweeper. Almost unbelievably, the carefully groomed feline won a first prize.

Hughes' only outstanding failure was his own fault because he spilled his secret before judges at the Madison Square Garden horse show had a chance officially to pass on the merits of Orphan Puldeca, Sire Metropolitan, dam Electricity, purchased by Hughes for eleven and a half dollars, from the Metropolitan Street Railway Company which was changing from horse to electric power. The animal could not be started until Miss Clara Hughes, its rider, jingled a little bell. Its name meant "Often Pulled a Car."

HUGH TROY [2]

For sheer originality in practical jokes, a zany named Hugh Troy takes the cake. Troy's career began innocently enough when he bought a bench identical with the ones that have adorned the paths in Central Park, New York, for generations, and sneaked it into the park when no cop was looking. When he attempted to carry it out with him, he was arrested for stealing city property, but confounded the cop and the police lieutenant by producing a bill of sale that proved the bench was actually his. Troy made the mistake of trying the same trick in Prospect Park the next night. The police were laying for him this time and gave him three days in the hoosegow for "disturbing the peace."

Troy next bought twenty-dollars' worth of fake jewelry at neighborhood five-and-tens and spent hours taking out the vari-colored bits of glass that passed for diamonds, rubies, and emeralds. He gathered all of them into a small valise, and sauntered up Fifth Avenue. Directly in front of the old Tiffany's he released the catch on the valise. A cascade of "precious stones" spilled out on the pavement, and it took police reserves a full half hour to quell the resultant stampede.

Troy's third exploit was to dress up a squad of accomplices as workmen and dig a two-foot-wide trench across Thirty-fourth Street. The police obligingly helped him hang red lanterns at the edge of the ditch, and diverted traffic for two days before they discovered the whole thing was a hoax. Oxford students duplicated this project with signal success at the busiest crossing in Regent Street, London, the following season.

Troy's farewell Manhattan appearance was made in the Wall Street district. He parked an ancient model-T jalopy in front of the Sub-Treasury Building and surreptitiously approached a score of idle taxi-cab drivers, one by one. To all of them he gave identical instructions: "When you see me start that old Ford over there, just follow me." The result was a strange procession, led by Troy, with twenty cursing cabdrivers trying to jockey their way into line directly behind him. A half mile up Broadway, just below City Hall, a traffic cop stepped into the picture and halted the parade. At this point, Troy deemed it wise from the standpoint of health to transfer his interesting activities to other climes, and I lost track of him. . . .

DREW BERKOWITZ [3]

Speaking of gullibility . . . Broadwayites are easier suckers than the hayseeds in my home town of Rockford, Ohio.

[2] From *Shake Well Before Using*, A New Collection of Impressions and Anecdotes, Mostly Humorous, by Bennett Cerf, pp. 62-63. Copyright 1948, by Bennett Cerf. New York: Simon and Schuster, Inc.

[3] From *Pikes Peek or Bust*, by Earl Wilson, pp. 242-243. Copyright, 1940, 1943, 1944, 1945, by the New York *Post*; 1945, 1946, by the New York Post Corp. Garden City, New York: Doubleday & Company, Inc.

Sitting around the Stork Club one night, George Frazier, the writer, and Al Horwits, the publicist, speculated about who would land the $50,000-a-year public relations job that had just been vacated at Twentieth Century-Fox.

"Personally," said Frazier, "I think Drew Berkowitz will snag it."

"Drew Berkowitz!" exclaimed Horwits. "Really?"

In low voices they discussed Drew Berkowitz's excellent qualifications and decided he was indeed the man who should get it. Of course they couldn't be sure that Twentieth Century-Fox would prefer Drew Berkowitz; still . . .

They told a few friends what they thought.

Everybody they talked to had an opinion about Berkowitz. "He's not a big enough man for the job," said one. . . . "Berkowitz?" said another. "I knew him in Hollywood. We lunched together a couple of times and he had me to his house. He's a pet of Daryl Zanuck's. He's a cinch to get it." . . . "Drew Berkowitz?" cried a third. "Used to call himself Andrew Berkowitz. Big fellow, played a lot of golf. Comes from St. Louis, my home town. In fact, we used to be pals."

In less than forty-eight hours everybody in the industry was agog. Drew Berkowitz *was* the man for it, or *wasn't!* He was one of the best-known men in his field. Some liked him, some didn't. Naturally the word reached the columnists, and one of them scooped the field by printing that Drew Berkowitz had the inside track. Berkowitz's old friends phoned the Sherry-Netherland, where he was said to be hiding out, to congratulate him. Berkowitz was paged in Toots Shor's and at 21. A rival movie company started steps to hire him before Twentieth Century-Fox could sign him up.

Drew Berkowitz was, however, a myth.

He was a mere name invented by the mischievous Frazier and Horwits that night when out of deviltry they concocted the tale that Drew Berkowitz would get the job.

To them the most interesting thing was that nobody on Broadway would admit not knowing Drew Berkowitz.

Everybody knew him; nearly everybody knew him intimately.

CINCINNATI'S THREE-MONTH WONDER [4]

[In September 1944] advertising trade papers carried stories that Byron Keating had opened an advertising agency. When he landed his first account—the Little Tot Food Products Co.—such trade papers as *Broadcasting* carried the news. Then *Advertising Age* bulletined that Byron Keating Co. ("Cincinnati's fastest growing agency") was planning a new campaign for Soyscuits, a soybean biscuit mix.

But Keating made his biggest splash in the report of his talk before the Cincinnati Businessmen's League. Said Keating: "Agencies are doomed unless they establish totalitarian principles . . . with clients. Businessmen should keep their fingers out of advertising. Many agencies are producing inferior

[4] From *Time*, Vol. 44 (December 25, 1944), No. 26, p. 80. Copyright, 1944, by Time, Inc.

advertising, against their better judgment, for fear of losing lucrative accounts and because account executives 'butter-up' the client."

From frustrated copywriters all over the country, this speech brought Keating high praise, along with requests for jobs. Commented *Advertising Age,* "It's things like this that reaffirm our occasionally wavering faith that it's fun to be in the advertising business." Worldly-wise *Variety* headlined the talk "Just Let 'em Pay the Tab—Keating."

[In November] advertising trade papers carried news of the death of "Byron Keating, 59, after a heart attack attributed to overwork." Actually, Byron Keating was killed by his own parents—the two Cincinnati copywriters from whose lively imaginations he had sprung to hoax the advertising world.

Keating's creators were small, witty James B. Hill and big, sandy-haired John L. Eckels, advertising-agency copywriters. They dreamed up Keating to win an argument that political bigwigs are built by publicity, that they could create a tycoon in their own business out of thin air. They spent $4 on letter-heads, sent publicity releases to newspapers and magazines, invented companies and clubs for Keating to address. When the American Newspaper Publishers Association and Dun and Bradstreet Inc. requested financial statements, Authors Hill and Eckels decided the hoax had gone far enough.

[In December] the remains of Byron Keating—piles of news clips—were decently interred in Keating's "office," the middle drawer of Hill's desk. Hill and Eckels have only one regret: "We had a corker planned. We were going to phony up a foundation-garment account for Byron Keating. We were going to have the phony company pick a Miss Uplift from clerks behind brassière counters."

WHEN WALL STREET CAME TO PONCA CITY [5]

Dan J. Moran was born to the oil business. His father was a field man for the Standard Oil Company. . . . In his school days and college days [he] supplemented theoretical and technical education by employing his summer vacations in practical work as telegrapher, gauger, pumper, connection foreman, rig helper, tool dresser and field clerk. As one of a family of nine children he learned the practical art of human relationships. When he was graduated from the Case School of Applied Science he was thoroughly equipped to apply science, labor and personality alike to his job. His advance to responsibilities of field engineering, refinery construction engineering and so forth was as swift as it was inevitable. Twenty years after his entry into the business he was president of the Marland Oil Company. With the Marland's absorption by Continental the following year he moved into similar responsibility in that vast corporation.

There is a story attached to that deal which throws an illuminating light upon the character and ability of Dan Moran. Mergers of many millions of dollars, of companies holding a million and a half acres of oil lands under lease

[5] From *Then Came Oil,* The Story of the Last Frontier, by C. B. Glasscock, pp. 283-287. Copyright, 1938, by C. B. Glasscock. Indianapolis and New York: The Bobbs-Merrill Company, Inc.

and producing oil from more than three thousand wells, are worth a story. This one has a human element which makes it a favorite tale of Claude V. Barrow, oil editor of the *Daily Oklahoman*. As Barrow told it to me the proposed merger was held up in New York by directors of the Continental Oil Company who questioned the value of assets of the Marland company. The House of Morgan, heavily interested in Conoco, was in favor of the merger, but the Conoco directorate was not unanimous. Some of the directors demanded to be shown. Dan Moran undertook to show them. He invited the whole group out to Ponca City to make a tour of the oil fields, oil wells, refineries, pipe lines and other properties of the Marland company. It promised to be an interesting junket for the New Yorkers. They accepted the invitation.

When they descended from the train at Ponca City, the baggagemaster had more work to do than he had ever encountered with the arrival of a single train before. Trunks, Gladstones, golf bags, cases of guns and fishing tackle, overnight bags and so forth made a small mountain on the station platform. Dan Moran looked them over. There must have been a twinkle behind his eyes if not in them.

"Gentlemen," he said, or words to this effect, "I am delighted to see you. I am delighted to recognize this evidence of your understanding and appreciation of the possibilities of life in the West. I am sorry to disappoint you for the moment, and will be happy to show you the best of golf courses, trout streams and shooting country at your leisure. But first we must have our business trip. The Marland company is operated on a strictly efficient business basis. Its assets cover a large area. I assume that you have accepted our invitation primarily to inspect those assets. Kindly designate the bags which you will need for a few overnight stops and the porters will load them in these cars."

And before the jovial representatives of Wall Street on a holiday rightly realized what was going on they found themselves, with a single bag apiece, headed out through the Marland wells, refineries, pipe lines and so forth around Ponca City, onward through the other fields of the state in which it had holdings, on into the Texas fields, on into New Mexico, on into Colorado, back into Kansas and back again into Oklahoma.

Days of bumping over dusty or muddy roads, climbing out of cars at a hundred stops a day to examine producing wells, refineries, tank farms or pipe lines, nights of discomfort in outlandish hotels or bunkhouses, hasty meals at tables with oil-smeared and sweat-soaked workmen at company boarding houses followed with impressive speed and monotony. Dan Moran was unrelenting. They had questioned the extent of the Marland assets. He would show them, to the last derrick on the last acre of leases in the entire mid-continent field.

Soiled and disheveled, stiff and sore, red-eyed and hollow-eyed with weariness in the unaccustomed physical strain of the days and discomfort of the nights, the weaklings began to plea for relief.

"Oh, no, gentlemen! You've only seen a fraction of the Marland assets. Tomorrow we have to do three hundred miles through the last of the Texas fields and on into New Mexico. We have to see two hundred and eighty-seven wells producing in that area. There are five big tank farms, three refineries, two hundred and eighty-five miles of pipe line, twenty-seven drilling rigs in operation, eight hundred and seventy-two employes, nineteen company boarding houses, three company hospitals, one hundred and eleven thousand barrels of crude with an average gravity of thirty-seven coming out of the ground every day, and company trucking fleets and supply fleets of one hundred and nineteen cars in operation, with seven garages manned by thirty-nine mechanics to keep the cars operating at maximum efficiency and minimum cost. You must go on. This is quite an organization. You ain't seen nothin' yet."

At least it sounded that way to the visiting directors. They quailed. Some agreed that they were convinced. Some sneaked out with their bags and boarded the first available train back to New York. They would do anything, vote for anything, to get away from the terrific demonstration of the Marland company's wealth, diversification and extent which was being staged by the indefatigable Dan Moran.

The junket was what might be termed a howling success. By the time the remains of the party was dismissed at Ponca City to reclaim golf bags, guns, fishing tackle, riding breeches, dinner jackets, etc., and totter stiffly to a Pullman car bound back to Wall Street the deal was as good as completed. That, according to Mr. Barrow's delighted telling of the story, was Dan Moran—both a product and a producer of the oil business. That was Ponca City energy, effectively applied.

THE GOVLINS [6]

Something new has been discovered in Government offices. It's the Govlins. These strange little creatures are at large in the offices of the Co-ordinator of Inter-American Affairs in the Commerce Department Building. Employees have been warned to be on the lookout for them in an office memo. But by the memo's description, the Govlins have moved in and taken over choice spots in about every Federal office. It says that Govlins aren't related to Gremlins as they (gremlins) are "figments of the imagination and as such are not recognized by Government agencies." The memo then gives all available information on the Govlins.

"Govlins," the memo says, "make their home in filing cabinets. They live on Scotch tape and paper clips, not to mention staples. In hot weather they wear pointed foolscap made of interoffice memos and playsuits cut out of the very finest blue sheets. They have their own idea on how material should be filed and are apt, for instance, to switch Brazilian projects to Argentine press reports. Or else, they'll fish out a dispatch and place it on an official's desk. When the official bawls out his secretary for not being able to produce the dispatch, she can point out that it is under his nose. This makes the official look silly.

"Their favorite sport is a game which consists of bouncing on typewriter

[6] From "The Federal Diary," by Jerry Klutz, The Washington *Post*, Washington, D.C., Saturday, June 12, 1943.

keys, a point being scored for every wrxnj k?p which is struck by the person using the typewriter. An intriguing variation of this game may be played on the National War Agencies switchboard, with points for wrong numbers, disconnections and conversations overheard by ears for which they were not intended. The highest score obtainable is made when a Govlin manages to interject, 'That's what you think, you jackass' into a parley between two important officials, leaving each one under the impression that the offensive words were uttered by the other.

"The head Govlin is known as the Discombobulator of Inter-office Affairs, with headquarters on the third floor. He is assisted by an assistant discombobulator, who, in turn, is assisted by a deputy assistant discombobulator to the assistant discombobulator. Their special function is to suggest screwy policies to the executives. Govlins hold civil service rank and are promoted according to their ingenuity in devising chicaneries to confuse the personnel."

The final bit of advice to employees is that "Govlins should be severely ignored."

E. R. A. HOWLERS [7]

My husband has worked about one shift two months ago and now he has left me, and I ain't had no pay since he has gone, nor before either.

Please send me my elopement as I have a four months old baby and he is my only support and I kneed all I get every day to buy food and keep in close.

I am a poor woman and all I have is gone.

Both sides of my parents is very poor and I can't expect anything from them as my mother has been in bed for one year with one doctor and she won't take another.

Do I get more than I am getting?

Please send me a letter and tell me if my husband has made application for a wife and child.

I have already wrote to the President and if I don't hear from you, I will write to Uncle Sam both of you.

This is my eight child, what are you going to do about it?

I cannot get sick pay, I got six children, can you tell why this is?

Mrs. Brown has no clothes for a year and has been visited regularly by the clergy.

I am glad to say that my husband who has been missing is now deceased.

Sir, I am forwarding my marriage certificate and two children, one of them is a mistake.

I am writing to say that my baby was born two years old. When do I get my money?

Please find out for certain if my husband is dead, as the man I am living with now can't eat or do anything until he knows for sure.

[7] Excerpts from letters received by ERA Farmers Rehabilitation Project. Communicated by Louise Jones DuBose, Columbia, South Carolina.

I am very annoyed to find that you have branded my oldest child as illiterate. It is a dirty shame and a lie, as I married his father a week before he was born.

You have changed my little girl to a boy, will this make any difference?

I have no children as yet as my husband is a bus driver and works day and nite.

In accordance with your instructions I have given birth to a boy that weighs 101 pounds, I hope this is satisfactory.

The lady came into my office and reported this: "I have had no relief since they cut my husband's project off."

I have two children and my husband cannot supply enough milk.

In accordance with your instructions I have given birth to twins in the enclosed envelope.

MIZNERISMS [8]

. . . Conversation was Wilson [Mizner's] hobby, profession, and neurosis. His fame as a wit has grown steadily since his death, at the age of fifty-seven, in 1933. Although he wrote practically nothing, he is probably more quoted than any other American of this century. His chance remarks have been organized into a literature by his disciples. . . . Scores of men have won recognition as sparkling conversationalists because they have made small private collections of Mizner's sayings.

*   *   *   *   *

As a wit, Mizner belonged to two distinct schools—the scientific and the O. Henry. His scientific method consisted of bringing a calm spirit of inquiry to bear on boiling emotion. When an excited man rushed up to him exclaiming, "Coolidge is dead," Mizner asked, "How do they know?" The O. Henry school was the school of fantastic exaggeration. During Mizner's formative years, smart conversation consisted mainly of tired hyperboles. A majority of the familiar quotations from Mizner are extravagant figures of speech. He described a thin man as "a trellis for varicose veins." He told a conceited motion-picture producer, "A demitasse cup would fit over your head like a sunbonnet." Regarding a long-nosed Hollywood magnate, he said, "He's the only man who can take a shower and smoke a cigar at the same time," and "I'd like to take him by the feet and plow a furrow with him." Telling of a Klondike pal who had frozen to death in the act of tying his shoelaces, he said, "We had to bury him in a drum." A strutting little fellow went through bankruptcy and then strutted more than ever. "Failure has gone to his head," said Mizner. Describing his own flight from a madman armed with a revolver, he said, "I got up enough lather to shave Kansas City."

A man with a flourishing head of hair once joined his table at the Brown

[8] From *The Legendary Mizners,* by Alva Johnston, pp. 64-68, 71-72. Copyright, 1953, by Evelyn Johnston; 1942, 1950, 1952, by the New Yorker Magazine, Inc. New York: Farrar, Straus and Young, Inc.

Derby restaurant in Hollywood, uttered several solemn platitudes and left. "Now I know," said Mizner, "that hair can grow on anything."

A famous stage beauty, who had risen by five marriages to wealth and a title, attempted to bandy insults with him. "You're nothing but a parlayed chambermaid," he said. "You've compromised so many gentlemen that you think you're a lady," he added.

Talking about Tom Sharkey, the great heavyweight prize-fighter, who kept a saloon with the old-fashioned swinging doors, Mizner said, "He was so dumb that he crawled under them for two years before he found out that they swung both ways."

He disapproved of San Francisco at the time when Hiram Johnson was sending grafters to jail in large numbers. "They learn to say 'Guilty' here before they can say 'Papa' and 'Mama,'" he said.

He was asked by Lew Lipton, stage and screen writer, if a certain actress wasn't a little "mannish." "Mannish!" he said. "Not at all. I understand it took her all winter to color a meerschaum pipe."

Many of Mizner's lines have passed into the language. Some, like "Life's a tough proposition, and the first hundred years are the hardest," are passing out again after long and hard service. His rules, "No opium-smoking in the elevators" and "Carry out your own dead," which he put into effect as manager of the Hotel Rand, in New York, in 1907, have become standard hotel practice. Among his philosophical maxims were "Be nice to people on your way up because you'll meet 'em on your way down," "Treat a whore like a lady and a lady like a whore," and "If you steal from one author, it's plagiarism; if you steal from many, it's research." H. L. Mencken, in his New Dictionary of Quotations, attributes to Mizner "I respect faith, but doubt is what gets you an education" and "A good listener is not only popular everywhere, but after a while he gets to know something." Mizner's comment on Hollywood, "It's a trip through a sewer in a glass-bottomed boat," was converted by Mayor Jimmy Walker into "A reformer is a guy who rides through a sewer in a glass-bottomed boat" and has since become a shop-worn jewel of stump oratory. Two of Mizner's thirty-year-old lines have recently had revivals in the movies. A magistrate asked him if he was trying to show contempt of court. "No, I'm trying to conceal it," muttered Mizner. A friend argued that a certain Broadway producer "must have a head" to be so successful. "They put better heads on umbrellas," said Mizner.

"I may vomit," the smash line in *The Man Who Came to Dinner,* is a Miznerism. Mizner was seated at his regular table at the Brown Derby in Hollywood, when a young stranger introduced himself as a novelist and said he had a big idea. The trouble with Hollywood, he said, was lack of literary conversation. He asked Mizner to join him in founding a club that would meet an evening or two a week for literary conversation. "Have I offended you?" asked the author, noticing the expression on Mizner's face. "Do you want me to leave?" "No, but you might move over a little," said Mizner, adding the statement that went so big on Broadway.

Among his miscellaneous lines are "You sparkle with larceny," "He'd steal a hot stove and come back for the smoke," "You're a mouse studying to be a rat,"

"Another pot of coffee, waiter, and bring it under your arm to keep it warm," "I've had better steaks than this for bad behavior," and "If you [a radio chatterer] don't get off the air, I'll stop breathing it."

Mizner usually avoided slang, although he had a few special words of his own, such as "croaker" for "physician," "heart trouble" for "cowardice," and "trap" for a "bank." He disliked puns, although a play on words was worth about $10,000 to him on one occasion. It made a jury laugh and saved him from a verdict for damages. After the Florida real-estate crash, a man had sued him to recover the purchase price of a barren plot, asserting that Mizner had falsely informed him that he could grow nuts on it. "Did you tell the plaintiff that he could grow nuts on the land?" Mizner was asked. "Oh, no," he replied. "I told him he could go nuts on it." He perpetrated a sort of physical pun once when playing poker with a man whose credit was not too good. The man threw his wallet on the table and said, "I raise five hundred dollars." Mizner pulled off a shoe and threw it on the table. "If we're betting leather, I call," he said.

GOLDWYNISMS

I [9]

[Samuel Goldwyn's] greatest fame . . . is based on Goldwyn sayings and Goldwyn jokes. Sam's words built much of Hollywood, but he mispronounces them and uses them in the wrong places. Nouns, verbs and adjectives are Goldwyn's tools; he is more celebrated for broken tools than for what he accomplished with them. He is unrivaled today, as an unconscious humorist, or wit, through no fault of his own. Sam does not wholly enjoy his pre-eminence, although at times he has deliberately promoted it. Henry Ford collected Ford jokes and printed them as advertising matter; on that precedent Goldwyn's publicity department formerly collected and invented Goldwyn gags and circulated them. The trend had already been so well established, however, that any dazzling flash of ignorance or any startling disarrangement of words would ultimately be attributed to Sam without any help from his press representatives. Today it takes an expert to pick the genuine Goldwyn lines from the spurious. More people are counterfeiting on Goldwyn than on Uncle Sam.

Some of the true Goldwyn lines are a credit to him. He can often put things more forcefully in his own medium of expression than they could possibly be said in the king's English. An ordinary man, on deciding to quit the Hays organization, might have turned to his fellow producers and said, "Gentlemen, I prefer to stand aloof," or "Gentlemen, I have decided to go my own way." Sam said, "Gentlemen, include me out." It would be impossible to make a more pointed remark than Goldwyn's, "A verbal contract isn't worth the paper it's written on." One day, after slicing five or six golf balls, he made a beautiful drive; he turned to the caddy and asked, "What did I do right?" The true Goldwyn line is seldom a boner or a howler. It is usually a plain statement with a

[9] From The Great Goldwyn, by Alva Johnston, pp. 15-17. Copyright, 1937, by Random House. New York.

slight twist; as, for example, his exclamation at the beach one lovely Sunday morning, "What a wonderful day to spend Sunday!"

Sam commands legitimate attention by thinking strange thoughts rather than uttering strange words. The absolute-monarch psychology causes him to feel that his problems are world problems. When he meditates, he thinks that everyone should, by some telepathic process, be listening in. He awakened an assistant at midnight once and started a telephone conversation by saying, "The woman must die in the end." "What woman?" the man asked. Goldwyn had been thinking out the plot of a picture; the employee was expected to know by thought transference all that had gone before. Sam was as annoyed as if the man had gone to sleep in a conference. He expects employees to have a sixth sense and to render supernatural service. Again and again, Sam starts conversations without telling the other man what the subject is.

One day he stopped every man he met on the Goldwyn lot, asking: "Do you think it is raining tonight?"

Several said, "No."

II [10]

Anybody who goes to a psychiatrist ought to have his head examined.

So this is a sundial and with it you can tell time by the sun! What won't they think of next?

This is positively the best pie I have ever tasted in my whole mouth.

So you think you can do it? I say to you in two words, it is IM-POSSIBLE!

When he asked a director to look over a movie script and then to express a frank opinion, the director replied: "I wouldn't dare—it's too caustic." Said Sam: "To hell with the cost—if you say it's a good movie, we'll make it anyhow!"

I never put on a pair of shoes unless I have worn them for five years.

Every time I don't agree with somebody, they say we have a disagreement.

III [11]

A cousin told him he had named his new baby William. "What did you do that for?" disapproved Goldwyn. "Every Tom, Dick, and Harry is named William."

He asked a newly signed actor where he hailed from. "Idaho," said the youngster. "Out here, young man," Goldwyn advised him, "we pronounce it Ohio."

[10] From "New York Close-Up," by Tex McCrary and Jinx Falkenburg, the New York *Herald Tribune*, January 29, 1950, Section 5, pp. 1, 4. Copyright, 1950, by the New York Herald Tribune, Inc.

[11] From *Try and Stop Me*, A Collection of Anecdotes and Stories, Mostly Humorous, by Bennett Cerf, p. 45. Copyright, 1944, by Bennett Cerf. New York: Simon and Schuster, Inc.

Some of the sayings are undoubtedly authentic; more of them are pure inventions by Hollywood wits like Howard Dietz and Jock Lawrence, who pinned remarks on Mr. Goldwyn that he probably hasn't heard to this day. Gradually he became a legend.—B.C., p. 43.

"DO THE STORY MY WAY" [12]

There is the [Hollywood] producer who walks around his office with his shoes off, and insists that in the movies every time a husband comes home he must kiss his wife on the forehead "or else the audience won't believe they're married."

There is the titan who declared that a melodrama "has to be full of airplanes." ("Before the airplane was invented, a melodrama had to be full of automobiles.")

There is the man who judged all stories by their resemblance to his ideal tale: "A story about two brothers in love with the same girl, or two sisters in love with the same boy."

There is the philosopher who insisted, "You can't do pictures about married people. Married people don't like them, and single people don't want their illusions broken."

There is the executive who spent $20,000 preparing to re-shoot an entire scene because one of the characters used the word "din": "The public won't understand the word 'din.' "

There is the producer who, when told that a set would cost $40,000, lamented: "Forty thousand here—forty thousand there. Say, it adds up!"

*   *   *   *   *

There is the producer who rejected a script "because Bing Crosby falls in love with the girl. In his last two pictures, the girl fell in love with Crosby! The public won't go for Bing falling in love with the girl."

There is the producer to whom a writer, in telling a story, used the word "frustrated." The producer requested an explanation, and the writer resorted to this analogy: "Take a bookkeeper, a little man earning twenty-five bucks a week. He dreams of getting a big, beautiful boat and sailing to the South Seas. But he can't fulfill his dreams—so he's frustrated." To which the producer cried: "I like that! Put a boat in the picture."

There is the producer who, at the climax of an argument about a story, called his writer to the window and said: "You see that big black car down there—the seven-passenger Lincoln with the chauffeur. That's mine. Which one's yours?" The writer pointed to a coupé. The producer said: "A Plymouth, huh? Okay, we'll do the story *my* way."

There is the producer who urged a writer to criticize a script "absolutely

---

[12] From *Hollywood: The Movie Colony, The Movie Makers*, by Leo C. Rosten, pp. 29, 240-241. Copyright, 1941, by Harcourt, Brace and Company. New York.

Hollywood still boasts an abundance of egomaniacs, buffoons, semi-literates, and persons of surpassing obnoxiousness. Its life is still syncopated. The inanities of movie production could still fill a hilarious volume. The malicious can select facts and anecdotes to lend verity to even the more outlandish yarns about Hollywood, and the visitor can quote producer-malapropisms. . . . And there are the other kind: men of great insight and occasional wit, men with an instinct for what is dramatically true, men with an urgency to put their visions on the screen.—L.C.R., pp. 28-29.

frankly; don't pull your punches. I want the truth!" When the writer began to comment, the producer cried: "Why, that's just your personal opinion!"

There is the producer who for years has refused to allow any of the characters in his films to speak German: "If they really *are* Germans, have them speak French."

There is the producer who—when the writer said, "The hero is walking down a dark alley; he has a terrible sense of disaster; he's frightened!"—declared that the audience wouldn't understand the hero's fright because "anything I don't see I'm not afraid of."

There is the producer who kept remarking that a director was stubborn. The director objected, "What do you want me to do—be a yes-man?" The producer replied, "No, no, no—but you could at least agree with me."

There is the executive of whom an associate said, "If he understands what you're talking about, he thinks he thought of it himself."

There is the producer who wouldn't allow his director to show a character entering a room without removing his hat (even reporters, detectives, etc.), because "the women in the audience resent it."

HISTORY OF THE SHAGGY DOG [13]

During the early 1920's, when Prohibition was profoundly affecting American life, it was also leaving its mark on humor. It led to widespread drunkenness, and the "stewed fruit" gag, comic dialogue involving an intoxicated individual, swept the country.

> Didn't I meet you in Buffalo?
> I was never there in my life.
> Neither was I. Must have been two other fellows.

Another famous gag of this sort and period took place between a cop and a barfly on Times Square. The cop asks the questions and the barfly answers:

> What are you looking for?
> I lost a ten-dollar bill on Thirty-Eighth Street and Sixth Avenue.
> Then what are you looking around here for?
> There's more light here.

These nonsense souse gags were called *shaggy jokes* during the early 1920's, and it was not until the next decade that they became known as *shaggy dog stories*. It is not clear how the term originated. The most plausible guess is that of verbal transference, since drunks and tramps were often described as shaggy, and sometimes called ragshags, shag-nasties, etc. The shift from shaggy to shaggy dog resulted from the popularity of one of these "alcohological" stories which actually dealt with a shaggy dog.

In 1916 a joke appeared in England about a Skye terrier. It was copied in *Youth's Companion* of that year and thence reproduced in the old comic *Life* magazine. Thereafter the original story occasionally reappeared in various

[13] From *The Humor of Humor,* by Evan Esar, pp. 255-258. Copyright, 1952, by Evan Esar. New York: Horizon Press.

versions with only minor changes—the only shaggy story about a shaggy dog popular in the 1920's. One of the variants describes two tipsy men who were at a dog show and stopped before a woolly Skye terrier. They stared at the small dog with the long shaggy hair and were puzzled. "Which end is the head of that animal?" asked one. "Damned if I know," replied the other. "Let's find out," suggested the first. "I'll stick a pin in it and you watch to see which end barks."

A number of other stories have been advanced as the prototype of the shaggy dog, but these are either nonsense stories of non-alcoholic content or claimants after the fact. Like the one popular in the early 1940's, when the rage of these stories demanded an original, which was given acceptance by Bennett Cerf's superlative bestseller, *Try and Stop Me*. This describes an individual who travels all the way from America to England to return a lost shaggy dog for which a reward has been offered, only to be told by the snobbish owner that her lost animal isn't *that* shaggy.

Another incorrect fictional claimant describes a lush who got home very late one night, removed his shoes and clothes in the foyer, slipped into the bedroom, and began to slide into bed. Whereupon his wife stirred in her sleep and thought it was their shaggy dog that used to crawl into bed with them on cold nights. She pushed him on the head, murmuring: "Get down, Rover, get down!" The lush was not too drunk to realize the situation, so he licked her hand—and she dozed off again.

By the mid-1930's in America the shaggy dog story ran a close second to the off-color story in oral acceptance and was far ahead of any other type in printed literature of polite society. Walter Winchell, Leonard Lyons, and other syndicated columnists began to reproduce more and more specimens, and *Esquire* and other magazines featured articles which were little more than collections of such jokes. They were still chiefly devoted to the nonsense of intoxication, rumhound rather than shaggy dog stories really, but by the end of this decade an increasing number of animals became the *dramatis canes*. Even among these animal stories only one in five or so was a dog, the others being horses, cats, parrots, pigeons, and other members of the animal kingdom. And even among the dog stories, the shaggy species was extremely rare.

During the next decade, the 1940's, the shaggy dog curve of popularity rose higher than ever. Never before in the history of jocular literature had nonsense attained such widespread public favor. This ascendancy encouraged all kind of nonsense and soon the shaggy dog story diverged into several old and new types of absurdity—the illogic of insanity, the comic behavior of d. t. creatures, wacky absent-mindedness, etc. Especially significant was the deviation into the *talking animal* story which is more satiric than absurd. It also hastened the admission into popular humor of the *mad psycho* story, the caricature of the demented psychoanalyst.

The shaggy dog story is really a counterpart of the [animal] fable. The fable points up a moral for human conduct whereas the shaggy dog story, like other jokes, is intended merely to amuse. In the fable animals talk and act as human beings for satiric purposes whereas in the shaggy dog story they do so merely to show the nonsense of such personifications. Perhaps the most famous of all such stories is the tale of the horse who can pitch and field baseball superbly but who, when asked by the team manager if he can bat, replies: "Who ever heard of a horse that can bat?" . . . For the sake of the record, here are a couple of famous American originals which went round the world and were translated into a number of foreign languages:

A man went to visit a friend and was amazed to find him playing chess with his dog. He watched the game in pop-eyed astonishment for a while. "I can hardly believe my eyes," he exclaimed. "That's the smartest dog I've ever seen." "Aw, he's not so smart," the friend replied. "I've beaten him three games out of five."

A horse walked up to a bar and asked for a martini with a dash of horseradish. The bartender mixed it and handed it to him. The horse drank it and smacked his lips. "I suppose you think it strange," said the horse, leaning over the bar, "that I should come in here and ask for a martini with horseradish in it." "Hell, no," said the bartender, "I like it that way myself."

By stimulating all varieties of nonsense the shaggy dog story resulted in making its name a descriptive title for virtually every kind of absurd and zany joke. At present the term is also loosely used to designate every funny drunkard and animal story, thus making it inclusive almost to the point of meaninglessness.

MORE SHAGGY DOGS [14]

American raconteurs . . . delight in telling two . . . stories about dogs whose exploits take place in raffish surroundings.

A dog goes into a saloon and asks the bartender for a gin, which he drinks without fuss or delay. The dog quietly leaves. The bystanders have been gaping at this civilized performance, and after the dog's departure one of them says to the bartender, "That's *quite* a dog! Does he always do that?" "Oh, no. He usually drinks whisky." (A variation has it that the bartender replies, "Oh, no. He usually comes in at seven o'clock.")

The other story concerns a dog and a parrot brought into a bar one day by a regular customer, who, having ordered his drink, says to the dog, "Now, fella!" And the animal starts a lively conversation with the bird. The performance ends. One of the other customers turns to the owner of these remarkable creatures: "Say! That's really something." "Well, it's not as cute as all that. You see, the act isn't on the level." "No?" "No. The dog is a ventriloquist."

*   *   *   *   *

It would be interesting to know how many "shaggy dogs" have originated in vestigial memories of "funny stories" or "tall stories" popular a generation, perhaps two generations earlier. The following American story . . . is pure "shaggy dog":

One day a man came into a saloon and produced a mouse from his pocket and set it down on the bar in front of him. When the ordered drink arrived—the bartender and the other customers were meanwhile in a virtual coma—the mouse, standing on tiptoe, sipped it and then, in a fine bass voice, sang "Annie Laurie." The neighboring customer asked the mouse's owner to sell him. "Hell!" said the owner. "Buy me a drink and I'll *give* him to you." The amazed and gratified neighboring customer bought the drink, pocketed the mouse, and departed rejoicing. "You must be nuts, man," expostulated the bartender. "Why did you give a gold mine like *that* away?" "Hell!" replied the ex-owner, "the only song that mouse *can* sing is 'Annie Laurie.'"

THE SAILOR AND HIS MOUSE [15]

Not long ago I was pulling a liberty in Baltimore, Maryland. While I was wandering around town I was putting forth my share of stopping at all the

[14] From *The "Shaggy Dog" Story, Its Origin, Development, and Nature* (with a few sundry examples), by Eric Partridge, pp. 66-67, 78-79. London: Faber and Faber Limited; New York: Philosophical Library, Inc., 1953.

[15] From "Some 'Whoppers' from the Armed Forces," by Norris Yates, *Journal of American Folk-lore*, Vol. 62 (April-June, 1949), No. 244, p. 175. Philadelphia: The American Folk-lore Society.

Told by Marine Corporal Richard T. Davis of Camp Lejeune, N.C. . . . I had heard practically the same version while serving with a National Guard battery in 1940. . . . In the National Guard version the locale was "some little California town" and the protagonist was a Regular Army man.—N.Y.

local hooch joints. I had been in quite a few that day and had seen quite a few sights. By sights I mean the local characters and out-of-town ones as well. This one dump topped them all though. I was sitting there downing my third bourbon and ginger when in walks this short swabbie (sailor). He was so short that he had to stand on his tiptoes to see over the bar. The bartender walked over to him and quoted "What's yours, sailor?" The sailor looked up at the bartender, who was a great big six-foot-six giant and said out of the corner of his mouth, "Give me a beer and a shot of whisky." The bartender walked away and brought the drinks. Without a word the swabbie drank the beer and to the amazement of every one poured the shot of whisky in the breast pocket of his blue jumper. As soon as this was done, the sailor turned to the bartender and said, "One more beer and one more whisky." The bartender hated to see good whisky go to waste, but he hurriedly refilled the short sailor's order. Again without a word the sailor drank his beer and into the pocket went the shot of whisky.

By this time the sailor was the center of attraction and all the customers in the place had him as their center of attraction. The bartender went red as he saw the sailor repeat his mysterious actions. For the third time the sailor asked for the same order as before, not aware that all of the eyes in the place were focused on him. This time the bartender asked him not to waste the whisky. The sailor merely gave him a dirty look and drank his beer and poured the entire contents of the shot glass again into his pocket. This time the huge bartender just couldn't stand it. He rushed over to the swabbie and started reading him off. He asked the swabbie just what satisfaction he was getting by pouring good whisky into his pocket. With this the little sailor reached out to his full extent and grabbed the big bartender by the front of his shirt and pulled him to where he wasn't any more than six inches away from his nose. Then he says, "You're pretty damn nosey, aren't you? If you bother me once more about how I drink, I'll personally take you outside and beat the living hell right out of you." With that a little white mouse with a very red nose stuck his head out of the sailor's pocket and said, "Yeah, and that goes for your goddam cat too."

THE TALKING HORSE [16]

We have only one authentic record of the actual remarks of a horse in the archives of Broadway. The horse in question was the cab horse driven by "Mississippi," a wizened up little ex-prize fighter who had his stand in front of Rector's at 48th and Broadway. "Mississippi" wore a battered old plug hat that Ted Lewis, then a young band leader in Rector's, won from "Sippy" in a crap game and made the most famous trademark in show business.

Joe Frisco, the great dancer, was feeding the old cab horse doughnuts one Broadway dawning and at the same time talking to the horse. Joe's remarks have

[16] From *Short Takes*, Readers' Choice of the Best Columns of America's Favorite Newspaperman, by Damon Runyon, pp. 174-175. Copyright, 1931, 1932, 1933, 1934, 1935, 1936, 1937, 1938, 1939, 1940, 1941, 1942, 1943, 1944, 1945, 1946, by King Features Syndicate, Inc. New York and London: Whittlesey House, McGraw-Hill Book Company, 1946.

been lost to history and were probably not important. The horse ate two doughnuts, then nuzzled Joe's ear, and Joe turned and started to dash into Rector's. The doorman stopped him.

"I saw that horse speak to you, Joe," he said. "What did he say?"

"He s-s-said he w-w-wanted a c-c-cup of coffee with his d-d-doughnuts," reported Joe. . . .

THE CHILD IN THE SUBWAY [17]

A friend of mine was riding in the subway one day. It must have been several years ago—at the time of the Coronation in England. Anyhow, my friend was sitting opposite a woman and child, and the child had a bandaged head, enormous, with what seemed to be rolls and rolls of bandages wound around it. All of a sudden, the woman started slapping the child and yelling, "So a king you would be! A king yet!"

Finally my friend couldn't stand it any more. "What's the idea?" he demanded. "This child appears to be in agony. What's the idea of slapping him?"

So the woman started unrolling the bandage. It covered up a chamber pot into which the child had stuck his head, and she explained that they were on their way to a doctor to get it removed. "A king he would be!" she said. "They were playing coronation, and my son, he insisted on being king."

THE LOVER'S GIFT [18]

This woman was a very good friend of a friend of a friend of my sister, who told her the story. The woman had a lover, about whom she of course did not want her husband to learn. The lover was eager to give her a fur coat, and she wanted it very much, but the problem was: how could she suddenly acquire a fur coat without her husband getting suspicious? Finally they hit on the idea of his buying the coat and leaving it in a locker at Grand Central station. He would then give her the key to the locker, and she could pretend to her husband that she found it on the street.

All went according to plan. One day she said to her husband, "Darling, look what I found! A key to one of those lockers at Grand Central."

"Oh really," said he.

"Why don't you go down and claim whatever is in it?"

He protested it wasn't honest, and so forth, but finally he agreed to go down on his way to work and bring home what was in the locker.

[17] By Samuel Gallant. From *New York Folklore Quarterly*, Vol. II (November 1946), No. 4, Special New York City Number, edited by Elaine Lambert Lewis and James O'Beirne, pp. 276-277. Copyright, 1946, by New York Folklore Society. Ithaca, New York.

The coronation theme is unusual. Sometimes the story is told of a goldfish bowl. Sometimes the covering over the bowl or pot is a paper bag, and the locale a trolley car. Oddly enough, it always seems to be a doctor who is to do the removing.—E.L.L. and J.O.

[18] By Irwin Shapiro. *Ibid.*, pp. 277-278.

He went to Grand Central, got the coat, and brought it to the office with him. He threw it down over a table, and his secretary came in and saw it.

"Darling!" she cried, kissing him. "Is this for me? After all these years? How wonderful!"

"Why—er—of course, of course," he said. "Sure it's for you. I just bought it." She was overjoyed.

So that night his wife met him at the door all excited. "What was in the locker?" she said, "Where is it?"

"Here," he said, and handed her a second-hand umbrella he had bought at a pawn shop on the way home.

THE MAN IN THE MIDDLE [19]

It was nearly one o'clock in the morning when Harry Wesson got on a subway train at Times Square, bound for Washington Heights. He was sleepy, and barely able to note, without being much interested, that the car was nearly empty, and that an elderly lady across the aisle was staring at him with apparent disapproval. Why? He had had a few drinks, it was true. But——

This vague line of thought was broken at the next stop, when three men came in arm-in-arm; if Wesson had looked dissipated, as he suspected he did, these men looked drunk, and the old lady transferred her unfavorable attention to them. For this, or some other reason, they sat down beside her. Two of them stared at Wesson; the man in the middle seemed too drunk to stare at any one. His companions talked across him, but they seemed to be speaking some foreign language. Wesson could not understand a word, but he felt that they were talking about him. Odd—but it didn't matter.

At Fifty-Ninth Street several people got out; nobody got on, and Wesson noticed that he, the old lady, and the three men were alone in the car. The old lady now appeared fidgety, and the drunk had passed out. The other two continued their unintelligible conversation, and again it seemed to Wesson that they were talking about him. As the train slowed down at Seventy-Second Street, the old lady rose decisively and marched toward the door, brushing against Wesson.

"You follow me, young man!" she muttered. "Mind that, now!"

Somewhat dazed, Wesson obeyed. On the platform, as the train moved away, he said, annoyed: "What can I do for you, madam?"

The old lady snorted.

"Young man, I should think I've done something for you. Didn't you see that the middle man was dead?"

[19] By Ben C. Clough. From *The American Imagination at Work,* Tall Tales and Folk Tales, edited by Ben C. Clough, p. 355. Copyright, 1947, by Alfred A. Knopf, Inc. New York.

This story, in essence, has drifted about New York for decades, not changing very much, though sometimes Wesson is a young girl, the old lady an old gentleman, and so on. The underlying mystery is never solved.—B.C.C.

Print by Fritz Eichenberg, from *American Stuff,* An Anthology of Prose & Verse by Members of the Federal Writers' Project, with Sixteen Prints by the Federal Art Project (New York, The Viking Press, Inc., 1937).

SLEEP by FRITZ EICHENBERG

THE WATCH WITH THE RADIUM DIAL [20]

. . . In the days when radium watch and clock dials were a novelty, a gentleman living in the hotel won first prize at a bridge tournament, the prize a wrist-watch with radium dial.

[20] From *Tales of a Wayward Inn*, by Frank Case, pp. 57-60. Copyright, 1938, by Frank Case. Philadelphia and New York: J. B. Lippincott Company.

"Do you suppose," says the wife, arriving home from the party, "that you can actually see the figures in the dark."

"Let's try."

So they put out all the lights in the living-room but are unable to make it sufficiently dark because of the lights from outside coming through the window.

Presently the man in the adjoining room, which we will call 907, telephones down to the office that his neighbors are making so much noise he cannot sleep; so up goes the watchman to listen at the door of 906, but all is quiet as a church and down he goes and so reports. For the second time 907 complains and up again goes the watchman, and again all is quiet. The third time 907 says he is going to get up and leave if something isn't done; so this time the watchman takes his pass-key and gently opens the door of 906, to discover a living-room all in darkness and quiet. As he is about to close the door very gently, a terrific pounding comes from the clothes-closet which opens off the living-room. The watchman opens the cupboard and out stagger Mr. and Mrs. Radium.

What had happened was that as the living-room wasn't sufficiently dark for a satisfactory demonstration of the new watch, they had gone into the clothes-closet, forgetting that they had installed their own lock, a snap lock, that opened only from the outside, and had locked themselves in. The reason the watchman had not heard them on his first two or three investigations was that they were exhausted from pounding and hollering, and their rest periods synchronized with the watchman's trips, so that while he was listening they were lying on the closet floor waiting for their strength to come back, returning to the attack while he was downstairs reporting that 907 only imagined he heard noises.

So he lets them out and all is well—but only for a little time. They prepare for bed, she in night-dress, he in pajamas, when she suddenly thinks of blaming the hotel for the misadventure.

"It seems very funny to me that someone didn't hear us hammering and pounding on the wall! This closet is right next to the public hall and certainly any one passing could hear us!"

"Oh, I don't know," yawns the husband, who wants to go to bed and forget the whole thing.

"Not at all!" says Mrs. Radium. "I'm sure you can hear in the hall! You go out and I'll go in the cupboard and pound and see if you can hear."

So in she goes again and closes the door and out he goes in pajamas and closes the hall door, which also has a spring lock. And there they are, she pounding on the closet door, he pounding on the hall door. So he rings the elevator bell and up comes the elevator, but it is full of people and he in his night clothes and bare feet in the public hall, so he ducks into the maid's pantry and the elevator man looks up and down the hall and, seeing no one, goes on about his business. And this can be carried on indefinitely, they may be there yet, locking themselves in and out and pounding on doors to learn if you can really see radium watch dials in the dark, although it is many years ago and they are probably too old now to be interested in science.

THE WHITE SATIN DRESS [21]

In Cincinnati there was a pretty girl who had just been engaged to be married. To look her best at a country-club dance to be given shortly after the engagement had been announced, she bought a beautiful white satin gown at one of the leading department stores. On the night of the dance she and her fiancé were much admired. She was very happy because of her popularity and her approaching wedding. Although the evening was a warm one in summer, she never missed a dance and, of course, was happiest when dancing in the arms of her lover.

After a couple of hours, however, she began to feel faint but could not resist the excitement of the dance. Suddenly she collapsed unconscious in her fiancé's arms. When a doctor arrived, he found her dead. The autopsy showed that she had been strangely poisoned by an embalming fluid that somehow had entered her body. Small traces of the fluid were discovered in the girl's white satin gown, from which it must have penetrated her skin during the heat and exertion of the dance.

When the officials of the store where she had bought the dress were threatened with the police, they finally admitted they had allowed a wealthy family to rent the dress for the funeral of their daughter, after which it had been returned to the store and sold. The lingering fluid from the dead body had embalmed alive the happy girl who had proudly worn her white satin gown.

"LAVENDER" [22]

A few years ago the postmaster in a village that lies beside the lonely waters of the Ramapo River, dappled by light and leaf shadow in the morning and darkened by hill shadows in the afternoon, talked often about a lithe tawny girl with hyacinth eyes and wheat-yellow hair. He was a sophisticated gentleman, traveled and urbane, a member of a distinguished family in those parts. To atone for his sins, he said, he taught a boys' class in a Sunday school that was in session on the first day of each week after the preaching in a tiny, weathered church back in the Ramapo hills.

From the summits of those hills, on a clear day washed by recent rain, the slim gray towers on Manhattan Island seem to advance into sight and hang, like figures long ago worked into the tapestry on the old blue sky wall. None of the boys in Sunday school had ever entered the city on the horizon and only a few

[21] From "'Embalmed Alive': A Developing Urban Ghost Tale" by J. Russell Reaver, *New York Folklore Quarterly*, Vol. VIII (Autumn 1952), No, 3, pp. 219-220. Copyright, 1952, by New York Folklore Society. Cooperstown, New York.

This story was first told me by a fellow college student, who was from Cincinnati, in a dormitory "bull session." Fantastic as its central motif is, college students accepted it at the time as fact.—J.R.R.

For a New York variant, see Bennett Cerf, *Famous Ghost Stories* (New York, 1944), pp. 359-360.

[22] From *Dark Trees to the Wind*, A Cycle of York State Years, by Carl Carmer, pp. 306-311. Copyright, 1949, by Carl Carmer. New York: William Sloane Associates.

of them had been to Hillburn or Sloatsburg in York State or any of the New Jersey towns to the west. They were a shy lot but wild as woods animals are wild, and they found the simple lessons in Christian ethics the postmaster was trying to teach difficult at best and impossible at those times when that girl was around.

She went through his class, the postmaster said, like a slow pestilence. A boy would be gone for a month, sometimes two months, and then he would come back on a Sunday, glowering and sheepish, and one of his schoolmates would be absent for a while. The Sunday-school teacher would sometimes see him and the girl picking wild blackberries on a hillside or, on a Saturday night, walking the road shoes in hand to a country dance.

There was much talk about the girl among the hill-folk gossips, and the postmaster, whose job gave him speaking acquaintance with most of these, gathered from what they said that she was gay and hot tempered and amoral—feeling that the general admiration gave her the privilege of disobeying the somewhat eccentric conventions of her own community. The only time he had a good look at her was during a Wednesday night prayer meeting at which, according to an announcement the previous Sunday, the contents of three barrels of old clothes from the members of a New York City church would be distributed. The girl came in after the service and just as the preacher beat in the head of the first barrel. She was barefoot and it was obvious that she wore only a stained and patched calico-check dress much too small for her. She sat in the back pew and paid no attention as the usual pathetic garments that are contained in such shipments were displayed and granted to those who could argue the greatest need.

There was a gasp when the preacher pulled from the middle of the second barrel a lavender evening dress covered with sequins that glinted like tiny amethysts. It was cut low off the shoulders and as soon as the preacher saw that he rolled it up into a shapeless bundle holding it helpless and waiting for some one to speak for it. No one did but the girl stood up and padded swiftly down the aisle. Without saying a word she grabbed the dress from the good man's hands and raced out of the church.

From that time on, the postmaster said, no one ever saw the girl in other costume. Rain or shine, day or night, she was a brush stroke of lavender against the brown of dirt roads, the green of hill slopes, the khaki-colored shirts and pants of whatever boy strode beside her.

Frost came early that year and leaves dropped. The air was clear and the New York towers came nearer and stayed longer. The hill people were all talking about a letter that had come to the girl from cousins in Jersey City. The postmaster had told one of his Sunday-school boys that the letter had come and the next day she had stood before his window and quietly asked for it, the sequins glinting purple in the shadowy room. People who dropped in the next day said her cousins had invited her to visit them and they had sent the money for her bus fare. A week later, a witness regaled the postmaster with a description of the expressions on the faces of the bus passengers down on the asphalt highway twelve miles away when the girl climbed aboard, holding her long skirt about her waist.

In mid-December came a cold snap and the thermometer outside showed eighteen degrees below zero when the postmaster opened his window for business. The people in the line of waiters-for-mail were more eager to give him the news than to receive their letters. The body of the girl in the lavender dress had been found frozen and stiff on the road a few miles above the bus stop. Returning from Jersey City, she had left the bus and begun the long walk home, but the evening dress proved too flimsy wear for such a night.

The postmaster said that after this tragedy all the students in his class came regularly to Sunday school, and that was the end of the story of the girl.

The girl froze to death about 1939 and for a decade nothing reflected doubt on the postmaster's conclusion. But now a growing number of people feel that his narrative, the truth of which is easily provable by many witnesses, has had an inexplicable consequence, overtones that have transcended his matter-of-fact realism. For a strange report recently began its round of upstate towns and, particularly, colleges. It had many variants, as such tales do, but in none of them was it in any way connected with the account of the girl, her dress, and her death, a factual record known only in the vicinity of her Ramapo home, and the suggestion of such a connection is made here possibly for the first time.

As I heard it, two Hamilton College juniors motoring to a dance at Tuxedo Park after sunset of a warm Indian summer Saturday on the road that runs through the valley of the little Ramapo River saw a girl waiting. She was wearing a party dress the color of the mist rising above the dark water of the stream and her hair was the color of ripe wheat. The boys stopped their car and asked the girl if they could take her in the direction she was going. She eagerly seated herself between them and asked if they were going to the square dance at Sterling Furnace. The thin, tanned face with high cheekbones, the yellow hair, the flashing smile, the quicksilver quality of her gestures, enchanted the boys and it was soon a matter of amused debate whether they would go along with her to Sterling Furnace or she would accompany them to the dance at Tuxedo. The majority won and the boys were soon presenting their new friend to the young couple who were their hosts at the Park. "Call me 'Lavender,' " she said to them. "It's my nickname because I always wear that color."

After an evening in which the girl, quiet and smiling, made a most favorable impression by her dancing, drifting dreamily through the waltzes in a sparkling cloud of lavender sequins, stepping more adeptly than any of the other dancers through the complications of revived square dances—Money Musk—Hull's Victory—Nellie Gray—the boys took her out to their car for the ride home. She said that she was cold and one of them doffed his tweed topcoat and helped her into it. They were both shocked into clichés of courtesy when, after gaily directing the driver through dusty woodland roads she finally bade him stop before a shack so dilapidated that it would have seemed deserted had it not been for a ragged lace curtain over the small window in the door. After promising to see them again soon, she waved good night, standing beside the road until they had turned around and rolled away. They were almost in Tuxedo before the chill air made the coatless one realize that he had forgotten to reclaim his property and they decided to return for it on their way back to college the next day.

The afternoon was clear and sunny when, after considerable difficulty in finding the shack, the boys knocked on the door with the ragged lace curtain over its window. A decrepit white-haired woman answered the door and peered at them out of piercing blue eyes when they asked for Lavender.

"Old friends of hers?" she asked, and the boys, fearing to get the girl into the bad graces of her family by telling the truth about their adventure of the day before, said yes they were old friends.

"Then ye couldn't a-heerd she's dead," said the woman. "Been in the grave-yard down the road fer near ten years."

Horrified, the boys protested that this was not the girl they meant—that they were trying to find some one they had seen the previous evening.

"Nobody else o' that name ever lived round here," said the woman. " 'Twan't her real name anyway. Her paw named her Lily when she was born. Some folks used to call her Lavender on account o' the pretty dress she wore all the time. She was buried in it."

The boys once more turned about and started for the paved highway. A hundred yards down the road the driver jammed on the brakes.

"There's the graveyard," he said, pointing to a few weathered stones standing in bright sunlight in an open field overgrown with weeds, "and just for the hell of it I'm going over there."

They found the stone—a little one marked "Lily"—and on the curving mound in front of it, neatly folded, the tweed topcoat.

THE TELL-TALE SEAWEED [23]

This is the story just as I heard it the other evening—a ghost story told me as true. It seems that one chilly October night in the first decade of the present century, two sisters were motoring along a Cape Cod road, when their car broke down just before midnight and would go no further. This was in an era when such mishaps were both commoner and more hopeless than they are today. For these two, there was no chance of help until another car might chance to come by in the morning and give them a tow. Of a lodging for the night there was no hope, except a gaunt, unlighted, frame house which, with a clump of pine trees beside it, stood black in the moonlight, across a neglected stretch of frost-hardened lawn.

They yanked at its ancient bell-pull, but only a faint tinkle within made answer. They banged despairingly on the door panel, only to awaken what at

[23] From *While Rome Burns*, by Alexander Woollcott, pp. 83-86. Copyright, 1934, by Alexander Woollcott. New York: The Viking Press, Inc.

More recently, the Curator of the Botanical Museum in St. Louis has assured me that this tale, whispered from neighbor to neighbor across the country, has become distorted in a manner offensive to students of marine vegetation. According to him, the visitor from the sea was seen in a house in Woods Hole, Mass. He was a son of the house who had been drowned during his honeymoon off the coast of Australia. The seaweed picked up off the dusty floor of that New England mansion was of a variety which grows only off the Australian coast. The Curator even presented me with the actual seaweed. I regard it with mingled affection and skepticism, and keep it pressed between the pages of Bullfinch's Mythology.—A.W.

first they thought was an echo, and then identified as a shutter responding antiphonally with the help of a nipping wind. This shutter was around the corner, and the ground-floor window behind it was broken and unfastened. There was enough moonlight to show that the room within was a deserted library, with a few books left on the sagging shelves and a few pieces of dilapidated furniture still standing where some departing family had left them, long before. At least the sweep of the electric flash which one of the women had brought with her showed them that on the uncarpeted floor the dust lay thick and trackless, as if no one had trod there in many a day.

They decided to bring their blankets in from the car and stretch out there on the floor until daylight, none too comfortable, perhaps, but at least sheltered from that salt and cutting wind. It was while they were lying there, trying to get to sleep, while, indeed, they had drifted halfway across the borderland, that they saw—each confirming the other's fear by a convulsive grip of the hand—saw standing at the empty fireplace, as if trying to dry himself by a fire that was not there, the wraithlike figure of a sailor come dripping from the sea.

After an endless moment, in which neither woman breathed, one of them somehow found the strength to call out, "Who's there?" The challenge shattered the intolerable silence, and at the sound, muttering a little—they said afterwards that it was something between a groan and a whimper—the misty figure seemed to dissolve. They strained their eyes, but could see nothing between themselves and the battered mantelpiece.

Then, telling themselves (and, as one does, half believing it) that they had been dreaming, they tried again to sleep, and, indeed, did sleep until a patch of shuttered sunlight striped the morning floor. As they sat up and blinked at the gritty realism of the forsaken room, they would, I think, have laughed at their shared illusion of the night before, had it not been for something at which one of the sisters pointed with a kind of gasp. There, in the still undisturbed dust, on the spot in front of the fireplace where the apparition had seemed to stand, was a patch of water, a little, circular pool that had issued from no crack in the floor nor, as far as they could see, fallen from any point in the innocent ceiling. Near it in the surrounding dust was no footprint—their own or any other's—and in it was a piece of green that looked like seaweed. One of the women bent down and put her finger to the water, then lifted it to her tongue. The water was salty.

After that the sisters scuttled out and sat in their car, until a passerby gave them a tow to the nearest village. In its tavern at breakfast they gossiped with the proprietress about the empty house among the pine trees down the road. Oh, yes, it had been just that way for a score of years or more. Folks did say the place was spooky, haunted by a son of the family, who, driven out by his father, had shipped before the mast and been drowned at sea. Some said the family had moved away because they could not stand the things they heard and saw at night.

A year later, one of the sisters told the story at a dinner party in New York. In the pause that followed a man across the table leaned forward.

"My dear lady," he said, with a smile, "I happen to be the curator of a museum where they are doing a good deal of work on submarine vegetation. In your place, I never would have left that house without taking the bit of seaweed with me."

"Of course you wouldn't," she answered tartly, "and neither did I."

It seems she had lifted it out of the water and dried it a little by pressing it against a window pane. Then she had carried it off in her pocketbook, as a souvenir. As far as she knew, it was still in an envelope in a little drawer of her desk at home. If she could find it, would he like to see it? He would. Next morning she sent it around by a messenger, and a few days later it came back with a note.

"You were right," the note said, "this is seaweed. Furthermore, it may interest you to learn that it is of a rare variety which, as far as we know, grows only on dead bodies."

And that, my dears, is the story as I heard it the other evening, heard it from Alice Duer Miller who, in turn, had heard it five-and-twenty years before from Mrs. George Haven Putnam, sometime dean of Barnard College and author of that admirable work, *The Lady*. To her I must go if—as I certainly did—I wanted more precise details. So to Mrs. Putnam I went, hat in hand and, as an inveterate reporter, showered her with questions. I wanted the names of the seaweed, of the curator, of the museum, of the two sisters, of the dead sailor, and of the nearby village on Cape Cod. I wanted a roadmap marked with a cross to show the house in the grove of pines. I wanted—but the examination came to a dead stop at the sight of her obvious embarrassment. She was most graciously apologetic, but, really, what with this and what with that, she had forgotten the whole story. She could not even remember—and thus it is ever with my life in science—who it was that had told it to her.

EMILY STORIES [24]

There are three apparently indestructible anecdotes, which have been coming in [to the *New Yorker*] at least once a week ever since I can remember. They are always garnished with what scholars call a wealth of corroborative detail: the incident in question happened last Tuesday to the contributor's Cousin Emily in Pelham Manor, and the editors have permission to check with her if they don't believe it.

EMILY'S CAT

Last Tuesday Cousin Emily's cat died. After puzzling for a long time about what to do with the tiny corpse, Emily wrapped it up in a shoe-box and took it in to New York, planning to drop the box into the first refuse basket she came upon. Before she found one, however, a man snatched her parcel and ran.

[24] From *It's Still Maloney*, or *Ten Years in the Big City*, by Russell Maloney, p. 44. Copyright, 1945, by Russell Maloney. New York: Dial Press.
The Emily stories are localized, by Russell Maloney's telling, in New York, but they are told elsewhere as true. I have told one of them as an incident occurring in Providence, and gullibly thought I was narrating a fact. (I even knew the heroine—I thought!)—Ben C. Clough, *The American Imagination at Work* (New York, 1947), p. 692.

Emily's Hat

1. Emily wore her new hat to luncheon at a smart restaurant. Seated across the room was a woman wearing an exact duplicate of the hat. Being a good sport about the whole thing, Emily caught her eye, pointed to her own head, and made a rueful face. The woman merely looked alarmed, finished her meal hastily, and left. Later, in the powder room, Emily looked in the mirror and discovered she *hadn't* worn the new hat that day, after all.

2. Emily had to go to a funeral at one of the big Fifth Avenue churches. Arriving in town a little early, she went shopping at Saks and bought a small, flowered hat. At the door of the church a man offers to take her parcel, and Emily, supposing this to be the custom at this particular church, gives it to him. Later, as the casket is carried out, she sees on top if it, in the company of several small floral pieces, her flowered hat.

TRUE LOVE IN TULSA [25]

[A Tulsa youth] was in the Slough of Despond—the whole world had become utter darkness; life was not worth the living—his girl "that was the one thought of his waking moments, the radiant image of all his dreams," had turned him down cold, spurned his one great passion. He would put an end to it all, and perhaps when she looked on his rigid face, she would realize her cruelty. Yes, he would bring the tears to her beautiful eyes. So he procured a bottle of carbolic acid, a rope, a pistol, and some gasoline. He rushed to the Arkansas River, jumped into his canoe—first tying one end of the rope to a stout tree limb, the other end around his neck. He drank the carbolic acid, poured the gasoline over his clothes, set fire to them, and jumped from the canoe, shooting his gun at the same time. The shell, missing his head, cut the rope in two, sousing him into the river, which quenched the flame. He swallowed so much water, in his excitement—up came all of the carbolic acid—and "If I hadn't been a darned good swimmer," he says, "I surely would have drowned." But the best part, his lady love was waiting at the shore, saying "You big boob, if you want to use this license with me get into some dry clothes. Won't you ever learn that when a woman says 'No,' she means 'Yes'—sometimes?"

MATCHMAKER STORIES [26]

The *shadchen* has remained one of the ever-popular figures of Jewish folk humor. He is a type with which even the Gentile has become familiar. These stories deal with the matchmaker in action. The action follows a traditional pattern. The *shadchen* lands a prospect and proceeds to build him [or her] up either to the virtues of marriage or to the matchless qualities of his [or her] merchandise.

[25] From *Tulsa—The City Beautiful,* by Mrs. Dan Morris, [p. 10]. [Tulsa, Oklahoma: 1927.] [No pagination or publisher.]

[26] From *Meet the Folks,* A Session of American-Jewish Humor with Sammy Levenson, pp. 58, 59-60. Copyright, 1946, 1947, 1948, by the Citadel Press. New York.

The shadchen went into ecstasy over the abundance of remarkable attributes of a particular lass. She had everything a man could ask for: beauty, culture, money, family, wisdom.

"Isn't it true," broke in the *bocher* [young man], "that she has a broken leg?"

"A broken leg! Some people don't appreciate anything," the *shadchen* snapped back. "Look! Suppose you get a girl with two good legs. You marry her, you are happy, you have three beautiful children, you buy a two-story mansion. One day your wife falls down the grand staircase and breaks a leg. There are doctors, hospital bills, the children are left stranded without their mother, sleepless nights. . . . And here am I, offering you *a ready-made broken leg!*"

The *shadchen* was rehearsing the interview.

"Don't talk too much. Let him do the talking. Don't giggle. And if he asks you your age, for heaven's sake, answer with *saichel!* [horse sense]."

They sent her off and waited impatiently for the results. . . .

She came back—in tears. It was a failure.

"What happened? Did you blabber? Did you behave like a fool? Nu!"

"Tell us already!"

"He asked me my age. . . ."

"So what did you say?"

"So I said 38!"

"38? Didn't I tell you to answer with *saichel?*"

"Oy, *shadchen!* 38 was already with *saichel!*"

BOP JOKES [27]

From the world of jazz musicians and bebop players has come a new brand of humor: the bop joke. Until the last few months bop jokes have been limited, perhaps mercifully, to people in show business. But now bop humor is becoming something of a fad, and *Life,* feeling its readers should be warned of this wayward form of wit, offers a few examples which can be understood by referring to the glossary of bop terms. . . .

The essence of bop humor lies in the fact that its creators, carried away by their music, are often in a dopey state of ecstasy known as "gone." Their sense of time is so cockeyed that racing or falling objects seem to be floating by. Violent events become sweet and lovely. The bopster views his world with wonder and joy, and nothing is ever quite what it is. Like boiled snails, bop jokes certainly are not everybody's dish, but those who acquire the taste for them feel cool, gone, crazy, and stoned.

Bop Vocabulary

Cool: tasty, pretty
Crazy: new, wonderful, wildly exciting

[27] From "That Crazy Bop Joke Craze, With Glossary One Can Understand, If Not Appreciate, Musicians' Gags," *Life,* Vol. 33 (September 29, 1952), No. 13, pp. 67, 69-70. Copyright, 1952, by Time, Inc. New York.

Dig: to understand, appreciate the subtleties of

Flip: to react enthusiastically

Gone: the tops—superlative of crazy

Goof: to blow a wrong note, or to make a mistake

Hipster: modern version of hepcat

Stoned: drunk, captivated, ecstatic, sent out of this world

ALL ABOARD A CLOUD

Two bopsters are stoned in a hotel penthouse. One says, "Man, I feel so great I could walk right out on that cloud!" He steps out the open window. When police arrive, one asks the second bopster why he let his friend jump. "Man," he replies, "I thought he could make it!"

STONE-COLD LOVE ON PARK BENCH

Heading homeward from a party, two hipsters, completely stoned, pause to snuggle on a park bench. A fire engine roars by, bells clanging, sirens screaming. The boy flips. "Solid, doll," he murmurs, "they're playing our song!"

THEY GET GOING ON PIE

Two bopsters go into a hash joint. One orders a piece of pie. "Sorry," says the waitress. "The pie is gone." "Oh, that crazy pie!" cries the bopster. "I'll take *two* pieces!"

NO LOITERING ON THIS CORNER

Standing on a street corner, a couple of hipsters see a motorcycle roar past them at 90 mph. "Man," says one, "I thought he'd *never* leave!"

MUSIC HATH CHARMS

Bopsters, sightseeing in India, listen to a snake charmer. "Just dig that cool arrangement!" one exclaims. "Never mind the arrangement," says his pal, ogling the wriggling cobra. "Dig that crazy music stand!"

BURLESQUE BITS

I. From Bit to Skit [28]

Bits furnish the bulk of the material on which most burlesque dialogue and action is based, and often these very same bits furnish the material for a large percentage of the sketches and black-outs used in present-day revues. Only the limited number of book shows dared to trust their fortunes to new dialogue and even these retained some bits intact, to insure stock laughs.

[28] From *Burleycue,* An Underground History of Burlesque Days, by Bernard Sobel, pp. 162-165, 166, 264-265. Copyright, 1931, by Bernard Sobel. New York: Rinehart & Company, Inc.

The bits, considered technically, have a basic pattern, a kind of formula. . . . The typical bit always contains a menacing situation—like a man caught with another man's wife. This situation, because of its universal applicability, is open to innumerable deviations. The second man can kill the first, all three can commit suicide, or turn the whole incident into a joke. J. P. McEvoy, for instance, has the woman pick up the man, lead him into her home, introduce him to her husband, and then say: "There John, I've brought this man home because he's wearing just the kind of spats I wanted you to buy."

The humor of these situations is rarely evident in the printed script. For the laughs must be acted out and visualized. The personality of the players, the action and the phrasing created the laughs, and thus it was that burlesque companies could present perpetually the same old bits classifying these by a single term like the "lemon bit." Experienced burlesquers can describe an entire show by merely inspecting the properties. If there's a gavel back stage, then there's a court room bit; and so on indefinitely. Burlesque companies present their whole show by following a catch word diagram which lists bits. . . .

So fearful was the comic of the theft of his bits that he retained them by memory only, never trusting them to paper. . . . Yet the material, as a matter of fact, was original only in so far as personal presentation was concerned.

* * * * *

Because a comic possessed a bit for seasons, he felt he took on with it the accretion of ownership. But very few bits were the original works of burlesquers. They were merely inheritances, often formulas from minstrel show and medicine man, who were, in turn, the partial heirs of traveler and mediaeval troubador and perhaps a few crusaders. "Body bits" for instance were redressed old Negro acts like "Lawyer Smart," "Mr. and Mrs. Brown," "Ike and Mike in Honolulu," "Ike and Mike in the Mountains," "Man Who Look Like Me," "Parson Milks," "No More Beans." Among the best known bits were "Razor Jim," "Oh Ma Look at Him," "Kiss in the Dark," "Murder at the Toll Gate," "Ghost in the Pawn Shop" and "The Coming Man."

The theatrical value of the bits never occurred to the burlesquer until around the 1900's when the Broadway shows began to use black-outs and skits; that is, bits redressed with settings, costumes, effects, and much detail, assuming the importance of a substantial scene, three or four supplying most of the risible entertainment of the evening. Thus the burlesquers suddenly realized that they had been tossing away two or three times as much material in a single performance as was necessary to fill up two or three shows.

* * * * *

The following specimen "bits" reveal their humor range and compactness:

The straight man, dressed like a judge, comes out and says:

"Hear ye. Hear ye. The court is now open. All divorce proceedings will now be taken care of. We'll hear the first case on the docket."

At these words, a comic comes out dressed as an Indian, with his back to the audience so that his identity is withheld.

The judge says:

"What is your trouble?"

"When Indian plant corn," says the comic dolefully, "Indian gets corn. When Indian plants rye, Indian gets rye. But when Indian plants Indian and gets Chinaman, he wants a divorce."

*   *   *   *   *

. . . The straight man working with the second or third comic would bet that the Irishman could not pick up the suitcase without saying "Ouch." As the comedian reached down over the suitcase, the straight man would give him a kick in the trousers whereupon he would cry "ouch" and lose the bet.

*   *   *   *   *

The tramp says to the Irish comic:

"My wife's going to have a baby."

"Isn't that nice."

"Here comes the nurse now. She's going to take care of her."

The nurse enters and says:

"Is there anything I can do for you?"

"Yes," says the prospective father. "Let me know right away if it's a girl or a boy."

"All right. I will. If it's a girl, I'll blow a horn once; if it's a boy, I'll blow twice."

"Very good. Hurry up. And don't forget."

A minute later the horn blows once. Whereupon the tramp and the Irishman shake hands. Then the horn blows again to the consternation of both. Then it blows four times continuously. Finally a peddler walks in blowing a fish-horn and yelling "fresh fish."

II. Top Banana[29]

. . . Three comedians divide two bananas. The one who gets left out on the count is told, "You get the third banana." The lowest buffoon became known as the "third banana"; hence the head comic was "top banana."

III. The Philanthropist[30]

. . . Bowery tramps [scratch] out their fleas to an orchestral accompaniment, *crip, crap, bom.* A middle-aged dandy in evening dress appears to take pity on them, wishes to make them heirs to his millions. Various other street characters appear, among them a weatherbeaten drab. She reminds him of his mother. He becomes very sentimental and tells at great length of the

[29] From "Top Banana: Burlesque Not Dead Yet," by Johnny Mercer, New York *Herald Tribune,* October 28, 1951. Copyright, 1951, by the New York Herald Tribune, Inc.

[30] From *New York Nights,* by Stephen Graham, p. 145. Copyright, 1927, by George H. Doran Company. New York.

Cf. City Lights, with Charles Chaplin.

change he is going to make in all their lives. They seem to believe him and are all ready to be taken in a limousine to his country house, when his keepers arrive and take him away to the asylum whence he has escaped—back to the "bug house."

IV. The Unco-operative Cop[31]

. . . A man finding he has no money left and no shelter for the night decides that he will commit an offence against the law and so get a free bed in prison. "Now what shall I do? I know, I'll pick a quarrel." He does so. A cop comes and parts him from the man he has begun to assault, addressing fatherly remarks to the one who was to blame and warning the innocent party very sternly. So that device will not do. "I know, I'll insult a lady." He does so. He insults her very ribaldly. The lady screams for protection. A cop hurries up and asks her how many times he is going to find her making a disturbance in that street, and he winks knowingly at the homeless man. That also has failed. He simulates being drunk. But this only produces affectionate concern on the part of the police, whose chief desire is for a share of the "stuff." In despair the homeless man rings a fire [alarm]. A woman rushes out and says, "You've saved my home. You splendid man! You hero!" and hands him a hundred dollars, and the woman leaves him standing bewildered with the notes fluttering in his hand. Then a policeman comes up and snatches the money from him, declaring it to be counterfeit. . . .

[31] *Ibid.*, p. 144.
Cf. "The Cop and the Anthem," by O. Henry.

XV. Suburbia

A suburbanite or commuter has been described as a man who shuttles back and forth from a place where he would rather not live to a place where he would rather not work. This cynicism points to a new kind of schizophrenia that began to afflict Americans as soon as the city dweller discovered that he did not have to put up with the inconveniences of the city and was free to substitute for them the inconveniences of the suburbs. In other words, the city is a nice place to work in, but he won't live there if you give him the place. But inasmuch as the city is still his bread and butter and still has a monopoly on commercialized entertainment, the suburbanite is still tied to the apron strings of the city, commuting to its theaters and night spots as well as to its shops and offices. Now with business following city dwellers to the suburbs, in the latest stage of the flight from the city—the decentralization of industry—some suburbanites have ceased to live a double life, while some city dwellers have become reverse commuters from the city to the suburbs.

A familiar symbol of the flight from the city is the commuter racing for his outbound train in the evening, only to race the other way again, on the rebound, for the morning train. But the suburbanite has more positive reasons for moving to the suburbs than merely escaping from the city and running for trains. In a survey of new suburban homeowners by Lee McCabe in the *New York Times*, "Suburbia's V.I.P.'s" said that "what they most enjoyed about living in a house after spending all or part of their lives in an apartment" was:

(1) The baronial splendor of going upstairs to bed and coming downstairs to breakfast. (Something the ranch-house owner wouldn't know about.) (2) The ability to get up in the middle of the night and give the baby his two-o'clock feeding without having the neighbors complain. (3) The wonder of it all, going out and clipping the grass, listening to the birds. (4) Sitting on the terrace and relaxing with a mint julep. (5) Being able to throw the kids out in the back yard and not having to worry about them. (6) Watching the mortgage principal go down twenty cents every month.

But combining and transcending all these joys is the satisfaction of being neighbors as well as having them. True, city neighborhoods have their neighborhood spirit and relationships, reproducing the small-town atmosphere of "everybody knows everybody else." But there is not the same sense of community solidarity and home-town pride that small-towners know and have missed ever since they moved to the city. In this respect, however, as in others, Suburbia is not all alike. It ranges all the way from average, down-at-the-heels to exclusive country-club communities, from garden-apartment developments to the mass-produced suburbs. Suburbia varies too in the amount and rate of change in folkways and attitudes, change from rugged individualism to a new kind of collective living.

While the individual homeowner or conventional housing-development dweller tends to go it alone, the mass-produced suburbs like Levittown, New York, and Park Forest, Illinois (as studied by Harry Henderson and

William H. Whyte, Jr.) approve and encourage the joining of organizations, from churches and P.T.A.'s to clubs of all kinds. Thus the ambition to become a "wheel" and pride in one's own home tend to offset the inevitable transiency and sense of transience characteristic of these new communities of young veterans and junior executives. At the same time there is a refreshing casualness in dress (causing qualms to clothing manufacturers) and attitudes, as in the attitude toward pregnancy (with jokes about "our major industry," the "Levittown look" and "Fertility Acres").

The growing pains of these cities in the making, with their problems of dogs and children, afford valuable training in citizenship and may help new communities avoid the mistakes of the old.

That the commuter and the suburbanite are subjects of sociological study as well as of books of humor (*Slightly Cooler in the Suburbs, Daily except Sunday, Larks in the Popcorn*) is a sign that they are becoming a serious threat to the city. As more and more business firms follow the trend to the suburbs and more and more regional shopping centers are built (a trend started in the 1930s when the big city department stores began to open branches in the swankier suburbs and summer resorts), the more the city will feel the pinch on its pocketbook, from loss of taxes, rents, etc., as well as the chill of the commuter's indifference to the city's welfare. But it is to be hoped that the movement away from the city will lead ultimately, not to the cities' becoming satellites of the suburbs, but to a new regional balance and better understanding between the two. Then when a New Yorker tells a waitress in a New Hampshire hotel that he is thinking of buying a house there because "it's nice up here where you live and it's much quieter," she will not (as William Chapman White tells it) reply, slightly aghast: "Well, if you'll excuse me sir, I heard New Yorkers were crazy sometimes but I never thought any of them were that crazy."

THE UPTOWN COMMUTER [1]

. . . Residences were following one another farther north, and northward followed also the retail stores. . . . A cartoon [of the Nineties] showed the average New Yorker with all his goods packed on a camel, starting out on a road marked "Farther north."

* * * * *

This was the time of the cable-cars which swooped around "Dead Man's Curve" at Broadway and Fourteenth Street, of the "Gibson Girl" and the "Floradora Sextette" and also of the growing pressure of city transportation. "The rapid transit problem," wrote Mayor Gilroy in his message of 1894, "is no nearer solution than it was two years ago." Two years earlier had been born the story of the Uptown Commuter—that famous Mr. Brown who came home from business one day and met his offspring at the dinner table. "This is your father," Mrs. Brown is reputed to have said. "I am very glad to meet you, sir," responded the son with formal dignity. "I have often heard my mother speak of you." . . .

[1] From *"Manna-Hatin," The Story of New York,* pp. 186-187. Copyright, 1929, by the Manhattan Company. New York: The Manhattan Company of New York.

SUBURBAN CAMARADERIE ON THE CHICAGO AND NORTH WESTERN [2]

The camaraderie that you used to find aboard transcontinental trains when the journey from Chicago to San Francisco took three or four days is still a part of suburban travel. Everybody rides the same train every weekday for years on end. By a sort of squatter's right he establishes title to his own seat, and this is respected by people who have laid similar claim to seats of their own. In due time he gets to know everybody aboard and all about his family. There is no such clearing-house for gossip in the world.

A card game got started on the Waukegan run thirty years ago and it's been going on ever since. The cards aren't the same, or the card table supplied by the conductor—who isn't the same either—or the upholstery on the plush seats. The game that started out as cinch has gone through some metamorphoses— whist, auction bridge, contract—but the players haven't changed, nor apparently have they ever finished a rubber.

The society of the suburban trains develops its pets and bores just like other societies. The late Lew Ferguson, who established a record for endurance as a conductor on the North Shore haul, recalled one old lad who was virtually ostracized because of one bad habit.

Ferguson observed: "He read his paper too early."

Amplified, this meant that he was the sort of man who combines his reading with buttered toast and soft-boiled eggs and so had finished his absorption of the morning's news by the time he got to the station. With nothing much to do between Evanston and Chicago it was his custom to flop down alongside somebody who hadn't read his paper and engage in sprightly conversation about his grandchildren or his setter dog.

"He was shunned like the plague by everybody," said Ferguson. "until finally he had nobody to talk to but me. Then I shunned him too."

The conductors, like the commuters, are *sui generis*. They are people of great tact, patience, and friendliness. And they get to learn more about human beings than would ever be possible on one of those long runs where they see the passenger only when he gets on and six hours later when he gets off. There have been times when this intimate knowledge of how people behave has soured them. But usually they are philosophically tolerant. Sometimes the urge to do something for people whose lives are spent shuttling to and from work overpowers them. And on at least one occasion this impulse took a novel form. One conductor on the Milwaukee division figured out that the operating corporation had a lot more money than the poor people who rode the trains. Therefore, it seemed logical that the corporation ought to pay the fare. So, for a couple of years, he made a practice of letting everybody travel free. He would snap his punch at a commutation ticket—but never a ride came off.

[2] From *Pioneer Railroad*, The Story of the Chicago and North Western System, by Robert J. Casey and W. A. S. Douglas, pp. 278-279. Copyright, 1948, by the McGraw-Hill Book Company, Inc. New York and London: Whittlesey House.

Eventually the corporation caught up with him and disagreed with his theory.

Many articles reach the lost and found department from the suburban runs. Since the first time a North Western engineer safely piloted his train back from Waukegan, the inbound traveler has heard the conductor bawl his last warning: "Chicago—remember your parcels!" It is as much a slogan of the North Western as "Safety first." But there's more to it than that. The conductor, who knows everybody on his train, is sometimes his own lost and found department. If you forget anything going into town, you get it back on your way home.

LOST AND FOUND [3]

. . . A commuter stopped in the [Grand Central] terminal for a shoeshine one morning and took off his galoshes to discover he had forgotten to put on his shoes; he had pulled the galoshes over his bedroom slippers when he went out to shovel snow after breakfast. Since the slippers were leather, he got a shine anyway—and said he was looking forward to the most comfortable day in the office in years.

One rainy noon I passed the coach lost-property window and saw that 33 raincoats and 30 umbrellas had already been brought up from trains. Actually, 96 per cent of the items passengers report as lost turn up behind the Lost and Found counter.

One such article was a 16-pound bowling ball in a specially made canvas bag, which showed up not once but six times, always on a Thursday. It belonged to a stockbroker who had a weekly bowling session that day and brought in his own ball from his home in South Norwalk, Connecticut. Each morning he would get on the local train at his home station, ride to Stamford, and transfer to an express. The bowling ball would ride the local into town. Thursday evenings the broker would call at Lost and Found and pick up his ball.

But the brakeman on the local who had been carrying that 16 pounds up the stairs from the tracks each week had been doing a little figuring. He noticed there was a big bowling alley right next to Grand Central. Maybe, he guessed, the broker was using him for a little free redcap service.

The sixth Thursday, when the broker appeared with his usual apologies, there was a message waiting for him.

"The brakeman says to tell you," the boys said, "that the next time he finds that ball on the local this side of Stamford he's going to drop it off in Cos Cob Creek."

And that was the last we saw of the South Norwalk stockbroker's 16-pound bowling ball.

Another commuter came in one day and asked if a book had been found. What was the name of the book? He didn't know.

"My wife tucks a book under my arm every morning to impress the neighbors," he said. "I never read them. I sleep all the way in."

[3] From "Everything Happens at Grand Central Station," by Edward G. Fischer, with Wayne Amos, *Collier's*, Vol. 133 (March 5, 1954), No. 5, pp. 87-88. Copyright, 1954, by the Crowell-Collier Publishing Company. New York.

THE BIG SNOW [4]

At 5:32 P.M. on the day of the Big Snow, December 26, 1947, the New York Central's suburban local-express No. 241 left Grand Central Terminal, New York City, for Harmon, New York—a run of thirty-three miles—due to arrive at 6:30. At Dobbs Ferry, twenty miles out, on account of the heavy drifts, the shoes of the multiple unit train failed to make contact with the third rail. This was about 8:00 P.M., and it was not until 3:00 the next morning that a Diesel locomotive finally arrived from Harmon and pulled out No. 241, together with another stalled train coupled to the head end. Before the train started, one of the conductors announced that no stops would be made between Dobbs Ferry and Harmon and that passengers for Tarrytown, the next regularly scheduled stop, would have to ride to Harmon and catch a south-bound train back to Tarrytown. Whereupon the Tarrytown passengers, including one pregnant woman, consulted, and one of their number calmly pulled the emergency cord as the train passed Tarrytown station. The heavy load and the sudden stop snapped a coupling and broke the double train in two, leaving the rear cars stalled until about 8:00 A.M., when another Diesel locomotive came to its rescue.

I was a passenger on No. 241, in one of the cars left behind at Tarrytown. Some twenty-five of us passed the night (seventeen hours all told between Grand Central and Harmon) in acute discomfort and boredom, relieved by the following good-natured and not so good-natured kidding and kibitzing. All our social and cultural differences were temporarily leveled or forgotten in our common plight. As we fought cold, hunger and weariness, we made folklore, like a pioneer community "laughing off" hardships and hard times.

FOOD AND DRINK, ETC.

Imaginary conversations in the dining car: "Waiter, no mushrooms on the steak, please." "Don't turn over the eggs."

A nice steak, now—oh, boy!

Anyone have a ham sandwich?

Nice train—diner and everything—cocktails.

Fruit juice, coffee and lots of buttered toast.

There goes a freight, full of nice cattle and chickens.

The aristocratic grandmother from Scarborough, on her Italian meat-ball sandwich bought at Tarrytown: "This bread is good. It helps to fill you when you're feeling gaunt. I'll keep this piece for breakfast."

One of her grandchildren, a little girl of eight or ten: "When I get home I'm not going to wash my face or brush my teeth. I'm going to eat last night's dinner, this morning's breakfast and today's lunch."

Black market prices: one dollar a cigarette.

The drinks are on me, boys!

[4] By B. A. Botkin.

HEAT AND LIGHT

Let's pile up the chairs in the smoker [club car] and set fire to it.

Passengers ready to retire? The conductor will make up the berths.

If the lights and heat go off, we'll all freeze to death. Finally the feet freeze and gangrene sets in. The ice water comes out of your veins.

The Red Cross girls will be waiting for us at the station with doughnuts and hot coffee.

(Someone burned paper in a spittoon. A man and a woman covered with a coat, sat with a train lantern between them. Someone stood on a seat and warmed his hands on an electric bulb. In the morning they all came into our car to keep warm by huddling together.)

MISCELLANEOUS QUIPS

Next station, Tarrytown—I hope.

As we filed back into the train at Dobbs Ferry at 3:00 A.M. to be pulled out: "Is this the 5:32 or the 5:44?" "Tickets, please. Show your passport. Show your birth certificate."

To conductor: "You'll have to give us a note to prove to our wives we were on this train." "Say, we were held up—get it? We had a 'holdup.' "

I know I should have gone to church four times Christmas.

Negro in back of car: This ain't true. This ain't supposed to happen at Christmas.

GRIPES

One of the little girls: "I'm going to write to the company and say, 'Your service is definitely vulgar.' "

If there was any way we could shoot a railroad!

"Is one of the fifty-two vice-presidents of this road on this train?" "They're all home in bed." "They're ashamed to be seen."

Once a commuter pays for his ticket, that's all they care.

The people you can meet when a train is stuck like this! (Jesting)

Wake me up if anything interesting happens.

Blast this snow!

On suing the railroad: "The conductor would say it was an act of God." "I wish an act of God would get us home."

Gradually we became more and more group conscious and unified, and more resentful. We resented the fact that for a time at least the limiteds were passing us on the express track, while we were stalled. The commuters, we said, are the mainstay of the railroad (that's what *we* think!) and yet we weren't being given a thought. The railroad could at least have seen that we were supplied with coffee and sandwiches and taken to a warm place to wait. We were so close to Harmon—and yet so far—that a Diesel engine could have gone back and forth pulling out trains. Or we could have been removed to another train on another track. We even resented the brakemen and conductors, on whom we pinned some of the blame. At first they seemed indifferent or vague in their answers to our questions. "The brakeman's and conductor's delight," someone said, fallaciously, "double time overtime." But later we began to sympathize with them as obviously victims of the same accident. They were just as anxious as we to get home, we figured, and tired from their long day. One conductor lived in Brooklyn.

As a futile gesture, to relieve our gripes, we circulated a petition to send to the company to protest against the whole business and to ask for a refund of our fares. But in it we were careful to pay tribute to the train crew as courteous and deserving of commendation for trying to keep up our spirits. The petition was never sent. I still have it.

For a few days the "mass" effect of our experience lingered, as we related incidents and quoted wisecracks. On subsequent trips I looked closely at my fellow passengers to see if I could recognize any of my erstwhile partners in misery. But gradually we relapsed into our class differences and complacency and the callous monotony of commuting, secretly wishing, perhaps, for a renewal of the camaraderie without the crisis.

COMMUTER'S LAST RIDE [5]

Arthur Corbin is known far and near as a very nice chap. He's a lawn-mowing, hedge-trimming solid citizen—pillar of society type, and all that. He is the last man on earth who willfully would lead his fellow man astray. And so, with not a little perplexity, Mr. Corbin today was assaying his responsibility for the tipsy condition in which whole droves of his fellow commuters (lawn-mowing, hedge-trimming, equally solid citizens all) arrived at their homes last night.

Mr. Corbin was as innocent as the driven lamb, if that's the correct simile. True, it was in his honor that last night's 5:32 New Haven Railroad train out of Grand Central Station—normally a bone-dry run—had a bar car. True, his name figured in hundreds of spirited toasts. But he didn't plan it that way.

The only thing that Mr. Corbin planned was that last night's commutation should be his last one, after 31 years of riding the New Haven. Some days earlier, he had mentioned that fact casually to the folks with whom he plays bridge.

Because Mr. Corbin IS such a nice chap, a farewell party seemed in order. So a conspiratorial committee was formed.

The upshot was that when Mr. Corbin stepped aboard the 5:32 he found it gaudily decked out with flowers, and he was greeted with shouts of "Surprise! Surprise!" And there was this bar car. Normally the bar car rolls eastward on the 4:30 P.M. train. But last night, at the request of the committee, the railroad added it to the 5:32.

And so, at Darien, Westport, Fairfield and other outposts, the stillness was

[5] From "Dry Train Runs Wet for Farewell," by Allan Keller, New York *World-Telegram and Sun*, February 25, 1954, p. 3. Dateline: Westport, Conn., February 25. Copyright, 1954, by the New York World-Telegram and Sun.

shattered by offkey singing whenever the 5:32 came to a halt. And wives, long accustomed to greeting sober husbands, found themselves rounding up an extraordinarily jovial lot.

The honor guest is 74-years-old. He retired yesterday after 53 years as an automobile salesman. . . .

"SPRUCE MANOR," NEW YORK [6]

Twenty miles east of New York City as the New Haven Railroad flies sits a village I shall call Spruce Manor. The Boston Post Road, there, for the length of two blocks, becomes Main Street and on one side of that thundering thoroughfare are the grocery stores and the drug stores and the Village Spa where teen-agers gather of an afternoon to drink their cokes and speak their curious confidences. There one finds the shoe repairers and the dry cleaners and the second-hand stores which sell "antiques" and the stationery stores which dispense comic books to ten-year-olds and greeting cards and lending library masterpieces to their mothers. On the opposite side stand the bank, the Fire House, the Public Library. The rest of this town of perhaps four or five thousand people lies to the south and is bounded largely by Long Island Sound, curving protectively on three borders. The movie theater (dedicated to the showing of second-run, single-feature pictures) and the grade schools lie north, beyond the Post Road, and that is a source of worry to Spruce Manorites. They are always a little uneasy about the children, crossing, perhaps, before the lights are safely green. However, two excellent policemen— Mr. Crowley and Mr. Lang—station themselves at the intersections four times a day and so far there have been no accidents.

Spruce Manor in the spring and summer and fall is a pretty town, full of gardens and old elms. (There are few spruces but the village Council is considering planting a few on the station plaza, out of sheer patriotism.) In the winter, the houses reveal themselves as comfortable, well-kept, architecturally insignificant. Then one can see the town for what it is and has been since it left off being farm and woodland some sixty years ago—the epitome of Suburbia, not the country and certainly not the city. It is a commuter's town, the living center of a web which unrolls each morning as the men swing aboard the locals, and contracts again in the evening when they return. By day, with even the children pent in schools, it is a village of women. They trundle mobile baskets at the A & P, they sit under driers at the hairdressers, they sweep their porches and set out bulbs and stitch up slip-covers. Only on weekends does it become heterogeneous and lively, the parking places difficult to find.

Spruce Manor has no country club of its own, though devoted golfers have

[6] From "Suburbia: Of Thee I Sing," in *A Short Walk from the Station*, by Phyllis McGinley, pp. 9-16, 17-18, 20-22. Copyright, 1933, 1934, 1935, 1936, 1938, 1939, 1940, 1941, 1943, 1944, 1945, 1946, 1947, 1948, 1949, 1950, 1951, by Phyllis McGinley. New York: The Viking Press, Inc.

Drawing by Carl Rose from *Slightly Cooler in the Suburbs*, by C. B. Palmer (Garden City, New York, Doubleday & Company, Inc., 1950).

"Spruce Manor" is Larchmont, New York.

their choice of two or three not far away. It does have a small yacht club and a beach which can be used by anyone who rents or owns a house here. The village supports a little park with playground equipment and a counselor, where children, unattended by parents, can spend summer days if they have no more pressing engagements.

It is a town not wholly without traditions. Residents will point out the two-hundred-year-old Manor house, now a minor museum; and in the autumn they line the streets on a scheduled evening to watch the Volunteer Firemen parade. That is a fine occasion, with so many heads of households marching in their red blouses and white gloves, some with flaming helmets, some swinging lanterns, most of them genially out of step. There is a bigger parade on Memorial Day with more marchers than watchers and with the Catholic priest, the rabbi, and the Protestant ministers each delivering a short prayer when the paraders gather near the War Memorial. On the whole, however, outside of contributing generously to the Community Chest, Manorites are not addicted to municipal get-togethers.

No one is very poor here and not many families rich enough to be awesome. In fact, there is not much to distinguish Spruce Manor from any other of a thousand suburbs outside of New York City or San Francisco or Detroit or Chicago or even Stockholm, for that matter. Except for one thing. For some reason, Spruce Manor has become a sort of symbol to writers and reporters familiar only with its name or trivial aspects. It has become a symbol of all that is middle-class in the worst sense, of settled-downness or rootlessness, according to what the writer is trying to prove; of smug and prosperous mediocrity—or even, in more lurid novels, of lechery at the country club and Sunday morning hangovers.

. . . I have yet to read a book in which the suburban life was pictured as the good life or the commuter as a sympathetic figure. He is nearly as much a stock character as the old stage Irishman: the man who "spends his life riding to and from his wife," the eternal Babbitt who knows all about Buicks and nothing about Picasso, whose sanctuary is the club locker room, whose ideas spring ready-made from the illiberal newspapers. His wife plays politics at the P.T.A. and keeps up with the Joneses. Or—if the scene is more gilded and less respectable—the commuter is the high-powered advertising executive with a station wagon and an eye for the ladies, his wife a restless baggage given to too many cocktails in the afternoon.

* * * * *

. . . We came here from an expensive, inconvenient, moderately fashionable tenement in Manhattan. It was the period in our lives when everyone was moving somewhere. Farther uptown, farther downtown, across town to Sutton Place, to a half-dozen rural acres in Connecticut or New Jersey or even Vermont. But no one in our rather rarefied little group was thinking of moving to the suburbs except us. They were aghast that we could find anything appealing in the thought of a middle-class house on a middle-class street in a middle-class village full of middle-class people. That we were tired of town and hoped for children, that we couldn't afford both a city apartment and a farm, they put down as feeble excuses. To this day they cannot understand us. You see, they read the books. They even write them.

. . . As for [Spruce Manor's] being middle-class, what is wrong with acknowledging one's roots? And how free we are! Free of the city's noise, of its ubiquitous doormen, of the soot on the windowsill and the radio in the next apartment. We have released ourselves from the seasonal hegira to the mountains or the seashore. We have only one address, one house to keep supplied with paring knives and blankets. We are free from the snows that block the countryman's roads in winter and his electricity which always goes off in a thunderstorm. I do not insist that we are typical. There is nothing really typical about any of our friends and neighbors here, and therein lies my point. The true suburbanite needs to conform less than anyone else; much less than the gentleman farmer with his remodeled salt-box or than the determined cliff dweller with his necessity for living at the right address. In Spruce Manor all addresses are right. And since we are fairly numerous here, we need not fall back on the people nearest us for total companionship. There is not here, as in a small city away from truly urban centers, some particular family whose codes must be ours. And we could not keep up with the Joneses even if we wanted to, for we know many Joneses and they are all quite different people leading the most various lives.

The Albert Joneses spend their weekends sailing, the Bertram Joneses cultivate their delphinium, the Clarence Joneses—Clarence being a handy man with a cello—are enthusiastic about amateur chamber music. The David Joneses dote on bridge, but neither of the Ernest Joneses understands it and they prefer staying home of an evening so that Ernest Jones can carve his witty caricatures out of pieces of old fruit wood. We admire one another's gardens, applaud one another's sailing records; we are too busy to compete. So long as our clapboards are painted and our hedges decently trimmed, we have fulfilled our community obligations. We can live as anonymously as in a city or we can call half the village by their first names.

On our half-acre or three-quarters, we can raise enough tomatoes for our salads and assassinate enough beetles to satisfy the gardening urge. Or we can buy our vegetables at the store and put the whole place to lawn without feeling that we are neglecting our property. We can have privacy and shade

and the changing of the seasons and also the Joneses next door from whom to borrow a cup of sugar or a stepladder. Despite the novelists, the shadow of the Country Club rests lightly on us. Half of us wouldn't be found dead with a golf stick in our hands, and loathe Saturday dances. Few of us expect to be deliriously wealthy or world-famous or divorced. What we do expect is to pay off the mortgage and send our healthy children to good colleges.

For when I refer to life here, I think, of course, of living with children. Spruce Manor without children would be a paradox. The summer waters are full of them, gamboling like dolphins. The lanes are alive with them, the yards overflow with them, they possess the tennis courts and the skating pond and the vacant lots. Their roller skates wear down the asphalt and their bicycles make necessary the twenty-five mile speed limit. They converse interminably on the telephones and make rich the dentist and the pediatrician. Who claims that a child and a half is the American middle-class average? A nice medium Spruce Manor family runs to four or five and we count proudly, but not with amazement, the many solid households running to six, seven, eight, nine, even twelve. Our houses here are big and not new, most of them and there is a temptation to fill them up, let the *décor* fall where it may.

Besides, Spruce Manor seems designed by providence and town planning for the happiness of children. . . .

*   *   *   *   *

Spruce Manor is not Eden, of course. Our taxes are higher than we like and there is always that eight-eleven in the morning to be caught and we sometimes resent the necessity of rushing from a theater to a train on a weekday evening. But the taxes pay for our really excellent schools and for our garbage collections (so that the pails of orange peels need not stand in the halls overnight as ours did in the city) and for our water supply which does not give out every dry summer as it frequently does in the country. As for the theaters—they are twenty miles away and we don't get to them more than twice a month. But neither, I think, do many of our friends in town. The eight-eleven is rather a pleasant train, too, say the husbands; it gets them to work in thirty-four minutes and they read the papers restfully on the way.

*   *   *   *   *

Some of the ladies are no doubt painting their kitchens or a nursery; one of them is painting the portrait, on assignment, of a very distinguished personage. Some of them are nurses' aides and Red Cross workers and supporters of good causes. But all find time to be friends with their families and to meet the 5:32 five nights a week. They read something besides the newest historical novel, Braque is not unidentifiable to most of them, and their conversation is for the most part as agreeable as the tables they set. The tireless bridge players, the gossips, the women bored by their husbands live perhaps in our suburb, too. Let them. Our orbits need not cross.

And what of the husbands, industriously selling bonds or practicing law or editing magazines or looking through microscopes or managing offices in the city? Do they spend their evenings and their weekends in the gaudy bars of 52nd Street? Or are they the perennial householders, their lives a dreary round of taking down screens and mending drains? Well, screens they have always with them, and a man who is good around the house can spend happy hours with the plumbing even on a South Sea island. Some of them cut their own lawns and some of them try to break par and some of them sail their little boats all summer with their families for crew. Some of them are village trustees for nothing a year and some listen to symphonies and some think Milton Berle ought to be President. There is a scientist who plays wonderful bebop, and a corporation executive who has bought a big old house nearby and with his own hands is gradually tearing it apart and reshaping it nearer to his heart's desire. Some of them are passionate hedge-clippers and some read Plutarch for fun. But I do not know many—though there may be such—who either kiss their neighbors' wives behind doors or whose idea of sprightly talk is to tell you the plot of an old movie.

It is June, now, as I have said. This afternoon my daughters will come home from school with a crowd of their peers at their heels. They will eat up the cookies and drink up the ginger ale and go down for a swim at the beach if the water is warm enough, that beach which is only three blocks away and open to all Spruce Manor. They will go unattended by me, since they have been swimming since they were four and besides there are life guards and no big waves. . . . Presently it will be time for us to climb into our very old Studebaker—we are not car-proud in Spruce Manor—and meet the 5:32. That evening expedition is not vitally necessary, for a bus runs straight down our principal avenue from the station to the shore, and it meets all trains. But it is an event we enjoy. There is something delightfully ritualistic about the moment when the train pulls in and the men swing off, with the less sophisticated children running squealing to meet them. The women move over from the driver's seat, surrender the keys, and receive an absent-minded kiss. It is the sort of picture that wakes John Marquand screaming from his sleep. But, deluded people that we are, we do not realize how mediocre it all seems. We will eat our undistinguished meal, probably without even a cocktail to enliven it. We will drink our coffee at the table, not carry it into the living room; if a husband changes for dinner here it is into old spotty trousers and more comfortable shoes. The children will then go through the regular childhood routine—complain about their homework, grumble about going to bed, and finally accomplish both ordeals. Perhaps later the Gerard Joneses will drop in. We will talk a great deal of unimportant chatter and compare notes on food prices; we will also discuss the headlines and disagree. (Some of us in the Manor are Republicans, some are Democrats, a few lean plainly leftward. There are probably anti-Semites and anti-Catholics and even anti-Americans. Most of us are merely anti-antis.) We will all have one highball and the Joneses will leave early. Tomorrow and tomorrow and tomorrow the pattern will be repeated. This is Suburbia.

But I think that some day people will look back on our little intervals here, on our Spruce Manor way of life, as we now look back on the Currier and Ives kind of living, with nostalgia and respect. In a world of terrible extremes, it will stand out as the safe, important medium.

CHANGES ALONG PHILADELPHIA'S MAIN LINE [7]

Among the quiet valleys west of Philadelphia lies . . . the Main Line. It is an undefined region, five to ten miles wide, straddling the tracks of the Pennsylvania Railroad as it heads west for Pittsburgh. It may not be the only residential area named for a freight track, but here there is no wrong side of the tracks. It's all good, all fashionable, all exclusive.

The people of the Main Line prize stability, wealth and gracious living. Its well-to-do leaders have built a way of life that wins the envy of all who see it. All things considered, the Main Line represents suburban America at its best. The people are decent, the homes friendly, and the beauty of the land is something rare.

The region's reputation for glamour and glitter goes back to its golden era, the years from about 1900 to 1929, when the Main Line was one of the best-known social centers of the world. The great names of Philadelphia society, names rich in the lore of Pennsylvania history, clustered about the Main Line. The Cadwaladers, Cassatts, Chews, Biddles, Robertses and Drexels maintained a kind of court in their immense manor houses, and to it they grudgingly admitted wealthy newcomers like the Wideners (traction money), the Dorrances (Campbell's soups), the Strawbridges (department stores) and the Pews (oil and politics). Life in the golden era was just about perfect, if one had a lot of money. The winter was spent in Florida. In summer a few families moved to Newport, but most preferred the more sedate and rural life of Bar Harbor. Most families kept a city dwelling in Philadelphia's famed Rittenhouse Square. And the rest of the time they lived in their palaces along the Main Line. These massive and sprawling homes were fabulous. The Foerderer mansion was built in Spanish style, with fittings acquired from a Spanish cathedral. The Percival Roberts home, with its magnificent sunken gardens, resembled a French master-piece. The Gibson mansion was Gothic and seemed like a brooding castle surrounded by dark trees. The Brock home was Elizabethan, with cross-timbered overhangs. The old Griscom estate (now a Dorrance property) was Norman down to the smallest cobble in the courtyard. Even the railroad followed European models, announcing in 1879: "Some of our new stations are perfect little gems that look as if they were brought bodily over from the castles of the Rhine or the cottages of Switzerland."

But to the average Main Liner, English ways were the ones to be copied. Tea was a ritual with the ladies. Main Line males fancied the British derby and the Chesterfield coat. They liked to be outfitted by Jacob Reed's, where the trouser waist was high. One Jacob Reed tailor warned his customer: "I can make the trousers a bit more British, sir, but if I do, you'll strangle." They preferred

[7] From "The Main Line," by James A. Michener, *Holiday*, Vol. 7 (April 1950), No. 4, pp. 34-35, 37, 39, 43-44, 50-52, 54, 134. Copyright, 1950, by the Curtis Publishing Company. Philadelphia.

cricket to baseball, and the Merion Cricket Club, now famous for tennis and squash, originally specialized in the English sport. The Main Line's oldest college, Haverford, played no baseball until 1915, but sent a cricket team to England several times to play Eton and Harrow.

Many roads are called lanes, after the English fashion. When a collection of medium-priced houses was proposed for Love's Lane, there was objection until it was discovered that they would all look like English cottages. The most popular style of architecture for the great estate was always English—"It looks at home on the Main Line"—and the private schools and colleges of the area were built upon English models. The quiet pattern of life lived by nine tenths of the population had its inspiration in English country habits.

But the region's fame has usually rested upon its gaudier social fiestas. In the golden era the great houses saw a round of famous parties. When Mrs. George W. Childs Drexel entertained at Wootton, her lavish estate in Bryn Mawr, people came from Europe to attend. A dinner at Percival Roberts' might seat a hundred and fifty guests. Thousands of dollars were spent on lawn parties, and each year some baronial family would give a memorable dance at the Bellevue-Stratford with a make-believe Niagara Falls or a replica of Versailles.

Today the Main Line is changed. New Deal legislation has made the old way of life impossible, and few couples can amass enough money under present tax laws to maintain big estates. The old mansions of the Main Line are being torn down. The Brock establishment, with seven chimneys, leaded windows, timbered front, octagonal turret and confused architecture, has gone. Morris Clothier's immense Clairemont has been torn down to save taxes. J. Kearsley Mitchell's handsome mansion has been demolished. The show place of them all, Percival Roberts' palace, was demolished by the owner because from its windows he could see the tip of the smokestack of a newly installed public garbage incinerator. But the marvelous gardens with their French stairs remain, and in the evening shadows the Roberts ruins are majestic.

Instead of a huge pile of masonry costing millions, the Main Line aristocrat now prefers a $40,000 house; and in place of thirty servants he tries hard to find—and keep—one. Numerous families have followed the example of Mary K. Gibson, who has abandoned her millionaire father's castle to live most comfortably in the garage. Gate houses are especially popular, with their nine or ten convenient rooms.

A new pattern of aristocratic life has developed. When young couples entertain, they skip the soup and serve the food themselves. Families have two cars instead of seven. Men still like to buy their suits at Jacob Reed's, but instead of spending the entire summer at Bar Harbor, they are likely to go there for shorter vacations, with some of the young men flying up for week ends; others prefer the nearby Pocono Mountains. Years ago an ambitious family would have hesitated at the idea of sending a son to the University of Pennsylvania. Princeton was a must. But now scions of the old families attend Penn and live at home to cut expenses.

Daughters, too, go to college and take jobs. They say, "It's no fun to be just a débutante and stay in bed all morning if you haven't been to a dance the night before. All the boys work for a living and they won't go to parties except on week ends."

Today the Main Line has become the stronghold of the good, average citizen, and the change pleases most of its residents. As one of them explained it to me, "Certainly the rich families have been hard hit. But it's better for the community when we're all reasonably well off. Today we don't figure things with the millionaire in mind. We shoot for the man with his life insurance paid up and maybe a few thousands in the bank."

This average Main Liner makes considerably more than $100 a week, has a small inheritance and two children, lives in a home that cost more than $20,000, plays golf at the Merion Golf Club (where Bobby Jones completed his grand slam in 1930), knocks around such pleasant hostelries as the Covered Wagon or the Conestoga Mill on Saturday nights, drives a medium-priced car, sends his children to the best schools he can afford, sees to it that his daughter's wedding takes place in the fashionable Church of the Redeemer, in Bryn Mawr, votes Republican, and is proud of living on the Main Line.

For, even shorn of its old social glory, this community is still one of the most exclusive in the land. "Even in Alcoholics Anonymous," one native said proudly, "a man from a good Main Line family is known as carriage trade."

*   *   *   *   *

Along the Main Line, Lower Merion seems to be the choice community in which to live. It has rolling hills, plunging streams, a wide river, famous private schools, excellent colleges, spacious homes and a good group of citizens. It is one of the wealthiest townships in America and its public schools rank with the best.

The township lies right against Philadelphia. It contains only twenty-four square miles and about 48,000 people. It is composed of thirteen separate communities, none of which has its own government (though right in the middle of the township, engulfed on all sides, sits the town of Narberth, which governs itself and is not a part of Lower Merion).

The two best-known towns in the township are Bryn Mawr and Ardmore. Each name means "high hill," the former in Welsh and the latter in Gaelic, Ardmore having belatedly discovered that it had a spot some ten feet higher than Bryn Mawr's best.

Among the more exclusive new communities are Gladwyne and Penn Valley, especially the latter. Only families of some wealth can afford to buy land in Penn Valley, for restrictions are enforced both by custom and by law.

*   *   *   *   *

To catch the real flavor of the Main Line one must attend a meeting of a hunt club. The Radnor Hunt is perhaps the finest. Unlike clubs in some other parts of America, which drag a trail of anise seed along the ground, the Radnor chases live foxes. Its aristocratic leaders wear "pink" coats on special occasions, and ride across some of the most expensive real estate in the land, while other socialites tag along in rich tweeds that look stunning in the picture sections of the Sunday papers.

Life along the Main Line would be perfect if it were not for the constitutional disturbances that go with it. Having fled the strains of city life, the suburbanite's first interest is in insulating himself against all shock. He surrounds himself with men of his own thinking, those who take pride in land ownership, in club life and in restrained behavior. He becomes conservative, and this is especially true along the Main Line, where he has more to protect. He is apt to say, "We have good government out here because it's in the hands of the right people. You know, the Republicans."

The Main Line found it difficult to forgive one of its own privileged sons, George Earle, for becoming governor of Pennsylvania on a New Deal platform. That was something that just shouldn't have happened. "And he lived here too. He was one of us."

*   *   *   *   *

There is one quirk of the suburban mind that must be respected in Lower Merion. If you buy more than an acre of land, don't, for heaven's sake, call it a home or a farm; it's an estate. You have an estate wagon, an estate fence, an estate keeper, and you buy rhododendron of "estate size." In most American communities this attitude would seem pretentious, but on the Main Line it seems to grow naturally, planted there by the baronial families that ran the genuine blue-chip estates.

*   *   *   *   *

When the Paoli Local leaves Philadelphia at night, it carries with it much of the city's wealth. The fortunes of the Wideners, Cassatts and Reas were founded on profits from transportation routes. The Gibsons, Strawbridges, Dorrances and Clothiers made their money in trade. Editors, lawyers, brokers and even college professors earn their income in the city and spend it in the suburbs. They are the "daylight citizens" of Philadelphia, the group who do not pay their full share of its taxes nor help carry the burdens of its government.

Alarmists cry that if the flight of wealth to the suburbs continues, Philadelphia may one day become a ghost town. If the prediction should ever come true, the suburbs will have killed themselves, for suburban life is good only so long as the parent city is strong and vital. Few would be satisfied with Main Line life if there were no city theaters, libraries, orchestra, zoo, art museums and wholesale centers.

*   *   *   *   *

The next twenty years should tell the story of Philadelphia and its suburbs. If city operations can be streamlined, if taxes can be adjusted, and above all if suburban citizens continue to help govern the city of which they are actually a part, Philadelphia and its beautiful surroundings should both improve with age.

But there is an essential goodness in Main Line life, taken all by itself. When people across the world yearn for a home in America, they must often picture the middle-class home such as those along the Main Line. It is secure. It is quiet, clean, filled with modern gadgets. Children from this home go to fine schools, enjoy unusual benefits. There is a healthy social life, an enviable political efficiency. Justice keeps guard at every corner, and there remain opportunities for enterprise. It is a good life. That it is also wealthy, tightly organized, set in beauty, and jealously guarded pleases the solid citizen, and he is determined that it shall remain that way.

REVERSE COMMUTERS [8]

Reverse commuting came into its own in Westchester today when the New York Central added Train No. 465 to its Harlem Division schedule. Marking the line's recognition of a trend toward industrial dispersion from New York, the new train left Grand Central Terminal at 8:02 A.M. and reached here at 8:35.

. . . The 186 passengers on the Central's new train—sixteen came aboard at Mount Vernon—included men and women who had never commuted before. They were employes of the General Foods Corporation, which began moving here yesterday from mid-Manhattan.

The payload also included veteran commuters to whom No. 465 was just a way of getting to work two minutes earlier. . . .

And the three cars under Conductor T. J. Powers also carried: Lots of new or recent reverse commuters, mostly women, who loved the route to their jobs because "you breathe fresh air for a change." Others, mostly men, who did not love it quite so much because "you have to eat less for breakfast and watch the clock all the way." Still others who, having commuted to New York at other times in their lives, were in a position to compare the two processes.

*   *   *   *   *

"I think New Yorkers are much more easy-going in their commuting," [George S. Barth] summed up. "They're not so much in a rush as the people who come into New York."

Fred Schonert, a Brooklynite on his first commuting trip, had another slant. "I'm the kind of a fellow," he said, "who's always too early for everything. I'm usually forty-five minutes early in the office. So now I'll use up that time commuting and I won't have to get up any earlier anyway."

Five other neophytes sat three-and-two in facing seats and agreed with yawns and grimaces that they wished they had stayed in bed. "Confidentially," said one, an uncontradicted spokesman, "this stinks."

When the train arrived, there was a localized dispersal from the station. General Foods had buses lined up for its people. One woman edged through the crowd and asked rather grandly, "Where can I get a taxi?" Three men with a few minutes to kill sized up the town. One of them spoke a timeless paraphrase: "It's a nice place to visit," he said, "but I wouldn't live here for the world."

[8] From "Rail 'Switch' Aids New Commuters: Central Adds Train to Haul General Foods Employes Shifted to Westchester," by Milton Bracker, The New York Times, March 16, 1954, p. L-31. Copyright, 1954, by The New York Times, Inc. Dateline: White Plains, March 15, 1954.

XVI. Something to Sing About

For every phase of city life represented in this book—civic pride and local rivalry, hicks and greenhorns vs. city slickers, local characters (whether heroes or stereotypes), local legends and sagas (especially disasters), the gay and wicked city—there are songs, running the gamut from pathos to bathos. If the city produces more popular songs than folk songs, it is because the city is still too new. But the popular songs of today may become the folk songs of tomorrow. For the test of a folk song, after all, is its history and whether the people like it, no matter by whom or how it is written.

As the home of Tin Pan Alley, New York became the song maker not only for the city but for the nation and the world. "The best songs came from the gutter in those days," writes Edward B. Marks of his New York song-plugging experiences in the Nineties, when the city's "lowest dives" would make or break the latest popular song. As street lore is the heart of city lore, so street songs from children's game songs and chants to street cries, are the heart of city songs. Among the earliest city songs were "street ballads," often written and printed a few hours after the event, and hawked in the street like newspapers.

Songs about individual cities celebrate their charms and scenes and those of individual streets and neighborhoods. In the 1850s, J. Gairdner's "New York, Oh, What a Charming City," set the tone for innumerable nostalgic songs of the "take me back to the old home town" variety:

In Bowery, in Broadway, he rambled up and down,
Took by-way and odd-way, resolved to see the town;
And as he went, he sang this song, "Now, is it not a pity
I should have stayed away so long from such a charming city."

In the Library of Congress' collection of sheet music under the head of "Civic Songs" one finds such gems as "Atlanta, the Queen of Dixie Land," "The Beautiful Hills of Ann Arbor," "Atlantic City Is Calling You," "Beans, Beans, Beans (Boston's My Home Town)," "They Don't Know Brooklyn Like I Do," "Chicago, the Gem of the Shore," "Cleveland on Lake Erie's Beautiful Shores," "Corpus Christi, Texas, on the Bay," "Detroit, Always R'arin' to Go," "El Paso, Where Sunshine Spends the Winter," "Minneapolis Makes Good," and so on down the alphabet.

A list of "Songs about New York City" in the Music Division of the New York Public Library comprises 200 titles, forty-seven about Broadway alone. Among the Bowery songs one misses "I Put Him on the Cheese," which, according to Roy L. McCardell in "When the Bowery Was in Bloom," was heard only in McGurk's. "The popularity of this song was due to the fact that it was understood to be a recital of one of the earliest activities of the bouncer of this establishment, a merciless, abysmal brute whose talent accounted for his sobriquet of Eat-'Em-Up Jack McManus."

A fresh guy came in the restaurant
And ordered a kidney stew;
"And keep your fingers out," he said,
"And get on a hurry too!"

He was looking for trouble, he wanted a row,
    Says I, "You might say please;
Don't get gay with your sassy play
    Or I'll put you on the cheese!"

Chorus:

    "Kick his slats in!" cried the gang,
    And quickly gathered round.
    I'm always perlite, I'm a favor-ite,
    They wouldn't see me downed.
    The omnibus slipped me a pair of knucks,
    But I had no need of these;
    I gave him a swipe with a piece of lead pipe,
    And it put him on the cheese!

In the whole range of city songs, none are more characteristic than the "melting-pot" songs (often in dialect) dealing with the comic stereotypes of the "stage" Irishman, German, Italian and Negro. Often mere libels, however good-natured, these "immigrant" songs have their sympathetic and serious side, as in "No Irish Need Apply." Of all these "minority" songs, Negro songs, beginning with the "coon songs" (the urban equivalent of the older "darky" or plantation songs) and culminating in the blues, are both the most folkloristic and the most socially significant. In his autobiography, *Father of the Blues* (with Arna Bontemps, New York, 1942), W. C. Handy tells how much of his life in St. Louis went into the writing of the blues classic, "The St. Louis Blues."

First there was the picture I had of myself, broken, unshaven, wanting even a decent meal, and standing before the lighted saloon in St. Louis without a shirt under my frayed coat. . . . While occupied with my own miseries during that sojourn, I had seen a woman whose pain seemed even greater. She had tried to take the edge off her grief by heavy drinking, but it hadn't worked. Stumbling along the poorly lighted street, she muttered as she walked, "Ma man's got a heart like a rock cast in de sea."

Negro migration from the South to the cities of the North produced not only blues but "bad man" songs like "Bully of the Town," "Stagolee," and "Brady."

After he had been shot down in a saloon by Black Duncan with his gatling gun,

    Brady went to hell, lookin' mighty curious,
    The devil says, "Where you from?" "East St. Louis."
    "Well, pull off your coat and step this way,
    For I've been expecting you every day."

    When the girls heard Brady was dead
    They went up home and put on red.
    And come down town singing this song—
    "Brady's struttin' in hell with his Stetson on!"

The same urban conditions that produced "Brady"—migration and overcrowding, accompanied by police brutality—are still producing songs of homelessness and homesickness, like this Spanish song of present-day Puerto Ricans in New York City—a long and yet not so long way from the humor and pathos of "early miseries." (This is from a Spanish jukebox record in Tony Schwarz's *New York 19*, Folkways Album No. FP 58.)

I wouldn't change my hut, my *choza,* by the entire state
In this country of such a cold weather.
The Puerto Rico mountains—the birds sing there.
They sing from way down to up the peaks of the mountains.
I wouldn't change Puerto Rico by sixty New Yorks.

The country in which I was born—we're suffering many, many
    bad economic things.
Even though I feel terrible there,
In my country there are always flowers—
That is my paradise.
I wouldn't change Puerto Rico by sixty New Yorks!

I wouldn't change Caguas, a city in Puerto Rico, or San Juan,
By Albany, the capital of the whole state of New York.
To be a peasant, an *jíbaro,* is an honor.
Even though I have to go through a number of things,
I wouldn't change Puerto Rico by five hundred New Yorks!

I wouldn't change Puerto Rican chickens by frozen chickens in
    the ice boxes here.
When I saw the snow coming down like coconut flakes from heaven,
I was crazy seeing that kind of stuff coming down.
My soul was very disconsolate.
I wouldn't change Puerto Rico by four thousand New Yorks!

PATRIOTIC DIGGERS [1]

Johnny Bull, beware! keep at your proper distance,
Else we'll make you stare at our firm resistance.
Let alone the lads who are freedom tasting;
Recollect our dads gave you once a basting.

Chorus:

Pickaxe, shovel, spade, crowbar, hoe, and barrow,
Better not invade; Yankees have the marrow.

To protect our rights 'gainst your flints and triggers,
See on yonder heights our patriotic diggers.
Men of every age, color, rank, profession,
Ardently engaged, labor in succession.

[1] Text from *The Rough and Ready Songster,* pp. 195-196. (Copyright date established by the New York Public Library as 1848[?]) New York and St. Louis: Nafis and Cornish, Publisher.

Tune from *Early American Ballads,* sung by John and Lucy Allison with choral accompaniment, Record No. 533A, Keynote Album K-102. New York: Keynote Recordings, Incorporated.

Transcribed by Evelyn Modoi.

According to a note in the clipping file of the Music Division of the New York Public Library, this song, by Samuel Woodworth, author of *The Old Oaken Bucket* and *The Hunters of Kentucky,* was copyrighted in 1814 and was widely sold in the trenches that were dug in defense of the cities of Baltimore and New York against threatened invasion by the British fleet. The tune is that of *Great Way Off at Sea,* or *Rob and Joan.*

According to the Allisons' note, this is "one of the nation's first labor songs," written at a time when "labor was in great demand and the trades flourished," when "Americans began to realize the vastness of their empire and sang bragging songs," when "new frontiers were rapidly being pushed forth, expansion was taking place, towns were rising, cities growing."

Johnny Bull, beware! keep at your proper distance

Else we'll make you stare at our firm resistance.

Let alone the lads who are freedom tasting;

Recollect our dads gave you once a basting.

Chorus:

Pickaxe, shovel, spade, crowbar, hoe, and barrow,

Better not invade; Yankees have the marrow.

Grandeur leaves her towers, poverty her hovel,
Here to join their powers with the hoe and shovel;
Here the Merchant toils with the patriotic Sawyer,
There the Laborer smiles, near him sweats the Lawyer.

Here the Mason builds freedom's shrine of glory,
While the Painter gilds the immortal story;
Blacksmiths catch the flame, Grocers feel the spirit.
Printers share the fame and record their merit.

Scholars leave their schools with their patriotic Teachers,
Farmers seize their tools, headed by their Preachers.
How they break the soil; Brewers, Butchers, Bakers;
Here the Doctors toil, there the Undertakers.

Bright Apollo's sons leave their pipe and tabor,
Mid the roar of guns, join the martial labor;
Round the embattled plain in sweet concord rally,
And in Freedom's strain sing the foe's finale.

Plumbers, Founders, Dyers, Tinmen, Turners, Shavers,
Sweepers, Clerks, and Criers, Jewelers, Engravers,
Clothiers, Drapers, Players, Cartmen, Hatters, Tailors,
Gaugers, Sealers, Weighers, Carpenters, and Sailors.

Better not invade; recollect the spirit
Which our dads displayed and their sons inherit;
If you still advance, friendly caution slighting,
You may get by chance a bellyful of fighting.

"NO IRISH NEED APPLY" [2]

I'm a dacint boy, just landed from the town of Ballyfad;
I want a situation—yis, and want it mighty bad.
[I have seen employment advertised—" 'Tis just the thing," says I;]
But the dirty spalpeen ended with—"No Irish need apply."

I'm a da - cint boy, just land - ed from the
town of Bal - ly- fad; I want a sit - u - a - tion --yis, and
want it might-y bad. I have seen em- ploy-mint ad- ver-tised, "Tis
just the thing," says I; But the dir- ty spal-peen end- ed with "No
I-rish need ap-ply." "Whoo!" says I, "but that's an in-sult, though to
get the place I'll try"; So I wint to see the blag-gard with his "No
Chorus
I-rish need ap- ply." Some do count it a mis- for-tune, to be
christ - ened Pat or Dan, But to
me it is an hon-or to be born an I - rish-man!

[2] An original song by John F. Poole. From *Tony Pastor's New Irish Comic Songster*, pp.
5-6. New York: Tony Pastor, 1865.
Written for and sung with immense success by the great Comic Vocalist of the age,
Tony Pastor.
Tune from *People's Songs*, Vol. 3 (May 1948), No. 4, p. 5. Copyright, 1948, by
People's Songs, Inc. New York.

"Whoo!" says I, "but that's an insult—though to get the place I'll try";
So I wint to see the blaggard with [his] "No Irish need apply."

[*Chorus:*

Some count it a misfortune to be christened Pat or Dan,
But to me it is an honor to be born an Irishman!]

I started off to find the house, I got it mighty soon;
There I found the ould chap saited—he was reading the *Tribune.*
I tould him what I came for, whin he in a rage did fly:
"No!" says he, "you are a Paddy; and no Irish need apply."
    Thin I felt my dandher rising, and I'd like to black his eye—
    To tell an Irish gintleman, "No Irish need apply."

I couldn't stand it longer, so a hoult of him I took,
And I gave him such a welting as he'd get at Donnybrook.
He hollered, "Millia murther!" and to get away did try,
And swore he'd never write again, "No Irish need apply."
    He made a big apology, I bid him then good-by—
    Saying, "When next you want a bating, add, 'No Irish need apply.'"

Sure I've heard that in America it always is the plan
That an Irishman is just as good as any other man:
A home and hospitality they never will deny
The stranger here, or ever say, "No Irish need apply."
    But some black sheep are in the flock—a dirty lot, say I;
    A dacint man will never write, "No Irish need apply."

Sure Paddy's heart is in his hand, as all the world does know;
His praties and his whisky he will share with friend or foe;
His door is always open to the stranger passing by;
He never thinks of saying, "None but Irish may apply."
    And in Columbia's history his name is ranking high;
    Thin the divil take the knaves that write, "No Irish need apply."

Ould Ireland on the battle-field a lasting fame has made;
We all have heard of Meagher's men, and Corcoran's brigade.
Though fools may flout and bigots rave, and fanatics may cry,
Yet whin they want good fighting-men, the Irish may apply.
    And whin for freedom and the right they raise the battlecry,
    Thin the rebel ranks begin to think no Irish need apply.

THE LOYAL BOSTON MAN [3]

There was a man from Boston, Bostonian through and through,
Who just believed in Boston, as Boston people do;
And he so much loved Boston, his heart was filled full of pain
When sent from dear old Boston down to the State of Maine.
He landed far from Boston, and then he looked all around,
How different from Boston, this rough and rocky ground;
It was so unlike Boston, he couldn't call up a smile,
Away from Boston Common at least a hundred mile.

[3] Words by Charles F. Pidgin. Music by Louis Well. Copyright, 1891, by Charles F. Pidgin. From *Delaney's Collection of Songs*, No. 1, p. 2. New York: William W. Delaney, April 1892. Sung with great success by Miss Maggie Fielding.

Chorus:

Yes, 'tis Boston, 'tis Boston, 'round which the world revolves,
    Yes, 'tis Boston, 'tis Boston, where pork and beans are grub;
Yes, 'tis Boston, 'tis Boston, that one to leave resolves,
    But, no! he cannot do it, he cannot quit the Hub.
Because, when far away from Boston, no Boston joys I see,
Because the Boston music, Boston sights and Boston ways suit me;
Because the Boston culture, cranks, east winds, to me they all are prime,
Because 'tis Boston, Boston first and last, and Boston all the time.

He struck the supper table, 'twas not at all Boston style,
He'd not be false to Boston and taste such cooking vile;
For pork and beans called loudly, Bostonian bill-of-fare,
But as it was not Boston, no Boston beans were there.
No restaurants like Boston's, no Music Hall, beer, and 'pops,'
No musty ale and lobster, no Parkses' mutton chops;
No chance to sit when drinking, they had only open bars,
No Boston German bands and no Boston open cars.

He thought of Boston science, aesthetical Boston things,
The Boston angel maid, who can paint, and writes and sings;
Oh anything from Boston to pass such a night away,
Till nature's sun greets Boston in Boston's beauty bay.
No Boston nap could get, for the silence was thick and dense,
And so this Boston man went to roost upon a fence;
Not e'en a Boston newsboy to cheer him the livelong night,
With Erral, Globe, and Rekkid, to yell till morning light.

Next morning went to walk, with a hope that he'd something meet,
There was no Boston sidewalk, no kind of Boston street;
He wished to climb a mountain, but how he did not know,
No Boston elevator, and so he did not go.
No kind of Boston meeting, no Socialists with complaints,
To advocate that tramps and the scamps should share with saints;
He found no Boston pictures to cheer up his Boston heart,
Though nature pleases some, he was sound on Boston art.

No Boston man could stand it, with Boston so far away,
When Boston folks love Boston, in Boston they should stay;
He asked the road to Boston, the Boston road they did show,
And murm'ring 'Boston, Boston!' to Boston he did go.
Oh, Boston, Boston, Boston, thy children all love thee so,
They would not go to heaven, such earthly joys they know;
But if they go, they'll take Beacon street and the State House dome,
To make celestial Boston like Boston left at home.

HICKS AND CITY SLICKERS [4]

I. Rural Sentiment

The versatile [Harry] Von Tilzer also left his mark on the rural type
of song. Early in his career he composed a piece called *Where the Morning*

[4] From *Read 'Em and Weep*, The Songs You Forgot to Remember, by Sigmund Spaeth, pp. 237-238, 255-258. Copyright, 1926, by Doubleday, Page & Company. New York: Arco Publishing Company, Inc., 1945.

Glories Twine Around the Door, but did nothing with it until one day Howard Graham, brother of the composer of *Two Little Girls in Blue,* brought him a lyric called, *When the Harvest Days Are Over, Jessie Dear.* Von Tilzer bought this outright for the sake of the title alone and adapted it to the melody which he already had for the Morning Glory song. Later he gave this a new tune of its own, and used it as a follow-up. A third use of the idea appeared under the title *When the Goldenrod Is Waving, Annie, Dear,* and, as usual, there were imitations in plenty after the public taste for the rural had been thoroughly established.

Down on the Farm was another successful paean of agriculture, which found a war-time echo in *How you gonna keep 'em down on the Farm, after they've seen Paree?* There were various other "want to go back" songs, of hazy geography, one of which rhymed "wish again" with Michigan." (*My Old New Hampshire Home* was really the first great hit of this type, but Von Tilzer sold this outright for a pittance.)

II. RUBE SONGS

In addition to the steady stream of sentimentality about the advantages of living on a farm, fostered by song-writers who live in cities, there has been a significant school of rural realism in which the "rube" is given a consistent dialect and a naive philosophy comparable with that of the more widely exploited Negro. The stock farmer song is still *Wal, I Swan* (or *Ebenezer Frye*), by Benjamin Hapgood Burt, published by the Witmarks in 1907, and in constant demand both as a solo and as a rural quartet number. The interpretation is traditionally in a high-pitched, nasal voice, with a facial expression indicating toothlessness:

WAL, I SWAN! [5]

I run the old mill over here to Reubensville,
    My name's Joshua Ebenezer Frye.
I know a thing or two, you bet your neck I do,
    They don't ketch me for I'm too darn sly.
I've seen Bunco men, allus got the best o' them,
    Once I met a couple on the Boston train.
They says, "How be you!" I says, "That'll do!
    Travel right along with your darn skin game."

Chorus:

Wal, I swan! I mus' be gittin' on!
    Giddap, Napoleon! it looks like rain.
Wal, I'll be switched! the hay ain't pitched.
    Come in when you're over to the farm again.

I drove the old mare over to the County Fair,
    Took first prize on a load o' summersquash.
Stopped at the cider mill coming over by the hill,
    Come home "tighter" than a drum, by gosh!

[5] Copyright, 1907, by M. Witmark & Sons. Copyright renewed. Reprinted by permission.

I was so durn full I give away the old bull,
　Dropped both my reins clean out on the fill.
Got hum so darn late couldn't find the barn gate.
　Ma says, "Joshua, 'tain't possibil."

We had a big show here 'bout a week ago,
　Pitched up a tent by the old mill dam.
Ma says, "Let's go in to the sideshow,
　Jus' take a look at the tattooed man."
I see a cuss look sharp at my pocketbook,
　Says, "Gimme two tens for a five."
I says, "You durn fool! I be the constabule!
　Now you're arrested sure as yer 'live.[6]

I drove the old bay into town yesterday,
　Hitched by the track to the railroad fence.
Tied her good and strong, but a train came along,
　And I ain't seen the "hoss" or the wagin sense.
Had to foot it home, so I started off alone,
　When a man says "Hurry! yer barn's on fire."
But I had the key in my pocket, you see,
　So I knew that the cuss was a fool or a liar.

My son Joshua went to Philadelphia,
　He wouldn't do a day's work if he could.
Smoked cigarettes too, way the city folks do.
　What he's a-coming to, ain't no good.
He didn't give a darn 'bout stayin' on the farm,
　Keeps writin' hum he's a-doin' right well.
It seems sort of funny that he's allus out o' money,
　And Ma says the boy's up to some kind o' hell.

Miss Katharine Lane, who, after years of urbanizing, is still a country mouse at heart, contributes from an amazing memory this delightful reminiscence of the days when lightning-rods were lightning rods:

I'm a jolly old farmer, Ben Hastings is my name,
I come way down from Skowhicken, Maine.

Got forty acres of well-tilled land,
A barn full of hay and a bank full of sand.

Forty head of cattle and one big shoat,
Ten head of horses and a billy-goat.

Out in the garden, pulling up sod,
Along come a lady with a lightnin'-rod.

Slicker than a mink, quicker than a mouse,
Wanted to put the lightnin'-rod over our house.

"Put it all over, I don't care."
She put it all over, I dee-clare.

Five hundred dollars was her fee.
Sez I, "The house don't belong to me!"

[6] On the third chorus sing, "I'll be durned, the butter ain't churned."

MICHAEL ROY [7]

In Brooklyn city there lived a maid,
    And she was known to fame;
Her mother's name was Mari Ann,
    And hers was Mari Jane;
And ev'ry Saturday morning
    She used to go over the river,
And went to market where she sold eggs,
    And sassages, likewise liver.

[7] From *Heart Songs,* Dear to the American People and by Them Contributed in the Search for Treasured Songs Initiated by the *National Magazine,* [compiled by Joe Mitchell Chapple,] pp. 408-409. Copyright, 1909, by the Chapple Publishing Company, Ltd. Boston.

Chorus:

> For oh! for oh!
> He was my darling boy,
> [*Shouted*] FOR he was the lad with the auburn hair
> And his name was Michael Roy.

She fell in love with a charcoal man,
McCloskey was his name;
His fighting weight was seven stone ten,
And he loved sweet Mari Jane;
He took her to ride in his charcoal cart,
On a fine St. Patrick's day,
But the donkey took fright at a Jersey man,
And started and ran away.

McCloskey shouted and hollered in vain,
For the donkey wouldn't stop,
And he threw Mari Jane right over his head,
Right into a policy shop;
When McCloskey saw that terrible sight,
His heart it was moved with pity,
So he stabbed the donkey with a bit of charcoal,
And started for Salt Lake City.

THE SPIELERS [8]

I'll sing about some nobby girls I met the other night,
Who are very fond of dancing; in it they take delight.
They go to parties and soirees, and almost every ball;
You're sure to find the "spielers" there who take the shine of all.

Chorus:

> Graceful and so charming, they glide along so neat,
> Enchanted by the music, they time their busy feet.
> Their merry, ringing laughter, their faces with pleasure beam;
> While dancing in the mazy waltz the "spielers" reign supreme.

They dance the lancers and glide waltz, Mazourka and quadrille,
Polka and Virginia reel, it seems they can't keep still.
They're on the floor at every dance, all night they're sure to stay,
And when the dawn comes peeping in, they go home at break of day.

THE BABIES ON OUR BLOCK [9]

In the original "Mulligan Guard Ball" was . . . one of the best-loved
Harrigan and Hart songs, *The Babies on Our Block*, a forerunner of *The Sidewalks of New York* and all its tribe, with some actual quotations from old Irish
tunes. . . .

[8] By J. L. Feeney, to the tune of "Sweet Forget-Me-Not." From *Lost Chords*, The
Diverting Story of American Popular Song, by Douglas Gilbert, pp. 166-167. Copyright,
1942, by Douglas Gilbert. Garden City, New York: Doubleday & Company, Inc.
[9] From *Read 'Em and Weep*, The Songs You Forgot to Remember, by Sigmund Spaeth,
pp. 131-132. Copyright, 1926, by Doubleday, Page & Company. New York: Arco Publishing Company, Inc., 1945.
Copyright, 1879, by Wm. A. Pond & Co.

THE BABIES ON OUR BLOCK.

SONG AND CHORUS.

Words by ED. HARRIGAN.   Music by DAVE BRAHAM.

1. If you want for in-for-ma-tion, Or in need of mer-ri-ment, Come o-ver with me so-cial-ly To Murphy's ten-e-ment; He owns a row of hous-es In the First ward, near the dock, Where Ireland's rep-re-sent-ed By the Ba-bies on our Block. There's the Pha-lens and the Wha-lens From the sweet Dun-och-a-dee, They are sit-ting on the rail-ings With their chil-dren on their knee, All gos-sip-ing and talk-ing With their neigh-bors in a flock, Singing "Lit-tle Sal-ly Waters," With the Ba-bies on our Block. Oh, Lit-tle Sal-ly Wa-ters Sit-ting in the sun, A cry-ing and weep-ing for a young man; Oh, rise, Sal-ly, rise, Wipe your eye out with your frock; That's sung by the Ba-bies a-liv-ing on our Block.

2. Of a warm day in the sum-mer, When the breeze blows off the sea, A hundred thousand chil-der-en Lay on the Bat-ter-y; They come from Murphy's build-ing,—Oh, their noise would stop a clock! Oh there's no peram-bula-to-ry With the Ba-bies on our Block. There's the Clea-rys and the Lea-rys From the sweet Black wa-ter side, They are lay-ing on the Bat-t'ry And they're gaz-ing at the tide; All roy-al blood and no-ble, All of Dan O'Con-nell's stock, Singing "Grav-el, Green-y Grav-el," With the Ba-bies on our Block. Oh, Grav-el, Greeny Grav-el, How green the grass-es grow, For all the pret-ty fair young maidens that I see; Oh, "Green Grav-el, Green," Wipe your eye out with your frock; That's sung by the Ba-bies a-liv-ing on our Block.

3. It's good-morn-ing to you, landlord; Come, now how are you to-day? When Patrick Mur-phy, Es-qui-re, Comes down the al-ley way, With his shi-ny silk-en beav-er, He's as sol-id as a rock, The en-vy of the neighbors' boys A-liv-ing off our Block. There's the Bran-nons and the Gan-nons, Far down and Connaught men, Quite ea-sy with the shov-el And so han-dy with the pen; All neigh-bor-ly and friend-ly, With re-la-tions by the flock, Singing "Lit-tle Sal-ly Waters," With the Ba-bies on our Block. Oh, Lit-tle Sal-ly Wa-ters Sit-ting in the sun, A cry-ing and weep-ing for a young man, Oh, rise, Sal-ly, rise, Wipe your eye out with your frock; That's sung by the Ba-bies a-liv-ing on our Block.

If you want for information, or in need of merriment,
Come over with me socially to Murphy's tenement;
He owns a row of houses in the First Ward, near the dock,
Where Ireland's represented by the Babies on our Block.
There's the Phalens and the Whalens from the Sweet Dunochadee,
They are sitting on the railings with their children on their knee,
All gossiping and talking with their neighbors in a flock
Singing, "Little Sally Waters," with the Babies on our Block.
Oh, Little Sally Waters, sitting in the sun,
A-crying and weeping for a young man;
Oh, rise, Sally, rise, wipe your eye out with your frock;
That's sung by the Babies a-living on our Block.

Of a warm day in the summer, when the breeze blows off the sea
A hundred thousand children lay on the Battery;
They come from Murphy's building, oh, their noise would stop a clock!
Oh there's no perambulatory, with the Babies on our Block.
There's the Clearys and the Learys from the sweet Black Water side,
They are laying on the Battery and they're gazing at the tide;
All royal blood and noble, all of Dan O'Connell's stock,
Singing, "Gravel, greeny Gravel," with the Babies on our Block.
Oh, Gravel, Greeny Gravel, how green the grasses grow,
For all the pretty fair young maidens that I see;
Oh, "Green Gravel Green," wipe your eye out with your frock;
That's sung by the Babies a-living on our Block.

It's good morning to you, landlord; come, now, how are you to-day?
When Patrick Murphy, Esquire, comes down the alley way,
With his shiny silken beaver, he's as solid as a rock,
The envy of the neighbors' boys a-living off our Block.
There's the Brannons and the Gannons, far-down and Connaught men,
Quite easy with the shovel and so handy with the pen;
All neighborly and friendly, with relations by the block,
Singing "Little Sally Waters," with the Babies on our Block.
Oh, Little Sally Waters, sitting in the sun,
A-crying and weeping for a young man,
Oh, rise, Sally, rise, wipe your eye out with your frock;
That's sung by the Babies a-living on our Block.

NEW YORK CHILDREN'S STREET RHYMES AND SONGS [10]

Down in the meadow where the green grass grows,
There sat Glory along the road,
She sang, and she sang, and she sang so sweet,
Along came a fellow and kissed her on the cheek.

Oh, Glory, oh, Glory, you ought to be ashamed
To marry a fellow without a name!
When you are sick, he'll put you to bed,
Call for the doctor before you are dead!

In comes the doctor, in comes the nurse.
In comes the priest with a high, high hat.
Out goes the doctor, out goes the nurse,
Out goes the priest with a high, high hat.

[10] By Fred Rolland. From *New Masses*, Vol. XXVII (May 10, 1938), No. 7, Section Two, p. 109. Copyright, 1938, by Weekly Masses Co., Inc. New York.

Old Aunt Marie [Maria], she jumped into the fire.
The fire was so hot, she jumped into the pot.
The pot was so black, she jumped into the crack.
The crack was so narrow, she jumped into the marrow.
The marrow was so rotten, she jumped into the cotton.
The cotton was so white, she stayed there all night.

Minnie and a Minnie and a hot-cha-cha!
Minnie kissed a fellow in a Broadway car.
I'll tell Ma, you'll tell Pa.
Minnie and a hot-cha-cha!

Eeny, meeny, mony, mike.
New York subway strike.
Have it, frost it.
Ack-a-wack a-wee woe wack!

Nine o'clock is striking.
Mother, may I go out?
The butcher boy is waiting
For to take me out.
I'd rather kiss the butcher boy
On the second floor
Than kiss the ice man
Behind the kitchen door.

Kiss me cute,
Kiss me cunning,
Kiss me quick,
My mommie's coming!

Brass shines, so does tin;
The way I love you is a sin.

The Brooklyn girls are tough,
The Brooklyn girls are smart,
But it takes a New York girl
To break a fellow's heart!

House to let,
Inquire within.
A lady got put out
For drinking gin.
If she promises
To drink no more,
Here's the key
To Mary's door!

F and K is out on strike.
We will picket and we'll shout.
Don't buy! Don't buy!
Don't believe the bosses' lies!
Don't buy scab merchandise!
Scabbing is an awful sin.
Help us fight and we will win!

I won't go to Macy's any more, more, more!
I won't go to Macy's any more, more, more!
There's a big fat policeman at the door, door, door!
He will squeeze me like a lemon.
A chalachke zol em nehmen.
I won't go to Macy's any more, more, more!

My mother, your mother live across the way,
514 East Broadway.
Every night they have a fight,
And this is what they say:
Your old man is a dirty old man.
He washes his face with the frying pan.
He combs his hair with the leg of a chair.
Your old man is a dirty old man!

Gypsy, gypsy lives in a tent!
Gypsy, gypsy couldn't pay rent!
She borrowed one, she borrowed two,
And out goes Y-O-U!

One, two, three, four,
Charlie Chaplin went to war.
When the war began to fight,
Charlie Chaplin said, "Good night!"

Oi sweet mamma! Oi sweet mamma!
I'd like to see your nightie next to my pajama.
Now don't get excited, don't get red!
I mean on the clothes-line and not in bed.

STREET CRIES OF NEW YORK CITY [11]

With the passing of the street cry recently forbidden by Commissioner
Bingham's order for the suppression of unnecessary noises New York has lost

[11] "Street Cries Set to Music—Sounds Henceforth Forbidden in New York—Passing of
the Noises That for More than a Century Have Individualized the Trades of the Street
Venders—Each with a Character of Its Own." *The Sun*, New York, Sunday, September
20, 1908, Second Section, p. 3, Vol. LXXVI, No. 20. Copyright, 1908, by The Sun
Printing and Publishing Association.

one of the familiar activities of a bustling city, the thing which for more than a century has individualized its lower strata of commercialism.

Irrespective of conjecture as to the ultimate fate of the street venders and their calling, the fact remains that in the relegation to oblivion of their various methods of attracting attention to their wares and pursuits a quaint gamut has been wiped off the map of modern musical chaos. Beginning with the ole clo' man and proceeding down the line to the huckster and the cutlery grinder, it is remarkable to observe how each has characterized his trade with a peculiarly different cry.

In the category of at least threescore of these merchants of the lesser world no one cry has been duplicated, and many of those familiar with their odd sounds have never erred in a necessary distinction. Thus, the cry of the banana man in bringing the housewife to the door has never deceived her into answering the shriek of the umbrella mender; nor has the bell of the scissors grinder ever misled the maid into bringing a bundle of rags to the junkman's jingle.

Possibly the most varying sounds have been those of the vegetable huckster, for not infrequently he invades the territory of other pedlers of his kind, and combining his wares with those of his rivals he often originates a cry. Thus we have had a series of cacophonies strung out in nasal cadences with no general significance excepting that a combination of fruits and vegetables is offered:

'Ta-toes!   Peach-es!   'N cents a bask- et!

One would naturally suppose that in the spontaneity of the street cry, particularly in a given number of syllables, there would be a repetition of tones, in other words that a number of persons singing a musical phrase bearing the same number of notes would render similar melodies in part. But in three distinct instances in which venders were exploiting their calling none infringed upon the other's artificial or extemporaneous music. The following example demonstrates this peculiarity. In the following cry there is an original strain:

Um - brel-las to mend!

The inflection is upon the second syllable. In the second cry, "Kettles to Mend" there is a sonorous tune of weird fibre entirely unlike the preceding melody, with an emphasis upon the last word:

Ket-tles to mend!   Ket-tles to mend!

The chair mender has also an entirely different vocality. Neither is there any diatonic resemblance to those above named, the first syllable of his cry being slurred in expression, as follows:

Chairs to mend! Chairs to mend!

How many of us are there who in the late summer and early fall will miss the welcome yell of the hot corn man! His is a musical cry. In it he endeavors to depict as nearly as possible a luscious suggestion of the steaming grain he offers by a diapason of sounds that please the mind and aim to tickle the palate.

That he often succeeds is also true, for frequently at a late hour windows are hoisted and a coin is dropped into the outstretched palm containing the golden buttered vegetable. There is also a tinge of poetry in the methods of his extending it for sale, as is seen in the improvised verse of the "darky":

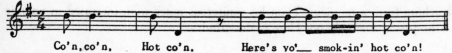

Co'n, co'n. Hot co'n. Here's yo'___ smok-in' hot co'n!

The barking dog and the shrill whistle of the peanut roaster, two disturbances comprised in the police ukase, lack every element of music. Possibly they have

THE
NEW-YORK CRIES,
IN RHYME.

Stereotyped by James Conner, New-York.

NEW-YORK:
PRINTED & SOLD BY MAHLON DAY,
AT THE NEW JUVENILE BOOK-
STORE, NO. 376, PEARL-
STREET.

HOT-CORN!

SCISSORS to GRIND!

LOCKS OR KEYS.

been foredoomed on this account. At any rate they are repellent on account of their monotony; and it is a coincidence that the bark of the mongrel is never novel, in that the similarity of rhythm with each restive canine is ever the same. Who has ever heard a different explosion in the midnight than this?

bow, bow,   bow, bow, bow, bow,   bow, bow,   wow!

A sepulchral call familiar to all, because of its guttural sonorousness, which also will no longer echo through the side streets is that of the broom man. He was wont to stroll along laden down with the household articles about his neck, arms, shoulders and head. At first hark one would imagine the tombs were belching forth a requiem. Then his soniferous notes were increased in volume as he passed sombrely on. Here is the grind:

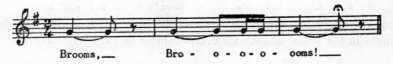

Brooms, —   Bro - o - o - o - ooms! —

At this juncture the gloom is partly dispelled by the tintinnabulating sound. It is the bell of the scissors grinder. The nasal abnormity which follows is an abomination, of course, but it is refreshing after the groans of its predecessor. The whirr of the grindstone is also a relief, although to some this sound grates upon the nerves like a rasping file upon metal. Still, the knife sharpener merrily paddles his feet while you sigh, and his cry rings thus:

Scis-sors to grind!   Scis-so- so- o- r-s to grind!

The line-up man, known as the backyard fiend, who is included in the forbidden category, and who is possibly the greatest invader upon rest and quiet, has the prerequisites in his yell of a genuinely Satanic sputterer. With ropes and hooks thrown over his shoulder he gains access into courts and areaways where the boldest intruder would fear to tread.

His temerity is only equaled by the gruelling discordances of his notes, and his tenacity has no counterpart. Incessantly this shout rings out, the musical quality of which is drowned in flat monotones, here and there relieved by a staccato exclamation:

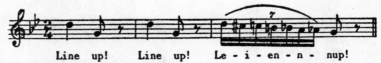

Line up!   Line up!   Le - i - en - n - nup!

Tugboat whistles have long been a source of discontent, and while these have been restricted in a measure by the new law it is unreasonable to suppose that they can ever be entirely repressed. This also applies to the toot and the chug

of the automobile. Neither of these possesses the least semblance to music, either
to soothe the savage breast or a policeman's heart!

Probably the most melodious euphony of any of the modern street cries that
have been suppressed has been that of the swarthy young banana pedler. In a
little handcart loaded down with the yellow fruit hidden in bunches beneath
layers of new weed, his cry, as he peers into basement windows, was not un-
musical and sometimes pleasant:

The allegation that the cry of the ole clo' man is not conducive to unrest may
have a few votaries, but these are in the minority, for while the fact exists that
the throat emittances from these collectors of discarded wearing apparel may not
be as earsplitting as those of some of their itinerant brethren, they possess about
as much melody as a hen's cackle. Noted strictly in musical writing the ole clo'
man's exhortation would read as follows:

Among other street cries prohibited under the new regime are those of the
shoe laces and suspenders men, the kindling wood man, the oyster and fish
pedler, the melon man and the strolling bootblack. The "wuxtra" newspaper
fiend is also a thing of the past. The assignment to obscurity of these nerve
destroying elements is a boon to many who welcome the city's progressive tenets
and its resultant quietude, and in another decade their extinction will have
become a memory.

"COME ON DOWN AND GATHER ROUND" [12]

These songs are not written down. I put the words to the tune, to fit
the occasion. I pick words to fit the occasion. Words that rhyme fast, and they
can understand them fast.

I usually sing songs to fit the neighborhood. If I get in a Jewish neighborhood, I sing songs like "Bei Mir Bist Du Schon." When I go in a colored neighborhood, they like something swingy. I might sing the same song but I put it in
a swing tune. I go into a Spanish neighborhood and I speak to them in Spanish.

[12] As told to Marion Charles Hatch and Herbert Halpert by Clyde ("Kingfish") Smith,
Harlem, New York, November 29, 1939. "Living Lore of New York City." Manuscripts
of the Federal Writers' Project of the Works Progress Administration in New York City.
   Several of Clyde Smith's fish cries are based on popular songs as follows: "Hi de Ho Fish
Song" and "Stormy Weather," based on the songs "Minnie the Moocher" and "Stormy
Weather," copyright by Mills Music, Inc., and used by permission; "Jumpin' Jive," based
on the song, "The Jumpin' Jive," copyright by the Edward B. Marks Music Corporation
and used by permission.

When I started peddling—that was in 1932—that's when I started singing them. "Heigho fish man, bring down your dishpan," that's what started it. "Fish ain't but five cents a pound." That "ain't" is the regular dialect. I found the people like it and it was hard times then, the depression, and people can hardly believe fish is five cents a pound, so they started buying. There was quite a few peddlers and somebody had to have something extra to attract the attention. So when I came around, started making a rhyme, it was a hit right away.

I found that my old songs wasn't going over so good so I had to get new tunes and new words—you know, just something new to attract attention.

"Come on down and gather round, I got the best fish in the town." That was the new development.

There was no peddlin' down in North Carolina, in that particular town where I grew up, so I did not hear such songs and rhymes when I was a boy. In Wilmington, North Carolina, there used to be a man say, "Bring out the dishpan, here's the fish man." I used to hear my father and them talking about it.

One of the first things I learned about peddling was: to be any success at all, you had to have an original cry. I know several peddlers that started out and they hollered, "Old Fish Man," but it doesn't work.

I've gone blocks where several fish men have gone already and sold fish like nobody had been there. When I sing, a certain amount of people will be standing around, looking and listening, and that attracts more people and whenever people see a crowd they think it's a bargain so they want to get in on it.

When I cry, it will be so loud that the people come to the windows, look out. They come down with bedroom shoes on, with bathrobes, and some have pans or newspapers to put the fish in.

When I first come in a block, nobody pays any attention. Then I start singing, get them to laughing, and looking, and soon they start buying. A lot of them just hang around to hear the song. I always try to give the best I can for the money, the best fish for the money, and that makes repeated customers. A lot of people wait for my individual cry.

The average day I cover about eight blocks and spend about an hour in each block, sometimes longer. Sometimes on Friday, it takes me about nine hours to cover what I would cover in seven hours another day.

When I have crabs the kids like to see the crabs jump and bite, so they stand around in big crowds.

Sometimes, when I sing, the kids would be dancing the Lindy Hop and Trucking. The women buy most of the fish. I find Home Relief and WPA people the best customers. They buy more. They have to budget more near than the average family.

In white and Jewish neighborhoods I feature the words, but in the colored neighborhoods I feature the tune. In the Jewish neighborhood they appreciate the rhyming and the words more, while in the colored neighborhood they appreciate the swinging and the tune, as well as the words. I put in a sort of jumping rhythm for the colored folks. That swing music comes right from old colored folks' spirituals.

In the street anything goes. Slap a word in there. The way I was this morning [at a recording session] I was very good. I didn't mess them up. On the street whatever comes to my mind I say it, if I think it will be good. The main idea is when I got something I want to put over I just find something to rhyme with it. And the main requirement for that is mood. You gotta be in the mood. You got to put yourself in it. You've got to feel it. It's got to be more an expression than a routine. Of course, sometimes a drink of King Kong [liquor] helps.

HI DE HO FISH SONG

(Tune: "Minnie the Moocher")

I'm the hi de hi de ho fish man,
And I can really sell fish, I can.
Some time I sell 'em high.
Hi de hi de hi de hi.
Some time I sell 'em mighty low.
Low, ho, ho, ho, ho, ho.
I sell 'em up,
I sell 'em down,
I sell 'em all around this town.
So hi de hi de hi
And hi de ho de ho,
Hi de hi de hi,
Hi de ho, ho, ho, ho.

STORMY WEATHER

(Tune: "Stormy Weather")

I can't go home till all my fish is gone,
Stormy weather,
I can't keep my fish together.
Sellin' 'em all the time.
If you don't buy 'em,
Old rag man will get me.
If you do buy 'em,
Your folks 'll kinda let me
Walk in the sun once more.
I don't see why
Your folks don't come and buy.
Stormy weather,
Come on, let's get together,
Sellin' 'em all the time.

* * * * *

[My song to the tune of "Bei Mir Bist du Schön"] goes over good in either Jewish or colored neighborhoods, but I have to swing it up a bit in the colored neighborhoods.

* * * * *

SHAD SONG

I got shad,
Ain't you glad?
I got shad,

> So don't get mad.
> I got shad,
> Go tell your Dad.
> It's the best old shad he ever had.
> I got shad,
> Caught 'em in the sun.
> I got shad.
> I caught just for fun.
> So if you ain't got no money
> You can't have none.
> I got shad,
> Ain't you glad?
> I got shad,
> Tell your great granddad.
> It's the best old shad he ever had.

I made that tune up myself.

*   *   *   *   *

TISKIT A-TASKET

> A-tiskit, a-tasket,
> I sell fish by the basket.
> And if you folks don't buy some fish,
> I'm gonna put you in a casket.
> I'll carry you on down the avenue,
> And not a single thing you'll do.
> I'll dig, dig, dig, all around,
> Then I'll put you in the ground.
> A-tiskit, a-tasket,
> I sell 'em by the basket.

A couple of years ago, when that song was popular, they liked it then. When a song is popular and I work up my tune to that, I work out words to fit the tune, and when the popularity of the song dies away, that song ceases to be a hit even with the fish customers. When a song is in its height of popularity, people will ask you to sing that fish song at that time. So that each of my songs represents a certain era of music.

FISH AND VEGETABLES

> I got vegetables today,
> So don't go away.
> Stick around
> And you'll hear me say,
> Buy 'em by the pound,
> Put 'em in a sack.
> Hurry up and get 'em,
> 'Cause I'm not coming back.
> I got apples, onions, and colored greens.
> I got the best string beans
> That I ever seen.
> I got oranges, tomatoes, nice Southern sweet potatoes.
> I got yellow yams
> From Birmingham.

> And if you want some,
> Here I am.
> And if you don't want none
> I don't give a
> Yam, yam, yam,
> I got green greens
> From New Orleans.

A song like this I'd just look on the wagon and rhyme up something to match with it. When I sang this song, this morning, I was just thinking of something to rhyme then.

JUMPIN' JIVE

(Tune: "The Jumpin' Jive")

> Jim, jam, jump, jumpin' jive.
> Make you buy yo' fish on the East Side.
> Oh, boy,
> What you gonna say there, Gates?
> Jim, jam, jump, jumpin' jive.
> When you eat my fish,
> You'll eat four or five.
> Pal of mine, pal of mine, Swanee shore.
> Come on, buy my fish once more.
> Oh boy, oh boy,
> Jim, jam, jump, jumpin' jive.
> Make you dig your fish on the mellow side.
> Oh boy, what you gonna say there, Gates?
> Don't you hear them hep cats call?

That means the music is in you and you're all livened up. You want to dance and swing it.

> Come on, boys, and let's buy 'em all.
> Oh boy, what you gonna say there, Gates?

In these jump joints, that means where they dance and drink and smoke marijuana weeds. The marijuana weed is a "jumping jive." The expression is "knock me a jive there Gates." That means, "Give me a marijuana cigarette." The jumping jive is supposed to make you do all these things. When you have the jumping jive on, you're supposed to do all these things, buy the fish.

*   *   *   *   *

AMERICAN STREET CRIES [13]

STRAWBERRIES

(Brooklyn)

> Strawberry! Strawberry!
> Oh, ten cents a quart, strawberry!
> A big, big, quart, a dime a quart, strawberry!
> Oh, ten cents a quart strawberry!

[13] *American Street Cries*, Chorus for Mixed Voices, A Cappella, arranged by Elie Siegmeister, pp. 1-5. The "American Ballad Singers" Series of Native American Folk-Songs. Copyright, 1940, by Carl Fischer. New York.

Straw-ber-ry! Straw-ber-ry! Oh, ten cents a quart, straw-

ber-ry!   A   big, big quart, a   dime a   quart, straw-

ber-ry!   Oh,   ten cents a quart, straw-ber-ry!_____

BLACKBERRIES
(New Orleans)

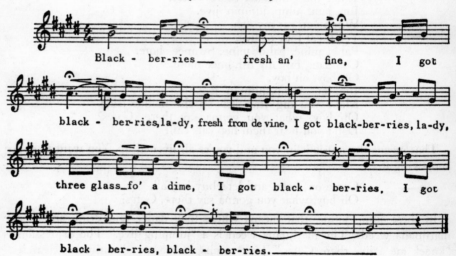

Black-ber-ries___ fresh an'   fine,   I got

black-ber-ries, la-dy, fresh from de vine, I got black-ber-ries, la-dy,

three glass_fo' a dime,   I got black-ber-ries,   I got

black-ber-ries, black-ber-ries._____

Blackberries fresh an' fine,
I got blackberries, lady, fresh from de vine,
I got blackberries, lady, three glass fo' a dime,
I got blackberries, I got blackberries, blackberries.

CHIMNEY SWEEP
(New Orleans)

Romanay, romanay, romanay, lady,
I know why yo' chimley won' draw.
Stove won' bake, an' yuh can' make no cake,
An' I know why yo' chimley won' draw.
Romanay, romanay, romanay, lady,
Romanay, romanay, romanay, lady.

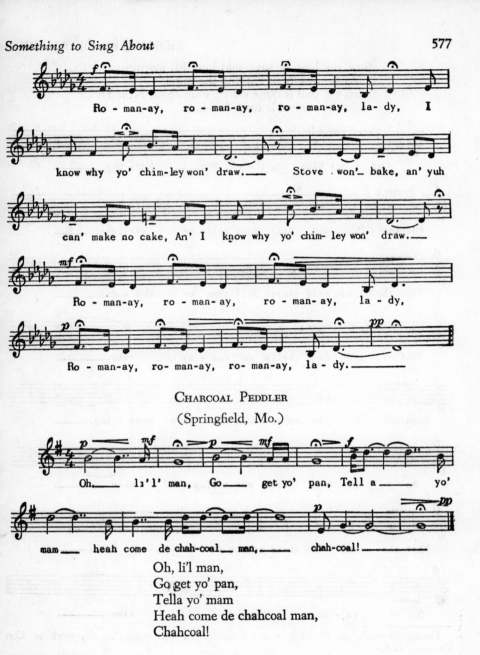

Ro - man-ay, ro - man-ay, ro - man-ay, la- dy, I

know why yo' chim-ley won' draw.___ Stove won' bake, an' yuh

can' make no cake, An' I know why yo' chim- ley won' draw.___

Ro - man-ay, ro - man- ay, ro - man- ay, la - dy,

Ro - man-ay, ro- man-ay, ro- man-ay, la - dy.___

CHARCOAL PEDDLER

(Springfield, Mo.)

Oh,___ lıʼlʼ man, Go___ get yo' pan, Tell a ___ yo'

mam___ heah come de chah-coal___ man, ___ chah-coal! ___

Oh, li'l man,
Go get yo' pan,
Tella yo' mam
Heah come de chahcoal man,
Chahcoal!

WHEN THE BREAKER STARTS UP FULL-TIME [14]

Our troubles are o'er, Mrs. Murphy,
For the Ditchman next door tells me straight,
That the mines will start full-time on Monday,
That's phat he tells me 'tanny rate.

[14] From *Minstrels of the Mine Patch*, Songs and Stories of the Anthracite Industry, by George Korson, pp. 29-30. Copyright, 1938, by the University of Pennsylvania Press. Philadelphia.
Transcribed by Melvin LeMon.

Sure the boss, he says, told him this morning,
  As he was 'bout ent'ring the mine,
That the coal is quite scarce 'roun' 'bout New York,
  So the rumors is work full-time.

Our trou-bles are o'er, Mrs.___ Mur-phy, _____

For the Ditch-man next door tells me   straight, _____

That the mines will start full time on   Mon - day, ____

That's   phat he   tells me 'tan - ny   rate. _____

Sure the   boss, he   says, told him this   morn - ing, ___

As   he   was 'bout en- t'ring the   mine, _____

That the coal is quite scarce roun' 'bout New   York, ____

So the ru - mors is work   full   time. _____

Daniel Brennan, of McAdoo, was my source for this song . . . the work of Con Carbon.—G.K.

The coal breaker, a straggling hulk of a building, is the most characteristic feature of the anthracite landscape. It is there that the amorphous lumps which the miner has extracted from the seam are cleansed and cracked into standard sizes for the market. Standing close to the mouth of a mine slope or shaft, it frequently may be found hugging a hillside.

Almost from the time that the first breaker cast its shadow, miners have invested it with symbolical significance.

'When the Breaker Starts Up Full Time' catches the mining folk in a happy mood. After prolonged unemployment the miners hear a rumor that their breaker is to resume production. All the good things sung of in the ballad represent so much wishful thinking because in the eighties when this ballad appeared, luxuries were beyond reach even when the mines were working full time.—G.K., notes for *Folk Music of the United States,* Issued from the Collections of the Archive of American Folk Song, Album 16, "Songs and Ballads of the Anthracite Miners," Record No. 79 A.1. Washington, D.C.: Library of Congress.

Chorus:

And it's boo-hoo if the news be true,
    Me store bill's the first thing I'll pay,
A stuff parlor shuit and a lounge I will buy,
    And an organ for Bridgie, hurray.
Me calico skirt I will throw in the dirt,
    In me silk one won't I cut a shine!
Cheer up, Mrs. Murphy, we all will ate turkey
    When the breaker starts up full-time.

I'll ne'er stick me fist in a washtub,
    The Chinese man he'll have me trade.
I'll ne'er pick a coal off the dirt bank;
    I'll buy everything ready-made.
We'll dress up our children like fairies,
    We'll build up a house big and fine,
And we'll move away from the Hungaries,
    When the breaker starts up full-time.

THE HOMESTEAD STRIKE [15]

The first attempt to organize the Pittsburgh iron- and steelworkers came in 1849, when four hundred puddlers rioted unsuccessfully against strike-breakers. Nine years later the ironworkers established a secret order called the Sons of Vulcan.

In the rapid expansion of the steel industry during the Civil War, labor and management clashed frequently. In 1865 the Sons of Vulcan came out into the open and negotiated the first wage scale in the iron and steel industry; and in 1876 the various craft unions merged into the Amalgamated Association of Iron and Steel Workers.

As the mills became bigger and more powerful, the struggle increased in intensity, culminating in the Homestead Strike—one of the bloodiest episodes in American industrial history.

Before dawn on the foggy morning of July 6, 1892, the whistle of the Homestead steel mills started to blow. This was a prearranged signal to warn the workers of trouble, and was reinforced by a horseman who galloped through the streets to call them out. Hugh O'Donnell, the steelworkers' leader, had received a telegram from the lookout on the Smithfield Street bridge in Pittsburgh, seven miles down the Monongahela River; it read: "Watch river. Steamer with barges left here."

Before long, O'Donnell and most of the 3,800 workers, armed with rifles, shotguns, pistols, and clubs, reached the mill in time to see the tugboat *Little Bill* emerge from the fog with two barges in tow. Their worst fears were realized when armed men in the uniform of the hated Pinkertons prepared to embark. These uniformed strikebreakers had been hired by the Carnegie Steel Company, which on June 20 had locked out the workers as the result of a wage dispute. Then the employees, backed by the Amalgamated Association, had retaliated by organizing on a military basis, and for five days had succeeded in preventing any one from entering the plant.

The stage was set for an epic battle. The company and the union were both powerful. Each had taken the law into its own hands. "This was no ordinary strike or lockout. It was revolution, sheer, stark, elemental." The *Little Bill* steamed away, leaving three hundred Pinkertons in the two barges, but opposed to them were thousands who now swarmed over the mill property to points of vantage. An all-day battle was on, mainly with small arms, but also with dynamite, burning oil and gas, and even obsolete cannon. When the Pinkertons finally surrendered, the toll on both sides was ten men dead and over sixty wounded.

The Homestead Strike inspired much verse and song. One of the most popu-

[15] From "Folk Songs of an Industrial City," by Jacob A. Evanson, in *Pennsylvania Songs and Legends,* George Korson, editor, pp. 443-446. Copyright, 1949, by University of Pennsylvania Press. Philadelphia.

Sung by Peter Haser at New Kensington, 1940. Recorded by George Korson. Notated by Jacob A. Evanson. Text from George Korson, *Coal Dust on the Fiddle* (Philadelphia, 1943), pp. 405-406.

lar sheet-music songs of the year was "Father Was Killed by the Pinkerton Men," a sentimental ditty typical of the melodramatic nineties. The real folk song of the bloody episode was "The Homestead Strike." It was sung everywhere, and oldtimers still sing it when a nostalgic mood takes possession of them. John Schmitt, from whom I obtained the tune, said he learned the ballad during the strike when he was sixteen.

Moderately fast

1. We are ask-ing one an-oth-er as we pass the time of day, Why

work-ing men re-sort to arms to get their pro-per pay, And

why our la-bor un-ions they must not be rec-og - nized, Whilst the

ac-tions of a syn-di-cate must not be crit-i - cized. Now the

trou-bles down at Home-stead were brought a-bout this way, When a

grasp- ing cor-po- ra-tion had the au-dac - i-ty to say:"You must

all re-nounce your un-ion and for-swear your lib-er - ty And

we will give you a chance to live and die in slav- er- y."

Chorus

Now the man that fights for hon-or, none can blame him,

May luck at-tend wher-ev-er he may roam.

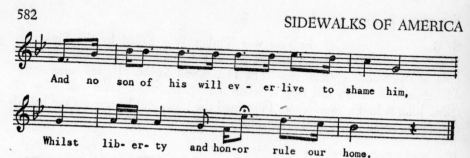

And no son of his will ev-er live to shame him,

Whilst lib-er-ty and hon-or rule our home.

We are asking one another as we pass the time of day,
Why workingmen resort to arms to get their proper pay,
And why our labor unions they must not be recognized,
Whilst the actions of a syndicate must not be criticized.
Now the troubles down at Homestead were brought about this way,
When a grasping corporation had the audacity to say:
"You must all renounce your union and forswear your liberty
And we will give you a chance to live and die in slavery."

Chorus:

> Now the man that fights for honor, none can blame him,
>   May luck attend wherever he may roam,
> And no son of his will ever live to shame him,
>   Whilst liberty and honor rule our home.

Now this sturdy band of workingmen started out at the break of day,
Determination in their faces which plainly meant to say:
"No one can come and take our homes for which we have toiled so long,
No one can come and take our places—no, here's where we belong!"
A woman with a rifle saw her husband in the crowd,
She handed him the weapon and they cheered her long and loud.
He kissed her and said, "Mary, you go home till we're through."
She answered, "No, if you must fight, my place is here with you."

When a lot of bum detectives came without authority,
Like thieves at night when decent men were sleeping peacefully—
Can you wonder why all honest hearts with indignation burn,
And why the slimy worm that treads the earth when trod upon will turn?—
When they locked out men at Homestead so they were face to face
With a lot of bum detectives and they knew it was their place
To protect their homes and families, and this was neatly done,
And the public will reward them for the victories they won.

THE JOHNSTOWN FLOOD [16]

No other tragedy touched the American people as did the Johnstown
flood. It produced many a legend and inspired much poetry and song. The
ballad given here, author unknown, is the most popular in the [Pittsburgh]
region's oral tradition about the flood.

This version is a composite. [Edwin] Hartz had learned the words from his
mother, Mrs. Etta Woods Hartz, a lifelong Pittsburgher, who was eighteen years
old at the time of the flood. . . .

On May 31, 1889, the South Fork Dam, four hundred feet above and sixteen

[16] *Ibid.,* pp. 456-459.

Sung by Mrs. Clara Bell Delaney, age 71, 1947. Text supplied by Edwin Hartz.
Notated by Miss Mary Means.

miles beyond Johnstown, broke. A roaring, forty-foot "ball" of water, a twenty-million-ton Niagara, rushed with incredible fury upon the city; it tore along with everything in its path—human beings, animals, trees, bridges, buildings: tossing locomotives around like cockle shells; piling up a mountain of debris at the railroad bridge below the town, which at once caught fire to become a funeral pyre for the living and dead trapped in it. Within a few hours 35,000 people were homeless, and 2,200 had been crushed, drowned, or burned to death in "the worst peacetime disaster of the nation's history."

Pittsburgh, eighty miles down the Conemaugh and Allegheny rivers, was the first to come to the rescue. Johnstown was an old steel town and thousands of its steel-mill "graduates" were in the Pittsburgh mills. The flood disaster struck them with special force and they made substantial contributions to Johnstown's relief. The Pittsburgh Relief Committee was in official charge of the stricken people of Johnstown for the twelve days before the state took over.

On a balm-y day in May, When na-ture held full sway,

And the birds sang sweet-ly in the sky a-bove; ____

A ____ cit-y lay se-rene, In a val-ley deep and green.

Where thous-ands dwelt in hap-pi-ness and love. ____

Chorus:

Now the cry of dis-tress Rings from East to ____ West,

And our whole dear coun-try now is plunged in woe ____

For the thous-ands burned and drowned In the cit-y of Johns-town.

All were lost in that great o-ver-flow. ____

On a balmy day in May,
When nature held full sway,
    And the birds sang sweetly in the sky above;
A city lay serene,
In a valley deep and green,
    Where thousands dwelt in happiness and love.

Chorus:

Now the cry of distress
Rings from East to West,
    And our whole dear country now is plunged in woe
For the thousands burned and drowned
In the city of Johnstown.
    All were lost in that great overflow.

Ah! but soon the scene was changed;
For just like a thing deranged,
    A storm came crashing through the quiet town;
Now the wind it raved and shrieked,
Thunder rolled and lightning streaked;
    But the rain it poured in awful torrents down.

Like the Paul Revere of old
Came a rider brave and bold;
    On a big bay horse he was flying like a deer;
And he shouted warning shrill,
"Quickly fly off to the hills."
    But the people smiled and showed no signs of fear.

Ah! but e'er he turned away—
This brave rider and the bay
    And the many thousand souls he tried to save;
But they had no time to spare,
Nor to offer up a prayer,
    Now they were hurried off into a watery grave.

Fathers, mothers, children all—
Both the young, old, great, and small—
    They were thrown about like chaff before the wind;
When the fearful raging flood
[Rushed in] where the city stood,
    Leaving thousands dead and dying there behind.

Now the cry of fire arose
Like the screams of battling foes,
    For that dreadful sick'ning pile was now on fire;
As they poured out prayers to heaven
They were burned as in an oven
    And that dreadful pile formed their funeral pyre.

THE MILWAUKEE FIRE [17]

'Twas the gray of early morning when the dreadful cry of fire
    Rang out upon the cold and piercing air,

[17] From *Wehman Bros. Good Old Time Songs,* No. 4, pp. 29-30. New York: Wehman Brothers. 1916.

Just that little word alone is all it would require
  To spread dismay and panic everywhere.
Milwaukee was excited as it never was before,
  On learning that the fire bells all around
Were ringing to eternity a hundred souls or more,
  And the Newhall House was burning to the ground.
The firemen worked like demons and did all within their power
  To save a life or try to soothe a pain;
It made the strongest heart sick, for in less than half an hour
  All was hushed and further efforts were in vain.

When the dreadful alarm was sounded through the oft-condemned hotel
  They rushed in mad confusion every way;
The smoke was suffocating and blinding them as well,
  The fire king could not be held at bay;
At every window men and women wildly would beseech
  For help, in tones of anguish and despair.
What must have been their feelings where the ladders could not reach,
  And they felt death's grasp around them everywhere?
Up in the highest window stood a servant girl alone;
  The crowd beneath all gazed with bated breath.
They turned away their faces, there was many a stifled groan,
  When she jumped to meet, perhaps, as hard a death.

In one place you could see a man, whose wife stood by his side,
  They say this man was a millionaire,
To save them from their dreadful fate they left no means untried,
  Gold or treasure had no value there.
A boy stood in a window and his mother was below,
  She saw him, and the danger drawing near.
With upraised hands, to pray for him, she knelt down in the snow,
  And the stoutest men could not restrain a tear.
She madly rushed toward the fire and wildly tore her hair,
  "Take me, oh, God, but spare my pride and joy."
She saw the flames surround him, and then, in dark despair,
  Said: "God have mercy on my only boy."

They tell us now that this hotel has been on fire before,
  And not considered safe for several years,
And still the men that owned it let it run on as before,
  And they are not to blame it now appears.
Incendiarism this time has been the cause they say,
  But who the fiend was they cannot tell;
So the people in Milwaukee will not rest by night or day
  Till the matter is investigated well.
Still this will be no benefit to those who've passed away,
  In this Milwaukee's greatest funeral pyre,
And peace be to their ashes is the best that we can say
  For the victims in this great and dreadful fire.

WILLIE THE WEEPER [18]

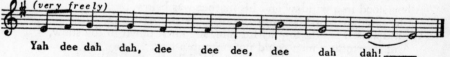

Did you ev-er hear the sto-ry 'bout Wil-ly, the Weep-er?

Made his liv-in' as a chim-ney sweep-er.

He had the dope hab-it an' he had it bad;

Lis-ten while I tell you 'bout the dream he had:

Teet tee dee dee dee dee,— toot too doo doo doo doo,—

(very freely)

Yah dee dah dah, dee dee dee, dee dah dah!—

Did you ever hear the story 'bout Willy the Weeper?
Made his livin' as a chimney-sweeper.
He had the dope habit an' he had it bad;
Listen while I tell you 'bout the dream he had:

Refrain:

Teet tee dee dee dee dee, toot too doo doo doo doo,
Yah dee dah dah, dee dee dee, dee dah dah!

[18] From *The American Songbag*, by Carl Sandburg, pp. 204-205. Copyright, 1927, by Harcourt, Brace and Company, Inc. New York.

R. W. Gordon in his editorship of the *Adventure* magazine department "Old Songs That Men Have Sung" received thirty versions of "Willy the Weeper," about one hundred verses different. Willy shoots craps with kings, plays poker with presidents, eats nightingale tongues a queen cooks for him; his Monte Carlo winnings come to a million, he lights his pipe with a hundred dollar bill, he has heart affairs with Cleopatra, the Queen of Sheba, and movie actresses.

As against versions of this heard in Detroit and New York, we prefer the one by Henry (Hinky) McCarthy of the University of Alabama. He gives it with pauses, with mellowed, mellifluous tones, with an insinuating guitar accompaniment. The lines "Teet tee dee dee dee dee," are lingering and dreamy, supposed to indicate regions where the alphabet is not wanted.—C.S.

For the original, see "A Hop Fiend's Dream," Louis J. Beck, *New York's Chinatown* (New York, Bohemian Publishing Co., 1898), pp. 165-166.

He went down to the dope house one Saturday night,
An' he knew that the lights would be burnin' bright.
I guess he smoked a dozen pills or mo';
When he woke up he was on a foreign sho'.

Queen o' Bulgaria was the first he met;
She called him her darlin' an' her lovin' pet.
She promised him a pretty Fohd automobile,
With a diamond headlight an' a silver steerin'-wheel.

She had a million cattle, she had a million sheep;
She had a million vessels on the ocean deep;
She had a million dollahs, all in nickels an' dimes;
She knew 'cause she counted them a million times.

Willy landed in New York one evenin' late,
He asked his sugar baby for an after-date.
Willy he got funny, she began to shout:
Bim bam boo!—an' the dope gave out.

I WONDER HOW I LOOK WHEN I'M ASLEEP [19]

I wonder, I wonder, I wonder
   How I look when I'm asleep!
I wonder, I wonder, I wonder
   How do I look when I'm through counting sheep!
Oh, tell me, oh, tell me, oh, tell me.
   The secret if you tell me I will keep.
I think I'll spend the day
In Philadelphi-a
   To find out how I look when I'm asleep.

A PERFECT DAY IN PHILADELPHIA

[19] Sung by Tom Glazer, Ossining, New York, July 25, 1954.

THE BOURGEOIS BLUES [20]

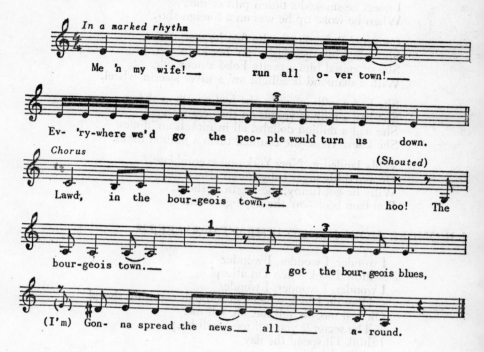

In a marked rhythm

Me 'n my wife!__ run all o- ver town!__

Ev- 'ry-where we'd go the peo- ple would turn us down.

Chorus

Lawd, in the bour-geois town,__ (*Shouted*) hoo! The

bour-geois town.__ I got the bour- geois blues,

(I'm) Gon- na spread the news__ all__ a- round.

Me 'n' my wife run all over town.
Everywhere we'd go the people would turn us down.

Chorus:

Lawd, in the bourgeois town, [*shouted*] hoo!
The bourgeois town.
I got the bourgeois blues,
[I'm] Gonna spread the news all around.

This is a parody of the chorus of the song *I Wonder How I Look When I'm Asleep*, which runs as follows:

I wonder, I wonder, I wonder
    How I look when I'm asleep!
I wonder, I wonder, I wonder
    How I look when I'm through counting sheep!
Oh, tell me, oh, tell me, oh, tell me.
    The secret if you tell me I will keep.
It's driving me to drink
And I haven't slept a wink
    From wondering how I look when I'm asleep!

(By B. G. DeSylva, Lew Brown and Ray Henderson. Copyright, 1927, by DeSylva, Brown and Henderson. New York.)
[20] Sung by Huddie Ledbetter (Leadbelly), Musicraft Album No. 227. Words and tune by Leadbelly.
Transcribed by Evelyn Modoi.

Me and Martha we was standing upstairs.
I heard a white man say, "I don't want no niggers up there."

Lawd, he's a bourgeois man, etc.

Home of the brave, land of the free.
I don't want to be mistreated by no bourgeoisie.

Me and my wife we went all over town.
Everywhere we go the colored people would turn us down.

The white folks in Wash'n't'n, they know how
To chuck a colored man a nickel just to see him bow.

Tell all the colored folks to listen to me:
Don't try to find no home in Wash'n't'n, D.C.

'Cause it's a bourgeois town, etc.

CHICAGO IN SLICES [21]

I have been to the North and been to the South,
    In traveling a man may a-far go
To the jumping off place before you will find
    A city to compare with Chicago.
If you never have altered your name in your life,
    Or never did up to a bar go,
Or never run away with another man's wife,
    They won't let you live in Chicago.

Some folks send by Adams express,
    And others put faith in old Fargo,
But if you want to go to the devil direct,
    Just enter yourself for Chicago.
The city with fast gals and gay gamboliers,
    Is as full as a ship with a cargo.
And it is truthfully said that the very best men
    Fight chickens and dogs in Chicago.

The infants they feed on whisky direct,
    And for liquor they to their Ma go.
And the muly cows give, as some might expect,
    Whisky punch in the town of Chicago.
They won't let the ministers live in the town,
    For on him they will put an embargo—
Unless he drinks wine with all his young friends,
    And then he may stay in Chicago.

[21] From *Lost Chords*, The Diverting Story of American Popular Song, by Douglas Gilbert, pp. 164-165. Copyright, 1942, by Douglas Gilbert. Garden City, New York: Doubleday & Company, Inc.

. . . The accent on pubs and prostitutes that enlivened the declining decade appears at its best, perhaps, in the song of Frank Lum, who was as well known for his topical songs as he was for the so-called "motto" songs which began in the late '80's and reached their zenith during the early '90's, "A Boy's Best Friend Is His Mother"—that sort of song. Although Lum was no better or worse than his colleagues in the matter of inept rhymes and faulty construction, he was an astute observer, and in his tours as a singer in the variety halls, all that touched him was grist for his creaking mill. His topical song that depicts the pub-and-wench expression of the period is "Chicago in Slices," but 'twill serve as a print of the general hellishness in any key city of the times.—D.G.

A PERFECT DAY IN CHICAGO

"HAST EVER BEEN IN OMAHA?" [22]

Hast ever been in Omaha,
 Where rolls the dark Missouri down,
And four strong horses scarce can draw
 An empty wagon through the town?

Where sand is blown from every mound
 To fill your eyes and ears and throat—
Where all the steamers are aground
 And all the shanties are afloat?

From *The Story of Omaha*, from The Pioneer Days to the Present Time, by Alfred Sorenson, pp. 460-461. Copyright, 1923, by Alfred Sorenson. Omaha: The National Printing Company.

Originally published anonymously in "The Drawer" department of *Harper's New Monthly Magazine*, September 1869, and attributed to John G. Saxe.

John G. Saxe was for many years editor of *The Albany Evening Journal* and died in 1887. He probably was never farther west than Buffalo. That he was not the author of the verses so accurately descriptive of Omaha at the time of the completion of the Union Pacific, was stoutly maintained by the late Dr. Victor M. Coffman, who told me that Frank Streamer wrote them. Streamer was a newspaper man who was employed in various capacities on the Omaha press for a few years prior to 1870. He was a brilliant and versatile writer, but, as is sometimes the case with such men, he was addicted to liquor and was his own worst enemy. One very rainy and muddy day he called at Dr. Coffman's office, and while waiting for the doctor he wrote the poem. When Dr. Coffman came in, Streamer read it to him and asked his opinion of it. "It's first class," replied the doctor, "and you ought to publish it." Streamer thereupon sent it to *Harper's Magazine*. This is the true story of "Hast Ever Been in Omaha?" Streamer was a wanderer, and when he departed from Omaha he was headed for the Pacific coast. What became of him no one in this city knows. . . . —A.S.

Where whisky shops the livelong night
    Are vending out their poison juice;
Where men are often *very* tight,
    And women deemed a trifle loose?

Where taverns have an anxious guest
    For every corner, shelf and crack;
With half the people going west,
    And *all* the others going back?

Where theaters are all the run,
    And bloody scalpers come to trade;
Where everything is overdone
    And everybody underpaid?

If not, take heed to what I say:
    You'll find it just as I have found it;
And if it lies upon your way,
    For God's sake, reader, *go around it!*

ABALONE SONG [23]

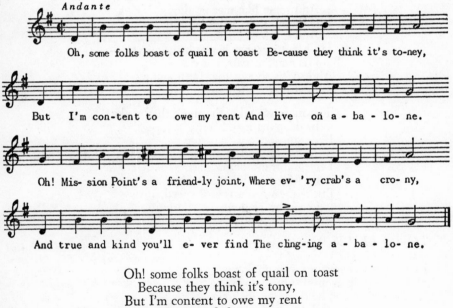

Oh, some folks boast of quail on toast Be-cause they think it's to-ney,

But I'm con-tent to owe my rent And live on a-ba-lo-ne.

Oh! Mis-sion Point's a friend-ly joint, Where ev-'ry crab's a cro-ny,

And true and kind you'll e-ver find The cling-ing a-ba-lo-ne.

    Oh! some folks boast of quail on toast
      Because they think it's tony,
    But I'm content to owe my rent
      And live on abalone.
    Oh! Mission Point's a friendly joint,
      Where ev'ry crab's a crony,

[23] By George Sterling, Jack London, Ambrose Bierce and Gelett Burgess. Music adapted by Sterling Sherwin. From *A San Francisco Songster*, An Anthology of Songs and Ballads Sung in San Francisco from the Gold Rush Era to the Present, Illustrative of the City's Metamorphoses from Camp to Metropolis, and Serving as Lyric Footnotes to Its Dramatic History, Cornel Lengyel, editor, pp. 128A-128B. Prepared with Assistance of the Works Progress Administration of California. Sponsored by the City and County [of] San Francisco. History of Music Project. [Works Progress Administration. Northern California.] San Francisco, 1930.

And true and kind you'll ever find
    The clinging abalone.

He wanders free beside the sea,
    Where'er the coast is stony;
He flaps his wings and madly sings—
    The plaintive abalone.
By Carmel Bay, the people say,
    We feed the lazzaroni
On Boston beans and fresh sardines,
    And toothsome abalone.

Some live on hope, and some on dope
    And some on alimony;
But my tom-cat, he lives on fat
    And tender abalone.
Oh! some drink rain and some champagne,
    Or brandy by the pony;
But I will try a little rye
    With a dash of abalone.

Oh! some like jam, and some like ham,
    And some like macaroni;
But bring me in a pail of gin
    And a tub of abalone.
He hides in caves beneath the waves,—
    His ancient patrimony;
And so 'tis shown that faith alone
    Reveals the abalone.

The more we take, the more they make
    In deep-sea matrimony;
Race suicide cannot betide
    The fertile abalone.
I telegraph my better half
    By Morse or by Marconi;
But if the need arise for speed,
    I send an abalone.

ST. LOUIS BLUES [24]

I hate to see de evenin' sun go down,
Hate to see de evenin' sun go down,
'Cause mah baby, he done lef' dis town.

Feelin' tomorrow lak I feel today,
Feel tomorrow lak I feel today,
I'll pack mah trunk, make mah get-away.

St. Louis woman, wid her diamon' rings,
Pulls dat man roun' by her apron strings.
'Twant for powder an' for store-bought hair,
De man I love would not gone nowhere.

[24] Words and music by W. C. Handy. Copyright, 1914, by W. C. Handy. Copyright renewed. Reprinted by permission. New York: Handy Bros. Music Co., Inc.

Chorus:

> Got de St. Louis blues, jes as blue as I can be,
> Dat man got a heart lak a rock cast in de sea,
> Or else he wouldn't have gone so far from me.

> [*Spoken*] *Doggoneit!*

Been to de Gypsy to get mah fortune tole,
To de Gypsy done got mah fortune tole,
'Cause I'm most wile 'bout mah Jelly-Roll.

Gypsy done tole me, "Don't you wear no black."
Yes, she done tole me, "Don't you wear no black.
Go to St. Louis, you can win him back."

Help me to Cairo, make St. Louis by mahself,
Git to Cairo, find mah ole friend Jeff.
Gwine to pin mahself close to his side.
If I flag his train, I sho can ride.

Chorus:

> I loves dat man lak a schoolboy loves his pie,
> Lak a Kentucky Col'nel loves his mint an' rye.
> I'll love mah baby till de day I die.

You ought to see dat stovepipe brown of mine,
Lak he owns de Di'mon' Joseph line.
He'd make a cross-eyed 'oman go stone blind.

Blacker than midnight, teeth lak flags of truce,
Blackest man in de whole St. Louis.
Blacker de berry, sweeter is de juice.

About a crap game he knows a pow'ful lot,
But when work time comes he's on de dot.
Gwine to ask him for a cold ten spot.
What it takes to git it, he's certainly got.

Chorus:

> A black-headed gal make a freight train jump de track,
> Said a black-headed gal make a freight train jump de track.
> But a long tall gal makes a preacher ball de jack.

Lawd, a blonde-headed woman makes a good man leave de town,
I said blonde-headed woman makes a good man leave de town,
But a red-headed woman makes a boy slap his papa down.

Oh, ashes to ashes and dust to dust,
I said ashes to ashes and dust to dust.
If mah blues don't get you, mah jazzing must.

Index

Caps and small caps indicate names of authors, editors, artists, musicians, singers, and informants who have contributed to the book.

Titles of songs are indicated by italics and first lines by quotation marks.